The Jesus Revolution

The Jesus Revolution

A Transformative Theology
of the New Testament

James M. Scott

CASCADE *Books* · Eugene, Oregon

THE JESUS REVOLUTION
A Transformative Theology of the New Testament

Cascade Books
An Imprint of Wipf and Stock Publishers
199 W. 8th Ave., Suite 3
Eugene, OR 97401

www.wipfandstock.com

PAPERBACK ISBN: 978-1-6667-4658-7
HARDCOVER ISBN: 978-1-6667-4659-4
EBOOK ISBN: 978-1-6667-4660-0

Cataloguing-in-Publication data:

Names: Scott, James M., author.

Title: The Jesus revolution : a transformative theology of the New Testament / James M. Scott.

Description: Eugene, OR: Cascade Books, 2023. | Includes bibliographical references and index.

Identifiers: ISBN 978-1-6667-4658-7 (paperback). | ISBN 978-1-6667-4659-4 (hardcover). | ISBN 978-1-6667-4660-0 (ebook).

Subjects: LCSH: Bible. New Testament—Theology. | Jesus Christ—Political and social views.

Classification: BS2417.P6 S368 2023 (print). | BS2417.P6 (ebook).

02/22/23

The author gratefully acknowledges permission to reprint the following journal articles and book chapters:

"The Speech-Acts of a Royal Pretender: Jesus' Performative Utterances in Mark's Gospel." *JSHJ* 20 (2021) 1–37. Leiden: E. J. Brill.

"Galatians 3:28 and the Divine Performative Speech-Act of Paul's Gospel." *ZNW* 112 (2021) 180–200. Berlin: de Gruyter.

"Second Corinthians 3–4 and the Language of Creation: The Citation of Genesis 1:3 in 2 Corinthians 4:6." In *Scriptures, Texts, and Tracings in 2 Corinthians and Philippians,* edited by A. Andrew Das and B. J. Oropeza, 51–69. Lanham, MD: Lexington Books/Fortress Academic, 2022.

For Kai, Liz, and Jordan

Beautiful world, where are you? Return again,
sweet springtime of nature!
Alas, only in the magic land of song
does your fabled memory live on.
The deserted fields mourn,
no god reveals himself to me;
of that warm, living image
only a shadow has remained.

—Friedrich Schiller

Contents

Preface

I HAVE LONG WANTED to write a biblical theology of the New Testament, and an academic publisher actually offered me a contract for such a project in the early 1990s, when I was still a freshly baked assistant professor. At the time, however, I did not feel that I was sufficiently ready, so I declined the offer and opted instead to pursue other projects that might help me to gain competency in the field and to build toward the eventual goal. Through the intervening years, I kept probing various possible approaches to constructing a New Testament Theology but was never satisfied with the results. It was only after the contested election of Joseph Biden as President of the United States that I found a new strategy and simultaneously experienced the decisive crisis point that motivated me to complete the project as quickly as possible. So, shortly before Christmas 2020, I set about to write my introduction to a biblical theology of the New Testament, all the while filled with an ever-increasing anxiety that the US's fragile democracy might finally collapse. The violent capitol insurrection on January 6, 2021, served to confirm my worst fears and propelled my writing into hyperdrive. I completed the first draft of the present volume in mid-April 2021 and called it *The Jesus Revolution* because of the convergence of three factors: my long-standing work on the New Testament; my new-found interest in the return to nonviolent revolution in the writings of Deleuze and Guattari which gave me a framework in which to think about New Testament theology; and my concern about the threat of violent revolution in the United States. Although the New Testament itself was the main driver of my endeavor, my goal in writing the present volume was to effect change.

The United States itself was born from revolution, the war of 1775–1783, in which the American colonists won independence from British rule. In 1782, toward the end of this revolution, Charles Thomas, secretary of the Continental Congress, designed what came to be known as the Great Seal of the United States. The Great Seal depicts a pyramid with an eye inscribed in it. This image and the whole seal evoke several of the pivotal concepts of this book.

First, the triangle shape recalls the Greek letter delta (Δ, δ), the first letter of *diaphora*, meaning "difference." Difference as the process of positive change or becoming informs our new approach to a biblical theology of the New Testament. Second, the seal is found on the obverse of the US dollar bill, a pillar of the capitalist system, which is the superpower "assemblage" of our modern times. As we shall see, there are three other kinds of "assemblage" that need to be discussed besides the capitalist: territorial, state, and revolutionary. Third, the seal contains the Latin motto *NOVUS ORDO SAECLO-RUM*—"a new order of the ages"—alluding to Virgil's *Fourth Eclogue* (line 5).[1] Virgil's poem was interpreted by later Christians as a prophecy of the coming of Christ,[2] and

1. Virgil's *Fourth Eclogue* is often called the "Messianic Eclogue": "The great order of the ages is born anew, now justice returns, . . . now a new lineage is sent down from heaven." The other motto on the Great Seal is *ANNUIT COEPTIS*, which is adapted from Virgil, *Aeneid* 9.624 (in a prayer to Jupiter in the mouth of Aeneas's son Ascanius at a critical moment in the Trojans' war in Italy) and is usually translated "[God] looks favorably on our undertakings." On the well-known Virgilian phrases used as American mottoes which appear on the Great Seal of the United States, see, e.g., Reinhold, *Classica Americana*, 233; Ziolkowski, *Virgil and the Moderns*, 19 with n45, 147.

2. Cf. Hardie, *Last Trojan*, 95, 128–29: "This riddling poem, dedicated to one of the Roman consuls of 40 BC, uses oracular language to express hopes for future political and social stability after years of Roman civil war. But its annunciation of the arrival of the final age foretold in the Sibyl's song, with the return of the Virgin (Justice), the return of the Golden Age of Saturn, and the descent from Heaven of a mysterious child, could be taken as a prophecy of a very different kind of order of things. The Church Father Lactantius [*c.* 240–*c.* 320], a friend of the first Christian emperor Constantine I (the Great), was the first to give the poem a Christian reading, seeing in it a reference by the Cumaean Sibyl, reported by Virgil, to the Golden Age that will follow the second coming of Christ. Constantine himself in a speech at the Council of Nicaea (AD 325) interprets the eclogue as a prophecy of the birth of Christ to the Virgin Mary. The 'death of the serpent' in the new Golden Age announced in the eclogue is taken to refer to the serpent in the Garden of Eden. Constantine says that Virgil himself was privy to the truth that the Sibyl foretold the birth of Christ, but deliberately obscured the message for reasons of safety. The belief that *Eclogue* 4 contained a prophecy of Christ, whether Virgil was conscious of the fact or not, and the idea that the Sibyls were pagan prophets of Christianity, had a long life." See further

we are suggesting in the present volume that Christ is the one who establishes the real new world order in the shell of the old. Fourth, the three corners of the pyramid evoke the idea of the three elements of an "assemblage." We shall have much more to say about that subject in our study. Finally, at the top, hovering above the body of the pyramid, is a giant eye, which we can relate the ever-present tendency of modern society to objectify. Our study seeks to eliminate the distinction between perceiver and perceived, virtual and actual, inside and outside, and subject and object.

Several preliminary comments are in order. First, our study does not begin from the position of any particular confession of faith,[3] and this can be disorienting for those who are used to thinking about Jesus Christ in traditional christological categories, such as the second member of the Triune God. When we say that Jesus Christ is an "abstract machine" or "condition" of the New Testament assemblage, we are referring to how he *functions* in relationship to the New Testament assemblage. This is not some kind of ultimate statement on who Jesus was or is ontologically.[4]

Second, we do not assume that the New Testament is a unity and that all its parts necessarily harmonize perfectly, and, again, this can be disorienting for those who are used to having everything nailed down and clearly defined.[5] From the perspective developed in this book, the New Testament is an "assemblage," that is, a diverse

---

Benko, "Virgil's *Fourth Eclogue* in Christian Interpretation," 646–705; Horsfall, "Virgil and the Jews," 67–80; Bremmer, "Virgil and Jewish Literature," 157–64.

3. See, however, Collins, "Is a Critical Biblical Theology Possible?," 17 (emphasis mine): "Critical method is incompatible with confessional faith insofar as the latter requires us to accept specific conclusions on dogmatic grounds. It does not, and cannot preclude a commitment to working within specific traditions, *and biblical theology is inevitably confessional in this looser sense.*" Markus Bockmuehl states that "it still remains de rigueur to assert . . . that Christian confessional and theological convictions have no place in serious study of the Bible" (*Seeing the Word*, 76; also 56). I want to make it clear, however, that the present study does not impugn confessional and theological convictions, which I myself happen to hold.

4. Cf. Bockmuehl, *Seeing the Word*, 191: "In the case of Jesus . . . , it is impossible to speak Christianly of his individuality without at the same time speaking of his metaphysical essence." The key here is that we are not speaking only of Jesus' *individuality*, but rather of his *function* with relation to the assemblage.

5. Unities of many kinds are the product of certain habitual ways of thinking that are common to Western culture. To take just one prominent example, we may think of "species": a group of living organisms consisting of similar individuals capable of exchanging genes or interbreeding. Cf., however, Conniff, "Unclassified," 52: "For three centuries, scientists have divided living things into tidy species. But the real world seems more slippery: a continuum in which one variety of life flows seamlessly into the next." Lichens are the ultimate example of a taxonomic nightmare: Lichens are lifeforms that defy classification because they seamlessly integrate multiple organisms across the kingdoms (i.e., a mutualistic symbiotic relationship between fungal, algal, and bacterial partners), thus becoming a type case of inter-kingdom collaboration. Cf. Sheldrake, *Entangled Life*, 70–93, here 89, citing the lichenologist Toby Spribille on the presence of more than two partners in lichens: "The 'basic set' of partners is different for every lichen group. Some have more bacteria, some fewer; some have one yeast species, some have two, or none. Interestingly, we have yet to find any lichen that matches the traditional definition of one fungus and one alga.'"

collection of writings, not a unity per se.[6] Assemblages are not unities but rather entities that are brought together for a particular purpose.[7] In this case, the coherence of the writings (i.e., the "concrete elements") is provided by Jesus Christ as the "abstract machine" or "condition" that suffuses the whole (the terms will be explained in due course).[8] This does not mean, however, that the writings will lie perfectly flat. Who Jesus was and how he was to be understood was a contested matter even in the New Testament (cf. Mark 8:27–29 pars.)[9] and certainly beyond.[10]

Finally, a word about the use of "revolution" in this book. It has *absolutely nothing* in common with the Capitol Insurrection pictured on the front cover. Indeed, the way we are using the term is emphatically opposed to the racism, lies, nationalism, and demagoguery which fueled the mob that stormed the Capitol in order to seize power through violent means on January 6, 2021.[11] What we have in mind instead

6. Here, we must consider that what we call the New Testament is only a selection of the writings that were available in early Christian circles during the first century and a half of the Jesus movement. The New Testament itself points to other writings that are either available or possible (cf. Luke 1:1–4; John 20:30; 21:25; 1 Cor 5:9; Col 4:16; 2 Thess 2:2). In addition, we have other collections of early Christian writings, including, for example, the "Apostolic Fathers" and the New Testament Apocrypha.

7. On assemblages, see further Nail, "What Is an Assemblage?" 21–37; Posteraro, "Assemblage Theory and the Two Poles of Organic Life," 402–32, esp. 404–16.

8. Another factor is that the collection of the assemblage was made by the church in a process that began in the middle of the second century CE and reached its final form in the fifth century. See further in the next chapter.

9. Whether or not Peter's confession of Jesus as Messiah at Caesarea Philippi (Mark 8:27–29 pars.) is deemed historical, it still provides evidence of the range of possible interpretations of who Jesus was: "and on the way he [sc. Jesus] asked his disciples, 'Who do people say that I am?' And they answered him, 'John the Baptist; and others, Elijah; and still others, one of the prophets.' He asked them, 'But who do you say that I am?' Peter answered him, 'You are the Messiah.'" See further Allison, *Jesus of Nazareth: Millenarian Prophet*, 67n251; Allison, *Constructing Jesus*, 41 (#27), 82–85, 133, 221–304.

10. The plethora of interpretations to which the New Testament has been subjected over the last two millennia can be compared to that to which Virgil's *Aeneid*, one of the most influential works in the Western canon, has been subjected over the same period of time. Cf. Hardie, *Last Trojan*, 19, who concludes after an extensive survey: "That the *Aeneid* should have been interpreted and assessed in such a bewildering diversity of ways, and appropriated by so wide a range of readers and writers, over the last two thousand years might be seen only as proof of the fact that 'meaning is only realized at the point of reception,' as the modern theory of reception will have it. On the other hand it might be taken as an index of the inexhaustible complexity of the *Aeneid* itself, a text to which could be applied Walt Whitman's defiant boast in *Song of Myself*: 'Do I contradict myself? | Very well then I contradict myself. | (I am large, I contain multitudes.)'" I fully endorse the view expressed by Bockmuehl, *Seeing the Word*, 232: "In reflecting on the possibility of finding a meeting place between the diversity both of biblical authors and of their interpreters, New Testament study in the twenty-first century will require a quantum leap beyond the tired clichés of the 'unity and diversity' problem as it was handled in the past. Advocates of easy harmonies of tension and contradiction, like those of relentlessly conflict-driven polarizations, routinely underrate their epistemologically sinister potential. Similarly, we are unlikely to advance our conversation with ideologically prescriptive developmentalism or, on the other hand, historically oblivious models of doctrinal and ecclesial assertion. Unity is impossible where truth is suppressed—but so is truth in the absence of difference." The present volume proposes that the "quantum leap" can be facilitated by what has been aptly called "the philosophy of difference."

11. Cf. Woodward and Costa, *Peril*, who report on Mark Milley's view on the January 6

is the nonviolent, peaceful *revolution* (the term "transformation" works just as well) inaugurated by Jesus Christ, which involves the prefigurative creation of the people to come and the world to come and is open to everyone equally.[12]

The following introduction to a biblical theology of the New Testament strains towards three interrelated outcomes: concepts, or new ways of thinking; percepts, or new ways of seeing and construing; and affects, or new ways of feeling.[13] As a result, we will find ourselves temporarily disoriented, our perceptions altered, our imaginations transformed.[14] All three outcomes are needed in order to effect change in the world.[15] This volume is ultimately about promoting change rather than merely describing phenomena.[16]

insurrection. Appointed Chairman of the Joint Chiefs by Trump in 2018, Milley summarized the event in an entry to his daily notebook dated January 9: "'Big Threat: domestic terrorism.' Some were the new Brown Shirts, a U.S. version, Milley concluded, of the paramilitary wing of the Nazi Party that supported Hitler. *It was a planned revolution.* Steve Bannon's vision coming to life. Bring it all down, blow it up, burn it, and emerge with power" (Woodward and Costa, *Peril*, 273–74 [emphasis mine]). In the Epilogue, Woodward and Costa return to Chairman Milley's interpretation of January 6: "Milley, ever the historian, thought of the little remembered 1905 revolution in Russia. The uprising had failed, but it had set the stage for the successful 1917 revolution that led to the creation of the Soviet Union. Vladimir Lenin, the leader of the 1917 revolution, had later called the 1905 revolution 'The Great Dress Rehearsal.' Had January 6 been a dress rehearsal? Milley told senior staff, 'What you might have seen was a precursor to something far worse down the road'" (Woodward and Costa, *Peril*, 415–16). See further Woodward and Costa, *Peril*, xviii–xix: "Milley believed January 6 was a planned, coordinated, synchronized attack on the very heart of American democracy, designed to overthrow the government to prevent the constitutional certification of a legitimate election won by Joe Biden. It was indeed a coup attempt and nothing less than 'treason,' he said, and Trump might still be looking for what Milley called a 'Reichstag moment.' In 1933, Adolf Hitler had cemented absolute power for himself and the Nazi Party amid street terror and the burning of the Reichstag parliamentary building. Milley could not rule out that the January 6 assault, so unimagined and savage, could be a dress rehearsal for something larger as Trump publicly and privately clung to his belief that the election had been rigged for Biden and stolen from him." Similarly, Nancy Pelosi, Speaker of the House of Representatives, regarded January 6th "a coup d'état against us [sc. the Congress] so he [sc. Donald Trump] can stay in office" (Woodward and Costa, *Peril*, xxiv).

12. When referring to nonviolent, political "revolution," it is necessary to acknowledge that "scientific revolutions" also occur, a term made famous by Kuhn, *Structure of Scientific Revolutions*. For Kuhn, "normal science" operates within an established scientific "paradigm" until the unexplained anomalies within the paradigm cause a crisis, leading to a sudden and irrevocable change of world view—i.e., a "paradigm shift," or "revolution" in ideas, knowledge, and research projects—whereby the world in which we live fundamentally changes; hence, a new paradigm replaces the old and poses a new set of problems to be solved. Our use of "revolution" has much in common with Kuhn's, but also some differences.

13. Cf. Deleuze, *Negotiations, 1972–1990*, 164–65.

14. As we shall see in chapter 4, Jesus himself is a teacher of signs who *disorients*.

15. Cf. Boundas et al., "Encounters with Deleuze," 166: "Deleuze defines philosophy as a creation of concepts, but creation has as its correlate the critique of concepts. In his *Theses on Feuerbach*, Marx famously complained that 'philosophers have hitherto only *interpreted* the world in various ways; the point is to *change* it.' But to create concepts is to change the world, if only in a minor way, since concepts are things of this world." As we shall see, Jesus' concepts are world-changing in precisely this way. Cf. also Stroumsa, *End of Sacrifice*, xvii, 123.

16. Of course, describing phenomena can indirectly promote change.

One of the new ways of thinking that will be entertained in the following pages is the concept that all things are interrelated.[17] This concept encourages us to see the connections between things and to prevent the siloization of knowledge that is so endemic to Western thinking.[18] As a result, we will not shrink from discussing issues outside of biblical studies per se.[19] In many cases, we will relate a topic to an analogous issue in the modern world or illustrate a point with a modern example. In this way, we will read biblical texts against a cultural horizon in line with our own rather than merely with that of antiquity, whether Greco-Roman or Jewish.[20]

17. Cf. Deleuze and Guattari, *Thousand Plateaus*, 3–25, who distinguish between two different methods: (1) arborescent: the traditional, tree-like style of thought and writing that has a center or subject from which it then expresses its ideas; this entails a hierarchy between ground and consequence, cause and effect, subject and expression; (2) rhizomatic: a de-centered, proliferating, mycelium-like style of thought and writing that can begin at any point and form a point of connection with any other. Deleuze and Guatarri do not use philosophy to interpret any other discipline, nor other disciplines to interpret philosophy. Instead, they allow disciplines to mesh, transform and overlay each other. We will speak more of these matters in the Introduction. Henceforth, *Thousand Plateaus* will be abbreviated *ATP*.

18. "To silo" in this sense means to isolate something (e.g., knowledge) in such a way that hinders communication and cooperation. For example, the very division of universities into administrative units (i.e., departments and faculties) that barely relate to one another and have constant financial and disciplinary pressure to "defend their turf" creates the conditions for siloization. The resultant loss of creative synergy is inestimable. Applied to the investigation of the New Testament, siloization is equally destructive, for it divides things that really do belong together. Hence, whereas scholars of yesteryear were busy decomposing the Gospels into layers based on whether the material seemed to reflect Judaism (in which case the material had some claim to an early date and perhaps authenticity) or Hellenism (presumably a later accretion and therefore unhistorical), it took a mammoth scholarly effort to demonstrate the interpenetration of Judaism and Hellenism by the time of the first century CE (a kind of "double helix" of religio-cultural influence), showing that the whole method was a nonstarter. Dividing things into apparently mutually exclusive categories (e.g., wisdom and apocalypticism or particularism and universalism) is what we Westerners do best, and when that happens, research is often stymied for a long period of time. Later, on the basis of further research, we discover that wisdom and apocalypticism are indeed compatible or that universalism does not exclude particularism. More on these subjects later.

19. Indeed, biblical studies itself is impossible without an interdisciplinary approach.

20. When I was a doctoral student in Tübingen in the 1980s, my *Doktorvater*, Prof. Dr. Peter Stuhlmacher, taught me many valuable lessons, besides of course the need for a *biblical* theology of the New Testament (a seminal impulse for the writing of the present volume, I gratefully acknowledge). One time, probably sensing that I had gone too far down the rabbit hole with my dissertation research and writing, he spontaneously asked me whether I had seen *Amadeus*. Just that much. No elaboration that *Amadeus* (1984) was a film about Amadeus Mozart that had just come out at the time. This was a pop quiz. When he could see that I clearly had no idea what he was talking about, he scolded me: "*Herr Scott, Theologie ist Sehen, Sehen, Sehen!*" ("Theology is [a matter of] seeing, seeing, seeing!"). What he was saying, I think, is that it is not enough for me to bury myself in the thought world of New Testament and in the overwhelming scholarly literature on the subject; I must also pay careful attention to the modern world all around me, and seek some way of bringing the two into conversation. As I discovered years later, Stuhlmacher was evidently giving me his own variation on a statement that another Tübingen professor of New Testament had made with respect to Theology as a scientific discipline. Cf. Schlatter, "Atheistische Methoden in der Theologie," 142 (emphasis mine): "As members of the university, we are absolutely obliged to engage in careful observation in each of our fields of study, whether they entail seeing that which has happened or is presently happening. That is the end-all for

If asking the right questions is fundamental to scientific investigation, the key to asking the right questions is finding the right perspective(s) from which to conceive them. And questions are always a political act.[21]

---

every endeavor of the university. *Science is, from first to last, seeing, seeing, seeing—and, ad infinitum, seeing* (*Wissenschaft ist erstens Sehen und zweitens Sehen und drittens Sehen und immer und immer wieder Sehen*)." My goal in the present volume is to observe this double sense of "*Sehen, Sehen, Sehen*" in order to be both culturally aware and scientifically grounded.

21. The artwork at the head of each chapter in this volume is meant to evoke the concept of mycelium and network that is constitutive of our biblical theology of the New Testament.

Abbreviations

AB   Anchor Bible

ABD   *Anchor Bible Dictionary*. Edited by D. N. Freedman. 6 vols.
            New York, 1992

ABRL   Anchor Bible Reference Library

AcT   *Acta theologica*

ATP   Deleuze, Gilles, and Félix Guattari. *A Thousand Plateaus: Capitalism
            and Schizophrenia*. Minneapolis, 1987

BCE   before the Common Era

BICS   *Bulletin of the Institute of Classical Studies*

BJS   Brown Judaic Studies

BDAG   Bauer, W., et al. *Greek English Lexicon of the New Testament
            and Other Early Christian Literature*. 3rd ed. Chicago, 1999

BZAW   Beihefte zur Zeitschrift für alttestamentliche Wissenschaft

CBQ   *Catholic Biblical Quarterly*

CBR   *Currents in Biblical Research*

CE   Common Era

CH   *Church History*

CRINT   Compendia rerum iudaicarum ad Novum Testamentum

CurTM   *Currents in Theology and Mission*

D&G	Deleuze and Guattari
EvT	*Evangelische Theologie*
FRLANT	Forschungen zur Religion und Literatur des Alten und Neuen Testaments
GRBS	*Greek, Roman, and Byzantine Studies*
HBT	*Horizons in Biblical Theology*
HSCP	*Harvard Studies in Classical Philology*
HTR	*Harvard Theological Review*
HvTSt	*Hervormde theologiese studies*
JAJ	*Journal of Ancient Judaism*
JBL	*Journal of Biblical Literature*
JETS	*Journal of the Evangelical Theological Society*
JHS	*Journal of Hellenic Studies*
JJS	*Journal of Jewish Studies*
JAJSup	Journal of Ancient Judaism Supplements
JSHJ	*Journal for the Study of the Historical Jesus*
JSJ	*Journal for the Study of Judaism in the Persian, Hellenistic, and Roman Periods*
JSJSup	Journal for the Study of Judaism Supplements
JSNT	*Journal for the Study of the New Testament*
JSNTSup	Journal for the Study of the New Testament Supplements
JSOTSup	Journal for the Study of the Old Testament Supplements
LNTS	Library of New Testament Studies
NovTSup	Novum Testamentum Supplements
NTOA	Novum Testamentum et Orbis Antiquus
NTS	*New Testament Studies*
NTTS	New Testament Tools and Studies
OED	*Oxford English Dictionary*
OGIS	*Orientalis graeci inscriptions selectae*. Edited by W. Dittenberger. 2 vols. Leipzig, 1903–1905
OTE	*Old Testament Essays*

QC	*Qumran Chronicle*
RAr	*Revue archéologique*
RC	Wells, C. Bradford. *Royal Correspondence in the Hellenistic Period: A Study in Greek Epigraphy.* New Haven, 1934
REA	*Revue des études anciennes*
RevQ	*Revue de Qumran*
SBLEJL	Society of Biblical Literature Early Jewish Literature
SBLRBS	Society of Biblical Literature Resources for Biblical Study
SBS	Stuttgarter Bibelstudien
SCI	*Scripta Classica Israelica*
SEG	Supplementum epigraphicum graecum
SJLA	Studies in Judaism in Late Antiquity
SJT	*Scottish Journal of Theology*
SNTSMS	Society for New Testament Studies Monograph Series
STDJ	Studies on the Texts of the Desert of Judah
SVF	*Stoicorum veterum fragmenta.* H. von Arnim. 4 vols. Leipzig, 1903–1924
TANZ	Texte und Arbeiten zum neutestamentlichen Zeitalter
TB	Theologische Bücherei
TSAJ	Texte und Studien zum antiken Judentum
VigChr	*Vigiliae christianae*
VTSup	Vetus Testamentum Supplements
WBC	Word Biblical Commentary
WMANT	Wissenschaftliche Monographien zum Alten und Neuen Testament
WUNT	Wissenschaftliche Untersuchungen zum Neuen Testament
ZAC	*Zeitschrift für Antikes Christentum*
ZNW	*Zeitschrift für die neutestamentliche Wissenschaft und die Kunde der älteren Kirche*
ZPE	*Zeitschrift für Papyrologie und Epigraphik*

INTRODUCTION

How to Construct a Biblical Theology of the New Testament

Introduction

How does one take an assemblage of *ancient* writings and show that they are relevant for *today*? And how do we demonstrate this relevance while remaining faithful to the actual content of those writings themselves?

I have struggled with the answer to these questions for many years. And as it turns out, I am not alone. As we shall see, the discipline of New Testament Theology itself has long been in a quandary on precisely these matters. What is the goal of New Testament Theology—understanding the text in its original meaning or understanding the text in its contemporary meaning? Or could it be both at the same time? In any case, the problem is an enormous one: How do we *bridge* the two-thousand-year gap between the first century CE and today?

Often, the answer to this question has been a twofold hermeneutic. First, understand the text in its original historical and literary contexts. Second, understand the text in our modern context.[1] In the words of the Swabian exegete Johannes Albrecht Bengel (1687–1752), which was the motto of the Nestle Greek New Testament up

---

1. This twofold approach is often associated with Krister Stendahl, who distinguished between the "two tenses" of "meaning"—"'What *did* it mean? And 'What *does* it mean?'"—or between exegesis (the task of description) and hermeneutics (the task of translation). Cf. Stendahl, "Biblical Theology, Contemporary," 418–32; Green, "Scripture and Theology," 32–35; Dinkler, "Beyond the Normative/Descriptive Divide," 127–45. The distinctions between the two tenses of biblical theology can be traced by to the foundational work of Johann Philipp Gabler. Cf. Stuckenbruck, "Gabler," 139–57.

to its twenty-fifth edition: "Apply yourself wholly to the text, and then apply the text wholly to yourself" (*Te totum applica ad textum . . . rem totam applica ad te*). Unfortunately, this leaves open a number of questions, including what "the whole thing" is and how the two horizons of ancient text and modern interpreter are to be bridged. How can New Testament Theology help us to find the normative meaning of the text for today, that is, its relevance in the context of modern readers? Are we on a quest for recondite and obscure knowledge about the distant past? Or can we find a way to let ancient texts speak afresh in our day and time?

The purpose of this book is not to provide a complete New Testament Theology (as if one could be written),[2] but rather to give a methodological introduction to the study of New Testament Theology.[3] Even this more limited objective is daunting, because there is no general agreement on how to construct a New Testament Theology. It's as if someone gave you a box of puzzle pieces but no box top with the picture on it, and told you to put the pieces together in some way. In the process of attempting to assemble the puzzle, you discover that the pieces don't fit together very well into an overall picture, or least you can't seem to find the right combination that will reveal a big picture.

Indeed, no instruction manual accompanies the twenty-seven books of the New Testament, telling us why they were included, how they are arranged, and what procedure we should use to access them. It took me a long time to figure out that the way I was approaching the New Testament was flawed. I was treating it primarily as an *object* of "scientific" investigation. My historical approach to the text meant that I was always encountering the New Testament in a way that created distance between those ancient texts and its modern readers.[4] That meant that I was always

2. There are plenty of thick books and even multi-volume works on New Testament Theology. As we shall see, however, a biblical theology of the New Testament in our sense of the term could never be completed, since the whole New Testament assemblage itself undergoes continuing transformation. That means, then, that New Testament Theology must likewise undergo continual revision. Of course, the other issue that we face is that "covering" too much material would threaten cognitive overload. A short, methodological introduction with plenty of illustrations, ancient and modern, will enable readers themselves to become involved in the theory and praxis of New Testament Theology (i.e., the aforementioned continual transformation of the New Testament assemblage). In short, what we are trying to supply here is not a pre-traced destiny, but rather more like a map, which encourages exploration in various directions, fosters connections between fields, and concentrates on *performance* and openness to the unknown. Our cartographic approach seeks to foster lines of flight in thinking— thought movements that will creatively evolve in connection with the lines of flight of other thought-movements, producing new ways of thinking rather than territorializing into the recognizable grooves of what passes for theological thought. Interpretations trace already established patterns of meaning; maps pursue connections or lines of flight not readily perceptible to the majoritarian subjects of dominant reality. *The Jesus Revolution* is such a map, hoping to elicit further maps.

3. The present volume stands in the tradition of other similar methodological introductions to "New Testament Theology." See, for example, Stuhlmacher, *How to Do Biblical Theology*; Dunn, *New Testament Theology: An Introduction*; Via, *What Is New Testament Theology?*; Räisänen, *Beyond New Testament Theology*; Hatina, *New Testament Theology and Its Quest for Relevance*.

4. "Distantiation" is the technical term for this distancing effect—the very opposite of an intimate,

trying to "recover" the historical Jesus or "rediscover" the historical Paul.[5] And the problem was further compounded, however, when I tried to relate that recovered/rediscovered figure to the modern world.

So, over the years, my question became: Is there a way to make the New Testament more directly intimate and personal rather than distant and "objective"? Is there, in other words, a way to avoid the gap between subject and object, text and interpreter? If so, this would help us all relate to the New Testament in a fresh and vital way.

My quest for a new approach to New Testament Theology has not been in vain. I found exactly what I was looking for in the modern philosophical discussion of *revolution*.[6] Today, we are witnessing a renewed interest in the return to (nonviolent) revolution, and the philosophical work of Gilles Deleuze and Félix Guatarri in particular has been instrumental in bringing about a resurgence of interest in this subject.[7] After

---

personal encounter. Modern biblical scholars have thought that "our history" (i.e., our way of reconstructing history) has little or nothing to do with that of the biblical writers, that our world is not their world. For a helpful approach to minimizing historical distance, see Martin Hengel's presidential address to the Society of New Testament Studies in 1993, which was published as "Aufgaben der neutestamentlichen Wissenschaft," 321–57, here 351n83, citing his Old Testament colleague Hartmut Gese: "Historical depth must open the text to the modern person. We probably experience that which is historical as something foreign to us, but if we embrace the historical as something that belongs to us, something that our fathers in the faith testified to and passed on to us, then we are emancipated from our confinement and isolation. Through their inheritance, we become whole people and 'with circumcised hearts and ears,' we avoid the worthless activity of merely looking at ourselves in the mirror. . . ." Along similar lines, as we shall discuss at length below, the agents/personae of a revolutionary/nomadic assemblage constitute the collective, *transhistorical* subject ("We") that connects together the condition/abstract machine and the concrete elements. Hence, our approach effectively eliminates historical distance altogether. See further also in chapter 9. Cf. Bockmuehl, *Seeing the Word*, 87–88. Note, however, that our approach does not eliminate the possibility that biblical texts produced different effects in different times and places. We are not talking here about universal or timeless ideas.

5. The job of the historian, it is claimed, is to *defamiliarize* us from the text. But the question soon becomes: How is it possible to relate to the text from which we have become so estranged?

6. Finding Deleuze and Guatarri was my "aha-moment," a moment of sudden insight or discovery for my years of work on New Testament Theology. I agree with the mathematician Ken Ono about the nature of such aha-moments in the life of the researcher. While on a day hike to Talhulah Falls, outside Atlanta, Georgia, Ono was able to solve one of the hitherto great unsolved problems in mathematics, viz., the divisibility properties of the partition numbers. Here is how he describes that experience: "What is an aha-moment? An aha-moment is something you can't really define; it just happens to you. But the way I think of it is, it's not something that happens to you instantly. It just happens to be the point in time when you realize the fruits of all of your hard work." Cf. Ono, "Nature of a Math 'Eureka!'" On the role of the aha-moment (also known as the Eureka effect) in creativity, see also Lynch, *Internet*, 174–77; Catmull, *Creativity*, 223.

7. It should be emphasized at the outset that I am not subscribing to everything that the philosophy of Deleuze and Guatarri stands for. My approach is very selectively focused on the implications of their work for the modern return to revolution. There may be other aspects of their philosophy that are also interesting or fruitful, but I am not dealing with these at all. Deleuze and Guattari provide us with *concepts* that enable us to think anew about New Testament Theology. As Jeremy Gilbert rightly points out, "The analytical resources offered by Deleuze's work [. . .] might be deployed from a range of political perspectives not necessarily limited to those which would seem to receive some explicit endorsement within it." Cf. Gilbert, "Deleuzian Politics?," 11. One of the major points with which we part company with Deleuze and Guattari is on the issue of transcendence. Their approach is so

the failure of so many recent revolutions (e.g., the Arab Spring,[8] Occupy Wall Street,[9] Hong Kong 2019,[10] the CHOP in Seattle[11]), it may seem incredible that there would be any appetite left for the subject. Nevertheless, the world has suffered so much damage in the last few decades that people are yearning for revolution—a new and better world—that remedies the massive problems we face today.

Here, I believe, New Testament Theology has something to contribute to the discussion of the modern return to revolution, even as the philosophical reflections on the modern return to revolution have something to contribute to our understanding of New Testament Theology. For if we can show that, as the New Testament gives witness, Jesus himself was a revolutionary and that he gave rise to a revolutionary movement that aimed at nothing less than opening up a new world in the here and now and not just in the sweet by and by,[12] then the ongoing relevance of the Jesus revolution can

---

exclusively focused on the "plane of immanence" that they actually disavow the transcendent. For a philosophical critique of this disavowal (i.e., an open system cannot posit being closed to transcendence), see Brassier, "Concrete Rules," 278. For the perspective that theology cannot be done with Deleuze and Guattari precisely because theology is anchored in the transcendent, see Boundas et al., "Encounters with Deleuze," 160–62. We shall have much more to say about Deleuze and Guattari's disavowal of transcendence in due course.

8. The Arab Spring (December 17, 2010–December 2012) was a series of anti-government protests, uprisings, and armed rebellions that spread across much of the Arab world in the early 2010s. It began in response to oppressive regimes and a low standard of living, starting with protests in Tunisia. From Tunisia, the protests then spread to five other countries: Libya, Egypt, Yemen, Syria, and Bahrain, where either the ruler was deposed (e.g., Muammar Gaddafi [Libya] and Hosni Mubarak [Egypt]) or major uprisings and social unrest occurred. A major slogan of the demonstrations in the Arab world was "the people want to bring down the regime." Cf. Sly, "Unfinished Business of the Arab Spring": "Ten years ago, the Arab world erupted in jubilant revolt against its dictatorial regimes. Today, the hopes awakened by the protests have vanished—but the underlying conditions that drove the unrest are as acute as ever." See further the four-part BBC series "My Arab Spring": https://www.bbc.co.uk/programmes/p035w97h/episodes/player.

9. From September 17 to November 15, 2011, Occupy Wall Street (OWS) was a protest movement against economic inequality that began in Zuccotti Park, located in New York City's Wall Street financial district. It gave rise to the wider Occupy movement in the United States and other countries. The OWS slogan, "We are the 99%," refers to income and wealth inequality in the US between the wealthiest 1 percent and the rest of the population. We will discuss OWS in more detail in chapter 5.

10. In 2019, the pro-democracy protests in Hong Kong brought dissenting voices into sharp focus. But the Chinese government introduced a National Security law brought a crackdown on the protests. Filmmaker Kiwi Chow's controversial documentary about the protests, "Revolution of Our Times," was screened at the Cannes Film Festival that year: https://www.youtube.com/watch?v=WbBU1AZS8HA. For an exposé of the situation of Hong Kong artists involved in producing protest art, see Harris and Rushton, "Hong Kong Artists: Should I Stay or Should I Go?"

11. From June 8 to July 1, 2020, the Capitol Hill Organized Protest (CHOP) was an occupation protest and self-declared autonomous zone in the Capitol Hill neighborhood of Seattle that envisioned a world without police. It was established on June 8 by George Floyd protesters who sought to defund the Seattle Police Department budget by 50 percent and to shift funding to community programs and services in historically black communities.

12. What we have heard consistently from modern (evangelical) Christianity is that "another world is coming," whether that means a renewed earth or heaven. But what we have not heard is, more positively, what this alternative world has to do with the present world. Beyond the mere statement

be in dialogue with modern return to revolution. The two can be engaged in a positive feedback loop with one another that is mutually transformative.

In taking this approach to New Testament Theology, I am cognizant that I am applying an *etic* (externally sourced) category to the study of the New Testament rather than *emic* (internally sourced) category.[13] But I am not wrong to apply the return to revolution to the New Testament, because although it may not be Cinderella's own slipper, it still fits remarkably well. Moreover, it allows us to interface with the modern world in an interesting, provocative, and culturally relevant way.[14]

---

of possibility, what is needed is a more constructive theology and practice of this "other world" in the present. I believe we can locate the beginnings of this emphasis on the present world—and not just "pie in the sky when I die"—in the writings of the New Testament, and indeed in the Scriptures in general. In short, we argue that actuality and virtuality coexist according to the New Testament texts. The aim of this book is threefold: (1) to provide a biblical-theological clarification and outline of the transformative strategies that both describe and advance the process of constructing real alternatives to the world as it is presently configured; (2) to do so by focusing on an assemblage of texts drawn from across the New Testament and understood in their literary, historical, and theological contexts; (3) more specifically, this work proposes practical strategies to enhance engagement in this world-changing transformation in the present. Hence, our goal in the New Testament Theology is not merely to interpret ancient texts but to encourage a modern revolution in accordance with its teachings. Our project is ultimately constructive: it aims to be a contribution to the creation of a new and better collective political body. It is explicitly interested in the revolutionary transformation of existing society. Thus the ultimate criterion of success for this book is not that it has simply described something, but that it will have been useful to those engaged in the present revolutionary task of changing the world.

13. Part of the reason for taking this particular approach to New Testament Theology is precisely because we live in a post-Christian era in which it is impossible to gain an audience simply by claiming divine authority. A public intellectual like Edward W. Said is quite explicit on this point. Cf., e.g., Said, *Representation*, 60, here 88–89: "In the secular world—our world, the historical and social world made by human effort—the intellectual has only secular means to work with; revelation and inspiration, while perfectly feasible as modes of understanding in private life, are disasters and even barbaric when put to use by theoretically minded men and women. Indeed, I would go so far as saying that the intellectual must be involved in a lifelong dispute with all the guardians of sacred vision or text, whose depredations are legion and whose heavy hand brooks no disagreement and certainly no diversity. Uncompromising freedom of opinion and expression is the secular intellectual's main bastion: to abandon its defense or to tolerate tamperings with any of its foundations is in effect to betray the intellectual's calling." Said, *Representation*, 120: "The true intellectual is a secular being." Given this state of affairs, it is sometimes wise for the biblical theologian to meet the secular world on common ground. As the theologian Bruce Ashford points out, Augustine (354–430 CE) could write in different modes, depending on his audience. On the one hand, when he was addressing fellow Christ-followers, Augustine was able to speak with the thick, theological discourse of Christian particularity, relying largely on Scripture for his points. On the other hand, when he needed to address the broader culture as a public theologian, the Bishop of Hippo, who was well-read in Greco-Roman philosophy, literature and rhetoric, was equally adept at speaking the thin discourse of translation, using language and nuanced philosophical arguments that were less specifically theological in nature. Cf. Ashford, "Augustine for the Americans."

14. For example, our approach to New Testament Theology as an explication of the Jesus revolution affords us an opportunity to dialogue with other revolutionary movements, both past and present. The purpose of such comparison is not simply interesting but also provocative, insofar as it allows us to interrogate whether—and, if so, the degree to which—the New Testament actually addresses some of the yearnings for a new and better world that have been—and currently are—the basis of revolutionary movements.

Perhaps most importantly, by looking at the New Testament through a very different lens, we can defamiliarize our approach to the New Testament so that we can reconnect with it in a fresh and vital way. Our goal in all this is not to overload readers with information, but rather to get them personally *involved* in the actual process of New Testament Theology as quickly as possible so that they can carry on independently.[15] As will be discussed, we are interested in what the New Testament can *do*, rather than in mere description.

One important caveat: In the following, we need to deal, to a certain limited degree, with unfamiliar philosophical concepts. Philosophy is of course not everyone's cup of tea. There will also be readers who question whether a book on New Testament Theology should be dealing with philosophical concepts at all.[16] Shouldn't we just focus instead on "the pure milk of the Word" (cf. 1 Pet 2:2) and the New Testament's own

15. To say that the biblical-theological side of my project is "theory" and that the world-transformation part is "practice" is to impose categories on the New Testament that are alien to it. Rather, the two sides of my project are intrinsic to the New Testament itself and are inextricable from it. They are not two heterogeneous actions, but rather components constitutive of the transformation espoused in the New Testament. This transformation is something truly revolutionary because it challenges the seeming givenness or inevitability of what we take to be an unchangeable reality. New Testament Theology (i.e., a description of the way we live in our world through theological ideas and concepts) exposes just how reactionary many of our fundamental concepts are, such that most of the time we fail to really think theologically at all, but rather simply soak in the stagnant pond of tried-and-tested ideas and methods. We do not need a New Testament Theology that will reinforce our prejudices; we need one that will enable us to enact the people to come and the world to come, to enter into a transformative process that anticipates the consummation of the ages brought about by God alone. Seen in this light, New Testament Theology goes beyond Deleuze's concept of a revolutionary *desire* that we need to think in ways that productively disrupt common sense and everyday life; we are talking about a revolutionary *anticipation* of what God has in store for humankind and the world. New Testament Theology is not something we apply to life. By thinking differently, we are created anew, no longer accepting ready-made norms and assumptions. We reject "common sense" and who we *are* (our present identity) in order to *become* something else entirely.

16. Our approach to New Testament Theology is unabashedly *political*, despite the fact that the conventional wisdom is that we should not "talk politics." Our whole lives are pervasively affected by politics in the broadest sense of the term. For Deleuze and Guatarri, "politics" is a broad-based term. It is not an expression of the majoritarian people but rather the creation of a "people to come." In this kind of minoritarian politics, life is the power or potential to produce relations, not a set of relations among already distinct entities. All effective politics, at any level of human interaction, is a becoming-minoritarian, not appealing to who we *are* but to what we might *become*. The way we think, speak, desire, and see the world is itself political; it produces relations, effects, and organizes our bodies. Therefore, our use of the term "political" with respect to New Testament Theology cannot be reduced to "empire criticism." Cf. McKnight and Modica, *Jesus Is Lord*, 17: "In brief . . . , empire criticism asks us to listen closer to the sounds of the empire and the sounds of challenging empire at work in the pages of the New Testament. This method has now extended to all books in the New Testament, and not just to Revelation, where it has played a role among scholars for longer than scholars care to count. It asks us to stand up and notice that the message of the gospel was at once spiritual and subversive of empire, that is was both a powerful redemptive message and a cry for liberation. Moreover, the New Testament, if we care to listen, is at times an assault on Caesar and calls Christians to form an entirely different society—one that listens to Jesus as its King and takes its orders not from Caesar or his laws but from Jesus and his moral vision, shaped by a cross that breeds sacrifice and self-denial. It calls us to worship King Jesus and not Caesar. This approach, if right, is breathtaking in its implications."

theological categories?[17] These are legitimate questions, and it's impossible to alleviate all the concerns up front. It should be noted, however, that the New Testament has often been approached philosophically,[18] and such approaches have been illuminating in the past.[19] For the moment, let us simply say, *the proof of the pudding is in the eating.* Therefore, it will not become clear how our approach to New Testament Theology is useful until after we are well into the discussion itself. Until we have a chance to get to that point, readers are urged to exercise patience and restraint. If you can work your way through the first few chapters, you will be glad that you hung in there. From that

17. On the role of philosophy in the construction of biblical theologies, see Collins, "Is a Postmodern Biblical Theology Possible?," 131–61.

18. As we noted in the preface, Deleuze and Guatarri themselves do not use philosophy to interpret any other disciplines, nor do other disciplines interpret philosophy. Instead, they allow disciplines to mesh, transform and overlay each other. This would be a good way to describe how the work of Deleuze and Guattari figures in the present volume. The fact that these philosophers are *French* is completely fortuitous; the present study puts no particular stock in an "academic fraternity with a French accent" (cf. Bockmuehl, *Seeing the Word*, 60).

19. Note that the most influential New Testament Theology, by Rudolf Bultmann, was built in part on the existentialist philosophy of Martin Heidegger. Cf. Longenecker and Parsons, *Beyond Bultmann*, 84–85, 103–6, 108, 116, 124–25, 134, 137, 139, 175–76, 235–37, 258; Baasland, *Theologie und Methode*, 58, 77–79, 81–83 et passim; Macquarrie, *Existentialist Theology*; Dreyfus and Wrathall, *Companion to Heidegger*, 23, 25. We shall return to this matter at a later point, but Bultmann was concerned to make his New Testament Theology relevant to modern humankind. While our approach to the New Testament Theology is also motivated by a quest for modern relevance, it could not be more different from Bultmann's methodology. To mention just one example, Bultmann's existentialist approach focuses on the individual as divorced from universal history, whereas our revolutionary approach is inherently communal in orientation and universal in scope. Another approach to the New Testament that has been extremely influential is the use of Hegelian dialectic by the theologian Ferdinand Christian Baur (1792–1860). See further in chapter 3. Lest someone think that the Christian church has formulated its most fundamental theological concepts without philosophical reflection, let us recall, for example, that the Nicene Creed, which speaks of Christ as being "of one substance" with the Father, was the result of trying to come to terms with the biblical witness as it existed in a predominantly Greek matrix. Cf., e.g., Beatrice, "*Homoousios*,'" 243–72. Moreover, Christian Platonism has been a very prominent approach to understanding the New Testament. The beginnings of an interweaving of Platonism with Christian thought go back to Clement of Alexandria and Origen. Augustine of Hippo was radically influenced by Platonic doctrines. And the list of theologians and philosophical influences could go on. The discussion of the New Testament and philosophy really needs to begin with early Judaism. For Judaism was viewed as a philosophy already from the mid-second century BCE (e.g., the Jewish philosopher Aristobulus, cited in Eusebius, *Praep. ev.* 13.12: "All philosophers agree that it is necessary to hold devout convictions about God, something which *our school* prescribes particularly well") and through the first century CE (e.g., Philo, *Embassy to Gaius* 245; *Mos.* 2.216; *Somn.* 2.127; Josephus, *Ag. Ap.* 1.54; 2.47). Cf. Collins, *Invention of Judaism*, 8–10. Many types of Judaism in the Second Temple period employed Greek philosophical concepts, and this was made possible—and perhaps necessary—by the fact that many of the Greco-Roman philosophical schools (especially Stoicism and Middle Platonism) had a strongly religious character, engaged in various theological debates, and criticized aspects of popular religion. The notion that the Jews were a nation of "philosophers" was common in the Hellenistic period, starting with Theophrastus (372–288/7 BCE). Cf. Stern, *GLAJJ*, I.8–11; also 45–46, 49–51, 94. See Stroumsa, *End of Sacrifice*, 54, who sees the relationship between theology and philosophy as "a turning point of decisive importance that would structure all of Western thinking from Philo to Spinoza, who put a final stop to the identification, or collusion, between philosophy and theology."

point onward, it will be much more appetizing as the ideas themselves continue to expand our taste buds in new ways.

By taking a revolutionary-assemblage approach to New Testament Theology, this is obviously not going to be your typical trudge through the writings of the New Testament, although the exegesis of texts will still play an important role. Nor will our approach be strictly thematic in nature, whether those themes are derived from the categories of systematic theology (e.g., Christology, pneumatology, ecclesiology, eschatology) or from some reductionistic scheme (e.g., reconciliation, covenant, apocalyptic).[20] That kind of approach to New Testament Theology is now superseded by our more comprehensive, integrative, and process-oriented approach. Finally, our approach to New Testament Theology will not devolve into a mere history of early Christianity, in other words, a description of the pure cause-and-effect change over time. Our approach is not only canonical in nature, thus setting some loose textual constraints on the study,[21] but it also entails a particular kind of processive change that entails self-referential self-generation (autopoesis), which usual historiography, with its focus on the chain of cause and effect, does not entertain.[22]

The following chapter is divided into three parts. In the first part, we introduce the reader to some of the problems of New Testament Theology as it is currently practiced and attempt to define the discipline. In the second part, we explore the modern return to revolution. In the final part, we attempt to compare and contrast the modern return to revolution to the New Testament. As we shall see, this comparison of the New Testament to the modern return to revolution holds an important key to understanding the New Testament in *both* its context of generation *and* its ongoing modern relevance.

New Testament Theology in Theory and Practice

What is "New Testament Theology"?[23] At first glance, this question appears to be straightforward. Some might say that New Testament Theology is simply the theological or religious ideas found in the New Testament writings. Others might answer that it is the authoritative repository of "essential" Christian teaching, apart from

20. Cf., similarly, Bockmuehl, *Seeing the Word*, 103–4, 114 ("the attempt to find a single overarching theme of biblical theology"), 115 ("grand unified theories").

21. Note, however, that these so-called "textual constraints" will be severely qualified in the following.

22. This is what Deleuze and Guattari call "reverse causalities." More than a break or zigzag in history, they argue, what is to come already acts upon "what is" before the future can appear, insofar as it acts as a limit or threshold continually being warded off by the past's attempt to preserve itself. But once a new present emerges it is seen to have been on its way the entire time. See the note in chapter 1 "For Those Interested in History."

23. In this section, the work of my colleague Tom Hatina has been particularly helpful in clarifying a number of issues relating to how New Testament Theology has been conceptualized and practiced. Cf. Hatina, *New Testament Theology*.

later doctrinal formulations of the church. Still others might respond that New Testament Theology is the teachings of Jesus—or at least that which is grounded in the teachings of the historical Jesus—such as the kingdom of God. While these kinds of encapsulations have some merit, they are woefully inadequate. In fact, to limit New Testament Theology to the religious content of the corpus we call "the New Testament" is to omit much of what the discipline has sought to accomplish. Since its inception approximately two and a half centuries ago, New Testament Theology has certainly dealt with the "religious" content of the New Testament, but more particularly it has been concerned with *how* the "religious" content is to be identified, understood and interpreted within its own historical context and in the present.[24] The difficulty in defining the discipline of New Testament Theology has revolved around the question of *how* rather than the question of *what*.

The question of *how* New Testament Theology is to be understood and practiced is essentially a hermeneutical one, meaning that it is a product of particular interpretative methods, structures and sets of assumptions that stem from the person who attempts to formulate a New Testament Theology. When we read the New Testament, we do not find a ready-made New Testament Theology contained within it. We find various ingredients that might go into making such a New Testament Theology—biblical language, theological reflection, and faith conviction—but no unified theology per se. New Testament Theologies are books written by modern scholars attempting to make sense of the manifold witnesses to beliefs and practice found in the New Testament. Sometimes, scholars are content merely to describe what they see; at other times, they get involved in the modern actualization of the message(s) that they find in the New Testament. The present volume takes the latter approach.

From what we have already said, New Testament Theologies are going to be very different from one another, giving the impression that the discipline suffers from a methodological crisis.[25] But how could it be otherwise? On the one hand, we are

24. Later, we will problematize the idea that the New Testament should be understood exclusively or even primarily in "religious" terms. As we shall see, the theological and the political are inextricably bound together in the New Testament assemblage.

25. For a trenchant critique of the present state of New Testament Studies, including that of New Testament Theology, see especially Bockmuehl, *Seeing the Word*. The present project resonates substantially with Bockmuehl's assessment, although it will also be necessary in the following pages to differentiate our approach to the New Testament in important ways. I would almost say that the present volume turns out to be the photographic negative of Bockmuehl's book (I unfortunately did not think to consult it until long after completing the initial draft of the book). One of my main concerns, for example, is that, for Bockmuehl, New Testament studies can be unified and salvaged from self-destruction with just a bit more attention to the NT's early effective history (i.e., the "living memory" of its first 150 years) and the coherent synthesis that it can produce. In my view, such an approach is helpful but does not go nearly far enough in rebooting either the discipline in general or New Testament Theology in particular. This supremely challenging endeavor will entail seeing and experiencing how the individual "parts" of the transhistorical assemblage of the Jesus revolution (i.e., the abstract machine, the concrete elements, and the personae) engage each other in a mutually transformative process.

dealing with a collection of ancient texts that are culturally and linguistically alien to our modern culture and that were written over the course of many years to separate communities of faith under a number of specific circumstances in the Mediterranean world. Right there, we have the makings of great diversity just at the level of straight description. Add to that, on the other hand, the fact that New Testament theologians are attempting to write their New Testament Theologies from their own sociocultural location either for fellow scholars or for modern faith communities among the two billion followers of Jesus around the world, and you can readily appreciate how writing a New Testament Theology could become a very complex enterprise with widely divergent results. Hence, we cannot expect a definition of New Testament Theology by genus and species any more than we can find a definition of "species" in biology.[26] In both cases, attempts at rigid categorization have proven completely elusive. There is no one definition of "New Testament Theology" that can subsume all the possible attempts, and there is also no one way that a New Testament Theology can or should be written. This is a matter of scholarly discernment and purpose, although some attempts will clearly be more accurate or true to their subject matter than others.

The definitions of New Testament Theology that have emerged focus mostly on the historical-hermeneutical divide. In other words, some have argued that New Testament Theology is primarily a *historical* enterprise that seeks to understand the "original" meaning of the text, authors or traditions (such as the "historical Jesus") behind them. Others have argued that it is primarily a *hermeneutical* discipline that focuses on the meaning of the text (and/or the traditions behind it) for today. Still others have argued that it is a combination of these, in varying degrees of balance. The present volume comes down firmly in support of this third option.

It is important to point out that whichever approach to constructing New Testament Theology one takes—whether historically or hermeneutically oriented—*the construct is formulated outside of the New Testament and imposed on it.*[27] Here, for example, is the statement of Rudolf Bultmann in his highly influential *Theologie des Neuen Testaments:*[28]

> Because the New Testament is a document of history, and in particular, of the history of religion, its interpretation requires the work of historical investigation, whose methods were developed from the time of the Enlightenment, and which bore fruit in the investigation of early Christianity and the interpretation of the New Testament. Such work can only be carried out from two standpoints, either from that of reconstruction or that of interpretation.

26. This point was raised in the preface.

27. Yet, as we shall see, the frame of the canon is not, as is often claimed, the late and arbitrary imposition of order upon diversity and of conformity upon otherness. To some extent, the two-Testament Scripture's concrete elements (constituent "parts") already cohere with one another by virtue of the abstract machine/condition that independently animates them in the first place.

28. Bultmann, *Theologie des Neuen Testaments*, 600. See further Longenecker and Parsons, *Beyond Bultmann.*

> Reconstruction is concerned with past history, interpretation with the writ-
> ings of the New Testament; and clearly, one cannot be done without the
> other. They always work mutually together. But the important question is
> which of the two is the servant of the other. Either the writings of the New
> Testament can be treated as "sources" which the historian uses in order to
> reconstruct early Christianity as a phenomenon of the historical past, or the
> reconstruction serves the need of the interpretation of the New Testament
> writings, on the assumption that these writings have something to say to the
> present. The historical investigation involved in the picture that is presented
> here is put at the service of the latter view.

Bultmann presents two alternatives: either the biblical texts are used as "sources" for
the reconstruction of beliefs (early Christianity) as a phenomenon of the historical
past, or the reconstruction serves the need of the interpretation of the biblical texts on
the assumption that they have something to say to the present.[29] As we shall see, the
reality is more complex than this, but the alternatives are a useful starting point for
reflection upon the genre of New Testament Theologies and their purposes.

New Testament Theology in its modern form is an innovation of Protestant,
mainly Lutheran, German scholarship of the nineteenth century. It owed its rise to
the emancipation of biblical studies from subservience to dogmatic and systematic
theology, an emancipation that happened gradually from the time of the Reformation and which accelerated in the seventeenth and eighteenth centuries. Basically, this
involved a recognition that the worldview of the New Testament writers differed so
fundamentally from those of Enlightenment Europe that it was no longer possible for
the New Testament to support uncritically the use that had traditionally been made of
it in dogmatic and systematic theology.

The effect of all this on the writing of New Testament Theologies has been a
strong affirmation of the first alternative of Bultmann's dichotomy: that the biblical
texts should be used as sources for the reconstruction of religious beliefs of the past.
A major problem with this approach is that reconstructions of the past based on the
writings of the New Testament vary widely from each other. The ever-changing reconstructions of early Christianity leads to a sense of uncertainty. These shifting sands are
hardly the basis for modern relevance of the texts.[30]

29. In a similar way, Rogerson, *Theology of the Old Testament* is motivated by a strong concern for
trying to find a way of using the resources of historical criticism "in the service of the interpretation of
Old Testament texts, on the assumption that they have something to say to the present" (12).

30. Many theologians have not been keen about the quest for the so-called "historical Jesus," precisely because it has led to great uncertainty and indeed doubt about the historical reliability of the
Gospels. Karl Barth and Paul Tillich disagreed about much, but they concurred that theology should
pursue its appointed tasks without undue interference from Jesus scholars, such as Reimarus, Strauss,
and Schweitzer. From this perspective, to insist on the theological pertinence of modern assertions
about the historical Jesus is to make a sort of category mistake. How could proclamation of the gospel
or our ultimate concern ever rest securely on the provisional judgments of historical research? How
one can or whether one should build theologically upon an ever-changing body of diverse opinion is

However, solving the problem by affirming Bultmann's second alternative—that the reconstruction should serve the interpretation of biblical texts in today's world—is not without its challenges, either. How is this to be done? The "ugly ditch" that supposedly separates the world of the Bible from our world(s) cannot be bridged by simply concentrating on the necessary part played by modern interpreters and interpretations in bringing biblical texts to expression. We are still missing *the bridge itself* between the world of the text and the world of the modern interpreter. However hard scholars may strive for objectivity, however hard they may try not to read their own interests and assumptions into the way they organize their work, they will not be able to avoid the fact that they are situated in times and circumstances that inescapably affect and shape what they do. Some scholars openly acknowledge that their agenda in writing a New Testament Theology is set by their own concerns and interests. In other words, the agenda is set subjectively, not by themes drawn directly from the New Testament, but from the authors' intellectual predilections and their reflections on the plight of humanity living in today's world(s). They assume, with Bultmann, that the New Testament has something to say to today's world. This does not mean that the New Testament will be interpreted as though there were no such thing as biblical scholarship. Yet, the agenda is set by the scholars' perception of human conditions in today's world(s).

In my view, the exclusively historical and hermeneutical approaches to New Testament Theology present us with a false dichotomy. Although, as we shall see, understanding the New Testament in light of the aforementioned modern return to revolution does impose an outside construct on the New Testament, once we take this approach, the return to revolution becomes a hermeneutical key that illuminates the New Testament assemblage in important new ways, and all aspects of that assemblage are immanent and internal to it. In other words, the ancient text and the modern interpretive community are now *inside* the event and integral to it. No bridge is necessary. Let me explain further what I mean.

Those who look behind the New Testament to find the historical Jesus as the basis for revelation, and thus the locus which binds past and present meaning, can be placed within the historical approach to the discipline. Most historical Jesus scholars use historical criticism to peel back the early Christian interpretations to reconstruct the teachings, deeds and self-identity of Jesus. Once the rigorous historical program is exhausted and a confident (supposedly "objective" and not

---

perhaps far from manifest. We shall argue, however, that change is part and parcel of the whole New Testament enterprise—and necessarily so. If the discourse of New Testament scholars is Heraclitean in that everything keeps changing, that is in part because the New Testament assemblage itself is open-ended with respect to the dynamic relationship between its three components (i.e., condition/abstract machine, concrete elements, and agents/personae). There can be no "assured critical results." Moreover, we affirm that Jesus is indeed foundational to the construction of a New Testament Theology. Therefore, engagement with the Gospels and with scholarship on the Gospels and the "historical Jesus" is unavoidable, however much one would wish for firmer ground on which to build theologically.

theologically influenced) reconstruction of the so-called "facts" is established,[31] the hermeneutical potential of the reconstruction is considered. The New Testament primarily serves as the gateway to authority, rather than as an authoritative interpretation per se. The reconstructed Jesus becomes the ultimate authority for theology and thus the connector bridging past and present.

We see things somewhat differently. It is our contention that engagement with the Jesus of history does indeed enable a renewed dialogue with our world today, but the process is different. We are not suggesting a simplistic leap from the "historical Jesus" to the Jesus of faith today. Instead, we shall see how the two are already inextricably intertwined within the assemblage. *No "bridge" or "connector" is necessary.*[32] Moreover, we reject the notion that objectivity is possible with respect to the subject matter by means of historical distance and disinterested scholarly neutrality. The community of

31. Note how Dale C. Allison challenges the way Jesus scholars usually conceive of their enterprise by showing that they, no less than those who are more overtly theological in orientation, are motivated by theological considerations in their reconstructions of the "historical Jesus." Cf. Allison, *Historical Christ and the Theological Jesus.*

32. In other words, the exclusively historical approach to the discipline of New Testament Theology is oriented toward recapturing something that has been lost, such as a lost "historical Jesus" of Galilee or a lost "Paul the apostle." What the quests for the lost "historical Jesus" and the lost "Paul" have in common is the Enlightenment assumption that the world is divided up into autonomous "subjects" (biblical scholars) and their "objects" of inquiry (the New Testament writings). As we shall see, our approach to New Testament Theology as assemblage breaks down the subject-object dichotomy: there are no outside interpreters per se, but rather internal agents in the ongoing process of transformation of the assemblage. Markus Bockmuehl's *Seeing the Word* has a similar burden. Of course, an approach that seeks to break down subject-object dualism begs the question of whether it is necessary to be a part of the transhistorical community of faith in order to be an "inside" interpreter and what it might mean to be "inside" in this sense. Bockmuehl seems to limit proper interpretation to the community of faith (e.g., *Seeing the Word*, 70 [author's emphasis]: "the implied reader [of the New Testament] has undergone a religious, moral, and intellectual *conversion* to the gospel of which the documents speak"; 75: "there are limits to how much you can usefully say about the stained glass windows of King's College Chapel [Cambridge] without actually going to see them from the inside"; 79 [author's emphasis]: "The gospel . . . stresses the need for a Christ-shaped *transformation* of our minds if we are to discern and embrace the will of God [Rom. 12:1–2; Eph. 4:17–24]"; 92: "It is here that transformed reason and Spirit-given, Christ-centered wisdom are *essential* to the Christian interpreter's task" [emphasis mine]), although he also acknowledges and encourages other kinds of interpreters (e.g., *Seeing the Word*, 21 ["interpreters of all stripes"], 24, 64 ["a newly conceived task of studying the New Testament, both for those who may approach it from a deliberately Christian theological perspective and for those who do not"], 73, 231–32) in "a common or public endeavor" (62) about "public truth" (59) "for a 'joined-up' approach to New Testament study to operate on a rather larger canvas than we have been used to, whether we claim to operate from a position of Christian faith, of another faith, or of no faith at all" (90). My own approach to this issue would suggest that the ideal situation is to be "inside" the transhistorical assemblage of the Jesus revolution, where understanding of Jesus and his effects (both the NT writings themselves and their effective history) are a mutually reinforcing, communal activity that is irreducible to a single interpreting community delimited by identity politics. Yet, because the Jesus revolution entails *comprehensive* transformation, other readers can and should be encouraged to come alongside, in ad hoc ways, in accordance with their own interests and/or positively oriented, transformative agendas. Given the present state of our world, cooperation is not only desirable but urgently needed.

the New Testament assemblage is integrally involved in both the production of meaning and the transmission of the New Testament texts themselves.

New Testament Theology: A New Approach to Its Theory and Practice

In order to present a new approach to the theory and practice of New Testament Theology, and particularly one that overcomes the shortcomings of both the exclusively historical and the hermeneutically oriented approaches to the discipline, we must introduce the important philosophical concept of the assemblage as propounded by Gilles Deleuze and Félix Guattari. This concept will open up new vistas on how the various moving parts of the assemblage of the New Testament interact with each other and enable a relatively coherent New Testament Theology.

Assemblages

Earlier, we pointed out that whatever approach to constructing a New Testament Theology one takes—whether historically or hermeneutically oriented or both—*the construct is formulated outside of the New Testament and imposed on it*. We now want to return to this issue and elaborate on it by introducing a key term in our discussion of New Testament Theology—"assemblages."[33] An assemblage is a category imposed from the outside on the material we are considering. This category is not derived

---

33. For a brief overview of the concept of "assemblages," see Colebrook, *Understanding Deleuze*, xx: "All life is a process of connection and interaction. Any body or thing is the outcome of a process of connections. A human body is an assemblage of genetic material, ideas, powers of acting and a relation to other bodies. A tribe is an assemblage of bodies. Deleuze and Guattari refer to 'machinic' assemblages, rather than organisms or mechanisms, in order to get away from the idea that wholes pre-exist connections. . . . There is no finality, end or order that would govern the assemblage as a whole; the law of any assemblage is created from its connections. (So the political State, for example, does not create social order and individual identities; the State is the effect of the assembling of bodies. There is no evolutionary idea or goal of the human which governs the genetic production of human bodies; the human is the effect of a series of assemblages: genetic, social and historical.)" See further Nail, "What Is an Assemblage?," 21–37; Posteraro, "Assemblage Theory," esp. 404–16. Applied to certain kinds of biological organisms, assemblage theory has particularly important implications for our developing Biblical Theology of the New Testament. Cf. Posteraro, "Assemblage Theory," 425–26: "The idea of an abstract pattern of relations incarnated in particular host-microbe consortia recalls Deleuze and Guattari's position that every concrete animal assemblage realises an abstract machine that maps a set of relations without specifying how and by what means it is to be materialized. The holobiont might be understood as an assemblage, that is, a coordination among various parts sourced from elsewhere, acquired vertically, by heredity, and horizontally, through its symbiotic associations. The holobiont, as an assemblage, is the incarnation of an abstract machine, which is to say that it is structured on the basis of an abstract diagram that outlines possible parts and the functions that would enlist them. Modelled this way, the organism as assemblage anticipates the holobiont, and the abstract machine on whose basis the assemblage is effectuated and concretised anticipates, at least in part, the turn from the genome to the hologenome as well."

from or even intrinsic to the subject matter itself. Someone calls something an assemblage for a specific purpose.

At first, it may seem that imposing extrinsic categories on the New Testament is a bad thing because it can distort our vision of what is actually in those writings. This is the way that I was taught to think about etic categories as applied to the New Testament. In more recent years, however, I began to realize that practically all our thinking about the New Testament is based in one way or another on extrinsic or heuristic categories.

For example, take the terms "apocalypse," "apocalyptic," and "apocalypticism." These are common terms in biblical studies, but hardly anyone realizes that, although they obviously have Greek roots, the way they are used to explore the New Testament is not derived from the New Testament itself (or even from early Jewish literature!) but rather from the workshop of modern scholars who wanted to investigate the New Testament (and similar literature). The terms derive from the Greek word for "revelation" (*apokalypse*), and indeed the literature that scholars wanted to study put an emphasis on divine revelation.[34] Once the term was used, however, it came to be applied to many other phenomena which were not directly related to divine revelation (e.g., those writings that had a similar worldview to that found commonly in apocalypses). Using these categories has allowed scholars to group texts in a way that facilitates making observations about their shared characteristics. We should not be confused, however, that the ancients had our categories in mind when they wrote these texts. Indeed, there is growing concern among scholars that "apocalyptic" has closed our minds to other ways that texts share characteristics (e.g., the "wisdom" features that are often also in play in these same texts). In any case, scholars continue to devise etic categories that will help them analyze texts from various perspectives. It's like going to the optometrist and letting him or her try out different lenses in order to improve your vision. Sometimes the optometrist must try many different combinations of lenses before we can clearly read the fine print at the bottom of the eye chart.

In a word, scholars have used assemblages to construct categories that help them investigate phenomena. These are generative models. The concept of "assemblage" plays a crucial role in the philosophy of Deleuze and Guattari.[35] The term in English refers to a gathering of things together into unities,[36] whereas the French original

---

34. The generic use of the term "apocalypse" is based on the very beginning of the book of Revelation: "The revelation (*apokalypsis*) of Jesus Christ, which God gave him to show his servants what must soon take place" (Rev 1:1). Scholars noticed that there were other Jewish and Christian revelatory texts that were similar to the Apocalypse of John. See further in chapter 9.

35. The following discussion of "assemblages" is particularly indebted to the work of Thomas Nail. Cf., e.g., his "What Is an Assemblage?," 21–37.

36. Cf. *OED*, s.v., "assemblage": (1) A bringing or coming together; a meeting or gathering; the state of being gathered or collected; (1) The joining or union of two things; conjunction; (3) A number of persons gathered together; a gathering, concourse; (4) A number of things gathered together; a collection, a group, cluster.

(*agencement*) on which the English translation is based denotes an arrangement or layout of heterogenous elements.[37] There are at least two major philosophical consequences of this distinction that Deleuze and Guattari use to develop their general logic of assemblages: the rejection of *unity* in favor of *multiplicity*, and the rejection of *essence* in favor of *events* or *processes*.

The first major philosophical consequence of inventing a "general logic of assemblages" for Deleuze and Guattari is that it provides an alternative logic to that of *unities*. A unity is defined by the *intrinsic* relations that various parts have to one another in a whole. A unity is an organic whole whose parts all work together like the organs of the human body. Each organ performs a function in the service of reproducing its relations with the other parts and ultimately the harmony of the whole organism. A heart separated from a body does not survive as a "heart," since the function of a heart is to circulate blood through a body. By the same token, the organism does not survive without a heart, since it is the nature of the organism to have a heart. The unity of an organic whole is given in advance of the emergence of the parts and subordinates the parts to an organizing principle.

In contrast to organic unities, for Deleuze and Guattari, assemblages are more like machines, defined solely by their external relations of composition, mixture, and aggregation.[38] In other words, an assemblage is a *multiplicity*, neither a part nor a whole.

37. This is a possible meaning of the English term *assemblage* as well. Cf., e.g., Young, *Travels in France*, 13 (emphasis mine), referring to Young's initial perception of the palace of Versailles: "I view it without emotion; the impression it makes is nothing. What can compensate the *want of unity*? From whatever point viewed, it appears an *assemblage of buildings. . . .*"

38. The human body is an assemblage of 59 elements, of which carbon, oxygen, hydrogen, nitrogen, calcium, and phosphorous account for 99.1 percent, but trace amounts of other elements are also essential (e.g., molybdenum, manganese, tin, copper, cobalt, chromium, potassium, thorium, zirconium, niobium, samarium, selenium). Cf. Bryson, *Body*, ch. 1: "How to Build a Human." As Bryson remarks, "That is unquestionably the most astounding thing about us—that we are just a collection of inert components, the same stuff you would find in a pile of dirt." The situation is arguably even more complex: A human being is actually an assemblage of nested assemblages. In other words, to paraphrase the well-known expression of infinite regress ("It's turtles all the way down"), it's assemblages all the way down. Cf. Sheldrake, *Entangled Life*, 16–17: "For humans, identifying where one individual stops and another starts is not generally something we think about. It is usually taken for granted—within modern industrial societies, at least—that we start where our bodies begin and stop where our bodies end. Developments in modern medicine, such as organ transplants, worry these distinctions; developments in the microbial sciences shake them at their foundations. We are ecosystems, composed of—and decomposed by—an ecology of microbes, the significance of which is only now coming to light. The forty-odd trillion microbes that live in and on our bodies allow us to digest food and produce key minerals that nourish us. They guide the development of our bodies and immune systems and influence our behavior. If not kept in check, they can cause illnesses and even kill us. We are not a special case. Even bacteria have viruses within them (a nanobiome?). Even viruses can contain smaller viruses (a picobiome?). Symbiosis is a ubiquitous feature of life." Sheldrake (*Entangled Life*, 17–18) goes on to problematize the concept of the "individual," arguing that "'We' are ecosystems that span boundaries and transgress categories. Our selves emerge from a complex tangle of relationships only now becoming known." On the concept of what we are calling here nested assemblages of living organisms, see the discussion of "endosymbiosis" in *Entangled Life*, 80–82. See also *Entangled Life*, 88: "Lichens are places where an organism unravels into an ecosystem and where

If the elements of an assemblage are defined only by their external relations, then it is possible that they can be added to, subtracted from, and recombined with one another ad infinitum without ever creating or destroying an organic unity. The elements of the assemblage are like a "dry-stone wall, and everything holds together only along diverging lines."[39] Each new mixture produces a new kind of assemblage, always free to recombine again and change its nature. Thus, as Deleuze says, "in a multiplicity, what counts are not the terms or the elements, but what is 'between' them, the in-between, a set of relations that are inseparable from each other." The assemblage constructs or lays out a set of relations between self-subsisting fragments.

The second major philosophical consequence of the theory of assemblages is that it provides an alternative to the logic of *essences*. The essence of a thing is what uniquely and necessarily defines it—in other words, what it is about a thing that makes it what it is such that it is not something else, which endures despite all its unessential aspects. The problem with this sort of question is that the answer requires

---

an ecosystem congeals into an organism. They flicker between 'wholes' and 'collections of parts.' Shuttling between the two perspectives is a confusing experience. The word *individual* comes from the Latin meaning 'undividable.' Is the whole lichen the individual? Or are its constituent members, the parts, the individuals? Is this even the right question to ask? Lichens are a product less of their parts than of the exchanges between those parts. Lichens are stabilized networks of relationships; they never stop lichenizing; they are verbs as well as nouns." Sheldrake, *Entangled Life*, 90: "Lichens are dynamic *systems* rather than a catalogue of interacting components." *Entangled Life*, 91: "[Toby] Spribille describes lichens as the most 'extraverted' of all symbioses. Yet it is no longer possible to conceive of any organism—humans included—as distinct from the microbial communities they share a body with. The biological identity of most organisms can't be pried apart from the life of their microbial symbionts. The word *ecology* has its roots in the Greek word *oikos*, meaning 'house,' 'household,' or 'dwelling place.' Our bodies, like those of all other organisms, are dwelling places. Life is nested all the way down." *Entangled Life*, 92: "Some researchers use the term 'holobiont' to refer to an assemblage of different organisms that behaves as a unit. The word *holobiont* derives from the Greek word *holos*, which means 'whole.' Holobionts are the lichens of the world, more than the sums of their parts. Like symbiosis and ecology, holobiont is a word that does useful work. If we only have words that describe neatly bounded autonomous individuals, it is easy to think that they actually exist. The holobiont is not a utopian concept. Collaboration is always a blend of competition and cooperation. There are many instances where the interests of all the symbionts don't align. A bacterial species in our gut can make up a key part of our digestive system but cause a deadly infection if it gets into our blood. We're used to this idea. A family can function as a family, a touring jazz group can give a captivating performance, and both still be fraught with tension. Perhaps it isn't so hard for us to relate to lichens after all. This sort of relationship-building enacts one of the oldest evolutionary maxims. If the word *cyborg*—short for 'cybernetic organism'—describes the fusion between a living organism and a piece of technology, then we, like all other life-forms are symborgs, or symbiotic organisms. The authors of a seminal paper on the symbiotic view of life take a clear stance on this point. 'There have never been individuals,' they declare. 'We are all lichens.'" The quotations are from Gilbert et al., "Symbiotic View of Life," 336. For an attempt to define lichens, see Goward, "Twelve Readings on the Lichen Thallus V," 31–37: "The enduring physical byproduct of lichenization," that is, "the biological process whereby a *nonlinear system* comprising an unspecified number of fungal, algal and bacterial taxa give rise to a *thallus* [the shared body of the lichen] viewed as an emergent property of its constituent parts." See further Posteraro, "Assemblage Theory," 402–32.

39. Deleuze and Guattari, *What Is Philosophy?*, 23.

us to already assume the finished product of what we are inquiring into.[40] Assuming the thing to be the complete product, we simply identify the enduring features of its history and retroactively posit them as those unchanging and eternal features that by necessity must have preexisted the thing.

In contrast to this, Deleuze and Guattari do not ask, "What is . . . ?" but rather, how? where? when? from what viewpoint? and so on. These are not questions of essence, but questions of *events* or *processes*. An assemblage does not have an essence because it has no eternally necessary defining features, only contingent and singular features. In other words, if we want to know what something is, we cannot presume that what we see is the final product nor that this product is somehow independent of the network of social and historical processes to which it is connected. For example, we cannot extract the being of a book from the vast historical conditions of the invention of an alphabetic language, distribution of paper, the printing press, literacy, and all the social contingencies that made possible the specific book of our inquiry, with all of its singular features (color, lighting, time of day, and so on) and all the conditions under which someone is inquiring into the book. A vast network of processes continues to shape the book and thus there is no final product. We do not know what the book might possibly become or what relations it may enter into, so we do not yet know its universal or essential features. We know only its collection of contingent features at a certain point in its incomplete process.

An assemblage is not just a mixture of heterogenous elements; this definition is far too simplistic. The definition of the French word *agencement* does not simply entail heterogenous composition, but entails a constructive process that lays out a specific kind of arrangement. All assemblages may be singular and heterogenous but they also share three features that define their arrangement: their *conditions*, their *elements*, and their *agents* (or what Deleuze and Guattari call their "abstract machine," their "concrete assemblage," and their "personae," respectively). An assemblage is a conjunction of a number of persons, forces and circumstances capable of its own collective experiences and actions.[41]

40. This is precisely the problem that we will observe with respect to essentialist definitions of "Judaism."

41. We are nervous about the mechanical (or "machinic") nature of Deleuze and Guatarri's concept of an assemblage. Lichens may provide a more robust analogy for what we are trying to describe. Cf. Sheldrake, *Entangled Life*, 89–90, citing the lichen specialist Toby Spribille: "Spribille's findings [about varying numbers of partners—and not just the traditional two (fungal and algal)—within any particular lichen] are troubling for some researchers because they suggest that the lichen symbiosis is not as 'locked in' as it has been thought to be. 'Some people think about symbiosis as being like a package from IKEA,' Spribille explained, 'with clearly identified parts, and functions, and order in which it's assembled.' His findings suggest instead that a broad range of different players might be able to form a lichen, and that they just need to 'tickle each other in the right way.' It's less about the identity of the 'singers' in the lichen, and more about what they do—the metabolic 'song' that each of them sings. In this view, lichens are dynamic *systems* rather than a catalogue of interacting components. It's a very different picture from the dual hypothesis. Since [Simon] Schwendener's portrayal of the fungus and alga as master and slave, biologists have argued about which of the two

The first feature shared by all assemblages is that they all have *conditions*. The condition of an assemblage is the network of specific external relations that holds the elements together. Deleuze and Guattari's name for this set of conditioning relations is the "*abstract machine.*" The condition is "abstract" in the sense that it lays out a set of extrinsic relations in which concrete elements and agents appear according to processes of stratification and destratification. The condition is a "machine" insofar as it binds heterogeneous parts into a functional whole (rather than an organic unity).

Different assemblages are defined by different sets of relations; thus there are also different types of abstract machines that arrange their elements in one way or another. In every case, the abstract machine functions as a kind of local condition of possibility—a set of relations in which elements appear to be meaningfully related. It is in this sense that Deleuze and Guattari state that the abstract machine is that "which at every instant causes the given to be given, in this or that state, at this or that moment. But . . . itself is not given."[42]

The abstract machine is *designated by a proper name* (e.g., American Revolution, Angela Merkel, Albert Einstein) because, as a proper noun, it refers to a unique set of relations as opposed to common nouns, which refer to essentialist categories of things (e.g., revolutions, statespersons, scientists).[43] Concrete elements and agents speak through this proper name and use it to attribute their similarities and differences from each other. In this sense, the abstract machine does not "signify" or "represent" anything beyond the arrangement of concrete elements. Occurring only once, an abstract machine is thus an asignifying proper name like the names of military operations (e.g., Operation Desert Storm in 1991) or the names of hurricanes (e.g., Hurricane Katrina in 2005).[44]

---

partners is in control of the other. But now a duet has become a trio, the trio has become quartet, and the quartet sounds more like a choir. Spribille seems unperturbed by the fact that it isn't possible to provide a single, stable definition of what a lichen actually is. It is a point [Trevor] Goward often returns to, relishing the absurdity: 'There's an entire discipline that you can't define what it is that they study?'" Scientists are still trying to figure out what ties the whole lichen system together to get it to form something other than a blob on a dish, but it is theorized that some of the bacteria of which lichen are jam-packed might hold the answer.

42. Deleuze and Guattari, *ATP*, 265.

43. Cf. Lorraine, "Plateau," 208–9: "An abstract machine 'places variables of content and expression in continuity' (D&G 1987: 511). It (for example, the Galileo abstract machine) emerges when variables of actions and passions (the telescope, the movement of a pendulum, the desire to understand) are put into continuous variation with incorporeal events of sense (Aristotelian mechanics and cosmology, Copernican heliocentrism), creating effects that reverberate throughout the social field (D&G 1987: cf. 511). [. . .] An assemblage that multiplies connections approaches the 'living abstract machine' (D&G 1987: 513)."

44. An "asignifying" sign does not represent or refer to an already-constituted dominant reality; rather, it stimulates or pre-produces a reality that is not yet there. See further the journal issue devoted to the subject in Hauptmann and Radman, "Signifying Semiotics." We will return to the subject of "signs" in our discussion of Jesus in chapter 4.

The abstract machine does not cause or program the concrete elements in advance, nor does it give them a normative direction. Rather, the abstract machine supports a "conjunction, combination, and continuum" of all the concrete elements it conditions. Take, for example, a constellation of stars. The constellation Ursa Major does not inhere naturally or essentially in the sky, and it does not cause the stars within the constellation to exist. It is simply the proper name for the set of conditioning relations that arrange a set of stars. Without stars in the sky there are no relations between stars, but without relations between stars there is only radical heterogeneity. In this example, the abstract machine is the relational lines that connect the stars and the concrete assemblage is the stars that are connected. However, since new stars are born and old stars die out and all of them move around in relation to our point of view on Earth, there is no eternal essence of the constellation. The constellation is a singular event: a set of relations that change as the elements change in a kind of reciprocal feedback loop.

The second common feature shared by all assemblages is that they all have *concrete elements*. Just as all assemblages have a set of conditioning relations (an abstract machine), they also have specific elements that are arranged in these relations—what Deleuze and Guattari call the "*concrete assemblage*." The concrete elements of an assemblage are the existing embodiment of the assemblage. They are not abstract; they are the part of the assemblage that appears within the relations of distribution. The concrete assemblages are "like the configurations of a machine" that give it its degrees of consistency. They compose an "abstract machine of which these assemblages are the working parts." Thus the relationship between the abstract relations and the concrete elements is not pre-constructed but has to be constructed piece by piece. One does not transcend the other, but both are mutually transformative. The concrete elements are like a skeletal frame, whereas the conditioning relations are the breath that suffuses the separate parts. In the case of a revolutionary assemblage (to be discussed further below), the concrete elements includes all the actions, weapons, tools, interventions, slogans, demands, and occupations that come together to create a revolutionary sequence.

Since the abstract machine is not an eternal essence or a program given in advance of the concrete elements, when the concrete elements change so does the set of relations that they are in. There is therefore a reciprocal determination between the abstract and the concrete: when one changes, so does the other. As Deleuze and Guattari say, the two are in reciprocal presupposition. This is why the consequences of events cannot be known in advance. There is no essence of the event; there are only concrete elements that are defined by their external relations, i.e., what they are concretely capable of at any given point. If we want to understand how an assemblage works, we do not ask what its essence is, but rather what it can *do* under the circumstances. This is an empirical question. We do not know in advance what a concrete body can do. The answer "can only be resolved step by step." For example, who are the allies and enemies of the assemblage? What are the consequences and implications of this assemblage now? What can the assemblage accomplish and where are its limits in some particular instance? Since the concrete elements are always changing along with their conditioning relations, the assemblage is always becoming capable of different things.[45] This requires a constantly renewed analysis of the assemblage.

The third feature shared by all assemblages is that they all have *agents*, which Deleuze and Guattari call "*personae*." Personae are not autonomous rational subjects, nor are they simply decentered or fragmented subjects incapable of action. Rather, the agents of an assemblage are the mobile operators that connect the concrete elements together according to their abstract relations. In other words, agents do not transcend the assemblage but are immanent to it. Herein lies the difficulty of immanence in the assemblage: one cannot have personae without an assemblage of which they are a part, but one cannot have an assemblage without agents that bring it about. Since the conditions, elements, and agents are all immanent to one another, Deleuze and Guattari argue that all three occur together in mutual presupposition.

For Deleuze and Guattari, personae are not first-person-singular, self-knowing subjects ("I think, therefore I am"); rather, they are first-person-plural collective subjects ("we") of an assemblage to which it is immanent.[46] No one is subject to themselves alone; they are part of a larger first-person-plural assemblage that arranges the conditioning relations and concrete elements in which the world of the agent is meaningful.

An Analogy for Understanding Assemblages

All this abstract philosophical language can be bewildering. Therefore, before proceeding with our application of the concept of assemblages to the biblical canon, we will try to illustrate it with an example. The three elements of an assemblage can be likened to a concept drawn from recent work in forestry ecology: the "Wood-Wide Web" (an assemblage), which includes the "mother tree" (condition/abstract machine), the forest of trees (concrete elements), and the mycorrhizal fungi (agents/personae).[47] The

45. This is particularly true, as we shall see, of a revolutionary assemblage, which is all about transformation.

46. In an assemblage such as a lichen, the lichen—the "we"—truly *is* the *conversation* of which the constituent parts (i.e., the lichen fungus, the lichen algae, and the lichen bacteria) are the participants and the thallus (i.e., the shared body of the lichen) the outward physical manifestation. The name we give to lichen conversation is the *process* of lichenization, and it is here that the lichen truly resides. Cf. Goward, "Twelve Readings on the Lichen Thallus, V," 31–37. Something similar can be said of a human assemblage. Cf. Rich, "Notes Towards a Politics of Location," 217: "The problem was that we did not know whom we meant when we said 'we.'"

47. Note, however, that Sheldrake (*Entangled Life*, 211–15) objects to the use of the term "wood-wide web" as too plant-centered, and he discourages anthropomorphisms such as "mother tree," "community," and "cooperation." Sheldrake emphasizes the agency of the mycorrhizal fungi in regulating their environment as a form of self-preservation. For our purposes, it matters little whether the trees or the fungi set the agenda. The point is that, within the assemblage of the wood-wide web, all

research of Suzanne Simard, professor of forest ecology at the University of British Columbia, and her colleagues shows how heterogenous trees (e.g., Douglas fir and paper-bark birch trees) in a forest organize themselves into far-flung networks, using the underground web of mycorrhizal fungi which connects their roots to exchange information and even goods.[48] This "wood-wide web," as it has been dubbed, allows scores of trees in a forest to convey warnings of insect attacks, and also to deliver carbon, nitrogen, and water to trees in need. The resulting diagram of the forest network

---

the components occur together in mutual presupposition.

48. Cf., e.g., Simard et al., "Mycorrhizal Networks," 39–60. Our metaphorical use of mycorrhizal networks resembles Deleuze and Guattari's concept of the "rhizome," that is, any network of things brought into contact with one another, functioning as an assemblage machine for new affects, new concepts, new bodies, or new thoughts. The rhizome creates and recreates the world through connections. A rhizome has no structure or center, no graph or regulation. Deleuze and Guattari contrast the "rhizome" with an "arborescent structure," which has dominated Western thinking for centuries. Arborescence is a hierarchical, tree-like structure that orders epistemologies and forms historical frames and homogeneous schemata. In our metaphorical use of mycorrhizal fungal networks, tree-like structures are bound together interdependently by the underground network; they are not therefore totally disparate systems (hierarchical vs. horizontal, transcendent model vs. immanent process). Cf. Deleuze and Guattari, *ATP*, 15: "We're tired of trees. We should stop believing in trees, roots, and radicals. They've made us suffer too much. All arborescent culture is founded on them, from biology to linguistics. Nothing is beautiful or loving or political aside from underground stems and aerial roots, adventitious growths and rhizomes." Deleuze and Guattari do not mention physics as part of this "arborescent culture," but they could have done so if they had considered Albert Einstein, whom they barely mention in *ATP* (see merely 484, 501, 511). For Einstein's unrelenting faith in cosmic unity (i.e., that all of nature must be described by a single theory) that led him repeatedly to make *vertical* analogical category leaps from one frame of reference to another to yet another, each time with increasing generalization and abstraction. First, Einstein leaped from a narrow frame of reference (i.e., Galileo's principle of relativity, which applies only to mechanics under conditions of constant velocity) to a more general/abstract/hierarchical frame (i.e., Einstein's principle of special relativity, which applies to both mechanics and electromagnetism, but, again, only under conditions of constant velocity). Second, based on his first analogical leap, he made a meta-analogical leap (i.e., an analogy of an analogy) to an even more generalized principle of relativity (appropriately named "the principle of general relativity"), which subsumed both of the earlier principles of relativity (Galileo's and Einstein's), but the new generalized principle applied to *all frames of reference*, including accelerating frames (i.e., not just constant velocity but also change in velocity and/or change in direction). Clearly, then, Einstein's drive to unify the branches of physics was *arborescent* to the core. Einstein's analogical mode of thinking is thoroughly discussed in Hofstadter and Sander, *Surfaces and Essences*, 452–502, here 468 (emphasis mine): "Einstein's intuition told him that any such distinction [between mechanics and electromagnetism] was unnatural, since, in the end, any conceivable experiment in any conceivable *branch* of physics belongs to *the same unified tree of physics*." It will come as no surprise, then, that after making his earth-shaking discoveries, Einstein spent the next thirty years of his life seeking a unified field theory, the holy grail of his implacable faith in cosmic unity. Hofstadter and Sander refer to Einstein being "spurred on by his certainty that the laws of nature are pervaded by the deepest, most *divine beauty* of all" (*Surfaces and Essences*, 500 [emphasis mine]). This strikes a decisive blow against Deleuze and Guattari's disavowal of transcendence. Nevertheless, Einstein's mental process in formulating his principles of relativity can also be described, without contradiction, as developing in a *horizontal, rhizomatic* way. As Hofstadter and Sander show (*Surfaces and Essences*, 468), "In sum, in this case, as in many others, we see that there is no sharp line of demarcation between vertical category leaps and horizontal category extensions."

resembles an airline route map.[49] In one 30 x 30-meter plot of forest containing sixty-seven trees, the most highly connected tree was linked to forty-seven other trees through its underground network of mycorrhizal fungi.[50] Simard calls this a "mother tree," which uses the network to nourish shaded seedlings, including its own offspring (which can be recognized as kin), until they are tall enough to reach the light on their own.[51] And, in a striking example of interspecies "cooperation" (rather than competition), Simard found that fir trees were using the fungal web to trade nutrients with paper-bark birch trees over the course of the season. The evergreen species will tide over the deciduous one when it has sugars to spare, and then call in the debt later in the season. For the forest community, the value of this mutualistic underground economy appears to be better overall health, more total photosynthesis, and greater resilience in the face of common threats. In short, these trees are able to create scalable networks of self-maintaining, self-operating, and self-repairing units. Networked, decentralized, modular, reiterated, redundant, and green, trees are models of the kind of community (assemblage) that humans can definitely learn from.

If we think of the "wood-wide web" as the assemblage of heterogenous concrete elements (the various species trees in a forest), then the relationship between them is regulated by the highly connected "mother tree" (the condition/abstract machine) and the infinitely expandable, underground network of mycorrhizal fungi (the agents/personae), which exhibits a rhizomatic structure of collective subjectivity.[52]

Network theory has also been applied to what has been termed "the Greek Wide Web," the web of countless historical relationships between people, places, and cultural practices that led to the emergence of ancient Greek civilization.[53] This concept, although still under development, has potentially significant implications

49. Cf. Simard et al., "Mycorrhizal Networks," 51 (fig. 5).

50. Simard et al., "Mycorrhizal Networks," 51. Cf. Deleuze and Guatarri, *ATP*, 513: An assemblage that multiplies connections approaches the "living abstract machine."

51. For Simard's discussion of "mother trees," see http://www.youtube.com/watch?v=iSGPN m3bFmQ. Simard also has a longer TED Talk on the subject: https://www.ted.com/talks/suzanne_ simard_how_trees_talk_to_each_other?language=mg. See now Simard, *Finding the Mother Tree*.

52. Cf. Sheldrake, *Entangled Life*, 45–69, here 47: "Mycelium is conceptually slippery. From the point of view of the network, mycelium is a single interconnected entity. From the point of view of a hyphal tip, mycelium is a multitude." The *Armillaria ostoyae* (honey mushroom) in Oregon is estimated to be up to approximately 9,000 years old. The mycelial network of an individual *Armillaria ostoyae* in the Malheur National Forest in Oregon composes the world's oldest and largest known organism. In 2003, a single organism of *Armillaria ostoyae* was reported in a mixed-conifer forest in northeast Oregon. This fungus' mycelium was estimated to cover an area of 965 hectare (3.73 sq. mi.), with a maximum width of 3810 m (2.4 mi.), and its age was estimated to be between 1,900 and 8,650 years old (depending on the assumed rate of spread [1.0 m/year or 0.22 m/year, respectively]). Cf. Ferguson et al., "*Armillaria* Species," 612–23; Sheldrake, *Entangled Life*, 3–4, 56, 61–62, 231n4.

53. Cf. Brughmans, "Ancient Greek Networks," 146, 147. This journal article reviews Malkin, *Small Greek World*. For the term "the Greek wide web of identities," see Malkin, "Networks and the Emergence of Greek Identity," 60; cf. also Harder, "Spiders in the Greek Wide Web?," 259–71. For a helpful overview of terms and issues, see Müller, "Globalization, Transnationalism, and the Local in Ancient Greece."

for the study of historical processes that impinge on our assemblage approach to a biblical theology of the New Testament. In particular, network theory, combined with the assemblage approach pursued here, could help to construct a more nuanced and differentiated picture of the historical processes by which the early Jesus movement emerged within Judaism, grew and developed through self-organization, and expanded to other peoples and places via hubs, preferential attachment, decentralization, and clustering. That discussion must, however, remain a desideratum for now, since the present volume already pushes the limits of complexity for an introductory methodological overview.

The Biblical Canon as Assemblage

Seen as an "assemblage," the biblical canon is not a unity per se, but rather a heterogenous multiplicity defined solely by its external relations of composition, mixture, and aggregation. In that case, the elements of the assemblage can be added, subtracted, and recombined with one another without ever creating or destroying an organic unity.[54] In a multiplicity such as the canon, what counts are not the terms or the elements, but what is "between" them, the in-between, a set of relations that are inseparable from each other. As an assemblage, the canon constructs or lays out a set of relations between self-subsisting pieces.

As we have seen, assemblage theory provides an alternative to the logic of essences. As an assemblage, the canon does not have an essence because it has no eternally necessary defining features, only contingent and singular features. In other words, if we want to know what the canon is, we cannot presume that what we see is the final product, nor that this product is somehow independent of the network of social and historical processes to which it is connected.[55] A vast network of processes continues to

54. We do indeed find that various communities of faith have assembled canons of differing extents over the years. On the Dead Sea Scrolls and the canon of the Hebrew Bible/Old Testament, see VanderKam and Flint, *Dead Sea Scrolls*, 154–81. A related question is whether the Dead Sea Scrolls found at Qumran should be seen as a "library," which, of course, depends on the definition of the key term vis-à-vis other potentially applicable terms (e.g., "corpus," "collection," "clusters," "scroll storehouse," or simply "scrolls"). Cf. White Crawford and Wassen, *The Dead Sea Scrolls at Qumran and the Concept of a Library*, which emphasizes that the controversial question of whether or not the corpus of manuscripts unearthed in the Qumran caves constitute a "library" has important ramifications for how those scrolls are understood, the purpose of the settlement at Qumran, the identity of the inhabitants of Qumran, and when and why the scrolls were deposited in the caves (e.g., whether the scrolls represent the "library" of an Essene settlement or rather the depository of writings brought from Jerusalem and representing all of Jewish literature at the time). We would like to suggest that the issue could also be usefully reexamined in light of the "assemblage" theory of Deleuze and Guattari, which would provide a robust and comprehensive theoretical framework for understanding the function of scrolls.

55. Since the discovery of the Dead Sea Scrolls, there has been a "revolution" in our understanding of late ancient Jewish text-production and the development of scripture. Many biblical scholars now regard it as anachronistic to speak of "the (Hebrew) Bible"/"Old Testament"—and, accordingly, of "apocryphal" or non-biblical texts and traditions, and of "rewritten Bible"—during the Second Temple

shape the canon and thus the idea of a "final" product is an illusion.[56] We do not know what the canon might possibly become or what relations it may enter into, so we do not yet know its universal or essential features.[57] We know only its collection of contingent features at a certain point in its incomplete process. For this reason, Luke-Acts ends in Acts 28 with Paul in Rome, but there is no word of what happens next. The two-volume work is purposely left open-ended, because the story that Luke writes is ongoing. In a similar way, the abrupt and rather disturbing ending of Mark's Gospel has the women

---

period, and probably until some point in the Rabbinic or early Christian periods, certainly after the Bar Kokhba revolt (132–135 CE). There was no generally accepted canonical list of scriptural books in the Second Temple period. Moreover, the traditions that would later become the Bible and the Apocrypha did not exhibit textual fixity or canonical fixity. Instead, the situation has been characterized in terms of "pluriformity." This pluriformity characterized the textual situation in general, and no clear boundaries between center (e.g., Jerusalem) and periphery (e.g., Qumran) may be demarcated. This pluriform situation did not mean that, in the Second Temple period, just any text could be considered authoritative. On the contrary, it is equally clear that there was a notion of authoritative scripture, even if that notion was not applied exclusively to a canonized and fixed set of texts. Scriptural traditions were regarded as worthy of quotation and interpretation, and a principal way of composing new texts involved "rewriting" or, more generally, imitating textual traditions to which authority was already attached. Not every community may have agreed on a list of these traditions, let alone on their textual form, but there appears to have been a considerable amount of overlapping consensus. One of the greatest challenges confronting scholars is to maintain both of the fruits of the Dead Sea Scrolls research, the pluriformity of textual traditions, and the scriptural authority of many of these traditions. If, for present purposes, we continue to use the concept of "canon," it needs to be understood that we do so in full view of the Dead Sea Scroll "revolution." Our understanding of "assemblage" does not require textual or canonical fixity, but rather presupposes an open-ended approach, so we can proceed with a concept of "Bible" or "Scripture," even as we acknowledge that the exact scope of that collection cannot be known for the first century CE and may well have been variable within limits. One implication of this new way proceeding is that there is no longer a good reason to assume that, in general, texts that did not find their way into the Bible are later and less authoritative than texts that did. Consequently, there is no simple way to apply the distinction between works that are considered authentic and others that are pseudepigraphic.

56. Students often ask me whether this or that early Jewish writing is "canonical." They are concerned that we will let some foreign body intrude into our understanding of Scripture. They have been told that "Scripture interprets Scripture," which is a partial truth. It was never true, however, that the Bible could be understood without any "outside" consultation. Just on the purely semantic level, we cannot understand Scripture without recourse to lexical usage outside the confines of the canonical writings. Moreover, in our conception of Scripture as an assemblage, the exact extent of the concrete elements (i.e., individual writings) is indeterminate, and the number of contingent factors, including other bodies of literature, that influence the assemblage is practically unlimited. Therefore, we should not rule any comparative material out of bounds. To reappropriate the famous saying by the church historian Jaroslav Pelikan, who was taking a swipe at Protestantism, "The problem with *sola Scriptura* is that *Scriptura* was never *sola*." Cf. Pelikan, "Luther and the Liturgy," 50–51. We shall see many examples of this point in our study.

57. This perspective has much in common with the views expressed in Helmer and Landmesser, eds., *One Scripture or Many? Canon from Biblical, Theological, and Philosophical Perspective.*

fleeing in terror from the empty tomb (Mark 16:8).[58] The very open-endedness of the account suggests that the story continues on a new basis.[59]

As we have seen, however, an assemblage is not just a mixture of heterogenous elements. The French word *agencement* does not simply entail heterogenous composition, but requires a constructive process that lays out a specific kind of arrangement. As with all assemblages, the canon may be singular and heterogenous but it also shares three features that define its arrangement: condition, concrete elements, and agents.

Like all assemblages, the canon has a condition (abstract machine), that is, the network of specific *external* relations that hold the elements of the assemblage together. We do not expect that the canon goes together seamlessly and perfectly, as if it were an organic unity such as the human body. Rather, the canon is more like Ursa Major (the Great Bear),[60] one of the largest and most prominent northern constellations, the seven brightest stars of which form the familiar formation called the Big Dipper.[61]

58. The much-discussed ending of Virgil's *Aeneid*—the anticlimax in which Aeneas slays his archenemy Turnus—is similarly abrupt and disturbing (at least for modern scholars): "And saying this he ripped | Open the breast of Turnus, and Turnus' bones | Went chilled and slack, and his life, with a groaning shudder, | Indignant fled away to the shades below (*vitaque cum gemitu fugit indignata sub umbras*)" (*Aen.* 12.950–93 [trans. David Perry]). On recent approaches to the ending of the *Aeneid*, see Gaskin, "On Being Pessimistic about the End of the *Aeneid*." The comparison between the ending of Mark and that of the *Aeneid* deserves further exploration, insofar as both texts look forward to the establishment of an empire. The comparison between the two writings extends to the "longer ending" of both. The longer ending of Mark's Gospel (16:9–20) is of course well known (cf., e.g., Kelhoffer, *Longer Ending of Mark*), but the ending of the *Aeneid* was felt to be so disturbing that one fifteenth-century Italian poet added an extra book to the poem (in Latin verse) tying Virgil's loose ends into a neat bow (cf. Buckley, "Ending the *Aeneid*?," 108–37). Like the longer ending of Mark, the longer ending of the *Aeneid* was so popular that it was included in editions of the *Aeneid* for centuries afterward.

59. In a similar way, Deleuze and Guattari see Kafka's unfinished novels as the fulfillment of his project, the novels' supposedly defective plots actually being central aspects of their functioning as open-ended, perpetually moving machines. Cf. Deleuze and Guattari, *Kafka*, 73. We are dealing here with what Deleuze and Guattari call "minor literature," which they define as literature that is immediately social and political, that engages a "collective assemblage of enunciation," and that uses language with a "high coefficient of deterritorialization" (*Kafka*, 18, 16). Cf. Bogue, *Deleuzian Fabulation*, 7: "By engaging a collective assemblage of enunciation, minor writers strive to assist in the creation of a viable collective, which, unfortunately, does not yet exist. Although minor writers alone cannot create such a collectivity, they can offer interpretations in the political sphere that might enable the invention of such a genuine community in the future."

60. A "constellation" is a group of stars forming a recognizable pattern that is traditionally named after its apparent form or identified with a mythological figure. Modern astronomers divide the sky into 88 constellations with defined boundaries. Constellations are regions that the sky is divided into in order to help with identifying where objects are located in the sky. The name Ursa Major comes from the story in Greek mythology that the nymph Callisto was turned into a bear and placed as a constellation in the heavens by Zeus. Constellations had stories attached to them that were important for the transmission of traditional knowledge in many oral cultures. See, for example, "Songlines: Tracking the Seven Sisters," an Aboriginal-led exhibition at the National Museum Australia about the star cluster of the Pleiades: https://www.nma.gov.au/exhibitions/songlines.

61. Technically, the Big Dipper is an asterism (from Greek *asterismos*, from *astēr* ["star"]), a prominent pattern or group of stars, typically having a popular name but smaller than a constellation. At the outer edge of its bowl of the Big Dipper, the line extending from the two stars points toward Polaris,

Ursa Major does not exist inherently in the sky; it is simply the *proper name* given to the set of conditioning relations that arrange a set of stars in a readily recognizable form *when viewed from Earth*.[62]

In a similar way, the biblical canon is the proper name for the set of conditioning relations that arrange a set of writings. Without the writings there are no relations between the writings, but without relations between the writings there is only radical heterogeneity. Hence, the condition in this case is the relational lines that connect the writings and the concrete assemblage is the writings that are connected. When the relational lines that connect the writings are viewed together, a pattern emerges that forms a sort of unity.

The second common feature shared by all assemblages is concrete elements—which for the canon consists of the biblical writings. Just as all assemblages have a set of conditioning relations (an abstract machine), they also have specific elements that are arranged in these relations. The relationship between the conditioning relations and their concrete elements is not pre-constructed but has to be constructed piece by piece.[63] One does not transcend the other, but both are mutually transformative. The concrete elements are like a skeletal frame, whereas the conditioning relations are the breath that suffuses the separate parts. Of course, having spoken of breath that suffuses, we immediately think of the idea that scripture, as an assemblage,[64] is "inspired" (cf. 2 Tim 3:16).[65] Here it should be noted that whereas Deleuze and Guat-

---

the North Star. Ascertaining the constellation, recognizable by its familiar shape, had a practical function, too. For example, sailors could use the constellation, and particularly the North Star, to navigate.

62. Walter Benjamin uses the figure of the constellation as a philosophical concept describing the relationship between ideas and the phenomena. Cf. Sahraoul and Sauter, *Thinking in Constellations*. See, for example, Paula Schwebel, "Constellation and Expression in Benjamin and Leibniz," 51–81, here 67 (author's emphasis): "The constellation depends on a mental act, which unites the phenomena, based on the recognition of an affinity between distinct elements. Were it not for this mental act, the constellation would fall into dispersion. While the constellation's lack of *inherent* unity suggests that it is merely conventional or constructed, the constellation is no *arbitrary* construction, since the configuration of its elements is determined by the intrinsic structure and order of ideas. The constellation is a form of *expression*."

63. Indeed, the individual writings themselves were in the process of formation and redaction during the period under consideration. One of the major findings of the Dead Sea Scrolls was the pluriformity and fluidity of the biblical texts. Under such conditions, the search for the "original" text seems misplaced. Moreover, the fact that what we would call "biblical" texts were side by side with similar texts that did not happen to become "canonical" suggests that our whole notion of the formation of the biblical text needs an overhaul.

64. Although in 2 Tim 3:16, *pasa graphē* actually refers to "every scripture" (individualizing) rather than to "all scripture" (taken as a whole).

65. Here, we must be careful not to overload this singular text with too much meaning. First, even if 2 Tim 3:16 refers to the assemblage of texts that we call the Old Testament (see the previous note), this does not include the "New Testament," which was not even in existence at the time of writing. Second, the Greek term *theopneustos* (usually translated "inspired") is far from clear in its meaning. One often hears the term explained etymologically as "God-breathed," based on the component parts of the word: *theos* (God) + *pneustos* (breath/spirit). But this way of explaining terms has long since fallen into disrepute among careful interpreters of the New Testament. Actual usage in particular

tari thought of the condition/abstract machine as immanent to the assemblage on the plane of immanence, the inspiration of Scripture entails not just an integrating, horizontal relationship between texts but also a transcendent relationship between the canon assemblage and God.[66] As stated previously, this is an example of how our study of New Testament Theology parts company with the essentially materialistic and exclusively immanent philosophy of Deleuze and Guattari. On the other hand, there can be no doubt that, both individually and corporately, the biblical texts came together through historically conditioned human agency on the plane of immanence. It is a matter of both-and rather than of either-or.

Since, viewed immanently, the condition/abstract machine that defines the relationship between the concrete elements is not an eternal essence or a program given in advance of the concrete elements, when the concrete elements change,[67] so does the set of relations that they are in. There is thus a reciprocal determination between the abstract and the concrete: when one changes, so does the other. This is why the consequences of events cannot be known in advance. There is no essence of the event; there are only concrete elements that are defined by their external relations, i.e., what they are concretely capable of at any given point. If we want to understand how an assemblage works, we do not ask what its essence is, but rather *what it can do*.[68] As an assemblage, the

---

contexts is what we need. Alas, *theopneustos* is a *hapax legomenon*, that is, it occurs only this one time in the New Testament, thereby making it difficult to know exactly what was the term means in context without recourse to usage outside the New Testament. Cf., e.g., Keener, "2 Timothy 3:16," 217–31. On the other hand, the New Testament itself gives credence to the authority of either the individual writings themselves (e.g., John 21:24–25; Rev 22:18–19) or the words and traditions that lie behind the writings (e.g., 1 Thess 2:13; 1 Cor 2:6–16; Matt 28:19–20; John 20:30–31; Jude 14–15). The letter of Jude is a particularly important example of this phenomenon, because, as I have argued elsewhere, the influence of 1 Enoch is far more influential there than merely the well-known citation of 1 En. 1:9 in Jude 14–15; 1 Enoch is actually a mainstay of the letter. Cf. Scott, "Jude the Obscure."

66. Cf. Hengel, "Salvation History," 240 (author's emphasis): "However, can we still call this 'history'? Is it not simply a literary collection of texts of differing content and quality? Certainly: one could also speak of a *word-of-God-history* [cf. Rom 3:2–3; 9:4–5] and a *faith-history* [cf. Gal 3:23], for all these texts stand in a *historical* connection and seek to testify to God's action, i.e., what God does and says. It is the belief in the one God of Israel, who is confessed in primitive Christianity as the Father of Jesus Christ, that holds all these texts together." Nevertheless, there is a false sense of inspiration that must be resisted (Hengel, "Salvation History," 243): "Any apologetic fundamentalist biblicism which appeals to the verbal inspiration and inerrancy of the canonical Scriptures goes wrong. It is basically a disguised rationalism which contradicts the nature of Scripture as the testimony of human faith to God's words and actions that create salvation."

67. It may seem strange to think of a biblical canon as changing, but that is in fact what happened over time and from place to place in the history of the canon. For many scholars, to speak of a Jewish canon in the Second Temple period is an anachronism. The texts found in the caves of Qumran did not form a "library" and there is doubt that they even form an assemblage. Much remains unclear as to why and how those particular texts were assembled there. A number of the texts do not seem to be products of the Qumran community itself. Some are clearly biblical texts, albeit of widely varying types. Other texts were probably brought in from other parts of the Jewish landscape. The literature on these subjects has exploded in recent years, but for a summary see again Flint and VanderKam, *Dead Sea Scrolls*. On all these questions, see Collins et al., *Ancient Jewish and Christian Scriptures*.

68. For a similar approach to biblical texts, see Breed, "Nomadology of the Bible," esp. 315–20.

biblical canon is no different in this regard. The question is What are the consequences and implications of this assemblage now? What can the canonical assemblage accomplish and where are its limits in some particular instance? Since the concrete elements are always changing along with their externally determined conditioning relations, the canonical assemblage is always becoming capable of different things. This requires a constantly renewed analysis of the canonical assemblage.

The third feature shared by all assemblages is that they all have agents/personae.[69] Agents are not autonomous rational subjects, they are collectively immanent to the assemblage. In the case of the canonical assemblage, the agents are the communities that arrange the conditioning relations and concrete elements (individual writings) that are meaningful in the world where the agents live. One cannot have agents without a canonical assemblage, but one cannot have a canonical assemblage without agents that bring it about. Since the conditions, elements, and agents are all immanent to one another, they all occur together in mutual presupposition. The meaning of the texts for the communities is inherent in the canonical assemblage, and the hermeneutical, meaning-making moves are part of the ongoing process of canon-formation as such. This effectively eliminates all the hand-wringing of modern scholars who wonder how we can move from ancient text to modern relevance. In the assemblage model, *the movement is built-in automatically* by virtue of the continuing mutual relationship between the three elements of the canonical assemblage.[70] This act of connecting the concrete elements together is the theologizing *process*.[71]

In his *Traditions of the Bible: A Guide to the Bible As It Was at the Start of the Common Era*, James L. Kugel provides an insight that fits well with the canon as an

---

69. In this context, the term *personae* brings to mind *dramatis personae*, the characters of a play, novel, or narration. That idea fits well because the "persons of a drama" are seen as a *group* rather than as individuals per se. This group has a story arc involving change etc.

70. On the mutual role of the community and its "liturgical" practices in scripturalization, on the one hand, and of scripture in community formation, on the other, see Newman, *Before the Bible*, 142: "A liturgical habitus, to draw on the concept of Pierre Bourdieu, was cultivated through both individual and communal prayer, reading, and performance. Such ongoing performances were an integral feature of the transmission of cultural texts and their transformation into 'scriptural' texts. [. . .] The liturgical elements and aspects of performance that are represented in the texts themselves serve both to authorize the text as scripture and to establish a setting that enables its extension. In the late Second Temple period the ongoing interpretation of scripture in communal contexts, mediated in part through prayers, hymns, and other poetic texts, can help to explain its open-ended and pluriform character." On the role of the revelation to Enoch in forming the eschatological community of the saved, see Scott, "Comparison," 202–4.

71. Cf. Bockmuehl, *Seeing the Word*, 90 (emphasis mine): "In its historic ecclesial setting Christian thought has intrinsically been a movement of the exegesis of Scripture that, in the context of eucharistic fellowship, invigorates believers and interpreters with the One who is the very Bread of Life. [. . .] To understand *how the New Testament 'works'* requires one to take seriously where it resides, whom it addresses, and of what it speaks. There is no self-subsistent mellifluous dogma but a question open to public and interfaith engagement." For further statements that are amenable to assemblage theory as discussed here, see Bockmuehl, *Seeing the Word*, 91, 113, 114, 163–67.

assemblage in the sense that we are discussing it here.[72] As Kugel explains, one of the assumptions shared by all ancient interpreters was that "Scripture constitutes one great Book of Instruction, and as such is a fundamentally *relevant* text."[73] This description corresponds to the idea of the Jewish Scriptures, which were also influential in the formation of the New Testament, as an assemblage with a condition and agents. The condition is obviously that the assemblage functions as *wisdom* instruction.[74] The agents are the sages who arose after the Babylonian exile and became the authoritative interpreters of Scripture in the Second Temple period. Examining each of these elements of the assemblage in turn yields some important results.

First, the conception of Scripture—the heterogenous writings that arose in various times and places in a complex textual history over hundreds of years—as a Book of Instruction owes its condition to Wisdom tradition.[75] In Wisdom tradition, the sages of old had packaged their insights about the observable world in clever proverbs that

72. Cf. Kugel, *Traditions of the Bible*, 1–41.

73. Kugel, *Traditions of the Bible*, 15; cf. also 16–17 (author's emphasis): "Everything [in the Hebrew Bible] was held to apply to present-day readers and to contain within it an imperative for adoption and application to the readers' own lives. Paul's observation about the biblical narrative of the Israelites' wanderings in the desert, 'Now these things [that happened to the Israelites in the desert] happened to them as a warning, but they were written down for our instruction, upon whom the end of the ages has come' [1 Cor 10:11], is merely one formulation of an assumption that had long characterized ancient biblical interpretation. For Paul, as for all ancient interpreters, the Bible is not *essentially* a record of things that happened or were spoken in the past. That they happened is of course true; but if they were written down in the Bible, it was not so as to record what has occurred in some distant past, but 'for our instruction,' so that, by reading the sacred text whose material comes to us from the past, we might learn some vital lesson for our own lives." Cf. Collins, "Natural Theology," 101–3.

74. Paul is convinced that "whatever was written in former days was written *for our instruction*" (Rom 15:4). See also Rom 4:23–24: "Now the words, 'it was reckoned to him' (Gen 15:6), were written not for his sake alone, *but for ours also*. It will be reckoned to us who believe in him who raised Jesus our Lord from the dead." Cf. Hays, *Echoes of Scripture*, 166.

75. The term "wisdom tradition" is not unproblematic in biblical scholarship. In recent years, some interpreters have questioned the value of the "wisdom" designation as a generic category or even a useful descriptor when studying the Bible and related texts. Certain scholars argue that "wisdom" is a modern scholarly construct, and nebulous criteria and lack of clarity about the extent of the "wisdom" corpus should lead to an obituary for this designation. Others have claimed that instructional literature constitutes one of the oldest and clearest generic types in the ancient world, and the biblical writers of books like Proverbs drew directly from what might properly be called a wisdom tradition. These commentators argue that there is a remarkable coherence to the wisdom category. The whole controversy evokes our previous discussion of emic vs. etic categories on the example of "apocalypse," "apocalyptic," and "apocalypticism." On April 27, 2021, Union Presbyterian Seminary hosted a helpful symposium on "Wisdom as a Category for Studying Ancient Texts and Discourses," which included the following participants representing the full range of perspectives on the issue: Stuart Weeks of Durham University, Katherine Dell of University of Cambridge, Will Kynes of Samford University, and John Collins and Jacqueline Vayntrub of Yale Divinity School. For a video recording of the event, see https://www.youtube.com/watch?v=1xsRVXDGjTg. One of the most contentious issues in this discussion is the relationship between wisdom and apocalypticism in the Dead Sea Scrolls, especially in 4QInstruction. Cf. Goff, "Recent Trends," 376–416. This debate has consequences for our understanding of Jesus, because the Gospels present Jesus as having an emphasis on both wisdom and apocalypticism. See further in chapter 3.

often demanded scrutiny by later sages and students of wisdom in order to be fully understood. Schooled in these techniques, sages quite naturally brought them to bear on Scripture. The very conception of Scripture as a great corpus of divine instruction whose lessons, therefore, are relevant to every age—is a projection of the sages's assumptions about wisdom literature onto *all* of Israel's variegated corpus of ancient writings. If this is correct, the wisdom condition of the canonical assemblage is intimately connected to the activity of the sages as agents of the assemblage. And the corpus of what constitutes "Scripture" and what is therefore the object of interpretation changed over time and varied from one group of readers to the next.[76]

As Kugel explains, when the teachers of wisdom began to include Scripture among their subjects, the whole nature of their activity was changing. Where wisdom had previously consisted of contemplating the natural world and the social order and deducing from them the general plan by which God conducts the world, it was now more and more Scripture that was consulted to understand God's ways. Thus, it happened that the sage, who had previously walked about the world or stood at his window looking out, now sat down at his table and opened the Book. For, the Book, even more than the world, was the place in which God's will and God's ways were expressed—but much thought and contemplation (interpretation) were still needed if the sage was to understand fully God's sacred written messages. The interpreter, as mediator of the divine wisdom found in Scripture needed to peer deeply into words from the ancient past and explain their present application—how this or that law was to be observed, what the present implications of some ancient narrative were, or even how, in the words of some prophet long dead, there nonetheless lurked a message directed to a later day.[77] Clearly, then, the agents of the assemblage—i.e., the sages as authoritative interpreters—were singularly qualified to determine the ongoing, contemporary relevance of the Scripture because they were able, by virtue of their wisdom training, to approach the canonical

---

76. For his own part, Kugel's book is dedicated to creating "a snapshot, or a portrait at least, of the Bible as it was interpreted for a specific period—roughly speaking, from about 200 B.C.E. through the first century or so C.E." (*Traditions of the Bible*, 29–30). As Kugel (*Traditions of the Bible*, 30) readily acknowledges, however, "This required defining, in somewhat arbitrary fashion, what 'Scripture' would or would not include (since even within this period its contents varied over time and from group to group)." On the question of "canon" in the Second Temple period, see further above.

77. For example, Paul's observation about the biblical narrative of the Israelites' wanderings in the wilderness: "Now these things [that happened to the Israelites in the desert] happened to them as a warning, *but they were written down for our instruction*, upon whom the end of the ages has come" (1 Cor 10:11 [emphasis mine]). For Paul, as for all ancient Jewish interpreters, the Bible was not merely a record of things that had happened or were spoken in the past. That they happened is of course true; but if they were written down in the Bible, it was not so as to record what has occurred in some distant past, but "for our instruction," so that, by reading the sacred text whose material has come to us from the past, we might learn some vital lesson for our own lives. See again 2 Tim 3:16–17: "Every scripture is inspired by God and is useful for teaching, for reproof, for correction, and for training in righteousness, so that everyone who belongs to God may be proficient, equipped for every good work." Modern biblical interpreters have often failed to appreciate that biblical texts are not bound by the meaning of their original context; the texts continue to speak authoritatively in subsequent contexts as well.

assemblage in accordance with its generative condition (abstract machine) as a Book of Wisdom Instruction. Again, one cannot have personae without an assemblage of which they are a part, but one cannot have an assemblage without agents who actualize it. Since the conditions, elements, and agents are all immanent to one another, Deleuze and Guattari argue that all occur together in mutual presupposition.[78] In the case of the assemblage of Scripture, the time when this mutual presupposition occurred was in the Second Temple period. If we want to understand the process of scriptural canonization, we must immerse ourselves in the history and literature of the Second Temple period.[79] As we shall see, however, the situation becomes even more complex when we consider the separate wisdom traditions, including especially the Enochic, to which the Second Temple period gave rise (more on this later). Yet, this is the crucible in which the New Testament was formed.

The New Testament as Assemblage

Much of what we have already said about the canon of the Old Testament/Hebrew Bible can also be reaffirmed about the New Testament.[80] Therefore, we can forego a

78. As we have seen, the relationship between the abstract relations (conditions) and the concrete elements is not pre-constructed but has to be constructed piece by piece. One does not transcend the other, but both are mutually transformative. Seen from this perspective, the biblical texts are not self-contained meaning-makers but rather entities that are codependent on human agency for their actualization. Hence, the question becomes How do these texts function? What processes do they set in motion? Insofar as these processes are transhistorical as well, each historically and geographically distinct community needs to engage afresh with the text of Scripture.

79. If, as Deleuze and Guattari maintain, all life is a process of connection and interaction, and any body or thing is the outcome of a process of connections, then the developing assemblage of scripture is also created from its connections *both within and without*. In no way can scripture be seen as totally separate from its connections with other assemblages.

80. It should be noted that the philosophical work of Deleuze and Guatarri has seldom been applied to the New Testament. Cf. McLean, "What Does *A Thousand Plateaus* Contribute to the Study of Early Christianity?," 533–53, here 536–37: "In contrast to theology, the field of Christian origins has not yet encountered Deleuzian philosophy, at least not seriously. But if the discipline of theology actually *needs* Deleuzian philosophy . . . , then why does the discipline of Christian origins not have the same need? Perhaps the discipline's lack of interest can be traced back to its basic theoretical orientation. As a general tendency, the discipline of Christian origins seems to be oriented towards recapturing something which has been lost, such as a lost 'Paul the apostle', a lost 'historical Jesus' of Galilee, or Jesus' lost, original teachings. . . ." See, however, Whitlock, ed. *Critical Theory and Early Christianity*, Part II: Gilles Deleuze (ch. 5: "Gilles Deleuze and Early Christian Texts," by Matthew Whitlock; ch. 6: "The Deleuzioguattarian Body of Christ without Organs," by Bradley McLean; ch. 7: "The Many Acts of the Apostles: Simulacra and Simulation," by Matthew Whitlock and Philip Tite; ch. 8: "Facing the Nations: Becoming a Majority Empire of God—Reterritorialization, Language, and Imperial Racism in Revelation 7:9–17," by Sharon Jacob). For some examples of theology's recent engagement with Deleuze's philosophy, see Goodchild, "Theological Passion for Deleuze," 357–65; Adkins and Hinlicky, *Rethinking Philosophy and Theology with Deleuze*; Barber, *Deleuze and the Naming of God*; Justaert, *Theology After Deleuze*; Ben Simpson, *Deleuze and Theology*; Boundas et al., "Encounters with Deleuze," 160–62. Our project is not to write a new gospel, but rather to examine the original one and to explore its ongoing implications. Contrast the special issue of *The Bible and Critical Theory* 13

lengthy discussion at this point. One implication of what we have already stated, how-ever, is that a *Biblical* Theology of the New Testament is not only possible but really the only plausible way to discuss New Testament Theology within the paradigm we are setting forth.[81] By the same token, if we insist on examining the New Testament canon piecemeal,[82] we will never appreciate the function of the assemblage (in its various forms) for the life of communities of faith.[83]

The relevant question for the New Testament is what is the *condition* (abstract machine) of the assemblage. As we have seen, an assemblage has a condition, that is, the network of specific external relations that holds the elements together. Since the relations are immanent to the elements, the abstract machine is designated by a proper name *through* which concrete objects and agencies speak and attribute their similari-ties and differences from each other. The abstract machine is designated by a proper name because as a *proper noun* it refers to a unique set of relations (e.g., American

---

(2017), which engages with Blanton et al., *Insurrectionist Manifesto.*

81. Our decision to cut the Gordian knot in this way, rather than deal with the issues en bloc at this juncture, is not an attempt to deny that the concept of Biblical Theology is a contested concept and that it will likely remain such. On the major challenges of constructing a Biblical Theology, see, e.g., "Is a Postmodern Biblical Theology Possible?," in Collins, *Bible after Babel*, 131–61; Collins, *Encounters with Biblical Theology*; Motyer, "Two Testaments, One Biblical Theology," in Green and Turner, *Between Two Horizons*, 143–64; Dohmen and Söding, *Eine Bibel—Zwei Testamente: Posi-tionen biblischer Theologie*; Hafemann, *Biblical Theology: Retrospect and Prospect.* We have merely come to the conclusion that no amount of preliminary study will be able to deal with all the objec-tions to a biblical theology to the satisfaction of even most scholars. However, in the course of our study, we will endeavor to address some these issues, although our main focus will be on introduc-ing a biblical theology of the New Testament from an assemblage perspective, which necessarily includes the Hebrew Bible/Old Testament. Cf. "Is a Critical Biblical Theology Possible?," in Collins, *Encounters with Biblical Theology*, 17: "For biblical theology, the biblical tradition is a given and it is assumed to be meaningful and to have some continuing value, although the biblical theologian in-evitably works with some canon of Scripture (contrary to Wrede), although this does not necessarily imply a qualitative difference over against ancient literature but only a recognition of the historical importance of these texts within the tradition."

82. Here we are taking aim at the many attempts at constructing a New Testament Theology (or even a theology of Paul) by simply doing a theological analysis of the individual writings apart from their context in the canonical assemblage. See, for example, the series edited by James D. G. Dunn entitled "New Testament Theology" (Cambridge University Press): "This series provides a program-matic survey of the individual writings of the New Testament. It aims to remedy the deficiency of available published material, which has tended to concentrate on historical, textual, grammatical, and literary issues at the expense of the theology, or to lose distinctive emphases of individual writ-ings in systematised studies of 'The Theology of Paul' and the like. New Testament specialists here write at greater length than is usually possible in the introductions to commentaries or as part of other New Testament Theologies, and explore the theological themes and issues of their chosen books without being tied to a commentary format, or to a thematic structure drawn from elsewhere. When complete, the series will cover all the New Testament writings, and will thus provide an at-tractive, and timely, range of texts around which courses can be developed." Cf. Dunn, *Theology of Paul's Letter to the Galatians*, [iv].

83. That said, various parts of what became the New Testament canon(s) circulated at first as as-semblages in their own right. We will discuss the Gospels and the Pauline letters as assemblages in later chapters.

Revolution, Mahatma Gandhi, Albert Einstein) as opposed to common nouns, which refer to essentialist categories of things (e.g., revolutions, statesmen, scientists). The abstract machine is thus an asignifying *proper name*.

As an assemblage, the New Testament also has a condition or abstract machine, and its condition also has a name: Jesus Christ. This is not merely the so-called "histori-cal Jesus" of modern scholarly reconstruction, although such reconstructions certainly deserve consideration.[84] We are speaking instead of the Jesus who animates the whole New Testament. In other words, the New Testament is part of Jesus' effective history.[85] In the language of Paul, Jesus became a life-giving spirit, who moved into his early

84. The modern quest for the historical Jesus began with the European deists, who were interested in anti-ecclesiastical readings of the evidence. The deists doubted that the Church's Jesus was the real Jesus, and therefore they set about to separate truth from fiction—the truth about the Jesus of history, the real man from Galilee, as opposed to the later accretions of the Christian Church, which made Jesus out to be something bigger than life. The standard method of the quest for the "historical Jesus" is subtraction: it aspires to erase from the New Testament record that which comes from others or that which comes from after Jesus's death. But that method arguably leaves us with an eviscerated figure. If our argument that the New Testament constitutes a revolutionary assemblage is correct, then all of the layers and accretions of the Jesus tradition are part of the ongoing transformative process of the New Testament's formation. This is necessarily an open process in which the agents/personae and the constituent concrete elements creatively interact with one another and have the opportunity for further transformation of the assemblage.

85. Cf. Tuckett, "Does the 'Historical Jesus' Belong Within a 'New Testament Theology'?," 243–44: "The argument of this chapter is not to equate the teaching of the historical Jesus with a 'New Testa-ment theology' without remainder. The latter (in the sense taken here) will always go beyond the teaching of the historical Jesus to include reflections by others on the full significance of Jesus, his life, death and 'aftermath'; and in this, the views of the pre-Easter Jesus (insofar as we can recover them) may well be superseded, changed and developed. But in any theological process of doing more than simply describing the wide range of 'theologies' reflected in the New Testament, in any process of critically evaluating such differences and seeking to make theological value judgements about them, the historical Jesus may play an essential role as *part* of that process. In this sense, therefore, I suggest that the historical Jesus belongs inextricably within any attempt to engage in a 'theological' interpreta-tion of the New Testament, i.e., to produce a 'New Testament theology.'" Bockmuehl takes a similar position but puts even more emphasis on "effective history" and extends it to the first 150 years, the period of "living memory" (*Seeing the Word*, 22, 64–68, 117–18, 132, 134–35, 163–67, 187–88). See, e.g., Bockmuehl, *Seeing the Word*, 24: "My suggestion is that, during the first two centuries, living memory of the apostolic generation served as a kind of hermeneutical magnetism with the potential to orient a profusion of centrifugal particularities toward the New Testament's implied readings and readers—and thereby to the identity of the Jesus Christ of whom all its authors speak." Bockmuehl also uses other metaphors to describe this phenomenon: "that document's [i.e., the New Testament's] cen-tral concern—Jesus of Nazareth" (76); "a unifying canonical impulse" (112); "the integrating vision in the texts" (113); "the implied canonical consensus" (114); "the *central kerygma* of the New Testament" (115 [author's emphasis]); "a shared central kerygma" (115); "a common subject, which is the gospel" (132, cf. 108). For Bockmuehl, this effective history entails the unbroken and identifiable chain of personal recollection reaching back to the apostles and ultimately to Jesus Christ himself (183–84, citing Irenaeus, *Letter to Florinus*, ap. Eusebius, *HE* 5.20.5–7: Irenaeus → Polycarp → John [and other eyewitnesses] → the Lord; see also Bockmuehl, *Seeing the Word*, 156, 231). Hence, the *incarnate* Word of Israel's God is seen as the unifying subject matter of the New Testament whom readers are invited to perceive in the *written* word. It would seem, then, that faithfulness to Jesus Christ must take priority over any particular ecclesial expression his effects, although the two clearly presuppose one another.

followers and their texts, with their memories and their hopes, their agreements and their controversies. Jesus' life reached beyond itself, to live on in others.[86]

In the same way, the coherence of the New Testament canon as a whole is guaranteed by its presence as an assemblage. These writings were brought together because, in some way, they were seen to function together because of Jesus Christ.[87] Strange as it may seem, however, the idea of a New Testament canon is foreign to the New Testament itself. During the time of the composition of the separate writings of the New Testament, the writers themselves viewed the Jewish Scriptures as authoritative writings;[88] the New Testament as an assemblage of writings did not yet exist.[89] What we can say, however, is that some of the writings were already thought

86. In the book of Acts, the Holy Spirit is also called "the Spirit of the Lord" (Acts 5:9; 8:39) and "the Spirit of Jesus" (16:7), showing that the Spirit is one way in which Jesus Christ becomes the animating force (condition/abstract machine) of the revolutionary assemblage. Cf. also Rom 8:9 ("the Spirit of God"//"the Spirit of Christ"); 2 Cor 3:17 ("Now the Lord is the Spirit, and where the Spirit of the Lord is, there is freedom"); Gal 4:6 ("the Spirit of his Son" in the hearts of believers, "crying, 'Abba! Father!'"); Phil 1:19 ("the Spirit of Jesus Christ"); 1 Pet 1:11 ("the Spirit of Christ"). On the role of the Spirit of Christ in the transformative process, see chapter 8 on 2 Cor 3–4.

87. The formation of the New Testament was a long and controversial process. What was to be included in or excluded from the collection was a contentious issue. Hence, it is not surprising that different canons developed along the way, with the most extreme one being that of Marcion (d. ca. 160 CE), who rejected the whole Old Testament and accepted only a reduced version of Luke's Gospel and ten of the letters of Paul. See further McDonald, "Forming Christian Scriptures as a Biblical Canon," in Collins et al., *Ancient Jewish and Christian Scriptures*, 121–44. One significant contribution not discussed by McDonald is that of Trobisch, *First Edition of the New Testament*, who argues on the basis of the primary manuscript evidence (rather than merely the secondary testimonies of the church fathers) that "the New Testament, in the form that achieved canonical status, is not the result of a lengthy and complicated process that lasted for several centuries. The history of the New Testament is the history of an edition, a book that has been published and edited by a specific group of editors, at a specific place, and at a specific time" (6). For Trobisch, that specific time was "in the middle of the second century when the church in Asia Minor communicated with Rome" (105). Moreover, this earliest edition (*editio princeps*) already carried the title "New Testament" (*hē kainē diathēkē*), and was conceived from the beginning as the second part of the Bible, along with the "Old Testament." It should be noted that Trobisch makes a sharp distinction between the questions of how and when the New Testament came to be regarded as a closed canon (i.e., the acceptance of these writings individually as authoritative scriptures) and the questions of when and why these writings were first put together in a collection; his study is devoted exclusively to the latter set of questions. Trobisch's thesis is extensively evaluated and discussed in Heilmann and Klinghardt, *Das Neue Testament und sein Text im 2. Jahrhundert*.

88. On the Septuagint as "the Bible of the early Church," see Cook, "Septuagint as a Holy Text," 1–9. The translation the Hebrew Bible into a foreign language, which necessitates semantic and cultural adaptation, began in Egypt during the third century BCE. Hence, the Scriptures became detached from their original ethnic or cultural tradition. That process of what we might call "absolute positive deterritorialization" (on which see further in chapter 1) continued in the subsequent centuries. Cf. Stroumsa, *End of Sacrifice*, 53.

89. It was not until 367 CE that we first find a list of canonical writings (compiled by Athanasius, the bishop of Alexandria) that consists of the 27 books we now call the New Testament. The collection was finally acknowledged by the Council of Hippo (393 CE) and the Council of Carthage (397 CE). The compilation of lists of authoritative Christian writings was not new to the fourth century. Since the second century CE, a variety of groups calling themselves Christian compiled their own lists that included various writings—some that are in the New Testament and others that are not, such as the

of as authoritative in their own right because they came from leaders in the church. Paul claimed to be "an apostle of Jesus Christ" and an eyewitness to the resurrected Lord, which lent him an aura of authority that other leaders did not have. Nevertheless, even Paul often had difficulty with being accepted as authoritative, having to argue for it in some of his letters. However, the most important factor in the process of collecting the writings that would eventually become the New Testament assemblage is that Jesus Christ—as the condition who drives the whole revolutionary event—brings both the concrete elements (the writings of the New Testament) and the agents/personae (the heterogeneous communities of the Jesus movement) into a direct, creative, and ongoing mutual relationship which is intrinsic to the assemblage itself. Ironically, however, the effect of the heterogenous Jesus movement was ultimately *centrifugal*—to disperse its participants in ever-wider circles rather than to bring them together at one focal point.[90]

Jesus' Program of Revolutionary Transformation and Assemblages

Our discussion of assemblages with respect to the biblical canon in general and the New Testament in particular has enormous implications for our construction of a New Testament Theology, for now we are asking how the canonical assemblage *works*. This is a fundamentally *theological* question, and one that has an *empirical* answer. For if, as we have suggested, Jesus Christ is the condition (abstract machine) of the New Testament assemblage, then we must now go on to investigate how the New Testament functions with respect to Jesus Christ as the assemblage's condition.

Shepherd of Hermas and the *Epistle of Barnabas*. Cf. Pedersen, "New Testament Canon and Athanasius of Alexandria's 39th *Festal Letter*," 168–77.

90. This applies to the concrete elements of the assemblage as well. Cf. Hengel, *Four Gospels and the One Gospel of Jesus Christ*, 114: "Especially between AD 70 and 150 the thought and teaching of the church developed in a very lively, indeed sometimes almost too lively way; there was more and more 'experimentation' and there were often vigorous arguments. In his preface, already between 75 and 80 Luke quite deliberately refers to the prior work of the 'many.' He wants to improve it; however, he does not reject this work but builds on it. Thus 'plurality' does not necessarily mean chaos nor—as often today—a dismissal of the question of truth. In the development of the second century, when the mainstream church was being more and more consolidated by the *regula fidei* and the *monarchical episcopate*, the progressive *multiplicity* of Gospel-like writings also brought with it the danger that the tradition would run wild, that there would be splits, and that special subjective, indeed false, teaching would arise. At that time this was countered not least by a concentration on what for us are the four earliest 'apostolic' Gospels and on the traditions which stood behind them or were prompted by them." Another factor that promoted plurality and "de-globalization" was the proliferation of biblical translations, whereby the story of Jesus of Nazareth, and with him the entire *historia sacra*, was extended to humanity as a whole but also encouraged competition among different linguistic and cultural centers. Cf. Stroumsa, *End of Sacrifice*, 39–40; also 91: "I have referred, in speaking of the rise of the religions of the Book, to the 'de-globalization' of the Mediterranean world in Late Antiquity and the error of Constantine, who believed that Christianity offered him a spiritual basis to unify the empire, whereas the new religion encouraged the centrifugal energies of various cultures."

Here, we will suggest that, in terms of Deleuze and Guattari's taxonomy of abstract machines (i.e., territorial, state, capitalist, and revolutionary), Jesus Christ is a "revolutionary abstract machine."[91] If this seems like a surprising suggestion, it is because we are so used to thinking of Jesus and the New Testament in strictly "religious" terms that we have been blinded to the fact that "religion" and "politics" were inextricably intertwined in the ancient world. For example, the Hasmonean rulers were king-priests[92] and the Roman emperor was the Pontifex Maximus (i.e., the head of the principal college of priests).[93] However, in our modern push to analyze and categorize, we have separated that which had hitherto been joined together.[94] As we shall see, however, Jesus gave rise to a revolutionary movement that seamlessly combined what we so glibly call "religion" and "politics."[95]

Revolutionary events entail the *prefigurative* construction of another world— "the future anterior" or "that which will have been." Seen from the perspective of the Jesus tradition, we might formulate the Jesus revolution in the words of Dale C.

91. This section is indebted to Thomas Nail's summary of Deleuze and Guattari's philosophical reflections on the subject of the revolutionary abstract machine. Cf. Nail, *Returning to Revolution*.

92. During the century of Jewish independence after the Maccabean revolt, the Hasmonean kings also acted as high priests, despite the severe criticism from some parties, including the Zadokite priests whom the Hasmoneans usurped. Cf. VanderKam, *From Joshua to Caiaphas*, 240–393.

93. On the intertwined nature of religion and politics in the ancient world, see the various works by Simon R. F. Price, including, for example, *Rituals and Power* and "Rituals and Power," 47–71, here 70–71: "A Christianizing theory of religion which assumes that religion is essentially designed to provide guidance through the personal crises of life and to grant salvation into life everlasting imposes on the imperial cult a distinction between religion and politics. But a broader perspective suggests that religions need not provide answers to these particular questions, and the imposition of the conventional distinction between religion and politics obscures the basic similarity between politics and religion: both are ways of systematically constructing power." See also Koulakiotis and Dunn, *Political Religions in the Greco-Roman World*, 1: "Until the 1980s, historical treatments of ancient religion focused mainly on myth, cult and ritual as a way to interpret the mental structures or primary emotions of ancient peoples. In these early attempts to articulate practice, scholars too primarily functionalist or structural approaches that prioritized the social dimensions or religion over the political, but in the last few decades, a 'political turn' in the study of religion has taken hold. Awareness of the embedded nature of religion, together with the omnipresence of 'politics' in almost every aspect of public and private life, has led scholars to concentrate intentionally on the relationship between these two concepts—politics and religion—and the specific physical, mental and literary spaces in which they interacted. Despite this intellectual shift, however, the aspects of this diptych are far from being exhausted, particularly from a comparative or juxtapositional perspective." In addition to the secondary literature cited in *Political Religions*, see also, e.g., Doroszewski and Karłowicz, *Dionysus and Politics*.

94. This goes along with our above-mentioned critique of the siloization of knowledge in the Western tradition.

95. The modern distinction between the political framework and the religious community—that is to say, the separation between church and state—is foundational to John Locke's *De tolerantia* (1689). Many people believe that this bifurcation is the sole possible basis for peaceful coexistence in our multicultural pluralistic societies. Cf. Collins, "Temporality and Politics in Jewish Apocalyptic Literature," 140: "When the final kingdom is thought to have come, utopia becomes ideology and the revolutionary spirit of the apocalypses is betrayed." As we shall stress in subsequent chapters, the creation of the people to come in the prefigurative future anterior is a process of becoming-minoritarian rather than an accession to political power.

Allison: "Jesus wants some things even now to be the way they were in the beginning because that is how they are going to be in the kingdom of God."[96] This is not merely a transcendent, oppositional, or potential world, but rather an immanent and creative *process* from within the developing situation.[97] We might say that Jesus is the catalyst or founding condition for the ongoing process of transformation that effectuates the name of Jesus. Jesus himself is presented as having initiated the process through his performative language. For example, the catalogue of miracles that Jesus lists in Matt 11:2–5//Luke 7:18–23 (Q) is designed to call to mind oracles from Isaiah (cf. Isa 26:19; 29:18–19; 35:5–6; 42:18; 61:1–2) and thereby imply that the eschatological age, when illness will vanish and all wrongs will be made right, has begun to arrive in Jesus' ministry through his authoritative word.[98]

The abstract machine, according to Deleuze and Guattari, is an "asignifying proper name" that works within a logic of collective action. Proper names do not "represent" or stand in for something else; they are instead the markers of a real yet non-concrete, actual yet non-effectuated event whose being is all of the affects, elements and agents that constitute it. Thus, for example, according to the book of Acts, as Saul (also known from 13:9 onward as Paul) was engaged in a campaign of persecution against followers of Christ, the risen Lord Jesus Christ confronted him: "Saul, Saul, why do you persecute *me*?" (Acts 9:4 [emphasis mine]; cf. 22:7; 26:14). Of course, Saul was not actually

96. Allison, *Jesus of Nazareth: Millenarian Prophet*, 210. Whereas Bockmuehl emphasizes canonical intentionality as a hermeneutical key (cf. *Seeing the Word*, 49, 68, 113, 117, 118, 223, 230, 272), we are stressing Jesus Christ. In and of itself, Scripture does not have a *telos*; that is provided by the abstract machine/condition of the assemblage, "the author and finisher of our faith" (τῆς πίστεως ἀρχηγὸν καὶ τελειωτήν, Heb 12:2).

97. Once again, by focusing on the "plane of immanence" rather than the "plane of transcendence," we are not denying transcendence. To the contrary, we fully acknowledge God, the Spirit, revelation, inspiration, and a multitude of other important realities as the ultimate origin of difference (e.g., creation itself). For present purposes, however, we are trying to explore the assemblage as a historically contingent system, and this requires giving human beings agency in the process of producing difference. The plane of immanence is also the most accessible to historical investigation. Ultimately, these two planes are not at odds with one another (see further above on Einstein's two principles of relativity), and we shall see some examples of how they interface. If, for example, we take seriously that there is a God and that he sent his Son, then the two planes are integrated in this one incarnated human being (transcendence in immanence). Moreover, if, as we argue in chapter 2, Jesus was executed as a royal pretender on the plane of immanence, does this rule out the salvific effect of his death on the plane of transcendence? Or, to name another example, doesn't the process of undoing the hierarchical differences of race, class, and gender that currently prevail in society, thus making one new human being in Christ, require not only human engagement in a multitude of contingent situations on the plane of immanent difference but also a new creative act of God to initiate and complete the process (which is essentially the culmination of his first creative act) on the plane of immanence? See further in chapter 3 on Gal 3:28, which argues that the performative word of Christ, which Paul proclaims in the gospel, is nothing less than the performative word of God in a (re)new(ed) creation, thus effecting the fusing—or rather the enfolding—of the two planes into one univocal plane of being (see chapter 9 on the book of Revelation). Most of the issues we deal with in this book have both horizontal and vertical aspects, even though we focus largely on the former. As Paul expressed it, "I'm speaking *in human terms* (ἀνθρώπινον λέγω)" (Rom 6:19; cf. also Rom 3:5 and Gal 3:15 [κατὰ ἄνθρωπον λέγω]).

98. We shall have more to say about Jesus' performative language in chapter 2.

persecuting Jesus Christ himself, but rather his followers. Traditional interpretation, from Augustine to Karl Barth, has emphasized the implied unity between the head (Christ) and the members of the body (the Church).[99] Others have seen a connection between Acts 9:4 and Jesus' teaching in Matt 25:34–46, where, in the context of the final judgment involving "all the nations," a separation takes place between the sheep and the goats, depending on whether an individual has acted righteously toward the needy—the hungry, the thirsty, the stranger, the naked, the sick, and the imprisoned.[100] In each case, the Judge pronounces his verdict as if the deed had been done to him personally: "*I* was hungry and you gave me food, etc." or "*I* was hungry and you gave me no food, etc."[101] In the context of the book of Acts, however, Paul was persecuting those who were taking collective action "in the *name* of Jesus."[102]

In other words, as the abstract machine, Jesus acts as an attractor or horizon around which concrete actions and agents circulate, contest, and transform each other. As we shall see, this process of transformation by fits and starts is precisely how the Jesus movement becomes universalized according to the New Testament.

According to Deleuze and Guattari, a revolutionary abstract machine is characterized by several distinct features, which, we argue, are particularly applicable to Jesus Christ:

1. A Revolutionary Abstract Machine Is Both Singular and Absolute. The revolutionary abstract machine is "singular" in the sense that it is an unlawful or illegitimate deviation from the currently prevailing power structures. As such, the revolutionary abstract machine introduces *a unique and unstable condition* that ruptures the old order and begins to open a new field of the possible. This is a completely new condition for inclusion rather than merely a reformation or restoration of a prevailing condition. "No one puts new wine into old wineskins," Jesus is quoted as saying (Mark 2:22 pars.). As we shall see in chapter 2,

99. Cf. Col 1:18; Eph 5:23; 1 Cor 12:4–31.

100. Compare Jesus's command to love one's enemies (Matt 5:44//Luke 6:27 [Q], 35). In Mark 12:28–34, the greatest commandments are loving God and loving one's neighbor.

101. Cf. Prov 19:17: "Whoever is kind to the poor lends to the Lord, and will be repaid in full." In earlier scholarship, a passage like Matt 25:34–46 might be adduced as an example of "corporate personality" (H. Wheeler Robinson) or "representative headship" (Seyoon Kim). Cf. Robinson, "Hebrew Concept of Corporate Personality," 49–62; Kim, "'Son of Man'" as Son of God.

102. Indeed, in the book of Acts, "the name of Jesus" plays a major role in the spread of the early Jesus movement. For example, when Peter preaches the assembled diaspora Jews in Jerusalem at Pentecost, he exhorts them to "repent, and be baptized every one of you in the name of Jesus Christ" (Acts 2:38). Later, Peter heals "in the name of Jesus Christ of Nazareth" (Acts 3:6; cf. v. 16; 4:10). The authorities ordered the disciples "not to speak or teach at all in the name of Jesus" (4:18; cf. 5:40). Philip "was proclaiming the good news and the kingdom of God and the name of Jesus Christ" (8:12). For a similar idea, this time relating to the Gospel of John, see Bockmuehl, *Seeing the Word*, 154. On the collective action of Jesus' followers as his surrogates, see Luke 10:6 (par. Matt 10:40; John 13:20): "Whoever listens to you listens to me, and whoever rejects you rejects me, and whoever rejects me rejects the one who sent me."

Jesus was crucified as a royal pretender, someone whom the authorities viewed as subversive, even though his means of revolution were completely nonviolent. Yet this crucified royal pretender was the condition that opened up a prefigurative new world for his followers.

The revolutionary abstract machine is "absolute" in a twofold sense. First, it establishes *the self-referential basis* by which the body politic legitimates its own existence. Without reference to a superior political power to justify its emergence, the condition for a revolutionary body refers only to itself as the guarantor of its own existence. Jesus Christ clearly fulfills this role: He claimed his own authority for what he was doing.[103] The antitheses of the Sermon on the Mount provide a classic example of Jesus' self-authorizing approach. In each antithesis, Jesus states a scriptural principle ("You have head that it was said . . ."), followed by a declaration of the opposite based on his own authority ("but *I* say to you . . .").[104] Hence, the revolutionary Christ-event created a new existence.

Second, the revolutionary abstract machine is "absolute" in the sense that it is "a local absolute." For Deleuze and Guattari, a revolutionary abstract machine is a singular-universal, whose origins are contingent and local but whose consequences are potentially infinite.[105] As such, a revolutionary body politic is radically inclusive of anyone who wants to participate under its mutable and reinterpretable conditions, but only insofar as such participation changes the nature of the entire assemblage.[106] The absolute of this abstract machine, therefore, should not be confused with the absolutes or universals of *identity* that remain the same (and pre-given), while only adding on an increasing number of axioms or elements to be represented (as in reform movements that seek merely to prop up an existing regime or monetary system). Rather, when Deleuze and Guattari speak of a "becoming-everybody/everything" of revolution, what this means is that everybody and everything may participate in an effectuation and transformation

103. Note, however, that Jesus acted in concert with the will of the Father, thus bringing heaven and earth into realignment through his agency. See the Matthean version of the *Lord's* Prayer: "on earth as in heaven" (Matt 6:10).

104. Cf. Matt 5:21–44.

105. In that case, the Jesus movement envisioned universality from the beginning (cf. Matt 28:19–20). For a revolutionary body politic not only includes those who participate in its internal transformation, but also aims to include others not already part of the struggle. That is, the revolution is both inclusive and expansive. It has the capacity for internal transformation and external growth beyond its local construction. Jesus reached out, for example, to "tax collectors and sinners" (Matt 9:10, 13; Mark 2:15–17; Luke 5:30, 32; 15:1), for which Jesus received heavy criticism: "Look, a glutton and a drunkard, a friend of tax collectors and sinners!" (Matt 11:19//Luke 7:34 [Q]). This kind of radical inclusiveness would continue to characterize the Jesus movement. For in doing so, as Jesus enjoins, people imitate God, who overflows with loving kindness to the just and the unjust without distinction (Matt 5:43–48//Luke 6:32–35 [Q]).

106. This point has tremendous implications for our developing New Testament Theology. Rather than a static entity, New Testament Theology in the sense that we are developing it here entails our creative participation in the ongoing process of transformation in the New Testament assemblage.

of a revolution to the extent that they are also transformed by it and as they respond to the demands of the event. Thus, a condition for participation allows not merely for the possibility that everyone may become other than they are, it names a singular and absolute condition (in this case, Jesus Christ) under which everyone can participate in and shape the creation of another world alongside the old—or rather in the shell of the old.[107]

The revolution that Jesus catalyzed was located in Galilee, which corresponds to the idea that the contingent revolutionary abstract machine centered around him is "absolute local." At the same time, the consequences of Jesus Christ as a revolutionary abstract machine proved to be practically infinite in scope and open to all. The story of the New Testament is how a movement centered on Jesus—an obscure, almost invisible peasant operating in the rural backwater of Galilee—burst the bounds of its narrow confines, provocatively relocated to Jerusalem, where Jesus had been crucified under the Romans, and, from there, became a worldwide challenge eventually even to the Roman government itself. Seen as a two-volume work within the New Testament assemblage, Luke-Acts tells the story of the expansion of the Jesus movement in the most comprehensive and detailed way, ending with the apostle Paul under house arrest in Rome and proclaiming the transforming message of Jesus there. Centuries later, the fledgling Jesus movement would actually become reterritorialized as the empire itself.[108] This was not the new world that Jesus had envisioned and that his early followers had sought to create prefiguratively in the future anterior.[109] Such is the nature of revolutionary movements, however. They can start with high hopes and yet eventually fail to avoid reassimilation into the mundane.[110]

Jesus as condition/abstract machine of the New Testament assemblage can be compared to the aforementioned function of wisdom instruction as the condition/abstract machine in the formation of the biblical canon.[111] For the New Testament presents Jesus as the Wisdom of God.[112] However, Jesus is Wisdom

107. As we shall see, this new world will mirror the old in certain respects and yet outstrip it in others.

108. Cf. Stroumsa, *End of Sacrifice*, 92–93, 96–97, 107.

109. Jesus did not originate the concept of the future anterior. Pious Jews who were apocalyptically oriented had already understood themselves to be living in the time of God's proleptic establishment of control over evil which anticipates his ultimate triumph at the end. Cf. Stuckenbruck, "Overlapping Ages at Qumran and 'Apocalyptic' in Pauline Theology," 309–26.

110. George Orwell's *Animal Farm* springs to mind: In this spoof on Stalin's revolution, the farm animals who initially rejected their human overlords eventually become like the humans in their maltreatment of others. According to Mark 10:42–44 pars., Jesus had warned about falling into a similar scenario.

111. Cf. deSilva, *Jewish Teachers of Jesus*, who argues that the answer to the question about the source of Jesus' "wisdom" (Mark 6:2 par. Matt 13:54) is not only the Hebrew Scriptures but also writings of the Second Temple period such as the Wisdom of Ben Sira and 1 Enoch.

112. Cf., e.g., 1 Cor 1:24, 30. See further Bockmuehl, *Seeing the Word*, 80–81, here 81 (author's

not only in the sense of instruction, but rather in the Enochic sense of revealed saving wisdom.[113] This becomes clear from a reading of both Q (the hypothetical sayings source common to Matthew and Luke) and the letters of Paul. The Logos of John's Gospel is similar. These will be dealt with in due course.

2. A Revolutionary Abstract Machine Is the "Degree Zero" of Its Body Politic. The condition of a revolutionary body politic, or what Deleuze and Guattari call a revolutionary abstract machine, also marks the most minimal degree of existence within the body politic. In the sense that an emerging revolutionary condition or event is singular, it is not representable within the normal state of affairs. Because of this relative invisibility, Deleuze and Guattari say that such an abstract machine marks a "degree zero" or is the "most deterritorialized element" in the newly developing political arrangement.[114] In other words, the abstract machine offers the first hint of an actual, concrete political force offering an alternative to the competing processes of political representation (e.g., the established regime or economic system). This condition does not indicate a mere potential for transformation that cannot be realized in any particular transformation or whose realizations are only betrayals or ironies. This "zero degree" bears a particular name such that a political field can begin to gain consistency around it, creating a "vortex" or site of "circulating reference."

---

emphasis): "And this same Christ, the wisdom of God, is himself the message of the 'God-breathed' Scriptures: in the context of the faith in Christ they 'are able to *make you wise* for salvation' (2 Tim. 3:15)."

113. Enoch is the condition/abstract machine of the revealed-saving-wisdom tradition of the Enochic assemblage. As a condition/abstract machine, Enoch is a proper name and a datable event in the antediluvian period. Out of the almost incidental mention of Enoch in Gen 5:18, 21–24, Jewish devotees of the Second Temple period developed an enormous literature in Enoch's *name*, but that story need not occupy us at this juncture. See merely Reeves and Reed, *Enoch from Antiquity to the Middle Ages, Vol. I: Sources from Judaism, Christianity, and Islam.* On the idea that framing the Book of the Watchers (1 En. 1–36) as testamentary blessing discourse offers a possible explanation for the compositional development of the Enochic corpus as a whole, see Newman, "Participatory Past: Resituating Eschatology in the Study of Apocalyptic," 427–30.

114. Basically, territorialization is an understanding of life, politics, and philosophy based on territory, on conquering, occupying, living in, and defending a piece of ground. Deterritorialization is a breaking up of territory, which can lead to a reterritorialization in different terms. These notions of territory and territorialization refer to the earth and to how humans occupy and live on Earth. For example, traditional wealth has always been tied to ownership and production of land. But with capitalism you have a deterritorialization, where money as capital replaces the original value of land as territory. Land is no longer primary, but wealth has been deterritorialized as land and reterritorialized as capital. To extend deterritorialization "can be called the creator of the earth—of a new land, a new universe, not just a reterritorialization" (*ATP*, 509). Deleuze and Guattari envision the creation of a new world which is a creation of Earth. Not another Earth or a different Earth, but the creation of Earth itself as subject of its own events and humans and other territorial creatures as individuations of this new comprehension of Earth.

You can't get much more "deterritorialized" than Jesus of Nazareth.[115] Jesus says in effect, "No, I am not of your kind, I am the outsider and the deterritorialized." He may have been from Nazareth, but according to Matt 8:20//Luke 9:58 (Q), Jesus said of himself to a prospective disciple, "Foxes have holes, and birds of the air have nests; but the Son of Man has nowhere to lay his head."[116] This passage apparently alludes to Psalm 8, the only place in Jewish literature where "son of man" and "the birds of the air" are found together. This psalm, perhaps an inner-biblical exegesis of Gen 1:26–28, proclaims honor and glory of mortals ("son of man," Ps 8:4 LXX), who have dominion over the beasts of the field and "the birds of the air" (v. 9). Jesus, however, declares that the Son of Man is worse off than the birds and beasts, for he, unlike them, is without a home. So far from his head being crowned with glory and honor, Jesus finds no place to rest. He is the ultimate example of "deterritorialization" and as such forms the "degree zero" in the newly developing political arrangement that he inaugurated. Indeed, as we shall see, Jesus sets himself against all the contemporary forms of representational politics—territorial, state, and capitalist. "Representation" in this sense of the term entails an essentially moral view of the world, explicitly or implicitly drawing on "what everyone knows." Representation constitutes a particularly restricted form of thinking and acting, in accordance with fixed norms. Jesus definitely confronted the fixed norms and basic assumptions of his day.

However, the key to Jesus' success as a condition of a new political movement was not merely opposition to the status quo.[117] It also entailed internal

115. Deleuze and Guattari (*ATP*, 381–82) refer to the nomad as "the Deterritorialized par excellence." Cf. Lundy, "Call for a New Earth, a New People," 127 (emphasis mine): "The nomad is 'the deterritorialized par excellence'. . . , because their travelling is not for the sake of relocating from one territory to another (as is the case with migrants). Rather, their movement is itself *a way of life*, which is to say that with the nomad 'it is deterritorialization that constitutes the relation to the earth, to such a degree that the nomad reterritorializes on deterritorialization itself. It is the earth that deterritorializes itself'. . . ." As a way of life, then, nomadism, for Deleuze and Guattari, is not merely a literal movement between points on terra firma but rather an ideological movement in the in-between of the future anterior. In a similar way, people like Mary and Martha (Luke 10:38–42; cf. John 12:1–8) or Zacchaeus (Luke 19:1–10) can "follow" Jesus without leaving their home. On "The Unclear Boundaries of Discipleship: Supporters of Jesus Who Did Not Leave Their Homes," see Meier, *Marginal Jew*, 3:80–82.

116. This text does not support the view that Jesus had nothing to say about himself, other than that he had no permanent address, no bed to sleep in, no respect on his home turf. Such a view contradicts the broad testimony of the relevant sources. In words attributed to Jesus and in words assigned to others, in stories as well as in sayings, Jesus presents himself as having a starring role in the eschatological drama. Cf. Allison, *Historical Christ and the Theological Jesus*, 64–66. In terms of our developing New Testament Theology, Jesus is the abstract machine/condition of the whole assemblage.

117. Cf. "Temporality and Politics in Jewish Apocalyptic Literature," in Collins, *Encounters with Biblical Theology*, 129–41, here 140: "The 'no' of the apocalyptist is not a Barthian *Nein* to nature and this world as such. Rather, it is a political 'no,' a rejection of a particular world order. While it hardly offers a political program, its efficacy should not be underestimated. In the words of the long-time American activist Daniel Berrigan, 'it is the same no that has shaken thrones and the enthroned where they sit. It is Bonhoeffer's no, and Parks' . . . Mandela's and Vaclav Havel's.' It is not for nothing that the

political consistency. Political consistency, according to Deleuze and Guattari, thus not only requires a self-referential condition for its beginning, but it also requires this beginning point to bear some sort of marker to indicate its non-appearance from the perspective of the dominant political arrangement of laws and markets. Here is something really different.[118] Furthermore, the abstract machine is also invisible from within its own political arrangement; that is, it is practically inscrutable. No one knows entirely what it is or what it is capable of doing. This is why Deleuze and Guattari call it an "abstract" machine. A revolutionary condition is "abstract" in the sense that it does not appear as a concrete "thing." It is a real and contested moment whose name brings together a host of previously marginalized political desires.

Jesus was always an ambiguous figure, at least according to the Synoptic Gospels.[119] His own followers, let alone those outside the circle, did not understand who Jesus was and what he was about. Jesus' enigmatic teachings and actions needed constant clarification and still remained beyond reach for most. In particular, Jesus' teaching about the kingdom was difficult to pin down as a "thing." What was it? Where was it? It all seemed so abstract and nebulous. We will discuss Jesus' teaching about the kingdom in chapter 3.

There can be little question that Jesus was at the center of a real and contested moment. Both within and outside the fledgling Jesus movement,[120] there was constant strife over every aspect. Schweitzer ended his *Quest of the Historical Jesus* with these words:

> He comes to us as one unknown, without a name, as of old, by the lakeside, he came to those men who did not know who he was. He says the same words, "Follow me!" and sets us to those tasks which he must fulfil in our time. He commands. And to those who hearken to him, whether wise or unwise, he will reveal himself in the peace, the labours, the conflicts, and the suffering that they may experience in his fellowship, and as an ineffable mystery they will learn who he is.[121]

Emperor Augustus had oracles collected and burnt. The apocalyptic vision was a denial and contradiction of *Roma aeterna*, the official eschatology of empire."

118. Cf. Matt 12:41–42//Luke 11:31–32 (Q).

119. In John's Gospel, on the other hand, John the Baptist publicly announces Jesus' identity from the outset: "The next day he saw Jesus coming toward him and declared, 'Here is the Lamb of God who takes away the sin of the world!'" (John 1:29). In other words, the cat is out of the bag immediately, whereas in the Synoptic Gospels there is a general lack of understanding and only a gradual lifting of the veil.

120. A note on usage is necessary at this point. In the following, we will use terms such as "Christ-followers," "Jesus movement," or "assemblies." The term "assembly" not only correlates with our overarching term "assemblage" but also allows a comparison and contrast with "assembly" (*ekklēsia*) of the Greek city-state. We will return to this issue in chapter 8.

121. Schweitzer, *Quest for the Historical Jesus*, 487.

Although Schweitzer set out to find Jesus through historical-critical methods, and although he believed that he had indeed found him, he also recognized the limitations of his methods and conclusions. He understood that there is, in addition to all our inferences about the history behind texts, the firsthand experience of heeding and following Jesus, of personally and corporately participating in his vision for a new world. Without this personal and corporate participation, our knowledge of him is the less. As Matt 11:29 reports Jesus as saying, "Take my yoke upon you, and learn of me."

Our approach to New Testament Theology uses the philosophical system of Deleuze and Guatarri as a *tool* or *lens* to explore Jesus' revolutionary teaching and the impact he has had on the New Testament assemblage.[122] As we can already see, this entails personal participation in the process that he initiated and continues to sustain. It might seem strange to use a modern philosophical system as a tool that is fundamentally materialist and radically immanent. However, as I have shown elsewhere, the Jewish authors of the Enochic corpus did basically the same thing: They used concepts from early Stoicism in order to articulate their vision of a new world and a new people. In doing so, these Jewish writers did not accept the materialism and immanence of Stoicism holus-bolus; they selectively used various concepts without appropriating the whole Stoic philosophical system.[123] In availing ourselves of Deleuze and Guatarri's work as a resource to be utilized, we are not attempting to adjudicate the relative adequacy of metaphysical systems, which is, in any case, beyond our competence.[124]

122. As I. A. Richards famously stated in the preface to his *Principles of Literary Criticism*, 1: "A book is a machine to think with." A theory is a conceptual toolbox. If it is useful, then we can gain insight from it.

123. See further Scott, *Apocalyptic Letter to the Galatians*, chap. 2. A similar point can be made about another Jewish writing of the Second Temple period, the Wisdom of Solomon. Cf. "Natural Theology and Biblical Tradition," in Collins, *Encounters with Biblical Theology*, 119–20.

124. Cf. "Is a Critical Biblical Theology Possible?," in Collins, *Encounters with Biblical Theology*, 22: "Nonetheless, a biblical theology that adverts *only* to sociological and historical functions is reductionistic. The biblical texts must also be recognized as proposals about metaphysical truth, as attempts to explain the workings of reality. This aspect of the Bible is perhaps most obvious in the Wisdom literature but it is also a factor throughout the Bible, from the creation stories to the apocalypse. [. . .] The problem is that we lack any acceptable yardstick by which to assess metaphysical truth. It is possible to compare and contrast biblical worldview with a modern system, such as process philosophy, but philosophical systems too are traditions of discourse and there is no consensus on their validity in contemporary culture. It is not within the competence of biblical theologians as such to adjudicate the relative adequacy of metaphysical systems. Their task is to clarify what claims are being made, the basis on which they are made, and the various functions they serve."

1

Revolutionary Transformation Today

Some Key Concepts and a Way Forward

Introduction

So far, we have introduced our developing New Testament Theology in terms of Deleuze and Guattari's concept of "assemblages." Both the Old Testament/Hebrew Bible and the New Testament are assemblages that have three elements—abstract machine/condition, concrete elements, and agents/personae—that relate to each other in an ongoing process of transformation. This novel approach means that a Biblical Theology of the New Testament is neither a mere *description* of biblical content nor a secondary *actualization* of the normative meaning of the text for today. Instead, we are taking the position that the New Testament assemblage—with Jesus Christ as the condition who drives the whole revolutionary event—brings both the concrete elements (the writings of the New Testament) and the agents/personae (the heterogeneous communities of the Jesus movement) into a direct, creative, and ongoing mutual relationship which is intrinsic to the assemblage itself. The resulting Jesus revolution opens up a new world in the shell of the old. In short, we are presenting New Testament Theology not as a static entity, but as an ongoing participatory process of *becoming.*[1] We hereby explicitly invite readers, as full participants, into the feedback loop of that ongoing process of continual transformation.

1. In other words, we are aiming at more than a mere accurate description of the New Testament and its potential for transformation; our New Testament Theology should be used to construct

But it is not enough to argue that the New Testament is a revolutionary assemblage. By virtue of its role in a revolution, the New Testament assemblage constantly bumps up against other kinds of assemblages that are constructed on a very different basis and stand opposed to revolution. Therefore, to understand how the New Testament continues to unfold, we need an understanding of the forces and factors that impinge upon it. Here is where an explanation of Deleuze and Guattari's typology of assemblages is necessary.

Another matter that needs immediate attention is Deleuze and Guatarri's typology of *change* in the various kinds of assemblages. Obviously, everything is always changing; that's an inevitability. But assemblages can handle change in very different ways with major consequences. If we want to understand how the revolutionary New Testament assemblage engages with transformation, we must see it in juxtaposition to the other approaches to change.

The Typology of Assemblages

As we have seen, all assemblages have in common three features that define their arrangement: condition/abstract machine, concrete elements, and agents/personae. Each of the three features presupposes and is immanent to the others. However, there is not just one kind of assemblage. For Deleuze and Guattari, there are in fact four kinds of assemblage: territorial, state, capitalist, and nomadic/revolutionary. The analysis of these different types of assemblages is what Deleuze and Guattari call the politics of assemblages. For our purposes, the fourth kind of assemblage—the nomadic/revolutionary—is the most important, but the others are also interesting insofar as the nomadic/revolutionary stands in sharp contrast to them, and the actors in the New Testament constantly interact with the other kinds of assemblage. We may also note that any particular assemblage may incorporate elements of the other three while remaining *mostly* one sort. In other words, the following four types of assemblage are never absolutely pure; all assemblages are composed of a mixture of these four types to various degrees.[2]

In the first three types of assemblages (i.e., territorial, state, and capitalist), community members exist only within a pre-given scope of certain conditions and elements. They recognize, reflect, communicate, and represent within the generally

---

another world within the shell of the present one, at least in an anticipatory way.

2. Hence, the concept of a specifically topological theory of political history provides a way to consider political events as having several overlapping and contingent tendencies at once, each to a greater or lesser degree. This heterogeneity is not a matter of contradiction or exclusion. As we shall see, the individual writings of the New Testament exhibit this kind of heterogeneity as well. For example, Matthew's Gospel can be seen as, to some degree and without contradiction, both a territorial assemblage ("I was sent only to the lost sheep of the house of Israel" [Matt 10:6]) and a revolutionary assemblage (opening out to the inclusion of the gentile nations [Matt 28:19–20]). See also the discussion of Paul's relationship with the Roman Empire in chapter 6.

redundant parameters of a prior field of shared identity. This unifying process allows conflicting differences to be held together and mediated, depending on the type of assemblage, by either a territorially shared "way of life," a governmentally enforced system of "rights/contracts,"[3] or a profit-driven "market."[4] As Thomas Nail observes, "Political differences, according to the politics of representation [e.g., patriarchy, statism, capitalism], are always differences from the same and within the identical."[5] In other words, the differences within any one of these three assemblages do not involve a fundamental break with the shared identity. Only the nomadic/revolutionary assemblage breaks away from the politics of identity[6] and pre-given representation,[7] entering instead into a true process of participation and mutual transformation. If the primacy of *identity* is what defines an exclusivistic world of re-presentation (presenting the same world again), then *becoming* (i.e., becoming different/other than we are, transformation) redefines a radically inclusive world of presentation, across lines of race, gender, class, geography and so on.[8] Let us examine each type of assemblage in turn.

Territorial Assemblages

Territorial assemblages are arranged in such a way that the concrete elements are coded according to a natural or proper usage. In these assemblages, the mutational character of the conditions, elements, and personae are arbitrarily determined according to a set of specific limits. Territorial assemblages divide the world into coded segments. Each concrete element has a designated place and every person's life has a plan related to its place in the world, whether we are talking about family, school, army, or job.

3. For example, Canada is held together by its Constitution and Charter of Rights and Freedoms, and the United States of America by its Constitution and the Bill of Rights (the first ten amendments to the Constitution).

4. For example, the World Trade Organization (WTO) deals with global rules of trade between nations. Its main function is to ensure that global trade flows as smoothly, predictably and freely as possible.

5. Nail, *Returning to Revolution*, 113.

6. Identity politics refers to the tendency of people of a particular religion, race, social background, etc., to form exclusive political alliances (tribalism), moving away from traditional, broad-based party politics. In each of the first three assemblages (i.e., territorial, state, and capitalist), the politics of identity understands difference only as a difference of the same. In our media-saturated world of positive feedback loops, this sameness is merely amplified.

7. Habitual thinking and groupthink are endemic to our whole culture. The variety and change of the experienced world has been diluted by a limited conception of difference: difference-from-the-same (e.g., McMansions, Hollywood movies, social-media echo chambers, fashion, big-box stores). If the primacy of *identity* is what defines a world of re-presentation (presenting the same world again), then *becoming* (i.e., becoming different) defines a world of presentation anew.

8. In calculus, the first derivative of a point is not its position in space, but its propensity to change its position; not where an object *is*, but how it *moves* in space and time. This is an illustration of the difference between *identity* and *becoming*.

A good example of a territorial assemblage is India's nearly three-thousand-year-old caste system, one of the world's oldest social hierarchies, which divides Indian society into four distinct castes and a series of complex inter-castes within that structure. The Dalit community (considered "untouchable" in orthodox Hindu scriptures and practice) are so low in this social hierarchy that they are outsiders to the caste system, and historically they have faced severe discrimination as a result.[9] If you are a Dalit, there is nothing you can do about it; that is simply your lot in life.

Territorial codes define the "natural" norms of life. They express the pre-given, essential, and proper limits and usage of persons and objects in a given assemblage by explaining how the world is related to the past, to an inscription of memory—"this is how things are done, how they have always been done." According to Deleuze and Guattari, these "qualitatively different chains of mobile and limited code" are formed by three basic actions: (1) "a selection cut" allowing something to pass through and circulate, (2) "a detachment cut" that blocks part of that circulation, and (3) a "redistribution of the remainder" to begin a new chain of code.

The first synthesis of territorial coding—the synthesis of connection—attempts to ward off the chaos of a meaningless world—the shapeless jumble of life—by making a "selection cut" from fundamentally uncoded flows, allowing some of them to pass through while others are blocked. This primary repression wards off an absolutely chaotic world by deselecting some of its flows, and it puts into circulation and connection

9. For an unsettling, satirical novel about the massive inequities in Indian society, see Manu, *Serious Men*. The story follows Ayyan Mani, a middle-aged Dalit working as a lowly assistant to a brilliant Brahmin astronomer at the Institute of Theory and Research in Mumbai (Brahmins are members of the highest Hindu caste). Ayyan lives in a slum with his wife and son. Furious at his lot in life, Ayyan concocts a fantastic scheme to catapult his son to notoriety as a supposed mathematical genius (a trope redolent of the self-taught Indian mathematician Srinivasa Ramanujan). Here, for example, are a few selections from the book: "How beautiful that you've forgiven the people who brutalized your forefathers. The Brahmins, the kind of things they did. The things they do even now. In private, they still call you the Untouchables, do you know that? In public they call you 'Dalits,' but in private they call you such horrible things. [. . .] Hinduism is like that, Mr Mani. The Brahmins and the Untouchables. That can never change. People only pretend that it has changed." "The Brahmins were three thousands years in the making, Sister. Three thousand years. At the end of those cursed centuries, the new Brahmins arrived in their new vegetarian worlds, wrote books, spoke in English, built bridges, preached socialism and erected a big unattainable world. I arrived as another hopeless Dalit in a one-room home as the son of a sweeper. And they expect me to crawl out of my hole, gape at what they have achieved, and look at them in awe. What geniuses." "Buddha is our god. The other gods are gods the Brahmins created. In their deviant stories, those gods fought against demons which were us. Those black demons were our forefathers." "Ayyan laughed. Yes, yes, Indians were the oldest civilization on Earth, the greatest, the best. And only Indians had culture. Others were all dumb nomads and whores. Ayyan detested this moronic pride more than anything else about the country. Those flared nostrils, those dreamy eyes that people made when they said that they were once a spectacular race. How heaps of gems were sold on the streets, like berries. How ancient Brahmins had calculated the distance between the Earth and the Moon long before the whites; how Ayurveda had figured everything about the human body long before Hippocrates; something close to the heliocentric theory long before Copernicus. In this delusional heritage of the country, his own ancestors were never included. Except as gory black demons in the fables of valiant fair men."

the others to be coded. By marking a separation, the connective synthesis is able to organize things into a stable identity, or "coded stock." The "entry pole" of selection begins with a genealogical or hereditary line of hierarchically coded stock: codes of kinship, codes of worship, codes of communication, codes of exchange, codes of location (places of worship, places for eating, places for rubbish, and so on).[10] Everything has its proper code: the proper time, the proper place, and the proper people to do it.

In the first century, the territorially shared Jewish "way of life" was very much a matter of "selection cuts." Some things were prescribed and other things were proscribed—and these selection cuts applied to practically every area of life.[11] There

10. Compare the concept of "territorial assemblages" to Smith, *Map Is Not Territory*, who argues that there are two basic existential options (or symbolic systems) open to humankind—locative and utopian worldviews—which determine one's vision of place, along with a whole language of symbols and social structures. Smith emphasizes that these two stances are "coeval existential possibilities which may be appropriated whenever and wherever they correspond to man's experience of the world" (101). Hence, it is possible to change worldviews or even oscillate between them (132). "To change stance is to totally alter one's symbols and to inhabit a different world" (143), that is, "a concomitant shift from a cosmological to an anthropological view-point" (Smith, *Map Is Not Territory*, 128). On the one hand, *locative* worldviews (corresponding roughly to our "territorial assemblages") are concerned with proper emplacement of all things and persons (since being-in-place is what renders them sacred). The locative vision of the world (and its related religious activity) is centripetal and closed/bounded, with structures of center and conformity to place. Instead of a locative worldview, Smith can also refer to a cosmology, the "locative map of the world," "which guarantees meaning and value through structures of congruity and conformity" (292). For locative worldviews, according to Smith (134), "That which is open, that which is boundless is seen as chaotic, the demonic, the threatening. The desert and the sea are the all but interchangeable concrete symbols of the terrible, chaotic openness. They are the enemy *par excellence*. [. . .] Order is produced by walling, channeling, and confining the waters." As an example of a locative view of the cosmos, Smith (137–38) gives the caste system of India, which entails a total system of boundaries, limits, places, structures of order, and lack of freedom. In the locative worldview, humankind is defined by the degree to which it harmonizes itself to the cosmic pattern of order (139). On the other hand, *utopian* worldviews (using the term *utopian* in its strict sense: the value of being in "no place" [101]) valorize mobility as transcendence ("centrifugal" rather than "centripetal") and liberation ("open" rather than "closed," "rebellious" rather than "conforming"). See further below on "nomadic/revolutionary assemblages." On the development of the Roman state from a "locative" religion or "religion of place" in the early and middle Republic to a more "utopian" form in the late Republic and early Empire, see Orlin, "Augustan Religion: From Locative to Utopian," 49–59.

11. For example, the Mishnah, which was framed around 200 CE but incorporates earlier traditions, constitutes an authoritative assemblage that explicates and applies the Law of Moses in the Pentateuch. The Mishnah is divided into six sections or *Sedarim* dealing with practically every area of life (it has even been described as a comprehensive philosophical system in Neusner, *Judaism as Philosophy: The Method and Message of the Mishnah*: Zeraim ("Seeds"), dealing with the ritual laws of the cultivation of soil; *Moed* ("Season"), dealing with the ritual laws of the Sabbath, festivals, and fasts; *Nashim* ("Women"), dealing with the ritual laws of family life, marriage and divorce; *Nezikin* ("Damages"), dealing with civil and criminal law and with government; *Kadashim* ("Sacred Things"), dealing with laws on the clean and unclean as well as with Temple services and sacrifices; and *Taharoth* ("Purity"), dealing with ritual laws of cleanness and defilement. Then Mishnah was further codified when it was later included and commented upon in the two Talmuds. Stroumsa (*End of Sacrifice*, 47–48) argues that the Mishnah and the New Testament were collected at almost the same time and for the same reason—to provide a lens through which to view their respective communities' interpretation of the Scriptures.

was even a proper place to do those things: where to worship (and where *not* to worship),[12] where to conduct civil transactions,[13] and even where to relieve oneself.[14] Certain activities were incumbent upon Jews when they lived or traveled within the territorial bounds of the traditional land of Israel.[15] For example, the Mosaic Law required a particular way of life for the Israelites within the boundaries of the Land of Israel.[16] If the Israelites failed to keep the Law in that place, they would be exiled

12. The proper place for the true worship of Yahweh varied according to the period of Israel's history. Before the Deuteronomic reform (ca. 630 BCE), there were a number of legitimate sanctuaries, including Hebron, Bethel, Gilgal, Shiloh, and, above all, Jerusalem, whose foundation was ascribed to great figures of the past who are often said to have erected an altar to some other cultic object at the place and to inaugurate the worship of Yahweh there. Thus, Abraham founded Hebron (Gen 13:18); both he and Isaac are said to have founded Beer-sheba (Gen 21:23; 26:23–25); Jacob founded Bethel (Gen 28:18–22; 35:7, 14–15) and Shechem (Gen 33:18–20); Joshua erected the twelve stones marking the shrine at Gilgal (Josh 4:20–24); and David established Jerusalem as a sanctuary (2 Sam 24). In the contest between Elijah and the four hundred fifty prophets of Baal and the four hundred prophets of Asherah on Mt. Carmel (1 Kgs 18:19–40), Elijah sacrificed a bull on "the altar of the Lord that had been thrown down" (v. 30). The proper places for the worship of Yahweh are set in sharp contrast to the "high places," which are associated with pagan (Canaanite) forms of worship and are strictly proscribed.

13. The city gate was the place where the elders of the city met to adjudicate disputes (cf. Josh 20:4; Ruth 4:1–6, 10).

14. Cf. Deut 23:12–14: "You shall have a designated area outside the camp to which you shall go. With your utensils you shall have a trowel; when you relieve yourself outside, you shall dig a hole with it and then cover up your excrement. Because the LORD your God travels along with your camp, to save you and to hand over your enemies to you, therefore your camp must be holy, so that he may not see anything indecent among you and turn away from you." The Dead Sea Scrolls (specifically the War Scroll and the Temple Scroll) confirm the ongoing use of this law in writings of the Second Temple period, specifying the exact distance of the latrine from the camp.

15. Of course, this begs the question of what the territorial bounds of the Land of Israel were, and various answers are given in the Old Testament and early Jewish literature of the Second Temple period. Cf. Alexander, "Geography and the Bible (Early Jewish)," 985–87.

16. Cf., e.g., Deut 4:5, 14, 40; 5:31, 33; 6:1; 8:6–10; 11:8–12, 18–21; 18:9–13; 19:14 (on moving boundary markers within the land); 21:1, 23; 23:20; 24:1–4; 25:15; 26:1–11. See further Davies, *Territorial Dimension of Judaism*; Brueggemann, *Land*, 3: "Land is a central, if not *the central theme* of biblical faith. Biblical faith is a pursuit of historical belonging that includes. Sense of destiny derived from such belonging. In what follows I suggest that land might be a way of organizing biblical theology. The dominant categories of biblical theology have been either existentialist or formulations of 'the mighty deeds of God in history.' The existentialist approach has been concerned with the urgent possibility of personal decision-making in which Israel's faith has clustered. In both traditions of scholarship, preoccupation with the time-space problem and the identification of time categories as peculiarly Hebraic have made interpreters insensitive to the preoccupation of the Bible for placement. Either with raw, isolated *decisions* or with identifiable decisive *events*, the major emphasis has been upon the transforming discontinuities in which God has been discerned or made himself known to his people. Only now, with the new yearning in our culture and with the exhaustion of such motifs as fruitful lines of interpretive pursuit, is another perspective possible. No doubt the existential binge of contextless decision as a stance of interpretation has run its course, and we are forced to look again at the privatizing, ahistorical character of such an approach. No doubt fresh awareness of land as a central Jewish category in relation to the state of Israel has alerted even Christians to new interpretive possibilities." Cf. Weinfeld, *Promise of the Land*, xv: "The fate of the land is the focal point of Biblical historiography. Beginning with the patriarchal stories in Genesis and ending with the destruction of Jerusalem in

from the land (cf. Deut 28:15–68), or, in the parlance of Deleuze and Guattari, they would literally be "deterritorialized."

The second synthesis of territorial coding—the disjunctive synthesis or "detachment cut"—blocks some connections from attaching themselves to the assemblage, through code prohibitions, taboos, limits and so on, so that a finite stock of code may circulate within a qualitatively distinct territory. Examples of these are the borders to towns, prohibitions on kinship, and boundaries to racial, ethnic, and gender identities.

Let us consider a specific example of a detachment cut—a taboo, the violation of which precludes one from living in the land. Based on Lev 18:16, marrying one's sister-in-law is forbidden,[17] so when John the Baptist denounced King Herod Antipas for marrying his brother's wife (Herodias),[18] Antipas had the prophet executed (Mark 6:17–29). The death of John the Baptist, in turn, set the stage for the beginning of Jesus' work in Galilee: "Now after John was arrested, Jesus came to Galilee, proclaiming the good news of God . . ." (Mark 1:14). Indeed, John's death cast a pall over Jesus from beginning to end, because Jesus had been baptized by John in the Jordan (Mark 1:9). Hence, when Antipas became aware of Jesus' activity, he said, "John, whom I beheaded, has been raised" (Mark 6:14–16). Later, when Jesus asked his disciples, "Who do people say that I am?" they answered him with a variety of answers corresponding to the confusion that surrounded Jesus: "And they answered him, 'John the Baptist; and others, Elijah; and still others, one of the prophets'" (Mark 8:27–28). However,

---

the book of Kings, the historiography of Israel hinges upon the land. The patriarchal stories envision the promise of the Land to Israel, and the remainder of the Pentateuch—the Exodus, the giving of the Law at Sinai and at the Plains of Moab, and the wanderings in the desert—describe a kind of preparation for the entrance into the Land. The historiography of the books of Joshua through Kings was motivated by a need to answer three questions: Why did the Israelites not conquer the Land in its ideal borders? (Compare Josh. 1:1–4 with Josh. 23:4–5, 13; Judg. 2:11–3:4.) Why was the northern land taken away from the Israelites (2 Kings 17:1–23)? And what was the cause of the fall of Jerusalem (2 Kings 21:11–15)? In this study I attempt to consider all the aspects of the theme of inheritance of the land of Israel: literary, historical, geographical, ideological, and theological."

17. Cf. Lev 18:16: "You shall not uncover the nakedness of your brother's wife; it is your brother's nakedness." After Lev 18:6–23 lists a number of similar taboos relating to sexual relations with near kin, the text goes on in vv. 24–30 to give the penalty for violation: "Do not defile yourselves in any of these ways, for by all these practices the nations I am casting out before you have defiled themselves. Thus the land became defiled; and I punished it for its iniquity, and the land vomited out its inhabitants. But you shall keep my statutes and my ordinances and commit none of these abominations, either the citizen or the alien who resides among you (for the inhabitants of the land, who were before you, committed all of these abominations, and the land became defiled); otherwise the land will vomit you out for defiling it, as it vomited out the nation that was before you. For whoever commits any of these abominations shall be cut off from their people. So keep my charge not to commit any of these abominations that were done before you, and not to defile yourselves by them: I am the LORD your God."

18. On Josephus's disapproval of Antipas's proposal to Herodias, see *Ant.* 18.136: "They [Herod Philip and Herodias] had a daughter Salome, after whose birth Herodias, taking it into her head to flout the way our fathers, married Herod [Antipas], her husband's brother by the same father, who was tetrarch of Galilee; to do this she departed from a living husband."

once Peter identified Jesus as "the Messiah" (8:29), Jesus immediately began to speak about his death in Jerusalem (8:31–33; cf. 9:30–32; 10:33–34). It is not surprising, then, that when Jesus' authority was called into question after his Temple action, Jesus answered the question with a question: "Jesus said to them [sc. the chief priests, the scribes, and elders], 'I will ask you one question; answer me, and I will tell you by what authority I do these things. Did the baptism of John [to which Jesus himself had submitted!] come from heaven, or was it of human origin? Answer me!'" (Mark 11:27–33). The point here is that the fate of John the Baptist and Jesus are inextricably intertwined—and it all began with John's stance on a taboo relating to acceptable degrees of marriage within the Jewish territorial assemblage.

Another example of a detachment cut is the boundary to ethnic identity that divided the world into Jews/Judeans and non-Jews/Judeans.[19] One of the main limits that the early Jesus movement faced was with respect to non-Jews (or the gentiles).[20] This is a complicated subject because in the past, gentiles had been able to relate to Israel under certain conditions.[21] Now that the Jesus movement was expanding in a radically inclusive way, as characteristic of a revolutionary assemblage, how could the gentiles be incorporated—and on what basis? Did they need to conform with the Jewish way of life in order to share meals with Jews? Did non-Jewish males need to be circumcised? In other words, were gentile followers of Jesus being incorporated

19. It is a matter of scholarly debate whether the Greek word *Ioudaioi* should be translated "Jews" or "Judeans." The latter translation emphasizes the territorial connection of the ethnic people to a particular place (Judea). Cf. Collins, *Invention of Judaism*, 2–4; Mason, "Jews, Judaeans, Judaizing, Judaism," 457–512; Schwartz, "'Judaean' or 'Jew'? How Should We Translate IOUDAIOS in Josephus?," 3–28; Cohen, *Beginnings of Jewishness*, 69–106; Bloch, "Jew or Judean," 229–40. We will return to this issue in our discussion of Gal 3:28 in chapter 7.

20. Paula Fredriksen (*Paul, The Pagans' Apostle*) prefers the term "pagans." There is no completely satisfactory term for either "Jews" or "gentiles" (from Latin *gentilis* "of a family or nation"). The latter tries to capture the fact that the plural Greek word *ethnē* denotes either "nations" (people-groups seen as wholes) or individuals who are members of a people-group. Somewhat confusingly from our binary perspective, first-century Jewish writers who wrote in Greek could even use the singular *ethnos* of the Jewish/Judean people-group. This is true also in the Gospels (cf. Matt 21:43; Luke 7:5; 23:2; John 11:42–43). See further Bockmuehl, *Seeing the Word*, 218–19.

21. Cf. Hayes, *Gentile Impurities and Jewish Identities*. In her chapter on "Impurity, Intermarriage, and Conversion in Second Temple Sources" (*Gentile Impurities and Jewish Identities*, 68–91), Hayes shows that a shift took place during this period. Cf. Hayes, *Gentile Impurities and Jewish Identities*, 89–90: "Kugel . . . suggests that the idea of Israel as a distinct and holy seed arose at a time (fifth century) when self-definition could no longer be simply equated with geography. 'If the people of Israel were *not* necessarily coterminous with the people living in Israel's territory, then the issue of borders needed to be handled in some nongeographic fashion, and this is precisely what Ezra-Nehemiah, *Jubilees*, and other early texts seek to do. In the extreme, as we have seen, this led to the assertion that the people of Israel were radically discontinuous with the rest of humanity.' Jubilees and 4QMMT can be located at the extreme end of a process that began in postbiblical times, when the geographically (or nationally) based definition of Jewish identity gave way to a religiomoral definition that enabled a higher degree of assimilation of interested foreigners. The extension of a requirement for genealogical purity (in the sense of unmixed lineage) to all Israelites reflects a desire to prevent assimilation of foreigners, and it occurred in stages."

into the territorial assemblage of Israel, or were they part of an altogether new and different kind of assemblage, a revolutionary assemblage? These were major points of contention in the early Jesus movement, and there was much discussion and acrimony, starting with the question of the non-Jews in Christ-assembly at Antioch. As we shall see, the situation in Antioch was especially contentious because it could be looked at from several different points of view, depending on whether Antioch was understood as part of the Land of Israel that was expected to be restored to the nine and a half tribes that were exiled under the Assyrians in 722 BCE. We will return to this issue in our discussion of Gal 2:11–14.

In terms of violating boundaries, Paul was accused, according to the book of Acts, of bringing Greeks into the Jerusalem temple, thereby defiling that holy place (Acts 21:28). Non-Jews were prohibited from entering the temple beyond the court of the gentiles. An inscription was placed as a warning on the wall surrounding the inner precincts: "No alien may enter within the balustrade around the sanctuary and the enclosure. Whoever is caught, on himself shall he put blame for the death which will ensue" (OGIS 2.598; SEG 8.169).[22] Hence, the territorial limits between Jews and gentiles were firmly established in a number of ways in the first century. Ephesians 2:14 refers to the ethnic discord between Jews and gentiles as a "dividing wall" that separates the two groups. The meaning of this term has been contested, but it may refer to the balustrade that marked out the area in the Jerusalem temple beyond which the gentiles were prohibited to enter. If so, it is used in Eph 2:14 as a metaphor of the whole complex of ethnic exclusions that separate Jews and gentiles.

The third synthesis of territorial coding—the conjunctive synthesis or the "redistribution of the remainder"—wards off the fusion of all codes into a single qualitative stock by producing a residuum. But it also begins a new line of code by redistributing this surplus through an alliance. There are many different mechanisms for warding off the fusion of codes and redistributing surplus code through alliances with other lines of code: practices of potlatch (giving away wealth in order to gain prestige and power), practices of struggle (itinerant raids and theft eliminating accumulation), practices of dowry (giving away wealth and establishing alliances with other kinship lines), gifts and counter-gifts, and so on.[23]

This third synthesis of territorial coding—specifically, conjunctive synthesis—can be illustrated by the complex story of King Herod Antipas's marriages. We have already referred to Antipas's illicit marriage to Herodias, which was denounced by John the Baptist. However, Antipas's first wife was the daughter of King Aretas of

22. Cf. Orian, "Purpose of the Balustrade in the Herodian Temple," 487–524; Llewelyn and Van Beek, "Reading the Temple Warning as a Greek Visitor," 1–22.

23. The related first nations of the Pacific Northwest and coastal British Columbia are prime examples of territorial assemblages. See further Kirk, Tradition and Change on the Northwest Coast, which describes many of the practices being described here (albeit not using the terms "conjunctive synthesis" or "redistribution of the remainder"). On the Coast Salish peoples, I have found two dissertations particularly helpful: Thom, "Coast Salish Senses of Place"; Kennedy, "Threads to the Past."

Nabatea. Antipas probably married her for political reasons, that is, to solidify the alliance between two peoples—Jews and Nabateans—and thus to prevent Aretas from encroaching on Antipas's territory. In other words, the Nabatean princess at this point was a "residuum," an excess daughter who could be used to form a strategic alliance and redistribute excess wealth via her dowry. According to Josephus, on his way to Rome Antipas visited his brother Herod Philip, the tetrarch of Trachonitis, and the latter's then-wife Herodias. Antipas fell in love with Herodias and proposed marriage to her. She accepted on the condition that he divorce his present wife, the daughter of Aretas. Antipas agreed and set sail for Rome. When he returned, Antipas's Nabatean wife returned to her father, who responded by initiating a war with Antipas. As a result, Antipas's whole army was destroyed. He wrote to Emperor Tiberius about the defeat, whose reaction was to ask Vitellius, the governor of Syria, to bring Aretas to him alive in chains, or, if he were killed, to send him his head. Clearly, the conjunctive synthesis of territorial coding is not a trifling matter.

State Assemblages

The second type of assemblage is the "state assemblage." State assemblages are arranged in such a way that the conditioning relations attempt to unify or totalize all the concrete elements and agencies in the assemblage. Instead of the surplus code generated by territorial assemblages that would normally form an alliance with other concrete elements, a surplus of code may instead begin to form an unchecked accumulation—agricultural, social, scientific, artistic, and so on—requiring the maintenance of a specialized body. This special body of accumulation then reacts back on the concrete elements and brings them into resonance around a centralized point of transcendence.[24] According to Deleuze and Guattari, state assemblages

> make points *resonate* together . . . very diverse points of order, geographic, ethnic, linguistic, moral, economic, technological particularities. [. . .] It operates by stratification; in other words, it forms a vertical, hierarchized aggregate that spans the horizontal lines in a dimension of depth. In retaining given elements, it necessarily cuts off their relations with other elements, which become exterior, it inhibits, slows down, or controls those relations; if

24. Compare this concept of "state assemblage" to Ma, "Hellenistic Empires," 335–36 (emphasis mine): "The *basileia*, Hellenistic kingdom, can be described as *a bundle of institutions*—in the traditional senses of formal organs, bodies, rules, and practices that structured state power in its most official manifestations. The model for this approach is the classic work by E. Bikerman, *Les Institutions des Séleucides* (1938), which combined a clear survey of institutions with a clear set of (often legalizing) propositions about the core principles of the Seleukid state, and a sense of the Hellenistic state as *a multiplicity of bodies and constituencies*, thus avoiding the formalist-royalist fallacy of focusing too much on the king and putting the king and kingship as the central problem. . . . Personal monarchy was of course an *ideological construct*, dependent on the collaboration of many for the ruler's will to be implemented." Ma goes on to give a survey of the various institutions that constituted the Hellenistic kingdom ("Hellenistic Empires," 336–42).

the State has a circuit of its own, it is an internal circuit dependent primarily upon resonance, it is a zone of recurrence that isolates itself from the remainder of the network, even if in order to do so it must exert even stricter controls over its relations with that remainder.[25]

In state assemblages, the abstract machine attempts to cut itself off from and rise hierarchically above the concrete relations and personae of the assemblage. What Deleuze and Guattari call "state overcoding" is thus characterized by centralized accumulation, forced resonance of diverse points of order, "laying out a divisible homogeneous space striated in all directions," and by its vertical and redundant center (on top), scanning all the radii.[26] Striation is one of the fundamental tasks of the state; striation results from the overcoding, centralization, and hierarchization of territories.

In the ancient world, state overcoding was very common. The religion of the Romans, for example, was strictly regulated by the state: "No one shall have gods to himself, either new gods or alien gods, unless recognized by the State" (Cicero, *Leg.* 2.8.19).[27] The Romans used animal sacrifice as a tool for cultural and political integration of the various peoples under the hegemony of its empire, since the universal practice of animal sacrifice—"the quintessential ritual complex of ancient civilizations"—was taken for granted as a normative cross-cultural practice that could work to tie together the sociopolitical hierarchies throughout the empire.[28] As James B. Rives shows, "the practice of animal sacrifice formed part of the basic common cultural vocabulary that helped unite the disparate ethnic and religious traditions of the Empire."[29] Thus, the Jerusalem temple, along with its counterparts in various localities

25. Deleuze and Guattari, *ATP*, 433 (authors' emphasis).

26. The state is the bond or knot that deterritorializes the diverse political segments and forces them into a new regime of overcoding. In ancient Rome, this overcoding is illustrated very nicely on the frieze of the Ara Pacis Augustae ("Altar of Augustan Peace"), in which the central acanthus grows from the bottom up and sends out tendrils. Unnaturally grafted onto those tendrils are various plants from all over the Roman Empire, symbolizing the nations under the hegemony of Rome as well as the fertility of the Empire that Augustus founded. Cf. Caneva, "Augustus Botanical Code," 63–77; Caneva, *Augustus Botanical Code*. For photographs of the Ara Pacis, see https://sites.google.com/site/arapacisaugustae/home/north-wall. On State overcoding, see also on Rev 13:16–18 (the mark of the beast) in chapter 9 below.

27. Cf. O'Brien and Vervaet, "Priests and Senators," 85–106, here esp. 97–102.

28. The quote is from Graf, "What Is New about Greek Sacrifice?," 116. The idea that animal sacrifice is "the quintessential ritual complex of ancient civilizations" suggests that sacrifice is an assemblage in the sense that we are using the term here. Cf., similarly, Stroumsa, *End of Sacrifice*, xvi, who refers to the end of sacrifice in Late Antiquity as "obviously a synecdoche."

29. Rives, "Animal Sacrifice and Political Identity in Rome and Judaea," 109: "The core of my argument is that Judaean tradition was one of these; that animal sacrifice, as a cultic practice central to both Judaean and Graceo-Roman religious tradition, played an important role in integrating Judaeans into the Graceo-Roman world." Cf. Orlin, "Augustan Religion: From Locative to Utopian," 51, 55–56, here 57: "The imperial cult [which focused on the *person* of the emperor], just like the previously locative cults of Rome, helped to bind the inhabitants of the empire together in a religious community that could be shared anywhere in the empire." Conversely, when the officiating priests of the Jerusalem temple refused to perform the twice-daily sacrifices in the temple on behalf of the emperor and the

throughout the empire, offered sacrifices on behalf of the Roman emperor, effectively making the Jerusalem temple into an extension of the imperial cult.[30] It is one of the great ironies of history that the death of Jesus Christ as a royal pretender ("the King of the Jews") at the hands of the Romans was interpreted as a *sacrifice*.[31] For that sacrifice would occupy the same integrating function for the anti-imperial kingdom of God that Jesus inaugurated,[32] while simultaneously eliminating the need for sacrifice not only in the Jerusalem temple but everywhere else as well, for his death was seen as "once for all" (cf. Rom 6:10; Heb 7:27; 9:12, 26; 10:10; 1 Pet 3:18).[33] It is not surprising, then, that when the "Christianizing" empire ultimately had its turn at state overcoding, sacrifice was officially abolished.[34]

Roman people that had been instituted by Augustus, that refusal constituted the outbreak of actual hostilities between Judeans and Romans, that is, "the foundation of the war against the Romans," as Josephus puts it (*J.W.* 2.408–409). "The cessation of sacrifices on behalf of the Emperor [was] tantamount to a declaration of revolt" (Rives, "Animal Sacrifice," 124). Besides these daily sacrifices on behalf of the emperor, sacrifices on special occasions were considered a test of loyalty to the emperor. Therefore, when the Judeans were accused of disloyalty to Emperor Gaius at one point, they were able to point to the large special public sacrifices (hecatombs) that they had made on his behalf on several occasions—at his accession to power, upon his recovery from illness, and in support of his forthcoming German expedition (Philo, *Embassy to Gaius* 356). On the perceived relationship between the Jews' penchant for revolution and their refusal to participate in the ritual complex of animal sacrifice on which the unity of humankind depended, see Philostratus, *Vita Apollonii* 5:33–34 (Stern, *GLAJJ*, II.341), quoting the first-century philosopher Euphrates: "For the Jews have long been in revolt not only against the Romans but against humanity; and a race that has made its own life apart and irreconcilable, that cannot share with the rest of mankind in the pleasures of the table *nor join in their libations or prayers or sacrifices*, are separated from ourselves by a greater gulf than divides us from Susa or Bactra or the more distant Indies. What sense then or reason was there in chastising them for revolting from us, whom we had better have never annexed?" In a similar way, Christians are charged with violating Roman polity by their refusal to participate in state-sponsored cults and their secretive and seditious worship of Jesus. Cf. Origen, *Contra Celsum* 1.1; 7.66; 8.12, 24.

30. Rives, "Animal Sacrifice," 122–23. Cf. Müller, "Globalization," who refers to "(g)localism," a neologism referring to the variety of ways in which local communities and cultures adopt and adapt the global *koine*: "A very good example is the way civic societies absorbed and incorporated the idea of Roman domination through the creation of a cult for the goddess Roma in the second century BCE, then for some generals in the late republic, and finally for the emperors, following the very Greek tradition of the cult of Hellenistic rulers. Wherever the initiatives lie, such behaviors were responses to the *imperium Romanum*, and these very local manifestations would have enhanced 'the sense of the interconnectedness of the empire' for 'those who viewed the monuments and participated in the festivals'. . . ."

31. On the interpretation of Jesus' death as a sacrifice, see, e.g., Hengel, *Atonement*. Of course, as in animal sacrifices generally, Christ's sacrifice was understood as voluntary. On Jesus' crucifixion as a royal pretender, see chapter 2 below.

32. For the integrating function of Christ's sacrificial death, see Rev 5:9: "You [sc. the Lamb] are worthy to take the scroll and to open its seals, for you were slaughtered and by your blood you ransomed for God saints from every tribe and language and people and nation; you have made them to be a kingdom and priests serving our God, and they will reign on earth." Cf. John 1:29.

33. Cf., e.g., Theissen, "Sacrificial Interpretation of the Death of Jesus and the End of Sacrifice," 139–60. Theissen characterizes the early Christian abandonment of sacrifices as "a revolution in the history of religion" (139).

34. Cf. Stroumsa, *End of Sacrifice*, 57: "*Sacrificiorum aboleatur insania*: 'That the folly of sacrifices

An excellent example of state overcoding and striation in the modern world is the "wilderness" designation given to certain tracts of land. The US Wilderness Act of 1964 set aside certain places as "wilderness" to be forever "untrammeled by man." From a First-Nations, territorial-assemblage perspective, however, the notion of "wilderness," rooted in the Euro-American separation of nature and culture, is highly problematic and even ludicrous. In his novel *Wolfsong*, Louis Owens, himself of Native American and European decent, has a member of a fictional coastal Salish people explain to his nephew about the US Wilderness Act:

> "This is a good thing they did," Uncle Jim had said, "because now maybe they won't cut all the trees and build roads. But if you think about it, it's pretty funny. When our people lived here long ago, before the white folks came, there wasn't any wilderness and there wasn't any wild animals. There was only the mountains and river, two-leggeds and four-leggeds and underwater people and all the rest. It took white people to make the country and the animals wild. Now they got to make a law saying it's wild so's they can protect it from themselves."[35]

The novel unfolds in what the government designates as "Glacier Peak Wilderness" in the North Cascades of Washington State. The native name for the mountain that is the centerpiece of this region is *Dakobed*, which is commonly understood to mean "Great Mother" in Coast Salish.[36] As Owens explains in a separate essay,

> At the center of the Glacier Peak Wilderness . . . is the vastly beautiful mountain named on maps, most unimaginatively, Glacier Peak. We look at the peak and see glaciers, and the text of the mountain is laid bare. There are other names for the peak, however, one of which is Dakobed. . . . The local Indian people, the Suiattle, look at Dakobed and see the place from which they came, the place where they were born, the mother earth. Their stories tell them that

be abolished,' states a law of Constantius II [Theodosian Codex 16.10.2]." Although Stroumsa gives perhaps too much credit to the rabbinic sages for this "transformation" (the concept of the death of Christ as a sacrifice "once for all" [see above for references] was arguably more directly influential), nevertheless Stroumsa is correct that the destruction of the temple in 70 CE required a radical change for (temple-based forms of) Judaism, since the only place where sacrifices could be made was now gone (*End of Sacrifice*, 56–83; see further below on supersessionism). Of course, not all forms of pre-70 Judaism were temple-based. Cf. Ego et al., *Gemeinde ohne Tempel = Community without Temple*. On the historical importance of Christ's sacrificial death for the end of the sacrificial cultus in antiquity, see Stroumsa, *End of Sacrifice*, 72–83. Tying together the points being made in this paragraph, perhaps we can state the matter this way: The Jewish failure to sacrifice on behalf of the emperor led inexorably to the destruction of the Jerusalem temple and thus to the permanent cessation of sacrifice there, while the "sacrifice" of Christ at the hands of the Romans was understood to end the need for sacrifice altogether.

35. Owens, *Wolfsong*, 80–81.

36. Although this understanding of the mountain's name is widespread, I have not been able to document that "Great Mother" is the actual lexical meaning of the term. Cf. Bates et al., *Lushootseed Dictionary*, 223, which defines the term as "permanently snow-covered mountain" and relates it to a cognate term meaning "water" (cf. 193).

they are related in an ancient and crucial way to this magnificent peak. There is an important and invaluable message in this knowledge, for whereas a society may well mine the heart out of something called a natural resource, one does not violate one's mother. The future of that wilderness and, of course, the future of all life depends upon whose stories we listen to: the stories that tell us we are bound in a timeless and inextricable relationship with the earth which gives us life and sustains us, or the stories that tell us the earth is a resource to be exploited until it is used up.[37]

We are all too familiar with State assemblage and its overcoding, because in Western democracies, we have lived in this arrangement all of our lives. As of this writing, we have just emerged from one of the most contentious elections in United States history. A president who has authoritarian tendencies has sought to accumulate and concentrate power in himself. It is safe to say at this point that he *is* the Republican Party. His motto, "Make America Great Again," in the 2016 presidential election, and "Keep America Great," in the 2020 election, have resonated with a large portion of the American people, who willingly cede a portion of their independence in exchange for secure borders and the kind of policies that ensconce their own way of life and (predominantly white) privilege.[38]

In the first century CE, there was no notion of a democratically elected leader. The Roman Empire, ruled by a single omnipotent emperor, was firmly entrenched in virtually all the Mediterranean places to which the New Testament refers. Under the Roman Empire, provinces were ruled by leaders who were either under the jurisdiction of the emperor directly (imperial provinces) or the Roman Senate (senatorial provinces). In some cases, as we have seen, lands were ruled by client kings. In any case, "state overcoding" of all aspects of society from top to bottom was in place, and actors in the New Testament bump up against this state hierarchy on many occasions. As we will discuss further in chapter 2, Jesus himself will run afoul of the Roman government in Judea, resulting in his crucifixion. In Thessalonica, Paul and his companions were accused of "acting contrary to the decrees of the emperor, saying that there is another king named Jesus" (Acts 17:1; cf. 16:21). Later, Paul will use his Roman citizenship in order to get out of being flogged in Jerusalem (Acts 22:26–29, 27), and eventually he appeals to the emperor himself to hear his case (Acts 25:11–12). These are just a few of the incidents in which the actors in the New Testament come into the crosshairs of governmental officials. In a state assemblage, there is a strong tendency to unify or totalize all the concrete elements and agencies, so that any hint of a disruption to the prevailing arrangement meets with a swift and sure response on the part of the state. As Jesus told his disciples, "You know that among the Gentiles

37. Owens, "Mapping," 211. On the notion of so-called "wilderness" in Owens's work, see further Brande, "Not the Call of the Wild," 247–63.

38. Cf. Snyder, *Road to Unfreedom.*

those whom they recognize as their rulers lord it over them, and their great ones are tyrants over them" (Mark 10:42 pars.).

Capitalist Assemblages

Capitalist assemblages are arranged in such a way that the conditions, elements, and agencies of the assemblage are divested of their qualitative relations and codes in order to circulate more widely as abstract quantities. In the capitalist assemblage, it is no longer the concrete elements that drive the process of progressive itinerant change (as in the territorial assemblage), nor the abstract machine that centralizes the control over the concrete elements (as in the state assemblage), but the agent or persona that becomes disengaged from the assemblage and tries to force unqualified concrete elements into strictly quantitative relations in which the accumulation of wealth is the goal and money is the common coin, the globally exchangeable quantity.

Deleuze and Guattari define a capitalist assemblage by its processes of "axiomatization." Axioms operate by emptying flows of their specific meaning in their coded context (e.g., sex as the act of marriage, the meal as the center of family life) and imposing a law of general equivalence in the form of monetary value (commodification). Thus emptied of their primary meaning and abstracted from any sustaining context, entertainment and fast foods become commodities sustained by whole industries to satisfy the appetites that their marketing and advertising departments create. These industries continue to stoke desire until the market is completely saturated. Then another company will come along with a new way to exploit the situation and thereby create new desires and a new market. Capitalism is a ravenous beast that devours all aspects of an existing social landscape, eviscerated of meaning and memory, and expels them as business transactions.[39]

In capitalist assemblages, people are no longer viewed as members of a society or citizens of a state, but rather as productivity units (workers)[40] or in terms of per capita consumption (customers).[41] The goal is to keep labor costs as low as possible

39. Cf. Rooney, *Beautiful World, Where Are You*, 16. The title is derived from the first line of the poem by Friedrich Schiller, "Die Götter Griechenlands" (1788). For a citation of the full poem, see the epigraph to the present volume.

40. Unit labor costs are often viewed as a broad measure of (international) price competitiveness. They are defined as the average cost of labor per unit of output produced. They can be expressed as the ratio of total labour compensation per hour worked to output per hour worked (labor productivity). This indicator is measured in percentage changes and indices.

41. Per capita consumption is the yearly use of goods and services by each person, derived by dividing the quantity of goods and services used by the total population. Capitalist consumerism involves the over-indulgent consumption of resources. Our dopamine economy, or what historian David Courtwright calls "limbic capitalism," is driving compulsive overconsumption, from compulsive gambling and shopping to binge eating and opioid abuse. Multinational industries, often with the help of complicit governments and criminal organizations, have multiplied and cheapened seductive forms of brain reward, from junk food to pornography. Cf. Courtwright, *Age of Addiction*.

through high efficiency and externalization of costs[42] and to extract as much wealth as possible from consumers in the shortest time possible.[43] This maximizing process of quantification on both ends requires decoding qualitative relationships in favor of globally exchangeable quantities.[44]

In the ancient world, the situation is much the same, although the ability to achieve global scale is necessarily more limited. The New Testament has much to say about the accumulation of wealth. In Luke 16:19–31, Jesus tells the story of the rich man and Lazarus, in which the rich man "dressed in purple and fine linen" and "feasted sumptuously every day," whereas the poor man named Lazarus, was diseased ("covered with sores") and "longed to satisfy his hunger with what fell from the rich man's table" (today, we call this as the trickle-down theory of economics).[45] The problem with a capitalist assemblage is not only what it does to the marginalized of society, but also what it does to the self-centered rich people themselves. It turns out that the rich have all the wrong priorities. Hence, Jesus pronounces woes against the

42. On "externalization of costs," see the video "The Story of Stuff" (2007): https://www.storyof-stuff.org/movies/story-of-stuff/; for an annotated transcript of the video, see https://www.storyofstuff.org/wp-content/uploads/2020/01/StoryofStuff_AnnotatedScript.pdf.

43. Inevitably, the end product of the capitalist assemblage is the destruction of the world, because capitalism is built on the premise that consumption must be fast, quantitatively unlimited, and universal in scale. Hence, despite the governmental watchdogs that are supposedly in place to prevent collapse, capitalism is simply unable to restrain itself, so it will plunder natural resources (fish, lumber, fossil fuels, ores), pollute the environment, and contribute to global warming. We are now seeing the disastrous effects of this unbridled production and consumption.

44. The stock market is the quintessential example of the depersonalized exchange of axiomatized entities that are radically abstracted from their actual context in society. It's simply a matter of mechanically buying and selling in order to make a profit, with little or no concern for what the underlying stocks themselves represent. The high-tech, professional hedge funds can perform trades at ultrahigh frequency using computer algorithms, which many retail traders view as an unfair advantage. The week of January 25, 2021, was a wild one on the stock market. The professional hedge funds thought that GameStop (a video game, consumer electronics, and gaming merchandise retailer) would trade lower, so they shorted the stock, thinking that they could buy it back at the lower price and pocket the difference. Small investors, however, revolted, for they were not only fond of GameStop, they also wanted to give the behemoth hedge funds a taste of their own medicine. Therefore, exchanging intel on Reddit (a discussion website) and using Robinhood (a commission-free trading app), a large number of retail investors banded together to buy up huge quantities of GameStop, causing the stock to skyrocket in price, which forced the hedge funds to cover their shorts at a loss of billions of dollars. This is perhaps the logical conclusion of capitalism: The market becomes simply a high-stakes board game to settle old scores.

45. In the "trickle-down" economic system, the poorest gradually benefit as a result of the increasing wealth of the richest. Alas, as the recent study by David Hope of the London School of Economics and Julian Limberg of King's College London shows, tax cuts for the rich over the past 50 years have only really benefitted the individuals who were directly affected, and did nothing to promote jobs, economic growth, or income equality. Cf. Hope and Limberg, "Economic Consequences of Major Tax Cuts for the Rich." Here is the study's conclusion directly from the abstract on the basis of data from 18 OECD (Organisation for Economic Co-operation and Development) countries over the past 50 years: "We find that major reforms reducing taxes on the rich lead to higher income inequality as measured by the top 1% share of pre-tax national income. The effect remains stable in the medium term. In contrast, such reforms do not have any significant effect on economic growth and unemployment."

rich, according to Luke 6:24–25. The rich man, anxious for control and security, said, "Soul, you have ample goods laid up for many years; relax, eat, drink, be merry." But God said to him, "You fool! This very night your life is being demanded of you. And the things you have prepared, whose will they be?" (Luke 12:19–20). Jesus believes that one cannot serve God and mammon (Matt 6:24//Luke 16:9–13 [Q]). Therefore, Jesus exhorts: "Do not store up for yourselves treasures on earth, where moth and rust consume and where thieves break in and steal; but store up for yourselves treasures in heaven, where neither moth nor rust consumes and where thieves do not break in and steal. For where your treasure is, there your heart will be also" (Matt 6:19–21). Jesus urges his hearers to focus exclusively on the most important possible pursuit: "The kingdom of heaven is like a merchant in search of fine pearls; on finding one pearl of great value, he went and sold all that he had and bought it" (Matt 13:45–46). For Jesus, then, capitalist assemblages distract from all that is most important in life.[46]

Nomadic/Revolutionary Assemblages

The fourth type of assemblage is the "nomadic/revolutionary assemblage." This is the assemblage that best describes the early Jesus movement. Nomadic/revolutionary assemblages are arranged in such a way that the conditions, elements, and agencies of the assemblage are able to change and enter into new combinations without arbitrary limit or so-called "natural" or "hierarchical" uses and meanings.[47] Deleuze and

---

46. The story of the rich man in Mark 10:17–27 is a salient example of this point: "As he was setting out on a journey, a man ran up and knelt before him, and asked him, 'Good Teacher, what must I do to inherit eternal life?' Jesus said to him, 'Why do you call me good? No one is good but God alone. You know the commandments: "You shall not murder; You shall not commit adultery; You shall not steal; You shall not bear false witness; You shall not defraud; Honor your father and mother."' He said to him, 'Teacher, I have kept all these since my youth.' Jesus, looking at him, loved him and said, 'You lack one thing; go, sell what you own, and give the money to the poor, and you will have treasure in heaven; then come, follow me.' When he heard this, he was shocked and went away grieving, for he had many possessions. Then Jesus looked around and said to his disciples, 'How hard it will be for those who have wealth to enter the kingdom of God!' And the disciples were perplexed at these words. But Jesus said to them again, 'Children, how hard it is to enter the kingdom of God! It is easier for a camel to go through the eye of a needle than for someone who is rich to enter the kingdom of God.' They were greatly astounded and said to one another, 'Then who can be saved?' Jesus looked at them and said, 'For mortals it is impossible, but not for God; for God all things are possible.'"

47. Compare "nomadic/revolutionary assemblages" to *utopian* worldviews in Smith, *Map Is Not Territory*. As we have seen, *utopian* worldviews valorize mobility as transcendence and liberation, which is rebellious, centrifugal and open, over against the other coeval existential possibility, *locative* worldviews, which are conforming, centripetal and closed. According to Smith (*Map Is Not Territory*, 101), "While in this culture, at this time or in that place, one or the other view may appear the more dominant, this does not effect [*sic*] the postulation of the basic availability of both at any time, in any place." Indeed, Smith (*Map Is Not Territory*, 103) states, "The alternation, the discoveries and choices of and between these two views is . . . the history of man and the history of religions." Depending on worldview, then, the nomadism (and hence the openness and vastness) of the Scyths in classical sources is either idealized or disdained: "On the one hand, their mobility makes them shiftless, barbaric, frightening, perpetual exiles; on the other hand, they are free, uncontaminated, wise, lords of all

Guattari call this type of assemblage "nomadic" because it was invented by histori-cally nomadic peoples whose movement was not directed toward a final end (a static territory or state) but functioned as a kind of "trajectory." For the nomad, Deleuze and Guattari observe,

> every point is a relay and exists only as a relay. A path is always between two points, but the in-between has taken on all the consistency and enjoys both an autonomy and a direction of its own. The life of the nomad is the intermezzo. Even the elements of his dwelling are conceived in terms of the trajectory that is forever mobilizing them.[48]

The concept of "nomadicism" that Deleuze and Guattari develop refers less to place-less, itinerant tribes-people[49] than to groups whose organization is immanent to

---

the earth they so casually roam" (*Map Is Not Territory*, 131). In a utopian worldview, the structures of order in the cosmos are not the positive limits that they were meant to be; instead, they have become oppressive. In such a situation, Smith argues, "Man is no longer defined by the degree to which he harmonizes himself and his society to the cosmic pattern of order; but rather by the degree to which he can escape the patterns" (*Map Is Not Territory*, 139). Smith (*Map Is Not Territory*, 140) gives the example of Paul and the Law: "As Paul in Romans 7 was to discover about the Law of Yahweh, that it was good *once*, but that it had been captured by the Powers and turned upside down so that 'the very commandment which promised life proved to be death to me' (Rom. 7:10), so each locative culture was to discover that its cherished structures of limits, the gods that ordained and maintained these limits, and the myths that described the creation of the world as an imposition of limits were perverse. Each culture rebelled against its locative traditions, developing a complex series of techniques for escaping limitation, for achieving individual and cosmic freedom now." Smith (*Map Is Not Territory*, 308–9) juxtaposes "a locative map of the cosmos" to "a utopian map of the cosmos." The latter seeks to break out of the oppressive confinement and interconnectedness of all things, in order to take "flight to a new world and a new mode of creation" (*Map Is Not Territory*, 309; cf. 150–51). "Indeed, I should want to go so far as to argue that if the Temple had not been destroyed, it would have had to be neglected. For it represented a locative type of religious activity no longer perceived as effective in a new, utopian religious situation with a concomitant shift from a cosmological to an anthropological view-point" (*Map Is Not Territory*, 128).

48. Deleuze and Guattari, *ATP*, 380.

49. See, however, Deleuze and Guattari, *ATP*, 381–82: "If the nomad can be called the Deter-ritorialized par excellence, it is precisely because there is no reterritorialization *afterward* as with the migrant. . . . With the nomad, on the contrary, it is deterritorialization that constitutes the relation to the earth, to such a degree that the nomad reterritorializes on deterritorialization itself. It is the earth that deterritorializes itself, in a way that provides the nomad with a territory. The land ceases to be land, tending to become simply ground (*sol*) or support. The earth does not become deterritorialized in its global and relative movement, but at specific locations, at the spot where the forest recedes, or where the steppe and the desert advance." We may compare Deleuze and Guatarri's concept of the nomad to Zeno's dream (cited in Plutarch, *On the Fortune of Alexander* 329A–B), in which the *cos-mopolis* is likened to free-range cattle that graze together and are nurtured by universal law (*nomos*). It cannot be happenstance that *nomad* derives from the Greek *nomas* ("roaming in search of pasture"), or that, as Deleuze observes, *nomos* itself has etymological connections with pasturing livestock. Cf. Roffe, "Nomos," in Pars, *Deleuze Dictionary*, 189–91: "The Greek word *nomos* is normally translated as law. Deleuze notes, however, in one of the few instances of etymological consideration in his work, that it is derived from the root word *nem*, which means 'to distribute.' He gives the example of the related word *nemô*, which in ancient Greek meant to 'pasture livestock'—in other words, to send out the animals to an unbounded pasture according to no particular pattern or structure. [. . .] The sense

the relations composing them. For example, an improvisational jazz band forms a "nomadic" group, in contrast with a symphony orchestra: in the former, group coherence arises immanently from the activity of improvising itself, whereas in the symphony orchestra, it is imposed from above by a conductor performing a composer's preestablished score.

In contrast to the capitalist assemblage, which makes possible unlimited immanent transformation on the condition of global quantification, the revolutionary/ nomadic assemblage makes possible a truly unlimited qualitative transformation and expansion of the assemblage.[50] Without the abstraction and dominance of any part of the assemblage, a truly reciprocal change occurs. Thus, the revolutionary/nomadic assemblage constructs a participatory arrangement in which all the elements of the assemblage enter into an open feedback loop whereby the condition, concrete elements, and agents all participate directly and equally in the process of transformation. This kind of participation and self-management thus offers a political alternative that is incompatible with territorial hierarchies based on essentialist meanings, state hierarchies based on centralized command, and capitalist hierarchies based on globally exchanged generic quantities. A nomadic assemblage is a new type of body politic that is no longer predicated on the territorial-body of the "natural" hierarchy, the party-body of the nation-state, or the market-body of capital.

The English word "nomad" comes from the Greek *nomas* ("roaming in search of pasture"). Thus, the nomad is territorial in a deterritorialized sense. We have already seen that Jesus was deterritorialized in the extreme, having "nowhere to lay his head" (Matt 8:20//Luke 9:58 [Q]). Jesus and his disciples were itinerant,[51] but they did not abandon the world. Jesus and his followers went from village to village, not from deserted place to deserted place. Jesus does not retire to the wilderness, nor does he set up a community on the shores of the Dead Sea. In 1 Pet 2:11, the notion of itinerancy in the early Jesus movement continues when the author addresses his

---

of *nomos* as anarchic distribution can be understood in reference to the *nomad*. Rather than existing within a hierarchical structure like a city, nomadic life takes place in a non-structured environment where movement is primary." On Zeno's dream, see further Scott, *Apocalyptic Letter to the Galatians*, 129–38, where it is discussed that Zeno employs a similar etymology (i.e., a play on words between "the grazing of the herd together" [*agelē synnomos*] and "universal law" [*nomos koinos*]). On the influence of early Stoicism on Deleuze, see further Johnson, "Deleuze–Stoicism Encounter," 270–88; Johnson, *Deleuze, a Stoic*.

50. Similarly, Bruce Lincoln discusses how a religion of resistance can form a truly revolutionary movement only if the former can break out of its insularity, absorb other groups like itself, and attract new members from other sectors of society. Cf. Lincoln, *Holy Terrors*, 88–89.

51. Cf. Mark 10:28–31: "Peter began to say to him, 'Look, we have left everything and followed you.' Jesus said, 'Truly I tell you, there is no one who has left house or brothers or sisters or mother or father or children or fields, for my sake and for the sake of the good news, who will not receive a hundredfold now in this age—houses, brothers and sisters, mothers and children, and fields with persecutions—and in the age to come eternal life. But many who are first will be last, and the last will be first.'" Cf. Allison, *Historical Christ and the Theological Jesus*, 116.

readers metaphorically as "aliens and exiles." Or, as Paul expresses it, "our citizenship is in heaven" (Phil 3:20).

Much of the rest of our study will be unfolding the implications of the nomadic/revolutionary assemblage for understanding New Testament Theology. Before embarking on that task, we still need to understand the typology of change in assemblages.

The Typology of Change in Assemblages

Not only are there four different types of assemblages (territorial, state, capitalist, and revolutionary/nomadic), but also four different types of coexistent processes of change in those assemblages. In every assemblage, four different kinds of political change are at work, what Deleuze and Guattari refer to as "deterritorialization." Deterritorialization is the way in which assemblages continually transform, maintain homeostasis, and/or reproduce themselves. If we want to know how an assemblage works, we must ask, "What types of change are at work?" We are talking here about dynamic processes rather than static entities.[52]

The four kinds of deterritorialization or change that define assemblages are: (1) "relative negative" processes that change an assemblage in order to maintain and reproduce an established assemblage; (2) "relative positive" processes that are ambiguous insofar as they neither reproduce an established assemblage nor create a new assemblage; (3) "absolute negative" processes that do not support any assemblage, but undermine them all; and (4) "absolute positive" processes that do not reproduce an established assemblage, but instead create a new one. Let us look more closely at each of these types of change that can affect any assemblage.

---

52. Compare the typology of change in assemblages to Jonathan Z. Smith's notion of the change that is possible from locative to utopian worldviews: "The adoption of one or the other of these symbolic systems has the most profound implications for the question of social change" (*Map Is Not Territory*, 132). For Smith (*Map Is Not Territory*, 143 [author's emphasis]), "*social change is preeminently symbol or symbolic change*. At the heart of the issue of change are the symbolic-social questions: what is the place on which I stand? what are my horizons? what are my limits? I have suggested that there are two basic answers to these questions, that these two provide the description of a social or individual center of value and meaning, and that from such a center all other symbolizations derive their meaning. Thus when one adopts one or the other of these two basic stances, one adopts a whole symbolic universe which is, for the individual or culture, *the* Universe. To change stance is to totally alter one's symbols and to inhabit a different world. And finally, I have suggested that these two stances ought not to be looked upon as stages in social (or individual) evolution or growth, with maturity or modernity associated with the open or limitless. Rather I have insisted that these two stances are coeval possibilities. From this perspective, place (whether in an open or closed structure) ought not to be viewed as a static concept. It is through an understanding and symbolization of place that a society or individual creates itself."

Relative Negative Deterritorialization

Relative negative deterritorialization (RND) is the process that seeks to maintain and/ or reproduce an assemblage. This is the process by which preestablished assemblages adapt and respond to changes in their relations by incorporating those changes. For example, the demands of popular social movements against governmental policies can often be satisfied through the adaptation of state politics: legal reform, increased political representation, and party support. These processes allow the preestablished state assemblage to remain in place through modification. Popular movements against war, poverty, the exclusion of minorities, and so on are "lines of flight" or expressions of political realities different from the established ones. Relative negative deterritorialization aims to obstruct these lines of flight by offering them an increased incorporation of their desires into the existing state assemblage.[53] In doing so, these desires become normalized as part of the state itself.

53. There are various strategies that are used to accomplish RND in politics. Cf., e.g., Snyder, *Road to Unfreedom*, who describes two approaches—the "politics of inevitability" and the "politics of eternity"—that are used to prevent or discourage any real change and individual responsibility. The *politics of inevitability* entails "a sense that the future is just more of the present, that the laws of progress are known, that there are no alternatives, and therefore nothing really to be done" (*Road to Unfreedom*, 7). "The politics of inevitability is the idea that there are no ideas. Those in its thrall deny that ideas matter, proving only that they are in the grip of a powerful one. The cliché of the politics of inevitability is that 'there are no alternatives.' To accept this is to deny individual responsibility for seeing history and making change. Life becomes a sleepwalk to a premarked grave in a prepurchased plot" (Snyder, *Road to Unfreedom*, 15). When actual experience causes the belief that tomorrow will be worse than today, the collapse of the politics of inevitability ensues, and another experience of time takes over: the *politics of eternity*. Cf. Snyder, *Road to Unfreedom*, 8: "Whereas inevitability promises a better future for everyone, eternity places one nation at the center of a cyclical story of victimhood. Time is no longer a line into the future, but a circle that endlessly returns the same threats from the past. Within inevitability, no one is responsible because we all know that the details will sort themselves out for the better; within eternity, no one is responsible because we all know that the enemy is coming no matter what we do. Eternity politicians spread the conviction that government cannot aid society as a whole, but can only guard against threats. Progress gives way to doom. In power, eternity politicians manufacture crisis and manipulate the resultant emotion. To distract from their inability or unwillingness to reform, eternity politicians instruct their citizens to experience elation and outrage at short intervals, drowning the future in the present. In foreign policy, eternity politicians belittle and undo the achievements of countries that might seem like models to their own citizens. Using technology to transmit political fiction, both at home and abroad, eternity politicians deny truth and seek to reduce life to spectacle and feeling." Snyder, *Road to Unfreedom*, 257–58: "It is easy to see the appeal of eternity to wealthy and corrupt men in control of a lawless state. They cannot offer social advance to their population, and so must find some other form of motion in politics. Rather than discuss reforms, eternity politicians designate treats. Rather than presenting a future with possibilities and hopes, they offer an eternal present with defined enemies and artificial crises. For this to work, citizens have to meet eternity politicians halfway. Demoralized by their inability to change their station in life, they must accept that the meaning of politics lies not in institutional reform but in daily emotion. They must stop thinking about a better future for themselves, their friends, and their families, and prefer the constant invocation of a proud past." Snyder, *Road to Unfreedom*, 267: "The politics of eternity tempts with a cycle of nostalgia and delivers a cycle of conflict." In discussing these two alternative approaches to politics, Snyder is long on diagnosis but short on prescription. He give excruciating detail on the perils of the politics of inevitability and eternity, both of which lead us toward unfreedom,

Assemblages are thus never total or homogenous. All assemblages are always undergoing some kind of adaptation or change. The question is, What kind of process of transformation are they undergoing? Relative negative deterritorializations are the processes that simply maintain or reproduce an established territorial, statist, or capitalist assemblage.

Spotify as an Example of Relative Negative Deterritorialization

In order to illustrate RND, we will now adduce several examples from both the ancient and the modern world. We begin with an analysis of Spotify.[54] Founded in 2006, the music-and-podcast-streaming service Spotify has quickly become a ubiquitous presence on digital devices. Like all social phenomena, it is an assemblage, meaning that it is not a fixed, unified entity, but rather a relational construct comprised of heterogeneous and emergent component parts that are arranged together toward certain strategic ends. To understand how the Spotify assemblage functions, we will need to examine its structure, its political typology, and its typology of change. As we shall see, Spotify is a capitalist assemblage that uses RND in order to capture and keep its music-loving audience.

First, we examine Spotify's structure. Like any assemblage, Spotify has an abstract machine/condition, concrete elements, and agents/personae. The term Spotify itself is the abstract machine—a set of conditions that signify the concrete elements and agents of an assemblage in whatever configuration they are currently arranged. The *abstract machine* is dependent on exterior elements, that is to say the material and technical but also expressive and symbolic desires that produce subjectivity and agency to exist. In the case of Spotify, these exterior elements produce data (via the personae) that can then be fed into the algorithms that perpetuate the application. The *concrete elements* of the assemblage consists of the cache of music that is stored on Spotify's servers, essentially any music to which a person could want to listen. The *personae/agents* are the users of Spotify. However, we are not talking here about individuals per se, but rather about the collective choices of the users that bring the concrete elements of the assemblage and its algorithm into new relationships.

Next, we examine the *political typology* of the Spotify assemblage and its *typology of change*. In this case, it is clear that we are dealing with a predominantly *capitalist* assemblage, which quantifies music choices and seeks to monetize information. Its freemium model allows users to listen to music for free but with just

---

but he doesn't give us much help on how to respond to those enslaving forces. The little help that he does provide points in the direction of revolution, real change, and the key to that change is creating a "politics of responsibility," whereby "we become the makers of a [world] renewal that no one can foresee" (Snyder, *Road to Unfreedom*, 279). In this regard, Snyder highlights the need to restore the mutually reinforcing virtues of equality, individuality, succession, integration, novelty, truth, and trust (*Road to Unfreedom*, 277–79).

54. For the full report, see von Hacht, "Spotify Assemblage."

enough interruption through advertisements that they are gently coaxed into paying a subscription fee in order to enjoy advertising-free listening. Either way, the
whole system is able to perpetuate itself while paying musicians royalties. To this
end, Spotify employs RND in order to keep users listening ad infinitum. For example, the algorithm perpetually suggests songs that the listener might enjoy playing,
based on their own past choices and the choices of listeners with a similar profile. It
also ranks songs based on the collective valuations of the agents, which encourages
listeners to explore the unfamiliar or to select the top ranked. In this way, Spotify is
able to keep its customers happily listening to tunes without interruption. This may
not seem like a form of enslavement, but the algorithm that the platform uses seeks
to lock listeners into a feedback loop that exploits their psychological vulnerabilities
(i.e., what they want when they want it).[55] A similar analysis applies to any number
of Internet-based social media platforms.

TikTok as an Example of Relative Negative Deterritorialization

Our next example shows how RND applies to a state assemblage. A group of disaffected aboriginal voters in a state assemblage were vulnerable to being co-opted by
another group or system or to simply giving up on any system. So the question became, "How are you going to tell this group of Indigenous peoples to participate in the
State system that has oppressed them for so long, and tell them to trust it?" One Native
American politician had the bright idea of posting culturally relevant messages on
TikTok, which served either to keep her constituency in the fold or to recapture them.
In one video, for example, the politician zooms by on a scooter wearing a traditional
red outfit with white ribbons as she shouts, "Excuse me, I'm Indigenous. Coming
through!" More than one hundred thousand people watched the video, and the image
became a symbol of her ultimately successful campaign.[56]

The Incident at Antioch as an Example of Relative Negative Deterritorialization

Our third example of RND is drawn from the New Testament. According to Paul,
the Jewish Christ-followers in Antioch attempted to compel gentile believers in their
assembly to comply with a Jewish way of life in order to maintain table fellowship:

> But when Cephas came to Antioch, I opposed him to his face, because he
> stood self-condemned; for until certain people came from James, he used to
> eat with the Gentiles. But after they came, he drew back and kept himself sepa-
> rate for fear of the circumcision faction. And the other Jews joined him in this

55. Cf. Ward, *Loop*; Lembke, *Dopamine Nation*.
56. https://www.kcur.org/politics-elections-and-government/2020-12-16/young-state-lawmakers
-in-kansas-missouri-harness-the-strange-power-of-tiktok.

> hypocrisy, so that even Barnabas was led astray by their hypocrisy. But when
> I saw that they were not acting consistently with the truth of the gospel, I said
> to Cephas before them all, "If you, though a Jew, live like a Gentile and not
> like a Jew, how can you compel the Gentiles to live like Jews?" (Gal 2:11–14)

At first, the mixed assembly was meeting together in harmony and eating shared meals, implying perhaps also the Lord's Table. Then the "men from James" came. At that point Peter, under external pressure, withdrew from table fellowship with the gentiles, causing the rest of the Jewish Christ-followers to follow suit. Paul calls their move "hypocrisy." The Jewish pressure might have resulted in an irreparable split the community into two separate factions—Jewish and gentile—depending on whether the gentiles submitted to the demand that they "live Jewishly" (i.e., to observe Torah, including circumcision and dietary laws) or they followed Paul's admonition that Torah-observance was unnecessary for them. Paul denounced Peter and the rest of the Jewish believers in the assembly because the apostle to the nations did not want to see a rift. He advocated for unity because the new revolutionary assemblage, consisting of Jews and gentiles on an equal basis, was for him the actualization of the new humanity in Christ.[57] In contrast, Peter and the other Jewish Christ-followers were enforcing on the gentile believers a condition for communal inclusion that was tantamount to preserving or reproducing an established *territorial* assemblage—a form of Judaism based on the Mosaic Torah.[58] This is a case of RND.[59]

57. See the discussion of Gal 3:28 in chapter 7.

58. Seen in terms of assemblage theory, Second Temple Judaism was not a unified entity but rather as a multiplicity of forms of belief and practice. Moreover, despite attempts to identify the elements that define "common Judaism," there is no "essence" of Judaism. We would do better to see it as an evolving and multifarious process. See further below.

59. Cf. Lincoln, *Holy Terrors*, 77–92, who posits a typology of religion consisting of four basic types: religion of the status quo, religion of resistance, religion of revolution, and religion of counter-revolution. On *religion of the status quo*, see Lincoln, *Holy Terrors*, 79: the religious ideology of the dominant faction and institutional means of its propagation. On *the response of the religion of the status quo to a religion of resistance*, see Lincoln, *Holy Terrors*, 83: "Whereas there will be as a rule only one religion of the status quo within a given society at any given time, the variety of religions of resistance that may thrive simultaneously is well-nigh endless, and history attests to a rich variety of exemplars. They may be ascetic, libertarian, or orgiastic; impassioned, cathartic, or quietistic; utopian or nihilist; esoteric, mystical; militant or pacifist; authoritarian, egalitarian, or anarchist; and so on ad infinitum. No attempt to reduce them to a small number of 'ideal types' is possible without serious distortion. As a class, they are best characterized by a negative feature: their refusal to accept the religion of the status quo in part or in toto [e.g., values, ethics, membership, leadership, and rituals]. And however innocuous the doctrines or activities of such groups may seem, this refusal constitutes at the very least an implicit threat to the interests of the dominant faction—a threat that is regularly answered by their stigmatization or suppression." On *the difference between religion of resistance and religion of revolution*, see Lincoln, *Holy Terrors*, 85: "Religions of resistance define themselves in opposition to the religion of the status quo, defending against the ideological domination of the latter. Religions of revolution, on the other hand, define themselves in opposition to the dominant social faction itself, not its religious arm alone, promoting direct action against the dominant faction's material control of society." A religion of resistance can transform itself into a religion of revolution under the right sociopolitical circumstances (Lincoln, *Holy Terrors*, 86–89). On *religion of counterrevolution*, see

To understand the Jewish perspective on the matter, we need to recall that within the territorial bounds of the traditional land of Israel, certain practices were incumbent on all residents, including non-Israelites. Thus, in the Hebrew Bible the *ger* ("resident alien") was a non-Israelite who resides among the Israelites in the land of Israel and observes Torah while doing so, including dietary restrictions (Exod 12:19, 48; Lev 17:10, 12, 13, 15), circumcision (Exod 12:48–49), and proper observance of the Sabbath and holy days (Exod 12:10, 19; 23:12; Lev 16:29; Num 9:14; Deut 5:14; 16:11, 14; 26:11).[60] It will not go unnoticed that these are the very issues that Paul addresses in his letter to the Galatians and in Antioch. The borders of Israel are defined in various ways in the Old Testament and early Jewish literature, but some texts make the northernmost border extend to the Taurus Amanus mountains, the mountain range just to the north of Antioch on the Orontes.[61] In that case, Syrian Antioch itself would be part of the Land of Israel, and, as *gerim*, gentiles in the Antiochene Christ-assembly could be expected to observe Torah.[62] Even then, however, the gentiles would not be on equal footing with native Jews/Judeans.[63]

Lincoln, *Holy Terrors*, 91: "As for the defeated religion of the status quo, it too assumes a new form as a religion of resistance, albeit a very special one, which I would term the 'religion of counterrevolution.' Its marks are profound nostalgia, condemnation of the new order as usurpers, and—in its early years, at least—active attempts to restore the dominant faction with which it fell. . . ."

60. See further Hayes, *Gentile Impurities and Jewish Identities*, 21–22 et passim; van Houten, *Alien in Israelite Law*; Achenbach et al., *Foreigner and the Law*, esp. the contributions by Achenbach (29–52), Rainer Albertz (53–70), and Christophe Nihan (111–34); Mayshar, "Who Was the *Toshav*?," 225–46. Note that circumcision required of the *ger* in Exod 12:48–49 is *voluntary*, depending on whether he wants to celebrate Passover. This is not a matter of forced circumcision as in the Hasmoneans' policy of compelling conversion to Judaism in the gentile lands that they conquered under the assumption that these land lay within Israel's traditional boundaries (cf. Collins, *Invention of Judaism*, 97–99). The term used in some of these cases is ἀναγκάζω ("to compel"), the same verb that Paul uses in Gal 2:14 to describe the Jewish behavior toward the gentile believers in Antioch ("how can you compel the Gentiles to live like Jews/Judeans [πῶς τὰ ἔθνη ἀναγκάζεις ἰουδαΐζειν]?"). Cf., e.g., Josephus, *Ant.* 13.318: Aristobulus "made war against Iturea, and added a great part of it to Judea, and *compelled* (ἀναγκάσας) the inhabitants, if they wished to remain in their country, to be circumcised and to live according to the laws of the Jews/Judeans (περιτέμνεσθαι καὶ κατὰ τοὺς Ἰουδαίων νόμους ζῆν)." See also Josephus, *Life* 113.

61. Cf. Alexander, "Early Jewish Geography," 985–87.

62. Cf. Bockmuehl, "James, Israel and Antioch," 49–83; Siegert, "Vermeintlicher Antijudaismus und Polemik gegen Judenchristen im Neuen Testament," 85–86. On this interpretation, the men from James could have understood the Jesus movement primarily in terms of the restoration of the original twelve tribes of Israel, including "the lost sheep of the house of Israel" (i.e., the northern tribes exiled under the Assyrians in 722 BCE), within the northernmost extent of the traditional boundaries of the Land (i.e., the Taurus Amanus range), which would have included Antioch. If this is correct, then the early Jesus movement in its Pauline and Jamesian forms had vastly different visions of what the Christ event meant for the gentiles living in Antioch.

63. A text like Deut 14:21 makes it clear that *gerim* occupied a second-class status in the Land compared to that of native Israelites: "You shall not eat anything that dies of itself; you may give it to aliens residing in your towns for them to eat, or you may sell it to a foreigner. For you are a people holy to the LORD your God."

For Paul, the territorial assemblage of Mosaic Judaism based on Torah-observance was superseded by the Christ-event. The term "supersessionism" has received a bad name in recent discussions of Paul and Judaism. As I discuss elsewhere, however, Paul's supersessionism has parallels within the Old Testament and early Judaism.[64] Seen in light of the concept of assemblages, Paul continues the line of flight that Jesus initiated *within Judaism*, which can be characterized as an extension of a wisdom-apocalyptic-Enochic line.[65] The whole discussion of a "parting of the ways"—that is, between Judaism and Christianity, viewed as monoliths—is wrongheaded.[66] We must think, rather, of a number of partings of the ways (or even continual partings of the ways) between *mutations within Judaism*.[67] For the question is not what the assemblage *is*, but rather what the assemblage *does* and what it *becomes*. And what the assemblage does continues to change and transform in accordance with new lines of flight.[68] Whereas E. P. Sanders emphasizes sameness ("common Judaism" and its

64. Cf. Scott, *Apocalyptic Letter to the Galatians*, ch. 3.

65. We shall discuss Jesus as a "line of flight" *within Judaism* in the Conclusion to the present volume.

66. See further Schröter et al., *Jews and Christians—Parting Ways in the First Two Centuries CE?*; Gabrielson, "Parting Ways or Rival Siblings?," 178–204; Schnelle, *Die getrennten Wege von Römern, Juden und Christen: Religionspolitik im 1.Jahrhundert n.Chr.*; Schnelle, "Römische Religionspolitik und die getrennten Wege von Juden und Christen," 432–43.

67. Cf. Baron et al., *Ways That Often Parted*, 1–13. As we have seen, in his *End of Sacrifice*, Stroumsa refers to the radical rabbinic innovations in religious practice that were necessitated by the cessation of animal sacrifice in 70 CE. He calls these innovations a "paradigm shift" (2), a "transformation" (the term and its cognates appear 161 times), a "revolution" (30x), "*supererogation*" (69 [emphasis mine]), a "democratization and spatial explosion of Jewish worship" (65), and "a victory of the moderns over the ancients" (114). "What matters from the present perspective is that the Jews—a people whose ways of worship had been destabilized, and who in order to survive had to *practically reinvent their religion*, or at least their ritual—might offer under the High Empire the very example of a spiritualized religion, or a religion without blood" (65 [emphasis mine]). Stroumsa concludes (130): "The Jews seem to be at the origin of each of the transformations I have studied: personal identity, the place of the Book, the abandoning of sacrifices, the development of communities—Judaism seems to have experimented with all these aspects of the 'new' religion that emerges in Late Antiquity. [. . .] It is in large part thanks to its Jewish heritage that Christianity was able to invent new frameworks in which religion would redefine itself." Although he does recognize some precursors to these radical innovations (e.g., *End of Sacrifice*, 32, 70, 75, 113, 123), Stroumsa tends to downplay continuity between pre- and post-70 in favor of a thesis of rupture, such that the rabbinic sages become the main engines of innovation. As we have mentioned, however, the notion of community without temple is already found within various forms of Judaism before the destruction of the Jerusalem temple in 70 CE: e.g., the *Songs of the Sabbath Sacrifice* (4Q400–407, 11Q17) describes the heavenly worship on the first thirteen Sabbaths of a year and assumes a unity between the angelic worship offered in the celestial sanctuary and the worship offered by humans on earth. Paul has the concept of community *as* temple (cf. 1 Cor 3:16–17; 2 Cor 6:16; also Eph 2:21). Moreover, if Stroumsa had included the Enochic tradition in his study, he would have been able to keep his conclusion, that Jews seem to be at the origin of the transformations he has studied, but he would have had to backdate the source of the influence in several cases by as much as a half millennium.

68. Cf. Witte et al., *Torah, Temple, Land*, 1–8, here 1: "Distinctive political, cultural, and social constellations are associated with each of these [i.e., diverse forms of Judaism that have evolved in different geographical areas], in which Jewish communities developed their own conception of themselves

"laundry list" of unchanging characteristics), we are focusing on the emergence of difference (becoming-other). As stated earlier, we are dealing here not with static entities or essences, but rather with *dynamic processes*.[69]

Paul viewed the incident at Antioch as a make-or-break issue of solidarity for the Christ-assembly. He strongly opposed the attempt at RND by the Jewish adherents of Jesus there. According to Gal 2:11–14, Paul pushed for open table fellowship, without regard to social distinctions, and, in doing so, he effectively continued the creative unfolding of the Jesus revolution.[70]

Relative Positive Deterritorialization

Relative positive deterritorialization (RPD) is the process of change that does not reproduce an established assemblage, but it does not create a new one, either. The process is therefore completely ambiguous and indeterminate, a borderline phenomenon in an emergent situation. It is not yet clear whether the process will result in the new element being reincorporated into an already established assemblage through relative negative deterritorialization (see above) or the new element will go on to become an independent assemblage through radical transformation. There is still the possibility of either co-optation or a new world.

---

and how they were perceived by the outside world. Judaism saw itself confronted with the distinctive contexts and challenges presented by the Persian Empire, Egypt, Greek culture, the Imperium Romanum, and, not least, by emerging Christianity. Ancient Judaism existed, therefore, in a world which was permanently changing in terms of political, social, and religious parameters. Judaism itself was also subject to constant processes of change, both of its self-perception and its external perception. What was deemed to be 'Judaism' or 'Jewish' was fluid and often contested with a need for constant renegotiation. In the following, 'Judaism' and 'Jewish' are, therefore, not to be understood as designations for religious communities with a clearly defined profile, but as heuristic categories to be filled with content in different periods of time and diverse religious, social, and political constellations. As a consequence, current developments in research on ancient Judaism, which highlight the diversity and fluidity of the categories 'Judaism' and 'Jewish,' are taken into account and refined." The whole volume deals with the forms of appearance that Judaism took in antiquity. As is well known, ancient Judaism was a religion in constant change, with various perspectives on central categories such as Torah, Temple, and Holy Land. Therefore, that which was seen as "Judaism" or "Jewish" was not a fixed entity, but rather a dynamic process.

69. Cf. Tomson, "The Wars against Rome," in Tomson and Lambers-Petry, *Image of the Judaeo-Christians*, 1–31, here 3. Tomson ("The Wars against Rome," 15) also points out that in the pre-70 situation, the (Essene) community behind 4QMMT said of themselves, "we have separated ourselves from the majority of the people" (פרשנו מרוב העם). Can this not be seen as a "line of flight" from the dominant form of Judaism? On the declaration of separation in 4Q397 frag. 16, line 6 (and its textual and interpretive uncertainties), see further Hacham, "Exile and Self-Identity in the Qumran Sect," 3–21, here 14–15; Wearne, "4QMMT," 99–126; von Weissenberg, *4QMMT: Reevaluating the Text, the Function, and the Meaning of the Epilogue*, 201–3; Fraade, "To Whom It May Concern: 4QMMT and Its Addressee(s)," 507–26, here 512–13; Bar-Asher Siegal, "Who Separated from Whom and Why? A Philological Study of 4QMMT," 229–56.

70. Cf. Matt 22:1–14//Luke 14:15–24 (Q); Gos. Thom. 64; Matt 9:10–13; Mark 2:15–17; Luke 5:29–32. On Paul's creative unfolding of the Jesus revolution, see further in chapter 6.

The Galatian assemblies can be adduced as a case in point. In the previous section, we described the incident at Antioch (Gal 2:11–14) as an example of (attempted) relative negative deterritorialization. The Jewish Christ-followers in Antioch were attempting to compel the gentiles to maintain or reproduce an established territorial assemblage (i.e., a Mosaic form of Judaism based on Torah-observance). Paul does not indicate the outcome of that conflict, so it too remains ambiguous.

For Paul, the incident at Antioch is a direct analogy to the situation in Galatia. The Galatian gentile believers were being pressured by Jewish outsiders to submit to Torah-observance. As a result, the outcome of Paul's work among the Galatians hung in the balance: "I am afraid that my work for you may have been wasted" (Gal 4:11). The issue at stake is whether the Galatians will continue to accept the Pauline gospel and its process of new creation or they will be co-opted by the already-established territorial assemblage promoted by the Judaizers: "Formerly, when you did not know God, you were enslaved to beings that by nature are not gods. Now, however, that you have come to know God, or rather to be known by God, how can you turn back again to the weak and beggarly elements? You are observing special days, and months, and seasons, and years" (Gal 4:8–10). Paul sees a comparison here between Judaism and paganism as territorial assemblages.[71] Having been enslaved in one kind of preestablished territorial assemblage (paganism), with its devotion to territorial gods,[72] they are now in danger of being re-enslaved in another kind of territorial assemblage (a form of Judaism), with its devotion to Torah-observance.[73] Paul is worried that the Galatians are jumping out of the frying pan and into the fire. One way or the other, however, the outcome of the Galatians' process of transformation is completely ambiguous, so Paul confronts the situation in no uncertain terms: "Stand firm, therefore, and do not submit again to the yoke of slavery" (Gal 5:1).

71. This comparison has struck commentators as highly unusual and provocative. As we shall see, however, Paul's comparison has an important parallel in the Epistle of Enoch (1 En. 92–105), to which Paul's letter to the Galatians is also otherwise indebted.

72. In the Greco-Roman world, polytheism prevailed, although individual gods received special worship in various locations. At Rome, Jupiter was the chief god, and in Roman religious and political thought, it was Jupiter's favoring of Rome that in conjunction with Roman attention to religious matters led to the creation of the Roman Empire and Rome's ascendancy over the Mediterranean world. Unlike Jupiter at Rome, Zeus was not the chief god of every Greek city, each of which adopted a particular tutelary deity: at Athens (the only Greek or Roman city to be named for a god), this was Athena, at Sparta Apollo, and Aphrodite at Corinth. In addition, many local and minor deities tended to be associated with the twelve Olympian gods, with their local or regional name becoming an epithet of the Olympian god in question. Cf. Dillon, "Gods in Ancient Greece and Rome."

73. In Gal 4:8–10, Torah-observance is summarized in terms of observing "special days, and months, and seasons, and years," although, as we have seen, Paul's letter to the Galatians makes it clear that Torah-observance in general is at stake, including circumcision and dietary laws. Paul's generic reference to sacred calendars at this point facilitates his analogy between Judaism and paganism.

Absolute Negative Deterritorialization

Absolute negative deterritorialization (AND) is the process of change that does not support any political assemblage but rather undermines them all. These are lines of flight that escape preestablished assemblages but instead of being ambiguously split between the old and the new (as in relative positive deterritorialization), they are unambiguously against the old assemblage as well as any new assemblage. However, by rejecting all forms of preestablished assemblage, they become fragmented targets easily recaptured by the relative negative deterritorializations of territorial, statist, and capitalist assemblages. Deleuze and Guattari state, "Staying stratified—organized, signified, subjected—is not the worst that can happen; the worst that can happen is if you throw the strata into demented or suicidal collapse, which brings them back down on us heavier than ever."[74] This is what happens when rebels try to subvert a ruling assemblage without attempting to establish another one in its place.[75] The dominant assemblage will simply seek to quell the disruption and restore order. This was the fate of many insurrections in antiquity that attempted to subvert the status quo. The reaction of the ruling powers was swift and decisive.

Take, for example, the famous slave rebellion that occurred between 73 and 71 BCE.[76] This revolt was led by Spartacus, a former auxiliary soldier from Thrace who had fought on the side of the Romans only to end up a gladiator-slave. The rebellion began in Capua, not far from Naples, Italy, when approximately seventy gladiators escaped from their training school, using kitchen utensils as weapons. On the road, they discovered several wagons filled with gladiators' weapons, which they seized. Other slaves, many of them shepherds and herdsmen who had plenty of weapons of their own, quickly joined the runaways in the rebellion. The rebels became so numerous that Roman legions, under the command of Crassus, were sent against them. The rebels were desperate, because they knew that, if captured, they would be shown no mercy. They swiftly defeated the well-trained Roman troops in several battles. Each time they defeated a Roman legion, they took its weapons. In the end, however, the rebels were vanquished. Spartacus himself died fighting, but six thousand of his followers were captured. They were crucified on the Appian Way, the two-hundred-kilometer-long road from the city of Rome to Capua. Because the rebels were merely rejecting one system and not fighting for another (i.e., a new world without slavery),[77]

74. Deleuze and Guatarri, *ATP*, 161.

75. The French revolutionary, Maximilien de Robespierre (1758–94), understood this point well: "It is not enough to have overturned the throne: our concern is to erect upon its remains holy equality and the imprescriptible Rights of Man" (cited in Scurr, *Fatal Purity*, 230). In other words, a new revolutionary assemblage.

76. Cf. Schiavone, *Spartacus*; Shaw, *Spartacus and the Slave Wars*, 130–65.

77. Cf. Schiavone, *Spartacus*, 117: "He [sc. Spartacus] certainly did not want to abolish slavery: nothing authorizes us to think so." Schiavone, *Spartacus*, 120 (emphasis mine): "But the point . . . was that the success of a subversive solution fed by the lowest social orders . . . would have presupposed

they became fragmented targets susceptible to recapture by the relative negative deterritorialization of the dominant state assemblage.

Absolute Positive Deterritorialization

Absolute positive deterritorialization (APD) is the process of change that seeks not to maintain or reproduce a preestablished assemblage (as in relative negative deterritorialization), but rather to actually create a new one. The goal of this type of change is to "prefigure" a new world; that is, to create a new world in the shell of the old. Not only does this type of change escape the capture of established assemblages (territorial, statist, or capitalist), it also connects with other elements that have escaped capture. Their connection is not one that reproduces an alliance (as in a territorial assemblage), or totalization (as in a state assemblage), or commodification (as in a capitalist assemblage), but rather forms an entirely new kind of assemblage characterized by direct participation.

To give an example of APD in the Jesus tradition, let us consider Mark 3:31–35 pars:

> Then his mother and his brothers came; and standing outside, they sent to him and called him. A crowd was sitting around him; and they said to him, "Your mother and your brothers and sisters are outside, asking for you." And he replied, "Who are my mother and my brothers?" And looking at those who sat around him, he said, "Here are my mother and my brothers! Whoever does the will of God is my brother and sister and mother."

Here, Jesus explicitly rejects the natural kinship ties of his native Jewish territorial assemblage, in favor of a revolutionary assemblage characterized by absolute positive deterritorialization.[78] This was the creation of a new world in which kinship ties

---

the existence of ties, alliances, and cultures that only a class structure could have provided, and which, instead was totally missing in that world. And it was precisely this limit that proved the undoing of Spartacus . . . —*the inability to trigger something resembling an authentic revolution.*" Schiavone, *Spartacus*, 121 (emphasis mine): "Above all, though, it [sc. Spartacus' plan] was unrealistic because of the lack of a real political and social perspective to offer to the rebels, capable of going beyond a simple break with Rome . . . ; something with the power to hold together the urban and rural plebs and masses of slaves, not just with closeness brought by desperation but indicating *the possibility of a new beginning.*"

78. There are several points to be made here. First, the leader of a revolutionary movement could normally expect to have support from his own family. Cf. MacMullen, "How to Revolt in the Roman Empire," 201: "It would naturally be assumed that your relatives could be counted on for aid and cooperation. The assumption did not always work out. It would be supposed that anyone contemplating revolt would base himself in the region where he was born. Native sons started out with a special advantage. For that reason governors and legionary legates were not routinely sent out to the regions they knew best, their own home provinces; rather the reverse, as was affirmed by law in the wake of Avidius Cassius' revolt." However, second, instead of receiving support from his family, they accused him of being "out of his mind" (Mark 3:21; cf. John 10:20). Leaders of armed insurrections were routinely regarded as "out of their minds." Cf. MacMullen, "How to Revolt in the Roman Empire,"

are based not on heredity, but on doing the will of God, who is their only "Father."[79] The result is a radically open social reality that allows a practically unlimited number of people to be directly related to Jesus. This new world that Jesus speaks into existence through his performative word is part and parcel of the gradually expanding community that Jesus has been forming around himself throughout the Markan narrative, including the call of his disciples (cf. Mark 1:16–20; 2:13–14) and the appointment of the Twelve (3:13–19), again through his performative word.[80] Although the circle of Jesus' followers becomes as broad and accessible as possible, it still effectively excludes people who oppose him, such as the scribes (3:22–30) and Jesus' biological family (3:31, 32).[81] Jesus is creating the new world in the shell of the old.[82] He is calling people to the creation of new modes of existence that will connect up with others to construct a new revolutionary political body.

202: "A rash of armed uprisings were attempted in 218 among the eastern legions. Their leaders were all executed. They had never had a chance, and a contemporary (Did 80.7.2) judged 'they were out of their minds [ἐξεφρόνησαν],' like Avidius Cassius in the judgment of Herodes Atticus." Cf. Philostratus, *Lives of the Sophists* 563: "Moreover, the story is told that when Cassius the governor of the Eastern provinces was plotting treason against Marcus, Herodes rebuked him in a letter that ran thus: 'Herodes to Cassius. You have gone mad (ἐμάνης).'"

79. Notice how Mark 3:35 pars. omits mention of those who do the will of God being a "father." Cf. Matt 23:9: "And call no one your father on earth, for you have one Father—the one in heaven." Jesus famously teaches his disciples to prayer to "Our Father in heaven" (Matt 6:9; cf. Luke 11:2), even as he himself prays to "Abba, Father" (Mark 14:36 pars.).

80. On Jesus' performative utterances, see further in chapter 2.

81. Cf. Luke 14:26: "Whoever comes to me and does not hate father and mother, wife and children, brothers and sisters, yes, and even life itself, cannot be my disciple." See also Matt 12:30//Luke 11:23 (Q): "whoever is not with me is against me." On the other hand, we find this: "whoever is not against us is for us" (Mark 9:40//Luke 9:50). Jesus' radical inclusiveness tends to err on the side of openness rather than on circling the wagons.

82. After Jesus' death, his family do become followers of Jesus. Indeed, James the brother of Jesus later became the leader of the Jesus movement in Jerusalem (Acts 15 and following; Gal 2:1–12), and, according to the Jewish-Christian author Hegesippus (ca. 180 CE) as recorded in Eusebius (*Ecclesiastical History* 3.20.1–6), the descendants of Jesus' brother Jude were persecuted under Emperor Domitian (ca. 95 CE): "There were yet living of the family of our Lord, the grandchildren of Judas, called the brother of the Lord, according to the flesh. These were reported as being of the family of David, and were brought to Domitian by the Evocatus. For this emperor was as much alarmed at the appearance of Christ as Herod. He put the question, whether they were of David's kindred, and they confessed that they were. He then asked them what property they had, or how much money they owned. And both of them answered that they had between them only nine thousand denarii, and this they had not in silver, but in the value of a piece of land, containing only thirty-nine acres, from which they raised their taxes and supported themselves by their own labor. Then they began to show their hands, exhibiting the hardiness of their bodies, and the callouses formed by incessant labor on their hands, as evidence of their own labor. When asked also about Christ and his kingdom, what was its nature, and when and where it was to appear, they replied, 'that it was not a temporal nor an earthly kingdom, but celestial and angelic, that it would appear at the end of the world, when coming in glory he would judge the living and the dead, and give to everyone according to his works.' Upon which, Domitian despising them, made no reply, but treating them with contempt, as simpletons, commanded them to be dismissed, and by a decree ordered the persecution to cease. Thus delivered, they ruled the churches, both as witnesses and relatives of the Lord. When peace was established, they continued

Conclusion

We have been through some fairly deep water: assemblages, typology of assemblages, typology of change in assemblages. The good news is that we are through the most challenging part of our book in terms of the presentation of new concepts. Our next step is to apply these concepts to Jesus and the revolutionary movement to which he gave rise.

living even to the times of Trajan." According to this account, Jesus' relatives raised suspicion because they were of a the royal line of David and Jesus had proclaimed a message of the kingdom. See further Bauckham, *Jude and the Relatives of Jesus in the Early Church*; Lambers-Petry, "Verwandte Jesu als Referenzpersonen für das Judenchristentum," 32–52. As we shall see in chapter 2, the idea that Jesus was a revolutionary figure was not misplaced. Moreover, the reason for the prominence of Jesus' kin in the early Jesus movement will be discussed in chapter 5.

2

Jesus' Crucifixion as a Royal Pretender

Kingship [i]s a discursive, performative phenomenon,
manifested in speech-act. —John Ma[1]

Introduction

SO FAR, WE HAVE used the modern return to revolution in order to explore the ancient Jesus revolution. We have discussed the typology of assemblages (territorial, state, capitalist, and nomadic/revolutionary) as well as the typology of change (deterritorialization) that assemblages can undergo (relative negative, relative positive, absolute negative, and absolute positive). We have illustrated each of these concepts with examples drawn from both the ancient and the modern world. Now we are ready to delve more deeply into the revolution that Jesus inaugurated.[2]

The Jesus revolution inevitably provoked extreme responses from the Jewish and Roman authorities who ruled over the territorial and state assemblages, respectively.[3] One of the indisputable historical facts in the Jesus tradition is that, with the support of Jewish leaders in Jerusalem, the Roman government in Judea had Jesus crucified

1. Ma, "Kings," 179.

2. The following is based on Scott, "Speech-Acts of a Royal Pretender," 1–37, with supplemental material.

3. Insofar as Jesus frequently inveighed against the wealthy, his rhetoric also evoked a negative response from the rich, who included many of those in leadership of the territorial and state assemblages, as well as those involved in the capitalist assemblage.

78

as "the king of the Jews," that is, as a royal pretender and an insurrectionist. However, the historical question remains: What exactly did Jesus say or do that provoked his crucifixion?[4] Despite some claims to the contrary by modern scholars, it seems extremely unlikely that Jesus advocated the violent overthrow of the government. That was not the nature of Jesus' perceived sedition. We have already suggested that the reason that Jesus alone was crucified—and his followers were left unscathed—is that his was a nonviolent revolution; otherwise, his followers would have been crucified with him. What, then, was the probable cause for Jesus' crucifixion?

To answer this historical question, we turn now to a historical analysis of the Gospel accounts that give us some vital clues. As we shall see, Jesus' apocalyptic vision of the kingdom of God not only opposed territorial, state, and capitalist assemblages, he also said and did things that pointed to a new and better world, a world in which humankind would be liberated from many forms of oppression, both literal and figurative. Moreover, Jesus' performative utterances actually sought to create this new world in the shell of the old. We shall argue that it was these performative utterances that provoked the authorities to have Jesus crucified, because these utterances were recognized as indicative of his perceived royal pretensions. If this is correct, then Jesus was seen as following a pattern that was widespread in the ancient world among other royal pretenders.

The present study focuses on the presentation of Jesus in Mark's Gospel, particularly why both sympathizers and critics perceived he aspired to kingship and why he therefore ended up crucified as a royal pretender, "the King of the Jews." Scholars have had difficulty understanding how the charge against Jesus could have been sustained.[5] The thesis pursued here is that Jesus' discourse itself was understood as an attempt to construct power, on the model of Hellenistic kings and royal pretenders.[6]

4. As mentioned in chapter 1, our developing New Testament Theology would consider historical reconstruction of the Jesus tradition as part of the evidence that undergirds it. Assessing why Jesus was crucified must be regarded as one of the most important historical considerations in this regard.

5. Cf., e.g., Allison, *Constructing Jesus*, 238–40.

6. We have several reasons for focusing in this study on Hellenistic royal pretenders and kings. (1) If, as Allison argues, "Jesus seems to have conceptualized the divine rule in contrast to the tyrannical rule of the stereotypical monarch" (*Historical Christ and the Theological Jesus*, 105), then our focus on the Hellenistic royal pretenders and kings can concretize what the stereotypical monarch was like. (2) The Hellenistic period affords an abundance of literary and epigraphic material on royal pretenders and kings. (3) The Hellenistic material is relevant for our understanding the traditional land of Israel not only during the Hellenistic period but on into the Roman imperial era. This is in line with recent trends in the study of the Eastern Mediterranean world, in which the "long Hellenistic Age" is seen as a period extending from the reign of Alexander the Great through the reign of Hadrian. For the term "long Hellenistic Age," see Chaniotis, *Age of Conquests*, 3: "The study of the Hellenistic Age traditionally ends with the suicide of Cleopatra in 30 BC and the annexation of her Egyptian kingdom by Rome. This certainly is an important turning point in political history. It marks the end of the last great Hellenistic kingdom and the beginning of the principate—a form of monarchical rule that took shape after Augustus and his successors. The year 30 BC, however, is not a turning point in the history of society, economy, religion and culture. Trends that we observe in the Hellenistic Age continued in the two centuries after Cleopatra's death. In order to fully understand them, we need to consider

This thesis does not require that the local actors needed firsthand access to a royal court or intimate knowledge of such a court.[7] As we shall see, Palestinian Jews could have known about the speech-acts of Hellenistic rulers both directly through publicly displayed monuments and indirectly through received Maccabean tradition.[8] In other words, the present study proceeds from the imminently historical supposition that Jesus was interpreted on the basis of well-known cultural categories and expectations of the contemporary period.

---

sources that postdate that year. And vice versa, we cannot understand the political institutions, the social organization, the economy, the culture and the religion of the Graeco-Roman East in the first two centuries of the Imperial period without considering their Hellenistic roots. The period from Alexander's campaigns in the East to roughly the reign of Marcus Aurelius (AD 160–80) should be best studied as one single historical period, for which I introduce the term 'long Hellenistic Age.' One may recognise several distinct phases in this period of approximately 500 years . . . but the development was continuous." As Karen Radner states in the introduction to *State Correspondence in the Ancient World*, "The normative value of royal letters provides an obvious connection between Hellenistic practice and that of other states, earlier and later" (9). On imperial correspondence, see Millar, *Emperor in the Roman World (31 BC–AD 337)*, 213–28 et passim. Millar also emphasizes the continuity between Hellenistic royal correspondence and imperial letter-writing (*Emperor in the Roman World*, 213, 214, 221). See further Ma, *Antiochos III*, 183; Lavan, *Slaves to Rome*, 218–29, here 222 (emphasis mine): "The explanation for this continuity lies in the fact that these letters [i.e., Augustus's letter to the city of Sardis in Lydia (5 BCE) and the letter of Septimius Severus and his son and co-emperor Caracalla to the city of Nicopolis ad Istrum in Moesia Inferior (198 CE)] are following a script that was already well established in the time of Augustus. Like Republican magistrates before him, Augustus was not just writing in Greek but appropriating the forms and idioms of a long tradition of Hellenistic diplomacy. The structure of a dialogue articulated through city decrees and imperial letters, the letter form, and the rhetoric of benevolence and euergetism all *follow a pattern that had been established by the Hellenistic kings*." We shall see additional evidence of the continuity between Hellenistic royal pretenders and Roman imperial pretenders in MacMullen, "How to Revolt in the Roman Empire," 198–203.

7. Cf. Allison, *Constructing Jesus*, 245: "It may also matter that Jesus and his hearers had no access to a royal court, so that, unlike weddings and fathers, lilies and the birds of the air, their firsthand knowledge of kings was nil."

8. It is, of course, difficult to know how much illiterate Galilean peasants, living in an oral culture, would have known about kingship. Some could presumably have been apprised of the glorious Maccabean era and the Hasmonean period of independence. To that degree, it is possible that they would have known something about the interactions of the Jewish leaders with the Seleucid kings as described in the Books of the Maccabees. Such lore would have been "in the air" rather than taught in a formal educational setting based directly on literary sources. By the same token, documentary evidence could have been known as well, assuming that someone who was in a position to read the monuments could pass on that knowledge to the locals. In Maresha, located 40 km southwest of Jerusalem, copies of a royal letter were found on two stelae, in Greek, the so-called Heliodoros Stele (178 BCE), in which King Seleucus IV, writing to his viceroy (Heliodorus) appointed a high priest (Olympiodorus) as overseer over all the sanctuaries of Coele Syria and Phoenicia, including the Jerusalem Temple. The fact that the royal letter in question was found only in Maresha and Byblos is purely happenstance; it applied to the entire satrapy. Cf. Cotton-Paltiel et al., "Juxtaposing Literary and Documentary Evidence," 1–15; Yon, "De Marisa à Byblos avec le courrier de Séleucos IV," 89–105. Surely such a royal letter would have been well known, not only because it had such a wide geographical distribution and enormous religio-cultural significance, but because it was a letter whose performative utterance apparently had an adverse effect on the Jerusalem temple (cf. 2 Macc 3:13). See further below.

The following discussion consists of three sections: (1) a brief review of the evidence that, according to Mark's Gospel, Jesus was crucified as a royal pretender; (2) a survey of the performative utterances of Hellenistic kings and royal pretenders; and (3) an examination of Jesus' performative utterances as recorded in Mark.

Jesus as Royal Pretender

Mark's Gospel presents Jesus as having been crucified as a royal pretender.[9] According to Mark 15:26, "The inscription of the charge against him read, 'The King of the Jews.'"[10] Allison writes, "My contention about Jesus' self-conception [i.e., that he sees himself as the end-time king of restored Israel] can appeal to a second likely fact: he was crucified as 'king of the Jews.' The circumstance, according to John Collins, suggests that Jesus 'was viewed as a messianic pretender and that the kingdom he proclaimed was understood, at least by his followers, as a messianic kingdom.' This makes sense. If Rome executed Jesus for making himself out to be a king, then in all probability some people, including presumably some sympathizers, or maybe even Jesus himself, hoped him to be such."[11]

Let's briefly review how Mark presents this turn of events as having occurred during Jesus' final week in Jerusalem:[12]

9. The term "pretender" is used here in the sense of a person who claims or aspires to a title or position, especially a claimant to a throne (often when considered to have no just title). Mark's Gospel is sensitive to the possibility that there may be rival claimants to the Jewish throne in the future: "And if someone says to you at that time, 'Look! Here is the Messiah! or 'Look! There he is!'—do not believe it" (Mark 13:21; cf. Matt 24:23–24). This strongly implies that Jesus, who speaks the prophecy of false messiahs, is the true Messiah.

10. All four Gospels coincide: Jesus was sentenced and crucified as an alleged "king of the Jews," and the charge against him was stated on a placard, which, according to Matt 27:37 and John 19:19, was placed at the top of the cross. On the execution of Jesus as "King of the Jews," see Allison, *Constructing Jesus*, 233–40. As Allison (*Constructing Jesus*, 234–35) argues convincingly, "The formulation 'King of the Jews' stems neither from proof from prophecy nor from the Christology of the community. In general early Christians hesitated to use the title 'King' for Jesus. Would the formulation of the inscription, with its decidedly political ring, really rest on a historicization of a dogmatic motif? This is not very plausible." In an interesting thought experiment, Allison (392–423) examines what we can know about the death of Jesus based solely on the testimony of Paul's letters. Although the apostle does not say why Jesus was crucified, he nevertheless gives enough clues about Jesus' perceived identity that we would be able to surmise, even without the Gospels, that the Romans executed Jesus "because they perceived him to be a royal pretender" (398).

11. Allison, *Constructing Jesus*, 233–34, citing Collins, *Apocalyptic Imagination*, 257. Note that, with one major exception, Allison (*Constructing Jesus*, 231) declines to attempt showing that any story or event happened as told in the Gospels. That exception is the sentencing of Jesus by Pilate for the crime of being "king of the Jews."

12. For a much fuller accounting of the evidence that Jesus was crucified as an insurrectionist who was conducting anti-Roman activities and had royal pretensions, see Bermejo-Rubio, "Jesus and the Anti-Roman Resistance," 1–105. For example, cf. Bermejo-Rubio, "Jesus and the Anti-Roman Resistance," 25n85: "The convergent evidence [i.e., that Jesus did indeed make kingly (rebellious) claims] is overwhelming: the *titulus crucis*; the messianic entry in Jerusalem, full of royal signs (see B. Kinman,

- When Jesus appeared before Caiaphas, the high priest, the latter asked Jesus, "Are you the Messiah, the Son of the Blessed One?" to which Jesus unequivocally replied, "I am."[13] Jesus goes on to add, in terms of Dan 7:13–14 combined with Ps 110:1, "And 'you will see the Son of Man seated at the right hand of the Power,' and 'coming with the clouds of heaven'" (14:62; cf. 12:35–37). The first citation alludes to the scene of the last judgment in Daniel 7 (cf. also Mark 13:26); the second citation is a royal enthronement psalm in which the kingly figure sits at the right hand of Yahweh.

- According to the Markan account of Jesus' trial before Pilate, the Roman governor asked Jesus whether he is "King of the Jews" (15:2a). As Allison observes, Jesus did not say "No," but rather responds rather evasively, "You say so," after which he made no further reply (15:2b–5).[14]

- The handing of Jesus over to be crucified is set in the context of a choice between releasing Jesus as the "King of the Jews" or rather an insurrectionist named Barabbas (15:6–15). This episode adds to the narrative evidence that Jesus is crucified as a royal pretender or usurper.

- In the next scene, the Roman soldiers charged with carrying out the crucifixion first stage a mock coronation ceremony (15:16–20). Like a Hellenistic king, Jesus was invested with the visible and recognizable signs of kingship—the headdress and the purple cloak (15:17–18). Instead of the usual diadem (a cloth fillet worn about the head, the equivalent of the crown), however, Jesus was given a crown of thorns, which evidently emulated the radiate headdress of several Hellenistic kings. On coinage, Antiochus IV Epiphanes (who also uses the epithet *Theos Epiphanes* ["God Manifest" or "The God Who Appears"])[15]

'Jesus' Royal Entry into Jerusalem,' in Darrell L. Bock and Robert L. Webb [eds.], *Key Events in the Life of the Historical Jesus: A Collaborative Exploration of Context and Coherence*, WUNT 247 [Tübingen: Mohr-Siebeck, 2009], pp. 383–427, esp. 405–411); the charge specified by Lk. 23.2; Jesus' reference to 'my kingdom' (Lk. 22.29–30); the emphatic appearance of the title 'king' in Pilate's interrogation and in the following narrative (Mk 15); the mocking of Jesus by the soldiers; the request of James and John to Jesus (Mk 10.35–40), presupposing that Jesus will be enthroned as the king of the new age; Jn 19.12 and Acts 17.7, which also hint at the seditious nature of the claim; and so on. The conclusion that Jesus made kingly claims is hardly [sic] inescapable." Bermejo-Rubio argues trenchantly that "a convergent pattern pointing to a seditious Jesus" is "an undeniable textual fact" (Bermejo-Rubio, "Jesus and the Anti-Roman Resistance," 100) and that to disagree with this assessment is to offer a drastically distorted image of Jesus (104).

13. According to Mark 8:29, Peter had confessed Jesus to be "the Messiah," and, as Allison observes, "it is clear from the context that the Davidic Messiah or royal Messiah is meant, because the acclamation is offered as an alternative to the opinion of some that Jesus is 'one of the prophets'" (*Constructing Jesus*, 229; cf. 133). On Jesus as Davidic Messiah, see Allison, *Constructing Jesus*, 279–98.

14. Allison, *Constructing Jesus*, 230, arguing that Jesus' response was effectively a plea of *nolo contendere* (Latin, literally "I do not wish to contend"; i.e., a plea by which a defendant in a criminal prosecution accepts conviction as though a guilty plea had been entered but does not admit guilt).

15. Note that Mark 13:14 alludes to the "desolating sacrilege," that is, Antiochus IV's cultic intrusion into the Jerusalem temple (cf. Dan 9:27; 11:31; 12:11; 1 Macc 1:54; 2 Macc 6:2; Josephus, *Ant.* 12:253).

appropriated the complex symbolism of Apollo-Helios for his own epiphany, which included a portrait of the king with a radiate crown (i.e., a crown with rays fanning out from the king's head).[16] In the context of a mocking investiture with royal regalia, Jesus' crown of thorns is redolent of such a radiate crown:[17] "Then the soldiers led him into the courtyard of the palace (that is, the governor's headquarters); and they called together the whole cohort. And they clothed him in a purple cloak; and after twisting some thorns into a crown, they put it on him. And they began saluting him, 'Hail, King of the Jews!' They struck his head with a reed, spat upon him, and knelt down in homage to him. After mocking him, they stripped him of the purple cloak and put his own clothes on him. Then they led him out to crucify him." As Allison notes, "All of this assumes that he has made himself out to be a sovereign."[18]

If, as we have seen, Mark presents Jesus as having been crucified as a royal pretender, "The King of the Jews," the question becomes how anyone could have come to this conclusion on the basis of what Jesus had said and done. For Allison, the imminent eschatological expectation in the Jesus tradition is what "makes sense of why the Roman authorities executed him as a messianic pretender."[19] At another point, Allison offers a different approach: "Yet perhaps the strongest argument for Jesus having been in fact crucified as 'king of the Jews' is the lack of a better suggestion regarding his alleged crime."[20] I would like to add to these reasons for Jesus' crucifixion as a royal

---

16. Cf. Nawotka, "Apollo, the Tutelary God of the Seleucids," 261–84, esp. 261–62; Iossif and Lorber, "Celestial Imagery on the Eastern Coinage of Antiochus IV," 129–46; Wright, "Seleucid Royal Cult, Indigenous Religious Traditions, and Radiate Crowns," 67–82, esp. 78–80. On Apollo as featured on Seleucid coinage, see Ma, "Hellenistic Empires," 324–57, here 345–46: "In addition to local adjudication and ad hoc quasi-legislation, one area of consistent regulation by the state was currency. . . . The Hellenistic kingdoms struck coins in gold, silver, and bronze, marked with the king's name and usually, in the case of gold and silver, the king's face; the obverse bore motifs, often religious, linked with dynastic identity. A typical third-century Seleukid tetradrachm bore on one side the profile portrait of the king, physiognomically individualized and wearing a diadem, and on the other side a representative of Apollo, the ancestor of the dynasty, in a fixed pose that did not change from reign to reign (sitting on the *omphalos* and holding an arrow), and the king's title and name in the genitive ('of King Antiochos'). . . ." See also Ma, *Antiochos III*, 15, 61, 94, 146, 181, 230, 240, 254–59, 262, 274, 294, 295, 296, 308, 324.

17. Cf. Amedick, "'Iesus Nazarenus Rex Iudaiorum,'" 53–66; Coleman, "Fatal Charades," 47: "The crown of thorns, nowhere in the Gospels identified as an instrument of torture [first at Clem. Alex. *Paed.* 2.73–75], is plausibly interpreted as an imitation of the radiate crown of divine rulers, as depicted on contemporary coins; the purple robe likewise mocked the regalia of hellenistic rulers; Jesus so attired would be a parody of θέος [*sic*] as well as βασιλεύς, and hence an object of mocking *proskynesis*." See, however, Yarbro Collins, *Mark*, 726.

18. Allison, *Constructing Jesus*, 230. Cf. Dunn, *Christianity in the Making*, 1:86: "His [sc. Jesus'] execution on the charge of being a messianic pretender ('king of the Jews') is generally reckoned to be part of the bedrock data in the Gospel tradition." See further Dunn, *Christianity in the Making*, 1:627–47, 784–90.

19. Allison, *Constructing Jesus*, 137.

20. Allison, *Constructing Jesus*, 235.

pretender a new approach: Jesus' performative utterances, understood as pleas for recognition, gave credence to the case against him.

Performative Utterances of Hellenistic
Kings and Royal Pretenders

The British analytical philosopher J. L. Austin wrote the signally important book, *How to Do Things with Words*, which describes speech-acts called "performative utterances." A performative utterance performs an action in and by words that change the state of the world (e.g., I grant, I decide, I release [from taxation], I appoint, I decree, I promise, I curse).[21] Unlike statements of fact, such speech-acts are neither true nor false per se,[22] but rather either "felicitous" or "infelicitous," that is, they are either effective or they are not. Speech-acts are effective when they meet conventional expectations and are validated by the intended audience. For example, if a person is pronounced "dead" at 10:40 am, that pronouncement has legal force and is also generally accepted as authoritative, if it occurs under the right circumstances (e.g., by trained medical personnel in a hospital or at a crime scene); in that case, the person is officially "dead." If, under normal circumstances, an unauthorized individual makes the same pronouncement, the utterance has no practical consequences. Thus, a performative utterance is a sociopolitical act that depends on the institutional context in which it is performed, the manner in which it is performed, and the recognition with which it is received. The status-changing performative, "I now pronounce you husband and wife," must be said by the right person, in the right context, and be accepted by the intended audience in order to effect a marriage between two people, with all the rights and responsibilities attending to it.

For historians of the ancient world, speech-act theory provides a powerful tool for exploring, in a nuanced way, the meaning of words in context on multiple levels. Austin's seminal insight allows the historian to see the relationship between a speech-act, its accordance with a set of cultural conventions and expectations, and its (intended or actual) transformative effect on the world. Thus, speech-act theory helps the historian read textual evidence and provides a useful and powerful means for interpreting historical documents, enabling a thick description of how words affect the world by showing the relationship between power, language, and context. The result is more satisfying and complex readings of the textual evidence in its historical

21. Austin, *How to Do Things with Words*. The exact form of the performative utterance is not at issue. A declaration, for instance, can be performative if it actually enacts the event it proclaims (e.g., "You're fired!" or "All of you are one in Christ Jesus" [Gal 3:28]). On Gal 3:28 as a performative utterance, see further in chapter 7 below.

22. This is indeed one of the chief values of speech-act theory: It goes beyond the narrow confines of propositional truth and formal logic, exploring instead the realm of language effecting action.

context.[23] These readings are also quite generative insofar as they allow us to perceive relationships between texts that might otherwise remain hidden.

John Ma uses speech-act theory in order to investigate the interaction between the ruler and the ruled in the Hellenistic world, using the interplay between the Seleucid empire and the Jewish *ethnos* in Maccabean Judea (175–129 BCE) as a case study.[24] Ma argues that performative speech-acts (I give, I grant) were the language of imperial power, the Hellenistic king's main medium for vertical communication with his subjects.[25] The post-conquest situation confronted the affected populace with a clearly defined institution of kingship, which entailed the authority to make performative utterances and the recognized conventions to ensure their acceptance. The form of the speech-act assumes not only its felicity, but also its efficacy and success. Yet, this seemingly top-down, one-way flow of words autocratically effecting transformative actions on the ground—what Pierre Bourdieu[26] called "social magic" (*magie sociale*)—was actually much more complicated and unstable than it would at first appear: The subjects themselves not only initiated the interaction in many cases but also played a major role in determining the outcome of the interaction, for their consent and approval were crucial to the establishment and maintenance of the power structure.[27] Thus, the interaction between ruler and ruled reveals the

23. For a primer of speech-act theory for historians, see Ma, "Seleukids and Speech-Acts," 71–112, here 75–85.

24. For statements of the goals of his study, see Ma, "Seleukids and Speech-Acts," 72, 105.

25. Ma, "Seleukids and Speech-Acts," 108. Cf. Ma, "Hellenistic Empires," 345: "The state, by its control of performativeness (namely the legitimacy of speech with practical effects, such as orders or edicts), and its position as the ultimate holder of means of violence to enforce its will, found itself providing a whole range of services to the ruled, in terms of regulation, arbitration, and enforcement."

26. Bourdieu, *Ce que parler veut dire*, 125–26. Cf. Ma, "Seleukids and Speech-Acts," 89–90, 107–8: "Power imagines its transactions as simple Austinian illocutions: the speech-act is uttered, fulfils conditions, is accepted, and therein has effect on people and on things. To go further, it presents the unilateral efficiency of its utterances as a natural, unquestioned fact dependent on some god-like quality inherent to the uttering entity, rather than on acceptance by an audience. Unsurprisingly, it assumes that illocutionary uptake for its orders involves not only acknowledging the speech-act, but actually obeying the order. In contrast, the Maccabean example, characterized by transactions made ambiguous by the flux in the political situation, serves as a reminder that the magical, god-like effect of performative utterances depends on conditions outside and before the utterances: the effect is an eminently social construct, arbitrary and open to challenge or resistance—a fact which ideologies of domination try to obnubilate, by positing that arbitrary, historically determined systems of 'social magic' belong to the order of things." For more on "social magic" and performative utterances, see Ma, "Epigraphy and the Display of Authority," 133–58.

27. Cf. Ma, "Paradigms and Paradoxes in the Hellenistic World," 374: "The central medium for the expression of royal power, the 'performative utterance', is also disturbingly open to weakness—a phenomenon C. Préaux termed 'la faiblesse du droit', the odd powerlessness of the central authority: the very appearance of absolute authority, expressed in centrally issued diktats, means that local practice must be integrated by *post-eventum* pronouncements in which initiative is often local." See further Ma, *Antiochos III*, 384; Ma, "Seleukids and Speech-Acts," 107–8. As MacMullen discusses ("How to Revolt in the Roman Empire," 199–201), an insurrectionary movement needed support from three groups: wealthy landowners, the civilian population, and the army. Without this broad base of support, the uprising was doomed to fail.

contractual nature of power, which is more akin to a negotiation (or "euergetical dialogue")[28] than a simple, unilateral pronouncement, even though the conventionalized, published language of the king's performative utterance tends to mask the transactional, *do ut des* nature of the interaction and the behind-the-scenes political wrangling for concessions.[29] In a time of political instability caused, for example, by an external threat or and internal challenge to the throne, the subjects had even more ability to negotiate favorable terms from their ruler, because the ruler was motivated to pacify the populace and keep them within the fold.[30] Royal pretenders, however, could up the ante by using performative language to promise even more favorable terms for the subjects if they would accept his rule instead of the current regime's. As Ma shows, the Maccabees were skillful in repeatedly playing off Seleucid king against royal pretender and vice versa, negotiating a better and better deal for themselves in the process. As a result, the Seleucids had to relinquish ever more political control and tax revenue, in what became for them a race to the bottom and an eventual path to complete independence for the Jewish people. In the end, "the Seleukids had nothing more to offer but infelicitous speech-acts: these no longer had the context of authority and conventions that ensured uptake, and they were predicated on 'facts' (such as the existence of Seleukid power) that were manifestly untrue. Josephus tells us (*AJ* 13.274) the poignant end of the story which had started with the long, confident, imperial, letter of Antiochos III concerning the Jews: a century later, Hyrkanos simply responded with contempt for both Seleukid kings [i.e., Antiochos VIII Grypos and Antiochos IX Kyzikenos], ἀμφοτέρων κατεφρόνησεν."[31]

For our purposes, Ma's discussion of royal pretenders to Seleucid kingship is the most interesting instance of performative language, because, as discussed further

28. For the term "euergetical dialogue," see, e.g., Ma, *Antiochos III*, 79, 186, 187, 191, 204, 208, 235, 239.

29. Cf. Ma, "Seleukids and Speech-Acts," 85, 105: "The later Seleukids uttered formally correct speech-acts, as they made offers in the hope of securing support for their attempts on the throne or as they granted privileges which they had no power to refuse; but because of the ambiguous political situation and the lack of a clearly defined, stable power, their intended audience—the Maccabees—had considerable latitude in matters of choice, giving or refusing illocutionary uptake only on conditions that suited them. The situation could be analysed in the terms developed by Austin: the illocutionary acts ('I grant') also had a perlocutionary force ('I bargain')—except that this perlocutionary dimension was radically at odds with the appearance of power and authority which the illocutionary acts implied: these appear a mere veil for the 'real' bargaining going on. At any rate, awareness of the 'real,' perlocutionary transactions only makes the more remarkable the fact that the Seleukids and the Jews maintained the appearance of authoritative utterer and receptive subject, in a comedy of power played by each party for different reasons." See also Ma, "Seleukids and Speech-Acts," 108: "The concepts of speech-act theory, when applied to the Maccabean material, reveal that power rests not only on the exercise or the threat of violence, but also on some basic, invisible, contract between the rulers, whose speech-acts need acceptance to be translated into reality, and the ruled, whose consent ultimately decides on the felicity of the rulers' utterances."

30. Cf., e.g., Ma, "Seleukids and Speech-Acts," 94–95. The issue of royal pretenders is set in a broader context in Chrubasik, *Kings and Usurpers in the Seleucid Empire*.

31. Ma, "Seleukids and Speech-Acts," 104.

below, Jesus himself also employed performative utterances and was eventually executed as a royal pretender.[32]

Royal pretenders started to emerge in the Seleucid empire after the Seleucid dynasty split into two branches, both descended (or claiming descent) from a son of Antiochos III (i.e., Seleucus IV, on the one hand, and Antiochus IV, on the other). For example, when Demetrius I Soter (son of Seleucus IV) was challenged for the throne by Alexander Balas (who posed as son of Antiochus IV), the former sent a letter to Jonathan, the leader of the Jews, with the intention of making peace with Jonathan before he made peace with Alexander against him (1 Macc 10:3–4). The text goes on to state that Demetrius gave him a number of concessions and privileges to secure his assistance against the royal challenger: authority to recruit troops, to equip them with arms, and to become his ally; and he commanded that the hostages in Acra, the Seleucid citadel in Jerusalem, should be released to him (10:6). But the usurper Alexander Balas made a counteroffer in a letter:[33]

> King Alexander to his brother Jonathan, greetings. We have heard that you are a man powerful by his valor, and ready to be our friend. So we have made you today high priest of your nation and grant you the right to be called Friend of the king (and he sent him a purple cloak and a golden crown), so take our side and observe friendship toward us. (1 Macc 10:18–20)

32. We have already suggested a justification for our focus on the Seleucid evidence in the introduction. Clearly, it would be possible to expand the purview of this article to include further evidence (e.g., Hasmonean or Herodian rulers), but that remains a desideratum for a future study. One example must suffice here. Beginning with the death of their mother Alexandra in 67 BCE, the Hasmonean brothers, Hyrcanus II and Aristobulus II, engaged civil war with each other when the younger brother succeeded in wresting the Judean throne from Hyrcanus. In response, Hyrcanus appealed to the Arab king Aretas to help reinstate him on the throne: "Hyrcanus also promised him [Aretas] that if he were restored and received his throne, he would return to him the territory and the twelve cities which his father Alexander had taken from the Arabs" (Josephus, *Ant.* 14.18). The text continues: "Because of these promises which were made to him, Aretas marched against Aristobulus with an army of fifty thousand horsemen and foot soldiers as well, and defeated him in battle" (*Ant.* 14.19).

33. In the Roman Empire as well, usurpers used letters to attract supporters. Cf. MacMullen, "How to Revolt in the Roman Empire," 199 with n9, 200–202. These letters would have included performative language, promising a certain benefits (contingent upon success of the insurgency, of course). Note, however, that we have a lack of direct evidence for performative language used by insurrectionists. Cf. MacMullen, "How to Revolt in the Roman Empire," 199: "Direct, express testimony to the moment of suasion—'Join me and I will make you a governor'—is difficult to come by, even when the outlines of the participants' later careers are well attested. From an original inner membership, invitation then moves out tentatively to wider circles. Aspirant to the throne, the praetorian prefect Nymphidius Sabinus seeks candid advice from a well-informed friend, who 'did not think there was a single tenement house ready to call Nymphidius "Caesar."' So the prefect made no move. A wider canvass by letter was possible though dangerous. 'You are out of your wits' was the reaction of one correspondent when approached by Avidius Cassius. But Avidius was not deterred. We would give a good deal to know more about the delicate business of making soundings preliminary to armed uprisings. One could hardly ask people outright, 'Just how disloyal are you?'"

Although Alexander had not yet established himself as king when he wrote this letter, he took the royal title anyway.[34] Hence, his performative utterances—the appointment of Jonathan as the Jewish high priest and granting Jonathan the right to be called "Friend of the king"—were merely aspirational, since the usurper did not yet have the royal authority to grant them.

Not to be outdone by his rival, Demetrius responded by issuing another letter, pronouncing a whole series of grants, exemptions, and privileges in order to encourage the Jewish nation not to side with his enemies (1 Macc 10:25–45): exemption from all taxes and agricultural rent, the grant of sacred status to the Jerusalem temple, the surrendering of the Acra, tax-exemption for all Jews in the kingdom during Jewish festivals, the gift of the city of Ptolemais to subsidize cultic activity in the temple, and various subventions for the temple and for building work, both on the temple and on the walls of Jerusalem. Despite these concessions, Jonathan sided with Alexander against Demetrius, and so when the latter was killed in battle against Alexander, Alexander, now as king, rewarded Jonathan accordingly. Thus, his initially aspirational performative utterances had a genuine basis for being realized.

It is unnecessary to recount the rest of the story, in which the Jewish nation deftly maneuvered back and forth between rivals to the Seleucid throne in order to gain the best advantage for themselves. By the end of the process, the Jewish people had outmaneuvered the Seleucids so handily that although the people had rebelled against the weakened Seleucid king, Demetrius II gave the Jewish people the ultimate concession—their independence:

> King Demetrius to Simon, high priest, Friend of the kings, and to the elders and the nation of the Jews, greetings. We accept the golden crown and the palm, which you have sent, and we are ready to make a great peace with you, and to write the officials for the purpose of granting you exemptions. And all the grants we have made to you stay valid. And let all the fortresses, which you have built, remain in your power. And we forgive you the errors and offenses committed to this day (ἀφίεμεν δὲ ἀγνοήματα καὶ τὰ ἁμαρτήματα ἕως τῆς σήμερον ἡμέρας), and we release you from the crown-tax which you owe; and whatever tax was levied in Jerusalem, let it not be levied anymore. And if some of you were ready to join our forces, let them register, and let there be peace between us. (1 Macc 13:36–40)

This peace treaty in letter form pronounces forgiveness for the Jews' past offenses (i.e., siding with the usurper in rebellion against the Seleucid king). As Ma points

34. Other royal pretenders include, for example, Achaeus (223–213 BCE), the cousin of Antiochus III, who initially campaigned on behalf of Antiochus III in Asia Minor, but in 220 BCE Achaeus attempted to usurp the Seleucid kingship, assuming the diadem and the royal title at Laodicea in Phrygia and ruling over "all of the land on this side of Taurus" (i.e., cis-Tauric Asia Minor). Cf. Ma, *Antiochos III*, 28–29, 54–63 et passim.

out, the total exemption from tribute was equivalent to a state of independence.[35] The text explicitly states: "In the one hundred seventieth year the yoke of the Gentiles was removed from Israel, and the people began to write in their own documents and contracts, 'In the first year of Simon the great high priest and commander and leader of the Jews'" (1 Macc 13:41–42). Thus, in 142 BCE, the Jewish nation started a new formal "era," a dating system taking this year as its starting point.

The Seleucid letters embedded in 1 Maccabees can be viewed as efforts by successive Seleucid pretenders, then rulers, to integrate and constrain Maccabean Judea within imperial institutions, by congenial grants and privileges. As Ma observes, "When a pretender to the Seleukid throne writes a letter to Jonathan or Simon, he is formally uttering performative speech ('I confirm . . . I grant . . . I exempt from taxes . . . I renounce'), from a position reserved for a king. Nonetheless, he is not yet king: he will become so, if the subjects acknowledge his speech-act as performative, according it uptake to recognise its illocutionary force, then generally acknowledging or constituting his authority. *The pretender's proclamations are thus themselves attempts to seize the position of authority which will validate his utterances—including the initial one.*"[36]

Royal pretenders had to fulfill several conditions in order to pull off this attempt at self-legitimization:[37]

- First, the usurper had to achieve ultimate military victory over the incumbent Seleucid king. If the usurper failed to triumph in the end, his performative utterances would be exposed as merely aspirational and, in and of themselves, impotent, having no effect on the world.

- Second, the pretender's performative speech-acts needed to be accepted, despite their problematic, self-fulfilling nature. Ma calls them "'pseudo-performative' grants."[38] "The letters of pretenders may look like 'normal' performatives: in fact, they are *pleas for recognition, offers in a negotiating situation, or rather a kind of illocutionary market by auction, where the interlocutors at the receiving end of the royal performatives can make a choice.*[39] The capacity to work 'social magic,' this time, lies with the subjects: it is their choice which will make a king out of an adventurer writing to Jews on his landing in Syria and his attempt on the Seleukid throne triumphant."[40] Successive Seleucid royal pretenders used performative

---

35. Ma, "Seleukids and Speech-Acts," 100.

36. Ma, "Seleukids and Speech-Acts," 100–1 (emphasis mine).

37. Cf. Ma, "Seleukids and Speech-Acts," 101.

38. Ma, "Seleukids and Speech-Acts," 103.

39. Cf. MacMullen, "How to Revolt in the Roman Empire," 202: "It is no rash conjecture . . . to ascribe the partisan acts of whole cities for or against a pretender in terms of civic leaders bringing together neighborhood, trade, and cult groups (where all three were not identical). In turn, the leaders negotiated with the pretender."

40. Ma, "Seleukids and Speech-Acts," 101 (emphasis mine); cf. also 105.

utterances "*to create the appearance of power and authority out of weakness.*"[41] In reality, however, the construction of power was thoroughly contractual in nature—an eminently social construct.

- Third, in order to become king, the pretenders to the Seleucid throne had to offer legitimation and local consolidation to the Maccabees, who had once been rebels against the Seleucid empire. In the zero-sum game of empire, ceding power and authority to former enemies resulted in the concomitant relinquishment of their own power, thereby further weakening the empire.

Jesus' Performative Utterances

If, as discussed above, Jesus was crucified as a royal pretender, and if, as Ma shows, the Seleucid royal pretenders made performative utterances in an attempt to seize the position of authority that will validate their utterances in the first place, then reading Mark's presentation of Jesus may be enriched by an examination of Jesus' performative utterances. What speech-act theory allows us to do is to analyze the form of the exchanges and the tensions or ambiguities they carried. In the process, we will notice connections between parts of Mark's Gospel that have been partially hidden before. Examining Jesus' performative utterances will help us see that from the very inception of his proclamation in Galilee, Jesus is presented as asserting his kingship in a self-legitimizing move.[42] In fact, Jesus' performative utterances were pleas for recognition, offers in a negotiating situation, or rather a kind of illocutionary market by auction, where the interlocutors at the receiving end of the royal performatives can make a choice. It is their choice that will make a king out of Jesus. This is a more satisfying way to study the exchanges in the Gospel of Mark than merely paraphrasing them seriatim.

Austin's insights lead to a richer interpretation, and greater sensitivity to multi-layered interaction. Speech-act theory helps us understand how kingdom is created by royal pronouncement—that is, royal power as discourse. From this perspective, we can see that Jesus' numerous performative utterances as presented in Mark's Gospel were understood as Jesus' bid to claim the kingship.[43]

Jesus' first performative utterance in Mark's Gospel occurs in Mark 1:14–15, the summary of Jesus' proclamation in Galilee: "Now after John was handed over, Jesus went into Galilee, proclaiming the good news of God and saying, 'The time is fulfilled

41. Ma, "Seleukids and Speech-Acts," 108 (emphasis mine).

42. Most Hellenistic kings of the third and second centuries BCE were peripatetic; they spent the majority of their reign in constant motion on campaign. Cf. Chaniotis, *War in the Hellenistic World*, 61. Jesus was also peripatetic.

43. Some preliminary work on performative utterances in Mark's Gospel was done by Maxey, "Power of Words in Mark," 296–303. However, his study does not consider the thesis that we are developing in this chapter.

and the kingdom of God has come near/is at hand; repent and trust in the good news.'" Allison has made the case that "when the evangelists generalize in their editorial comments . . . , these are, notwithstanding the redactional agendas, the most reliable statements of all."[44] In that case, the précis of Jesus' message in Mark 1:14–15, which is surely redactional, should not be discarded for that reason. Jesus' proclamation as summarized here is not simply an impartation of information or a statement of fact; it is arguably a performative utterance—or rather, the "'pseudo-performative' grant" of the royal pretender—insofar as it seeks actually to effect the inauguration of the kingdom of God that it announces,[45] a kingdom that will be consummated only in the future.[46] In the rest of Mark's Gospel, Jesus' speech-acts entail the unfolding of this inaugural performative in concrete words and deeds.[47] From the perspective of Mark's Gospel, Jesus set about to create the kingdom of God by royal pronouncement. It was a matter of royal power as discourse, on the model of the Hellenistic kings.

Several aspects of Jesus' proclamation are illuminated by comparison with the interactions between the Seleucid empire and the Jewish nation. First, by saying that "the time is fulfilled," Jesus announces the beginning of a new "era," just as the reign of Simon Maccabeus established a new era of Jewish independence from Seleucid rule in 142 BCE (see above) and just as, before that, the reign of Seleucus I established a new era of his independent power in 311 BCE.[48]

44. Allison, *Constructing Jesus*, 19.

45. On the presence of the kingdom, see Allison, *Constructing Jesus*, 98–116, here 116: "The upshot of the preceding pages is this: there is no reason to tear asunder what the tradition holds together. If Jesus sometimes, as so many are convinced, proclaimed the presence of God's kingdom, this is insufficient reason to urge that he did not also proclaim its future, apocalyptic revelation." See further in chapter 4 below.

46. On the futurity of the kingdom of God in the Jesus tradition, see Allison, *Constructing Jesus*, 36–39, 41, 164–204. That this expectation was a *Naherwartung*, see Allison, *Constructing Jesus*, 44–48, 54–55, 65–66, 97. Luke 19:11, for example, reports that when Jesus neared Jerusalem, his disciples "supposed that the kingdom of God was to appear immediately ($\pi\alpha\rho\alpha\chi\rho\tilde{\eta}\mu\alpha$)."

47. See further below. Mark 1:14–15 has a possible parallel in Matt 11:2–4//Luke 7:18–23 (Q). In answer to John the Baptist's question about whether Jesus is the "coming one," Jesus responds: "Go and tell John what you have seen *and heard*: the blind receive their sight, the lame walk, the lepers are cleansed, the deaf hear, the dead are raised, the poor have good news brought to them." Jesus thereby alludes to Isa 61:1–2, along with several other Isaianic prophecies. Cf. Allison, *Intertextual JesusQ*, 109–14. This raises the question of whether Jesus' proclamation of the "good news" is related to the deeds of power that are listed. Certainty cannot be had, but 4Q521 (4QMessianic Apocalypse) foretells that "[the hea]vens and the earth will listen to his [sc. God's] Messiah" (משיחו) and possibly ascribes to this messianic figure a list of miracles very reminiscent of Matt 11:2–4//Luke 7:22–23 (Q), concluding with a citation of Isa 61:1: "He will heal the wounded, and revive the dead, and bring good news to the poor." Cf. Allison, *Constructing Jesus*, 266; Yarbro Collins and Collins, *King and Messiah as Son of God*, 171. Does this messianic figure perform these deeds of power by the word of his mouth? As we shall see, such a ruler is envisioned in Isa 11:1–12.

48. On the Seleucid era, see Kosmin, "Short Introduction to the Seleucid Era"; Kosmin, *Time and Its Adversaries in the Seleucid Empire*; Ma, "Hellenistic Empires," 324–25. On the creation of a "royal timespace," combining vivid involvement in the present and the local with broader scales and perspectives, which was "the very exercise of kingship and its deepest, most essential pleasure," see Ma,

Second, Jesus' announcement of the "kingdom of God" clearly shows that his intention is to establish an empire to usurp the current one(s).[49] The fact that this kingdom is "at hand" suggests that its coming is imminent; indeed, in and through Jesus' performative words, the kingdom was already beginning to dawn.

Third, Jesus' call for the people to "repent" has clear parallels to the Seleucid regime, which acknowledged repentance on the part of people who had rebelled against the empire and who were subsequently forgiven (see above on 1 Macc 13:36–40, esp. v. 39).[50] Jesus is saying that the people should desist from their former rebellion and side with him against his opponents, whoever they may be. Like the Seleucids, Jesus introduced new categories of relationship to symbolize alliance with himself. Whereas the Seleucids had categories such as "Friend of the king" and "brother,"[51] Jesus used similar terms of fictive kinship: "Here are my mother and my brothers! Whoever does the will of God is my brother and sister and mother" (Mark 3:31–35; cf. 10:29–30).[52] For the Seleucids,

---

"Kings," 193–94.

49. That Jesus was the central actor and main object of the "kingdom of God" is discussed in Allison, *Constructing Jesus*, 221–304, here 231: "From my point of view, all the texts that I have cited are closely related; they constitute a family of traditions that requires explanation. All of them, whether they use a formal title or not, are united in one particular: when they look into the future, they see Jesus, and indeed Jesus front and center." Allison, *Constructing Jesus*, 303: "There is no good reason to reject the main thesis of this chapter, which is that he [sc. Jesus] was the center of his own eschatological scenario. [. . .] Jesus did not envisage a 'brokerless kingdom.' Nor did he proclaim a 'kingless kingdom.' Rather, when he looked into the future, he saw thrones, including one for himself. What caused him to hold such a conviction is not subject to analysis. We can know only the fact, not the why."

50. Cf., e.g., Chaniotis, *War in the Hellenistic World*, 69: "Its [sc. Amlada's] inhabitants, part Greek, part native, had taken advantage of the Pergamene involvement during the Third Macedonian War and of a Galatian invasion in 168 BC, and had overthrown the Pergamene garrison. When their revolt was subdued, they had to provide hostages and pay substantial sums for reparations. A few years later (160 BC?) Amlada was in a desperate financial situation. When the city appealed to the king's benevolence, Attalos, acting on behalf of his brother Eumenes II, explained why he accepted their request, released the hostages and reduced the tribute (*RC* 54): 'because I saw that you have repented of your former offences [θεωρῶν οὖν ὑμᾶς μετανενοηκότας τε ἐπὶ τοῖς προημαρτημένοις] and that you zealously carry out our orders.' Through the publication of this letter on stone, the principle of *do ut des* became an example for future generations."

51. As we have seen, Seleucid kings and royal pretenders used the designations "brother" and royal "Friend" in an extended sense to refer to the leaders of subject communities, such as Jonathan and Simon. See above on 1 Macc 10:18–20; 13:36–40; see also 11:30–37 ("King Demetrius to Jonathan, his brother"). On royal "Friends," see Ma, *Antiochos III*, 8n12, 21, 27, 35, 36, 53–54, 71, 111, 215, 215, 217, 290, 310, 330; Ma, "Seleukids and Speech-Acts," 90–91, 98, 99, 101, 104. In a letter to Heliodorus (178 BCE), King Seleucus IV addresses his viceroy as "his brother." Cf. Cotton-Paltiel et al., "Juxtaposing Literary and Documentary Evidence," 1–15. Interestingly enough, Heliodorus later assassinated Seleucus IV and attempted to assume the Seleucid throne. Cf. Scolnic, "Heliodorus and the Assassination of Seleucus IV according to Dan 11:20 and 2 Macc 3," 354–84.

52. On the will of God, see further Mark 12:28–34. Jesus is the model of one who does the will of God, even to the point of death (14:36, 39). A pretender necessarily causes sharp division, since it is necessary for all levels of society (within families, within cities, between cities) to take sides either for or against the usurper. Cf. MacMullen, "How to Revolt in the Roman Empire," 201–202. Jesus understood that he would cause division. See, e.g., Luke 12:51–53//Matt 10:34–36 (Q): "Do you think that I have come to bring peace to the earth? No, I tell you, but rather division! From now on five in

the empire was patrimonial, a family business,[53] with their own biological relatives and fictive "relatives" (*syngenesis*) holding the highest offices.[54] For Jesus, too, the kingdom was patrimonial,[55] but he declared that his true kin were those associated with him on another basis and power structure.[56] Even if this particular example is not directly tied to Jesus' conception of "kingdom," it still deserves mention in the light of the Seleucid comparative material and the construction of empire in evidence there.

Fourth, Jesus exhorts the people to "trust in the good news." From the perspective we are developing here, this exhortation is analogous to a royal pretender making a performative utterance—ostensibly a bona fide royal grant—that is actually a plea for recognition.[57] Jesus is not a king—far from it. He often shows signs of profound weak-

---

one household will be divided, three against two and two against three, they will be divided: father against son and son against father, mother against daughter and daughter against mother, mother-in-law against her daughter-in-law and daughter-in-law against mother-in-law." Cf. Gos. Thom. 16. On the Old Testament basis of this logion (i.e., Mic 7:6), see Allison, *Intertextual Jesus*, 132–34; Allison, "Q 12.51–53 and Mk 9:11–13 and the Messianic Woes," 289–310.

53. On the patrimonial monarchy, see Ma, "Hellenistic Empires," 341–42: "The model [i.e., Bicker-man's classic model of the Hellenistic royal state] focuses on Hellenistic kingship. This is personal and charismatic, defined by military success: the kingdom is 'spear-won,' to use the contemporary termi-nology, and victory grounds the legal claim to ownership of territory and political control over com-munities, as expressed in the supposedly monopolistic performative utterances that define a variety of local statuses: freedom from taxes, or freedom *tout court*, was a grant from the king. The kingdom is hence patrimonial in nature: administrated as actual patrimony, or along metaphors of ownership, it produces rent and tax to the benefit of the king, his family, and his Friends. At the same time, the king-dom is centralized, bureaucratic (to manage the extraction of surplus on a large scale), and hierarchi-cal (for practical but also ideological reasons, to articulate ruled territories into geographies of power and rule). The workings of administration are ideological as well as practical, in that they project an imagined empire that seems natural, extensive, and effective." See also Ma, "Hellenistic Empires," 351.

54. On the hierarchy of relationships with the king in Hellenistic kingdoms, see Ma, "Hellenis-tic Empires," 336–37; Chaniotis, *War in the Hellenistic World*, 64: "For the administration of their kingdoms, the Hellenistic kings relied on a circle of 'friends' (*philoi*), who were advisors, teachers of the princes, good company in hunting and drinking parties, governors of districts and provinces, envoys, and—above all—commanders of important army units. . . . When in the early second century the honorary titles of the members of the highest administration of the Ptolemaic kingdom were standardized, these revealed the personal character of government, but also the military origin of the kings' collaborators. . . . The ranks began with those of the bodyguards (*somatophylakes*) and the 'followers' (*diadochoi*), and reached the higher levels of 'friends' (*philoi*), chief bodyguards (*archiso-matophylakes*), 'first friends' (*protoi philoi*), and 'relatives' (*syngeneis*)." Cf. also Strootman, "Hellenistic Court Society," 75–76, 85, 87.

55. For example, in the context of the "cleansing of the Temple," Jesus proclaims that this was the house of his Father (Mark 11:17, citing Isa 56:7). In Mark 12:1–12, the wicked tenants plot to take the patrimony from the heir, a thinly veiled reference to the Jewish leaders' attitude toward Jesus, as the text itself acknowledges (v. 12).

56. New power structures and alliances are formed on the basis of speaking and acting in Jesus' name (cf. Mark 6:14; 9:37, 38–41; 13:6 [falsely!], 13). The biological family is rejected in favor of the community of disciples (cf. Matt 8:22; 22:48–50; Mark 3:33–35; Luke 8:21; 9:59–60; 14:26; Gos. Thom. 55; 99; 101). God is the "Father" of this community (cf. Matt 6:9; Luke 11:2b; also Matt 23:9). We may compare the Essenes and the Therapeutic, since they too abandoned biological relations in favor of a new community as family.

57. Even the language of belief and trust belongs in this context. When a city is conquered by a

ness.[58] Yet, if the people acknowledge his speech-act as performative (i.e., they accord it uptake by recognizing its illocutionary force), that would reinforce Jesus' authority, his original offer of the kingdom would then have a basis for being enacted, and he would indeed become their king.[59] What was true of Seleucid royal pretenders is true of Jesus as well: "The pretender's proclamations are thus themselves attempts to seize the position of authority which will validate his utterances—including the original one."[60] As we can see throughout Mark's Gospel, however, Jesus' performative utterances cannot succeed unless people believe.[61] The reason for this inability is not immediately obvious

Hellenistic king (or capitulates preemptively), the people must "entrust" (πιστεύσαντες) themselves to their conqueror. Thus, the letter of Zeuxis (the viceroy of Antiochus III) to Amyzon (*RC* 38), written in the immediate aftermath of the conquest of the city (203 BCE), is framed in the wider context of "all those who have entrusted and handed themselves over to us" (α]ὐτοὺς πιστεύσαντες ἡμῖν ἐνεχείρισαν). Cf. Ma, *Antiochos III*, 179, 292–94 (no. 5, line 2). See also the Letter of the Scipio brothers to the Herakleians: "As for us, we happen to be well disposed towards all the Greeks, and we will try, since you have come over to our [faith] (παραγεγονότων ὑμῶν εἰς τὴν ἡμέτεραμ [πίστιμ]), to show solicitude as much as possible, always trying to be responsible for some advantage. We grant you your liberty, just as to other cities which have entrusted themselves to us, with the right to see all your own affairs conducted by yourselves according to your laws, and in all other matters we will try to assist you and always be responsible for some advantage." Cf. Ma, *Antiochos III*, 366–67 (no. 45, lines 7–14). Attalus I treated the Smyrnians well, because they had "preserved to the greatest extent their faith towards him (διὰ τὸ μάλιστα τούτους τετηρηκέναι τὴν τρὸς αὐτὸν πίστιν)" (Polybius 5.77.6). Cf. Ma, *Antiochos III*, 55n11.

58. Cf., e.g., Mark 6:5–6: "And he could do no deed of power there [i.e., in his own hometown of Nazareth], except that he laid hands on a few sick people and cured them. And he was amazed at their unbelief" (6:5–6). As Ma observes, the Hellenistic empires were large and supralocal political structures of control and extraction, headed by a monarch and his power elite, sustained by violence, negotiation, and legitimacy ("Hellenistic Empires," 324). Jesus' kingdom was hardly large and supralocal (although, according to Mark, it was expanding into contiguous areas); its leaders were a motley bunch and anything but a power elite; and even the legitimacy of Jesus' birth was called into question (cf. Mark 6:3, where Jesus is referred to as "the son of Mary" rather than the normal patronymic). If Judas was thinking about kingdom in its usual terms, then he might have imagined a Hellenistic state run by and for the ruling elite, which controlled and extracted rent, tribute, and tax (cf. Ma, "Hellenistic Empires," 340, 343–44, 346–47; Ma, "Kings," 183–84). Having finally perceived that Jesus' brand of "kingdom" would end badly, Judas opted for Plan B—to cash out. Cf. Ma, "Hellenistic Empires," 350 (emphasis mine): "The presence of competing states that can often make *alternative offers, ideological or material, to local actors.* [. . .] The institutional context of royal ownership and patronage further affected the individual powerholders within the state—the military colonists, officials, and high-ranking courtiers that constituted the state's apparatus were also bound to the state by *incentives*, namely the distribution of property and revenue extracted from below or generated by state activities such as warfare. *When these incentives were not fulfilled, the state's men could defect.*"

59. The kind of reception that Jesus hoped for is exemplified in part in the so-called "triumphal entry." When, in Mark 11:9–10, Jesus enters Jerusalem, the crowd hails him as a royal savior: "Hosanna! Blessed is the one who comes in the name of the Lord! Blessed is the coming kingdom of our ancestor David." In the immediately preceding context, blind Bartimaeus cries out to "Jesus, Son of David" (10:46–52). The fact that Jesus enters Jerusalem on a donkey implicitly fulfills Zech 9:9: "your king comes to you . . . humble and riding on a donkey" (cf. Matt 21:5; John 12:15). See further Le Donne, *Historical Jesus*, 121. On the Jesus' entry into Jerusalem, see also Catchpole, "The 'Triumphal' Entry," 319–34, who argues that the "triumphal" entry matches Peter's confession of Jesus as Messiah and has to do with the disclosure of Jesus' identity and status.

60. Ma, "Seleukids and Speech-Acts," 100–101 (emphasis mine).

61. Cf. Mark 2:5; 5:34, 36; 6:5–6; 9:23–24 (the plaintiff cry of the father whose son was possessed

in the text, so the nexus between belief in Jesus' performative utterance and the efficacy or inefficacy of that utterance can appear to be a kind of "magic." However, on the basis of our comparison with royal pretenders, we can see that this magic is actually "social magic": believing in Jesus' performative utterance reflects the reality that its enactment requires the acceptance by the audience.[62]

The transactional nature of the kingdom of God that Jesus proclaims is well illustrated by his teaching on reciprocity in Mark 4:24–25: "The measure you give will be the measure you get, and still more will be given to you. For those who have, more will be given; and from those who have nothing, even what they have will be taken away." Participation in the kingdom of God is contingent on reception of Jesus' performative message, thereby entering into a reciprocal relationship that links royal benefaction with individual response in a self-perpetuating spiral.[63] Failure to receive his message positively, on the other hand, results in exclusion from the kingdom (cf. 4:10–12).[64] Ultimately, Jesus' "good news" of the kingdom sets in motion a performative word that extends to "the whole world" and "all nations" in its effectiveness; for, according to Jesus' eschatological discourse (13:3–37), his words will not pass away (13:31). Thus, Jesus predicts that his followers will "stand before governors and kings" because of him, "and the good news must first be proclaimed *to all nations*" (vv. 9–10). In the context of his anointment by a woman (14:3–9), Jesus says, "Truly I tell you, whenever the good news is proclaimed *in the whole world*, what she has done will be told in remembrance of her" (v. 9).

The worldwide scope of Jesus' performative word of the "good news" can be compared to the Hellenistic royal correspondence, in which the ongoing euergetical dialogue between ruler and ruled—that is, the royal performative granting of gifts and the reciprocal giving of civic honors and gratitude by the people—can be

by an evil spirit: πιστεύω· βοήθει μου τῇ ἀπιστίᾳ), 42; 10:52; 11:22–24, 31; 15:31–32. Contrast Green, "Kingdom of God/Heaven," 468–81, here 468: "From this initial syntactical foray, we observe immediately that the kingdom of God, a central concern of the Gospels, does not depend for its existence on human activity; humans do not create, build, construct, extend or render present the kingdom. The kingdom originates with God, it draws its character from God, and it precedes any human response to it, even though its presence invites (or demands) human response."

62. The popular acceptance of Jesus' performative message would have been underscored by the story of the voice from heaven at Jesus' baptism (Mark 1:11 pars., "And a voice came from heaven, 'You are my Son, the Beloved; with you I am well pleased'"; cf. Mark 9:7 pars.). Potential pretenders to the throne typically consulted the gods. Cf. MacMullen, "How to Revolt in the Roman Empire," 198: "A favorable answer, if it were spread around, could provide validation of projects otherwise dubious. Any resort to seers or oracles was therefore liable to the severest punishment by the sitting emperor; but Lucian [*Alex.* 32] makes it sound as if consultation nevertheless went on all the time, 'hazardous and over-venturesome—you know what questions the rich and powerful are likely to ask.'" See further Potter, *Prophets and Emperors*; Tomasino, "Oracles of Insurrection," 86–110.

63. Cf. Ma, *Antiochos III*, 182–94, here 185: "In the [Hellenistic] royal letters, the contract clause . . . expresses reciprocity, linking royal benefaction and civic reaction in a self-perpetuating spiral." On this "spiral," see also Ma, *Antiochos III*, 209, 373.

64. Cf., similarly, Jesus' teaching on obedience and reward (10:17–22) and rewards for complete loyalty (10:28–31).

plotted along three axes, all of which contribute to a rhetoric of *generalization*. (1) Chronologically, individual acts of euergetism or gratitude are never presented as isolated in time; they are always presented against a background of past precedent and future prospect: "The present moment is extended back in time by references to earlier relations; but it is also projected forward by the promise of future benefactions, requested by the cities or promised by the king or his subordinates. . . ."[65] In other words, chronological indications in royal letters and civic honorary decrees extend the interaction between the interlocutors in time, beyond the present transaction: "they constructed a context of continuity for each round of euergetical dialogue, mirroring the latter's structural openness to indefinite repetition."[66]

(2) In addition to a generalization of the euergetical dialogue on a temporal axis *through time*, specific acts of euergetism either to or from a specific city could be generalized on an anthropological axis, so that they are placed in the context of constant beneficence to "all Greeks" or even "all men."[67] For example, in the First Teian decree for Antiochus III and Laodike III (probably 203 BCE), the citizens of Teos praised Antiochus III for making "a very great display of the trustworthiness (πίστις), which was his before, towards all men (πρὸς ἅπαντας ἀνθρώπους), and, after that, he consistently is responsible for many favours toward us, giving an example to all the Greeks (παράδειγμα πᾶσιν ἐκτιθεὶς τοῖς Ἕλλη[σι]ν) of the disposition he adopts towards those who are his benefactors and show goodwill towards him."[68] Hence, there is a tendency in the epigraphical evidence of euergetism toward generalization of the specific transaction to the broader pan-Hellenic community or even the entire human race. "In the abstract, actions were considered as performances before the world. . . ."[69]

(3) The language of euergetism strives at generalization along a third axis by making individual transactions into paradigmatic shows of virtuous character within the relationship between the ruler and the ruled.[70] Thus, the euergetical dialogue is not just about individual accomplishments (e.g., particular, concrete benefactions on the part of one party or the other), but also about character and behavior in accordance with appropriate moral norms that are either imputed, exhorted or avowed. "What a concept such as καλοκἀγαθία ['excellence in character and conduct'] did was to make explicit the assumptions which underlay the whole dialogue: the existence of moral norms, which dictated appropriate behaviour (caring for subordinates, returning gratitude), and according to which rational choices were made and approved."[71] Moreover, this is an intimate relationship whose atmosphere of interaction is regulated by

65. Ma, *Antiochos III*, 187.
66. Ma, *Antiochos III*, 187.
67. Ma, *Antiochos III*, 187–88; cf. 216.
68. Ma, *Antiochos III*, 308–11 (no. 17), here 309 (lines 24–26).
69. Ma, *Antiochos III*, 211.
70. Ma, *Antiochos III*, 188–91.
71. Ma, *Antiochos III*, 190.

mutual "goodwill" (εὔνοια), "zeal" and "enthusiasm" (ἐκτένεια, σπουδή, προθυμία), "gentle behavior" (συμπεριφερόμενος), and actions done "with familiar kindness" (οἰκείως) and "humanely" (φιλανθρώπως). All of this topped with a generous portion of "gratitude" (εὐχαριστία) on both sides.

In sum, any transaction by ruler or ruled expressed in terms of this highly conventional discourse of euergetism was thereby proclaimed "a continuous relation, each round open to indefinite exchange and repetition, the generalizing vocabularies located it always at the same point in time and space (present dealings mirroring the past and announcing the future, and typical of dealings with men in general), for the same reasons (the character of the participants, appraised in a shared moral vocabulary) and with the same outcome of εὔνοια."[72]

It is obvious that the Jesus tradition as reflected in Mark's Gospel contains these three generalizing elements in abundance. The second one, which led us into this discussion in the first place, is clearly in evidence. Jesus' performative word of the "good news" of the kingdom has concrete, local significance, but each instance of euergetism has implications for the whole world as well.[73]

The chronological aspect of Jesus' performative word of the "good news" is also present. Individual acts of euergetism or gratitude are never presented as isolated in time; in the context of Mark's Gospel as a whole, these individual acts are presented against the background of past precedent and future prospect. We have already seen evidence of the future prospect of Jesus' performative word, how it will continue to reverberate until the consummation of time at the Parousia. The past, however, is equally important for the Markan Jesus. This subject would require a separate treatment, but suffice it to say here that one important motif is the restoration of the status quo ante. As we have seen, royal performative utterances determine statuses of various kinds. One of the most important statuses for Hellenistic empires was the restoration of the status quo ante. As Ma discusses in thoroughgoing detail, "the Great Idea to which Antiochos [III] devoted his life"[74] was a program of reconquest of the patrimony,[75] i.e., the territory that he considered his inherited

72. Ma, *Antiochos III*, 191–92.

73. Insofar as Jesus gathered the Twelve, symbolizing the twelve tribes of Israel, Jesus was acting like Israel's leader, and, as such, he had a central role in establishing the kingdom of God. Cf. Allison, *Constructing Jesus*, 232–33. On the Twelve as signifying the restoration of all twelve tribes of Israel in the Land of Israel with Jerusalem as the center of a world empire, see Allison, *Constructing Jesus*, 67–76; Bockmuehl, *Seeing the Word*, 211–15.

74. Cf. Ma, *Antiochos III*, 32.

75. The concept was evidently common during the Hellenistic period. In the book of Jubilees (second century BCE), for example, the author uses essentially the same argument as that of the Seleucids in order to justify the conquest of the Land of Canaan: Israel was *reacquiring* their rightful patrimony, which stemmed from the division of the earth among the sons of Noah (recorded in a "book" [Jub. 8:11–12]) but was subsequently usurped by Ham's son Canaan (Jub. 10:37–42). Cf., without noting the Seleucid parallel, VanderKam, *Jubilees*, 1:420; VanderKam, "Putting Them in Their Place," 47–69, esp. 66–69.

right,[76] so that cities were restored to their former status under the Seleucids.[77] This was what Antiochus III was attempting to accomplish: the reduction of all cities of Asia Minor to "the ancient structure of sovereignty" (*in antiquam imperii formulam*, Livy 33.38.1).[78] Ma refers to "the palimpsestic history of Asia Minor,"[79] whereby the region was continually reconquered, each time erasing the claim of the previous regime and reasserting the ancestral claim of the new king.[80] As a result, the col-

76. Cf., e.g., Ma, *Antiochos III*, 217 (referring to *OGIS* 219.2–16): "The king seeks to restore the cities of the Seleukis to peace and original happiness, and to 'reacquire his paternal empire'; this duly (διό) happens, when the king's 'fine and just enterprise' results in the restoration of the cities to peace, and the kingdom to its original situation. . . ."

77. As we have seen, the performative utterance of the king himself was the sole determiner of (re)conquered city's status. Cf., e.g., Ma, *Antiochos III*, 100: "Local autonomy was a status he [sc. Antiochus III] could grant, within an imperial space where he held the monopoly of performative utterances . . . ; local resistance (actual or ideological) was an anomaly, which would soon be reduced and lead to assimilation within the Seleukid space (Liv. 33.38.1–2)."

78. Antiochus III's policy was broadly interpreted to include not only the parts of Asia Minor conquered by Seleucus I but, according to Appian (*Syr.* 1), also Coele-Syria, some parts of Ptolemaic Cilicia. Appian continues: "With ambitious plans of mind, he attacked the Hellespont, Aeolia, and Ionia as if they belonged to him because he was king of Asia and they had once been subject to the kings of Asia." See also Appian, *Syr.* 12. On these claims, see Ma, *Antiochos III*, 29n13: "Antiochos claims Ionia and Aiolis because they used to belong to the 'former kings of Asia,' presumably the Achaimenids; which is similar, but not quite the same as appeal to ancestral rights." In several cases, the Seleucid "reconquest" of a city was a pure fiction, which required the city to accept a rewriting of their local history in accordance with the official narrative of the conqueror. Cf. Ma, *Antiochos III*, 197–99, 230. On "the creation of 'instant memory' soon after a Seleukid takeover," see Ma, *Antiochos III*, 225–26. Antiochus IV used similar arguments to those of his father. Cf. Ma, *Antiochos III*, 31: "He referred to τὰ ἐξ ἀρχῆς δίκαια, his original rights to ownership (κτῆσις) over Koile-Syria, originating in the history of the Diadochs (Pol. 28.20.1–9). As Polybios observes, Antiochos IV, with these arguments, 'convinced not only himself, but also his audience that he was right' (Pol. 28.20.10)."

79. Ma, *Antiochos III*, 51, 81.

80. Cf. Ma, *Antiochos III*, 31 (emphasis mine): ". . . the legal underpinnings of the Seleukid empire: the right of conquest, and the right of inheritance. An epigraphical document, mentioning the establishment of Seleukid power in Asia Minor, succinctly mentions both principles: 'Seleukos having gained power (ἐπικρατήσαντος) in the battle against Lysimachos, Antiochos, his son, having succeeded to the kingship (διαδεξάμενος τὴν βασιλείαν)' [*OGIS* 335.132–33]. How could these two apparently contradictory principles coexist? Bickerman argued that rights to ownership were not established by mere takeover, but by *the utter defeat of an opponent, resulting in his extinction* (as in the case of Antigonos at Ipsos or of Lysimachos at Kouroupedion) or in the formal surrender of his title to ownership. Therefore, according to Bickerman, aggression followed by occupation, even for a length of time, did not create rights to ownership (in contrast, Roman law acknowledged occupation (*usucapio*) as a source for legitimate ownership). What mattered was not length or continuity of occupation, but *the antiquity of the claim*: for Bickerman, the claims of Antiochos III to the cities of Asia Minor and Thrace were justified within the framework of Greek legal thought, because *the rights established by the victory over Lysimachos still held true. . . .*" In time, of course, the Seleucid claim to Asia Minor was itself erased and replaced by the prior claim to the area by the Attalids. Cf. Ma, *Antiochos III*, 252 (emphasis mine): "The Roman settlement of Asia Minor in 188 BC did more than just debar Seleukid power from the region, using the Taurus, which had once been a feature of Seleukid administrative geography, as an international frontier. It was also an exercise in history-writing: *it undid Seleukid Asia Minor, by referring not to the Seleukid past as the* status quo *for local rights, but to the situation which had pertained under the Attalids* (in c. 226, then 218)—an 'Attalid past'. . . . The settlement of

lections of inscribed royal letters on display in Hellenistic temples cumulatively recorded "the local epigraphical narratives": e.g., "the *antas* of the temple of Athena at Herakleia, where the Seleukid letters were succeeded by the letter of the Scipios, or the 'epigraphical museum' of the Amyzonian Artemision, recording the life of the city under Ptolemies, Seleukids, Rhodians, and as a free community."[81]

Seen in this light, much of what Jesus was attempting to accomplish with his performative proclamation of the "good news" was to restore the patrimony to its original, pristine state,[82] whether that means the recovery of the true purpose of the temple ("my [sc. Yahweh's] house") as "a house of prayer for all nations" (11:17, citing Isa 56:7)[83] or the recapitulation of the way things were from the beginning of creation according to the traditional *Urzeit-Endzeit* correlation: e.g., Sabbath observance (2:27–28, evoking the creation account of Gen 1:1–2:4a)[84] and marriage (10:2–9, citing Gen 1:27 ["But from the beginning of creation, 'God made them male and female'"] and 2:24 ["For this reason a man shall leave his father and mother and be joined to his wife, and the two shall become one flesh"]).[85] We will discuss these matters further in chapter 3.

As mentioned above, Jesus' initial attempt at self-authentication, by proclaiming that the kingdom has come near / is at hand as a tacit plea for recognition and

---

188 consigned the Seleukid project to history—no longer a live reality in its manifestations and its ideology, but of interest only to the historian. . . ."

81. Ma, *Antiochos III*, 252. The *antas*—i.e., the posts or pillars on either side of a doorway or entrance of a Greek temple—were a common place to display royal letters. Cf., e.g., Ma, *Antiochos III*, 252, 287, 305, 340, 344, 367.

82. A similar idea is found, for example, in Matthew's Gospel. Cf. Pennington, "Heaven, Earth, and a New Genesis," 28–44.

83. Jesus' accusation that "you have made it [sc. the temple] a den of robbers" (again, as part of the citation of Isa 56:7) can be compared perhaps to the King Seleucus IV's creation of some new tax on temples in Coele-Syria and Phoenicia, which may lie behind the reference to confiscation of funds from the Jerusalem Temple by the king's viceroy, Heliodorus, in 2 Macc 3:13. Cf. Cotton-Paltiel et al., "Juxtaposing Literary and Documentary Evidence," 12. On the frequent plundering of temples by Hellenistic kings, see further Chaniotis, *War in the Hellenistic World*, 155–57. Note also that Jesus allegedly spoke about destroying "this temple that is made with hands, and in three days I will build another, not made with hands" (Mark 14:58). In this connection, as additional support for the contention that Jesus was seen as a messianic pretender by some, Allison draws attention to the extensive Jewish tradition (starting with 2 Sam 7:10–14) about a royal figure building or rebuilding the temple. "So if—I leave the issue open—Jesus ever said, as Mark 14:58 and John 2:19 have him say, that he himself would raise or build a new temple, the implication would be patent. Opponents could readily have moved from 'He claims he will destroy and rebuild the temple' to 'He claims to be king'" (*Constructing Jesus*, 237–38).

84. Note Jesus' authoritative pronouncement here in the context of its universal significance from the beginning of creation: "Then he said to them, 'The sabbath was made for humankind, and not humankind for the sabbath; so the Son of Man is Lord even of the sabbath.'"

85. Cf. Allison, *Constructing Jesus*, 32n7: "I maintain that Jesus was looking not for the literal 'end of the world' but instead for the restoration of a world in disrepair. . . ." See further Doering, "Marriage and Creation in Mark 10 and CD 4–6," 133–63; Doering, "'Much Ado about Nothing?' Jesus' Sabbath Healings and Their Halakic Implications Revisited," 213–41, esp. 236–41.

acceptance, continues to unfold in Jesus' performative utterances in the rest of Mark's Gospel. Jesus portrays himself as the sower who sows the performative word of the worldwide kingdom of God, which produces a tremendous harvest among those who accept it, "yielding thirty and sixty and a hundredfold" (4:1–9 [parable], 10–20 [explanation], 30–32 [further elaboration of the growth of the world empire on analogy with Nebuchadnezzar's world-tree in Dan 4:12, 21]).[86]

As concrete examples of Jesus' performative utterances in actual practice, we may adduce the following:

- A man with an unclean spirit: "Be silent, and come out of him!" (1:21–28).

- A leper: "Be made clean!" (1:40–45).

- A paralytic: "Son, your sins are forgiven!"; "I say to you, stand up, take your mat and go to your home" (2:1–12).

- A man with a withered hand: "Stretch out your hand" (3:1–6).

- The wind and the sea: "Peace! Be still!"; "Who then is this, that even the wind and the sea obey him?" (4:35–41; cf. 6:47–52).

- The Gerasene demoniac: "Come out of him, you unclean spirit!" (5:1–20).

- Jairus's daughter: "'Talitha cum,' which means 'Little girl, get up!'" (5:21–24a, 35–43).

- A hemorrhagic woman: "Daughter, your faith has made you well; go in peace, and be saved of your disease" (5:24b–34).

- A Syro-Phoenician woman: "For saying that, you may go—the demon has left your daughter" (7:24–30).

- A man who was deaf and mute: "'Ephphatha,' that is, 'Be opened!'" (7:31–37).

- An unclean spirit: "You spirit that keeps this boy from speaking and hearing, I command you, come out of him, and never enter him again!" (9:14–29).

- Blind Bartimaeus: "Go; your faith has made you well" (10:46–52).

- A fig tree: "May no one ever eat fruit from you again"; "In the morning as they passed by, they saw the fig tree withered away to its roots" (11:12–14, 20–24).

It is impossible to discuss all of these examples here, so we will focus on the performative utterances that define statuses. In terms of the euergetical dialogue we are presently discussing, performative utterances are found commonly in the grant of privileges and benefits by Hellenistic kings whenever they seek a corresponding positive response from the addressees. The whole process begins with the conquest of the city: "The most important transaction that followed the takeover by the Seleukids

86. Another example of the power of Jesus words comes from his eschatological discourse (13:3–37): "Heaven and earth will pass away, but my words will not pass away" (v. 31).

was the regulation of local statuses. Conquest entailed the momentary loss of the van-quished party's political existence, to be recreated by a unilateral pronouncement (a performative speech-act *par excellence*) of the conqueror, on terms of his choosing and subject to his goodwill."[87] This is the point at which the conquered peoples "entrust" (πιστεύσαντες) themselves to their conqueror. From there, the ruler's performative speech-act decides on both the degree of subordination (ranging from "free" [in name only] to subject) and the amount of spoliation (ranging from exemption from tribute and garrisoning to heavy tribute, taxes, levies, and/or fines).[88]

Of course, Jesus was not a military conqueror in the traditional sense; he did not wage war with spears and swords. But he did mount a campaign against the forces of evil that oppressed human beings. Jesus' exorcisms should be seen in this light.[89] The status-change that they effected through Jesus' performative utterance[90] was no less liberating than the "liberty" that Hellenistic rulers proclaimed over cities that they had conquered. Of course, in both cases, the liberation comes under the auspices of the new regime, so it is not independence in any absolute sense of the word. Yet, in the case of exorcisms, it means that person becomes free from the harm inflicted by the unclean spirits. Jesus describes this conquest of evil as entering the strong man's (i.e., Satan's) house, tying him up, and plundering it (Mark 3:22–30).[91] Hence, Jesus

---

87. Ma, *Antiochos III*, 111–12. On the king's power to define statuses, see Ma, *Antiochos III*, 100, 101, 104, 109, 113, 128, 149, 150–74, 175, 178, 238, 244, here 173: "All statuses must originate with a performative speech act by the king." Ma, *Antiochos III*, 93: "Empire was also constituted by royal discourse into a space where individual difference mattered less than the king's power to define statuses."

88. Cf. Ma, "Hellenistic Empires," 340–41: "The Hellenistic state controlled, in hegemonic fashion, various communities that were explicitly called 'free and autonomous': they proclaimed this liberty in very public forms (for instance on coinage), and in practical terms, they were not subject to tribute, taxation, services, garrisoning, or billeting. The free communities still may be considered as under royal control: They may have been bound by treaty obligations to supply military assistance against other imperial states, and, most importantly, their freedom was treated by the state as a status among others—dependent on the performative utterances by the king that characterized the royal state." On early official Roman correspondence as patterned on Hellenistic models, see Sherk, *Roman Documents from the Greek East: Senatus Consulta and Epistulae*, 186–97; this includes the granting of privileges and benefits (193–94).

89. Here it is interesting to note that the conquests of Hellenistic kings also operated on two levels: on the one hand, their conquests were understood as military operations with the usual sociopolitical consequences; on the other hand, however, they were also imbued with supernatural significance. For instance, the Greek Gigantomachy tradition served as political myth, allegorically portraying Greek victory over "barbarian" enemies. Cf., e.g., Massa-Pairault and Pouzadoux, *Géants et gigantomachies entre Orient et Occident*. Insofar as the Greek Giants, a mythological race of monstrous appearance and great strength, were sons of divine beings (cf. Hesiod, *Theog.* 185), they can be compared to the giants in the Enochic tradition, that is, the bastard offspring of the Watchers and the daughters of men who, after their death, continued to plague men as evil spirits. Cf., e.g., Stuckenbruck, "Giant Mythology and Demonology," 36–57. Therefore, the Enochic tradition might be a source of the conception of unclean spirits in the Jesus tradition. Cf. Macaskill, "Apocalypse and the Gospel of Mark," 61–62.

90. For performative utterances effecting exorcisms, see, e.g., Mark 1:21–28 (esp. vv. 25–26); 5:1–13 (esp. vv. 8, 13).

91. Cf. Shively, *Apocalyptic Imagination in the Gospel of Mark*.

appropriates the forms and methods of the royal pretender or the Hellenistic king but modifies them in significant ways.[92] Ultimately, Jesus' kingdom will be the actual inversion of the usual Hellenistic kingdom:[93] the last will be first and the first will be last;[94] children, among the weakest and most vulnerable members of society, are the model for this kingdom;[95] the wealthy cannot enter the kingdom;[96] and self-sacrificial service will be the hallmark rather than the oppression of others.[97] If giving or grant-

92. Cf. Allison, *Historical Christ and the Theological Jesus*, 106: "Jesus seems to have conceptualized the divine rule in contrast to the tyrannical rule of the stereotypical monarch." See further Bauckham, "Kingdom and Church according to Jesus and Paul," 1–27.

93. The world is topsy-turvy; therefore, the kingdom of God sets about to turn it right side up. Cf. Allison, *Historical Christ and the Theological Jesus*, 114: "Jesus proclaims the new because the old is not enough (Mark 2:21–22). He turns the world over because he thinks that it is upside down (Matt. 20:16; Mark 10:31; Luke 13:30). He disorients that he might reorient. This requires confronting the ordinary with the extraordinary, at which he is an expert." See also Allison, *Constructing Jesus*, 36 (no. 17). As Ma observes, "The Hellenistic world was largely a world of tributary states, *resting on an agrarian basis*, and structured by the redistribution patterns between the center, local elites in the periphery, and various metropolitan-like entities (Friends, colonists, powerholders)" ("Hellenistic Empires," 352 [emphasis mine]). What Jesus did was to turn all of this on its head, so that the tail became the head— the agrarian basis became destined to be the leaders of the new kingdom. Jesus exhorts his followers to imagine different—and to us, alien—conventions in terms of which apparently absurd performatives make sense (e.g., Mark 10:41–45 pars.).

94. Cf. Mark 9:35; 10:31, 44. See further Matt 10:39; Luke 17:33 (Q); Matt 23:12; Luke 14:11 (Q); Matt 25:29; Luke 19:26 (Q); Mark 4:25; Matt 13:12; Luke 18:14; Gos. Thom. 4.

95. Cf. Mark 10:14–15.

96. Cf. Mark 4:19; 10:23–27.

97. Cf. Mark 10:41–45: "When the ten heard this [i.e., that James and John wanted positions of honor in the kingdom], they began to be angry with James and John. So Jesus called them and said to them, 'You know that among the Gentiles those whom they recognize as their rulers lord it over them, and their great ones (οἱ μεγάλοι αὐτῶν) are tyrants over them. But it is not so among you; but whoever wishes to become great (μέγας) among you must be your servant, and whoever wishes to be first among you must be slave of all. For the Son of Man came not to be served but to serve, and to give his life a ransom for many.'" As Allison notes, "The first part of Mark 10:45 ('the Son of Man came not to be served but to serve') is an ironic reversal of Dan 7:14, where the one like a son of man comes and multitudes serve him" (*Constructing Jesus*, 81). Note, however, that, according to Mark 1:13, the angels did "serve" Jesus in the wilderness (καὶ οἱ ἄγγελοι διηκόνουν αὐτῷ), and they will accompany him when he returns in glory (Mark 8:38; 13:26–27; cf. 1 En. 1:9, which is cited in reference to Christ's Parousia in Jude 14–15). Mark's Gospel may reflect the Enochic tradition of heaven as a royal court, replete with courtiers. Cf. Esler, *God's Court and Courtiers in the Book of the Watchers*. Mark 10: The term that Jesus is reported to have used there (μέγας) was used by several Hellenistic kings in order to emphasize their conquering prowess. On Antiochus III "the Great" and "the Great King," see Ma, *Antiochos III*, 64 (App., *Syr.* 1), 71n68, 72n71, 73, 82, 83, 149, 221, 222, 230, 231, 232, 234, 240, 251–52, 253, 257, 262, 264, 272–76 (Appendix 4: Μέγας and βασιλεὺς μέγας), 324; Chaniotis, *War in the Hellenistic World*, 60. Cf. also Stevens, "Antiochus Cylinder, Babylonian Scholarship and Seleucid Imperial Ideology," 66–88. Stevens (table, p. 74) notes that Antiochus I, Assurbanipal, and Nabonidus were all referred to as "great king" (*šarru rabû*) in inscriptions. Stevens, "Antiochus Cylinder," 79: "Unlike earlier rulers of Babylon, Antiochus [I] lacks any epithets linking him directly to Mesopotamian deities. [. . .] Antiochus is king not because he is beloved of Nabû, but because he is great (*rabû*), powerful (*dannu*) and the son of a previous king; he rebuilt Esagil and Ezida simply because his own heart urged it."

ing was "one of the central gestures of [Hellenistic] kingship,"[98] then Jesus gives the ultimate gift—his own life as a ransom for the many. Moreover, people fall at Jesus' feet, which in a Roman context at least, is a gesture of submission in the context of *deditio in fidem* (which itself is similar to the aforementioned entrusting oneself into the hands of the Hellenistic conqueror).[99]

Those who entrust themselves into Jesus' hands find that he bestows benefactions upon them through performative language.[100] Thus we read in Mark 2:5 about the healing of the paralytic: "When Jesus saw their faith, he said to the paralytic, 'Son, your sins are forgiven.'" As we have seen, Jesus "forgives sins" in a similar way that a Hellenistic king or a royal pretender might, but he does so on the individual level, and the sin of rebellion pertains to God and his ways rather than to an earthly king's. Moreover, like a Hellenistic king, Jesus is a "savior," but the focus of his saving act is neither military protection nor material support,[101] but rather life-saving, physical healing.[102]

98. Cf. Ma, "Kings," 185.

99. Cf. Zack, "Forschungen über die rechtlichen Grundlagen der römischen Außenbeziehungen während der Republik bis zum Beginn des Prinzipats," 89–163, here 133 with n120. For another example of this form of submission (bowing down at Jesus' feet), see Mark 7:25. For another kind of gesture of submission in the context of *deditio*, compare the triumphal entry into Jerusalem and the presentation of palm branches as a sign of submission.

100. The feedings of the 5,000 (Mark 6:35–44) and the 4,000 (8:14–21) can be understood as royal benefactions on a lavish scale for the great crowd, which was "like sheep without a shepherd" (6:34). At the same time, these feedings contrast with the kind of conspicuous consumption that characterized Hellenistic kingship, which was for the ruling elite rather than for the producers at the very bottom of the socioeconomic hierarchy. Cf. Ma, "Kings," 183–84; Ma, "Hellenistic Empires," 332, 343–44, here 352: "The Hellenistic world was largely a world of tributary states, resting on an agrarian basis, and structured by the redistribution patterns between the center, local elites in the periphery, and various metropolitan-like entities (Friends, colonists, powerholders)." What Jesus did was to turn all of this (from his perspective, topsy-turvy world) on its head, so that the agrarian basis became the leaders of the new state. See further Ma, "Hellenistic Empires," 343: "The process of administration and extraction . . . allowed the state to carry out three core activities . . . : war making, conspicuous consumption, and gift-giving. [. . .] The extraction of wealth in the form of rent, tribute, and taxation allowed the state to carry out further demonstrations of its power, in the form of conspicuous consumption and spectacle. [. . .] More generally, royal style, and its settings, drew on a variety of traditions (Macedonian, Achaemenid, Near Eastern, Egyptian), to present the image of a qualitatively superior life experience, as an image of inherent marvel and desirability. This sublimated the presence of subordination and rule into the unashamed celebration of royal luxury and consumption as a metaphor for superiority." Ma, "Hellenistic Empires," 347: "Finally, the producers (especially the peasants of Asia Minor, Egypt, and Babylonia) are the basic foundation of the [economic] system [i.e., the processes of extraction, distribution, and expenditure], by providing the agricultural surplus to the state . . . , but they do not receive any return in the form of support from the state: their function is taken for granted by everyone in the system." On the stately consumption of the royal banquet, see Ma, "Hellenistic Empires," 332.

101. Cf. Chaniotis, *War in the Hellenistic World*, 70: "By rendering such services [i.e., protecting cities from enemies in wartime, from pirate attacks or from barbarian invasions], a Hellenistic monarch could justify his claim to the title of *Soter* ('Savior')." See also Chaniotis, *War in the Hellenistic World*, 73. As we have seen, Antiochus III wanted to be regarded as a "savior" because of his gifts (tax-exemption and material support). See also Ma, *Antiochos III*, 219, 310.

102. For other occurrences of σῴζω ("to save") in Mark's Gospel: 3:4 (in the context of the man

In Mark 3:1–6, Jesus heals a man with a withered hand by his authoritative word: "He said to the man, 'Stretch out your hand.' He stretched it out, and his hand was restored." What is particularly interesting about this performative utterance is that it provokes the Pharisees and the Herodians (i.e., supporters of the rule and policies of King Herod Antipas) to conspire against him, how to destroy him (v. 6). That means that, according to Mark's presentation, early on in his public phase in Galilee, Jesus showed signs of royal pretension through his status-changing performative utterances. Mark 3:6 may be redactional, but it very likely expresses the historical reality that Jesus' opponents were wise to him from an early period (see further below).

In Mark 12:13–17, we find the Pharisees and the Herodians once again conspiring against Jesus:

> Then they sent to him some Pharisees and some Herodians to trap him in what he said. And they came and said to him, "Teacher, we know that you are sincere, and show deference to no one; for you do not regard people with partiality, but teach the way of God in accordance with truth. Is it lawful to pay taxes to the emperor, or not? Should we pay them, or should we not?" But knowing their hypocrisy, he said to them, "Why are you putting me to the test? Bring me a denarius and let me see it." And they brought one. Then he said to them, "Whose head is this, and whose title?" They answered, "The emperor's." Jesus said to them, "Give to the emperor the things that are the emperor's, and to God the things that are God's." And they were utterly amazed at him.

Given Jesus' provocative performative utterances, it was only a matter of time before the royal pretender could have been expected to make a declaration of release from taxes.[103] As we have seen, this was the tact taken by previous royal pretenders as well

---

with a withered hand, ψυχὴν σῶσαι); 5:23 (Jesus can lay hands on Jairus's daughter, ἵνα σωθῇ καὶ ζήσῃ), 28 (the hemorrhagic woman thinks by touching Jesus' clothes, σωθήσομαι), 34 (Jesus says to the woman, θυγάτηρ, ἡ πίστις σου σέσωκέν σε· ὕπαγε εἰς εἰρήνην καὶ ἴσθι ὑγιὴς ἀπὸ τῆς μάστιγός σου); 6:56 (ὅσοι ἂν ἥψαντο αὐτοῦ [sc. the fringe of his cloak] ἐσῴζοντο); 10:52 (Jesus says to a blind man, ὕπαγε, ἡ πίστις σου σέσωκέν σε); 15:30–31 (the mocking of Jesus on the cross: σῶσον σεαυτὸν καταβὰς ἀπὸ τοῦ σταυροῦ. . . . ἄλλους ἔσωσεν, ἑαυτὸν οὐ δύναται σῶσαι).

103. On Mark 12:13–17 pars., see Udoh, *To Caesar What Is Caesars: Tribute, Taxes, and Imperial Administration in Early Roman Palestine (63 B.C.E.–70 C.E.)*, 223–38, who doubts that the Markan text and its parallel passages in Matt 22:15–22 and Luke 20:20–26 provide us with an accurate portrayal of the economic and social life of first-century Palestine (i.e., these texts do not enable us to reconstruct a system of taxation in force in Palestine during Jesus' time). Although this is not the place to review Udoh's evidence in any detail, one observation may be appropriate at this point. Given what we have seen about the continuity of Hellenistic institutions into the early Roman Empire up to the time of Hadrian (see above on the "long Hellenistic Age"), the evidence that Fergus Millar amasses for the transfer of functions from Hellenistic kings to Roman emperors during this period becomes significant here (cf. *Emperor in the Roman World*, 3–4, 111, 140–42, 174, 190, 198–99, 213, 221, 326, 329, 353, 361, 395–96, 448, 454, 492–93, 614–15), and this is indeed the context in which Millar views the statement about "rendering to Caesar" in Mark 12:13–17 pars. (199, 552–53). Moreover, in the Greek east the Roman emperor was widely seen as a king, but an authority was attributed to him even more general than that which he actually exercised (Millar, *Emperor in the Roman World*, 17, 553–54, 613–14). Therefore, even if there is a lack of evidence for direct taxation in Palestine, the *perception*

as Hellenistic kings in defining statuses of the ruled.[104] Exemption from taxation was a status over which the king's performative speech had sole prerogative,[105] and, even though it was really only an exemption, it was understood as an act of gift-giving.[106]

---

that the emperor personally controlled taxation, tribute, and other levies could have had wide credence. In any case, there was a universal practice in the region (whether voluntary or under compulsion is not always discernible) of sending the emperor gifts, including gold crowns (Millar, *Emperor in the Roman World*, 139–42). "But while actual gold crowns, or sums in lieu of them, continued to be voted on special occasions, the 'crown gold' was also a regular tax levied in addition to these" (Millar, *Emperor in the Roman World*, 142).

104. For example, Antiochus III the Great (*Megas*), the "Great King" of the Seleucid empire (reigned 233–186), in the immediate aftermath of the conquest of the ancient Ionian *polis* of Teos (204 BCE), entered the city, with his royal Friends and troops, gave a speech in the *bouleuterion* before the *ekklesia*, proclaiming the city "holy and inviolate and free from tribute," as confirmed by a follow-up interview and celebrated by the Teians in a long epigraphical dossier (ca. 203). Cf. Ma, *Antiochos III*, 308–11 (no. 17). The long, follow-up, honorific decree by the grateful Teians shows that the king's promised benefactions had indeed been implemented, from which we quote here merely the part pertaining to taxation: "the king brought us not only peace, but also an alleviation of the heavy and harsh taxes for the future, by releasing us from the *syntaseis* [i.e., the tribute-like 'contributions' previously exacted by Attalus I from the city on the proclaimed pretext of defending its territory]." Cf. Ma, *Antiochos III*, 311–17 (no. 18, lines 50–52).

105. Cf. Ma, *Antiochos III*, 100: Antiochos III "did not present his conquests under the heading of the 'liberation of the cities,' but rather appealed to dynastic legitimacy and euergetic solicitude; local autonomy was a status which he could grant within an imperial space where he held the monopoly of performative utterances." Ma, *Antiochos III*, 173 ("all statuses must originate with a performative speech act by the king"), 154 ("The most obvious form of domination was royal taxation, to support the 'royal economy'"), 195 ("The euergetical register called for the involvement and the acquiescence of the ruled. Gifts, or what was represented as gifts [often simply refraining from certain forms of exploitation], were presented as tokens of a more general characteristic, the ruler's kind concern for the ruled, his desire to benefit them, and the euergetic nature of the king"). For example, Antiochus III declared Teos *asylos* and tax-free, "so that after the increase of the matters of the city, he would receive the title (lit., 'inscription') not only of benefactor of the people, but also of its savior" (ἵνα γενομένης ἐπαύξεως τῶν κατὰ τὴν πόλιν μὴ μόνον εὐεργεσίας λάβη τὴν ἐπιγραφὴν τῆς τοῦ δήμου, ἀλλὰ καὶ σωτηρίας). See further Ma, *Antiochos III*, 184, 309. See also Ma, *Antiochos III*, 49, 50, 61–62, 110 (referring to tax-relief for Jerusalem under Antiochus III [Josephus, *Ant.* 12.142–144]), 112, 123, 130–35, 139–40, 150, 156 ("Royal pronouncements were often directly performative inside the political space of the city, dictating actions and norms: . . . in Seleukid Kolophon, the farming of the civic taxes was regulated κατὰ τὸ τοῦ βασιλέως διάγραμμα ['according to the king's decree']"), 157, 158, 171 ("Local statuses inscribed the cities in the ideology of the patrimonial empire, since by nature they are based on the assumption that the king holds the monopoly of performative utterances within the state; statuses are defined by his pronouncements, and can be represented as his benefactions . . . the king's refraining from exactions is described with the same vocabulary as an actual gift"), 195, 203, 219 (Antiochus III's "administrative action [tax-relief!] is described in terms fitting for divine power"), 237, 247, 264–65, 310, 315, 243, 245, 365.

106. Cf. Ma, "Hellenistic Empires," 344–45: "One particular form that royal magnificence could take was gift-giving, which constitutes the third main heading of state expenditure. [. . .] The epigraphic record shows that a major part of the interaction between Greek city and ruler was taken up by asking for such gifts, and reciprocating by symbolical honors (crowns, statues, or the cultic honors mentioned above as part of the religious culture of empire). Similar benefactions are attested in the case of the priestly community at Jerusalem, and it is likely that most shrines received benefactions and subsidies from the state, which explains the state's interest in local shrines and its supervision of their finances and administration. Gift-giving was an essential part of the royal image, celebrated for

As we have seen on the basis of 1 Macc 13:36–40, total exemption from tribute was considered equivalent to a state of absolute independence from Seleucid rule.[107] The Pharisees and Herodians, who had previously taken umbrage with Jesus' performative utterances (cf. Mark 3:1–6), tried to get Jesus to make such a pronouncement about freedom from Roman taxation, thereby pressing his perceived bid for kingship to its logical extreme.[108] If some of his other performatives were less explicitly subversive in their royal pretensions, declaring release from Roman taxation would have been an unequivocal act of insurrection,[109] a declaration that would have been guaranteed to be infelicitous because it would have led inexorably to Jesus' execution as a royal pretender.[110] This is what happened anyway.

If, as we are arguing, Jesus' performative utterances in Mark's Gospel reveal Jesus' royal pretensions, then our thesis would seem to run counter to William Wrede's famous theory of the "messianic secret" in Mark.[111] Wrede sought to answer

instance in the third-century Greek court poetry of Theokritos . . . ; it was also closely linked to the nature of the state, in a number of instructive ways. Gift-giving reflected the assumption of authority, so that a concession, such as the exemption of taxation, could be presented as a gift on par with a shipment of grain: the personal generosity of the ruler was predicated on the power of the state. Apart from its ideological (celebratory or controlling) force, gift-giving also performed structural roles in the state: it provided an outlet for revenues in ways that bound and controlled individuals, ensured the collaboration of communities, and furthermore worked toward their administrative integration within circuits of extraction and distribution. In other words, gift-giving and dependency strengthened the state."

107. Cf. Ma, *Antiochos III*, 155: "Royal taxation was synonymous with royal domination, to the point that the settlement of Asia by the Romans in 188 would define free cities as those exempt from paying tribute to anyone."

108. Cf. "Literary, Theological and Historical Problems in the Gospel of Mark," in Hengel, *Studies in the Gospel of Mark*, 31–63, here 42 (emphasis mine): "The question of authority (11.28) already indicates that the leaders of the people know of Jesus' claim and want to use it to *lure him out into the open*; the high priest's question (14.61) is no longer a surprise: it simply puts into words ideas that have long been in the air and could already have motivated the accusation connected with the saying about destroying and rebuilding the temple (14.58). The surprise was Jesus' clear, unsurpassable confession of his unique status." See also Dunn, *Christianity in the Making*, 1:627: "In short, the only obvious reason why the risen Jesus was hailed as Messiah was that resurrection was seen as a vindication of a claim which had been in play *before* Jesus' crucifixion and resurrection. But if the question of Jesus as Messiah was an issue during his lifetime, then the whole logic underpinning Wrede's central thesis begins to go into reverse."

109. In the lead-up to the Jewish revolt against Rome in 66–70 CE, Agrippa II addressed the rebellious Jewish in 66 CE about their refusal to pay taxes to Caesar: "But your actions are already acts of war against Rome, for you have not paid your tribute to Caesar. . . . If you wish to clear yourselves of the charge of insurrection, . . . pay the tax" (Josephus, *J.W.* 2.403–404). Cf. Udoh, *To Caesar What Is Caesar's*, 229. On the relationship between freedom and remission of tribute to Rome for Judea, see Udoh, *To Caesar What Is Caesar's*, 156, 157, 243.

110. Once again, we see that the conditions for the "felicitousness" of Jesus' performative utterances are linked with the distribution of power—the conditions that govern the authority or the perceived entitlement of the utterer.

111. Cf. Wrede, *Das Messiasgeheimnis in den Evangelien*; ET *The Messianic Secret*. The subject has been widely discussed. See, e.g., Hengel, "Literary, Theological and Historical Problems in the Gospel of Mark," 41–45; Räisänen, *"Messianic Secret" in Mark's Gospel*; Yarbro Collins, *Mark*, 170–72; Pesch,

the question, When Jesus was made known as Messiah or when he made himself known as such?[112] Wrede argued that Mark's Gospel contains a *unified* secrecy motif consisting of the following four elements: (1) the command to silence addressed to demons, those who had been healed, and to the disciples; (2) the so-called parable theory; (3) the lack of understanding by the disciples; and (4) certain individual features that betray a tendency against publicity.

On the basis of this unified "messianic secret," Wrede comes to the following conclusions about Mark's understanding: (1) Jesus kept his messiahship secret as long as he was on earth; (2) Jesus revealed himself to the disciples, in contrast to other people, but even the disciples did not understand the revelation of who Jesus was; (3) the real understanding of who Jesus is begins with his resurrection.[113] With respect to the latter point, Wrede found the key to the secrecy motif in Mark 9:9, where Jesus instructs his closest disciples not tell anyone what they had seen on the mount of transfiguration "until the Son of Man should have risen from the dead." It is in this passage that the heart of Mark's messianic secret is expressed. During the earthly life of Jesus, his messiahship remains hidden from all but the innermost circle. But the resurrection will alter the situation; with the resurrection the secret is revealed. During the era of the secret (i.e., during Jesus' lifetime), the lack of understanding of Jesus' messianic identity is only natural, even for the disciples.

Wrede tried to argue that the messianic secret stems neither from the historical Jesus nor from Mark, but from Mark's tradition. The messianic secret is a transitional idea by means of which an attempt is made to reconcile the old view that Jesus became Messiah only as of the resurrection (cf. Acts 2:36; Rom 1:4; Phil 2:6–11) with the later messianic interpretation of Jesus' life (e.g., John's Gospel presents Jesus' activity from the outset as an epiphany of the Son of God). Regardless of its origins, however, the main point of Wrede's thesis is that the messianic secret in its Markan form is a secondary, theological (and therefore unhistorical) construction.

There are a few problems with Wrede's thesis. As several scholars have noted, for example, the "messianic secret" is not a unified motif. The four points listed above cannot be combined into a single entity called the *Messiasgeheimnis*; they must be explained separately, on their own terms (e.g., the reason for the so-called parable theory [Mark 4:11–12] was different from the reason that Jesus did not allow the demons to identify him). More importantly for our purposes, Wrede himself recognized that a number of passages in Mark's Gospel actually *contradict* the messianic secret. For example, Jesus sometimes does miracles in full view of a large crowd (2:1–12); the parables are sometimes understood even by his opponents (12:1–12, esp. v. 12); and Jesus' authority on earth is openly demonstrated by his miracles

---

Markusevangelium, 2.36–47; Dunn, *Jesus Remembered*, 50, 624–27; Tuckett, *Messianic Secret*.

112. Wrede, *Messiasgeheimnis*, 5.

113. Wrede, *Messiasgeheimnis*, 114.

(2:10). Hence, Mark's Gospel displays a marked *tension* between hiddenness and openness with respect to Jesus' "messianic" identity.

Our thesis about Jesus' performative utterances opens up a new perspective on Wrede's work on the "messianic secret." If we look back at Jesus' performative utterances listed above, we discover that some of them are part of what Wrede has identified as constituting the "messianic secret" (e.g., 1:21–28; 4:35–41; 5:35–43) and even more instances are part of the contrary *openness* theme (e.g., 2:1–12; 3:1–6; 5:1–20, 24b–34; 10:46–52), with two cases being tweeners: Jesus' attempt to keep things under wraps served only to have his reputation spread all the more vigorously far and wide (1:40–45; 7:31–37). The fact that Jesus' performative utterances occur in both kinds of passages—hiddenness and openness—suggests is that Jesus' performativity cannot simply be relegated to pre-Markan tradition having a transitional function (à la Wrede) or to Markan redaction (as a number of scholars have argued on the basis of Wrede's "messianic secret").[114] This opens the possibility that performativity was remembered as characteristic of Jesus himself.

This conclusion agrees coincidentally with the argument of Anthony Le Donne about the effectiveness of Jesus' words.[115] He begins by observing that Isa 11:1–12 foresees a leader ("a shoot" from "the stump of Jesse") who would usher in a peaceful kingdom. This "Prince of Peace" (Isa 9:6) "wouldn't have need of handheld weapons because he would win his battles with his wisdom and the spoken word: 'The Spirit of the Lord will rest on him, the Spirit of wisdom and understanding. . . . With the breath of his lips he will slay the wicked' (Isa. 11:2–4)."[116] According to Le Donne, Jesus saw himself as precisely this expected royal figure, one to whom God had given "dominion, glory, and a kingdom" (Dan 7:14). Words were Jesus' weapon of choice because Jesus' words held the very power of God: "Jesus believed that, by the Spirit of God, he would slay the *source* of evil by casting out demons with his words. He claimed that 'if I cast out demons by the Spirit of God, then the kingdom of God has come upon you' (Matt. 12:28). God's kingdom could be achieved, not with physical violence, but with the 'Spirit of wisdom.' Once the spiritual power behind Rome was bound, God's peaceable kingdom would become a reality."[117] Moreover, Le Donne

114. On redaction-critical interpretations of Wrede's messianic secrecy motif, see Räisänen, *"Messianic Secret" in Mark's Gospel*, 55–71. Peter's confession of Jesus as ὁ χριστός (Mark 8:29) is crucial for the plot of the Markan narrative, because immediately after this confession, which took place at the northernmost geographical extent of Jesus' travels, he announced his way into suffering and death in Jerusalem and began the journey.

115. Le Donne, *Historical Jesus*, 89–90, 113, 133–34.

116. Le Donne, *Historical Jesus*, 89. Isaiah 11 is evidently also the basis for expecting that Jesus, as the self-proclaimed "Messiah" (Mark 14:61–62 pars.), would be able to prophesy while blindfolded: "Some began to spit on him, to blindfold him, and to strike him, saying to him, 'Prophesy!'" (Mark 14:65 pars.). Cf. Isa 11:3: "He shall not judge by what his eyes see. . . ."

117. Le Donne, *Historical Jesus*, 89 (author's emphasis). For a different view, see Allison, *Constructing Jesus*, 284; and especially Bermejo-Rubio, "Jesus and the Anti-Roman Resistance," 1–105, who argues that Jesus was actually involved in *armed* resistance against the Romans.

continues: "With his words, Jesus made a memorable impact upon each of his hearers. Some believed that his words healed them. Others were impacted by his redefinition of the kingdom. Still others were offended by his subversive message and saw him as an affront to Israel's proper political aspirations. In each case, the impact of his message varied from interpreter to interpreter. At the same time, the Jesus tradition maintained a stable core of memory. The message of God's kingdom was at the heart of this core."[118] Jesus' faith in the effectiveness of his Spirit-empowered, performative speech led him to claim that he could destroy the Jerusalem Temple and build another (cf. Mark 14:56–59; John 2:18–21). Le Donne argues that Jesus' claim was not merely idle chatter or bravado; Jesus actually believed that, like Joshua of old ("Jesus" in Greek!), he could bring down walls and the power structures that go with them.[119] The Jerusalem priesthood took this claim as seriously as the Romans did the similar claim of an anonymous Egyptian with royal aspirations who came to Jerusalem, declared he was a prophet, and claimed that he could command Jerusalem's walls to fall down: the Roman governor Felix (52–59 CE) attacked the Egyptian's movement, killing four hundred of his followers and taking two hundred prisoners (cf. Josephus, *Ant.* 20.169–72; *J.W.* 2.57–59).[120] The parallel to Jesus and his fate is clear.

Conclusion

Performative speech-acts were used by successive Seleucid pretenders and kings to create the appearance of power and authority out of weakness.[121] As we have seen on the basis of Mark's Gospel, Jesus used performative utterances in a similar way, and, for that reason, he was recognized as a royal pretender by both sympathizers and critics alike. From the perspective of Mark's Gospel, Jesus set about to create the kingdom of God by royal pronouncement. It was a matter of royal power as discourse. The sympathizers, although growing in number, could not match the countervailing power of the ruling elites who found fault with him precisely because he was gaining a significant following. In the end, therefore, Jesus was crucified as a royal pretender at the hands of the Romans. Speech-acts are effective when they meet conventional expectations and are validated by the intended audience. Jesus was crucified as a royal pretender precisely because he *did* meet conventional expectations for kingship, but his bid was not adequately validated by his intended audience. To the leaders of Jesus' day, both Jewish and Roman alike, Jesus represented, as a royal pretender, the presence of a competing state that can make alternative offers,

118. Le Donne, *Historical Jesus*, 89–90.

119. Le Donne, *Historical Jesus*, 131–32. See Josh 6:15–21.

120. The Egyptian was one of a number of what Josephus unsympathetically calls "imposters and deceivers" who arose at this time and led insurrections (Josephus, *Ant.* 20.168). See further Allison, *Constructing Jesus*, 260–61, 398–99.

121. Ma, "Seleukids and Speech-Acts," 108.

ideological and material, to local actors, thus threatening a shift in popular support from the current regime(s) to that of the pretender.

Ma argued that the complexities of the Maccabean test case arise within the framework defined by Austin's notion of speech-acts: It is only through this theoretical framework that we start to notice and interpret these complexities.[122] Something similar can be said of the Jesus tradition as exemplified in Mark's Gospel. What speech-act theory allows us to do is to take the Gospel accounts seriously, but within a political reality which forms the context for the documents as speech-acts. Taking the Gospel of Mark as *our* test case, we can study the precise process by which Jesus comes on the scene with the royal grant of the "good news," exhorting repentance and belief (acceptance) of the "good news." From there, we can trace how this performative utterance was either accepted or rejected, in various circumstances, all the way through Jesus' final week and his crucifixion at the hands of the Romans as a royal pretender. Austin's insights lead us to a richer interpretation, and greater sensitivity to multi-layered interaction and subtle correspondences. As Ma argued, "These should be the contribution of any theory, when applied to historical material: allowing the historian to see more things and offer more sophisticated descriptions of the sociopolitical transactions."[123]

The collective force of the material in Mark's Gospel about Jesus' status-changing performative utterances has not been appreciated. When seen against the backdrop of Hellenistic kings and pretenders, this material is united in one particular: It constitutes a family of traditions that help to explain how someone could view Jesus as a royal pretender. We have explored our thesis about Jesus as a royal pretender primarily on the basis of Mark's Gospel, although we have tried to show, in a preliminary way, how our approach dovetails with other parts of the Jesus tradition[124] and that Jesus' performativity cannot be relegated to Markan redaction. It remains to be seen how our approach can be fleshed out on the basis of a fuller comparison of the available evidence, including both the Jesus tradition itself and the Greco-Roman and Jewish material. It seems probable that such a comparison will prove to be a powerful tool to be added to those that already exist for exploring the Jesus tradition. From that generative point of view, we will be able to see previously concealed textual connections and make some inferences about the historical contours of the historical Jesus.

Every comparison is simultaneously a contrast, and the comparison between Jesus as royal pretender and Seleucid royal pretenders is no different. We have chosen here to focus mostly on the comparisons, but it is obvious that Jesus explodes the boundaries of the normal Hellenistic usurper. Moreover, a more nuanced approach

122. Cf. Ma, "Seleukids and Speech-Acts," 106–7.

123. Ma, "Seleukids and Speech-Acts," 107.

124. See above, for example, on the comparison of Mark 1:14–15 with Matt 11:2–4//Luke 7:18–23 (Q) and on the logion about destroying the temple and building another (Mark 14:56–59; John 2:18–21).

would appreciate how the Jewish context in which Jesus operated also colors the kind of royal pretender he was. However, most of that nuancing had to be ignored for the purposes of the present brief study.

Jesus' announcement that the kingdom of God was at hand and the admonition to repent and believe the good news (Mark 1:14–15) inaugurated the building of a new world within and alongside the old. However, his performative language projected that which "will have been" as an unfolding revolutionary event. As yet, it had no objective status, only a conditional and experimental one: If, despite "factual" evidence to the contrary, you believe that Jesus is ushering in the kingdom (i.e., that it *will have been* a revolutionary event), then that belief functions in the future anterior.[125] If, however, because of the significant counterfactual evidence, you do not believe Jesus' proclamation, then the Jesus movement is an inconsequential moment in the history of state-capitalism to be co-opted or crushed.

Judas, one of the intimate followers of Jesus, was co-opted, and Jesus himself was crucified as a royal pretender. But the Jesus revolution was not thereby extinguished. Instead, the Jesus revolution continued unabated, because it was a nonviolent revolution and therefore did not affect Jesus' followers. As the famous, first-century Jewish historian, Flavius Josephus, observed in his so-called "Testimonium Flavianum,"

> At this time there appeared Jesus, a *wise man* (*sophos anēr*),[126] if indeed one should call him a man. For he was a doer of startling deeds, a teacher of people who receive the truth with pleasure. And he gained a following both among many Jews and among many of Greek origin. He was the Messiah. And when Pilate, because of an accusation made by the leading men among us, condemned him to the cross, those who had loved him previously did not cease to do so. For he appeared to them on the third day, living again, just as the divine prophets had spoken of these and countless other wondrous things about him. And up to this very day the tribe of Christians, named after him, has not died out. (Josephus, *Ant.* 18.63–64)

Scholars have had misgivings about some parts of this statement, arguing that the original composition was redacted by a later Christian scribe in order to make Josephus a witness to the divinity, messiahship, and resurrection of Jesus.[127] Be that as it may, there is little doubt that Josephus himself referred to Jesus generically as a "wise man."[128] But that could hardly have been the reason for the "accusation made by the leading men among us [sc. Jewish people/Judeans]." You don't have someone executed simply because he is wise or popular. There must have been more to the story. And that something more seems to be wrapped up with the short statement

125. Above, we referred to "social magic" to describe belief in Jesus' message.

126. The Greek expression perhaps reflects the Hebrew ḥākām.

127. For the details of this controversy, see Meier, *Marginal Jew*, 1:56–88.

128. Cf. Meier, *Marginal Jew*, 1:61–62.

that Jesus was the Messiah, the end-time king of Israel. Even if Josephus did not say precisely, "He was the Messiah," he may well have said something similar. For example, in a parallel passage, the authenticity of which has not been questioned, Josephus refers to "the brother of Jesus who is *called* Messiah (*ton adelphon Iēsou tou legomenou Christou*), James by name" (*Ant.* 20.200). Hence, Josephus may have originally written that Jesus was "the *so-called* Messiah," thus distancing himself from the claim. It would have been relatively easy for a later Christian scribe to simply delete an attributive participle in the original Testimonium Flavianum. In that case, Josephus can be correlated with the Gospels that Jesus was executed as a royal/messianic pretender, but his nonviolent revolution was carried on by his followers after his death. And why, despite their leader's death, did the tribe of Christians not simply die out as a movement?[129] Was it because they continued to live in the "future anterior"?[130] And were they able to do so because, as Josephus and the Gospels attest, Jesus himself was believed to have been resurrected?[131]

Jesus' use of performative language explains two important aspects of his life simultaneously. First, because his performative utterances were essentially pleas for recognition, ending up crucified as a royal pretender, amid a jeering crowd, was a sign of utter defeat and rejection; hence, his "cry of dereliction" on the cross—"My God, my God, why have your forsaken me?" (Mark 15:34 par. Matt 27:46; *Gos. Pet.*

---

129. The fact that Jesus' revolution was non-violent is confirmed by the fact that his followers were not executed with him. In a paper presented at the Virtual Annual Meeting of Biblical Meeting of the Society of Biblical Literature in 2020, "Josephus and Nonviolent Resistance to Romanization: The Immediate Jewish Matrix of Jesus of Nazareth," John Dominic Crossan argued, "For *violent* resistance Rome crucified the leader together with many of his major supporters. In 4 BCE at Jerusalem, for example, the Syrian legate captured 'the authors of the insurrection . . . the most culpable, in number about two hundred, he crucified' (*JW* 2:75 = *JA* 17.295). For *nonviolent* resistance, Rome crucified only the leader on the presumption that his followers would scatter and the movement would disappear. In the early 200s, for example, the famous Roman jurist, Julius Paulus, nicknamed Prudentissimus by his contemporary emperor, made a compilation of the *opinions*—in the juridical sense—of Roman law. Under 'Title XXII: Concerning Seditious Persons' he gave this legal precedent: 'The authors of sedition and tumult, or those who stir up the people, shall, according to their rank, either be crucified, thrown to wild beasts, or deported to an island' (*The Opinions of Julius Paulus Addressed to His Son*, Book V, Title 22.1). [. . .] My second conclusion from Josephus alone is that Jesus was crucified for founding a *nonviolent* movement of resistance to Romanization."

130. Cf. Allison, *Constructing Jesus*, 64: "The end of Jesus, to state the obvious, was neither the end of the present world order nor the beginning of its end. Why, then, did early Christians speak as though it was?"

131. As we have seen, the condition/abstract machine of an assemblage is that which at every instant causes the given to be given, in this or that state, at this or that moment, but itself is not given. Jesus functions as the given for his movement. As such, the effect of Jesus' death on his givenness was an open question. His movement could have dissolved, as the Romans fully expected, or it could continue on if his death was somehow able to be assimilated to that givenness. According to the witnesses of the New Testament, as well as the Testimonium Flavianum, the post-resurrectional appearances of Jesus were the key to the movement's ongoing vitality. In other words, the risen Christ was seen as the (continued) presence of the future.

5:19)—becomes quite understandable and believable.[132] Second, because Jesus' performative language set in motion the dawning of the kingdom of God, which entails the renewal of the world and the future resurrection, Jesus presumably held fast to the belief that he himself would not only participate in the resurrection but actually inaugurate it.[133] For Jesus, then, kingship is indeed "a discursive, performative phenomenon, manifested in speech-act."[134]

132. Contrast Allison, *Constructing Jesus*, 410, 426–27, 432.

133. Cf. Allison, *Constructing Jesus*, 55–65.

134. See the epigraph to the present chapter.

3

Jesus' Proclamation of the Kingdom and Revolutionary Transformation

Introduction

THE MODERN RETURN TO revolution has been a fruitful way to investigate the New Testament as an assemblage. So far, we have noticed that Jesus' proclamation of the kingdom of God is a performative utterance that actually enacts the kingdom insofar as people repent and believe the good news of the kingdom. Thus, a fragile community began to gather around Jesus, albeit one that imperfectly understood his message and only tentatively believed it. At the same time, opposition from the dominant territorial and state assemblages began to grow as it became more and more clear that Jesus appeared to be using performative language in the same way that royal pretenders often did, in order to gain a following and make a bid for the throne. The result was that Jesus was understood as a royal claimant who had to be stopped before he gained any more popularity.

In this chapter, we explore in more detail Jesus' proclamation of the "Kingdom of God/heaven."[1] As we have already argued, Jesus' proclamation of the kingdom

---

1. In Matthew's Gospel, Jesus proclaims "the Kingdom of heaven," in which "heaven" is not, as commonly thought, a circumlocution for the divine name ("Kingdom of *God*"), but rather an indication of territory or space. As a genitive of source, the kingdom is one that comes *from heaven* and whose origin is *in heaven*. See further Pennington, *Heaven and Earth in the Gospel of Matthew*, 321: "Matthew's choice to regularly depict the kingdom as τῶν οὐρανῶν [*of heaven* or *of the heavens*] is designed to emphasize that God's kingdom is not like earthly kingdoms, stands over against them,

is a self-legitimating, performative utterance that relies on belief in the promised new world in the "future anterior" (that which will have been) for enactment of the generative process of transformation leading up to it (at least in the interim before the consummation brought about by God/Christ). To say that the Jesus movement is self-generating does not mean that it came about *ex nihilio* (out of nothing).[2] First, those who joined the Jesus movement (or rather, were captured by it) did so as escapees or rejects from other kinds of assemblages (territorial, state, capitalist, and even nomadic/revolutionary). As disaffected or abandoned individuals (the discontent, hopeless, fearful, outcasts), they were ripe for capture by the revolutionary Jesus movement.[3] By avoiding secondary reterritorialization by the dominant assemblages, these escapees began to connect up with other similar individuals to transform the dominant conditions through the creation of a new world, at least in an anticipatory way. To continue the revolutionary movement that Jesus began would mean broadening the geographical reach of the dawning kingdom of God, building connections and networks to strengthen their shared deterritorializations, and taking on others' struggles as their own (e.g., against poverty, discrimination, injustice, and all forms of bondage and oppression).

Second, although Jesus was the "degree zero" for the new movement (i.e., he presented an almost indecipherable break from the prevailing assemblages), his message nevertheless had significant lines of continuity with other apocalyptically oriented, Jewish revolutionary movements. Although we will discuss these revolutionary movements at a later point, we may briefly summarize their general apocalyptic worldview as follows: Although God created a good world, evil spirits have filled it with wickedness, so that it is in disarray and full of injustice. A day is coming, however, when God will repair the broken creation and restore scattered Israel. Before that time, the struggle between good and evil will come to a climax, and a period of great tribulation and unmatched woe will descend upon the world. After that period, God will, perhaps through the agency of one or more messianic figures (with or without the sword),[4] reward the just and requite the unjust, both living and

---

and will eschatologically replace them (on earth)." Cf. also Allison, *Constructing Jesus*, 181–82. Seen in this light, the kingdom of heaven in Matthew's Gospel puts an emphasis on the transcendence of the kingdom as an earthly phenomenon.

2. Although the present study emphasizes the this-worldly (horizontal) plane of immanence, the New Testament itself often highlights the transcendent (vertical) reason for the dynamic power and growth of the Jesus movement: the working of the Holy Spirit in and through the witnesses appointed by Jesus. This is a major theme of the book of Acts (cf., e.g., Acts 1:8; see further in chapter 5 below). Yet, this working of the Spirit is not separate from the plane of immanence; rather, the Spirit is an anticipation of the end time in the present and as such is part of creating the "future anterior" through human instrumentality (cf. Romans 8).

3. See further on latent "lines of flight" in the Conclusion to the present volume.

4. Cf. "Temporality and Politics in Jewish Apocalyptic Literature," in Collins, *Encounters with Biblical Theology*, 129–41, here 137; "Jesus and the Messiahs of Israel," in Collins, *Encounters with Biblical Theology*, 169–78; Pss. Sol. 17:21–46.

dead, and then establish divine rule forever, which entails the recapitulation of the originally intended will of God for the creation. In other words, before Jesus ever came on the scene, there were other revolutionary Jewish apocalyptic movements in existence that proclaimed a message promoting a life in the future anterior, in anticipation of God's full and final redemption.[5]

Jesus fits comfortably within such an apocalyptic worldview, even if his own brand of revolution, which was based on special divine revelation (*apokalypsis*), had its own unique characteristics. Jesus was not looking for the end of the world, but rather for the restoration of the broken, topsy-turvy world as we currently know it. Moreover, he called upon his followers to anticipate that future renewed world by embodying the prefigurative future anterior (that which will have been) *in thought, word, and deed*.[6] By believing that Jesus' performative proclamation of the kingdom is an event, that belief functions as an actualization of the new and better world in the prefigurative future anterior. From this perspective, time is not linear. Rather, political events are heterogeneous points on a one-dimensional folded surface of space-time, so that any event such as Jesus' proclamation of the kingdom can be directly connected to any other in any combination by spatial proximity: without mediation or causal unity. Hence, Jesus does not have two future horizons (i.e., an imminent expectation, of the destruction of Israel and its temple, and a long-range expectation, of the universal judgment), but rather *one*: the creation of a whole new space-time that both projects a new future and retrojects a new past. Moreover, it creates in the present the past and the future it aspires to see. It is not the inert hope that "another world is possible," but rather the actualization of the new and better world in anticipation of its full and final form. It is the actual construction of a new present in the future anterior, which is necessarily contingent and open-ended.

For several reasons, this revolutionary process is necessarily contingent and open-ended. First, because its continuation is always contested: the revolutionary prefiguration of the world to come faces dangers from succumbing to systems that attempt to co-opt it, systems of neutralization, or processes of implosion or self-destruction.[7] For example, in view of the forces and factors that were threatening the Galatian assembly, Paul wondered whether his work among them had been "in vain" (Gal 3:4; 4:11). Second, the revolutionary process is always contingent and open-ended because it must be worked out in actual practice, ensuring that the singular

5. For a helpful overview, see Collins, *Apocalyptic Imagination*; Collins, "Temporality and Politics in Jewish Apocalyptic Literature," 138–39.

6. Anticipation is therefore a key concept for our study of New Testament Theology (cf., e.g., Romans 8). Anticipation occurs between the "already" and the "not yet" (see further below). We anticipate or expect events that have not yet happened, or we can imagine what might happen, only because we have created a concept that extends beyond our current mundane experience to what we might expect or imagine. On the modern study of anticipation, see, e.g., Miller, *Transforming the Future: Anticipation in the 21st Century*; Poli, *Introduction to Anticipation Studies*.

7. See chapter 1 on the typology of change in assemblages.

processes are maintained by creatively articulating them in a work, a text, or a way of living with oneself or with others. Obviously, these external threats and internal uncertainties mean that the revolutionary movement is constantly subject to change as circumstances themselves change.

In the following, we shall survey the material in the Jesus tradition relating to Jesus' understanding of revolutionary transformation in the kingdom of God: (1) what has *already* been inaugurated and (2) what is *not yet* consummated. Most scholars who have written on the eschatology of Jesus have allowed that he thought and spoke of God's rule as somehow truly present. At the same time, they have not eliminated all the sayings of Jesus about the future coming of the kingdom. So the question remains: How, if at all, can these two sorts of sayings be brought together or held in tension at the same time? We have already outlined an answer to this question, but we will now go into further detail. The goal here is not to assume that each and every text in our survey necessarily goes back to Jesus, but rather to gain a general impression of the kinds of perspectives that are attributed to Jesus and that are formative to the movement that he founded (these two perspectives are inextricably intertwined). Thus, as in chapter 2, we are following the method recommended by Allison for authenticating the Jesus tradition.

The "Already": The Presence of the Kingdom

Luke 17:20–21 reads as follows: "Once Jesus was asked by the Pharisees when the kingdom of God was coming, and he answered, 'The kingdom of God is not coming with things that can be observed; nor will they say, "Look, here it is!" Or "There it is!" For, in fact, the kingdom of God is among [or *in*] you (*entos hymōn*).'" Similarly, the Gospel of Thomas 113 reads: "His disciples said to him, 'When will the kingdom come?' Jesus said, 'It will not come by expectation. It will not be a matter of saying "here it is" or "there it is." Rather, the kingdom of the Father is spread out upon the earth, and people do not see it.'"

These two sayings of Jesus were, according to members of the Jesus Seminar, foundational to their position that Jesus was a preacher of the *present* kingdom of God, and they meant that in the exclusive sense: Jesus did not have an apocalyptic expectation. For example, John Dominic Crossan, a cofounder of the Jesus Seminar, accepts that the two sayings faithfully represent Jesus and that they constitute a rebuttal of "the validity of apocalyptic eschatology."[8] We have seen, however, that Jesus' emphasis on the presence of the kingdom of God by no means rules out the future.[9] Instead, the present is simply the construction of *the future anterior*—the way things *will have been*.[10]

8. Crossan, *Birth of Christianity*, 316.

9. Indeed, the literary context of Luke 17:20–21 prefaces warnings about the approaching eschatological catastrophe (vv. 22–37).

10. Many today read Luke 17:20–21 as a statement of antithetical exclusion: because the kingdom

Matthew 12:28//Luke 11:20 (Q) declares that the kingdom of God "has come" (*ephthasen*), using a verb that could be understood as proleptic (i.e., the kingdom is so near that it can be spoken of as though it were already present). Others have suggested that this text is a declaration that the kingdom has in fact entered the present. This could be correct, but to affirm that the kingdom has arrived is not to say that it is already all that it will be.[11] Both Matthew and Luke, for their part, attest to an end-time scenario that is *not yet* (see further below).

The antithesis so often presumed between the kingdom as present and the kingdom as future fails to reflect adequate engagement with Jewish sources. Daniel, which has clearly influenced parts of the canonical Gospels,[12] announces that "in the days of those kings [of the Greek kingdom] the God of heaven will set up a kingdom that shall never be destroyed" (Dan 2:44). Here the kingdom is yet to come (cf. 7:14, 18, 22, 27). In 4:34, however, God's kingdom endures from "generation to generation"; that is, the kingdom is already a present reality (cf. 4:3). Hence, it seems plausible that Jewish hearers of Daniel—and of Jesus—thought God's kingdom to be both present and coming, or in heaven now and on earth in the future.[13]

In the book of Jubilees, a Jewish writing from the second century BCE, the world to come—which is actually the restoration of the original creation—comes about as *a gradual process* in the shell of the calamitous old world.[14] According to Jub. 23:26–27, "In those days, the children shall begin to study the laws, to seek out the commands, and to return to the right way. The days will begin to become numerous and increase, and mankind as well—generation by generation and day by day until their lifetimes approach 1000 years and to more years than the number of days (had been)." As Dale C. Allison points out, "This passage is particularly instructive for the study of Jesus because many have concurred with R. H. Charles that, for the author of Jubilees, 'the era of the Messianic kingdom had already set in.'"[15] Whereas the center of Jub. 23 is a depiction of the Maccabean revolt, the last few verses, including those just quoted, refer to the eschatological repristination of the world. Jubilees, however, sees the now and the not yet as one continuous process of change without clearly defined stages. The consummation is not yet, but it has already begun. Again Allison: "To borrow

of God is even now "among you," it cannot, someday down the road, be "coming with things that can be observed; nor will they say, 'Look, here it is!' or 'There it is!'" More likely, however, Luke 17:20 does not really deny that the kingdom of God will someday come "with things that can be observed"; rather, Jesus says that solely in order to emphasize the unexpected declaration that follows in 17:21: the kingdom is present among you.

11. On apocalyptic expectation in the hypothetical sayings source Q, see further below.

12. Cf. Evans, "Daniel in the New Testament," 490–527.

13. See further Hengel and Schwemer, *Jesus und das Judentum*, 406–11.

14. Cf. Scott, *On Earth as in Heaven*, 119–27.

15. Allison, *Constructing Jesus*, 109. It should be noted, however, that *Jubilees* gives no hint of having a messianic expectation at all. Not all Jewish writings of the Second Temple period had messianic expectations, and in any case they were not uniform.

a phrase that Joachim Jeremias used to characterize the teaching of Jesus, *Jubilees* displays 'an eschatology that is in the process of realization.'"[16]

The Apocalypse of Weeks (1 En. 93:1–10 + 91:11–17),[17] which is embedded in the Epistle of Enoch (1 En. 92–105), another Jewish writing of the Second Temple period, also envisions an extended eschatological process that is already underway. The Apocalypse of Weeks divides human history from creation to the new creation into ten mega-"Weeks," each of which is several centuries long:

Weeks	Events
1	From Adam to Enoch
2	From Enoch to Noah
3	From Noah to Abraham
4	From Abraham to Sinai
5	From Sinai to the First Temple
6	From the First Temple to its destruction: "All who live in it [sc. Week 6] will become blind, and the hearts of all will stray from wisdom; and in it a man [i.e., Elijah] shall ascend. And at its conclusion the Temple of the kingdom will be burned with fire, and in it the whole race of the chosen root [i.e., Israel] will be dispersed."
7 (the author's own time)	The elect will arise in the midst of an apostate generation and be given sevenfold (complete) wisdom and knowledge
8	Israel will be judged; "the Temple of the kingdom of the Great One will be built in the greatness of its glory for all the generations of eternity"
9	The world will be judged; the earth will be purged of evil; remaining humanity will convert to righteousness
10	The Watchers (rebel angels) will be judged; the heavens and its luminaries will be renewed

What is interesting to note from the Apocalypse of Weeks is that the eschatological finale is not just a single point in time but rather, as in Jub. 23, a prolonged *process* that

16. Allison, *Constructing Jesus*, 109.

17. The proper order of this text is confirmed not only by the consecutive numbering of the "weeks" but also now by Qumran fragments of the book of Enoch.

is both already and not yet. Already in the seventh week, which is the author's own time, "the chosen will be chosen" "from the everlasting plant of righteousness," and they be given (by God) "sevenfold wisdom and knowledge" (1 En. 93:10). This is the revealed, saving wisdom referred to in the introduction to the present volume. In the Enochic writings, everyone who is to be saved at the time of the final judgment must have received and embody this saving wisdom.[18] As of the seventh "week," God has started the redemptive *process*. This is the beginning of the eschatological reversal of the ordinary, mundane situation. And yet the new temple will not be built until the end of the eighth week, and the new heavens and new earth—the consummation of the whole process—will not appear until even later.

Another way to approach Jesus' orientation to the "already" and the "not yet" is in terms of the forces of evil. He sees his own work as a *process* of defeating Satan and the forces of evil, although the full and final defeat of evil will come only at the consummation. In Luke 10:18, Jesus announces, "I saw Satan fall like lightning from heaven."[19] In doing so, Jesus was living in the future anterior, because in actuality Satan was still very much active at that point.[20] In Matt 12:28//Luke 11:20 (Q), Jesus is reported as saying, "But if it is by the finger/Spirit of God that I cast out demons, then the kingdom of God has come upon you." In other words, the exorcisms that Jesus performs actualize the kingdom of God in the present. Hence, as the kingdom of God advances into the world, Satan's kingdom is in the process of being destroyed. The proclamation that Jesus commissions his disciples to preach in the towns and villages, "The Kingdom of God has come near (*ēngiken*) to you" (Matt 10:7//Luke 10:9 [Q]), can be interpreted in this sense, since, at least in the Matthean version, the proclamation is connected with casting out demons (Matt 10:8).

Finally, the concept of the presence of the kingdom can be seen in Magnificat, the hymn of the Virgin Mary in Luke 1:46–55 (L),[21] named for its opening words, which translate as "My soul magnifies the Lord" (in the Latin Vulgate, *magnificat anima mea Dominum*). In the Magnificat, Mary's hymn sets the revolutionary tone for the entire Gospel of Luke:

18. Cf. Scott, *Apocalyptic Letter to the Galatians*, chap. 2.

19. Alternatively, what Jesus announces in Luke 10:18 is not the vision of a *future* event but rather the defeat of Satan in the primordial *past*, when the rebellious "sons of God" in the Book of the Watchers were forcibly cast out of heaven (cf. 1 En. 6–16; cf. also 86:1, 3; 88:1, 3). In our discussion of the book of Revelation in chapter 10, we will see that the past, present, and future time frames are not mutually exclusive.

20. Cf. 1 Pet 5:8: "Discipline yourselves, keep alert. Like a roaring lion your adversary the devil prowls around, looking for someone to devour."

21. Lukan special material (L) includes, for example, the promise of the birth of John the Baptist (1:5–25); the Annunciation (1:26–38); Mary's visit to Elizabeth (1:39–56); the birth of John the Baptist (1:57–80); the circumcision and presentation of Jesus in the temple (2:21–38); the boy Jesus in the temple (2:41–52).

He [sc. the Lord/the Mighty One] has shown strength in his arm; he has scattered the proud in the thoughts of their hearts. He has brought down the powerful from their thrones, and lifted up the lowly; he has filled the hungry with the good things, and sent the rich away empty. He has helped his servant Israel, in remembrance of his mercy, according to the promise he made to our ancestors, to Abraham and to his descendants forever. (Luke 1:51–55)

In other words, Mary is presented as envisioning a major reversal of this topsy-turvy world, which is expressed in the past tense, as if it were already a present reality—well before her baby is even born.[22] Mary was constructing the present in the prefigurative future anterior (that which will have been). She imagines a new and better world unfolding in the shell of the old, and, importantly, this teenaged peasant girl from the rural Galilean backwater has a pivotal role to play in that transformative process. Actualizing the future anterior in the present is not a top-down process, but rather one arising *from the bottom up*. This is why Luke emphasizes first announcement of Jesus' birth—"good news of great joy which will come to all people"—was to lowly shepherds who were keeping watch over their flock by night (Luke 2:8–20//Matt 2:1–12 [Q]). Peasant women, smelly, inarticulate fishermen, the poor, the diseased, outcasts of all kinds—these will be the basic constituents of the new movement that Jesus forms around himself, opening out to the rest of the world. Hence, the kingdom that Jesus inaugurates is not merely the inversion of the present reality; it involves making connections and initiating tendencies that transform reality in new ways.

22. Whether the song was drawn from another context (for which there is no evidence, except for its general form), when it is placed in the context of Jesus' expected birth, it takes on the meaning that God's great deeds of salvation in the past are anticipated to be enacted in a new form through the birth, life, and career of Jesus. Jesus will bring about revolutionary transformation, turning the topsy-turvy world right side up (e.g., bringing down thrones and reversing the fortunes of rich and poor). A similar idea is found in Acts 17:1–9, where Paul and Silas (and their converts) are accused of sedition by the hostile crowd of Jews and gentiles in Thessalonica: "These people who have been turning the world upside down [or: *who have led the whole world in revolt*] have come here also, and Jason has entertained them as guests. They are all acting contrary to the decrees of the emperor, saying that there is another king (*basileus*) named Jesus" (vv. 6–7). The verb used in v. 6 (*anastatoō*) is found in a similar sense in Acts 21:38: "Then you [sc. Paul] are not the Egyptian who recently stirred up a revolt (*anastatōsas*) and led four thousand assassins out into the wilderness?" According to Acts 17:6–7, Paul and those aligned with him are allegedly acting contrary to imperial decrees (as the source of law) and attempting to set up a rival emperor. Such a notion could have been derived from the proclamation of Jesus and his followers about the kingdom (*basileia*) of God and about Jesus as "Messiah" (Acts 17:3). Jesus' trial before Pilate shows how provocative the proclamation of the kingdom of God could be: "Then the assembly rose as a body and brought Jesus before Pilate. They began to accuse him, saying, 'We found this man perverting the nation, forbidding us to pay taxes to the emperor, and saying that he himself is the Messiah, a king'" (Luke 23:1–2). The stark alternative between Jesus and the emperor is also found in John 19:12–16, where the crowd in Jerusalem is presented as crying out to Pilate, "If you release this man, you are no friend of the emperor; anyone who claims to be a king sets himself against the emperor" (v. 12). When Pilate brought Jesus out and presented him to the Jews, saying, "Here is your King!" the people would have none of it and called for him to be crucified. Pilate asked whether he should crucify their king, but the chief priests answered, "We have no king but the emperor" (v. 15).

In sum, the foregoing section finds it plausible and indeed likely that Jesus affirmed the presence of the kingdom of God. It is not just a future hope but rather "already" manifested in the here and now. Or, to put it another way, the future is already unfolding in the present.[23]

The "Not Yet": The Future of the Kingdom

If, as we have seen, Jesus proclaimed the presence of the kingdom of God, that is no reason to deduce that Jesus did not also proclaim the kingdom's future, apocalyptic revelation. Some scholars pull apart what is inextricably bound together in the Jesus tradition (and, as shown above, in Jewish sources of the Second Temple period as well). Jesus, we have suggested, affirmed the construction of the new world of the kingdom in the present which is conceived of as the prefigurative future anterior. Beyond these anticipations of the consummation, however, Jesus also affirmed the consummation

---

23. It seems likely that the emphasis on "realized eschatology" in John's Gospel is actually an expression of constructing the future anterior in the here and now, for Jesus—the one who has seen the Father (John 5:37) and makes the Father known—embodies the revelation of the heavenly mysteries that the standard Jewish apocalypses seek to disclose through their visions and revelations. Cf. Ashton, *Understanding the Fourth Gospel*, who calls John's Gospel "an apocalypse in reverse" (vii, 274, 328–29, 529). Contrast Allison, *Historical Christ and the Theological Jesus*, 99–100: "We are not, however, without any backing from tradition when we promote—for ourselves, not for Jesus—a less than literal interpretation of apocalyptic eschatology. John's Gospel gives us canonical precedent for this sort of hermeneutical move. While the book retains the concept of a 'last day,' it nonetheless represents a fundamental rethinking of Christian existence. It replaces the eschatological speech of Matt. 24–25; Mark 13; and Luke 21 with the intimate words of encouragement at the Last Supper (John 13–17), which mostly omits apocalyptic expectations. Written when the delay of the parousia could be felt (cf. 2 Pet. 3:1–10), the Gospel prudently focuses not on Jesus coming on the clouds of heaven in the future but on the Spirit coming to believers in the present. It emphasizes not that the dead will someday rise (although it does not deny that) but rather that the living can even now enjoy eternal life. It teaches not the impending defeat of evil in a cosmic judgment but the routing of the devil at Jesus' crucifixion. It is almost as though the Evangelist systematically set out to translate the literal into the figurative, sought to reinterpret, in terms of present religious experience, the apocalyptic mythology he found in the Jesus tradition. Even here, however, we must candidly acknowledge a hitch. The Gospel, at least in its canonical form, seems to deny what it is doing. It takes for granted, indeed asserts, that its thoughts are the thoughts of Jesus, and that its reinterpretation is really no reinterpretation at all. This appears not only from the attribution of its inspired meditations to Jesus but also from the secondary addendum in ch. 21. Here Jesus asks Peter concerning the Beloved Disciple, 'If it is my will that he remain until I come, what is that to you? Follow me!' This quotation explains, we are told, why 'the rumor spread in the community that this disciple would not die.' Yet the rumor is untrue: 'Jesus did not say to him that he would not die but, "If it is my will that he remain until I come, what is that to you?"' Obviously behind these verses is Christian anxiety: the Beloved Disciple had died but Jesus had not yet returned. Some saying such as Matt. 10:23 or Mark 9:1 or Mark 13:30, taken at face value, that is, understood to mean that not all of Jesus' disciples would die before the consummation, must lie in the background, and all the disciples must now be dead. John 21:22–23 responds by denying that Jesus ever said such a thing or that, if he did, he was misunderstood. But if following the quest has led us to an apocalyptic Jesus, we must, even if we find John's reinterpretation of the tradition hermeneutically instructive, respectfully disagree on this score with whoever wrote John 21. Jesus apparently did expect the coming of God sooner rather than later, and it is only natural that the passing of time witnessed, if not a far-flung crisis of faith, then at least some uneasiness here and there."

itself, the time when the final judgment would eliminate all evil and a new era of blessedness would prevail on earth, a kind of heaven on earth. In the following, we adduce some of the evidence for this future expectation in the Gospels.

The Hypothetical Sayings Source "Q"

We cannot know for sure whether "Q" exists or, if so, what its precise extent may have been. The sayings source Q is typically defined as a collection (assemblage) of Jesus' sayings that are common to Matthew and Luke but are not in Mark,[24] although part of what is usually considered "M" (Matthean special material)[25] and "L" (Lukan special material)[26] could be part of Q as well. We simply don't know. It would take us too far afield to delve into the complexities of the modern discussion of Q. Suffice it to say, that many scholars consider Q to have arisen in stages and that the first stage (some 84 verses) is thought to be bereft of apocalyptic material, such as the petition of the Lord's Prayer, "Your Kingdom come" (Matt 6:10//Luke 11:2 [Q]), which entreats God to speed the arrival of the kingdom in its full and final form. That will be the time when God's will shall be done "on earth as it is in heaven" (Matt 6:10). However, if the putative first stage of the Sayings Source is concerned with the present, it should be noted that even the sayings focused on the present have a future aspect as well. The Beatitudes (Matt 5:3–12//Luke 6:20b–23 [Q]) have a strong moral component insofar as they entail attending to the needs the poor and the hungry in the here and now, but they are simultaneously promises of dramatic reversal in the future, when God will rid the world of poverty, hunger, and sorrow.[27] We are dealing here, once

24. Cf. Robinson et al., eds., *Critical Edition of Q: Synopsis*. As an assemblage, Q has the three components that all assemblages do, and therefore Q can be classified according to the political typology of assemblages and the typology of change in assemblages. All this opens up a new way to investigate Q, but that cannot be pursued here. For a recent discussion, see Andrejevs, *Apocalypticism in the Synoptic Source*. Another assemblage of Jesus' sayings is the Gospel of Thomas, which is often compared with Q. Again, with our assemblage approach, we have a new opportunity to interrogate the sayings tradition in the Gospel of Thomas. For an introduction to and translation of the text, see Elliott, *Apocryphal New Testament*, 123–47.

25. Matthean special material (M) includes, for example, the flight of Jesus' family into Egypt and their return (2:13–21); Jesus' teaching on oaths (5:33–37); Jesus' teaching on almsgiving (6:1–4); the interpretation of the parable of the tares (13:36–43); the parables of the hidden treasure and of the pearl (13:44–46); the parable of the net (13:46–47). To see the full extent of the Synoptic sources, see, e.g., Aland, *Synopsis of the Four Gospels*.

26. For examples of Lukan special material (L), see the discussion of the Magnificat (Luke 1:46–55 [L]) above.

27. The Beatitudes (Latin, "blesseds") are declarations found in the Sermon on the Mount in Matthew (5:3–12) and the Sermon on the Plain in Luke (6:20–23). They are performative pronouncements that confer an end-time blessing upon persons who are characterized by what they are (e.g., the poor) or do (e.g., peacemakers). The blessing assures the addressees of the vindication and reward that attend the salvation of God's end-time rule and thus provides encouragement in a time of difficulty. Luke has four Beatitudes balanced by four woes (6:20–26), and all take the form of direct address in the second-person plural ("Blessed are you . . ."). Matthew has nine Beatitudes and no woes (5:3–12),

again, with the present creation of the future anterior, in anticipation of the final con-summation. Similarly, the imperative, "Judge not, lest you be judged" (Matt 7:1//Luke 6:37 [Q]) probably means "Judge not, lest you be judged [by God in the final judgment]," especially as the following sentence, "And with the measure you measure you will be measured" (Matt 7:2//Luke 6:38 [Q]), occurs in later Jewish literature with an eschatological sense.[28] In other words, we are dealing here with the present creation of that which will have been. Jesus' admonition not to "store up for yourselves treasures on earth" but rather to "store up for yourselves treasures in heaven" (Matt 6:19//Luke 12:33 [Q]) entails an ongoing present activity that anticipates the renewed world that the faithful will someday inherit (cf. Matt 5:12//Luke 6:23 [Q]). Thus, the supposed first stage of the hypothetical sayings source is not devoid of an eschatological aspect. These future-oriented sayings are concerned with the present practice of the future anterior, just the rest of the Q material is. Followers of Jesus are to practice anticipations of the new and better world in the here and now.

The Correspondence between *Urzeit* and *Endzeit*

A central feature of Jesus' proclamation of the kingdom and its construction of time in the future anterior is the correspondence between *Urzeit* and *Endzeit*. By their common use of *Zeit*, the German words *Urzeit* ("primeval period") and *Endzeit* ("end time") are used here to signal that there is a correspondence between origins (the original creation) and eschatology (the new creation). This correspondence occurs often in the Old Testament, early Jewish literature, and the New Testament.[29] The creation accounts of the Old Testament are effectively critiques of the world of human experience and human actions.[30] They set up the utopian ideals of later Jewish apocalyptic literature. We will delve into the Old Testament here because we are constructing a *biblical* theology of the New Testament, which, as we have stated, entails the whole assemblage of Scripture (however defined by a particular community).[31] This scriptural matrix is absolutely essential for understanding Jesus' own program of revolution.

---

and all but the last are in the third-person plural ("Blessed are the . . ." or "Blessed are those who . . .").

28. Rüger, "Mit welchem Maß ihr meßt, wird euch gemessen werden," 174–82. See, for example, several targumic texts that come in the context of the correspondence between what is done in this world and what will happen in the world to come: *Targum Neofiti I* on Gen 38:25 ("In the measure in which a man measures it shall be measured to him, whether it be a good measure or a bad measure"); *Targum Pseudo-Jonathan* on Gen 38:25 ("It is better for me to be ashamed in this world, which is a passing world, than to be ashamed in the presence of my fathers, the righteous ones, in the world to come; it is better for me to be burned in this life in inextinguishable fire than to burn in the world to come in inextinguishable fire. For this is measure for measure . . .").

29. See further Doering, "Urzeit-Endzeit Correlation in the Dead Sea Scrolls and Pseudepigrapha," 19–58.

30. Cf. Rogerson, *Theology of the Old Testament*, 42–63. The present section is indebted to Rogerson's insights and perspectives.

31. This assemblage of Scripture entails its interpretation in subsequent Jewish tradition, and this

The World That God Created (Genesis 1) Contrasted with
the World of Present Human Experience

The Genesis creation stories effectively criticize the marred world in which readers or hearers of the stories had to live out their daily lives. These stories inspired discontent with the world as they knew it, and stimulated a yearning for a restored world. For the world that Gen 1 describes is *not* the world of present human experience. Although the text affirms that the God of ancient Israel is the Creator of the universe, the world of present human experience had changed radically from what God had originally created.

The world that God originally created is described in Gen 1:29–30, which decrees that men and animals are to eat only plants and fruit:

> God said, "Look, I am giving you every plant that produces seed everywhere in the earth, and every tree whose fruit produces seed; they shall be your food. As for the wild beasts, the birds of the heavens and the reptiles, all living creatures, their food will be every green plant."

This text shows that God originally created a vegetarian world, mandating that both human and animals should eat plants.[32]

According to Genesis, the human race and other creatures were not permitted to eat meat until after the Flood.[33] This implies a sharp contrast exists between Gen 1:26–30 and 9:1–7. In Gen 1:26–30, the relationship between humans and animals is one of harmony.[34] In Gen 9:2, that harmony is lost: "Fear of you and terror shall come upon every wild beast, every bird of the heavens, all reptiles and all the fish of the sea; they are delivered into your power." The verb translated here as "delivered" (*natan*) is used elsewhere in the Old Testament to denote Israel's victory over its enemies.[35] This is a world in which the human race may kill and eat animals provided that they avoid eating their blood (Gen 9:4).[36] Not only will other creatures fear humans, humans

---

pertains to the *Urzeit-Endzeit* correspondence as well. It will come as a surprise to many readers of Scripture that the concept of the Fall is not a universal understanding of Genesis 2–3 in the Old Testament and early Jewish literature of the Second Temple period. Cf. Collins, "Before the Fall," 293–308; Anderson, *Genesis of Perfection*, 197–210; Stordalen, *Echoes of Eden*.

32. Cf. Westermann, *Genesis*, 223–28.

33. Cf., e.g., Gen. Rab. 34:13.

34. In Gen 1:26, God commands humankind to "be fruitful and multiply, and fill the earth and subdue it; and have dominion over the fish of the sea and over the birds of the air and over every living thing that moves upon the earth." In the modern world, this divine mandate has been interpreted to mean that human beings have the divine right to exploit the world however they see fit, without concern about the adverse environmental impact that exploitation may have on the world. As a result, we now have, for example, global warming, collapsed fisheries, rampant deforestation, indiscriminate pollution of our land, air and water. This is the very antithesis of the harmony that was established at creation.

35. Cf., e.g., Exod 23:31; Num 21:2, 34; Deut 2:24, 30; 21:10; 2 Chr 24:24.

36. Compare the "apostolic decree" in Acts 15:23–29, a letter that reimposes the Noachic

themselves will become enemies of each other, for Gen 9:6 envisages that humans will shed human blood, despite the fact that they are created in God's image. What is portrayed here is a world of violence, the world of present human experience, a compromise world born of human wickedness and necessarily adapted to the destructive creature that humankind had become.[37]

That violence is absent from Gen 1:26–30, and the difference between the two worlds is that one is vegetarian and the other is not.[38] Vegetarianism is a way of describing a world at peace with itself. For the Bible, peace between human beings is inconceivable without a corresponding peace between humans and animals.[39] According to the Old Testament scholar John Rogerson, "It is possible to describe the Old Testament as the story of the divine project to form a type of humanity that would be capable of living in the kind of world described in Genesis 1."[40] By holding out the ideal of God's originally intended will for creation, the biblical text confronts humanity with an intolerable contrast between its present experience of discord and

---

commandments of Gen 9 on gentile believers: "The brothers, both the apostles and the elders, to the believers of Gentile origin in Antioch and Syria and Cilicia, greetings. Since we have heard that certain persons who have gone out from us, though with no instructions from us, have said things to disturb you and have unsettled your minds, we have decided unanimously to choose representatives and send them to you, along with our beloved Barnabas and Paul, who have risked their lives for the sake of our Lord Jesus Christ. We have therefore sent Judas and Silas, who themselves will tell you the same things by word of mouth. For it has seemed good to the Holy Spirit and to us to impose on you no further burden than these essentials: that you abstain from what has been sacrificed to idols and from *blood* and from what is strangled and from fornication. If you keep yourselves from these, you will do well. Farewell." See further Bockmuehl, "Noachide Commandments and New Testament Ethics," 72–105.

37. Thus, the Animal Apocalypse (1 En. 85–90), a Jewish apocalyptic writing from the Second Temple period, is an allegory of human history in which humankind is portrayed as animals, and the vicious wild animals molest the less aggressive, domesticated animals such as the sheep (i.e., Israel). In other words, the Animal Apocalypse takes the cues about the human-animal relationship from the Genesis text and transposes them onto human history as a whole.

38. Cf. Gen 9:3: "Every moving thing that lives shall be food for you; and just as I gave you the green plants [cf. Gen 1:29–30], I give you everything."

39. Genesis 1 affirms a kind of trans-species egalitarianism as an ethical principle, which opens up the possibility of conceptualizing a return of humanity to its original design.

40. Rogerson, *Theology of the Old Testament*, 48. For a description of that "divine project" (i.e., to create humanity in the divine image or to create a humane humanity), see Rogerson, *Theology of the Old Testament*, 187–95. Here, we should briefly mention that approaches to Old Testament Theology are many and varied. The earlier Old Testament theologies of Walther Eichrodt, Ernst Sellin, and Ludwig Köhler argued that the theology of the Old Testament centered around a single theme. A later generation of scholars (Claus Westermann, Samuel Terrien, and James Sanders) abandoned this search for a "center of the Old Testament" and focused instead on a "bi-polar" approach to biblical theology. Gerstenberger moved even farther away from the search for a unifying center. Cf. Gerstenberger, *Theologies in the Old Testament*, 1: "The Old Testament cannot of itself offer any unitary theological or ethical view, since it is a conglomerate of experiences of faith from very different historical and social situations." Hence, Gerstenberger organizes his work around five different social constructions in Israel's history: family and clan, village (small-town) community, tribal alliance, monarchy, and post-deportation faith communities.

violence and a world of harmony and bliss. This stark contrast plants the seed of desire for a new and better world.

The prophetic visions for the future continue to stoke those desires for a new and better world. Isaiah 65:17–24 is a case in point. Here, the vegetarian world of Gen 1:29–30 resurfaces in the context of an expectation of a new heaven and a new earth:

> For I am about to create new heavens and a new earth; the former things shall not be remembered or come to mind. [. . .] I will rejoice in Jerusalem, and delight in my people; no more shall the sound of weeping be heard in it, or the cry of distress. No more shall there be in it an infant that lives but a few days, or an old person who does not live out a lifetime; for one who dies at a hundred years will be considered a youth, and one who falls short of a hundred will be considered accursed. They shall build houses and inhabit them; they shall plant vineyards and eat their fruit. They shall not build and another inhabit; they shall not plant and another eat; for like the days of a tree shall the days of my people be, and my chosen shall long enjoy the work of their hands. [. . .] Before they call I will answer, while they are yet speaking I will hear. *The wolf and the lamb shall feed together, the lion shall eat straw like the ox.* . . . They shall not hurt or destroy on all my holy mountain, says the LORD. (Isa 65:17, 19–22, 24–25)

A similar expectation is found in Isa 11:1–10, which refers to the anticipated ideal king in the peaceful eschatological future:

> A shoot shall come out from the stump of Jesse, and a branch shall grow out of his roots. The spirit of the LORD shall rest on him, the spirit of wisdom and understanding, the spirit of counsel and might, the spirit of knowledge and the fear of the LORD. His delight shall be in the fear of the LORD. He shall not judge by what his eyes see, or decide by what his ears hear; but with righteousness he shall judge the poor, and decide with equity for the meek of the earth; he shall strike the earth with the rod of his mouth, and with the breath of his lips he shall kill the wicked. Righteousness shall be the belt around his waist, and faithfulness the belt around his loins. *The wolf shall live with the lamb, the leopard shall lie down with the kid, the calf and the lion and the fatling together, and a little child shall lead them. The cow and the bear shall graze, their young shall lie down together; and the lion shall eat straw like the ox. The nursing child shall play over the hole of the asp, and the weaned child shall put its hand on the adder's den.* They will not hurt or destroy on all my holy mountain; for the earth will be full of the knowledge of the LORD as the waters cover the sea. On that day the root of Jesse shall stand as a signal to the peoples; the nations shall inquire of him, and his dwelling shall be glorious.

Once vain human striving for empire ends (Isa 10:34), a perfect Davidic king will reign in Jerusalem, and all the world will enjoy peace and equity (11:1–10). The ideal age will be manifested in jurisprudence (vv. 1–5). The king will be endowed with prophetic insight.[41] Jesse was King David's father; hence, the "shoot . . . out of the stump of Jesse" is a king from David's dynasty. The imagery of the previous section of Isaiah continues here: Whereas the high trees representing Assyria's imperial haughtiness will be cut down to size (Isa 10:33–34), ideal kingship will emerge from the stump of Jesse. The ideal ruler will be endowed with the Spirit of the Lord and render accurate and fair judgments. His verdicts are described as powerful performative speech-acts: "he shall strike the earth with the rod of his mouth, and with the breath of his lips he shall kill the wicked." In Isa 11:6–9, the ideal age is seen as manifested in natural harmony. The relationship between humans (even the most vulnerable, such as a little child) and animals is one of harmony.[42] Once again, the world reverts to a vegetarian state in which even top predators like the lion eat straw like a domesticated animal.

We have given some scope to the originally intended will of God for the creation as evidenced in Genesis 1 and other parts of the Old Testament. The correspondence between *Urzeit* and *Endzeit* entails a critique of the world of present human experience and engenders a desire for the creation of a new and better world. Here we see some of the biblical roots of the Jesus revolution, to which we now turn.

Creation and Jesus' Vision for the Kingdom of God

Jesus' vision for the kingdom of God entails the present creation of a new world in the prefigurative future anterior, at least in an anticipatory way before the final consummation. If the kingdom is at hand, then the renewal of the world is nigh; and if the renewal of the world is nigh, then paradise is about to be restored; and if paradise is about to be restored, then concessions to sin are no longer needed, nor indeed can they be countenanced.[43] As we have seen, Gen 9:1–6 portrays the world of present human experience as a compromise world born of human wickedness and necessarily adapted to the destructive creature that humankind had become. The mundane world was far from the unspoiled one that God had originally created. *Jesus inaugurates the fulfillment of the aforementioned divine project to form a type of humanity that would be capable of living in the kind of world described in Genesis 1.* This is the implicit logic of Jesus' prohibition of divorce in Mark 10:2–12 (par. Matt 19:3–12).[44] The Pharisees ask Jesus a question about divorce in order to

41. As we have noted, the notion that the ideal king will not judge by what his eyes see (Isa 11:3) is evidently the basis for blindfolding Jesus in the context of the mock obeisance before his crucifixion (Mark 14:65 pars.).

42. Jesus' being with the wild animals during his testing by Satan in the wilderness after his baptism by John (Mark 1:13) is often interpreted to mean that Jesus is living in the peaceful, paradisal harmony with the wild animals in accordance with prophetic expectation. Cf. Bauckham, "Jesus and the Wild Animals (Mark 1:13)," 3–21; Culpepper, *Mark*, 50–51. See, however, Heil, "Jesus with the Wild Animals in Mark 1:13," 63–78.

43. On the subject, see further Stroumsa and Bockmuehl, *Paradise in Antiquity*.

44. See further Doering, "Marriage and Creation in Mark 10 and CD 4–5," 133–63.

"test" him (Mark 10:2). Why divorce, of all things? Their question seems so random. Were they trying to get Jesus to say something about divorce that would get him into trouble with the authorities, just as had happened to John the Baptist when he opposed Herod Antipas's divorce from his royal Nabatean wife and his remarriage to his brother's wife, Herodias (see further above)? If so, Jesus skirts the issue by advocating the abolishment of divorce altogether and with it the Mosaic allowance for divorce (Deut 24:1–2), which Jesus regards as having been added as a concession to the human condition: "Because of your hardness of heart he [sc. Moses] wrote this commandment for you" (Mark 10:5). Instead, insisting on the correspondence between *Urzeit* and *Endzeit*, Jesus requires a prelapsarian ethic: "*From the beginning it* [sc. divorce] *was not so*" (Matt 19:8). However, since divorce is still the order of the day in the marred world of mundane human experience, to advocate the permanence of marriage in accordance with the originally intended will of God for creation (Gen 2:21–24)[45] requires living in the prefigurative future anterior, that is, the creation of the new and better world in the shell of the old. To quote Allison once again, "Jesus wants some things even now to be the way they were in the beginning because that is how they are going to be in the kingdom of God."[46]

Jesus' prohibition of divorce as a reaffirmation of the originally intended will of God for creation in marriage (Mark 10:2–12) stands in some tension with his authoritative pronouncement reported a few chapters later that in the future the saints will neither marry nor be given in marriage, but instead will be like the angels of heaven (Mark 12:18–27). In first-century Judaism, sexual intercourse was largely thought of as serving the purpose of procreation rather than pleasure, and angels (usually regarded as male)[47] were considered immortal and therefore did not need to procreate. It followed, then, that if angels indulged in intercourse, it was purely self-indulgent (and indeed some fallen angels did have intercourse with human women, resulting in a bastard race of giants and the perpetuation of much evil in the antediluvian world, which was a primary cause of the Flood).[48] It seems, then, that Mark 12:18–27 applies

45. In Mark 10:7–9 par., Jesus cites Gen 2:24, which is set in the context of the original creation of woman for man: "'For this reason a man shall leave his father and mother and be joined to his wife, and the two shall become one flesh.' So they are no longer two, but one flesh. Therefore what God has joined together, let no one separate."

46. Allison, *Jesus of Nazareth*, 210.

47. According to the book of Jubilees (15:26–27), angels were "born" circumcised on the day of their creation: "Anyone who is born, the flesh whose private parts has not been circumcised by the eighth day does not belong to the people of the pact, which the Lord made with Abraham, but to the people (meant for) destruction. Moreover, there is no sign on him that he belongs to the Lord, but (he is meant) for destruction, for being destroyed from the earth, and for being uprooted from the earth because he has violated the covenant of the Lord our God. For this is what the nature of all the angels of the presence and all the angels of holiness was like from the day of their creation. In front of the angels of the presence and the angels of holiness he sanctified Israel to be with him and his holy angels." Cf. VanderKam, *Jubilees*, 1:519–21.

48. Paul alludes to these fallen angels in 1 Cor 11:2–16, mandating that women cover their heads "because of the angels." The thought is evidently that angels can be sexually aroused by the beautiful

the same idea to the saints living in the future anterior. Intercourse will be no more. The saints will be like the immortal angels. As we can see, there is some tension in the Jesus tradition about the matter of marriage. One strand of the tradition has Jesus re-affirming the originally intended will of God for creation in marriage (Gen 2:21–24), whereas another strand has Jesus eliminating marriage and sex altogether. Amazingly, Mark's Gospel includes both perspectives practically side by side without even raising an eyebrow. How do we explain this phenomenon?

Perhaps the problem is our modern desire for everything to be totally consistent, when in fact things are not that tidy. The New Testament assemblage is more open-ended and contested than that; the corporate agents/personae are working out the implications of Jesus as the animating force and condition of the assemblage, and there are different ways of viewing the matter, even if they are coming from Jesus' fundamental perspective on the correspondence between *Urzeit* and *Endzeit*. Perhaps we could attempt to harmonize the two perspectives by suggesting that there are two stages in the future plan for marriage and sex: marriage during the interim (the future anterior) and then an abolition of marriage and sex altogether in the eternal aftermath of the consummation. In any case, the common thread is that Jesus is remembered as being concerned about sex and marriage in the future anterior as a prelude to the recapitulation of the original creation in the new creation. Moreover, it seems that the early Jesus movement continued to work out the implications of the Jesus revolution for the construction of the prefigurative future in the present with respect to sex and marriage. Paul, for example, sought to affirm *both* approaches to the subject, advocating marriage for those who can't constrain themselves sexually, but celibacy for those who have the "gift" (cf. 1 Cor 7). In no case, however, should one divorce if one is already married, and that coheres with Jesus' teaching about the ideal of marriage in the future anterior, corresponding to the originally intended will of God for creation.[49] Elsewhere, Paul states that "there is no longer male and female" (Gal 3:28), echoing Gen 1:26–27 and thus seeming to come down on one side of the contested issue of sex and marriage in the future anterior.[50] The Gospel of Thomas (114:1), on the other hand, quotes Jesus as saying that females must actually become males as a condition for entering the kingdom of God, thus eliminating marriage and sex altogether: "Simon Peter said to them [sc. Jesus' disciples], 'Let Mary leave us, because women

---

female body, which therefore needs to be covered. Paul explicitly refers to the original creation in this passage.

49. This could be a possible (admittedly harmonizing) solution to the conundrum: Jesus taught *both* not to marry if one has not yet married (Jesus himself fits this category) *and* to not divorce if one is already married. Both of these teachings of Jesus could be understood as going back to the originally intended will of God in creation, albeit to different textual bases (i.e., Gen 1:26–27, on the one hand, and Gen 2:21–24, on the other). Paul merely adds the practical concession of marriage if sexual continence is impossible.

50. We shall discuss Gal 3:28 further in chapter 7. Of course, Gal 3:28 stands in some tension with other passages on women in the Pauline corpus, most notably 1 Cor 11:2–16 and 14:32–36. The reason for this tension will be considered in chapter 7.

are not worthy of life.' Jesus said, 'Look, I shall lead her so that I will make her male in order that she may also become a living spirit, resembling you males. For every woman who makes herself a male will enter the kingdom of heaven.'"[51] The thought here may be similar to Mark 12:18–27, which, as we have seen, states that redeemed humankind will be like the angels of heaven (i.e., like males, since angels are conceived of as males). We may also note that the first human being to be created was a male. In early Jewish literature, Gen 1:26–27 was sometimes interpreted to mean that the original human being incorporated both male and female aspects (the so-called androgyne ["man-woman"]), until they were separated in Gen 2, and the woman, who was taken out of man, then became an independent creature. Therefore, the idea that everyone will eventually be male may be a reflection of the *Urzeit-Endzeit* correspondence, that is, the reversion to the originally intended will of God for creation (i.e., maleness once again incorporating both male and female aspects in one).

That concessions to sin are no longer needed in the future anterior also illuminates Jesus' prohibition of oaths in Matt 5:33–37.[52] The presupposition of the oath is lying, for if everyone always told the truth, there would be no need to take an oath. Oath-taking assumes there are two types of statements, one of which demands commitment—the oath—and one of which need not—the statement without an oath. But in a sin-free world, a world like Eden as originally created or paradise regained, human beings should be invariably committed to every statement; and if they were so committed, then oaths would be superfluous. As Allison rightly observes, "In short, Jesus' prohibition of swearing is akin to his prohibition of divorce. Both set forth a prelapsarian standard that revokes a temporary concession in the Torah. . . . Jesus formulated imperatives that leave behind the Mosaic law for the sake of life in the world to come."[53] Or to put the matter in the terms that we have been using, Jesus' prohibition of oaths is part of his program for creating the new world in the shell of the old, which anticipates the full and final recovery of God's original intention for creation.

Along similar lines, Mark 2:27 ("The sabbath was made for humankind, and not humankind for the sabbath") recalls the original purpose of a day of rest.[54] The idea that "the sabbath was made for humankind" recalls the creation story in Gen 1–2:

> Thus the heavens and the earth were finished, all their multitude. And on the seventh day God finished the work that he had done, and he rested on the seventh day from all the work that he had done. So God blessed the seventh

51. Cf., e.g., Vogt, "'Becoming Male': A Gnostic and Early Christian and Islamic Metaphor," 217–42; Vogt, "'Becoming Male': One Aspect of an Early Christian Anthropology," 49–61.

52. Cf. Allison, *Resurrecting Jesus*, 174, 186–87.

53. Allison, *Resurrecting Jesus*, 186–87.

54. Cf. Marcus, *Mark 1–8*, 245, 246: "It may be that Mark thinks that Jesus restores the compassionate aspect of the original Sabbath, which in the interim has been effaced by a human hardheartedness that has transformed the good Sabbath into a source of destruction." On Mark 2:23–26, see further Doering, *Schabbat*, 409–16.

day and hallowed it, because on it God rested from all the work that he had done in creation. (Gen 2:1–3)

The implicit logic of Mark 2:27 seems to be that when God's purpose in establishing the Sabbath is rightly understood, it can override the prohibition of work in the Mosaic Law. This is analogous to Mark 10:6, where, as we have seen, Jesus also trumps an imperative (the divorce commandment of Deut 24:1–2) by appealing to the beginning of creation (citing Gen 1:26–27 and 2:24).

Jesus' Knowledge of the Future Was Necessarily Indeterminate

As stated earlier, the revolutionary process of creating the new and better world in the shell of the old is necessarily contingent and open-ended due to internal and external factors. Is the time of the consummation itself indeterminate? Indeed, according to Matt 24:36 and Mark 13:32, Jesus explicitly denies having knowledge of the date of the consummation: "But about that day and hour no one knows, neither the angels of heaven, nor the Son, but only the Father." Although the meaning of this sentence seems fairly straightforward, many interpreters find it difficult to accept that Jesus would lack knowledge of the future or that his perspective on the future was essentially open-ended.[55] Nor were they able to square the indeterminate perspective of Mark 13:32 par. with the expectation that the time of the end was to be soon.[56]

Both the indeterminate perspective and the immanent expectation may not be incompatible after all. As discussed in chapter 2, Jesus' performative proclamation of the kingdom is *contingent* on the repentance and belief of those who hear his message. In other words, his message is performative *if it is felicitous*.[57] The rabbis had a similar conception of time: The Messiah will come *today* if people will obey his voice:

He [sc. Joshua b. Levi] said to him [sc. the Messiah], "When is the master coming?" He said to him, "*Today*." He went back to Elijah, who said to him,

---

55. Explaining Mark 13:32 par. entailed some mental gymnastics among the church fathers. Cf. Allison, *Historical Christ and the Theological Jesus*, 82–83: "The great Origen, like Gregory the Great after him, observed that the church is the body of Christ and then wondered whether Jesus might not be referring to the ignorance of Christians. Bishop Ambrose of Milan, so admired by Augustine, attributed 'nor the son' to an Arian interpolation. Gregory Nazianzen, an important figure in the conquest of Arianism, offered that Jesus knew the eschatological date in his divine nature but not in his human nature. Ephrem the Syrian, overindulging his imagination, said that Jesus did not want to be pestered by people who thought he knew the time of the second coming, so he told a white lie, declaring that he did not know when he really did. Cassiodorus, the sixth-century Roman monk, contended, like Augustine before him, that 'I do not know' really meant 'I have not made you to know.' How could the judge of the last day not know when his own court would be in session?"

56. Note that the apocalyptic predictions attributed to Jesus in the Gospels were to be fulfilled within "a generation" (cf., e.g., Matt 12:41–42, 45; 23:36; 24:34; Mark 9:1; 13:30; Matt 23:34–35//Luke 11:49–51 [Q]).

57. As we have seen, speech-acts are *felicitous* (i.e., effective) when they meet conventional expectations and are validated by the intended audience.

"What did he tell you?" He said to him, "Peace be unto you, son of Levi." He said to him, "He [thereby] promised you and your father the world to come." He said to him, "But he lied to me. For he said to me, 'I am coming *today,*' but he did not come." He said to him, "This is what he said to you, '*Today, if you will obey his voice*' (Ps 95:7)." (b. Sanhedrin 98a)

The perspective we are developing here eliminates the scholarly hand-wringing about the so-called "delay of the Parousia,"[58] the notion that Jesus' disciples *invented* the Second Coming of Christ in order to continually defer the fulfillment of Jesus' expectations to the indefinite future.[59] Our approach affirms that Jesus was indeed apocalyptically oriented, looking forward to the final judgment and the elimination of evil, followed by the full and final culmination of the kingdom of God on earth, but that in the interim, he had inaugurated a revolutionary event that set in motion the actualization of the kingdom in the prefigurative future anterior. None of this is simply a return to precritical ecclesiastical tradition about Jesus' proximal and distal expectations; rather, we are attempting to understand Jesus within his own sociocultural location as a revolutionary figure who has a nuanced program of comprehensive transformation. The contingency of Jesus' performative proclamation of the kingdom entails a necessary uncertainty about the ultimate outcome of the process itself, let alone the precise date of that outcome.[60]

58. The Greek term *parousia* ("coming, advent") is regularly applied to the Second Coming of Christ.

59. For a helpful overview of positions on the question of the Parousia, from the traditional Christian perspective to modern critical perspectives, see Allison, *Historical Christ and the Theological Jesus*, 90–91.

60. The contingency of Jesus' performative proclamation of the kingdom raises the related issue of what constitutes a faithful unfolding of Jesus' proclamation. We may note, for example, that the details about the kingdom of God were left fairly sketchy, whether by Jesus himself or his followers or both. This lack of detail provides an opportunity for the agents/personae of the assemblage to think creatively about how to enact the kingdom in the here and now under ever-changing conditions. The situation is much the same in the ancient philosophical schools. Zeno of Cition, the founder of Stoicism, left behind a philosophical system whose details were fairly sketchy, but this allowed the successors of his school of thought to claim that they were merely following in the founder's footsteps with their innovations. The way of doing philosophy in each of the philosophical schools of thought concentrated more and more, as time progressed, on "creative exegesis" of the founders' writings, whereby they claimed no originality for themselves in the process. As David Runia comments, "For the Stoics Zeno's role was primarily inspirational, allowing his successors to fill in the gaps and construct a coherent body of doctrine" ("Philo of Alexandria and the Greek *Hairesis*-Model," 122). We may also think of the contingency of Jesus' teaching about the kingdom in terms of a constitution that is designed to guide a new nation for centuries: The principles of the founding document are purposely written in somewhat general and vague language so that they can be applied to any number of contingent situations that may arise, thus ensuring the document's ongoing relevance for the future. Differences of interpretation will of course occur, including split decisions and charges of "legislating from the bench," but the constitution itself is still perceived to be the source authority. Finally, we may think of the contingency of kingdom of God that Jesus inaugurated in terms of the famous Ship of Theseus. Among the questions asked by the Delphic Oracle was this enigma: If we consider a boat make of planks, what is it that makes the boat a boat? This question is more than

Given the inherent uncertainty about the outcome of the Jesus revolution, his "cry of dereliction" on the cross seems eminently understandable: "My God, my God, why have you forsaken me?" (Mark 15:36, quoting Ps 22:1).[61] Again, some interpreters immediately want to explain away the possibility that Jesus could have despaired at the end of his life, imposing on the text their own conception of Jesus and what he is capable of saying or doing. Indeed, I myself have often explained the quotation of Ps 22:1, the very first verse of the psalm, as a way of alluding—*pars pro toto*—to the rest of the psalm, which ends on a triumphal note of expected celebration after the psalmist emerges from the current crisis (Ps 22:21–26). For Jesus, that would mean resurrection after crucifixion, which, according to the Gospels, he had predicted (cf. Mark 8:31; 9:31; 10:33–34 and parallels). Nevertheless, we should give Jesus' anguished cry its full weight as an expression of a person who feels totally abandoned in the face of his impending death. When Jesus celebrated the Last Supper with his disciples and had drunk his last cup of wine, he predicted, "Truly I tell you, I will never again drink of the fruit of the vine until the day when I drink it anew in the Kingdom of God" (Mark 14:25 par.). When did he think that day would come? His cry from the cross can be interpreted as an indication that he had thought the kingdom would come immediately.

---

just a mind game: As time passes, some of the boat's planks are damaged and need to be replaced. There comes a time when not one of the original planks is left. The boat still looks like the original one, but in material terms it has changed. Is it still the *same boat*? The owner would certainly say, "Yes, this is my boat." Yet none of the material it was originally built from is still there. If we take the boat to pieces, it is reduced to a pile of planks—but they are not the same ones as at the beginning. If we were to analyze the components of the boat, we would not learn very much—a boat made from planks of oak is different from a boat made from planks of pine, but this is fairly incidental. What is important about the material of the planks, apart from their relative stability over time, is the fact that it allows them to be shaped, so that they relate to one another in a certain way. The boat is not the material it is made from, but something else, much more interesting, which organizes the material of the planks: The boat *is the relationship* between the planks. If you hammer a hundred strips of wood atop each other, you get a wall; if you nail them side by side, you get a deck; only a particular configuration of planks, held together in particular relationship, in a particular order, makes a boat. In terms of assemblage theory, what matters are not the elements of the assemblage but the relations between them. Genes operate in the same manner. Individual genes specify individual functions, but the relationship among genes allows physiology. The genome is inert without these relationships. That humans and worms have about the same number of genes—around twenty thousand—and yet the fact that only one of these two organisms is capable of painting the ceiling of the Sistine Chapel suggests that the number of genes is largely unimportant to the physiological complexity of the organism. It's not what you have; it's what you *do* with it. Cf. Mukherjee, *Gene*, 196, 316–17.

61. The accounts of Jesus' crucifixion are full of quotations from, and allusions to, Ps 22: "they divided his clothes, casting lists for them" (Mark 1:24) is a quotation from Ps 22:18; "wagging their heads" (Mark 15:29) is from Ps 22:7; and Jesus' cry "My God, my God, why have you forsaken me" (Mark 15:34) is from Ps 22:1.

The Politics of the Kingdom of God Is Not the Politics of Earth

Jesus conceptualizes the kingdom of God in sharp contrast to the tyrannical rule of the typical monarch.[62] According to Mark 10:42–43 pars., Jesus admonishes his disciples:

> You know that among the Gentiles those whom they recognize as their rulers lord it over them, and their great ones are tyrants over them. But it is not so among you; but whoever wishes to become great among you must be your servant.

The Jesus revolution entailed being radically inclusive and non-hierarchical. Rejection of oppressive lordship also appears in Mark 10:45, where the Son of Man, a royal figure in the Gospels, comes not to be served but to serve (an ironic reversal of Dan. 7:13–14, where peoples "serve" the "one like a son of man"). Here we see evidence that Jesus—particularly in his servanthood, suffering, and death—is understood as the condition/abstract machine of the entire revolutionary assemblage, especially in the construction of the future anterior. As such, he is the very antithesis of the typical ruler, who is self-serving, exploitative, and oppressive.[63] It should be noted, however, that in his trial before the Sanhedrin, Jesus predicts, according to Mark 14:62 pars., that he will come as Son of Man to judge his accusers, this time alluding to the Daniel passage in the original sense of the Son of Man as a potentate: ". . . and 'you will see the Son of Man seated at the right hand of the Power' (Psalm 110:1), and *coming with the clouds of heaven*' (Dan 7:13)." At the Parousia, therefore, the suffering Servant will be revealed as the sovereign Lord.

---

62. Cf. Bauckham, "Kingdom and Church according to Jesus and Paul," 1–27.

63. Cf. Matt 17:24–27, where Jesus, in discussing the temple tax, asks, "From whom do kings of the earth take toll or tribute? From their children or from others?" Although the paragraph assumes that God is a king, Peter's answer—"from others"—and Jesus' response—"then the sons are free"—indicates that God relates to the disciples not as the usual ruler to his exploited subjects but rather as a father to the privileged members of his family. To declare that "the sons are free" seems subversive for the reasons discussed in chapter 2. For in the ancient world, declaring people free from taxation by their overlords was tantamount to a declaration of independence. Of course, Jesus' words are ambiguous enough to avoid the charge of insurrection, especially since he goes on to encourage the payment of the tax "so that we do not give offense to them [sc. the authorities]" (v. 27). Nevertheless, for those who have ears to hear, Jesus' performative words can be understood to create the prefigurative future anterior, in anticipation of the time when God the Father rules supreme and his children are "free" indeed.

Conclusion

Jesus saw that the world of present human experience was in disarray on all levels,[64] from the individual,[65] to the family,[66] to the broader society.[67] Therefore, Jesus proclaimed a new and better world and then set about to actualize that vision in the present by beginning to restore the world to its original condition.[68] "Go and tell John what you have seen and heard: the blind receive their sight, the lame walk, the lepers are cleansed, the deaf hear, the dead are raised, the poor have good news brought to them" (Luke 7:22). Far from retreating from the present world of woe, Jesus' vision of the world to come drove him all the more into the present reality in order to actually create that new and better world in the shell of the old, at least in an anticipatory way.[69] In the Matthean version of the Lord's Prayer, Jesus teaches his

64. Cf. Matt 20:16; Mark 10:31; Luke 13:30.

65. On the level of the individual, pain, sorrow, poverty, disease, persecution, and demonic oppression were the order of the day.

66. On the level of the family, children are set against parents and, as Jesus well knew, parents were set against children (Matt 10:34–36//Luke 12:51–53 [Q]). "Brother will betray brother to death" (Mark 13:12).

67. On the level of the broader society, Pilate ruthlessly executes Galileans (Luke 13:1–2), and, as we saw, rulers lord it over their subjects (Mark 10:42–43 pars.).

68. To accomplish this goal, Jesus challenges the status quo in sometimes unexpected and radical ways. Cf. Allison, *Historical Christ and the Theological Jesus*, 114–15: "The tradition has him doing any number of peculiar things. He shares meals with people who might well be shunned, including, according to his critics, robbers for the state (Matt 11:19; Mark 2:16; Luke 7:34). He calls Peter and others to forsake their livelihoods, indeed to break off work in the middle of their labors to follow him (Matt 8:18–21; Mark 1:16–20; 2:13–14; Luke 9:57–62). He heals people on the Sabbath, no doubt intending to provoke debate and opposition, at which he succeeds (Mark 2:23–28; 3:1–6; Luke 14:1–6). He turns tables over in the Temple, declaring no more business as usual (Mark 11:15–19; John 2:13–17). His speech is equally suffused by oddities. There are his startling imperatives—'Leave the dead to bury their own dead' (Matt 8:22; Luke 9:60); 'Hate your father and your mother (Luke 14:26); 'Love your enemies' (Matt. 5:44; Luke 6:27); 'Greet no one on the road' (Luke 10:4). There are his unexpected generalizations—'Blessed are those who mourn' (Matt 5:4); 'The last will be first' (Matt 20:16; Mark 10:31; Luke 13:30); 'I have come not to bring peace but a sword' (Matt 10:34; Luke 12:51); 'There are eunuchs who have made themselves eunuchs for the sake of the kingdom of heaven' (Matt 19:12). And there are the memorable stories with unanticipated turns. We read of the Samaritan who, unlike his pious Jewish counterparts, displays charity (Luke 10:29–37); of the irrational employer who pays all laborers the same wage, regardless of hours worked (Matt 20:1-16); of the dishonest manager who earns praise for his flagrantly sinful actions (Luke 16:1-13); and of the long-suffering father who welcomes home the prodigal without a word of reprimand (Luke 15:11-32). 'Jesus,' in [Robert] Funk's words, 'detypifies' and 'defamiliarizes common perceptions. He says the unexpected. He confounds by contradicting what everybody already knows, by reversing those commonplaces his audience has just endorsed with their assent to his opening lines.'"

69. Cf. "Control and Becoming: Gilles Deleuze in Conversation with Antonio Negri," *Futur Antérieur* 1 (Spring 1990), translated by Martin Joughin; https://www.uib.no/sites/w3.uib.no/files/attachments/6._deleuze-control_and_becoming_0.pdf: "What we most lack is a belief in the world, we've quite lost the world, it's been taken from us. If you believe in the world, you precipitate events, however inconspicuous, that elude control, you engender new space-times, however small their surface or volume. It's what you call *pietas*. Our ability to resist control, or our submission to it, has to be assessed at the level of our every move. We need both creativity and a people." On Deleuze's concept of "believing

disciples to pray "Your kingdom come" (in the future), but that entails doing God's will "on earth as in heaven" (Matt 6:10), which begins in the here and now with forgiving our debtors (v. 12). For Jesus, the kingdom of God is both "already" and "not yet." To conceptualize the virtual reality of the kingdom in the future anterior, Jesus looks back to the future, meaning that the way forward is the way back to the originally intended will of God for creation. In following Jesus, the agents/personae of the new revolutionary assemblage are therefore committed to the creation of new modes of existence, no matter how small, that will connect up with others to construct a new revolutionary body politic. Moreover, their creative engagement with the world shows that the Jesus revolution coheres with a central tenet of ancient wisdom tradition—the concept that "human beings are to be caught up in the task of cocreating, participating in the continuing becoming of the world."[70] As we will discuss later, Jesus is identified with wisdom in the Gospels, and therefore the movement that he founded entails the unfolding of divine wisdom.

---

in the world," see further Saldanha, *Space After Deleuze*, 8, 43–44, 73–74.

70. Cf. Fretheim, *God and the World in the Old Testament*, 215–16 (emphasis mine): "The effect of such an understanding would be that God does not create in an unmediated way but works in and through Wisdom in bringing the creation into being. Wisdom is thus appropriately described as a created cocreator. This role for Wisdom in creation would be parallel with the way in which creation is sometimes depicted in Genesis 1, where among the 'modes' of God's creating is that of acting through already existent creatures, such as the earth (1:11–13) but especially the 'us,' the divine council, in 1:26. This understanding fits with the relational model of creation we have noted; God chooses not simply to be independent in creative activity. God chooses to be dependent upon wisdom, not only in creating the world but in continuing the relationship with that world. To be an observant and discerning member of such an interdependent creation will then entail hearing both the voice of Wisdom and the voice of God in and to that world—but then proceeding to act on what they hear. *The goal for human beings is to be caught up in the task of cocreating, participating creatively in the continuing becoming of the world.*"

4

The Hermeneutics of the Jesus Revolution, or Jesus as a Teacher of Signs

We learn nothing from those who say: "Do as I do." Our only teachers are those who tell us to "do with me," and are able to emit signs to be developed in heterogeneity rather than propose gestures for us to reproduce. —Gilles Deleuze[1]

Introduction

THE GOSPELS PRESENT JESUS as a master teacher who both enthralled and baffled his audiences.[2] He is often addressed as "teacher"[3] and sometimes even refers to himself as "teacher."[4] But Jesus' teaching should not be divorced from his proclamation. The two went together hand in glove. Of course, Jesus could adapt his message to his audience, whether that entailed teaching in the synagogues, debating scribes and Pharisees, addressing the masses, or instructing his disciples. Our goal here is to explore the hermeneutics of the Jesus revolution by examining how Jesus taught. As

1. Deleuze, *Difference and Repetition*, 23.

2. See, e.g., the crowd's reaction in Capernaum after he had taught in the synagogue and exorcised a man with an unclean spirit: "They were all amazed, and they kept on asking one another, 'What is this? A new teaching—with authority! He commands even the unclean spirits, and they obey him'" (Mark 1:27).

3. Cf. Matt 8:19; 12:38; 19:16; 22:16, 24, 36; Mark 4:38; 9:17, 38; 10:17, 20, 35, 51; 12:14, 19, 32; 13:1; Luke 3:12; 7:40; 9:38; 10:25; 11:45; 12:13; 18:18; 19:39; 20:21, 28, 39; 21:7.

4. Cf. Matt 10:24–25//Luke 6:40; Mark 14:14 pars.; John 13:13–14.

we shall see, Jesus was a teacher of signs that presented his hearers with conundrums, problems to be solved. His wisdom teaching encouraged reflection on the natural world, sometimes in ways that presented a witty reversal of scriptural texts. This, too, made for puzzlement and provocation. Finally, against this background, we suggest that Jesus is so imbued with Scripture that when he speaks we also hear a polyphony of other voices blending with it, producing a novel combination.

Jesus' Teaching in Terms of Signs

There is much that can be said about Jesus as master teacher.[5] In this section, we will focus on just one aspect—Jesus' teaching in terms of signs and how those signs reinforce his performative utterances and their revolutionary agenda.[6] The fact that Jesus taught in terms of signs is emphasized in John's Gospel, where Jesus does a series of "sign" (*sēmeion*) miracles, which point beyond themselves to his glory, his divine sonship, even his identity with the Father.[7]

For Jesus, learning was not just the acquisition of a preformed body of knowledge, along with a mere hint of something new ("new wine in old wineskins");[8] rather, Jesus' pedagogy of signs entailed first a critique of codes and conventions, an undoing of orthodox connections ("the [new] wine will burst the [old] wineskins"), and then a reconnection of elements, such that gaps between them generate problems that cry out for a solution. To learn what Jesus had to teach was to encounter signs, to undergo the disorienting jolt of something completely new, different, truly other, to unfold the differences that this new teaching enfolded. Genuine learning

5. Cf. Dunn, *Christianity in the Making*, 1:177: "The relation between Jesus and his disciples was remembered as one between teacher and taught, with the implication that, as such, the disciples understood themselves to be committed to remember their teacher's teaching." See further Dunn, *Christianity in the Making*, 1:698–702; Riesner, *Jesus als Lehrer*; Riesner, "Jesus as Preacher and Teacher," 185–210.

6. The following section is indebted, in part, to Bogue, "Deleuze's Apprenticeship in Signs and Pedagogy of Images," 53–67.

7. Cf. John 2:18; 4:54; 6:14, 30; 12:18. It should not be controversial that Jesus is remembered as performing miracles. Cf. "Miracles Here, There, and Everywhere," in Allison, *Historical Christ and the Theological Jesus*, 66–78, here 77: "What we can confidently infer about the miracles of Jesus on the basis of modern historical criticism is that he was reputed to be and thought himself to be a successful exorcist, healer, and wonder-worker and that some who knew him believed that they had witnessed truly extraordinary events." Even if Jesus was remembered as performing miracles, the character and number of miracles in the Synoptic Gospels are very different from the presentation and number of the "sign" miracles in John's Gospel. On the one hand, there is minimal overlap between the Synoptics and John: the Feeding of the Five Thousand (Mark 6:35–44 pars.//John 6:5–13) and Jesus Walks on the Water (Mark 6:48–51 par.//John 6:19–21). Other the other hand, five miracles are unique to John's Gospel: Water into Wine at the Wedding Feast at Cana (2:1–11); Official's Son at Capernaum (4:46–54); Sick Man at Pool of Bethesda (5:1–9); Raising Lazarus (11:1–44); Second Catch of Fish (21:1–11). See Twelftree, "Miracles and Miracle Stories," in Green et al., *Dictionary of Jesus and the Gospels*, 594–604.

8. Cf. Mark 2:22.

entails the accession of a new way of perceiving and understanding the world, which is never an easy endeavor, since our default setting is always to rely on stock notions, natural or habitual modes of comprehending reality. Jesus had to do something to rend that knowledge, because the only profound meaning is the one that is enveloped, implicated in an external sign.

Jesus knew that he could not teach the truly new in its stark newness; instead, he attempted to induce an encounter with the new by emitting signs, by creating problematic objects, experiences, or concepts. For signs are not transparent media for the communication of information, as if—lecture-style—a student could be filled up with knowledge like a vessel. Rather, signs are hieroglyphs, enigmas that point beyond themselves to something hidden. Signs are enfolded differences that impinge on thought and force thought to unfold those differences through explication. Signs are that which provoke the thought of difference, and only through an involuntary confrontation with something other does thought engage difference. Thus, when Jesus spoke in terms of new wine and wineskins, he confronted his hearers with an enigma. His audience was, of course, thoroughly familiar with the two physical objects under discussion,[9] but not with the underlying concept of "new wine" that Jesus was teaching. Hence, by discussing these objects in the context of his provocative behavior, Jesus simultaneously burst asunder the familiar, preformed connections of orthodoxy and thereby provoked his hearers to make the intended connections for themselves. For every sign has enfolded within it something "other," which must be unfolded if it is to be understood.[10] Only through such an encounter will the object of thought cease to be arbitrarily selected and attain the necessity of something that itself chooses thought, that constrains thought and sets it in motion.[11] Signs cause problems through their disorienting shock, forcing thought to deal with experiences that disrupt common,

9. Any sugary liquid, such as grape juice, that is left for more than a day will start to ferment by itself, that is, convert the sugars to ethyl alcohol.

10. Cf. Deleuze, *Difference and Repetition*, 22–23: "Learning takes place not in the relation between representation and an action (reproduction of the Same) but in the relation between a sign and a response (encounter with the Other). Signs involve heterogeneity in at least three ways: first, in the object which bears or emits them, and is necessarily on a different level, as though there were two orders of size or disparate realities between which the sign flashes; secondly, in themselves, since a sign envelops another 'object' within limits of the object which bears it, and incarnates a natural or spiritual power (an Idea); finally, in the response they elicit, since the movement of the response does not 'resemble' that of the sign. The movement of the swimmer does not resemble that of the wave, in particular, the movements of the swimming instructor which we reproduce on the sand bear no relation to the movements of the wave, which we learn to deal with only by grasping the former in practice as signs."

11. For example, Chagall's *White Crucifixion* (https://www.artic.edu/artworks/59426/white-crucifixion) causes the viewer to think about the relationship between Jesus' death and the persecution of the Jewish people throughout history, particularly in the wake of Kristallnacht in 1938 when the painting was made. The painting constitutes a sign that thoroughly subverts a Christian interpretation of Jesus' death and the Jewish role in it (e.g., "his blood be upon us and on our children" [Matt 27:25]), replacing it with a Jewish reclamation of Jesus, in which Jesus is seen as a representative Jew who suffers and dies as a result of state-sponsored oppression of the Jewish people.

coordinated functioning of the senses and faculties, thought that is bound to its preconceptions and entrenched modalities of life. Each problem is at once both the site of originary truth and the genesis of a derived truth.

Jesus' parables are the prime example of these kind of signs. The parables are seemingly simple stories, with thoroughly familiar images from everyday life, but they enfold enigmatic meaning that confronts the hearer with profound truth that destroys preconceptions even as it unfolds a new virtual reality. The point of Jesus' parables is frequently not easy to grasp; indeed, it is often illusive even for his most intimate followers. These stories use images that pose challenging problems, since the scenarios are not readily assimilable within standard interpretive schemas. Jesus' parables must be interpreted within their proper context. The audience is thereby asked to make its own connections, construed though an active interrogation of the forces connecting the images within a new and unfamiliar matrix. The challenge is to learn to see afresh in order to open themselves to Jesus' teaching. As Klyne Snodgrass aptly remarks, "The parables inform, but their primary purpose is to elicit a response. The response will be to move positively toward Jesus and his message or negatively away from him and his concerns."[12]

The goal of teaching is to think otherwise, to engage the force of that which is other, different and new. The search for truth always begins with a disruptive event that compels thought into action, and Jesus is a master at instigating such disruptive events. He defamiliarizes in the tradition of ancient wisdom.[13] All four Gospels portray Jesus as making provocative statements that jolt the hearer into paying attention and either accepting or rejecting.[14] In John's Gospel, for example, Jesus is reported as saying to Nicodemus, "Very truly, I tell you, no one can enter the kingdom of God without being born *anōthen* ('from above' or 'again, anew')," to which the Pharisee responds incredulously: "How can anyone be born after having grown old? Can one enter a second time into the mother's womb and be born?" (John 3:3–4). Moderns, too, lampoon such ideas, ridiculing the people who call themselves "born again," but in their original setting, Jesus routinely made provocative statements precisely in order to set people's wheels in motion, to get them to think outside timeworn channels. And, accordingly, Nicodemus is portrayed as engaging with Jesus in a sincere dialogue about the teacher's meaning. To learn, then, is to immerse oneself within an alien element and thereby open oneself to an encounter with signs.

12. Snodgrass, *Stories with Intent*, 565.

13. On the function of defamiliarization in wisdom literature, see Collins, "Proverbial Wisdom and the Yahwist Vision," 105–16, here 111–12.

14. Jesus' aphorisms (pithy sayings) are particularly jarring. Cf., e.g., Mark 9:45 ("And if your foot causes you to sin, cut it off; it is better for you to enter life lame than with two feet to be thrown into hell"); 10:25 ("It is easier for a camel to go through the eye of a needle than for a rich man to enter the kingdom of heaven"). See further "Aphorism," in Aune, *Westminster Dictionary of New Testament and Early Christian Literature and Rhetoric*, 36–41.

Jesus' Teaching on Becoming-Other

Jesus' revolutionary teaching in terms of signs is well illustrated with the anti-Wisdom saying in Luke 12:22–31//Matt 6:25–34 (Q).[15] As is typical in the Wisdom tradition, Jesus here encourages the listener to observe the natural world and to engage in becoming-other on the basis of what one sees. However, Jesus gives a surprising twist to the Wisdom tradition by encouraging consideration of different natural phenomena and then deriving the completely opposite point from the one made in the Wisdom tradition.[16]

Prov 6:6–11 LXX	Luke 12:22–31//Matt 6:25–34 (Q)
First Illustration (vv. 6–8)	First Illustration (v. 24)
"Go to the ant . . . and see (ἰδών)."	"Look (ἐμβλέψατε) at the ravens."
It prepares its "food" (τροφήν)	They do not reap or harvest.
And makes abundant storage in the harvest.	"God feeds (τρέφει) them" (cf. the use of "food" [τροφή] in v. 23).
Second Illustration (vv. 8a–b)	Second Illustration (vv. 27–28)
"Go to the bee and learn."	"Consider the lilies."
It works earnestly.	"They neither toil nor spin."
Its produce is used by kings, and the bee has respect.	Solomon was not arrayed like them.
Moral (vv. 9–11)	Moral (vv. 29–31)
Be diligent,	Seek the kingdom,
and poverty will flee from you.	And you need not worry about food or drink or clothing.

It seems plausible that the Q text is meant to echo and invert one particular passage of Solomonic wisdom, Prov 6:6–11 LXX. Q encourages disciples not to be anxious about their lives, about what they will eat or wear. As supporting evidence, Jesus refers (1) to the ravens, who do not sow or reap or use storehouses and yet are fed by God, and (2) to lilies, which neither spoil nor spin but are beautifully arrayed. Proverbs 6:6–11 also appeals to nature, but makes the opposite point: "Go to the ant, O sluggard, consider

15. For details, see Allison, *Intertextual Jesus: Scripture in Q*, 172–74.

16. On the failure of analogy in traditional Wisdom literature (i.e., the impossibility of using analogical reasoning to understand the ways of the Most High) and thus the need for "anti-wisdom wisdom" (i.e., divine wisdom that God shows the chosen and transcends human understanding), see Najman, *Losing the Temple and Recovering the Future*, 136–42.

its ways, and be wise. . . . It prepares its food in summer, and gathers its sustenance in harvest." The Old Greek translation adds a complementary illustration: "Or go to the bee, and learn how diligent it is, and how earnestly it is engaged in its work, whose labors kings and private citizens use for health, and it is desired and respected by all; although weak in body, it is advanced by honoring wisdom." Thus, whereas the Septuagint translation of Proverbs has the natural world offering two parables promoting the rewards of diligent work, Q has the natural world offering two examples of flourishing through divine benevolence *without the need for work*.[17]

This is not the only instance in which Q portrays Jesus as engaging in a witty reversal of scriptural texts in order to make a startling point.[18] And this is also not the only time that Q portrays Jesus as extolling the virtue of relying on God for one's sustenance in the context of seeking the kingdom. The Lord's Prayer (Luke 11:2–4//Matt 6:9–13 [Q]) teaches Jesus' disciples to pray, "Your Kingdom come. . . . Give us this day our daily bread." The latter petition alludes to the well-known story in Exod 16:1–36, where God is the source of manna (called "bread" in Num 21:5 and elsewhere and "angels' bread" in Ps 78:25) for the day to come.[19] In Jewish sources, manna was not only a memory of God's providential provision during Israel's wilderness wanderings but also a future hope of a transformed earth. Thus, according to 2 Bar. 29:8, "the treasury of manna will come down again from on high, and they will eat of it in those years because these are they who have arrived at the consummation of time." Hence, praying for one's "daily bread" is tantamount to praying for the coming of the kingdom. But as we have seen, "Jesus wants some things even now to be the way they were

17. The inversion of the Wisdom tradition by Jesus may be a function of his "Wisdom–apocalyptic–Enochic" line of flight. In effect, this move constitutes the eschatologization of Wisdom. Instead of observations on how the world works as in traditional Wisdom, Jesus promotes insights into how the world ideally works in the kingdom of God. To understand Jesus' perspective, we need to delve into apocalyptic writings of the Second Temple period. See, for example, the important comments in Kugel, *How to Read the Bible*, 656–57: "Apocalyptic writings are in some sense a continuation of late biblical prophecy, but scholars also point out its affinities with wisdom writing. It is certainly striking that the anonymous writers of apocalypses often choose not a prophet but an ancient sage or other worthy as the alleged author of their work: Enoch (described as the 'scribe/sage of heaven'), Ezra, or Baruch (both sages). Like earlier wisdom writing, apocalyptic texts hold that there is a great, divine plan governing all of reality, a plan whose rules were established long ago. And like wisdom writings, they hold that wisdom is basically hidden and requires deep contemplation in order to be revealed. Daniel and his fellow visionaries are thus *interpreters*. They interpret both dreams and texts (using, surprisingly, the same techniques for both). [. . .] The whole mentality of this period is that something is happening, but it is not seen by the naked eye. Eloquent indeed are Daniel's words of thanks to God after He has revealed him to the king's dream: 'Blessed be the name of God from age to age, for wisdom and might are His. He changes times and seasons, deposes kings and sets up kings; He gives wisdom to the wise, and knowledge to those who have understanding. He reveals deep and hidden things; He knows what is in the darkness, and light dwells with Him' (Dan. 2:20–22). The great patterns of history are like the weather: God changes kings the way He replaces spring with summer and summer with fall. But what is really going on is not visible to all, precisely because the patterns are so big. It is only to the wise and 'those who have understanding' that He reveals 'deep and hidden things.'"

18. Cf. Allison, *Intertextual Jesus*, 192–97.

19. Cf. Allison, *Intertextual Jesus*, 51–53.

in the beginning because that is how they are going to be in the kingdom of God." Jesus wants his disciples to live in the future anterior, that which will have been. In this case, that entails depending on God for one's sustenance.

For Jesus, the key to adopting the proper perspective is, as in Wisdom tradition, becoming-other through involved, intersubjective observation. Instead of being an anxious, always-striving human being on the model of the busy bee (as in the original Proverb), one should become a carefree creature that basks in security of divine providential care. Crucial to the perspective is denying human exceptionalism and an exclusively anthropocentric perspective and instead adopting the perspective of other creatures.[20] We shall have occasion to return to Jesus' teaching on becoming-other. For, as it turns out, he is also reported to have encouraged becoming-minoritarian, specifically becoming-child (cf. Matt 18:3; Mark 10:15; Luke 18:17; John 3:3, 5).

Jesus and Free Indirect Discourse

As we have seen, Jesus frequently cites or alludes to Scripture in his discourse, and Scripture has been identified as the concrete elements of an assemblage. In other words, Jesus' first-person speech is produced from this "collective soup."[21] Expressed in Deleuze and Guatarri's terms, Jesus' discourse is a "collective assemblage of enunciation."[22] The present section explores this phenomenon in more detail.

20. A particularly striking modern example of this kind of approach to the natural world is found among those who are looking to "fungal wisdom" for the future of the planet, including food security, medicines, pollution mitigation, and new human networks imitating mycelia. Oliver Hillenkamp argues that "becoming fungal" entails learning to "think like a mushroom," which will cause humans to "be inoculated with fungal ways of being." Cf. Hillenkamp, "Becoming Fungal," 1–6. It is interesting to see how even a trained mycologist like Merlin Sheldrake comes to similar perspectives with respect to his own scientific work on fungi: "I never behave more like a fungus than when I'm investigating them, and quickly enter into academic mutualism based on an exchange of favors and data. [. . .] To study a flexible network [i.e., fungi], I had to assemble a flexible network. It is a recurring theme: Look at the network, and it starts to look back at you." Sheldrake, *Entangled Life*, 215–16.

21. Cf. Costa Malufe, "Free Indirect Discourse and Assemblages," 261–71, here 269: "At stake here is that first-person speech is produced from this collective soup. And this at the point that the philosophers affirm there is no individual discourse, no subject of enunciation, 'all discourse is indirect'; thus, there is always a multiplicity of voices. [. . .] Or, as Deleuze and Guattari put it: 'My direct discourse is still the free indirect discourse running through me, coming from other worlds or other planets.'" As we saw in the preface, Walt Whitman defiantly boasted in *Song of Myself* (emphasis mine): "Do I contradict myself? | Very well then I contradict myself. | (I am large, *I contain multitudes*.)"

22. Cf. Deleuze and Guattari, *ATP*, 80: "The social character of enunciation is intrinsically founded only if one succeeds in demonstrating how enunciation in itself implies *collective assemblages*. It then becomes clear that the statement is individuated, and enunciation subjectified, only to the extent that an impersonal collective assemblage requires it and determines it to be so. It is for this reason that indirect discourse, *especially 'free' indirect discourse*, is of exemplary value: there are not clear, distinctive contours; what comes first is not an insertion of variously individuated statement, or an interlocking of different subjects of enunciation, but a collective assemblage resulting in the determination of relative subjectification proceedings, or assignations of individuality and their shifting distributions within discourse. Indirect discourse is not explained by the distinction between subjects; rather it is

We have emphasized that Jesus' proclamation is performative: it actually creates the reality that it expresses. For Deleuze and Guattari as well, language creates reality and does not merely represent or encode it. Language produces potencies affecting bodies and unexpected modes of living. As such, language has a narrative function in which concepts create a drama in real life. As an assemblage, language produces the real movement, always in connection with the assemblage of bodies in the real world in real time. Both assemblages—the *machinic assemblage of bodies* (content) and the *collective assemblage of enunciation* (expression)—are always working together, putting things in motion, changing things, producing a new reality.[23]

Jesus puts his voice together with that of Scripture as an implicit dialogue with scriptural ideas. Oftentimes, Jesus merely alludes to a biblical text without referring to the source; nevertheless, one feels the intervention of a new voice. We have seen evidence of this phenomenon in the previous section.[24] The technique in modern literature of free indirect discourse is apposite here. Free indirect discourse refers to a modality of reported speech based on the mutual interference between the voices of the author and the characters.[25] Similarly, if you listen to Jesus at any one point, you will hear a multi-

---

the assemblage, as it freely appears in this discourse, that explains all the voices present within a single voice. . . . The notion of collective assemblage of enunciation takes on primary importance since it is what must account for the social character." See further Deleuze and Guattari, *ATP*, 7, 22, 23, 78.

23. Cf. Deleuze and Guattari, *ATP*, 88: "On the first, horizontal, axis, an assemblage comprises two segments, one of content, the other of expression. On the one hand it is a *machinic assemblage* of bodies, of actions and passions, an intermingling of bodies reacting to one another; on the other hand it is a *collective assemblage of enunciation*, of acts and statements, of incorporeal transformations attributed to bodies. Then on the vertical axis, the assemblage had both *territorial sides*, or reterritorialized sides, which stabilize it, and *cutting edges of deterritorialization*, which carry it away." Graphic portrayals of these axes can be found in de Assis and Giudici, *Machinic Assemblages of Desire*, 15, 16, 62, 64.

24. See further Allison, *Intertextual Jesus*.

25. Cf. Costa Malufe, "Free Indirect Discourse and Assemblages," 263–65. The example of free indirect discourse that is given from Deleuze (Costa Malufe, "Free Indirect Discourse and Assemblages," 263–64) involves an allusion to one of Samuel Beckett's characters, Winnie, in the play *Happy Days* (1961): "The time is coming when it will hardly be possible to write a book of philosophy as it has been done for so long: 'Ah! The old style. . . .'" (citing Deleuze, *Difference and Repetition*, xxi). Costa Malufe ("Free Indirect Discourse and Assemblages," 264) comments: "Thus, in Deleuze's text, the expression 'Ah! The old style . . .' could be read as an example of free indirect discourse that puts Deleuze's voice together with Beckett's, as an implicit dialogue with Beckett's ideas. Even if between quotation marks—or, perhaps because of it, as the expression makes no reference to where it was extracted from—we can note and feel the intervention of a new voice. Let us recall that, as an expedient that began being used in modern literature, free indirect discourse refers to situations where the character's speech isn't reported, neither *directly*—as when one uses a dash to report what the characters say literally—nor *indirectly*, as when a narrator adopts the third person to paraphrase, in his or her own words, what is said by the character. [. . .] Far from being a mix between direct and indirect discourse, at stake here is a modality of reported speech based on mutual interference between the voices of the narrator and of the characters. The narrator adopts the character's tone, while also giving his or her own tone to them. [. . .] Thus, by laying hands on Winnie's Beckettian motto, 'Ah! The old style . . . ,' which even supposes a certain orality (as it's being said rather than written), Deleuze triggers a modulation in the sentence, making a new tonality intervene, as if a different voice traversed it. The result is a sentence

plicity of voices enmeshed, most often unmarked, in his discourse. In the process, a new assemblage is produced from the heterogeneous assemblage of Scripture. The concept of assemblage allows us to conceive a complex relationship of forces—a collectivity—that acts behind the constituted forms. Thus, there is always a multiplicity in movement, acting as a motor behind an enunciate. Jesus' direct discourse is still the free indirect discourse running through him, coming from other worlds.

Conclusion

The foregoing chapter shows that Jesus teaches from the Old Testament assemblage but he does so in new and provocative ways. His approach is to burst the bounds of the ordinary, subverting the normal channels and upsetting the status quo. To that end, he challenges his listeners to think with him in new ways. The goal of Jesus' teaching is not merely to impart knowledge but to change reality. This shows that, like his performative proclamation of the kingdom of God, Jesus' teaching is an integral component of his broader revolutionary aims to transform the world.

---

in which different tonalities coexist in intermodulation."

5

The Actualization of the Jesus Revolution through the Jesus Movement

Introduction

JESUS INAUGURATED A REVOLUTIONARY process based on his performative proclamation of the kingdom of God. In both word and deed, Jesus began to bring about what he proclaimed. Although his life was cut short, his execution at the hands of the Romans did not spell the end of the revolution that had been set in motion. For already during his lifetime, Jesus had sent out his disciples on several occasions in order to act as his surrogates and extend the reach of his performative message of the kingdom.[1] Therefore, even after his death, the revolution continued to be actualized by his followers as they believed in Jesus' message and sought to embody it in the future anterior.

In order to make the continuing construction of the kingdom in the future anterior as comprehensible as possible, we turn first to a concrete example from the modern return to revolution as a point of comparison. The Occupy Wall Street (OWS) movement is a relatively defined revolutionary event to which we have ready access in the recent past (September 17–November 15, 2011). If we can capture the general contours of that movement, we can use it as basis for comparing the more distant beginnings of the revolutionary Jesus movement as it continued to unfold after Jesus' death. Our goal here, however, is not merely to describe analogous revolutionary

1. Cf. Mark 6:7–13 pars.; Luke 10:1–12//Matt 9:37–38; 10:7–16 (Q).

events, but rather to open up new vistas that will be able to spark the imagination of what can be done in our own time.

The Occupy Movement

Our first task is to illustrate the modern return to revolution with a concrete example. Revolutionary theory is helpful, but it is not enough. We need to see how the theory translates into the *actuality* of revolution, that is, a set of concrete, embodied practices. Referring to the French Revolution, Josiah Ober writes, "If the proof of the pudding is in the eating, the proof of the revolutionary speech act is in the rebellion."[2] We can affirm this concept even if we are more interested in an example of *nonviolent* revolution to compare to the *nonviolent* Jesus revolution. Jesus provided the revolutionary speech-act and the beginnings of its actualization; the movement that Jesus set in motion was the ongoing proof of the revolution. Something similar can be said of the Occupy movement.[3] The actualization of revolution is the process that *gives a body* to a revolutionary idea: a body that is articulated and transformed by local and concrete struggles. The Occupy movement exemplifies the emergence of new revolutionary strategies that further elaborate and transform the idea of revolution. As we shall see, there is a widespread and deep-seated sense that the present course of the world is fundamentally wrongheaded; we are headed for catastrophe on multiple fronts. Hence, the desire for radical transformation among a large number of people worldwide is stronger than it has ever been in living memory.

The Origins of the Occupy Movement

At a time of cascading crises across the world, OWS, the largest global protest movement in world history, arose to challenge the rise in global unemployment, poverty, housing foreclosures, aggressive defunding of social services, environmental degradation, corporate greed, and the ineptitude of established political systems. As Slavoj Žižek put it in a speech at Zuccotti Park (the site of the Occupy movement, near Wall Street in New York City), "the taboo is broken, we do not live in the best possible world. But there is a long road ahead. There are difficult questions that confront us. We know what we do not want. But what do we want? What social organization can replace capitalism? What type of new leaders do we want." Thus, OWS broached the idea of revolution: Is a new and better world possible and, if so, how can the revolutionary idea be realized in actual practice? The influence of the Occupy movement was not limited to New York City; as a *translocal* grassroots movement, it spread to

---

2. Ober, "Athenian Revolution of 508/7 B.C.," 47.

3. The following description of OWS in terms of Deleuzian assemblage theory is based on Nail, "Deleuze, Occupy, and the Actuality of Revolution": https://muse.jhu.edu/article/501858. For a similar approach, applied to another situation, see Conio, *Occupy*.

over 2,556 cities across 82 countries, and over 600 communities in the United States. Clearly, then, the movement had unleashed a profound desire for radical transformation that had been bubbling beneath the surface for a long time.

The Idea of Revolution *in Concrete Action*

OWS was a revolutionary movement in that it aimed at creating a completely new world rather than reforming the present political and economic system. It was understood that negotiating with the powers that be might lead to mere mollification or possibly to co-optation rather than to any real change (recall our discussion of relative negative deterritorialization [RND]—the process by which a territorial, state or capitalist assemblage attempts to maintain or reproduce itself and thwart lines of flight, people who would try to escape from the assemblage and form something new by linking up with other escapees). Hence, instead of demanding reforms from political representatives or even trying to create its own representatives and leaders, the Occupy movement seized public space and tried to create its own form of direct democracy based on consensus decision-making, equality, and mutual aid. In societies that had failed to provide many of its members with the basic necessities of life and had refused to listen to their demands, the Occupy encampments around the world decided to provide these things for each other through direct political participation and consensus decision-making. They created kitchens, libraries, clinics, and media centers open to everyone who needed them. Thus, the Occupy movement not only expressed the popular acknowledgment that we do not live in the best of all possible worlds, it also started creating the alternative to the current socioeconomic system. Taking matters into their own hands, they refused to wait around for political representatives or corporations to fix the problems that the latter had created. For the Occupy participants, a new and better world was no longer merely possible, it was becoming a reality.[4]

As a revolutionary event, OWS was susceptible to several kinds of political deterritorialization (change): relative negative deterritorialization (tweaks to the system that allow the dominant political assemblage to maintain itself, thus neutralizing or reabsorbing the revolutionary event [see above]); relative positive deterritorialization (ambivalent change that neither reproduces the dominant political power nor

---

4. Compare the popular, nonviolent revolution against the Yanukovych government that took place in Kyiv's Independence Square (known as the Maidan) between November 2013 and February 2014. Cf. Snyder, *Road to Unfreedom*, 127–31, here 127: "Those who remained on the Maidan could do so only because they found new ways to organize themselves. The Maidan brought four forms of politics: the civil society [i.e., defense of the rule of law, horizontal networks, radical inclusion, self-organization], the economy of gift [i.e., extraordinary generosity], the voluntary welfare state, and the Maidan friendship [i.e., people that one trusted because of common trials, risking their vary lives for the sake of the revolution]." There can be little doubt that the Ukrainians' successful experience of solidarity in 2014 has made them a formidable foe against the resurgence of Russian aggression in 2022.

supports a revolutionary event and is thus unsustainable); and absolute negative de-territorialization (self-destructive change that does not support any political situation but rather undermines them all). Thomas Nail details the specific ways in which the Occupy movement was susceptible to these challenges to its very existence. Nevertheless, OWS was predominantly characterized by a fourth kind of political change—absolute positive deterritorialization (APD)—the kind of change that does not maintain or reproduce the dominant political assemblage but rather creates a breakout revolutionary event based on pent-up demand within the dominant assemblage. APD is the kind of transformation that not only escapes the dominant political order, but also connects up with an increasing number of other escaped or freed elements, because all other forms of social organization have their own ADP going on at any particular point in time. Hence, revolutionary events, far from being fashioned ex nihilo, simply harness the changes that are already underway in society. The Occupy movement was *translocal* in scope, ranging well beyond New York City to connect up with a global group of allies from across the political spectrum.

The collective aim of those involved in a revolutionary event is the creation of a new and better world. However, this ultimate goal is accomplished incrementally in the interim through the *prefigurative* construction of the new world. The Occupy movement did not just reject state-capitalism but rather created an alternative to it. Politicians and corporations had failed to serve the public interest, and so the people tried to prove that they can do it better themselves without the intervention of politicians and capitalists. By occupying public spaces and organizing the world they wanted to see (based on direct democracy, consensus decision-making, equality, trust, and mutual aid), the Occupy movement prefigured a new politics. The Occupy movement actualized the revolution in the future anterior as that which *will have been* the beginning of a new form of political assemblage.

As we have seen, however, any particular assemblage—whether territorial, state, capitalist or revolutionary—is never absolutely pure; it has elements of the other three kinds of assemblage while remaining *mostly* one sort. This heterogeneity is not a matter of contradiction or exclusion; it's an inherent part of the political typology of assemblages. As a result, political events like the revolutionary OWS have several overlapping and contingent tendencies all at once. We will repeatedly see the same kind of tension and mixture of tendencies in the early Jesus movement, to which we now turn.

The Early Jesus Movement as Portrayed in the Book of Acts

As we transition from this brief description of the actuality of revolution based on the concrete example of the Occupy movement to the early Jesus movement, we need to tamp down expectations. There is no direct or one-to-one correspondence between the two movements under discussion. OWS arose at a very different time and place and under vastly different conditions than the early Jesus movement. Nevertheless, juxtaposing the two movements can serve as a starting point for understanding the actuality of revolution in the early Jesus movement.

This move is a difficult one, because the New Testament confronts us with the Four Gospels, which detail the beginnings of the Jesus revolution,[5] and the rest of the New Testament, which gives us an impression of the unfolding of the Jesus revolution at various times and places and under diverse circumstances after Jesus' death and resurrection. In terms of the Occupy movement, we can express it this way: The Four Gospels tells us about the Zuccotti-Park-like beginnings of the early Jesus movement in Galilee and Judea (Jerusalem), while the rest of the New Testament details the explosive expansion of the early Jesus movement to the rest of the inhabited world of the first century CE, which is comparable to the global reach of Occupy movement. Clearly, it would overload the present section of this chapter to try to provide even a cursory account of the expansion phase of the early Jesus movement. The best that we can do here is to give a brief glimpse, and for that purpose the book of Acts plays a crucial role within the New Testament assemblage.

The Swing Function of the Book of Acts: From the Beginning of the Jesus Revolution in the Gospels to Its Further Unfolding in the Rest of the New Testament[6]

The story narrated in the book of Acts begins right where Luke's Gospel left off, with the community of Jesus' disciples gathered one last time around the resurrected Lord

---

5. The present short introduction to a biblical theology of the New Testament cannot deal adequately with the Four Gospels either individually or as an assemblage. Nevertheless, a few preliminary remarks are in order here. Regardless of whether the Gospels were originally written in isolation for local communities of Christ-followers (e.g., in the influential centers of Antioch, Rome, Caesarea, and Ephesus) or they were composed from the start for the wider *oikoumenē*, the revolutionary assemblage that Jesus inaugurated necessarily called into being a worldwide movement, thus making it practically inevitable that all four Gospels would soon assume a prominent function among the concrete elements within the assemblage. For the argument that the Gospels were written for all Christians everywhere from the beginning, see Hengel, *Four Gospels and the One Gospel of Jesus Christ*, 106–15; Bauckham, "For Whom Were Gospels Written?," 9–49. For the contrary argument that the Gospels were each written for local communities, see Sim, "Gospels for All Christians," 3–27. Hengel has an unique theory about how the Four Gospels came to be a collection (or what we might call an assemblage): the Gospels were stored in a book cupboard or community archive, where they were kept in a relatively fixed order, ready to hand, and provided with titles (cf. *Four Gospels*, 118, 121–23, 125, 130, 134, 136–40, 245, 279–80, 286). The cover of Hengel's volume portrays an example of such a book cupboard: detail from a mosaic in the Mausoleum of Galla Placidia, Revenna, replete with codices of the Four Gospels clearly labeled on the two shelves (Mark and Luke on the top shelf; Matthew and John on the lower shelf).

6. The following is indebted to Wall and Nienhuis, *Compact Guide to the Whole Bible*, which has been adapted for our assemblage approach to a biblical theology of the New Testament. The *Compact Guide*'s approach is not completely satisfactory, since it relies on the placement of Acts

to receive his final instructions (Luke 24:36–53; Acts 1:1–11). Jesus tells his followers to wait there in Jerusalem for the power of God to come upon them in the form of the Holy Spirit, for through this Spirit God would enable them to be Jesus' "witnesses in Jerusalem, in all Judea and Samaria, and to the ends of the earth" (Acts 1:8). The indwelling Spirit would provide the continuity between Jesus as the initiating and animating force of the revolution and the subsequent unfolding of the revolutionary event by his followers. At the end of John's Gospel, which comes directly before Acts 1 in the canonical assemblage, the resurrected Lord commissions his disciples with these words: "'As the Father has sent me, so I send you.' When he had said this, he breathed (*enefusēsen*) on them and said to them, 'Receive the Holy Spirit [*breath, (life-)spirit*]'" (John 20:21–22). Jesus breathes on them the Spirit, just as in the original creation God "breathed (*enefusēsen*) into his [sc. the first man's] face the breath of life, and the man became a living being" (Gen 2:7 LXX). Here, then, is a graphic portrayal not only of Jesus himself as the aforementioned animating force of the movement (i.e., the condition/abstract machine) but also of the new creation thereby effected that will enable the continuance of the revolutionary transformation of the world in accordance with the originally intended will of God for creation.

Revolution is not too strong of a term for what happens next in the book of Acts. According to Acts 2, when the Spirit of God comes down upon them soon after Jesus' ascension into heaven, the callow group of disciples is instantly transformed into Spirit-impelled powerhouses who are enabled to proclaim Jesus' performative proclamation of good news to the great crowd of Diaspora Jews who had gathered in Jerusalem for the Festival of Pentecost, fifty days after the first day of Passover (cf. Lev 23:15–16).[7] The result was nothing short of spectacular. First, the assembled Jews "from every nation under heaven" heard the proclamation, each in their own language, thus reversing the confusion of languages at Babel (cf. Gen 11:1–9) and signaling that God's restoration project—returning humanity to his originally intended purpose from creation—was now in full swing. Second, the efficacy of the performative proclamation of the gospel was demonstrable, insofar as about three thousand people accepted the disciples' message and were baptized on that day (Acts 2:41).

The early leaders of the church, called "apostles" (from Greek, "sent-out ones"), who had been commissioned by the risen Lord to carry his message abroad, soon took the good news beyond the traditional boundaries of Israel, resulting in the

---

in modern editions of the New Testament, which in turn go back to the order in Byzantine manuscripts. In the oldest Greek manuscript tradition, however, Acts is always combined with the general epistles (i.e., James, 1–2 Peter, 1–3 John, and Jude), and thereby functions as an introduction to *them* (rather than as an introduction to the letters of Paul [see below]). James, Peter and John were leaders of the earliest Christ-assembly in Jerusalem, so it would be appropriate to have their letters introduced by a book whose early chapters describes their activities. In either case, the book of Acts occupies a swing function.

7. Jesus' death and resurrection took place during the Passover season, although the exact timing of events varies in the sources (cf. Luke 22:1, 7, 13, 15; John 13:1; 18:28, 39; 19:14).

establishment of new assemblies in other regions of the Mediterranean (Acts 9–28). As they traveled about, they kept in touch with the assemblies that they had formed through letters. As emissaries of King Jesus, their letters were understood to be authoritative writings analogous to the royal letters written by and in the name of earthly kings.[8] Therefore, these letters—i.e., the twenty-one letters of Romans through Jude—were eventually collected and distributed among all the scattered assemblies. This very act of collection and distribution became the basis of further theological reflection and distillation, which had already been underway from the very beginning. For though the Christ-followers were spread throughout the Mediterranean world and made up of many different types of people (Jews and Greeks, slaves and free persons, males and females [cf. Gal 3:28]), all of them were animated by the same Spirit as the new humanity in Christ, a community whose words and deeds would actualize the divine ideal in the here-and-now, at least in an anticipatory way. Thus, starting with the narrative in the book of Acts, the unfolding of the Jesus revolution in the rest of the New Testament calls believers to embody Jesus' performative proclamation, to create a new and better world in the shell of the old. This is not just to see a reality filled with God's redemptive *potential* but rather to actually effect the future that is already present virtually. This is the life of the Spirit in the prefigurative future anterior.[9]

Taken together, Acts and the twenty-one letters comprise about half of the New Testament assemblage, with the Gospels making up the other half. Heterogeneous though its components may be in origin, the collection as a whole displays a semblance of organization, pointing to a transition from Jesus as the animating condition of the revolutionary event to the further unfolding of the Jesus revolution in the rest of the New Testament.[10] In mediating this transition, the book of Acts plays a crucial, transitional role within the canonical assemblage, enabling readers to look back to the Gospels and also to look forward to the letters. Here are some of the ways in which Acts performs this swing function:

(1) On the one hand, Acts carries on the *name* of Jesus from the Gospels. In John's Gospel Jesus told his disciples, "Very truly, I tell you, the one who believes in me will also do the works that I do and, in fact, will do greater works than these, because I am going to the Father. I will do whatever you ask *in my name*, so that the Father may be glorified in the Son" (John 14:12–13). As we have seen, Jesus is the *named* condition that animates the New Testament assemblage. Hence, as you read Acts, notice how Jesus' "name" functions in the life of the community: they teach in his name (e.g., 4:17–18; 5:28), they perform miracles in his name (e.g., 3:6, 16; 4:30),

8. Recall our discussion of the Hellenistic royal correspondence in chapter 3. We shall return to the issue of royal letters in chapters 5, 7, and 8.

9. As noted in chapter 3, the Spirit is an anticipation of the end time in the present and as such is part of creating the future anterior through human instrumentality.

10. As we have noted previously, the book of Acts underscores the ongoing function of Jesus Christ in the community that he founded by referring to the Spirit as "the Spirit of the Lord" (Acts 5:9; 8:39) and "the Spirit of Jesus" (16:7).

they cast out demons in his name (e.g., 16:18), and salvation and the forgiveness of sins are offered in his name (e.g., 4:12; 10:43). As the idea repeats throughout the book, the reader gets the clear impression that Jesus is continuing his own kingdom work in and through his followers who explicitly and collectively do their work in his name. This observation dovetails with our earlier concept of Jesus as the *named* condition of the New Testament assemblage.

(2) In Acts, therefore, the followers of Jesus actually mirror the activities and experiences of Jesus in the Gospels. Just as the Spirit descended on Jesus while he was praying (Luke 3:21–22), so also the believers are filled with the Spirit while they are praying (Acts 1:14; 2:1–4). Just as Jesus heals a paralytic early in his ministry (Mark 2:1–12 pars.), so also Peter heals a paralytic early in Acts (Acts 3:1–10). Just as the hemorrhagic woman touched Jesus' garment in order to be healed (Mark 5:27–30 pars.), so also those afflicted with various diseases who touch articles of Paul's clothing receive healing (Acts 19:11–12). Just as religious and political leaders persecute Jesus, so also those same people persecute the believers (e.g., Acts 4:1–22; 5:17–42). Just as Jesus, dying on the cross, prays, "Father, forgive them; for they do not know what they are doing" (Luke 23:34), and at the moment of his death, "crying out with a loud voice, 'Father, into your hands I commend my spirit'" (v. 46), so also Stephen, in the process of being stoned to death, prays, "Lord Jesus, receive my spirit" and, at the end "cried out in a loud voice, 'Lord, do not hold this sin against them'" (Acts 7:59–60).

(3) On the other hand, Acts also prepares the reader in several ways for the twenty-one apostolic letters that follow in the New Testament assemblage (i.e., Romans through Jude). Although much ink has been spilled in describing Luke-Acts as a single two-volume work by the same author, and indeed the two accounts seem to interlock with one another quite well,[11] nevertheless Luke and Acts do not appear side by side in the New Testament. If Luke originally designed Luke-Acts as a single two-volume work, Luke's Gospel became detached as a separate entity, which then, at a fairly early date, became the Third Gospel in the Fourfold Gospel assemblage (Matthew, Mark, Luke, and John). Hence, during the subsequent process of New Testament canon formation, Acts was free to take up its swing function between the Gospels and the apostolic letters.

One of the de facto functions of Acts is to provide a kind of prosopography for the authors of the letters. A prosopography is a description of a person's social and family connections, career, etc. Of course, readers of the Gospels would already be familiar with some of the authors of the subsequent letters, such as Peter and John. But they would need an introduction to the Paul who wrote the letters that come directly after Acts in the canonical order of the New Testament assemblage. Paul is

---

11. The events described at end of Luke overlap with those at the beginning of Acts. Moreover, both volumes are addressed to Theophilus (Luke 1:3; Acts 1:1), and Acts 1:1 explicitly states, "In *the first book*, Theophilus, I wrote. . . ." The Greek word translated here "book" is *logos*, a term used for the separate books of a work (cf. BDAG, s.v., 600 [1b]).

a major focus of the book of Acts. Hence, Acts provides an easy glide to Romans. By reading Acts first, we come to Romans knowing that Paul was a Pharisee and a former persecutor of Jesus' followers. We understand from Acts' three accounts of Paul's conversion experience that the persecutor had a dramatic encounter with the risen Lord on the way to Damascus whereby he was called into the Lord's service to proclaim the gospel (cf. Acts 9:1–22; 22:4–16; 26:9–18).

Another New Testament author who needs some clarification is James. James was a common name in the first century because it was the Greek form of the Old Testament patriarch Jacob (aka Israel), who was the father of twelve sons (the Israelites). As a result, quite a number of people named James are mentioned in the Gospels, the most important of whom is James the brother of John. That particular James is executed by Herod at the beginning of Acts 12. At the end of that chapter, when Peter is miraculously delivered from prison, he instructs his astonished allies at Mary's house to "tell this to James and to the believers" (Acts 12:17). Obviously, this is a different James. As it turns out from reading further in the book of Acts, this James is the leader of the Christ-assembly in Jerusalem; he provides the concluding judgment at the Apostolic Council that meets to decide the momentous and highly contentious issue of whether gentiles must abide by the Mosaic Law (Acts 15:13–21).[12] Turning to the Pauline letters, we find that the apostle Paul identifies this James as "the Lord's brother" (Gal 1:19; cf. Mark 6:3 par.), the one who received a special appearance of the resurrected Lord (1 Cor 15:7) and was subsequently named the first of three "pillars" of the Jerusalem Christ-assembly (Gal 2:9). James, the Lord's brother, must have been among the brothers of Jesus who, according to Acts 1:13–14, were with the disciples at Pentecost: "When they had entered the city, they went to the room upstairs where they were staying, Peter, and John, and James, and Andrew, Philip and Thomas, Bartholomew and Matthew, James son of Alphaeus, and Simon the Zealot, and Judas son of James. All these were constantly devoting themselves to prayer, together with certain women, including Mary the mother of Jesus, *as well as his brothers*." We have already discussed how Jesus' family had a lot of pull in the early Jesus movement. By the time we finally reach the Letter of James, toward the end of the canonical assemblage of the New Testament, we understand why the author presumes the authority to be able to write a royal encyclical letter "To the twelve tribes in the Diaspora" (Jas 1:1).[13] But is that authority based on his family connections, and, if so, is it at odds

12. We have already discussed the analogous treatment of this issue in Gal 2:11–14, the Peter-Paul conflict in Antioch. As we have seen, the issue can be viewed from two different perspectives: Paul's and that of "the men from James."

13. Our discussion of the Hellenistic royal correspondence in chapter 3 comes in handy here. Although we cannot develop the idea here, James, as the chief representative of Christ (his brother), writes an authoritative circular letter in the tradition of Hellenistic royal correspondence (and the Epistle of Enoch). Many aspects of the letter become understandable from this perspective, whether or not it is accepted that James, the brother of Jesus, is the true author of the letter. The related letter of Jude is another example of this phenomenon, again regardless of whether it is accepted that Jude, the brother of Jesus and James, is the true author. For a preliminary study in this direction, see Scott,

with the Jesus revolution itself, insofar as it seems to hold on to the old territorial assemblage that Jesus avowedly escaped by denying that his biological family was his true family based on doing the will of God (Mark 3:31–35)?[14] Or does James's authority depend rather on his new relationship with Jesus in the family of God?[15] As previously mentioned, James received a direct appearance of the resurrected Lord (1 Cor 15:7), which—much like Paul's "conversion" experience on the way to Damascus—must have led James to radically transform his perspective on his brother Jesus. It is entirely possible, therefore, that James, like Paul, rose to prominence in the early Jesus movement because of that special resurrection appearance. As you can see, thinking in terms of assemblages suggests interesting, new questions as we reexamine the New Testament using a different set of lenses.

(4) The book of Acts prepares the reader for the twenty-one apostolic letters not just prosopographically but also chronologically. Without the narrative framework provided by Acts, it would be difficult to place the letters into a chronological sequence of events. Even with Acts, this is not always an easy or straightforward task, since the correlation between Acts and the letters (the relative chronology) is often uncertain, and the events in Acts are difficult to correlate with chronologically certain events based on external evidence (the absolute chronology).

Despite the many uncertainties,[16] Acts supplies much of the essential backstory that is merely assumed in the letters. An important example of such a backstory is the fact that the Jesus revolution, which aimed at creating a new and better world for renewed humankind in the future anterior, nevertheless consisted of Jewish and gentile wings that, as we have intimated, struggled to remain together. According to Acts, the movement began with a more localized movement headed by Jewish believers (especially Peter and John) and directed toward Jewish people in and around Jerusalem (Acts 1–7). These were Jesus' witnesses "in Jerusalem, in all Judea and Samaria" (Acts 1:8a). Before long, however, that Jewish movement began attracting non-Jews (Acts 10), and soon thereafter a new phase of the original Jesus movement began, with Paul leading the effort to proclaim the gospel to the non-Jewish nations (Acts 15–28). These were Jesus' witnesses "to the ends of the earth" (Acts 1:8b). As we turn to the letters, we find that the shape of the letter collection reflects the same bifurcation of Jesus revolution: the first fourteen letters (i.e., Romans through Hebrews) are associated with the pioneering work of Paul among the non-Jewish nations,[17] and the next seven letters

---

"Jude the Obscure."

14. See the discussion of Jesus' biological family in chapter 1. As noted there, according to Hegesippus (as recorded in Eusebius, *Ecclesiastical History* 3.20.1–6), Jesus' relatives were of "the family of David." In other words, they were reputedly a royal family, which attracts the attention of Emperor Domitian.

15. See further below.

16. The historicity of Acts has been much disputed by modern scholars. We will not try to adjudicate this controversial issue; all we're after here are some general contour lines.

17. Note that Hebrews is included at the end of the Pauline letters because it was widely considered

(i.e., the letters of James, Peter, John, and Jude) are associated with the leaders of the Jesus movement among the Jewish people. Note that the order, excluding the name of Jude, reflects Paul's ordering of those whom he calls "pillars" of the Jerusalem assembly in Gal 2:9.[18] When the Letter of Jude identifies its author as "Jude . . . brother of James" (Jude 1), we recall that Jesus had one brother named James and another named Jude (Mark 6:3 par.). Hence, the final seven letters of the New Testament assemblage are all written in the name of the "pillar" apostles of the Jerusalem assembly, thus implying that their collective appearance (traditionally called the "Catholic Epistles") is meant to be received as though it was handed down to us with the imprimatur of Jesus' biological family members (note the bracketing of this seven-letter collection by the letters of Jesus' brothers, *James* and *Jude*).[19] Hence, we are confronted once again with the question that we posed above: If Jesus' biological family is so strongly in play in the Jerusalem assembly and in the final seven letters of the New Testament, what role does the territorial assemblage of traditional Jewish family ties still hold in the Jesus revolution, given that the latter is such a different kind of assemblage on a completely new and more inclusive basis? Here it is difficult to ignore that there are also otherwise some significant tensions between the Pauline letters and the Catholic Epistles, especially the standoff between Paul and James on the relationship between faith and works.[20] Do these apparent tensions reflect a difference in the outworking of the different assemblages and their respective typologies of change? In other words, do we find (a *more* revolutionary) *absolute positive deterritorialization* at work in the Pauline letters and (a *more* conservative) *relative negative deterritorialization* at work in the Catholic Epistles? We use the word "more" here because Jewish leaders such as James, Peter, John, and Jude were clearly members of the Jesus revolution. As discussed above, however, the different types of assemblages are never purely one type or another but are rather always a mixture, with one type being more prominent than the rest.

---

a letter of Paul, despite the fact that Hebrews does not explicitly name Paul as its author.

18. Cf. Lockett, *Letters from the Pillar Apostles.*

19. The use of "imprimatur" here is inspired by Martin Hengel's argument that James was "the first 'pope,'" meaning that James became the first leader of the Jerusalem church. This implies that James— and not Peter—was the "first among equals" (*primus inter pares*) in that assembly, which is very different from Roman Catholic dogma. Cf. Hengel, "Jakobus der Herrenbruder—der erste 'Papst'?," 71–104. On the prominence of James, see further Bauckham, "James and the Jerusalem Church," 415–80; Pratscher, "Der Herrenbruder Jakobus bei Hegesipp," 147–61, who discusses James's unique high-priestly function (148–50).

20. Contrast, for example, Jas 2:14–26 with Gal 3:6–14; 5:6; Rom 4:3–25. Even in Paul's own day, many misunderstood what he was trying to say. Some thought he was preaching an obedience-free gospel: since we are made right with God entirely by grace, why should we obey God's commands (Rom 3:8; cf. 6:1, 15)? Others, both friends and foes, thought Paul had rejected his Jewish past (Acts 21:20–21), since he sometimes drew a polarized distinction between God's law and gospel in a way that seemed to suggest, they claimed, that Christ had completely abolished the need for the law (Eph 2:15; cf. Matt 5:17–18). Some even thought that Paul was the only real, true apostle of Christ (see, e.g., 1 Cor 1:12–13, and also Marcion [second century CE], who rejected both the Old Testament and the apostles other than Paul).

Moreover, the four typologies of change within a given assemblage are always also at work. We should not understand the early Jesus movement as a changeless and totally unified entity; rather, we are dealing with a dynamic process that is being played out without a preestablished script. Hence, James, Peter, John, and Jude could well be Jesus revolutionaries but still hold onto some of their older traditional values in the territorial assemblage of their native Jewish heritage, which would make them to want to see things as they had always been *to some degree*. The answer to this question must await further investigation of the individual letters, but the existence of a possible fault line in the New Testament presents us all with a fascinating additional question: How does the New Testament deal with disagreements within the assemblage? The very fact that the New Testament juxtaposes the tensions, without trying to eliminate them by means of a harmonizing synthesis,[21] suggests that disagreement, whether real or apparent, need not be seen as catastrophic for the Jesus movement; indeed, it can be complementary and constructive. On the other hand, the very act of juxtaposing the differing views may be a way of effecting amelioration or correction, since no position is allowed to claim ultimate victory over the other.

Finally, Acts provides a narrative introduction to the issues and conflicts reflected in the letters. For instance, Acts tells the story of a Jesus movement that originates within Judaism but ends up becoming composed primarily of gentile believers. Many of the New Testament letters (most especially those of Paul) struggle with the question of how a predominantly gentile church is to keep faith with the God of Israel revealed to the world in the Jewish Scriptures and principally in the Jewish Messiah, Jesus. After all, Jesus insisted his mission was directed to Israel (Matt 15:24), and that "salvation is from the Jews" (John 4:22); and Paul maintains the priority of Israel by repeatedly insisting that salvation is offered "to the Jew first and also to the Greek" (Rom 1:16; cf. 2:9–10; 3:9; 10:12) and that the Messiah comes from the Israelites (Rom 9:5). Acts, in turn, maintains this same prioritization: The Jesus revolution begins as a localized, Judean movement (Acts 1–7), which then expands worldwide to the non-Jewish nations (Acts 8–28). Here as elsewhere in the New Testament, particularism and universalism are not mutually exclusive alternatives.

---

21. According to some scholars, the book of Acts itself was an attempt at a synthesis between rival factions within the early Jesus movement. The discussion started with the seminal work of Fredinand Christian Baur (1792–1860), who used Hegel's teleological schema of dialectic to argue that second-century Christianity represented the synthesis of two opposing theses: Jewish Christianity and gentile Christianity. The scheme can be summarized as follows: thesis (Peter/Law)—antithesis (Paul/gospel)—synthesis (early catholicism/the book of Acts). Although our revolutionary approach to New Testament Theology in terms of the typology of change in assemblages might be seen as reviving the specter of Baur, we have stressed that the Jesus revolution was not merely oppositional; it simultaneously initiated something radically new. On Deleuze's almost unrelentingly negative evaluation of Hegelian philosophy, see Baugh, "G. W. F. Hegel," 130–46; Hyatt, "No-where and Now-here: Utopia and Politics from Hegel to Deleuze." On the pernicious uses to which Hegelianism has been put in the twentieth century by both the Right ("Christian" fascist totalitarianism) and the Left (Marxism), see Snyder, *Road to Unfreedom*, 30–31.

Comparison of the Early Jesus Movement
with the Occupy Movement

Now that we have briefly examined both the Occupy movement and the early Jesus movement, we are in a position to compare the two. Again, although there is no one-to-one correspondence between the movements, their similarities are nevertheless illuminating. In both cases, we witness how the actuality of revolution is the process that embodies a revolutionary idea, but an embodiment that is also shaped by local and concrete struggles.

If the Occupy movement was based on popular outrage at the growing disparity of wealth and power between individuals and corporations, as well as the failure of political representatives to resolve their problems, does a similar scenario apply to the beginnings of the Jesus revolution? Was there a similar popular outrage in Galilee at the time of Jesus? Helen Bond surveys the relevant evidence.[22] Some scholars have attempted to portray the first-century Galilee in which Jesus lived as a society characterized by economic and political oppression leading to a violent insurrection by the populace.[23] There is some truth to this depiction, but its may be somewhat overstated. To be sure, at some periods in Galilee, King Herod the Great sought to put down the brigands who had been terrorizing the region (Josephus, J.W. 1.304–16).[24] After Herod's death in 4 BCE, uprisings erupted throughout the land, and a number of royal aspirants tried to seize the throne (cf. J.W. 2.56–65), perhaps inspired by stories of David as the head of a band of brigands in 1 Sam

22. Cf. Bond, *Historical Jesus*. On Jesus as a social revolutionary in the context of Galilee, see further, e.g., Freyne, "Jesus in Jewish Galilee," 197–212; Richardson, "Jewish Galilee," 213–26.

23. The social-scientific model employed by Horsley is based on modern, Eurocentric assumptions (such as class consciousness) rather than the values of Galilean villagers (where the territorial assemblage of kinship was more important). Cf. Bond, *Historical Jesus*, 24–25, 76.

24. Cf. Russell, "Roman Counterinsurgency Policy and Practice in Judaea," 248–81, here 261–65. See, e.g., Russell, "Roman Counterinsurgency Policy and Practice in Judaea," 261: "If conventional war was out of the question, was a large-scale insurgency still possible? Simply put, it already existed. Parts of Palestine (Galilee is particularly well attested) had been in an almost perpetual state of banditry (*lesteia*) for the last century. This had been of some concern to the Romans, but we can infer from the small scale of their military commitment that they had not seen it as a serious danger." Russell, "Roman Counterinsurgency Policy and Practice in Judaea," 262: "As a Hasmonean, descended from kings, and once favored by Rome, Antigonus was hardly what we might picture as a bandit chieftain. Were the *lestai* of regions like Galilee politically and socially motivated, and capable of a more broadly based insurrection in the 60s? Part of the difficulty in discussing the nature of rural insurgency is the ambiguity inherent in the Greek word often translated 'bandit,' *lestes* (pl. *lestai*). According to [Benjamin] Isaac, 'the term "bandit" could be applied to anyone who used force to attain his ends, whether they were part of the imperial establishment or belonged to its enemies.' This definition is a start, but rather general. More specifically, Josephus characterized independent armed groups as *lestai*, and attributed their motives to a desire for lawlessness, perhaps because of his own political sympathies, which tended to oppose their social base and goals. *Lestai* in Judaea included bands of people who were thieves and thugs, or who were rebelling against economic oppression, or who were rebelling against political oppression from within or without the state, or some combination of the three."

22–30.[25] Rome did not delay in reacting with brutal force. Under Varus, the Roman governor of Syria, two legions invaded Galilee, eliminating all opposition. The city of Sepphoris, about 5 km (3 mi.) northwest of Jesus' hometown of Nazareth, was razed to the ground and its inhabitants enslaved. When Judea was turned into a Roman province in 6 CE, a census was taken by Quirinius, the legate of Syria, to determine the appropriate levels of taxation for the inhabitants. According to Josephus, this prompted a Galilean named Judas to incite the people to revolt, declaring that God alone was their master (*J.W.* 2.118; *Ant.* 18.23–25). The revolt was quickly crushed, but it demonstrates once again how volatile the situation had become. Judas was the founder of what Josephus calls the "fourth philosophy" (the Pharisees, Sadducees and Essenes being the other three), and some scholars have taken this to mean that the Galilean founded a revolutionary movement, known as the Zealots,[26] which was active throughout the first century, culminating in the war with Rome in 66–70 CE. However, this interpretation has been called into question, since the Zealots as a group are first attested only during the war itself. The evidence suggests that even if no *sustained* and *organized* resistance can be documented during the first century CE, it is highly likely that sporadic pockets of insurgency broke out against Rome, even in the relatively stable period when Jesus was active (i.e., the 20s and 30s CE). To a certain degree, then, the volatile situation in Galilee during the time of Jesus can be compared to the outrage that gave rise to the Occupy movement, which was similarly short-lived and subject to government crackdown.

In other respects, however, the differences between the two movements are significant. Galilee was of course no New York City. Far from a densely populated, cosmopolitan city and cultural center, Galilee was sparsely populated and relatively insular, a self-contained region with little connection with the wider world, a backwater consisting predominantly of rural village life. As an agrarian society, the vast majority of Galileans were engaged in working the land. There is evidence in both Josephus and the Gospels that the people in Jerusalem thought of Galileans as rather unsophisticated and backward (John 7:41, 42; Acts 4:13). Nevertheless, when the center of the early Jesus movement relocated to Jerusalem after Jesus' crucifixion, the situation changed. Although on the frontier of the Roman Empire, Jerusalem was nevertheless considered an important city in the ancient world, and the constant connection between Jerusalem and the rest of the Mediterranean world was

25. Cf. Smith-Christopher, "Outlaw David Ben Jesse," 757–77.

26. The Zealots' name presumably derived from the *zeal* of a biblical hero like Phinehas in Num 25:13 (cf. Sir 45:23; 1 Macc 2:54; 4 Macc 18:12). Indeed, the outbreak of the Maccabean revolt is explicitly associated with Phinehas's zeal. Cf. 1 Macc 2:24–26: "When Mattathias saw it [sc. a fellow Judean offering pagan sacrifice on the altar in Modein], he burned with zeal and his heart was stirred. He gave vent to righteous anger; he ran and killed him on the altar. At the same time he killed the king's officer who was forcing them to sacrifice, and he tore down the altar. Thus he burned with zeal for the law, just as Phinehas did against Zimri son of Salu." On the Fourth Philosophy and other revolutionary groups of the period, see Feldman and Reinhold, *Jewish Life and Thought among Greeks and Romans*, 259–62.

maintained by the annual pilgrimage festivals (we have already referred to Passover and Pentecost), which brought streams of Diaspora Jews to the city, along with their funds for the temple. Therefore, when comparing the early Jesus movement and OWS, we must focus on Judea and Jerusalem, which was much more susceptible to political volatility and insurrection.[27]

The Occupy movement seized public space and tried to create its own form of direct democracy based on consensus decision-making, equality, and mutual aid. The picture developed in the book of Acts of the early Jesus movement in Jerusalem is somewhat similar. The public space that they "occupied" was the temple: "Day by day, as they spent much time together in the Temple" (Acts 2:46; cf. 3:1; 5:11, 20–21, 25, 45).[28] The assembly is characterized by a community of goods: "All who believed were together and had all things in common; they would sell their possessions and goods and distribute the proceeds to all, as any had need" (Acts 2:44–45).[29] "Now the whole

27. On the Jewish revolt against Rome as emanating from Judea and Jerusalem, see Popović, *Jewish Revolt against Rome*; Goodman, *Ruling Class of Judaea*.

28. Acts 21 portrays James, the leader of the Jerusalem church, as continuing his devotion to the temple. When Paul arrives in Jerusalem, James and the elders of the church with him express concern about the rumor that Paul teaches all Jews living among the gentiles "revolt from Moses" (*apostasian apo Mōüseōs*), and that he tells them not to circumcise their sons or observe the (Mosaic) "customs" (vv. 17–21). James and the other leaders instruct Paul to publicly demonstrate his piety by purifying himself, paying the expenses for four men under a (Nazirite) vow: "Thus all will know that there is nothing in what they have been told about you, but that you yourself observe and guard the law" (v. 24). Why would Paul need to purify himself? Because he is returning to the traditional Land of Israel from Gentile territory? In any case, Paul is said to have complied with their instructions: "Then Paul took the men, and the next day, having purified himself, he entered the Temple with them, making public the completion of the days of purification when the sacrifice would be made for each of them" (v. 26). This passage is a good example of the aforementioned tension among Christ-followers about the ongoing role of the Mosaic Law in the revolutionary assemblage. Are we to think of a (total or partial) abrogation of the Law (see on Gal 2:11–14) or rather of some compromise solution such as that already portrayed in Acts 15? Does the use of the term "customs" (*ethē*) in Acts 21:21 not indicate that the author of Acts recognizes Paul relegated the Mosaic Law to the realm of the territorial assemblage which had been superseded? The whole incident raises more questions than it answers, since, despite Paul's statement in 1 Cor 9:19–24, Paul could hardly be understood as giving unqualified support for the Mosaic Law as the ongoing basis for the new community's faith and practice. According to Acts 21:25, even the leaders of the Jerusalem church acknowledge that the gentiles are exempt from observance of the Law.

29. Because of the modern rhetoric against "socialism," many North Americans reject any notion of social welfare, regarding it as Marxist or communist ideology. It must be stressed, however, that the idea of a community of goods was not invented by Karl Marx, who advocated violent class war leading to a society in which all property is publicly owned and each person works and is paid according to their abilities and needs. The idea of a community of goods was already well known in the ancient world as portrayed in many different ideals of the return of the Golden Age. Cf. Gatz, *Weltalter, goldene Zeit und sinnverwandte Vorstellungen*, 162, 163, 169, 197. Some ancient Jewish groups, such as the Essenes and the Therapeutae, did more than just dream about a Golden Age; they set about actualizing it in the future anterior, and this included the practice of community of goods that enabled their members to have the necessities of life. For the Judean cultural context of this ideal, which is the most relevant for our understanding of the practice of the community of goods in Acts 4–5, see Capper, "Judaean Cultural Context of Earliest Christian Community of Goods, Parts I–V." Note Capper's emphasis on the continuity between Jesus' own practice with his disciples and

assembly (*tou plēthous*) of those who believed were of one heart and soul, and no one claimed private ownership of any possessions, but everything they owned was held in common" (Acts 4:32).[30] Thus, the community of goods was not an absolute requirement for membership in the new group, but people participated voluntarily (Acts 4:34–5:11). When some widows were being neglected in the daily distribution of food, the problem was immediately addressed through an open discussion in the "full assembly" (Acts 6:1–6). The result? "What they [sc. the Twelve] said pleased the whole assembly (*enōpion pantos tou plēthous*), and they chose Stephen, a man full of faith and the Holy Spirit, together with Philip, Prochorus, Nicanor, Timon, Parmenas, and Nicholaus, a proselyte of Antioch" (Acts 6:5). Hence, like the Occupy movement, the early Jesus movement responded to practical problems that arose among its constituents. For the early Jesus movement in Jerusalem, as for the OWS participants in NYC, another world was no longer merely possible, it was actually becoming a reality.

Like the Occupy movement, the early Jesus movement expressed, or risked, all four kinds of political transformation to at least some degree (i.e., relative negative deterritorialization, relative positive deterritorialization, absolute negative deterritorialization, and absolute positive deterritorialization). Ultimately, however, what makes the early Jesus movement distinctive is that it *most strongly* expresses revolutionary transformation characterized by absolute positive deterritorialization. Let us consider two of the dangers that the nascent Jesus movement faced and then how it nevertheless exemplifies APD most prominently.

The Danger of Relative Negative Deterritorialization

Despite being characterized most prominently by revolutionary transformation (see further below on ADP), the nascent Jesus movement did risk RND if it allowed itself

---

the earliest community of goods among Christ-followers in Jerusalem. Does Paul's collection for Jerusalem relate to the community of goods in Jerusalem? Cf. 1 Cor 16:1–4; 2 Cor 8–9; Gal 2:10; Rom 15:25–29. Paul makes his appeal to the Corinthians to resume the collection for Jerusalem: "for the purpose [of the collection] is not that there [should be] relief for others and affliction for you, but rather [it should be] out of equality. In the now time, your abundance should supply their lack, in order that their abundance may supply your lack, so that there may be equality" (2 Cor 8:13–14). Paul implies that the Corinthians are obligated to the Jerusalem saints, because they have received a spiritual gift from them, and because of their own material abundance. Paul promotes something radical: "the equalization of resources between persons of *different* social classes through voluntary redistribution." Moreover, he goes so far as to suggest that the donation for Jerusalem constitutes the submission of the Achaians to Jerusalem (2 Cor 9:13). The obligation is more expressly stated in Rom 15:26–27, and in Romans, Paul introduces a new term in referring to the collection: it is not only a "ministry," it represents "the offering of the nations" which it is Paul's priestly service to present (Rom 15:16). The conception goes back to prophetic expectations in the Old Testament, according to which the nations will bring gifts and wealth to Jerusalem (cf. Isa 18:7; 45:14; 60:5, 11).

30. The Greek term *plēthos* is used here in Acts for the first time in Acts of the whole Christ-assembly in Jerusalem. The term occurs often in Luke-Acts (8x in Luke and 16x in Acts, out of a total of 31 occurrences of the term in the New Testament as a whole).

to be captured by a new party leader or by creating a vanguard that speaks for the movement. In other words, a new hierarchy, which would have been a throwback to a more traditional territorial assemblage.[31] We see this possibility inherent in the prominence of the Twelve who took up where Jesus left off. These were men who could claim a particular authority because they had been with Jesus. Peter in particular was an early standout among this inner circle of Jesus' former disciples. According to Acts 1:15-26, it was Peter who "stood up among the believers (together the crowd numbered about one hundred twenty persons)" and advocated the need for filling the position vacated by Judas who had betrayed Jesus and subsequently committed suicide. The goal was to restore the full complement of the Twelve with "one of the men who have accompanied us all the time that the Lord Jesus went in and out among us, beginning from the baptism of John until the day when he was taken up from us— one of these must have become a witness with us to his resurrection" (Acts 1:21-22). Obviously, Peter regarded the Twelve as the natural leaders of the movement that Jesus had founded. The fact that most of the Twelve are little known, except as bare names in lists of the disciples, suggests perhaps that things did not work out as Peter had imagined.[32] In time, other leaders would emerge as need arose in the commu-

31. Matthew's Gospel has this tendency insofar as it has Jesus state that "I was sent only to the lost sheep of the house of Israel" (Matt 15:24; cf. 10:6), and further on Jesus promises the disciples, "Truly I tell you, at the renewal of all things, when the Son of Man is seated on the throne of his glory, you who have followed me will also sit on twelve thrones, judging the twelve tribes of Israel" (Matt 19:28//Luke 22:30 [Q]; see further Allison, *Intertextual Jesus*, 137-40, who discusses the possible allusion to Dan 7:9-14 here). Moreover, the Matthean Jesus directly prohibits missionary work among the gentiles: "Go nowhere among the Gentiles, and enter no town of the Samaritans, but go rather to the lost sheep of the house of Israel" (Matt 10:5-6). By the end of Matthew's Gospel, however, Jesus predicts that the "good news of the kingdom will be proclaimed throughout the world, as a testimony to all nations" (Matt 24:14), and the risen Lord famously pronounces the Great Commission, which instructs the eleven disciples to "Go therefore and make disciples of *all nations* (*panta ta ethnē*). . ." (Matt 28:19-20). In between, Jesus does have encounters with gentiles along the way (i.e., the centurion [Matt 8:5-13] and the "Canaanite" woman [Matt 15:21-28]).

32. According to the Gospels, Jesus selected the Twelve. It is possible that the idea behind the number twelve was the *anticipated* restoration of the twelve tribes of Israel, whereby the Twelve would assist Jesus in governing restored Israel, just as Moses and Aaron had originally appointed twelve phylarchs (tribal leaders), one for each tribe, to help them with governing Israel in the wilderness (cf. Num 1:4, 44). See Allison, *Constructing Jesus*, 232-33; Meier, "Jesus, the Twelve, and the Restoration of Israel," 365-404; Horbury, "Twelve and the Phylarchs," 503-27. If anticipating the restoration of Israel is the reason for selecting *twelve* disciples, is Jesus thereby portrayed as living in the future anterior? For at no point did Jesus actually come to power in Israel, nor did the Twelve ever rule on his behalf (cf. Matt 19:28//Luke 22:28-30 [Q]; see Allison, *Constructing Jesus*, 42-43). All this raises significant questions about the extent to which the revolutionary assemblage of the Jesus movement embraced aspects of the territorial assemblage of Israel and its expected restoration. It would take a separate study to deal with this question adequately. Suffice it to say at the moment that the question is a point of controversy and confusion both in the ancient Jesus movement and in modern scholarship on the subject. Allison's discussion of Matt 19:28//Luke 22:29-30 (Q) provides a salient case in point (*Constructing Jesus*, 186), "where Jesus avows that some of his followers will sit on thrones and judge or rule the twelve tribes of Israel. The prediction assumes the end of exile and the return of those tribes to the land of Israel. Other sayings in which the kingdom has a local sense probably presuppose the sort of territorial eschatology that these two Q sayings exhibit. Many or most ancient Jews would not

nity (e.g., Stephen and his fellow Hellenistic Jewish believers); Jesus' family members would come to prominence in the movement (see further above); and still other leaders—those who had *not* known Jesus personally and were at first avowed enemies of the movement—would stake revelatory claims to leadership (e.g., Saul/Paul). Under these diverse circumstances, leadership struggles were practically inevitable. Would the nascent movement overcome factionalism, escape political representation, and retain its countercultural character and radical inclusiveness? Or would leadership battles and internal dissension enable reactionary attitudes to prevail which would threaten the movement's revolutionary roots and its forward momentum?

The countercultural and forward-thinking character of the early Jesus movement was vital for its success, yet there was always a contrary tendency in the movement to remain unchanged or to default to the standards of the dominant culture. For example, the Corinthians assembly was composed mostly of gentiles along with some Jews (Acts 18:1–17; 1 Cor 1:14). First Cor 1:26–29 describes the sociocultural diversity within the Corinthian assembly: "Consider your own call, brothers and sisters: not many of you were wise by human standards, not many were powerful, not many were of noble birth. But God chose what is foolish in the world to shame the wise; God chose what is weak in the world to shame the strong; God chose what is low and despised in the world, things that are not, to reduce to nothing things that are, so that no one might boast in the presence of God." By stating that there were "not many" wise, powerful, or of noble birth, Paul implies that there were at least *some* who ticked one or more of these boxes according to the standards of the world.[33] Perhaps among the elite members of the Corinthian assembly was Erastus, "the city treasurer (*oikonomos*) of Corinth" (cf. Rom 16:23).[34] If some members of the Corinthian assembly were more powerful and better off than the rest, the social gradient very likely contributed to socioeconomic inequality in the assembly itself. Thus, Paul condemned how this inequality expressed

---

have distinguished clearly between God's kingdom and David's kingdom, and the latter was inevitably a political and territorial reality. If Jesus ever spoke of the kingdom of God as a place, as the Synoptics more than suggest that he did, we can be sure that his Jewish hearers would have thought in terms of the land of Israel, its capital, and the temple, which together 'were the sacred centre of the earth' that 'would one day attract all peoples.' *Once his sayings became the property of Gentile churches, alternative, nonterritorial readings could and did come into being. That, however, tells us next to nothing about the historical Jesus.*" If, as we are arguing, Jesus inaugurated a revolution that took a line of flight from the territorial assemblage of the dominant form of Judaism toward a more universal approach, that does not necessitate that he completely abandoned a restoration eschatology (cf. the Animal Apocalypse [1 En. 90:28–38] and the Apocalypse of Weeks [1 En. 93:9–10 + 93:11–14]). Nor should we necessarily assume that the Gentiles are responsible for all nonterritorial Jesus material. For any assemblage, including a revolutionary one, will contain some mixture of the other three types of assemblage. We should be particularly open to such a possibility insofar as Hebrew, Aramaic, and Greek words for "land, territory" (i.e., ארץ, ארק/ארע, γῆ) can also be translated "earth, inhabited world." Could Jesus have played on this semantic ambiguity in order to speak about both "land" and "earth" either simultaneously or at different times? Compare Brueggemann, *Land*, xiii, xv–xvi, xix, xx.

33. Cf. Theissen, *Social Setting of Pauline Christianity*; Meeks, *First Urban Christians*.

34. See further Brookins, "(In)frequency of the Name 'Erastus' in Antiquity."

itself during the community's celebration of the Lord's Supper, because the wealthier members ate the meal without regard to the poorer members who came late to the celebration or who could not afford to bring their own food (1 Cor 11:17–24). In terms of the typology of change in assemblages, the Corinthians' celebration of the Lord's Supper had devolved into a clear case of RND, whereby the revolutionary assemblage was in danger of being stripped of its countercultural distinctiveness and reabsorbed into the dominant culture. During the very meal that was meant to bring the whole heterogeneous community together as a united "We," the richer members were effectively reinforcing the stratification characteristic of the society at large. In other words, the very celebration that was meant to amalgamate the past, the present and the future of the revolutionary event in order to create a new and better world in the prefigurative future anterior was effectively being undermined:

> What should I say to you? Should I commend you? In this matter I do not commend you! For I received from the Lord what I also handed on to you, that the Lord Jesus on the night when he was betrayed took a loaf of bread, and when he had given thanks, he broke it and said, "This is my body that is for you. Do this in remembrance of me." In the same way he took the cup also, after supper, saying, "This is the new covenant in my blood. Do this, as often as you drink it, in remembrance of me." For as often as you eat this bread and drink the cup, you proclaim the Lord's death until he comes. Whoever, therefore, eats the bread or drinks the cup of the Lord in an unworthy manner will be answerable for the body and blood of the Lord. Examine yourselves, and only then eat of the bread and drink of the cup. For all who eat and drink without discerning the body, eat and drink judgment against themselves. For this reason many of you are weak and ill, and some have died. But if we judged ourselves, we would not be judged. But when we are judged by the Lord, we are disciplined so that we may not be condemned along with the world. (1 Cor 11:17–24)

The Corinthians failed to embody the truth that the celebration of the Lord's Supper has an eschatological horizon *"until he comes."* Appropriately, therefore, Paul ends the letter with the Aramaic cry, "Our Lord, come!" (*Marana tha*, 1 Cor 16:22). These words are the cry of the early Jesus movement as it lives out the implications of Jesus in the future anterior in anticipation of the final consummation.

For another example of the contrary tendency in the Jesus movement to remain unchanged or to default to the standards of the dominant culture, we may return to the story of the Apostolic Council in Acts 15. As we have seen, James was the most prominent leader in the Jerusalem community of believers at the time. Although the whole Council considered the issue at hand (i.e., whether the gentiles must be circumcised and keep the Mosaic Law), it was James who unilaterally pronounced the final verdict: "Therefore I rule (*dio egō krinō*) that we should not trouble those gentiles who are turning to God" (Acts 15:19). Although his decision was subsequently ratified by the whole assembly—"Then the apostles and the elders, *with [the consent of] the whole assembly* (*syn holē tē ekklēsia*), decided to choose men from among their members and to send them to Antioch with Paul and Barnabas [who had originally brought the issue to the Council's attention]" (15:22)—nevertheless, the Jerusalem Christ-assembly is still a step away from the kind of consensus decision-making that characterized the General Assembly of the Occupy movement, that is, a non-representational form of direct political participation.

The danger of RND was not only internal but also external. Like the Occupy movement, the Jesus revolution resisted neutralization and co-optation by the dominant assemblages. For example, the participants refused to be silenced even when the Jewish authorities threatened the speakers with violence (Acts 4:1–22; 5:17–42).

The Danger of Relative Positive Deterritorialization

Another danger for the nascent Jesus movement was relative positive deterritorialization (RPD), that is, deterritorializing too far and thereby self-destructing. The refusal to work with others who do not share all of one's own commitments can become an absolute principle, leading to a radical self-marginalization and possible eventual self-destruction of the movement. Jesus himself was confronted with this issue. According to Mark 9:38 par., John reported to Jesus, "Teacher, we saw someone casting out demons in your name, and we tried to stop him, because he was not following us." But Jesus wisely said in response, "Do not stop him; for no one who does a deed of power in my name will be able soon afterward to speak evil of me." Similarly, Acts depicts exorcists from outside the Jesus movement using the name of Jesus to cast out demons; these are itinerant Jewish exorcists, identified as "seven sons of the high priest Sceva." Unlike the portrayal in Mark, these exorcists are unsuccessful, because the evil spirit recognizes that they have no connection with Jesus (Acts 19:13–17). Nevertheless, Luke 9:49–50 follows Mark 9:38–40 in portraying Jesus as approving the use of his name by exorcists who have no relation to him and as supporting this approval with the same saying. Luke also preserves the saying that makes the opposite point, which the author apparently found in Q (Luke 11:23//Matt 12:30).

What would have happened to the early Jesus movement if it had refused to make common cause with Jewish people who were not originally part of their little enclave? What, for example, if they had refused to extend the right hand of fellowship to Saul/Paul, once he was turned from being a persecutor of the Christ-assemblies (Gal 2:9)? What if they had declined to admit gentiles of all social strata on an equal basis into the nascent movement? The answer is obvious. If they had decided to think in such a parochial way, they would have remained small, local, and utterly vulnerable to suppression. Simply put, their self-marginalization, their exclusiveness, their "purity," their hidebound lack of creative vision and spontaneity, would have threatened the very existence of the Jesus revolution.

Absolute Positive Deterritorialization

This is the kind of transformation that not only escapes the dominant political order, but also connects up to a growing number of other escaped or freed elements whose ultimate collective aim is the prefigurative creation of a new and better world in the shell of the old. The intermediate means of accomplishing this goal is through harnessing and recomposing the changes that are already happening in society, especially through assembling a new, revolutionary people—the people to come.

Just as the Occupy movement was *translocal* in scope, connecting itself up with a global allies across the political spectrum, so also the early Jesus movement was *translocal* and variegated in constitution. Starting in Jerusalem, the grassroots movement burst the bounds of its original base of operations, made significant inroads into new territories (e.g., Judea and Samaria), and established outposts (e.g., Syrian Antioch), which in turn could serve as staging points for further expansion to regions beyond (e.g., Asia Minor and Europe). Above all, however, it was the Johnny-come-lately apostle Paul who not only attempted to strengthen a meaningful connection between Jerusalem and the Christ-assemblies that he had established in Asia Minor and Europe,[35] but also reached out to the home-based Christ-assemblies in Rome—assemblies that he had not even founded—in order to solicit cooperation for his planned westward campaign all the way to Spain. One of the reasons for Occupy's success was that it did not reject groups with differing political aims. In a similar way, radical inclusiveness was critical for the success of the early Jesus movement. The resulting heterogeneity was a decisive strength of the movement, but its largely successful escape from territorial, state, and capitalist forms of power and representation also occasioned many growing pains. The movement would continue to struggle with the issue of boundaries and stratification.

Just as the Occupy movement was *translocal* in scope, it also had *localized* manifestations of the revolutionary body politic. A revolutionary body politic is a continually transformed condition and set of concrete consequences, but it is the collective revolutionary subject ("We") that connects the two together. The political personae are the agents of an operation that connects the abstract event to the concrete consequences. The Occupy movement produced a very specific type of collective subjectivity exactly along these lines and called themselves "the Occupiers." Piece by piece, "the Occupiers" showed the concrete consequences of the Occupy movement by effecting specifically appropriate actions. In the same way, the early Jesus movement produced a very specific type of collective subjectivity—their name "Christians"—which directly connected with the Christ-event that they were endeavoring to embody and express the consequences of. The term "Christian" (*Christianos*) is found three times in the New Testament.[36] Acts 11:25–26 reads: "and it was in Antioch that the disciples

35. Paul sought to make this connection primarily through the collection for Jerusalem.

36. For a full discussion of the term, see Trebilco, *Self-Designations and Group Identity in the New*

were first called 'Christians'"; Acts 26:28: "Agrippa said to Paul, 'Are you so quickly persuading me to become a Christian?" And 1 Pet 4:16: "Yet if any of you suffers as a Christian, do not consider it a disgrace, but glorify God because you bear this name." There has been much discussion on whether the term was first coined by outsiders (i.e., gentile opponents) to designate the believers in Antioch or rather it was a self-designation of the mixed Jewish and gentile community itself. Scholarship has come down decisively on the former possibility for a variety of reasons. In light of our discussion of the Jesus revolution, however, it does not really matter too much who first designated Christians as such. What is significant is that believers readily adopted the term as a self-designation, and the reason is obvious: the name "Christian" dovetailed perfectly with their relationship to the Christ-event, the *named* condition and raison d'être of their movement. The use of this self-designation recognizes that the evental condition of the Christ-event transforms the "Christians," who must in turn redeploy new concrete effectuations based on this change.

The other corporate term for Christ-followers in the New Testament is *ekklēsia*, which is usually translated "church."[37] This translation completely obscures the cultural connections of the term in the first century CE. We immediately think of steeples and crosses, pews and baptistries, etc. A better translation of the Greek term is "assembly." Why did early Christ-followers call themselves collectively *ekklēsia*, and what it is the significance of this term?

In the Greco-Roman context, *ekklēsia* was used for the "assembly" of citizens of the *polis* (city-state), who met to make a range of decisions affecting their common life. In this context, *ekklēsia* had the quite specific meaning of a "coming together," or a meeting, rather than the body of people that assembled. It was only when the citizens actually assembled from time to time that there was an *ekklēsia*. By contrast, the *boulē*, or city council, was a body that continued in existence, managing day-to-day affairs, and could be referred to even when it was not actually meeting. If, we have argued, the Jesus revolution sought to create a new world in the shell of the old, it might be significant that the new world order was understood using a term derived from the old world order.[38] The main difference would be that the whereas the Greco-Roman

---

Testament, 272–97. As Trebilco's study makes clear, "Christian" was not the only name for Christ-followers, nor even the most common. We are featuring this name here because it illustrates the intimate connection between Christ and his followers.

37. For the following, see Trebilco, *Self-Designations*, 164–207.

38. Cf. van Kooten, "Ἐκκλησία τοῦ θεοῦ," 522–48, here 522: "I argue that its [i.e., the Christian self-designation ἐκκλησία] Graeco-Roman political meaning in the sense of 'civic assembly' was decisive in its adoption by Paul, and that Paul wished to portray his communities as alternative organizations existing alongside the civic assemblies. . . . Through a sustained analysis of ἐκκλησία in the Hellenistic and Roman periods I show that, in many respects, the functioning of the Christian ἐκκλησίαι mirrors the operations of the civic assemblies." Note particularly the use of *ekklēsia* in reference to assemblies of Christ-followers in specific cities: "the *ekklēsia* in Jerusalem" (Acts 11:22); "the *ekklēsia* in Cenchreae" (Rom 16:1); "the *ekklēsia* of God that is in Corinth" (1 Cor 1:2); "the *ekklēsia* of the Thessalonians" (1 Thess 1:1; 2 Thess 1:1); "the *ekklēsia* in Ephesus" (Rev 2:1); "the

ekklēsia in Smyrna" (Rev 2:8); "the *ekklēsia* in Pergamum" (Rev 2:12); "the *ekklēsia* in Thyatira" (Rev 2:18); "the *ekklēsia* in Sardis" (Rev 3:1); "the *ekklēsia* in Philadelphia" (Rev 3:7); "the *ekklēsia* in Laodicea" (Rev 3:14). These examples show that the term is meant to be understood in light of Greco-Roman usage of an "assembly" in a *polis*. Cf., however, Last, "*Ekklēsia* outside the Septuagint and the *Dēmos*," esp. 967–69. The notion of a new *ekklēsia* of Christ-followers existing alongside the established civic *ekklēsia* is not as strange as it may sound, considering that in the ancient world the idea of a new named settlement within or alongside an established one was known. Cf. Thonemann, "Pessinous and the Attalids," 111–28, who points out, in addition to his main quarry (i.e., Pessinous [the indigenous temple-state], alongside Kleonnaeion [the secondary Greco-Macedonian *polis*]), "in the mid-170s, a new πόλις named Antiocheia was established by favour of the Sekeukid Antiochos IV at Jerusalem. The town and civic community of Jerusalem did not thereby cease to exist. Instead, a Greek-style πόλις of Antiocheia, inhabited by citizens designated with the ethnic *Antiocheis*, was established *alongside* of the older Jewish community of Jerusalem, which continued to exist *alongside* it" (125 [emphasis mine]). See further Ma, "Re-examining Hanukkah"; Kennell, "New Light on 2 Maccabees 4.7–15," 10–24. On the mimicry of civic structures, practices, and terminology, see Kloppenborg, "Associations, Christ Groups, and Their Place in the *Polis*," 1–56; Kloppenborg, *Christ's Associations*. The paper presented by Paddock, "Βασιλεία τοῦ θεοῦ and ἐκκλησία τοῦ θεοῦ: Boundary Markers for the Corinthians Believers," is relevant here (from her abstract):

> In the creation of sacred space, group members need to be able to identify themselves as insiders so as to determine who can be admitted into the sacred space without potentially profaning it. For the first century Corinthian believers, Paul sets forth boundary markers to help define insiders vs outsiders. Two boundary markers that play an important role within First Corinthians are the βασιλεία τοῦ Θεοῦ and the ἐκκλησία τοῦ Θεοῦ. For a believing community that most likely met in a variety of mundane spaces for worship, boundaries enabled the group to create sacred space when they congregated ἐν ἐκκλησίᾳ. In his 2003 book, *Putting Jesus in His Place: A Radical Vision of Household and Kingdom*, Halvor Moxnes bemoaned the fact that Kingdom of God studies has not experienced a spatial turn: "a one-sided focus on time has marginalized the question of place" (p. 110). While he focused on Gospel studies, the spatializing of the Kingdom of God can also play an important role in the Apostle Paul's letter to the Corinthians. Three times Paul mentions the Kingdom of God in 1 Corinthians: 4:20, 6:9-10, 15:50. In 4:20, Paul makes clear the Kingdom is not an intellectual manifestation created by words, but a place of power in which believers currently dwell and experience. In 6:9, Paul asks if the Corinthians understand their identity has changed once they passed through the kingdom boundary. Having become insiders, wrongdoers (outsiders) have no power over them nor do they have a place in this sacred realm. Finally, in 15:22, Paul looks to the future, arguing that the Kingdom of God is not a place that can be inherited by flesh and blood. Instead, insiders need to undergo a transformation—passing through another boundary, if you will, in order to experience the eschatological Kingdom of God. Throughout First Corinthians, Paul understands the kingdom as a boundary separating believers from non-believers. The Kingdom of God is a place in which insiders dwell, both now and, hopefully, in the future. Another boundary Paul creates to separate outsiders from insiders is the ἐκκλησία τοῦ Θεοῦ. First and Second Corinthians are the only Pauline epistles addressed to the ἐκκλησία τοῦ Θεοῦ. From the beginning, Paul sets the tone in identifying his audience, conjuring up both Jewish and Greco-Roman images for his audience. His first century audience is like those who assembled before the Tabernacle as well as those who assembled for civic duty. Each group was well-defined and had certain rules to follow, enabling them to participate in the assembly. So too, the Corinthian believing community, even when not assembled, needed to act in a way becoming of those who live in the sacred realm of the Kingdom of God, who have undergone the initiation rites to become members of the ἐκκλησία τοῦ Θεοῦ.

ekklēsia convened only sporadically and then disbanded, the *ekklēsia* of the new world order, continued in existence like a *boulē*—it never disbanded. Moreover, this new *ekklēsia* included not just males but females as well, and anyone could be full-fledged citizen and therefore part of the *ekklēsia*.

In the Jewish context, *ekklēsia* occurs frequently in the Septuagint and other Jewish literature of the Second Temple period for the assembly of the people of Israel.[39] In some cases, the term refers to an actual "assembly" of people when they gather (e.g., Deut 4:10; Sir 21:17). In a few cases, the term may be a self-designation for a group regardless of whether it was actually "assembling" or not. Trebilco argues that the use of *ekklēsia* can be traced back to the Hellenists in Jerusalem and that its use aligned the Jesus movement with the coveted tradition of Israel as the people of God. On this reading, *ekklēsia* was used as a collective name for their "assembly" because of its use in the Septuagint, showing the continuity with the Old Testament "assembly" without claiming that they alone were the heirs of that people. If this is the correct interpretation, then we must be cautious. For as in the case of the Greco-Roman context discussed above, the reuse of a designation from a particular cultural context may signify that a new world is being built in the shell of and alongside the old. In other words, the term may not indicate continuity with the old, but rather discontinuity (i.e., the new and better *ekklēsia* embodying universality, equality, and solidarity). We shall return to this important issue in chapter 8.

Conclusion

Comparing the early Jesus movement to the modern Occupy movement has been an illuminating exercise. Although there is no one-to-one correspondence between the two, their similarities are nevertheless striking at points. In both cases, we witness how the actuality of revolution is the process that *gives a body* to a revolutionary idea: a body that is transformed by local and concrete struggles. For both movements, creating another world in the shell of the old was no longer merely possible, it was becoming a reality in the here and now. Why, then, did the Occupy movement end in disillusionment, whereas the Jesus revolution continued to flourish? Such a way of putting the matter is perhaps overly simplistic. Surely, the popular outrage that originally sparked the Occupy movement did not suddenly disappear when the police forcibly cleared the Occupiers from Zuccotti Park. If anything, the outrage of "the 99%" has only increased in recent years. During the COVID-19 pandemic, for example, the 1 percent made billions of dollars not despite the crisis but actually *because of the crisis*, while many of the most vulnerable—millions of workers—lost their livelihood and with it their job-based access to healthcare just when they needed it most. Moreover, as I write this paragraph, the official moratorium

39. See Korner, *Origin and Meaning of Ekklēsia in the Early Jesus Movement*.

on foreclosures and evictions has just ended, with the result that millions of people who are behind on their payments because of the pandemic are about to lose the roof over their heads. Clearly, then, the ideal world of the Occupiers is farther away today than ever before; indeed, it seems to be moving away at warp speed as enormous structural problems compound themselves. The conditions are ripe for further revolutionary movements, perhaps even more aggressive ones that are willing to violently seize what they regard as rightfully theirs.

By the same token, to say that the Jesus revolution continued unabated seems like an overstatement. True, Christ-assemblies continued, grew, and spread in subsequent centuries. No amount of local persecution could crush the movement once and for all. But what about the movement's original commitment to the ongoing creation of the prefigurative future anterior? As time went on, the tendency of Christ-assemblies to accommodate to culture was strong, particularly since the revolutionary course brought Christians into conflict with the dominant society. Hence, the desire to work within established systems was not only the path of least resistance but also a survival technique for most Christ-followers. Nevertheless, from time to time a minority of Christ-followers would continue to intensely feel the massive disparity between their revolutionary New Testament roots and their present mundane reality, thereby creating an unquenchable thirst for something more and better not just as a vague future hope or possibility but more importantly as a present reality. This means that the modern trajectory of both the attenuated Jesus movement and the disbanded Occupy movement (to name just one example) is essentially the same—a revolutionary yearning for the creation of a new world in the here and now.

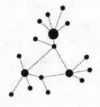

6

The Jesus Revolution as Creatively Unfolded by Paul

Introduction

As we have seen, Jesus' proclamation that the kingdom of God is at hand called upon people to repent and believe the good news, that is, to accept the creation of the kingdom in the shell of and alongside the old world. On the basis of the evidence from Acts, we have observed that the early Jesus movement continued to actualize Jesus' revolutionary vision, and that the movement grew and spread. Do the letters of Paul support this understanding of the continuity? Did Paul continue the Jesus revolution, or, as many scholars reckon, did he begin a separate movement?[1] Is Rudolf Bultmann correct that Jesus is not part of New Testament Theology but rather

1. In the previous chapter, we elected to deal with the expansion of the Jesus movement on the basis of the book of Acts. It should be acknowledged, however, that the letters of Paul, which are the focus of the present chapter, constitute the chronologically earliest writings of the New Testament. Therefore, many scholars would argue that Paul's letters should be handled first. Moreover, Paul's letters are primary sources from one of the main players of the early Jesus movement, whereas Acts is a more derivative source, in the sense that it is generated at the interface of two historical moments—the past of the earliest Jesus movement and the present within which the author of Acts narrates and theologizes. This is a thorny issue, to say the least. As stated previously, however, starting with Acts provides some of the backstory that helps with the contextualization of the letters, so it does have heuristic value. And as we stated from the outset, we are not interested in a reconstruction of history that pits "our history" against that of the authors of the New Testament. Seeing the New Testament as an assemblage enables us to understand it as our history.

its presupposition, with Paul leading the charge in the formation of a new religion called "Christianity"?[2] We shall argue here that Paul did not begin a separate religion or even a separate movement, but rather continued to creatively unfold Jesus' original vision of revolution.[3] However, this does not mean that Paul is simply a carbon copy of Jesus. We have made the case that every time the named condition (Jesus Christ, in this case) interacts with changes in the agents/personae (the expanding and spreading community of Christ-followers), this changes the revolutionary assemblage. For example, the urbanization of the originally rural Jesus movement, as it expanded to Jerusalem, and then onward into Syria, Asia Minor and Europe, could not help but contribute to significant changes in important respects. Of course, the different geographical locations themselves played a substantial role in changing the character of the movement. Despite these changes, however, the common tread was the construction of the prefigurative future anterior—a new and better world in the shell of and alongside the old—in anticipation of the final consummation. It is not a matter of Jesus *or* Paul, but rather of Jesus *and* Paul.

We learn from Paul's letters how the apostle tries to encourage local assemblies, most of which he himself had founded, to live in the future anterior.[4] These were Christ-followers who were struggling with all sorts of issues, including persecution, internal rivalries, misunderstandings, poverty, and even derailment. The letters also give us a window into Paul's own personal struggles as he continued to carry out his mandate from the risen Lord to preach the gospel to the nations. Referring to his time in Macedonia, Paul writes, "Our bodies had no rest, but we were afflicted in every way—disputes without and fears within" (2 Cor 7:5). What kinds of situations is Paul referring to? Second Cor 11:23–33 provides a salient example of these "disputes without and fears within":

> Are they [sc. Paul's opponents] ministers of Christ? I am talking like a mad-
> man—I am a better one: with far greater labors, far more imprisonments, with
> countless floggings, and often near death. Five times I have received from the
> Jews the forty lashes minus one. Three times I was beaten with rods. Once I
> received a stoning. Three times I was shipwrecked; for a night and a day I was
> adrift at sea; on frequent journeys, in danger from rivers, danger from bandits,
> danger from my own people, danger from Gentiles, danger in the city, danger

2. Cf., e.g., Wedderburn, "Paul and Jesus," 189–203; Wenham, *Paul*.

3. An important antecedent to the present endeavor is the work of Ernst Käsemann, who not only elucidated the message of Paul with motifs from the ministry of Jesus (cf. Käsemann, *On Being a Disciple of the Crucified Nazarene*), but also engaged in a political reading of Paul that kept the "revolutionary fire" burning, "in the face of a theology of history which has lost its past revolutionary fire (*das revolutionäre Feuer ihrer Vergangenheit*) and is now planting conservatively laid-out gardens on the lava that has turned to cold, hard stone." Cf. Käsemann, "Rechtfertigung und Heilsgeschichte im Römerbrief," 125.

4. For another approach to some of the same issues that we deal with in this chapter, see Smith, *Paul and the Good Life*.

in the wilderness, danger at sea, danger from false brothers and sisters; in toil and hardship, through many a sleepless night, hungry and thirsty, often without food, cold and naked. And, besides other things, I am under daily pressure because of my anxiety for all the churches. Who is weak, and I am not weak? Who is made to stumble, and I am not indignant? If I must boast, I will boast of the things that show my weakness. The God and Father of the Lord Jesus (blessed be he forever!) knows that I do not lie. In Damascus, the governor under King Aretas guarded the city of Damascus in order to seize me, but I was let down in a basket through a window in the wall, and escaped from his hands.

From this description, it is clear that the aforementioned "fears within" are due to Paul's constant anxiety over his churches (which were being influenced by the "false brothers and sisters"). The source of the "disputes without" is equally obvious: Paul keeps bumping up against the two dominant assemblages of his day—the state assemblage of the Roman Empire and the territorial assemblage of early Judaism. Being beaten with rods (cf. Acts 16:22–23) was a Roman form of punishment;[5] receiving "forty lashes minus one" was a Jewish form of punishment based on Deuteronomy (25:2–3), and being stoned (cf. Acts 14:19–20) was a Jewish form of capital punishment prescribed in Deuteronomy (17:5–7; 22:22–24).

Our next step, then, is to see how Paul's interactions with these dominant political assemblages shaped the Jesus revolution as the apostle continued to unfold it. Right away, however, we hit a hurdle. In contrast to Jesus, Paul refers to the "kingdom of God" only sporadically (1 Cor 4:20; 6:9–10; 15:24, 50; Gal 5:21; Col 4:11; 1 Thess 2:12; cf. 2 Thess 1:5; 2 Tim 4:1, 18). If, as we are contending, Paul continues to unfold the Jesus revolution, how is it possible that he fails to emphasize one of Jesus' key terms for the project?[6] We must acknowledge, however, that outside the Synoptic Gospels, the term "kingdom of God/heaven" is relatively rare. It occurs, for example, only twice in John's Gospel (3:3, 5) and a mere seven times in the twenty-eight chapters of book of Acts (1:3; 8:12; 14:22; 19:8; 20:25; 28:23, 31). However, most of the occurrences in Acts record *Paul's* preaching of the "kingdom of God" (Acts 14:22; 19:8; 20:25; 28:23, 31). Hence, Paul was remembered as having preached the kingdom, and his own letters also bear testimony to that fact. We should not, then, overly concentrate on the sparsity of one term, for Paul extensively uses the other key term of Jesus' proclamation—the "gospel" or "good news"—which, as we have seen, Jesus used in connection with his proclamation of the kingdom of God (cf. Mark 1:14–15).[7]

---

5. Cf. Thrall, *II Corinthians VIII–XIII*, 739–42.

6. Another issue is whether Paul was the one who influenced the Jesus tradition rather than vice versa. See, e.g., Díaz, *Mark*.

7. On Mark 1:14–15, see further in chapter 2. On the continuity between Jesus and Paul with respect to the "gospel," see Stuhlmacher, *Gospel and the Gospels*; Hengel, *Four Gospels and the One Gospel of Jesus Christ*.

Paul vs. the Roman Empire as State Assemblage

As we have seen, Jesus was crucified as a royal pretender, so an activist like Paul, who carried on the message of this publicly executed political subversive, automatically came into the Romans' crosshairs.[8] According to Acts 17:3, when Paul was in Thessalonica, he began to proclaim Jesus as "the Messiah" (i.e., the end-time king of Israel). As a result, he and his companion Silas were accused of sedition: "These people who have been turning the world upside down [or: who have led the whole world into revolt] have come here also. . . . They are all acting contrary to the decrees of the emperor, saying that there is another king named Jesus" (Acts 17:6–7).[9] Such accusations could bring Paul into serious trouble with the Roman authorities.

Romans 13:1–7

The only time that Paul refers to the Roman Empire in his extant letters is in Rom 13:1–7, where the apostle emphasizes that the Christ-followers in the imperial capital Rome must "be subject to the governing authorities."[10] But how can submitting to the dominant state assemblage of the time square with unfolding the revolutionary Jesus assemblage? Surely the two are mutually exclusive.[11] After all, Christ-followers cannot, without severe reservation, support the very regime that crucified the Lord Jesus Christ. Perhaps our assemblage approach to New Testament Theology can help us to resolve this seeming paradox. We have described a revolutionary movement as creating

8. On the political reading of Paul in the context of the Roman Empire, see the overview in Elliott, "Paul and Empire 1," 143–64; Elliott, "Question of Politics," 203–43; Horsley, *Paul and Empire*. See also more broadly Carter, "Question of the State and the State of the Question," 197–211.

9. Cf. Rowe, *World Upside Down*. As previously stated, however, a better translation of Acts 17:6 would be "who have led the whole world into revolt" (cf. 21:38). On the book of Acts, see further Strait, "Proclaiming Another King Named Jesus?," 130–45.

10. Even here, however, the reference to the Roman Empire is quite general. Cf. also 1 Cor 2:6, 8, which refers to "the rulers of this age" who "crucified the Lord of glory."

11. Cf. Collins, *Apocalyptic Imagination*, 335: "In the late twentieth and early twenty-first centuries there has been a trend to emphasize the political implications of Paul's thought and to construe his view of the Lordship of Jesus as a challenge to the ideology of the Roman empire. It is indubitably true that Paul's claim of absolute sovereignty for Jesus was incompatible with Roman imperial ideology. It is also true that he unambiguously identifies Jesus as the Jewish messiah, a title that normally had political implications. But Paul does not point up the political implications of his message. Rather, as Paula Fredriksen, has argued [*From Jesus to Christ*, 173], he 'denationalizes Christ' and 'shrinks the significance of contemporary politics.' Paul did not need to foster rebellion. Divine intervention was at hand, and the form of this world was passing away. Most telling is the statement in Rom 13:1-2: 'Let every person be subject to the governing authorities; for there is no authority except from God, and those authorities that exist have been instituted by God. Therefore whoever resists authority resists what God has appointed, and those who resist will incur judgment.' An apocalyptic perspective could lead to fierce criticism of earthly empires, as we shall see in the Book of Revelation, but it is not deployed in that way in the Pauline epistles." For a critique of "empire criticism," see further McKnight and Modica, *Jesus Is Lord, Caesar Is Not*.

a new and better world in the shell of and alongside the old. In this case, the Roman Empire is clearly running the old world that is in the process of passing away (cf. 1 Cor 7:31). It is Paul's firm conviction that worldly empire will eventually give way to the kingdom of God in a full and final way (cf. 1 Cor 15:24–28). In the meantime, however, Christ-followers must live in a dual reality in the present.[12] On the one hand, they are still under the dominion of the state assemblage, with all its apparatuses of government (reward and punishment, taxation). As a state assemblage, the Roman Empire is all about maintaining internal order and keeping chaos at bay.[13] So, Christ-followers cannot and should not be anarchists; they must obey the existing authorities or suffer severe consequences.[14] But before this text is lifted out of context and used for nefarious means by unscrupulous politicians (the Nazi regime springs to mind), let us emphasize that Christ-followers are also in the process of creating a new and better world in the shell of the old. They are already living in the prefigurative future anterior. They are thereby anticipating the final consummation when God will be all in all. Therefore, Christ-followers will always live in tension, and it will not always be easy to negotiate between their two lived realities.[15] It is clear from Paul's life and letters, however, where his own ultimate allegiance lay. He was willing to face all the aforementioned trials and tribulations in order to advance the gospel; in this matter, he refused to acquiesce to illegitimate displays of imperial power and authority.

12. In terms of the assemblage theory of Deleuze and Guattari, we can express this dual reality in the present as the difference between "the plane of immanence/consistency" and "the plane of organization." Cf. Bogue, *Deleuzian Fabulation and the Scars of History*, 25: "In the tenth section of *A Thousand Plateaus*, '1730: Becoming Intense, Becoming-Animal, Becoming-Imperceptible. . . ,' Deleuze and Guattari speak at length about becoming, and in that discussion the virtual is most often characterized as a 'plane of consistency' (or plane of composition, or plane of immanence), whereas the actual is called a 'plane of organization' (or plane of development). Becomings take place on the plane of consistency."

13. As we have seen, the state assemblage operates by stratification; in other words, it forms a vertical, hierarchized aggregate that spans the horizontal lines in a dimension of depth. In state assemblages, the abstract machine attempts to cut itself off from and rise hierarchically above the concrete relations and personae of the assemblage. This is what Deleuze and Guattari call "state overcoding," which is characterized by centralized accumulation and forced resonance of diverse points of order.

14. Here it is interesting to note that the English term "the powers that be" is actually an allusion to Rom 13:1. Cf. *OED*, s.v. "power" (II.8b).

15. As we have seen, any particular assemblage—whether territorial, state, capitalist or revolutionary—may incorporate elements of the other three while remaining *mostly* one sort. In other words, the four types of assemblage are never absolutely pure; all assemblages are composed of a mixture of the four types of assemblages to various degrees. Hence, the concept of a specifically topological theory of political history provides a way to consider political events as having several overlapping and contingent tendencies at once, each to a greater or lesser degree. This heterogeneity is not a matter of contradiction or exclusion. See further below.

Paul's Roman Citizenship

Paul's letters mention nothing about him being a Roman citizen. According to Acts, however, Paul was a citizen of both Rome (Acts 22:25) and Tarsus (21:39).[16] Indeed, he was *born* a Roman citizen (22:28). A Roman citizen was required to register the birth of his children within thirty days before a Roman magistrate, and the person received a wooden diptych (a writing tablet consisting of two hinged leaves) recording the declaration of citizenship, which acted as a certificate of citizenship for the rest of their life.[17] Presumably, then, Paul had such a diptych—and could produce it when he ran into difficulties with Roman officials.[18] When Paul was arrested in Jerusalem and ordered to be examined by flogging, Paul was able to thwart the plan by asking a pertinent question: "Is it legal for you [sc. a nearby centurion] to flog a Roman citizen who is uncondemned?" (Acts 22:25). Alarmed at this news, the centurion reported Paul's comment to the tribune, a Roman legionary officer.

> The tribune came and asked Paul, "Tell me, are you a Roman citizen." And he said, "Yes." The tribune answered, "It cost me a large sum of money to get my citizenship." Paul said, "But I was born a citizen." Immediately those who were about to examine him drew back from him; and the tribune also was afraid, for he realized that Paul was a Roman citizen and that he had bound him. (Acts 22:27–29)

This fascinating account furthers our discussion of assemblages in two important ways. First, Paul's strategic use of his Roman citizenship is instructive. By virtue of his being a card-carrying member of the state assemblage, Paul could use citizenship to shield himself from harsh interrogation techniques.[19] Later in the book of Acts, Paul will use

---

16. On Paul's citizenships in Rome and Tarsus, see further Hengel, *Pre-Christian Paul*, 1–17.

17. Cf. Sherwin-White, *Roman Citizenship*, 6.

18. Cf. Acts 16:35–40, referring to Paul's incarceration in the Roman colony of Philippi in Macedonia (emphasis mine): "When morning came, the magistrates sent the police, saying, 'Let those men go.' And the jailer reported the message to Paul, saying, 'The magistrates sent word to let you go; therefore come out now and go in peace.' But Paul replied, 'They have beaten us in public, uncondemned, men who are *Roman citizens*, and have thrown us into prison; and now are they going to discharge us in secret? Certainly not! Let them come and take us out themselves.' The police reported these words to the magistrates, and they were afraid when they heard that they were *Roman citizens*; so they came and apologized to them. And they took them out and asked them to leave the city. After leaving the prison they went to Lydia's home; and when they had seen and encouraged the brothers and sisters there, they departed." See also Acts 23:25–26, recording the words of a Roman tribune in a letter to the Roman governor about Paul's pending case: "Claudius Lysias to his Excellency the governor Felix, greetings. This man was seized by the Jews and was about to be killed by them, but when I had learned that he was a *Roman citizen*, I came with the guard and rescued him."

19. One practical implication of Paul's maneuver is that he was not adverse to using his natal connection with the state assemblage (i.e., his Roman citizenship) to his own advantage, even though he was simultaneously constructing the future anterior—the new and better world in the shell of the old (i.e., the Roman Empire). Engagement in constructing the future anterior does not mean disengagement with the world that is passing away. Cf. Hengel, *Pre-Christian Paul*, 8: "The important thing for

his Roman citizenship again, this time to appeal his case all the way to the emperor in Rome (Acts 25:10–12).[20] Paul had wanted to extend his mission to Rome, and so even under arrest, he found a way to accomplish his goal. Membership has its privileges. Second, the interchange between Paul and the tribune is interesting with respect to our discussion of assemblages. Two different pathways to Roman citizenship are presented in this text: by birth (Paul) and by purchase (the tribune). There are, in fact, other ways that citizenship was conferred as well, for example, by performative declaration. Citizenship was the collective assignment of a status. As Myles Lavan observes, "In the earliest phases of Roman expansion, naturalization was employed as a means of organizing and controlling populations. It was a status imposed on rebellious, not loyal, aliens—a striking inversion of later practice."[21] In the terminology of state assemblages, granting or imposing citizenship is a prime example of "state overcoding" to produce a hierarchized aggregate that spans the horizontal lines in a dimension of depth. Or, to put it still another way, granting citizenship was a means of constructing the Roman world. Seen in this light, Paul is a microcosm of the collision of two empires under construction—the Roman Empire and the kingdom of God. He is a model of the aforementioned tension produced by dual lived realities in the present.

Yet, Paul's lived reality was arguably much more complex than a mere duality. Who Paul *was* does not admit of a simple answer. Like most people, he was many things at once without contradiction or exclusion, and the relevance of those "circles of identity" shifted according to circumstances (cf. 1 Cor 9:19–23).[22] Paul never disavowed his Jewish identity,[23] although what he was *becoming* in Christ eclipsed everything else (cf. Phil 3:7–11).

Christians was not the privilege of an earthly citizenship but the fact that they were brothers and sisters. So we can certainly say that Paul did not attach any special value to his citizenship. However, that does not exclude the possibility that he was a Roman citizen who made use of that fact in particular circumstances, especially when he was being threatened."

20. Note, however, that being a Roman citizen and declaring, "I am a Roman citizen (*Civis Romanus sum*)," were not always a guarantee of favorable treatment by the Roman authorities. Cf. Beard, *SPQR*, 254, who states that "the most famous ancient use [of this declaration] was as the unsuccessful plea of an innocent victim [i.e., Publius Gavius] under a sentence of death imposed by a rogue Roman governor [i.e., Gaius Verres]."

21. Lavan, "Foundation of Empire?," 21–54, here 24.

22. Cf., e.g., Malkin, "Between Collective and Ethnic Identities," 283–92, who describes "the *simultaneity* of circles of identity and their shifting relevance. For example, Dorieus, a Diagorid from the polis of Ialysos in Rhodes, dedicated a statue at Olympia presenting himself as 'Rhodios,' a Rhodian. This man had several circles of belonging to a collective identity: a Diagorid (family); a citizen of Ialysos (*polis*); a Rhodian (regional-island identity); a Dorian colonist who probably saw himself as a descendent of the original migrants who had come with Tlepolemos (sharing in a pan-Dorian *ktisis*, an *exodus*-type story of migration and settlement); a member of the Dorian Pentapolis in Asia Minor, *qua* Ialysian; a member of the *emporion* at Naukratis, *qua* Rhodian; finally, a 'Greek' at Olympia. What is important is that he could 'plug into' any one of those according to context and no process of elimination could privilege any of those circles of collective identity" (Malkin, "Between Collective and Ethnic Identities," 290–91).

23. Cf. Rom 11:1; 1 Cor 7:17–19; 2 Cor 11:22; Gal 1:13–14; 2:15; Phil 3:4–6; also 2 Tim 1:3; Acts

Paul vs. Judaism as Territorial Assemblage

The second major assemblage that impinged on Paul was the territorial assemblage of early Judaism. As discussed in a previous chapter, territorial assemblages are not merely a matter of territory (i.e., a particular geographical location), but rather how that territory is qualitatively organized into an identity or "coded stock," which defines codes of kinship, codes of worship, codes of communication, codes of exchange, codes of location (places of worship, places for eating, places for rubbish, and so on). Territorial codes define the "natural" norms of life. They express the pre-given, essential, and proper limits and usage of persons and objects in a given assemblage by explaining how the world is related to the past, to an inscription of memory—"this is how things are done, how they have always been done." Homeostasis is the goal. In early Judaism, too, the territory (Judea) is qualitatively organized into an identity or "coded stock" based on the Mosaic Law (Torah). For Jews/Judeans,[24] obedience to the Law and its way of organizing every detail of life is the condition for occupying the Land.[25]

18:18; 20:16; 21:20–26; 21:39–22:5; 23:1, 6; 24:14–21; 26:2–8; 28:17–20. Emphasizing Paul's Jewish identity is the burden of the "Paul within Judaism" perspective. Cf. Nanos and Zetterholm, *Paul within Judaism*.

24. As we have seen, there is intense scholarly debate on how best to translate the Greek *Ioudaios*, whether in religious ("Jew") or in ethnic/geographical terms ("Judean"). There is no single correct answer. Much depends on the context in which the word occurs. When discussing Judaism as a territorial assemblage, *Ioudaios* in the ethnic/geographical sense comes to the fore. To a greater or lesser degree, even Diaspora Jews/Judeans had a relationship with the territorial assemblage, although whether that relationship should be described merely as "center versus periphery" should perhaps be called into question. The work that has been done on the "Greek Wide Web" suggests the possibility of a complex, variegated, and dynamic "network" approach may be a more fruitful metaphor for the historical processes at work in Jewish/Judean identity as well. Cf. Malkin, *Small Greek World*; Malkin, "Between Collective and Ethnic Identities," 283–92; Harder, "Spiders in the Greek Wide Web?," 259–71; Müller, "Globalization." Any discussion of these matters must begin with Barclay, *Jews in the Mediterranean Diaspora from Alexander to Trajan (323 BCE–117 CE)*, esp. 413–28.

25. Davies, *Territorial Dimension of Judaism*. Davies discusses "The Land" as "the essence of Judaism": "We have sought in the preceding pages to do justice to the theological role of territory in Judaism. *Jewish theology, as revealed in its major witnesses, points to The Land as of the essence of Judaism*. In strictly theological terms, the Jewish faith might be defined as 'a fortunate blend of a people, a land and their God.' But in any blend, an ingredient may be submerged, and in this formula, it has been claimed, the essential and distinctive significance of The Land may be lost sight of" (53 [emphasis mine]; cf. 116). According to Davies, for the land to be "essential" means that it is "an aspect of Judaism without which Judaism would cease to be itself" (*Territorial Dimension of Judaism*, xv). Note, however, that toward the end of his study, Davies distances himself from the notion of "The Land" as "the essence of Judaism." See Davies, *Territorial Dimension of Judaism*, 104 (cf. 121–26):

> In the preceding pages we have pointed to attitudes and historical realities which make it clear that there was before 70 C.E., and immediately after in the early Tannaitic period, no uniformity of territorial doctrine. And despite the overwhelming dominance of the rabbinic form of Judaism since then, the history of the Jews, although not to the same degree, reveals the same fissiparous, amorphous, and unsystematized doctrinal character. The concept of an adamant, uniform "orthodox" Judaism, which was not stirred by dissident movements and ideas or by the mystical, messianic yearnings which expressed themselves outside of, or in opposition to, the main, strictly

With assemblages, however, things are rarely straightforward. As we have seen, any particular assemblage—whether territorial, state, capitalist or revolutionary—may incorporate elements of the other three while remaining *mostly* one sort. In other words, the four types of assemblage are never absolutely pure; all assemblages are composed of a mixture of the four types of assemblages to various degrees. We have also discussed how the heterogeneous collection of writings in the Old Testament assemblage lacks unity; for alongside the Torah, there are other concrete elements of the assemblage—the Wisdom tradition being the prime example—that are not oriented on the Mosaic Law. Hence, we may expect—and do find—that early Judaism, which is based in large part on the Old Testament assemblage, is not a unified entity, either. Indeed, during the course of the Second Temple period, early Judaism changed and adapted in a variety of ways. For example, John Collins shows that, like the changing notions of what it meant to be "Greek," the understanding of Jewish ethnicity became dislodged in the Hellenistic period from a necessary connection to blood and descent by focusing on a comprehensive way of life as the distinguishing characteristic.[26] In terms of our discussion of the political typology of assemblages,

---

rabbinic, tradition, is no longer tenable. To define the place of Eretz Israel in Judaism requires recognition that the place has changed—or, more accurately, has received different emphases among various groups and at different times. However persistent some views of, and attachments to, The Land have been, and however uniform the testimony of the classical sources, there has not been one unchangeable, essential doctrine universally and uniformly recognized by the whole of Judaism.

26. Cf. Collins, *Invention of Judaism*, 8–10. According to Josephus (*Ant.* 13.257–58), for example, when John Hyrcanus conquered the Idumeans, about 128 BCE, he "permitted them to remain in their country so long as they had themselves circumcised and were willing to observe the laws of the Jews/ Judeans (*Ioudaiōn*). And so, out of attachment to their ancestral land, they submitted to circumcision and to having their manner of life in all other respects made the same as that of the Jews/Judeans (*Ioudaiois*). And from that time on they have continued to be Jews/Judeans (*Ioudaious*)." In a similar way, when Aristobulus conquered the Itureans in 104–103 BCE, "he compelled the inhabitants, if they wished to remain in their country, to be circumcised and to live in accordance with the laws of the Jews/Judeans (*Ioudaiōn*)" (*Ant.* 13.318). In other words, Judaism was imposed on the conquered peoples who were now part of Judean territorial assemblage. As Collins observes (*Invention of Judaism*, 98), "the Hasmoneans did this by taking a constructivist, or even instrumentalist, view of Judean ethnicity." Moreover, as Collins goes on to state (99), "the Hasmoneans were guided by an ideal but loosely defined sense of the traditional boundaries of Israel. 1 Macc 15:33–34 has Simon Maccabee declare: 'We have neither taken any man's land, nor do we hold dominion over other people's territory, but only over the inheritance of our fathers. On the contrary, for a certain time it was unjustly held by our enemies; but we, seizing the opportunity, hold fast to the inheritance of our fathers.'" The parallel to our earlier discussion of the incident at Antioch (Gal 2:11–14) is palpable, insofar as the territorial dimension of Judaism evidently motivated the Jewish Christ-followers to withdraw from table fellowship with their Gentile fellow believers, thus effectively compelling the latter to "Judaize." Bockmuehl's extensive discussion of the conflict between Peter and Paul in Antioch—and its import for F. C. Baur's massively influential, Hegelian hypothesis of the dialectical progress of early church history (*Seeing the Word*, 112, 121–36)—is extremely important, especially since, as Bockmuehl affirms, "one's exegetical judgment of that episode largely determines one's view of early Christian history as a whole—and vice versa" (*Seeing the Word*, 126). I would like to return to this issue in more depth on another occasion. Suffice it to say at the moment that our assemblage approach to a biblical theology of the New Testament can account for the tension between these two apostles of Jesus Christ without denying Judaism

we are dealing here with territorial assemblages that change their criteria for inclusion over the course of time. The world is still divided into coded segments that are deemed either natural or proper, but what counts as natural or proper itself changes. The lack of unity within early Judaism also expressed itself in a revolutionary line of flight that broke loose from the established territorial mold altogether, taking off in the direction of a modified Wisdom tradition.[27] Seen in light of Deleuze and Guattari's concept

(see the following note). As previously mentioned, all assemblages include elements of the other three kinds of assemblage, so tension is an inescapable part of assemblages in general. Jesus' revolutionary impulses were latent within the Judaism of his formative years, which helps to explain why he would continue to practice his ancestral way of life even as he started becoming a line of flight from it, a royal pretender inaugurating the radically different kingdom of God, which intended to turn a topsy-turvy world right side up (see chapter 3). We must not think of the formation of this new, revolutionary assemblage as occurring all at once or in hard-and-fast terms; a messy transitional phase was inevitable. And, to be clear, the transition in question was not from Judaism to "Christianity" (which does not even exist as a separate entity at this early stage of the Jesus movement), but rather from a Mosaic form of Judaism to another form of Judaism (quasi-Enochic). This is the same kind of *inner-Jewish* "supersessionism" that Bockmuehl himself finds expressed in Mark 12:1–9 (*Seeing the Word*, 218–19; on supersessionism, see further Scott, *Apocalyptic Letter to the Galatians*, chap. 3). Hence, we have no difficulty in affirming, on the one hand, that Peter was a fervent proponent of the solidly *Jewish* Jesus revolution and an unequivocal partner with Paul in the gospel of Jesus Christ (cf. Gal 2:7–9; Bockmuehl, *Seeing the Word*, 130–32), and, on the other hand, that the apostle to the circumcision (Gal 2:7–8) would of course consider whether—and, if so, to what extent—his ancestral way of life was meant to be continued on some basis, both for himself and for anyone else who joined the Jesus movement. By announcing the arrival of the kingdom, Jesus was creating a new world in the shell of the old (i.e., the return to the originally intended will of God for creation), yet Peter was still clinging to the old world that was in the process of passing away. A. A. Michelson, whose famous experiment disproved the existence of the ether as the medium through which light travels, did not immediately accept the results of his own experiment, although he reluctantly did so eventually. However, even in 1927, in his last paper published before his death, he referred to the ether in the following nostalgic words: "Talking in terms of the beloved old ether (which is now abandoned, though I personally still cling a little to it). . ." (cf. Holton, "Einstein, Michelson, and the 'Crucial' Experiment," 139). This, despite the fact that Michelson's experiment had long since helped to verify a new revolutionary assemblage, Einstein's Special Theory of Relativity (1905). It appears that Bockmuehl, in attempting to find common ground between Peter and Paul (which is completely supportable by the evidence he adduces), ends up affirming a Baur-like *synthesis* between the two figures—"the charismatic politics of innovation ('Paul')" versus "the episcopal politics of an authorized establishment ('Peter')" (*Seeing the Word*, 132)—which underestimates the degree to which Jesus inaugurated a truly revolutionary assemblage: "Still, we must note that *the synthetic view* adopted by the emerging consensus of the *catholic* rule of faith came to be the strongest of those earliest trajectories" (*Seeing the Word*, 136 [emphasis mine]). From our perspective, however, such a synthesis is impossible, and Paul was right, not just to look for a compromise (or "creative negotiation . . . between charismatic and episcopal polity," 133), but rather to denounce Peter and the other Jewish Christ-followers in Antioch, because, as Paul asserted, they were not going straight with respect to the truth of the gospel at that point (Gal 2:14). If, as Bockmuehl states in this regard, "To dismiss one in favor of the other is always to court tyranny of convention or the tyranny of revolution" (133), then the latter is ineluctable for the faithful follower of Jesus. Paul, for his part, calls this "tyranny" *freedom*.

27. For the most part, Davies, in *Territorial Dimension of Judaism*, treats Judaism as a monolith which is inexorably oriented on the Land and the Mosaic Law that regulates it. See above on his notion of "the Land" as "the essence of Judaism." At one point, however, he does acknowledge that "some expressions of Judaism itself" (i.e., later rabbinic circles) did abandon the traditional territorial dimension of Judaism through "deterritorialization" (132n10; on Davies's use of the term

of assemblages, Paul continues the line of flight that Jesus initiated *within Judaism*, which can be characterized as an extension of a wisdom-apocalyptic-Enochic line.

"deterritorialization," see also 93–94, 129–36). Davies fails to consider that already in the Second Temple period, this process of deterritorialization was underway in a form of Judaism that can rightly be called "Enochic." Yet, as Davies himself almost grudgingly points out (77), "The Wisdom literature . . . has, as we should now put it, a curiously 'international' flavour (and indeed draws upon Egyptian and other non-Jewish sources)." By saying that Wisdom literature has a "curiously 'international' flavour," does Davies mean that the Wisdom literature is inconsonant with the view that "The Land" is "the essence of Judaism" (53)? Bockmuehl's treatment of Jesus and Judaism suffers from much the same problem. Although he acknowledges that first-century Judaism was highly variegated (cf. *Seeing the Word*, 203–4, 220–21), Bockmuehl fails to examine whether another form of Judaism, such as the Enochic, might have affected Jesus' aims and teaching. Hence, Bockmuehl effectively operates with an essentialist definition of Judaism, which is equated with its territorial and particularistic Mosaic form. Anything that deviates from this is deemed "the de facto de-Judaizing of Jesus's aims and teaching" (197), which is tantamount to "a denial of Judaism" (222–23) and is aligned with "the depressingly familiar litany of patristic anti-Judaism" (224). This gratuitous assumption has far-reaching ramifications for Bockmuehl's study: (1) He regards universalism and particularism—both of which are represented in the Jesus tradition—to be mutually exclusive alternatives. Cf. Bockmuehl, *Seeing the Word*, 199–200: "And so we seem to arrive at the logical conclusion of a process that has been a hallmark of post-Enlightenment scholarship and that arguably has deep roots even in patristic thought [i.e., the very effective history on which Bockmuehl otherwise puts so much emphasis]. We are therefore inevitably caught between the horns of a dilemma: even allowing that it is historically plausible, can a Christian point of view affirm the essential Jewish particularity of Jesus's identity without thereby denying a part of its own heritage?" Bockmuehl, *Seeing the Word*, 204: "Making Jesus more of a Jew may seem to have the effect of making him less of a Christian—or at any rate less of a Western Enlightenment Protestant." Bockmuehl, *Seeing the Word*, 223. (2) As a result, in order to highlight the essential Jewishness of Jesus' identity (e.g., 193, 195, 203–4, 208–9, 221–22), Bockmuehl feels that he must correspondingly downplay any universalistic strains: "Ever since antiquity, theologians have tended to privilege universalizing abstractions about Jesus's person and teaching over the Jewish particularities of his dress, his diet, and his disputes with fellow Jews. One could debate why this has been so, or indeed whether it may be a necessary consequence of the New Testament's own universalizing witness. That it occurred is an uncontroversial matter of historical record—as is the fact that the wedge driven between Jesus and Judaism by Jews and Christians alike has, from antiquity to the period of living memory, trough consequences of incalculable horror" (194); "his general avoidance of Gentiles, at least to the extent that the two apparent exceptions in the Gospels attract special attention (see Mark 7:24–30 ‖ Matt. 15:21–28 and Matt. 8:5–13 ‖ Luke 7:1–10)" (208); "It is particularly significant that the preservation of such obsolete elements in the Gospels arguably runs against the grain of redaction: they have become politically incorrect for evangelists committed in every case to the gospel's post-Easter outreach to *Gentiles*" (210 [author's emphasis]; cf. 131); "His ministry signally touched a handful of individual Gentiles, and his message included the promise that a (perhaps deliberately ambiguous) mass of otherwise unspecified exiles would arrive from the east and the west to join with Abraham, Isaac, and Jacob in the messianic banquet (Matt. 8:11 ‖ Luke 13:29)" (222). However, if, as we are suggesting, Jesus is coming from an Enochic perspective, we don't need to play off particularism against universalism, or Judaism against Christianity (indeed, we shouldn't even be talking about the latter in the pre-70 situation). The Enochic tradition makes clear that the focus on the remnant of Israel expands to a worldwide, indeed cosmic, perspective, which includes the Gentile nations in its purview. Even the destiny of the Twelve to sit on twelve thrones, which Bockmuehl uses to bolster his case for the particularity of Jesus' Jewishness (211–15), also inadvertently makes the case for universalism, insofar as "these thrones, surrounding the Son of Man's 'throne of glory,' also evoke the heavenly thrones of the saints around that of the Ancient of Days in Daniel 7:9" (215); for the Son of Man "was given dominion and glory and kingship, that all peoples, nations, and languages should serve him" (Dan 7:14).

This revolutionary line was not oriented primarily on the Mosaic Law and the Land of Israel, but rather on more universal strains pertaining to the creation of a new and better world. We shall return to this issue presently.

Against this general backdrop, we can appreciate how Paul could still be *within Judaism* (broadly conceived) and yet not partake of the dominant form of Judaism which is oriented on the land of Israel and the Torah that regulated Israel's relationship to it. Although Paul is regularly regarded as the founder of "Christianity," in truth he is not outside of the range of possible forms of Judaism in the first century CE. The kind of Judaism that Paul came to embrace in connection with his encounter with the risen Lord already had some of the revolutionary ingredients pertaining to the creation of a new and better world in prefigurative future anterior. This explains how Paul dovetails with Jesus, without the apostle being merely a carbon copy of Jesus. Paul appropriates Jesus and the related Enochic tradition and then proceeds to unfold them in his own unique way, in accordance with his own background as a Pharisee and his own set of consequent circumstances. Hence, the change that took place in Paul's life when he met the risen Lord was indeed transformative, but it was not a break with Judaism. It was more like sliding into a parallel track within the same rail yard. Still, the change was significant, for it set Paul off in a different direction.

We have suggested that Paul had a complex relationship with the state assemblage of the Roman Empire: It produced a tension of dual lived realities in the present, as Paul lived under the factual domination of worldly empire, even as he lived in the virtual freedom of the kingdom of God in the future anterior. In a similar way, Paul had a complex relationship with the territorial assemblage of his traditional, Mosaic form of Judaism ("the tradition of the fathers" [Gal 1:14]). It, too, produced a tension of dual lived realities in the present, as Paul continued to uncouple from his former way of life in Judaism, even as he lived a new life in Christ, in a new, revolutionary assemblage.

Paul and Palestinian Judaism

Since Judaism is so foundational to our understanding Paul, we need to take a closer look at some of the ideas that have just been discussed in the preceding paragraphs. For this purpose, we will interact with the seminal work of E. P. Sanders on Palestinian Judaism (or "common Judaism"), which has become widely accepted in New Testament studies and the basis for further developments which we cannot go into here (i.e., "the New Perspective on Paul" and the "Paul within Judaism" perspective).[28] According to Sanders, Palestinian Judaism can be defined in terms of "a 'laundry list' of practices and beliefs from monotheism through Sabbath observance to sacrifice in the temple in

28. We broached this subject in chapter 1 (in conjunction with the Incident at Antioch as an example of Relative Negative Deterritorialization), but it comes in for more thorough discussion here.

Jerusalem (while it still stood)," which includes "covenantal nomism."[29] In other words, according to Sanders's description, Judaism is what we have called an assemblage, and more particularly a *territorial* assemblage (*Palestinian* Judaism). The problem with Sanders's conception of Judaism is that it tries to apply an essentialist definition to an assemblage.[30] As we have seen, the theory of assemblages provides an alternative to the logic of essences.[31] Assemblages are heterogeneous collections for a particular purpose, but such collections are not fixed entities. They are subject to transformation according to changes in any or all of their components—their abstract machine/condition, their concrete elements, and their agents/personae. Therefore, we need to deal with Judaism as a dynamic *process* rather than as a fixed entity.[32]

The difficulty with Sanders's approach to "common Judaism" becomes apparent when we consider 1 Enoch, a heterogeneous collection of Jewish apocalyptic writings from the Second Temple period, which developed primarily over the course of the three centuries before the turn of the era (and to a certain extent on into the first century CE).[33] Taken together, these Enochic writings have a *named* abstract machine/ condition—i.e., the antediluvian patriarch Enoch—which is different from the *named* abstract machine/condition that determines the Mosaic form of Judaism that Sanders describes—i.e., Moses himself.[34] As is well known, what we now regard collectively

29. See, most recently, E. P. Sanders's essay on "Covenant Nomism Revisited," 51–83. For a summary of what "covenant nomism" entails, see Sanders, *Paul and Palestinian Judaism*, 422: "(1) God has chosen Israel and (2) given the law. The law implies both (3) God's promise to maintain the election and (4) the requirement to obey. (5) God rewards obedience and punishes transgression. (6) The law provides for means of atonement, and atonement results in (7) maintenance or reestablishment of the covenantal relationship. (8) All those who are maintained in the covenant by obedience, atonement and God's mercy belong to the group which will be saved."

30. For Sanders's attempt to deny the claim (made by Jonathan Z. Smith and Philip Alexander) that he was "someone who sought the *essence* of Judaism," see "The Origin of the Phrase 'Common Judaism,'" in Sanders, *Comparing Judaism and Christianity*, 31–49, esp. 35–36, 46–49. However, his conclusion (49) speaks for itself: "In my own view, I have been in quest of historically ascertainable characteristics of a religion, which I distinguish from an essence. One of the things that I like most about 'covenantal nomism' as a theological lowest common denominator is that it has a lot of content. It actually depends on the idea of *loyalty*. It is as theological as von Harnack's 'core' of Christianity [i.e., *das* Wesen *des Christentums*], but it is much better suited to historical proof, because loyalty to the people of Israel and to the law can be supported by evidence. 'Common Judaism,' of course, puts more meat on those bones and is more obviously descriptive. Thus I do not think that I know what the essence of Judaism was. I think that there were *basic* and *common* observances and beliefs that served to identify some people as Jews in the ancient world and that gave the group a firm identity."

31. Cf. Nail, "What Is an Assemblage?," 21–37, here 23–24; Nail, "Kinaesthetics," in de Assis and Giudici, *Machinic Assemblages of Desire*, 179–96, here 182.

32. Cf. Witte et al., *Torah, Temple, Land*.

33. Specialists in the Enochic literature will, of course, point out that our main access to the collection of writings that we call 1 Enoch is through much later transmission in manuscripts written in Ethiopic, although the Aramaic Qumran fragments of the Enochic writings show that they stem from the Second Temple period. Cf. Drawnel, *Qumran Cave 4*.

34. Interestingly enough, although the Enochic writings contain no Mosaic laws, they do use Mosaic language in order to enhance the primacy of Enoch over Moses. Cf. Nickelsburg, "Nature and

as 1 Enoch rarely refers to the Sinaitic covenant and the Mosaic Law. In the words of George W. E. Nickelsburg, "one looks in vain in 1 Enoch for formal parallels to the laws and commandments found in the Mosaic Pentateuch and the Book of Jubilees, nor can one find references to issues like Sabbath observance, the honoring of one's parents, the rite of circumcision, and the full range of cultic laws."[35] In short, Sanders's definition of "common Judaism" is far too narrow and restrictive to encompass 1 Enoch.[36] Moreover, the Enochic corpus is a revolutionary assemblage with an apocalyptic outlook.[37] As such, 1 Enoch not only looks forward to but also advocates the present actualization of a new and better world in the shell of and alongside the old. It seems highly likely that the old world that the Enoch corpus is leaving behind for the new one is precisely the world described by the Moses and the Mosaic Law. For example, the Animal Apocalypse (1 En. 85–90), which adumbrates human history from creation to new creation, glosses over the whole subject of the Mosaic Law (1 En. 89:28–35), looking forward to the final transformation of humankind in the eschaton, when—through the revealed saving wisdom mediated by Enoch—humankind reverts to its original pristine purity in which God created it. In the analogous Apocalypse of Weeks (1 En. 93:1–10 + 91:11–17), the ten-"Week" course of human history culminates in the eschaton, which is a prolonged period beginning in Week 7, that is, the real Jewish author's own time in the Second Temple period: "At its [sc. the seventh Week's] conclusion, the chosen will be chosen, as witnesses of righteousness from the everlasting plant to whom will be given sevenfold wisdom and knowledge" (93:10).[38] It will be a very long time between Week 7 and Week 10, when "sin will never again be mentioned" (91:17), that is, it will be eradicated forever. In the meantime, those who have received revealed wisdom through Enoch are to live in the future anterior, in anticipation of the consummation of history.

Function of Revelation in 1 Enoch, Jubilees, and Some Qumranic Documents," 91–119, here 101. See further Scott, *Apocalyptic Letter to the Galatians*, ch. 2.

35. Nickelsburg, "Enochic Wisdom," 123–32, here 126. For a full discussion of the matters presently under consideration, see Scott, *Apocalyptic Letter to the Galatians*, ch. 2.

36. For Sanders's strongest statement on his least-common-denominator approach to "common Judaism," see Sanders, *Comparing Judaism and Christianity*, 43 (emphasis mine): "Thus, diversity and the creation of subgroups do not necessarily destroy unity. The Pharisees, the Sadducees, the Essenes, the members of the 'fourth philosophy,' the common people, and Hellenistic Jewish philosophers such as Philo all disagreed on lots of points. They all belonged, however, to Judaism. *Where most of them agree* is where we find 'common Judaism.'" With this approach, the Enochic corpus seems to fall through the cracks.

37. The significance of this insight should not be overlooked. In describing Judaism, we need to emphasize how things connect as unfolding forces rather than how they "are," and tendencies that could evolve in creative mutations. Seen as unfolding forces rather than as static essences, the multiple forms of Judaism in the first century CE could follow a path of mutation precipitated through actualization of connections among entities that were previously only implicit, thus releasing new powers in the capacities of those entities to act and respond. In the case of the Enochic form of Judaism, apocalyptic and wisdom traditions have forged new connections that go beyond Mosaic forms.

38. See the summary of the Apocalypse of Weeks in chapter 3 above.

We are arguing that instead of thinking of Judaism in terms of Sanders's fixed, essentialist definition, we regard Judaism as an assemblage that is flexible and changeable enough to encompass the Enochic corpus, just as Judaism is later elastic enough to include the rabbinic Judaism, which underwent a "religious revolution/transformation."[39] The Enochic corpus arose evidently as a consequence of one or more breakdowns or exclusions from standard wisdom tradition,[40] which focuses on the observable, static world, where the general, ethereal and eternal is the order of the day.[41] During the Hellenistic period, under pressure from Hellenistic overlords and under influence from early Stoicism, like-minded scribes immersed in wisdom tradition began to imagine a different world than the one that was currently observable, a new and better world in which those endowed with *sevenfold (perfect) wisdom* would become ascendant (cf. 1 En. 93:10 [cited above]). No sage could discover this new and better world through empirical observation—a world that was once again in synch with heaven—because that world is not the world of present human experience and therefore could only be *revealed* through their hero Enoch, the antediluvian patriarch who, according to Gen 5:24, "walked with God (*'Elohim*)" (or, as the Enochic tradition understands the text, "with the *'elohim* [understood as a plural] = angels"). Enoch was very well connected and had learned practically everything there is to know from his heavenly interlocutors. Moreover, despite their marginalized existence in the present world, the Jewish

39. As we have seen, this is the thesis of Stroumsa, *End of Sacrifice*, esp. 56–83.

40. There is absolutely no reference in standard wisdom tradition—that is, the wise sayings of Proverbs, Job, or Ecclesiastes (Qohelet)—about anything from the Bible, let alone from Israel's illustrious ancestors Abraham, Isaac, and Jacob, nor of Moses or the great Sinai revelation. The relative silence on these matters in the Enochic tradition as well is not happenstance. First Enoch comes out of—or is an offshoot from—wisdom tradition.

41. Cf. Kugel, "Wisdom and the Anthological Temper," 10: "Wisdom usually designated things known. Those things, however, were neither infinite nor random. For, in the ancient world, knowledge was conceived to be *an altogether static thing* [emphasis mine]: whatever a person might come to know belonged to a *defined* corpus of things; it was this finite body that 'wisdom' *designated*. This defined corpus of insights was deemed to play a special role in the world: it underlay all of reality, constituting the great set of master plans by which the world—the natural world, of course, but also human society—was governed. In biblical Israel, as indeed elsewhere in the ancient Near East, this meant that wisdom had a divine character. Wisdom was, in an oft-stated biblical view, the set of plans with which God had created and continued to run the world: 'By wisdom the Lord founded the earth, by understanding He established the heavens' (Prov. 3:19). [Ps. 104:24; 92:6–7] God, in other words, had established a set of highly detailed rules by which His world would be governed: the sun would rise in the east and set in the west, precious metals would be hidden inside rocks and extracted therefrom with fire, storks would roost in fir trees, and so on. Such rules as these three were obvious enough. Other parts of the divine plan, however, were hidden; however finite, the totality of wisdom, of the divine plan, was somehow beyond the grasp of any human being. In alluding to this circumstance, the Bible offers various explanations for it. One, certainly, was that God had intentionally *hidden* the rules by which the world worked, leaving it up to this or that sage to discover individual pieces of the puzzle: 'It is the glory of God to conceal things, and the glory of kings to find them out' (Prov. 25:2)." The kind of sage I have in mind as an example of the breakdown or exclusion from standard wisdom tradition is a disillusioned old man like Qohelet, who "*is* a sage, irredeemably so, yet he frequently holds the received wisdom of sages up to the light and finds it wanting" (Kugel, "Wisdom and the Anthological Temper," 25).

scribal sages who looked to Enoch for the truth began to create that new and better world in the prefigurative future anterior, by living out the life of the sage in perfect harmony with the universe in the here and now. In other words, these Jewish scribal sages were already living in anticipation of their future angelomorphic existence, for which their forebear, Enoch himself, was the model, since he had already undergone the transformation that they all hoped to experience one day.

The importance of all this for our interpretation of Paul and his letters cannot be overstated. For the form of Judaism that we find in Paul and his letters is more like that 1 Enoch than anything else. Like the Enochic corpus, in other words, Paul cannot be subsumed under a Mosaic form of Judaism (so-called "common Judaism").

Paul and the Jesus Revolution

So far, we have been considering Paul with respect to the dominant assemblages of his day—the territorial assemblage of Judaism and the state assemblage of the Roman Empire. What about Paul and the Jesus revolution? In the following, we approach this question in terms of the Enochic wisdom that is at root of both Jesus and Paul and thus something that brings Jesus and Paul together. We also discuss how both Jesus and Paul promoted a nonviolent revolution. In the end, we argue that in his own way, Paul continued to creatively unfold the Jesus revolution.[42]

How are we to understand the relationship between Jesus and Paul? We have already identified Jesus Christ as the abstract machine/condition of the whole New Testament assemblage, which includes the Pauline letters. However, by saying that Jesus Christ is the condition of the Pauline letters as well, that does not necessarily mean that there is a lot of Jesus tradition in Paul. To the contrary, we are struck with how little the Jesus of the Gospels actually comes to expression even tangentially in Paul's letters.[43] We are arguing instead that Jesus' performative proclamation of the

42. One mechanism by which Paul ensured that Jesus Christ as the named condition/abstract machine of the revolutionary assemblage would remain a "living memory" was through ritual connected with the celebration of the Lord's Table (which is functionally similar to the recollection of the exodus from Egypt in the Passover Haggadah). Cf. Bockmuehl, *Seeing the Word*, 181: "Remembrance (*anamnēsis*; Luke 22:19; 1 Cor. 11:24–25) of *Jesus* was of course at the heart of corporate Christian worship from the start. [...] Still, the story of Christian origins is the more remarkable for attaching its founding memory not only to a saving event but also, explicitly, to a saving *person*: 'Do this in memory of me [*eis tēn emēn anamnēsin*]'. ..."

43. On echoes of the Jesus tradition in Paul, see, e.g., Allison, *Constructing Jesus*, 305–86; Dunn, *Theology of Paul the Apostle*, 189–95; Wenham, "Jesus Tradition in the Letters of the New Testament," 2041–57. Paul may have learned about Jesus through his early and extensive contact with Peter (and James) in Jerusalem: "Then after three years [dating from his call/conversion] I did go up to Jerusalem to get to know (*historēsai*) Cephas and stayed with him fifteen days; but I did not see any other apostle except James the Lord's brother" (Gal 1:18–19). On the debate over the use of the verb *historeō* here (which occurs only this one time in the New Testament), see Dunn, *Theology of Paul the Apostle*, 188; "Gal 1,18: ἱστορῆσαι Κηφᾶν," in Hofius, *Paulusstudien*, 255–67, here 262 (author's emphasis): "Zutreffend und einzig möglich ist für ἱστορῆσαι Κηφᾶν Gal 1,18 die Übersetzung: 'um Kephas

gospel of the kingdom[44] and his inauguration of the prefigurative future anterior are what animate and suffuse Paul's approach.[45] Here we are concerned not so much with an exact one-to-one correspondence between Jesus and Paul as with Paul's general

[persönlich] *kennenzulernen.*"' Although the verb itself does not denote "to get information from," it is nevertheless probable that Paul and Peter would have discussed Jesus and his proclamation during that two-week period: "Natürlich ist es denkbar (wenn auch nicht beweisbar), daß Paulus sich bei seinem zweiwöchigen Aufenthalt im Hause des Petrus unter anderem auch über Jesu Erdenwirken und seine Verkündigung hat berichten lassen" (267).

44. Cf. Dunn, *Theology of Paul*, 190: "We may note again the uniqueness of the coinage (singular *euangelion*) and possible allusion to Jesus' words in Rom. 1.16 ('I am not ashamed of the gospel'). Together these observations make quite a strong case for the conclusion that wrapped up in Paul's use of the term was a memory of Jesus as the one 'who preaches the good news (*euangelizomenou*) of peace' (Isa. 52.7), one who was sent 'to bring good news (*euangelisasthai*) to the poor' (Isa. 61.1), and that Paul was a least sometimes aware of this (Rom. 1.16). A second allusion can be recognized in the rather striking but not much commented on parallel between Jesus' and Paul's teaching on the kingdom (of God). That the kingdom of God was a central feature of Jesus' preaching is well known. We would expect anyone who knew or cared about Jesus' ministry to be aware of this. Paul, however, says very little about the kingdom. Where the term does occur, it usually appears in the formulaic talk of 'inheriting the kingdom' [1 Cor 6:9–10; 15:50; Gal 5:21; cf. Eph. 5:5; Matt 5:5; 19:29], or with similar future eschatological reference [1 Thess 2:12; 2 Thess 1:5; cf. Col 4:11; 2 Tim 4:1, 18; of Jesus' eschatological but present reign, 1 Cor 15:24; cf. Col 1:13]. This suggests that the category of 'the kingdom of God' lay to hand in the common stock of early Christian tradition. Paul took it up as occasion demanded, as an obviously familiar theme. In contrast to Jesus, however, Paul made much more of the term 'righteousness.' Indeed, the inverse ratio between the two uses has suggested to some that Paul, with some deliberateness, replaced Jesus' emphasis on the kingdom with his own emphasis on righteousness." See further Stuhlmacher, *Gospel and the Gospels*.

45. Cf. Bockmuehl, *Seeing the* Word, 42–43, who advocates reexamining "the 'Paul and Jesus' question—not merely from the old-fashioned source-critical perspective of 'how much Paul knew,' but by genuine comparison of Paul and Jesus on newly topical issues like God, Messiah, Israel, Jerusalem, law, ethics, kingdom, resurrection, and eschatology." Contrast Welborn, *Paul's Summons to Messianic Life*, xv: "Crucially, the temporality that Paul posits as a creation of the messianic event stands opposed to every philosophical teleology; there is no room in Paul's 'now time' for the future. I shall argue that Paul's concept of the 'now time' can only be understood when it is located in proximity to Jesus' proclamation of the nearness of the kingdom of God." Welborn, *Paul's Summons to Messianic Life*, xvi: "I will argue below that Paul's eschatology underwent significant development from his first epistle (1 Thessalonians) to his last (Romans), and that this development had the character of an intensification: that is, the future hope of Paul's early years became, in the crucible of his suffering, a present reality. This is a crucial contribution to my dialogue with the philosophers, since even the best of Paul's philosophical interpreters are captive to the traditional notion that Paul decomposed the messianic event into two times—resurrection and *parousia*—and that Paul continued to await the Second Coming of Jesus at the end of time. I will argue below that those who are waiting for the inevitable to happen, remain enthralled by the future, and so never enter with Paul into the 'today of salvation.'" Welborn, *Paul's Summons to Messianic Life*, xvii: "In this midnight of the twenty-first century, we must hold fast to the memory of Paul, who did not despair of glimpsing in the little groups of mainly oppressed persons who had joined his messianic assemblies the vanguard of the sons and daughters of God, who would awaken and take responsibility for the redemption of the world (Rom. 8:19)." Alas, it is unnecessary to deny that Paul is oriented ultimately on the *Parousia* even as he emphasizes creating the future anterior in the here and now. On Welborn's understanding of the Pauline concept of "the now time" by locating Paul's usage in relation to Jesus's proclamation of the "nearness" of the kingdom of God (Mark 1:15; Luke 10:9, 11//Matt 10:7 [Q]), see further Welborn, *Paul's Summons to Messianic Life*, 17–21; cf. Allison, *Constructing Jesus*, 124 with n424.

orientation and trajectory.[46] We have already observed that Paul admonishes obedience to the state assemblage of the Roman Empire, not least in the matter of paying taxes (Rom 13:1–7). On this particular issue, Paul seems quite similar to Jesus, who enjoined paying taxes to Caesar: "Give to the emperor the things that are the emperor's, and to God the things that are God's" (Mark 12:13–17).[47] Jesus and Paul sought to pursue their revolutionary agenda without unduly antagonizing the Roman government. For Paul, Christ is a model to imitate in a general sense, which does not involve strict copying.[48] Paul describes himself as an "ambassador for Christ,"[49] that is, one who speaks semi-autonomously on behalf of his Lord, creatively adapting his approach to each contingent situation.

As it turns out, the general contours of what Paul says and does in the spirit and power of Christ have much in common with the Enochic tradition. For in all three cases, the revelation of saving wisdom is understood as key to constructing life in the future anterior.[50] In other words, belief in the good news of the kingdom, which Jesus

46. Take, for example, 1 Cor 13, as aptly described in Allison, *Historical Christ*, 27–29. Although the words in v. 2, "if I have all faith so as to move mountains, but do not have love, I am nothing," may echo Jesus' promise about the power of faith (Matt 17:20; 21:21; Mark 11:23), the Love Chapter is entirely Paul's own work; it does not claim to derive from Jesus. Yet, as early Christian commentators on the passage well recognized, it is Jesus' influence, his vision, his teaching that animated Paul to write as he did. Like Jesus, Paul makes love the chief virtue (e.g., Matt 5:43–48; 19:19; 22:34–40). Like Jesus, Paul says that matters of the heart are more important than all outward show (e.g., Matt 6:22–23; 12:33–35; 15:7–20). Like Jesus, Paul calls for patience, kindness, and long-suffering (e.g., Matt 5:21–26, 38–42, 43–48). To put the matter in assemblage terms, Jesus is the abstract machine/ condition for Paul's Love Chapter. Jesus was a real person and a real memory, and he became a living tradition that encouraged some construals and discouraged others. Clearly, however, in writing the Love Chapter, Paul exercised considerable creativity in his unfolding of the Jesus revolution, and particularly Jesus' emphasis on revolutionary love.

47. In his *Apology* addressed to Emperor Antoninus Pius, Justin Martyr asks that Christians not be condemned for the "name" alone (7.1–5); he defends them against the charge that the kingdom (*basileia*) which they awaited was an earthly one (11:1–2); and he emphasizes the law-abidingness of Christians and their long-established acceptance of paying taxes (17.1–4).

48. Cf., e.g., 1 Cor 11:1; 2 Cor 8:8; Phil 2:5–11; Eph 5:2.

49. Cf. 2 Cor 5:20: "So we are ambassadors for Christ, since God is making his appeal through us; we entreat you on behalf of Christ, be reconciled to God." On reconciliation in 2 Cor 5:18–20 as a political metaphor denoting the cessation of hostilities between warring parties, see Breytenbach, *Versöhnung*. The fact that the first person plural (*presbeuomen*) is juxtaposed to "you" (i.e., the Corinthians) shows that the "we" refers primarily to Paul himself, in keeping with the defense of his apostleship in 2 Cor 2:14–7:4. On ancient ambassadorship, see further Savalli-Lestrade, "Ambassadeurs royaux, Rois ambassadeurs," 695–718; Bash, *Ambassadors for Christ*. On the use of the first-person plural in official/royal correspondence, see chapter 8 below. For examples from the late Republic and early Imperial periods, see Sherk, *Roman Documents from the Greek East: Senatus Consulta and Epistulae to the Age of Augustus*. As Sherk points out (*Roman Documents from the Greek East*, 193), "The general agreement between the phrases and modes of expression of the Hellenistic letters and those in the Roman is striking. Diplomatic courtesy and chancery procedure had developed a pattern to be followed in the opening remarks of official Greek letters. The Romans took up this pattern, consciously or unconsciously, and used it in their own correspondence." Seleucid officials usually used the first-person plural. Cf. Ma, *Antiochos III*, 271, 298, 294.

50. On Jesus' intimate connection with wisdom, we can appeal to any number of texts. For example,

proleptically proclaims, is the basis for Paul's gospel message as well. This is a message that makes one wise unto salvation, that is, enables one to successfully come through the final judgment, but that wisdom is needed in the here and now to create the future anterior, in anticipation of the consummation.

Paul contrasts the wisdom of the world with the saving wisdom of God, for according to God's wisdom, of which Jesus is the embodiment,[51] the world is currently upside down and needs to be turned right side up. The means by which God chooses to accomplish this revolution are, from the world's point of view, utterly foolish: the performative message about a crucified royal pretender. Thus, we read in 1 Cor 1:18–25:

> For the message about the cross is foolishness to those who are perishing, but to us who are being saved it is the power of God. For it is written, "I will destroy the wisdom of the wise, and the discernment of the discerning I will thwart." Where is the one who is wise? Where is the scribe? Where is the debater of this age? Has not God made foolish the wisdom of the world? For since, in the wisdom of God, the world did not know God through wisdom, God decided, through the foolishness of our proclamation, to save those who believe. For Jews demand signs and Greeks desire wisdom, but we proclaim Christ crucified, a stumbling block to Jews and foolishness to Gentiles, but to those who are the called, both Jews and Greeks, Christ the power of God and the wisdom of God. For God's foolishness is wiser than human wisdom, and God's weakness is stronger than human strength.

Paul goes on to say that the divine wisdom revealed in the crucified Christ was—and continues to be—incomprehensible to the "rulers of this age" who "crucified the Lord of glory" (1 Cor 2:6, 8).[52]

Not only is the wisdom of God itself foolishness to the world, but the people who are being saved by this wisdom are utterly contemptible from a worldly perspective.

Paul identifies Jesus Christ as "the wisdom of God" (1 Cor 1:24); Christ Jesus "became for us wisdom from God" (1 Cor 1:30). In Christ "are hidden all the treasures of wisdom and knowledge" (Col 2:3). The sheer number of aphorisms in the Jesus tradition suggests that Jesus was a sage and teacher of wisdom. Cf. Aune, "Oral Tradition and the Aphorisms of Jesus," 211–65, here 240–41. However, Jesus as wisdom teacher is often seen as a mutually exclusive alternative to his apocalyptic focus. See the discussion in chapter 3. Cf., e.g., Vorster, "Jesus," 526–43. It is now widely recognized, however, that this is a false alternative. Jesus' sayings in the Q material, for example, must be seen as mingling wisdom and apocalypticism. Cf. Andrejevs, *Apocalypticism in the Synoptic Source*, 23–58. See further Allison, *Constructing Jesus*, 31–220. Whereas the wisdom passages in the double tradition (Q) emphasize Jesus' message rather than the relation of Jesus himself to divine wisdom (cf. Matt 12:42//Luke 11:31; Matt 11:16–19//Luke 7:31–35; Matt 23:34–36//Luke 11:49–51; Matt 23:37–39//Luke 13:34–35), Matthew's presents Jesus not just as wisdom's messenger but as wisdom itself (Matt 11:2–19, 25–30; 23:34–39). See further Burnett and Bennema, "Wisdom," in Green et al., *Dictionary of Jesus and the Gospels*, 995–1000.

51. Cf. 1 Cor 1:30: "He [sc. God] is the source of your life in Christ Jesus, who became for us wisdom from God, and righteousness and sanctification and redemption."

52. On "anti-wisdom wisdom," see Najman, *Losing the Temple and Recovering the Future*, 136–42.

Hence, in calling the Corinthians to faith, God "chose what is foolish, . . . weak, . . . low and despised in the world, things that are not, to reduce to nothing things that are" (1 Cor 1:26–29).[53] This completely subverts the stratified world order, in which those on top are always the strongest, the greatest, the richest, the most intelligent, and the most beautiful. In thereby espousing the very opposite of cultural expectations, Paul, in his own way, unfolds the implications of Jesus' call in Mark 10:42–45 for a complete overturning of the status expectations of normal leadership. The new standard is servanthood based on the model of the Son of Man who serves and gives his life as a ransom for many. At the same time, we should recognize that all this is a work in progress. Although "the present form of the world is passing away" (1 Cor 7:31), "every ruler and every authority and power" has not yet been destroyed, as will happen at "the end" when God subjects "all things" to Christ (1 Cor 15:24–28). Hence, from a worldly perspective, the minuscule evidence of any tangible world renewal at present, let alone the sorry condition of some of Paul's own communities and the persecution that Paul continues to suffer, can be used as a further reason to deride Paul's proclamation of the Jesus revolution as a fool's errand. Undaunted, Paul declares that current circumstances, counterintuitive though they may be, allow the power of God to be demonstrated all the more clearly (2 Cor 12:8–10).

Conclusion

In this chapter, we have been exploring how Paul takes up the Jesus revolution and continues to actualize it in the here and now in anticipation of the consummation at the Parousia. As we have seen, Jesus' faith in the world to come did not take him out of the world *but rather all the further into it*. In a similar way, the process of actualization that the apostle undertakes is not a preprogrammed path, but rather a creative unfolding. But it is a creative unfolding that pertains to the present in light of the expected future.

In 1 Cor 6:1–8, for example, Paul worries about the Corinthians' commitment to the Jesus revolution and about their being recaptured by the mundane state system (relative negative deterritorialization) when they sue each other in court:

> When any of you has a grievance against another, do you dare to take it to court before the unrighteous, instead of taking it before the holy ones (*tōn hagiōn*)? Do you not know that the holy ones will judge the world? And if the world is to be judged by you, are you incompetent to try trivial cases? Do you not know that we are to judge angels—to say nothing of ordinary matters? If you have ordinary cases, then, do you appoint as judges those who have no

53. Compare Deleuze's description of the revolutionary people—"the people to come": "This is not exactly a people called upon to dominate the world. It is a minor people, eternally minor, taken up in a becoming-revolutionary. Perhaps it exists only in the atoms of the writer, a bastard people, inferior, dominated, always in becoming, always incomplete." Cf. Deleuze, *Essays Critical and Clinical*, 4.

standing in the church? I say this to your shame. Can it be that there is no one among you wise (*sophos*) enough to decide between one brother and another, but a brother goes to court against a brother—and before unbelievers at that? In fact, to have lawsuits at all with one another is already a defeat for you. Why not rather be wronged? Why not rather be defrauded? But you yourselves wrong and defraud—and brothers at that. (1 Cor 6:1–8)

According Paul, Christ-followers are to live in the future anterior by judging each other in the present Christ-assembly in the same way that they will judge the angels at the consummation. Because they are constructing the prefigurative new world in the shell of and alongside the old, law courts of the mundane world that is passing away are irrelevant for believers on the "plane of consistency" (where becomings take place). Their autonomous judgment of each other takes place within the purely immanent criterion, which is conditioned by Christ. Based on the above discussion of 1 Corinthians, we are now able to add that Paul identifies Christ with Wisdom (*Sophia*), so being "wise" (*sophos*) enough to judge each other within the Christ-assembly (1 Cor 6:5) is clearly a function of Christlikeness. Alas, insofar as the Corinthians are presently taking each other to secular courts, they are only virtually the people to come.

Paul's perspective in 1 Cor 6:1–8 can be compared to the Enochic/Stoic tradition in which civil law courts play no role for sages/"holy ones" and gods/angels are structural components of the cosmos.[54] The Enochic tradition also prominently features the judgment of the rebel angels (the Watchers) in the eschatological future.[55] In his essay on "Why Should Women Cover Their Heads Because of the Angels? (1 Corinthians 11:10)," Loren T. Stuckenbruck interprets Paul's concern for women's head coverings in light of the Enochic tradition of the fallen angels.[56] Once again, those seeking to construct the future anterior must be careful of redeterritorialization by the powers that be.

---

54. Cf. Scott, *Apocalyptic Letter to the Galatians*, chap. 2.

55. Cf. Stuckenbruck, *Myth of the Rebellious Angels*, 12–17, 22–24. Insofar as the Enochic tradition foresees the eschatological judgment taking place *on earth* (116), this may be the source of Paul's concept of human involvement in the event. See further Davis Bledsoe, "Throne Theophanies, Dream Visions, and Righteous(?) Seers," 85–86.

56. Stuckenbruck, *Myth of the Rebellious Angels*, 257–80.

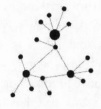

7

Paul's Vision of the Personae in the Revolutionary Assemblage

The New "We" (Gal 3:28)

Introduction

IN THE PREVIOUS CHAPTER, we gained an overview of how Paul and his letters challenge us to rethink how the Jesus revolution can be actualized in the here and now. We were introduced to a creative process of becoming-other that extends to new modes of existence in every area of life. For Paul, one of the key components of this ongoing, comprehensive process of transformation is becoming the people to come. This people does not yet exist, but in at least two ways, it is in the process of becoming.[1] First, those who are in the revolutionary process of becoming the people

---

1. Cf. Lundy, "Call for a New Earth, a New People," 119–39, here 132: "The people who are missing, who are yet to come, are not and cannot be known in advance, even by those who bring them forth, for they are not a possible people. Rather, and most importantly, *they must be created*. In the context of art, *where* does an original piece of work reside before it is created? Nowhere. It is created in the act of creation—line by line, paint stroke by paint stroke; and in most cases the created can only be retrospectively identified as such, including the possibility that such a thing could be created. When an artist creates an earth-shattering work, they often do not even 'know' what it is they are doing (or how), let alone know in advance the precise features of the work as a 'possibility.' To borrow another example from Bergson, where did *Hamlet* reside before Shakespeare wrote it . . . ? The suggestion that *Hamlet* existed in the ether as a fully-formed possibility before it was created is absurd. So too with the people to come."

to come are breaking down the social stratification, the hierarchical structures, imposed by the usual standards of the mundane world. This is the vertical dimension of the transformative process. Second, those who are in the process of becoming the people to come are committed to making new connections with any and all Christ-followers, in order to construct a new revolutionary body politic in a new and better world. This is the horizontal dimension of the transformative process, which makes the Jesus revolution translocal or cosmopolitan. Taken together, these two dimensions of the transformative process mark out a new "We" that creates the prefigurative future anterior. Galatians 3:28 illustrates this new mode of existence better than practically any other Pauline text.[2] Therefore, an extended treatment of this important text is essential to our project.

In his recent article on "Paul the Cosmopolitan?" Christopher D. Stanley disputes the idea that Paul espoused a "cosmopolitan" ideal:

> The apostle Paul has been viewed by many as a cosmopolitan thinker who called Christ-followers to embrace the ideal of a single humanity living in harmony with a divinely ordered cosmos. A close comparison of Paul's apocalyptic theology with various interpretations of "cosmopolitanism" over the centuries, however, shows few points of agreement. Paul was fundamentally a Jewish sectarian whose vision for a better world embraced only Christ-followers and involved the cataclysmic end of the present world order. Those who accepted and lived by this vision were effectively relegated to the same marginal position in civic life as the local Jewish community.[3]

There are several difficulties with this approach to the issue at hand. First, although he mentions Gal 3:28 as a text that has been thought to express Paul's "cosmopolitanism," Stanley does not discuss it at any length: "Verses such as Gal 3.28, Eph 2.19 and Col 3.11 are often cited as evidence that Paul envisioned (and perhaps even sought to create) a world in which all merely local attachments and identities are relativised and transcended by the loftier ideal of a single humanity living in harmony with a unified, divinely ordered cosmos."[4] Stanley argues that "these interpretations represent a serious misreading of Paul's rhetorical strategies," and "underestimate the extent to which Paul was embedded in a Jewish symbolic universe that required non-*Ioudaioi* Christ-followers to renounce central elements of their own world-view and social identity that relegated them to a peripheral social location in the *polis/colonia* similar to that held by Diaspora Jews. In short, Paul remained a Jewish sectarian even as he laboured to bring non-*Ioudaioi* into the nascent Christ-movement, which he regarded

---

2. The following is based in large part on my article, "Galatians 3:28 and the Divine Performative Speech-Act of Paul's Gospel," 180–200, to which has been added further insights from our developing Biblical Theology of the New Testament.

3. Stanley, "Paul the Cosmopolitan?," 144.

4. Stanley, "Paul the Cosmopolitan?," 144. There is only one other brief mention of Gal 3:28 in his study. Cf. Stanley, "Paul the Cosmopolitan?," 154n27.

as a thoroughly Jewish project."[5] My contention, however, is that before such a perspective can be accepted, Gal 3:28 deserves a much more nuanced discussion.[6] As we shall see, Paul's perspective was indeed thoroughly Jewish, but it was nonetheless "cosmopolitan" in a certain sense of the word.[7]

This leads to a second problem with Stanley's approach: the way he defines "cosmopolitanism." Based on a brief and selective overview of the various ways in which the term "cosmopolitanism" has been understood from ancient times to the present,[8] Stanley seeks "to demonstrate that Paul does not fit well under any of these rubrics, and that he in fact stands far removed from any 'cosmopolitan' vision of human social life, with the partial exception of the ancient Cynics."[9] Nevertheless, Stanley also rejects the comparison with Cynic cosmopolitanism because of his conviction that Paul is a Jewish sectarian: "His identity was inseparably tied to a particular people, not to humanity in general. . . ."[10] As we shall see, however, it is Stanley's definition of "cosmopolitanism" that is problematic here.

The following discussion will deal with these issues in reverse order. First, we will consider recent research into ancient "cosmopolitanism" in order to secure a working definition of the term for our purposes. This will help us to ascertain whether—and, if so, in what sense—Gal 3:28 can be categorized as "cosmopolitanism." Second, we will examine Gal 3:28 itself—its context and interpretation, including the textual support for εἷς ("one") in verse 28d, which is crucial if this verse can be described in terms of "cosmopolitanism."

Definition of "Cosmopolitanism"

Whereas Stanley focuses largely on ancient *philosophical notions* of "cosmopolitanism,"[11] we will concentrate here on ancient political practice of "cosmopolitanism." Our

5. Stanley, "Paul the Cosmopolitan?," 145.

6. For example, Stanley does not recognize the citation of Gen 1:27 in Gal 3:28c, which is crucial for the interpretation of the passage in context. Stanley's only mention of Gen 1:27 is in reference to 1 Cor 11:7 (cf. Col 3:10). Cf. Stanley, "Paul the Cosmopolitan?," 157n31.

7. For a helpful overview of interpretive approaches to Gal 3:28, see Tolmie, "Tendencies in the Interpretation of Galatians 3:28 since 1990," 105–29. For other recent studies of Gal 3:28, see, e.g., Breytenbach, "Taufe als räumliche Metapher in den Briefen des Paulus," esp. 133–35; Neutel, *Cosmopolitan Ideal*; Martin, "Queer History of Galatians 3:28," 77–90; Yarbro Collins, "No Longer 'Male and Female' (Gal 3:28)," 27–39; Hogan, *No Longer Male and Female*; Uzukwu, *Unity of Male and Female in Jesus Christ*.

8. Stanley, "Paul the Cosmopolitan?," 146–54.

9. Stanley, "Paul the Cosmopolitan?," 145. For a comparison of Paul's letters with each of the cosmopolitan models surveyed by Stanley, see "Paul the Cosmopolitan?," 154–61.

10. Stanley, "Paul the Cosmopolitan?," 156; cf. also 155: "Only those who are devoted to Christ at his coming will share in this world [to come]; it is sectarian to the core."

11. As Stanley discusses, the term "cosmopolitan" has its origins in Greco-Roman philosophical traditions that can be traced back to the fourth century BCE. Diogenes of Sinope is said to have called

approach is guided by the book edited by Myles Lavan, Richard E. Payne, and John Weiswiler, *Cosmopolitanism and Empire: Universal Rulers, Local Elites, and Cultural Integration in the Ancient Near East and Mediterranean*, which aims to reclaim the term "cosmopolitan" for historical analysis.[12] The editors explain their method: "Like other analytical terms derived from Greco-Roman traditions, such as 'political,' 'imperial,' or 'urban,' the usage of 'cosmopolitan' should be rooted in our own contemporary political-theoretical discourse, rather than Hellenistic or Roman thought. The aims of historical analysis differ from those of the philosophers, political theorists, and literary scholars who have developed and debated cosmopolitanism in recent decades. It is the value of the concept in elucidating social and political structures and changes rather than its abstract meaning that is of concern to historians."[13] In other words, the editors are involved in the "etic" side of the historical project (i.e., second-order, professional, external meta-interpretations of first-order data), in contrast to an "emic" exploration of the ancients' categories (i.e., first-order, sociocultural, internal interpretations concerning any society's own origin stories, worldviews, etc.).[14] The genre "apocalypse," for example, is a modern *etic* category rather than an ancient *emic* one, but it has enabled fruitful comparison of a wide variety of ancient texts.[15]

---

himself a *kosmopolitēs*, "a citizen of the cosmos." Subsequent thinkers, notably the Stoics, articulated a form of citizenship that transcended the bounds of the *polis*—hitherto thought to constrain human political possibilities—in order to encompass all of (sage) humanity in a universal community ordered by universal law. We may add that according to Plutarch (*On the Fortune of Alexander* 329A–B [*SVF* 1.262, part]), Zeno of Kition originated this vision for humanity: "The much-admired *Republic* of Zeno, the founder of the Stoic school, is aimed at this one main point, that we should not dwell in cities or peoples, each one marked out by its own notions of what is just, but we should regard all human beings (*pantas anthrōpous*) as our fellow members of the populace and fellow-citizens (*politas*), and there should be one way of life and order, like that of a herd grazing together and nurtured by a common law. Zeno wrote this, picturing it as if it were a dream or image of a philosopher's well-regulated society, but it was Alexander who gave effect to the idea." For a full discussion of this text and its comparison to the eschatological finale of the Animal Apocalypse (1 En. 90:37–38), see Scott, *Apocalyptic Letter to the Galatians*, ch. 2. There, it is argued that, like the Stoic concept of citizenship in the universal cosmic city, the Enochic vision entails an alternative to ethnicity that transcends ethnic boundaries. The Animal Apocalypse does not envision a different race or ethnic group. Rather, it represents a return to the originally intended condition of undifferentiated humankind, before it disintegrated into mutually hostile ethnic groups governed by their own separate systems of positive law.

12. Lavan et al., *Cosmopolitanism and Empire*, 2.

13. Lavan et al., *Cosmopolitanism and Empire*, 10.

14. Cf., e.g., Harris, "History and Significance of the Emic/Etic Distinction," 329–50.

15. Cf. Collins, "Genre Apocalypse Reconsidered," 21–40, who reflects on the definition of the genre "apocalypse" that emerged from the SBL working group in 1979 (23–24): "We viewed the genre as an etic category: 'It is important to note that the classification "apocalyptic" or "apocalypse" is a modern one. Some ancient Jewish, Christian and Gnostic words are entitled *Apokalypsis* in the manuscripts . . . However, the title is not a reliable guide to the genre.' . . . our definition was at a higher level of abstraction than the self-presentation of individual texts . . . while I do not dispute the value of emic analysis of the self-presentation of texts, this does not invalidate the use of analytic categories, based on the commonalities we now perceive between ancient texts, whether their authors perceived them or not." For a critique of the genre "apocalypse" as an etic category, see Newman, "Participatory Past," 418–21, 423–24.

The editors of the volume go on to define the key term:

> *Cosmopolitanism* designates a complex of practices and ideals that enabled
> certain individuals not only to cross cultural boundaries but also to establish
> an enduring normative framework across them. The historically particular
> ideals that led certain groups to transcend distance and difference also com-
> pelled them to develop practices that could integrate geographically and
> culturally disparate populations. Cosmopolitanism might thus be defined as
> theoretical universalism in practice. Whether a conqueror, a monk, or a mer-
> chant, the cosmopolitan regards an encounter with a politically, linguistically,
> ethnically, and/or religiously distinct group as an opportunity to incorporate
> its members into their network of political, religious, or economic communi-
> ties. Recognition of the legitimacy of groups qua groups has therefore been a
> feature of all historical cosmopolitanisms, but, as only the cosmopolitan had
> the capacity to recognize, this had the effect of enforcing the subordination
> of the recognized. Once the encountered group had accepted the terms of
> integration, the cosmopolitan found himself in an incommensurably superior
> position, as the author of their shared norms. Such relations were established
> against the backdrop of disparities of power, with the cosmopolitans in pos-
> session of superior political, military, ideological, or economic resources.[16]

The editors of *Cosmopolitanism and Empire* offer four general conclusions that emerge
from the volume as a whole.[17] First, cosmopolitan practices and interactions were
essential for imperial cohesion. Second, elite integration operated through the formation of common cultures (assimilation) or the management of differences within a
shared normative framework (subordination) by imperial authorities, usually in some
combination. Third, cosmopolitanism never entirely effaced local differences despite
its ecumenical message. Fourth, integrative approaches highlight how empires could
interact or borrow institutions, ideas, or practices from one another.

The book's emphasis on the dialectic between translocal culture and local accommodation, on the one hand, and between rhetoric and reality, on the other, is instructive for the interpretation of Gal 3:28. Paul's letters are replete with the language
of empire.[18] Indeed, the letter form itself, particularly in Galatians, can be seen as a
reflection of similarly styled royal and imperial letters from the Hellenistic and early
Roman empire, respectively, as shaped by the apocalyptic Epistle of Enoch (1 En. 92–
105).[19] Paul's apocalyptic perspective is already oriented on the worldwide spread of

16. Lavan et al., *Cosmopolitanism and Empire*, 10. The work of Iran Malkin on networks and the
emergence of the Greek-speaking world complements this understanding of "cosmopolitanism." Cf.
Malkin, *Small Greek World*.

17. Lavan et al., *Cosmopolitanism and Empire*, 2–4.

18. The literature on this subject has become voluminous over the past several decades. See chapter 6 above.

19. Cf. Scott, *Apocalyptic Letter to the Galatians*, ch. 4.

God's kingdom.[20] Hence, insofar as the aforementioned dialectic of empire is already present in Jewish apocalyptic literature of the Second Temple period as well,[21] joining these insights about early Judaism with those of the editors and their Cambridge working group on cosmopolitanism will provide cogent arguments in a nuanced, coherent picture of Paul's thinking in Gal 3:28.[22]

Text, Form, Structure, and Context

The text of Gal 3:28 can be set forth as follows in order to show its component parts:

a. οὐκ ἔνι Ἰουδαῖος οὐδὲ Ἕλλην,

b. οὐκ ἔνι δοῦλος οὐδὲ ἐλεύθερος,

c. οὐκ ἔνι ἄρσεν καὶ θῆλυ·

d. πάντες γὰρ ὑμεῖς εἷς ἐστε ἐν Χριστῷ Ἰησοῦ.

The relationship between the whole and the parts in Gal 3:28 is difficult to ascertain. Clearly, the first three pairs belong together in some way. The third pair, however, differs from the other two in its linguistic form. Rather than the form "there is neither Jew nor Greek" and "there is neither slave nor free," the form of the third pair is "there is no male *and* female." The different form of the phrase "male and female" (ἄρσεν καὶ θῆλυ) indicates that it is most likely a citation from Gen 1:27: "And God made the man/human being (τὸν ἄνθρωπον), in accordance with the image of God he made him, *male and female* (ἄρσεν καὶ θῆλυ) he made them." Our interpretation of Gal 3:28 proceeds on the premise that v. 28c is a citation of Gen 1:27. As Karin B. Neutel comments, "Scholars generally agree that the wording of the third pair preserves a quote

20. Cf., e.g., Scott, "Comparison," 193–218. On geographical aspects of Paul's universal vision, see Scott, *Paul and the Nations*; Scott, *Geography in Early Judaism and Christianity*. In a similar vein, see now Fredriksen, *Paul, the Pagans' Apostle*.

21. Cf. Portier-Young, *Apocalypse Against Empire*. As an example of the aforementioned dialectic between translocal culture and local accommodation, we may cite the eschatological expectation of the Enochic literature in which the gentile nations worship of God of Israel without themselves becoming Jews/Judeans. Cf. Stuckenbruck, "Eschatological Worship of God by the Nations," 188–206.

22. A number of authors writing on cosmopolitanism from various angles include a reference to Paul, and particularly Gal 3:28. Cf., e.g., Badiou, *Saint Paul*, 9, 73, 104; Long, "Concept of the Cosmopolis in Greek and Roman Thought," 57; Richter, *Cosmopolis*, 66; Appiah, *Cosmopolitanism*, xiv.

from the creation story in Genesis (1.27), where the same phrase occurs."[23] Seen in this light, Paul's framework is strongly creational.[24]

The fourth part of Gal 3:28 is a declaration that, from a purely syntactical perspective, grounds the negation of the three pairs in v. 28a–c: "*for* you all one in Christ Jesus" (πάντες γὰρ ὑμεῖς εἷς ἐστε ἐν Χριστῷ Ἰησοῦ). Functionally, however, verse 28d expresses the goal of the three negations in v. 28a–c, that is, unity and equality in Christ.[25]

This understanding of Gal 3:28d assumes the Greek text of Nestle-Aland[28], which represents the majority of the witnesses and a broad geographical distribution.[26] This is also the lectio difficilior—and therefore the presumptively stronger reading—insofar as the use of the masculine numerical term εἷς is unique in Paul.[27] Nevertheless, Jens Herzer calls the majority reading into question and argues instead for an (Alexandrian) reading which is represented by P[46] (the earliest witness of the text, *ca.* 200 CE) and Codex Alexandrinus (fifth century): ὑμεῖς ἐστε Χριστοῦ Ἰησοῦ.[28] If Herzer's suggestion is correct, then εἷς (and therefore the potential interpretation of the passage in terms of cosmopolitanism) would be seen as a secondary development that has nothing to do with Paul's original point in context. It is impossible to go into detail on the textual problem at this point. Suffice it to say that if a plausible explanation for Paul's use of εἷς can be found in the immediate context (see below), then the case against the majority reading will be severely weakened.

Is there a progression or "hierarchy of values" within the three pairs of Gal 3:28a–c?[29] At first glance, it might appear that there is a progression from general (Jew-Greek) to specific (male-female), with the middle pair (slave-free) giving the range of possibilities within any given society. However, Adela Yarbro Collins takes another tack:

> The question of a hierarchy of values is difficult to answer with regard to Gal 3:28. If there is a movement from lowest to highest, the male-female pair would be the most important. The rest of the letter to the Galatians, however,

23. Neutel, *Cosmopolitan Ideal*, 187. See also Yarbro Collins, "No Longer 'Male and Female' (Gal 3:28)," 29. For a dissenting voice, see, e.g., Uzukwu, *The Unity of Male and Female in Jesus Christ*, 17–23. Interestingly, many scholars pass over the citation of Gen 1:27 in Gal 3:28c in silence. Cf., e.g., Herzer, "'Alle Einer in Christus'—Gal 3,28b und kein Ende," 124–42, who at first summarizes believers' new status in Gal 3:28 as "jenseits ethnischer, sozialer und *anthropologischer* Unterschiede" (126 [emphasis mine]), but later as "in ethnischer, sozialer und *schöpfungsgemäßer* Hinsicht" (142 [emphasis mine]). The latter seems to presuppose that "male and female" in Gal 3:28c refers to Gen 1:27, but that connection is never made explicit.

24. Cf. Campbell, *Quest for Paul's Gospel*, 98, 101–2.

25. Cf. Yarbro Collins, "No Longer 'Male and Female' (Gal 3:28)," 29.

26. For an exhaustive discussion of Gal 3:28d, see Matthes, *Die Taufe auf den Tod Christi*, 145–50.

27. The closest parallel in the Pauline corpus is Eph 2:15: ἵνα τοὺς δύο κτίσῃ ἐν αὐτῷ εἰς ἕνα καινὸν ἄνθρωπον. See further below.

28. Cf. Herzer, "Gal 3,28b," 124–42.

29. The term "hierarchy of values" comes from Zimmermann, *Die Logik der Liebe*, 58–61.

suggests a different view. The Jew-Greek pair is clearly the most important for Paul, at least in this context. It makes sense to infer that the slave-free pair is next in importance, since he uses metaphorical slavery extensively in the letter. The male-female pair would seem to be the least important for Paul.[30]

In other words, instead of interpreting the pairs in Gal 3:28a–c as a progression from least important (Jew-Greek) to most important (male-female), a contextual reading of Gal 3:28 might lead to the very opposite interpretation: from most important (Jew-Greek) to least important (male-female).

In our view, however, the progression in the three pairs of Gal 3:28a–c is best described as that from general to specific. Moreover, as will be developed further below, the male-female pair in verse 28c, with its different linguistic form and as a citation of Gen 1:27, occupies a pivotal position as a bridge to the declaration of unity in verse 28d.

In terms of form and function, Gal 3:28 is often understood as part of a baptismal liturgy, which may extend to all or part of verses 26–28.[31] 1 Cor 12:13 can be seen as another allusion to the same baptismal tradition: καὶ γὰρ ἐν ἑνὶ πνεύματι ἡμεῖς πάντες εἰς ἓν σῶμα ἐβαπτίσθημεν, εἴτε Ἰουδαῖοι εἴτε Ἕλληνες εἴτε δοῦλοι εἴτε ἐλεύθεροι, καὶ πάντες ἓν πνεῦμα ἐποτίσθημεν.[32] For our purposes, the most important aspect to observe about the form and function of Gal 3:28 is that it is a performative utterance. As Yarbro Collins argues, "The ritual [i.e., baptismal] context give verse 28 a *performative force*: The saying is intended to create the social reality that it declares is the case."[33] On this understanding of the text, "the words expressed in Gal 3:28 during the baptismal ritual would have been meant as an actual enactment of what they express: all baptized persons are qualified to be full members of the church, and no group defined by gender, ethnicity, social, or legal status may be excluded from being 'in Christ.'"[34]

In support of the interpretation of Gal 3:28 as a performative utterance, we may point out that Gen 1:27, which, as we have seen, is cited in Gal 3:28c, is a report on the result of the divine performative in Gen 1:26: "And God said, 'Let us make

30. Yarbro Collins, "No Longer 'Male and Female' (Gal 3:28)," 35. Yarbro Collins ("No Longer 'Male and Female' (Gal 3:28)," 35) goes on to discuss why Paul did not mention the male-female pair in his use of the baptismal formula in 1 Cor 12:13 (cf. also Col 3:10–11). On Col 3:11 and its comparison to Gal 3:28, see also Bormann, "Barbaren und Skythen im Lykostal?," 161–98.

31. Cf., e.g., Breytenbach, "Taufe als räumliche Metapher in den Briefen des Paulus," 133–35; Yarbro Collins, "No Longer 'Male and Female' (Gal 3:28)," 28; Betz, *Galatians*, 184. Betz also argues that Gal 3:28 is a beatitude, even though the term "blessed" is missing (*Galatians*, 183, 185). J. Louis Martyn defines the unit of thought as Gal 3:26–28 and as a baptismal formula. Cf. Martyn, *Galatians*, 373–79. Richard Longenecker refers to Gal 3:27–28 as a "baptismal confession." Cf. Longenecker, *Galatians*, 155.

32. Note, however, that Herzer ("Gal 3,28b," 127–28, 129, 132, 133–34, 141–42) seeks to distance 1 Cor 12:13 from the interpretation of Gal 3:28 on the grounds that many of the entailments in that passage are not present in Galatians.

33. Yarbro Collins, "No Longer 'Male and Female' (Gal 3:28)," 28 (emphasis mine).

34. Yarbro Collins, "No Longer 'Male and Female' (Gal 3:28)," 27; cf. 37.

man/humankind according to our image and likeness' (καὶ εἶπεν ὁ θεός Ποιήσωμεν ἄνθρωπον κατ᾽ εἰκόνα ἡμετέραν καὶ καθ᾽ ὁμοίωσιν)." Through his powerful word, God called humankind into existence. We shall have more to say about this matter below when we discuss how the citation of Gen 1:27 in verse 28c serves as a bridge to the performative utterance in verse 28d.

Hence, even if James D. G. Dunn, among others, is correct in calling into question the hypothesis of Paul's use here of a "baptismal liturgy,"[35] the declaration is most likely performative, as part of Paul's own gospel message.[36] J. Louis Martyn has pointed out that Paul's gospel itself is a performative utterance.[37] According to Martyn, the primary concern of the letter to the Galatians is "to repreach the gospel in place of its counterfeit."[38] In this repreaching of the gospel, Paul begins not from a common rhetorical and thus human point of departure, but from "the divine and thus nonrhetorical point of departure" of Christ's death and resurrection,[39] an event that marks God's apocalyptic invasion into the world to liberate human beings from enslavement to cosmic powers.[40] In Paul's "evangelistic argument,"[41] rhetoric may have its place, but "the gospel itself is not fundamentally a matter of rhetorical persuasion (1:10–12)."[42] Paul is not trying to persuade the Galatians that faith is to be preferred to the law; rather, he is "constructing an announcement designed to wake the Galatians up to the real cosmos, made what it is by the fact that faith has now *arrived* with the advent of Christ" (Gal 3:23–25).[43] Paul's rhetoric is thus "more revelatory and *performative* than hortatory and persuasive," since it "*presupposes God's action through Paul's words*."[44]

35. Cf. Dunn, *Galatians*, 201: "That such a liturgy [i.e., Gal 3:26–28] fitted his argument so neatly is by no means impossible, thought the existence of such elaborate liturgies at this early stage is questionable. . . ; and when the key evidence is from the Pauline letters themselves, it becomes methodologically difficult to distinguish more widespread patterns from characteristic Pauline themes and forms." For further arguments against Gal 3:28 as part of a pre-Pauline baptismal liturgy, see Uzukwu, *Unity of Male and Female in Jesus Christ*, 23–30; Herzer, "Gal 3,28b," 125n3, 141.

36. Cf. Campbell, *Quest for Paul's Gospel*, 95: "correctly understood, it [sc. Gal 3:28] is an excellent summary of the Pauline Gospel."

37. Cf. Martyn, *Galatians*, 23. Paul's gospel is performative because, as the apostle states in Romans, "the gospel is the power of God unto salvation for those who believe, to the Jew first and also to the Greek" (Rom 1:16). Indeed, the gospel that Paul preaches is ultimately based on the "word of Christ (ῥῆμα Χριστοῦ, Rom 10:17), which Paul received through revelation." Cf. Hofius, "Wort Gottes und Glaube bei Paulus," 153–54. Compare, for example, 1 Thess 2:13: "And we also thank God constantly for this, that when you received the word of God that you heard from us, you accepted it not as the word of men but *as what it really is* (καθώς ἐστιν ἀληθῶς)—the word of God, which is at work (ἐνεργεῖται) in you believers."

38. Martyn, *Galatians*, 23.

39. Martyn, *Galatians*, 148.

40. Martyn, *Galatians*, 23.

41. Martyn, *Galatians*, 22, 148.

42. Martyn, *Galatians*, 22.

43. Martyn, *Galatians*, 23 (author's emphasis).

44. Martyn, *Galatians*, 23 (emphasis mine). A striking example of performative language in the

Galatians 3:28 as a Performative Speech-Act

The nature of Paul's performative declaration of the gospel in Gal 3:28 can be further explained in terms of the speech-act theory developed by Angela Esterhammer on the basis of Gen 1–3.[45] This, in turn, will show more clearly the connection of Gal 3:28 with political cosmopolitanism. For as we have seen, the latter entails a dialectic between translocal culture and local accommodation, on the one hand, and between rhetoric and reality, on the other. The same kind of dialectic is found in Esterhammer's description of performativity in Gen 1–3.

According to Esterhammer, there are two types of performative utterance in Gen 1–3: "sociopolitical" and "phenomenological" (although in the latter case, we will use the term "divine/sovereign" instead). The most common performative utterances are embedded in established conventions that derive their primary performative force from their position within sociopolitical institutions (e.g., ethnicity, state, cult, class, education).[46] For this reason, Esterhammer calls them "sociopolitical" performatives.[47] Clearly, the world as we know it operates on the basis of a vast, hierarchical network of such sociopolitical performatives in which the historical, political, and/or cultural context of the speaker or audience shapes meaning. These performative utterances are "political" in the broad sense of being concerned with

---

context of baptismal liturgy is the issue that became public in January 2022: A priest of the Diocese of Phoenix, Arizona, was found to have changed just one word of the ritual, which thereby invalidated a large number of baptisms over a twenty-year period. For the Diocese's official statement, see https://dphx.org/valid-baptisms/, which explains the matter as follows: "The word in question is the use of '*we*' in place of '*I*.' It is not the community that baptizes a person and incorporates them into the Church of Christ; rather, it is Christ, and Christ alone, who presides at all sacraments; therefore, it is Christ who baptizes. The Baptismal Formula (the words used in the Rite) has always been guarded for this reason: so it is clear that we receive our baptism through Jesus and not the community. If you were baptized using the wrong words, that means your baptism is invalid, and you are not baptized. You will need to be baptized." The website also gives the Vatican's statement on using the proper words when conferring the sacrament: "In 2020, the Congregation for the Doctrine of the Faith (CDF) responded to questions about the validity of baptisms if any words are changed. They authoritatively ruled that to say '*We* baptize you in the name of the Father and of the Son and of the Holy Spirit' does not convey the sacrament of baptism. Rather, ministers must allow Jesus to speak through them and say, 'I baptize you in the name of the Father and of the Son and of the Holy Spirit.'" The website explains what happens in baptism: "When you are baptized, your sins are forgiven and your soul is wiped clean!" Since "baptism is the basis of the whole Christian life, the gateway to life in the Spirit (*vitae spiritualis ianua*), and the door which gives access to the other sacraments," all sorts of ramifications follow from the invalidated baptisms, including the validity of marriages in the Church: "Does this [invalidated baptism] affect my marriage? Maybe! Unfortunately, there is no single clear answer. There are a number of variables when it comes to valid marriages, and the Tribunal is here to help."

45. Esterhammer, *Creating States*, 42–64. Esterhammer's approach to performative speech-acts is based, in turn, on the pioneering work of Austin, *How to Do Things with Words*.

46. By the same token, "Societal institutions only exist insofar as they are created by speech acts (charters, vows, declarations of independence) and kept in existence by the exercise of verbal performativity." Cf. Esterhammer, *Creating States*, 27.

47. Cf. Esterhammer, *Creating States*, 12 et passim.

power, knowledge, ascendency, and subordination.[48] This forges another connection with our discussion of political cosmopolitanism.

In her discussion of performatives in Gen 1–3, Esterhammer regards the "Jahwist" version of the creation story in Gen 2:4b—3:24 as representing sociopolitical performatives, which are oriented toward communal order, emphasizing the contractual language of law, which institutes a new order" with marked hierarchy.[49] In Gen 2:19–20, for example, the man, acting as subcreator, names the animals whom God had brought to him, just as God himself had named the things that he had created, according the previous chapter of the received form of the text. The man's performative speech-act thereby establishes his dominion over the animals. In a similar way, God brings the woman to the man, and he names her.[50] The resulting hierarchical relationship between the sexes is reinforced and institutionalized by the divine speech-act of the curse on the woman for her role in the disobedience: "yet your desire shall be for your husband, and he shall rule over you" (Gen 3:16).

The second type of performative utterance is independent of all sociopolitical conventions and institutions. What can be called "divine" or "sovereign" performatives[51] refers to utterances in which the speaker creates a new or alternative reality that is not directly or exclusively dependent upon the sociopolitical context. Rather, such utterances derive their performative force from the sovereign authority of the speaker. The prototype for "divine/sovereign" performatives is the act of creation by the divine word in the "Priestly" account of creation in Gen 1. According to the Genesis text, the ultimate performative speech-act from a biblical perspective was the series of divine utterances, which effected the creation of the world.[52] Here, the sovereign word of

---

48. Cf., Esterhammer, *Creating States*, 95.

49. Esterhammer, *Creating States*, 55.

50. The fact that the woman is said to be derived from the man (Gen 2:21–22) is perhaps a further indication of the woman's subordination to the man. Cf. 1 Cor 11:2–16. On sexual differentiation in creation, see van Ruiten, "Creation of Man and Woman in Early Jewish Literature," 34–62.

51. Our use of the term "divine/sovereign" performative focuses on the speaker's will. However, Esterhammer herself calls this kind of performative "phenomenological," that is, the ability of language to create a world of phenomena by reflecting the consciousness and intentionality of the speaker. For Esterhammer, the "phenomenological performative" is exemplified in God's "Let there be light" (Gen 1:3): "the belief that words can be instruments of meaningful action is nowhere more forcefully imagined than in a myth in which a deity creates the world through acts of speech." Esterhammer, *Creating States*, 48; cf. also 12–13, 42–64, 94.

52. Cf. Bollobás, "Biblical Word Power from a Performative Perspective," 87–88; Esterhammer, *Creating States*, 42–64. Andreas Wagner recognizes several performative speech-acts in Genesis 1 (i.e., 1:22, 28, 29), but does not deal with the acts of creation through the divine word themselves. Cf. Wagner, *Sprechakte und Sprechaktanalyse im Alten Testament*, 66–67, 97, 109, 126, 272, here 159–60: "Einen Sonderfall stellen Jahwes Schöpfungsworte (etwa Gen 1) dar, die hier nicht weiter behandelt werden sollen. Sie müssen natürlich als DEKLARATIVA gelten, die schaffen, was sie beinhalten; zur Qualität als Jahwe-Wort kommt hier noch eine bestimmte Vorstellungswelt des religös-mythischen Kontextes ins Spiel (Vorstellung des Schöpfung durch das Wort), die von der Exegese bereits eingehend beschrieben ist."

God, which acts prior to the existence of any sociopolitical institutions,[53] is the means of bringing a completely new reality into existence.[54]

In Gal 3:28, Paul uses both types of performative utterance as two poles of a dialectic that drives his proclamation of the gospel toward its teleological goal. That is, Gal 3:28a–c implies the results of *sociopolitical* performatives, and verse 28d constitutes a reiteration of the *divine* performative through Paul's proclamation of the gospel. These "two poles" are clearly related to the "dual reality" in which Christ-followers must live in the present (see chapter 5). Or in terms of Deleuze and Guatarri's nomenclature, we are dealing with "the plane of organization" (i.e., the actual sociopolitical situation) and "the plane of consistency" (where becomings take place). We turn now to a fuller discussion of these two poles.

Galatians 3:28a–c represents the results of sociopolitical performatives, conventional utterances that are rooted in sociocultural institutions, where power, domination, ascendency, and subordination are the order of the day. Paul uses the binary opposition between Jew and Greek, slave and free, male and female to illustrate this hierarchical framework, proceeding from general to specific. Clearly, to be a slave puts one at the bottom of the social hierarchy, a hierarchy in which it is much better to be free. The institution of slavery declares some people to be subservient and others to be their masters.[55] The same institution also allows, by various means, for some slaves to attain their freedom through a process of manumission. In any case, the binary

53. God's act of speaking the world into existence in Genesis 1 would seem to have little in common with Austin's concept of "performative utterance," since this divine speech-act preexists and transcends social convention (i.e., extra-linguistic institutions). Nevertheless, Austin's student, John R. Searle, made room for the "supernatural performative" (e.g., Gen 1:3, "And God said, 'Let there be light'; and there was light") in his taxonomy of illuctionary acts, in a section on "declarations." Cf. Searle, *Expressions and Meaning: Studies in the Theory of Speech Acts*, 16–20. For Searle, declarations are cases where one brings a state of affairs into existence by declaring it to exist, cases where, so to speak, "saying it makes it so" (e.g., "I resign," "You're fired," "I excommunicate you," "War is hereby declared"). Declarations "bring about some alteration in the status or condition of the referred to object or objects solely in virtue of the fact that the declaration has been successfully performed" (Searle, *Expressions and Meaning*, 17). "There are two classes of exceptions to the principle that every declaration requires an extra-linguistic institution. First there are supernatural declarations. When, e.g., God says 'Let there be light' that is a declaration. Secondly there are declarations that concern language itself, as for example, when one says, 'I define, abbreviate, name, call or dub.'" See also Searle, "How Performatives Work," 549.

54. Cf. 1 En. 14:22, which describes part of Enoch's vision of the heavenly throne scene: "Ten thousand times ten thousand stood before him, but he needed no counselor; *his every word was deed*." See further Nickelsburg, *1 Enoch 1*, 258n22a, 265, who adduces as a parallel the reference to the creative word of God in Psalm 33(32):9: "he spoke, and it came to be" (הוא אמר ויהי; αὐτὸς εἶπεν καὶ ἐγενήθησαν); see also v. 6 ("By the word of the Lord the heavens were made, and all the host by the breath of his mouth"); Prov 8:22–31, where God creates by means of Wisdom.

55. The economic system in Paul's world relied heavily on the institution of slavery. Slaves worked in mines, fields, and households, where they managed household affairs (family finances, caring for children, etc.). There were various ways in which one could end up becoming a slave: the slave trade, being taken captive as a prisoner of war, being born the child of slaves, and incurring debt that could not be repaid in any other way. Cf. Chaniotis, *Age of Conquests*, 337–43.

opposition between slave and free had major legal, social, and economic ramifications. A slave had few, if any, legal rights, and could be exploited with impunity by the owner. There is no doubt as to which classification—slave or free—is to be preferred. Compare Aristotle's report on the position of the Sophists:

> Others, however, maintain that for one man to be another man's master is contrary to nature, because it is only *convention* that makes the one a slave and the other a freeman and there is no difference between them *by nature*, and that therefore it is unjust, for it is based on *force*. (Arist. *Pol.* 1253b20–23)[56]

The sociopolitical performatives that declare one person to be a Greek and another a Jew, along with the hierarchy and value judgments that go along with these performative utterances, are more equivocal. The value of one ethnicity over another is ultimately a matter of perspective. To some, being or becoming a Jew/Judean is the highest good,[57] and worth considerable personal sacrifice in order to attain or maintain it. The conversion of the royal family of Adiabene (Josephus, *Ant.* 20.17–96) is a salient case in point.[58] To others, being Greek was the ideal. Added to this perspectival issue is the fact that ethnicity can be assigned, manipulated, or forced. Paul charges Peter with "compelling the Gentiles to Judaize" (Gal 2:14), a sociopolitical performative forcing the non-Jews to adopt Jewish ways (or act like Jews) in order to be accepted as members of the community.[59] The institutionalization of these designations meant that they could be applied to different people for different reasons, depending on the circumstances (e.g., citizenship and other political rights, taxation, conscription, political districting).[60]

---

56. Quoted in Betz, *Galatians*, 193n95 (emphasis mine). The Greek text reads: τοῖς δὲ παρὰ φύσιν τὸ δεσπόζειν (νόμῳ γὰρ τὸν μὲν δοῦλον εἶναι τὸν δ' ἐλεύθερον, φύσει δ' οὐθὲν διαφέρειν)· διόπερ οὐδὲ δίκαιον· βίαιον γάρ. Cf. also Chaniotis, *Age of Conquests*, 339, who points out that in the early third century BCE, Epicurus and his contemporary Zeno, the founder of the Stoic school of philosophy, criticized slavery, attributing its existence not to nature but to human convention.

57. Galatians 3:28a refers to the distinction between Jew and Greek, which, in his former Pharisaic worldview, Paul would have considered a fundamental binary defining all social interaction. There is an in-group (Israel—or rather a subset of Israel) and an out-group (the rest of humankind).

58. Cf. Barclay, "Ἰουδαῖος: Ethnicity and Translation," 46–58; Mason, "Jews, Judaeans, Judaizing, Judaism," 506–7.

59. On the meaning of the verb ἰουδαΐζω in Gal 2:14, see the differing perspectives of Steve Mason and Daniel R. Schwartz. Cf. Mason, "Jews, Judaeans, Judaizing, Judaism," 457–512; Schwartz, "Appendix: May We Speak of 'Religion' and 'Judaism' in the Second Temple Period?," in *Judeans and Jews*, 91–112.

60. For example, the issue of who was a Jew/Judean became crucial in establishing liability to the *fiscus Iudaicus*, the tax of two denarii on Jews that went toward the rebuilding of the temple of Jupiter Capitolinus in Rome. Cf. Goodman, "Nerva, the *Fiscus Judaicus* and Jewish Identity," 40–44. In the Roman Empire, it was possible to become a Roman citizen in a number of ways, including by birth or by declaration. Citizenship was the collective assignment of a status. Cf. Lavan, "Foundation of Empire?," 24: "In the earliest phases of Roman expansion, naturalization was employed as a means of organizing and controlling conquered populations. It was a status imposed on rebellious, not loyal, aliens—a striking inversion of later practice."

Gentiles had long been regarded as the Other in Jewish history.[61] The biblical narrative is replete with examples in which Israelite identity is set in sharp contrast with "the Other"—the menacing foreign peoples round about them. The allegorical Animal Apocalypse (1 En. 85–90) portrays Israel as sheep who are continually ravaged by foreign nations, which are depicted as vicious wild animals. Identification of the gentile as the Other reaches its zenith in the daily prayer of thanksgiving recorded in a later rabbinic text: "R. Judah says, 'A person must recite three blessings every day: "Praised are you, O Lord, who has not made me a gentile (גוי)," "Praised are you, O Lord, who has not made me a slave (עבד)," and "Praised are you, O Lord, who has not made me a woman (אשה)"'" (b. Men. 43b).[62] All three of these elements are reflected already in Gal 3:28 (cf. Col 3:11).[63]

Of course, from a Greek perspective the Jew-Greek binary in Gal 3:28a looks quite different. In a text that may be a precursor to the rabbinic passage just cited, Diogenes Laertius (1.33) reports that Socrates used to say that there were three blessings for which he was grateful to Fortune: "that I was born a human being and not an animal, a man and not a woman, a Greek and not a barbarian."[64] Yet, who counted as "Greek" was more complicated than simply a matter of kinship, although it should be noted that the earliest Hellenic explanations had Greeks themselves, not Trojans, as the ancestors of Rome, and the notion of Rome as a "Greek city" persisted for centuries.[65] The development of Greek identity went hand in hand with the consciousness of the "otherness" of barbarians, although the Greek concept of barbarism and "the other" changed over time, with a concomitant prioritization of culture over ethnicity as the primary marker of identity.[66]

As previously mentioned, the male-female binary in Gal 3:28c occupies a pivotal position in what we have termed the two poles of a dialectic. On the one hand, Gal 3:28c harks back to the original divine performative in Gen 1:26–27. From this perspective,

61. Cf. "Jews and Greeks as Philosophers," in Gruen, *Construct of Identity*, 133–52, here 133.

62. Cf. Kahn, *Three Blessings*.

63. Cf. Goldenberg, "Scythian-Barbarian," 87–102. See, however, Uzukwu, *Unity of Male and Female in Jesus Christ*, 8–16.

64. The Greek text reads: πρῶτον μὲν ὅτι ἄνθρωπος ἐγενόμην καὶ οὐ θηρίον, εἶτα ὅτι ἀνὴρ καὶ οὐ γυνή, τρίτον ὅτι Ἕλλην καὶ οὐ βάρβαρος.

65. Cf. "Cultural Fictions and Cultural Identity," in Gruen, *Construct of Identity*, 7–20.

66. Cf. Hall, *Hellenicity*. On the changing notions of "Greekness," see further Jensen, *Barbarians in the Greek and Roman World*, 5, 8, 40, 87–91, 96–97, 111–15; Malkin, *Ancient Perceptions of Greek Ethnicity*; Malkin, "Between Collective and Ethnic Identities," 283–92. Cf. Collins, *Invention of Judaism*, 4–8, who discusses the "constructivist" approach to ethnicity, which emphasizes the malleability of communal identity, and the role of discourse in shaping it. Collins goes on to show that, like the changing notions of what it meant to be "Greek," the understanding of Jewish ethnicity became dislodged in the Hellenistic period from a necessary connection to blood and descent by focusing on a comprehensive way of life as the distinguishing characteristic (8–10). In terms of the political typology of assemblages, we are dealing here with territorial assemblages which change their criteria for inclusion over the course of time. The world is still divided into coded segments that are deemed either natural or proper, but what counts as natural or proper changes.

"male and female" are complementary rather than hierarchical, just like the rest of the binaries in Gen 1.[67] Seen in this light, Gal 3:28c forms a bridge to the divine performative in v. 28d: the new and improved status of unity and equality "in Christ Jesus."[68] This new status is similar to the *divine* performative in Gen 1:26–27 that called "male and female" into existence, because in both cases the relationship between the entities is one of equality rather than hierarchy.[69] Moreover, by virtue of the citation of Gen 1:27 in Gal 3:28c, the new community that the divine performative of Gal 3:28d calls into existence "in Christ" can be seen as the teleological goal of the Pauline gospel—the recapitulation of the originally intended will of God for creation.

On the other hand, Gal 3:28c must also be read in light of what "male and female" became as a result of the *sociopolitical* performatives in Gen 2:4b—3:24 (and, of course, throughout the rest of human history as well). In Gen 2, the already created male *names* the newly formed female who is derived from part of his own body; the male thereby occupies a position of authority over the female, a position that is institutionalized sociopolitically by the subsequent divine curse (another performative) on the woman: "your desire shall be for your husband, and he shall rule over you." In view of the reality of being a female in the first century CE,[70] the binary in Gal 3:28c signifies a hierarchical, male-dominated institution. Only verse 28d unequivocally

67. Cf. Esterhammer, *Creating States*, 54 (author's emphasis): "When the God of Genesis 1 distinguishes between day and night or land and sea, he establishes a type of difference in which opposites are assigned their proper places *as contraries*, but one is not defined in terms of, or as the *negation* of, the other (i.e., darkness is 'darkness' rather than 'non-light,' and vice versa). [. . .] Each member of a pair of terms complements the other, as established in the chapter's ritual refrain, according to which the evening and the morning together make up a unit of time." Note, however, that there is a possible exception to this general pattern: "the two great lights—the greater light to rule the day and the lesser light to rule the night" (Gen 1:16). Nevertheless, both lights are regarded as "great" in their own right, with the difference between them being that of intensity rather than hierarchy.

68. This unity in Christ does not mean uniformity. Individuals are still diverse, but the categories that are used to classify them are broken down.

69. Herzer ("Gal 3,28b," 131–32) is correct that the connection between vv. 28a–c and v. 28d is crucial for the meaning of the latter; however, as previously mentioned, he does not consider the citation of Gen 1:27 in v. 28c ("male and female"), which does provide a basis for understanding the issue in v. 28d as one of unity and equality (oneness) in Christ. Cf. Herzer, "Gal 3,28b," 134 (author's emphasis): "Hier [sc. in Galatians] geht es nicht um die Einheit der Gemeinde als Leib Christi, die dann in dem maskulinen εἷς als einer—wie auch immer zu erklärenden—'Einheitsaussage Gestalt gewänne. Ausweislich vor allem von 3,28a [= vv. 28a–c] geht es nicht um die Einheit, sondern vielmehr um die *Gleichheit* der an Christus Glaubenden unabhängig von ihrem ethnischen, sozialen und genderbezogenen *Status* und auch unabhängig von den Kategorien, die unter den gegebenen gesellschaftlichen, kulturellen und religiösen Umständen alles andere als eine Gleichheit zum Ausdruck bringen. Ähnliches gilt für die Gal 3,28b [= v. 28d] folgende Aussage in V.29 von der Erbschaft der Verheißung Abrahams: Auch hier is nicht die Einheit der Gemeinde das Grundanliegen, sondern ihre Gleichheit im Hinblick auf die Partizipation an diesem Erbe: Sie alle sind insofern 'in Christus' gleich, als sie darin alle—wie Christus (vgl. 3,16)—als Kinder Abrahams gelten." See further below.

70. Cf., e.g., Osborne et al., "Polarities in Religious Life and Inclusions/Exclusions," 247–82, which includes essays on "Male/Female" in the Greek World" (247–61) and "Male/Female in the Roman World" (270–82).

escapes the conventional, sociopolitical performativity and pronounces a new and vastly improved status for *all* those who are "in Christ Jesus."[71]

The swing function of Gal 3:28c points first and foremost to the original divine performative utterance of Gen 1:26–27, which accomplished the creation of humankind as male and female. Galatians 3:28d, in turn, entails a new divine performative utterance—the creation of a new humanity in Christ. Insofar as Paul addresses the declaration to ὑμεῖς, the assemblies of Galatia,[72] which stand pars pro toto for worldwide "assembly" that is being created,[73] the simplest interpretation of the masculine singular εἷς is that Paul is still thinking about Gen 1:26–27, where, as we have seen, the masculine singular noun ἄνθρωπος occurs twice in a generic sense.[74] This generic sense of ἄνθρωπος and the use of εἷς in reference to it is prepared for in the previous context of Galatians by the collective term σπέρμα and the use of εἷς in reference to it: τῷ δὲ Ἀβραὰμ ἐρρέθησαν αἱ ἐπαγγελίαι καὶ τῷ σπέρματι αὐτοῦ. οὐ λέγει· καὶ τοῖς σπέρμασιν, ὡς ἐπὶ πολλῶν ἀλλ' ὡς ἐφ' ἑνός· καὶ τῷ σπέρματί σου, ὅς ἐστιν Χριστός (Gal 3:16). In its original context in Genesis, the "seed" of Abraham is obviously a collective term meaning "offspring."[75] Although Paul initially restricts the "seed" of Abraham to "one" (Christ), he subsequently expands it to include all those who belong to Christ or are part of Christ: εἰ δὲ ὑμεῖς Χριστοῦ, ἄρα τοῦ Ἀβραὰμ σπέρμα ἐστέ, κατ' ἐπαγγελίαν κληρονόμοι (3:29).

Thus, through the use of εἷς in Gal 3:16 and 28, Paul is able to bring several strands of his proclamation together. The God who spoke the world and humankind into existence speaks once again in a new creative act: God speaks through the apostle's gospel

71. On Gal 3:28 in the context of "apocalyptic egalitarianism," see Allison, "Apocalyptic Ethics and Behavior," in Collins, *Oxford Handbook of Apocalyptic Literature*, 295–311, here 307.

72. Cf. Gal 1:2 ταῖς ἐκκλησίαις τῆς Γαλατίας.

73. On the concept of a worldwide "assembly" in Paul's letters, see Trebilco, *Self-Designations and Group Identity in the New Testament*, 179–80. On the relationship between the local and the global, see Müller, "Globalization, Transnationalism, and the Local in Ancient Greece." Particularly important in this regard is the thesis of Malkin, *Small Greek World*, 5: "Greek civilization as we know it emerged, in my view, not in spite of distance but because of it. I will suggest that it was distance and network connectivity that created the virtual Greek center." In a similar way, the emergence of the translocal Jesus movement can be explained as an assemblage that created a virtual center via network connectivity. Hence, the activities that facilitated this connectivity—personal visits, the substitutes for personal visits (letters), the collection for Jerusalem, etc.—are of paramount importance. Indeed, as we shall see in chapter 8, the Spirit-directed lives of individual Christ-followers constitute exemplars of the "letter of Christ" (2 Cor 3:3), that is, substitutes for the personal parousia of Christ for all to read.

74. Given the aforementioned bridge function of Gal 3:28c and the familiarity of the Gen 1:27 text cited there, Paul does not need to express the ἄνθρωπος in order for it to be understood in context. This observation explains how the absolute usage of the masculine εἷς can be both unique in Paul and yet readily explicable on the basis of Gal 3:28 itself. Our interpretation does not require an appeal to the parallel passage in Eph 2:15 (ἵνα τοὺς δύο κτίσῃ ἐν αὐτῷ εἰς ἕνα καινὸν ἄνθρωπον), although the connection there between creation and "one new man" may suggest that the author of Ephesians also thought in terms of Gen 1:26–27.

75. Cf., e.g., Gen 12:7; 13:15–16; 15:5.

message in order to bring about a new creation—the transformation of human beings and indeed the whole world.[76] According to Gal 3:8, however, this performative gospel was preached beforehand to Abraham, explicitly promising that "All nations shall be blessed in you [sc. Abraham]" (citing Gen 12:3).[77] Hence, the means to new creation and universal blessing is by incorporation into Abraham's "seed" through Christ.

Perhaps, however, we are not dealing here with a *new* creative act at all, but rather with the unfolding of the original divine fiat in creation (Gen 1).[78] Judith H. Newman has shown that blessing speech, whether divine (as in Gen 12:1–3) or human (as in Gen 49 and Deut 33), is "potent speech" (i.e., what we have referred to as *performative* utterance):

> Blessings are the only kind of prayer speech that is used both by the deity and by humans. Humans can bless other humans, as we see in the case of testamentary blessings, but they can also offer blessings to God. In that way, human blessings provide an index of divine immanence, of the awe-filled experience of the Creator as potent and privileged creator of time and space, as revealer of heavenly wisdom and cosmic mysteries. Yet these blessings are pronounced by a human mouth using the same faculty of speech in which God created and blessed animals, humans, and even sabbatarian time itself.[79]

---

76. On Paul's conception of the renewal of the world, see Hahne, *Corruption and Redemption of Creation*. Moreover, as a status-changing divine act effecting a new creation, the declaration in Gal 3:28d should not be seen merely as an extension of the baptismal and clothing metaphors in the immediately preceding context (vv. 26–27). Cf. Breytenbach, "Taufe als räumliche Metapher," 134: "Wie die Glaubenden in das Wasser eingetaucht wurden, wurden auch die Galater metaphorisch 'in Christus eingetaucht,' sind damit von ihm umkleidet und haben ihn insofern 'angezogen.' Die Metaphorik wird weitergeführt, sie sind jetzt Juden und Griechen, Sklaven und Freigeborenen, männlich und weiblich gleich gekleidet."

77. Gal 3:8 (citing Gen 12:3; cf. 18:18): προϊδοῦσα δὲ ἡ γραφὴ ὅτι ἐκ πίστεως δικαιοῖ τὰ ἔθνη ὁ θεός, προευηγγελίσατο τῷ Ἀβραὰμ ὅτι ἐνευλογηθήσονται ἐν σοὶ πάντα τὰ ἔθνη.

78. As we have seen, the unfolding of the original divine creative act through human instrumentality is a theme of the Wisdom tradition. Cf. Fretheim, *God and the World in the Old Testament*, 215–16 (emphasis mine): "The effect of such an understanding would be that God does not create in an unmediated way but works in and through Wisdom in bringing the creation into being. Wisdom is thus appropriately described as a created cocreator. This role for Wisdom in creation would be parallel with the way in which creation is sometimes depicted in Genesis 1, where among the 'modes' of God's creating is that of acting through already existent creatures, such as the earth (1:11–13) but especially the 'us,' the divine council, in 1:26. This understanding fits with the relational model of creation we have noted; God chooses not simply to be independent in creative activity. God chooses to be dependent upon wisdom, not only in creating the world but in continuing the relationship with that world. To be an observant and discerning member of such an interdependent creation will then entail hearing both the voice of Wisdom and the voice of God in and to that world—but then proceeding to act on what they hear. *The goal for human beings is to be caught up in the task of cocreating, participating creatively in the continuing becoming of the world.*"

79. Newman, "Participatory Past," 415–34, here 432. On "potent speech," see Newman, "Participatory Past," 432, 433.

Moreover, the divine promise of blessing in Gen 12:1–3 is in effect an open-ended promissory note, which receives a partial fulfillment within the Pentateuch itself and also has an anticipatory function for future fulfillment. "The divine promises are both realized, partially fulfilled at pregnant times and unrealized, awaiting realization at some unanticipated point."[80] In that case, Paul's performative proclamation of the gospel based on Gen 12:3 should be seen in the light of this dual fulfillment scheme: partial fulfillment now and complete realization later.[81] Is it possible that Paul understands Gen 12:3 as one of those "pregnant times" that is actually a further unfolding of the divine performative utterance in the original creation of the world (Gen 1)? This possibility presents itself because Paul identifies the gospel that he preaches as *both* the promise to Abraham *and* God speaking through the apostle's gospel message in order to bring about a new (or renewed) creation. Our discussion of 2 Cor 3–4 in chapter 8 will elaborate on the latter aspect. What is important to consider is whether Paul sees the promise to Abraham and to his "seed" within a creational framework rather than as a completely separate speech-act.

Conclusion

In sum, Gal 3:28 is a performative speech-act containing two poles of a dialectic that drives Paul's proclamation of the gospel toward its teleological goal—the re-creation of humankind according to the originally intended will of God. This involves a form of "political cosmopolitanism" that is both similar to and different from that of empire-builders in the ancient Near East and the Mediterranean.

On the one hand, Paul's form of political cosmopolitanism is *similar* to the others insofar it is dialectical in nature: the declared unity and equality between all those who are in Christ Jesus stands in tension with the hierarchical world as it is known to exist at present. The new world order is, in part, aspirational or virtual, a process that is still underway until its consummation at the Parousia.

On the other hand, Paul's form of political cosmopolitanism is also *different* from the others insofar as the whole basis for the formation of the new humanity in Christ is the performative word of God in an act of new creation effected through the gospel that Paul preaches. The resulting status-change is unlike anything that other political cosmopolitanisms have on offer,[82] for those who are assimilated by faith into the es-

80. Newman, "Participatory Past," 429. In the previous part of the present volume, we have described a similar phenomenon as "the folding of space-time." In chapter 9, we will attempt to bring both of these ideas together in describing the book of Revelation.

81. Compare the aforementioned types of performative utterance as two poles of a dialectic that drives his proclamation of the gospel toward its teleological goal.

82. The a fortiori argument of Stoic philosopher Epictetus (mid-first to second century CE) illustrates just how extraordinary becoming the adopted son of a Caesar would be for commoners in the Roman Empire. Cf. Epictetus, *Discourses* 1.3.1–2 (LCL): "From the thesis that God is the father of mankind how may one proceed to the consequences? If a man could only subscribe heart and soul,

chatological people of God become "sons of God," on par with the unique Son of God, the Lord Jesus Christ, whose identity and heirship they appropriate.

As sons of God, the new humanity in Christ is not a *genos* in the sense of a "third race" in addition to Jews and gentiles,[83] but rather a newly created, undifferentiated humankind corresponding to the originally created humanity (Gen 1:26–27),[84] which subsequently disintegrated into the situation that prevails in "the present evil age" (i.e., rival ethnicities, social stratification, and hierarchical gender differences).[85]

Ultimately, as we have seen, Gal 3:28 is rooted in Paul's Jewish apocalyptic worldview, especially as exemplified in the Enochic tradition, which had already been interacting with the political cosmopolitanism of pagan empires for centuries.

Galatians 3:28 encapsulates Paul's gospel in a wonderfully compelling way, proclaiming the new, unified "We" of humankind that is being re-created "in Christ." In terms of our discussion of the political typology of assemblages and the typology of change in assemblages, what Paul is declaring here is clearly a revolutionary assemblage that is undergoing absolute positive deterritorialization (i.e., the process of revolutionary change to a new form of existence). This is a new type of body politic that is no longer predicated on established norms (i.e., the territorial-body of the vanguard, the party-body of the nation-state, or the market-body of capital).[86] The revolution-

---

as he ought, to this doctrine, that we are all primarily begotten of God, and that God is the father of men as well as of gods, I think that he will entertain no ignoble or mean thought about himself. Yet, if Caesar adopts (εἰσποιήσηται) you no one will be able to endure your conceit, but if you know that you are a son of Zeus (τοῦ Διὸς υἱός), will you not be elated?" See further Scott, *Adoption as Sons of God*, 91–92.

83. On "Christians" as a "third race" separate from Jews/Judeans and gentiles, see, e.g., Harnack, *Die Mission und Ausbreitung des Christentums in den ersten drei Jahrhunderten*, 1.259–81; Kimber Buell, *Why This New Race*; Zetterholm, "Paul within Judaism," in Nanos and Zetterholm, *Paul within Judaism*, 31–51, esp. 47–51; Lieu, *Neither Jew nor Greek? Constructing Early Christianity*, 52–60.

84. It is interesting to note that the Lukan genealogy of Jesus (Luke 3:23–38) culminates in "Adam, son of God" (Ἀδὰμ τοῦ θεοῦ).

85. Paul's understanding of new creation in Gal 3:28 should also be distinguished from the ancient controversy over the propriety of treating the universal "man" like an individual. Cf. Sextus Empiricus, *Against the Professors* 7.246 (*SVF* 2.65, part): "Neither true nor false [impressions, according to the Stoics] are the generic ones. For of things whose species are of this kind or that kind, the genera are neither of this nor of that kind. For example, of men (τῶν ἀνθρώπων) some are Greeks, others barbarians; but the generic man (ὁ γενικὸς ἄνθρωπος) is neither Greek (since then all specific men would be Greek) nor barbarian (for the same reason)." Long and Sedley, *Hellenistic Philosophers*, 1.180 (English translation); 2.184 (Greek text).

86. As an example of the norm-shattering process of transformation in the unfolding Jesus revolution, we may cite the unusual position of women. The book of Acts portrays the Holy Spirit as coming upon both men and women equally (cf., e.g., Acts 1:14; 2:1–4, 17–18; 10:44–47). Thus, from the very beginning, women were present alongside their male counterparts when the Spirit was poured out (Acts 1:14), and then both men and women began to prophesy at the prompting of the Spirit (2:14–18). Whereas women were generally in a position of subjugation in the ancient world (i.e., they were considered property under the authority of fathers and husbands), woman have agency in the book of Acts, independently taking decisive action and leading their homes without consulting a male figure (16:14–15, 40). In the case of one of the only couples mentioned in Acts, the wife Priscilla is named *before* her husband, Aquila, more often than he is named before her (18:2, 18, 26), suggesting

ary assemblage at work here makes possible a truly unlimited qualitative transformation and expansion of the assemblage, allowing for maximal political inclusion and participation. Galatians 3:28 constructs a participatory arrangement in which all the elements of the assemblage enter into an open feedback loop in which the condition (Jesus Christ) and the agents/personae (Christ-followers) all participate equally in the process of transformation. One's ethnic origin is irrelevant. One's social status is immaterial. One's gender is inconsequential. All that matters now is becoming a new creation in Christ along with all that it entails. Specifically, what counts is the extent to which, as they continue to undergo comprehensive transformation both individually and communally, they elude established forms of knowledge and the dominant forms of power. Since, as we have seen, no assemblage exists in a pure form (i.e., all assemblages are composed of a mixture of the four types of assemblages with one type being dominant), a revolutionary assemblage can expect to find tensions within it created by remnants of other ways of forming the body politic. Moreover, the process of change that the revolutionary assemblage undergoes will not be free from a dialectic in lived experience between present realities and the creation of the future anterior. We do find these kinds of tensions in the Pauline assemblies, for example, pertaining to women. Nevertheless, we must keep in mind the anticipated telos of the revolutionary assemblage as proclaimed in Gal 3:28.

The goal of the type of change that the community is undergoing (i.e., absolute positive deterritorialization) is to prefigure a new world; that is, to create, in an anticipatory way, a new world in the shell of the old. We are dealing with a process that creates something new from the subjects and objects that are continually escaping from other assemblages. Or to put it in Pauline terms, those who have been liberated from the present evil age (Gal 1:4). The Pauline assembly is constructive insofar as it builds an alternative, irreducible to the preestablished assemblages of the past. As such, ADP is not just a transfer from an established assemblage to a revolutionary one, but also an ongoing process of transformation that continues until the consummation.

Finally, Gal 3:28 helps Christ-followers to understand why it is important not to regard other people as "the Other," that is, that which is distinct from, different from, or opposite to themselves. That is the root of nationalism, ethnic superiority, class consciousness, and gender inequality. All this fades away when believers

that she was more prominent than he was. In Paul's letters as well, women are portrayed in leadership roles in house-based Christ-assemblies, and they are engaged in ministry alongside men. In Rom 16:3, for example, Paul greets Prisca (i.e., Pricilla) before Aquila, although he quickly adds about them both: "who work with me in Christ Jesus, and risked their necks for my life, to whom not only I give thanks, but also the churches of the Gentiles" (16:3–4). Even more countercultural is the possibility that Paul refers to one of the female addressees of Romans as an "apostle" (*apostolos*): "Greet Andronicus and Junia, my relatives who were in prison with me; they are prominent among the apostles (*tois apostolois*), and they were in Christ before I was" (Rom 16:7). Much ink has been spilled on whether the Greek form *Jounian* in the text should be read as a man's name (Junias) or a woman's name (Junia), but the NRSV translation given here reflects the latter possibility. See further, e.g., Lin, "Junia," 191–209.

consider that they themselves are called to be "the Other": They are *becoming* the new, recreated humanity in Christ. And, it should be noted, as "the Other," they will be regarded as inferior, dominated, always in becoming, always incomplete (cf. 1 Cor 1:26–29; 4:8–13).[87]

---

87. Cf. Deleuze, *Essays Critical and Clinical*, 4 (cited in chapter 6). On persecution in the early Jesus movement, see, e.g., Ste. Croix, *Christian Persecution, Martyrdom, and Orthodoxy*; Gassman, "On an Alleged *Senatus Consultum* against the Christians," 1–8; Schnabel, "Persecution of Christians in the First Century," 525–47; Ehrman, *Triumph of Christianity*, ch. 7; Goodman, "Galatians 6:12 on Circumcision and Persecution," 275–79; Cook, "Chrestiani, Christian, Χριστιανοί," 237–64; Dunne, *Persecution and Participation in Galatians*. On persecution in Galatians, see Scott, "Comparison," 214–16.

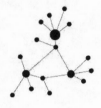

8

The Role of the Spirit of Christ in the Transformative Process

(2 Corinthians 3–4)

Introduction

IN THE PREVIOUS TWO chapters, we have examined Paul's creative unfolding of the Jesus revolution—the construction of a new and better world in the prefigurative future anterior. After securing an overview of the matter in chapter 6, we focused on a particular Pauline text in chapter 7, showing that Paul's performative proclamation of the gospel, like that of Jesus before him, actually enacted the reality that it expressed. Specifically, we explored how Paul's declaration in Gal 3:28, as a reiteration of the gospel that he preached, performatively called a revolutionary body politic into a completely new existence in Christ. This new humanity in Christ recapitulates the originally intended will of God for creation, thereby breaking down all forms of hierarchical stratification that characterize the mundane world, particularly respect to gender, class, and race. We were careful to add, however, that, this side of the Parousia and the ultimate renewal of the world, the process of transformation that is currently underway in the Christ-assemblies is never fully and finally complete. Life in the future anterior is more of an anticipatory trajectory that proceeds by fits and starts than a fixed destination.

In the present chapter, we continue to explore Paul's creative unfolding of the Jesus revolution on the basis of an extended treatment of another Pauline text.[1] Specifically, we examine, on the basis of 2 Cor 3–4, the role of the Spirit of Christ in the aforementioned process of creating the new humanity in Christ through the performative preaching of the gospel. This brings us back full circle to our earlier discussion of Jesus Christ as the condition/abstract machine of the revolutionary assemblage. In the introduction, we noted that the Holy Spirit—variously also called, for example, "the Spirit of Jesus" (Acts 16:7) and "the Spirit of Jesus Christ" (Phil 1:19)—is one way in which Jesus Christ becomes the animating force of the whole movement. Importantly, this also brings us back to Jesus' emphasis on the recapitulation of creation— the process by which "Jesus wants some things even now to be the way they were in the beginning because that is how they are going to be in the kingdom of God."[2] For Paul, as for Jesus before him, the present process of transformation entails a correspondence between *Urzeit* and *Endzeit*. In other words, the end toward which all creation is inexorably moving will have been the re-creation of the world. What 2 Cor 2–3 allows us to see with particular clarity is that the re-creation of the world takes place in the shell of and alongside the old. This passage also shows how the apostle bases his conceptions on the Old Testament. Once again, our project of constructing a *Biblical* Theology of the New Testament comes into focus.

To be more specific, the present chapter explores the meaning and purpose of Paul's citation of the Old Testament in 2 Cor 4:6 in the context of chs. 3–4. In 2 Cor 4:1–6, Paul ends the section with a summary of the nature of his preaching (v. 5) and the glory of his ministry's gospel (v. 6). Of particular interest is the wording in v. 6: "For it is the God who said, 'Let light shine out [or: *Light will shine out*] of darkness' (ἐκ σκότους φῶς λάμψει), who has shone in our hearts to give the light of the knowledge of the glory of God in the face of Jesus Christ." Most scholars think that Paul is citing a modified form of Gen 1:3 LXX here: "And God said, 'Let there be light, and there was light.'" Another possibility is that Paul conflates Gen 1:3 with Isa 9:1, the only other time that φῶς λάμψει occurs in the Septuagint. Considering the wider context of 2 Corinthians in which the citation occurs helps to clarify Paul's point. This chapter consists of two interrelated parts. The first part, on Paul's use of the royal-letter tradition in 2 Cor 3:3, is meant to establish the essential context in chapters 3–4 for understanding the use of Gen 1:3 in 2 Cor 4:6 in the second part.

---

1. The following chapter is based in part on a paper that was presented at the Annual Meeting of the Society of Biblical Literature in November 2020 and is reprinted here from Scott, "Second Corinthians 3–4 and the Language of Creation," 51–69.

2. Allison, *Jesus of Nazareth*, 210.

Part I: Paul's Use of the Royal-Letter Tradition in 2 Cor 3:3

In 2 Cor 2:17, Paul identifies himself[3] as a minister who is "sent from God" (ἐκ θεοῦ) and "stands before God's presence" (κατέναντι θεοῦ).[4] The apostle stands before God not just metaphorically, but rather literally[5] as an Enoch-like figure who shuttles between earth and heaven,[6] with heaven conceived of as a royal court replete with courtiers.[7] In this way, Paul distinguishes himself from his opponents: "For we are not, like so many, peddlers of God's word" (οὐ γάρ ἐσμεν ὡς οἱ πολλοὶ καπηλεύοντες τὸν λόγον τοῦ θεοῦ). Tzvi Novick argues that the image of the peddler here is linked directly to the notion of aroma or fragrance in verses 15–16: "Paul's reference to peddlers in v. 17 depends, I suggest, on the prominence of spices in the inventory of goods furnished by peddlers."[8] As Novick recognizes, however, "the odor imagery of 2 Cor 2:15–16 undoubtedly develops the reference to the triumph in 2:14," although he still insists that "this imagery *also* looks forward to the peddler of 2:17."[9] The problem with this interpretation is that the text does not state that the peddlers are hawking aromatic wares; they are peddling "the word of God" (τὸν λόγον τοῦ θεοῦ). Paul evidently has in mind here something more like the χρησμολόγοι ("collectors/reciters of oracles"), who are often referred to pejoratively as "oracle-mongers."[10] In Aristophanes's *Birds* (957–991) the anonymous *chrēsmologos* is portrayed as a "charlatan" (ἀλαζών) peddler of oracles, which he quotes from a papyrus roll and bogusly attributes to a legendary Boeotian seer named Bacis. As Albert Henrichs points out, the dialogue in *Birds* suggests that "written collections of traditional oracles existed, that they were in the hands of self-appointed religious experts who competed with one another, that these oracles

3. Interpreting the first-person plural (ἐσμεν) as an apostolic "we," which refers to Paul himself. In the 2020 Virtual Annual Meeting of the SBL, J. Andrew Doole delivered a paper entitled "Could Paul Refer to Himself in the Plural?" Doole answered the question with a categorical no. Cf. Nasrallah, "Paul's Letters," 85–104. However, as Doole himself reported, first-person plurals are commonly employed in the Hellenistic royal correspondence. Cf. also Ma, *Antiochos III*, 26, 62, 141, 168, 204n79, 271, 284–88, 289–91, 317–18, 340–41, 350, 354–56, 360–62, 363. Kings and queens were not the only ones who used the first-person plural; royal officials such as Zeuxis (the governor of cis-Tauric Asia) did as well. Cf. Ma, *Antiochos III*, 30, 66, 128, 179, 185, 230, 289–90, 294, 304–5, 327–29, 341–42. On Paul as a royal figure who writes in the tradition of royal correspondence, see further below.

4. Here we may ask whether the comparative particle ὡς weakens the sense in which Paul stands before God's presence, thus breaking the direct similarity to Enoch's rather more realistic experience before God. We may note, however, that when Paul speaks about his encounter with the divine, he speaks rather reluctantly and demurely (cf. 2 Cor 12:1–4). In that case, the ὡς may represent a similar form of apostolic humility.

5. Cf. Renwick, *Paul, the Temple, and the Presence of God*, 44, 50, 61–74.

6. Cf., e.g., 2 Cor 12:1–4. On Paul as an Enoch-like figure, see my *The Apocalyptic Letter to the Galatians*, ch. 4.

7. Cf. Esler, *God's Court and Courtiers in the* Book of the Watchers.

8. Novick, "Peddling Scents," 544.

9. Novick, "Peddling Scents," 549 (emphasis mine).

10. Henrichs, "*Hieroi Logoi* and *Hierai Bibloi*," 216–222. See further Zimm, "*Chrēsmologoi* in Thucydides," 5–11.

were of dubious authenticity, and that oracles in general were susceptible to forgery."[11] The *chrēsmologos* quotes an oracle of Bacis referring explicitly to Cloud-Cuckoo-Land (i.e., the birds' city in the air) as a place between Corinth and Sicyon inhabited by wolves and crows (*Birds* 967–68; cf. 969).[12] Not to be outdone, Peisetaerus, the oracle-monger's partner in dialogue who had recently founded Cloud-Cuckoo-Land, appeals to a higher authority than Bacis when he quotes, allegedly from direct, personal experience, an oracle of the Delphic god Apollo (982). In a similar way, Paul contrasts the peddlers of the word of God with his own experience as one who speaks with sincerity, as one who is sent from God and stands in the unmediated presence of God (cf., e.g., 1 En. 14:8–16:4; 2 Cor 12:1–4).[13]

The message that Paul proclaims on the basis of this direct access to divine revelation has a different effect on those who hear it, depending on whether they are being saved or are perishing: "to one a fragrance from death to death, to the other a fragrance from life to life" (2 Cor 2:16). We may compare Enoch in his role as the revelatory mediator par excellence. For on one of his celestial journeys, with Michael as interpreting angel, Enoch learns firsthand about the extraordinarily fragrant tree of life from which the righteous will eat with salvific effect in the eschaton: "Its fragrances will be in their bones, and they will live a long life on the earth, such as your fathers lived also in their days" (1 En. 24:2–25:7, here 25:6).[14] As the archangel explains, however, "no flesh has the right to touch" the fragrant tree until "the Great Holy one, the Lord of glory, the King of eternity" descends to earth and conducts "the great judgment, in which there will be vengeance on all and a consummation

---

11. Henrichs, "*Hieroi Logoi* and *Hierai Bibloi*," 218. Cf. Yu, "The Divination Contest of Calchas and Mopus and Aristophanes' *Knights*," 910–34, who argues that Aristophanes casts politicians and rogues as purveyors of oracles (*chrēsmologoi*) who abused divination for political advantage and personal gain. Such seers are often set within the Greek tradition of dueling oracles.

12. If Corinth and Sicyon are contiguous cities, then Cloud-Cuckoo-Land as a place "between" them is literally a utopia (i.e., "no place"). The references to "Corinth" (968) and the "Corinthians" (969) suggest perhaps that Paul had the oracle-monger scene in mind when he wrote 2 Cor 2:17.

13. Insofar as Paul has in view itinerant peddlers of divine oracles in 2:17, we may perhaps compare Paul's opponents in 2 Cor 10–13, who are characterized as interlopers in Paul's divine sphere of action (cf. 10:13–16). Alas, this would entail a decision about the compositional unity of the letter, which is beyond the scope of the present chapter. The possibility is intriguing, however, because Paul explicitly refers there to his letters that are "weighty and strong" (10:9–10), perhaps alluding to the royal letter tradition (see further below).

14. The extraordinary fragrance of this tree is mentioned no less than five times in the text: Cf., e.g., 1 En. 24:3b–6: "And fragrant trees encircled it [sc. the mountain that resembled the seat of a throne]. Among them was a tree such as I had never smelled, and among them was no other like it. It had a fragrance sweeter smelling than all spices, and its leaves and its blossom and the tree never wither. [...] Then I said, 'How beautiful is this tree and fragrant....' [...] and he [sc. the archangel Michael] said to me, 'Enoch, why do you inquire and why do you marvel about the fragrance of this tree...?'" On the fragrant tree of life in 1 En. 24:2–25:7, see further Bautch, *Study of the Geography of 1 Enoch 17–19*, 122–25; Nickelsburg, *1 Enoch 1*, 314–16. On the tree of life of which the victorious Christ-follower is given the privilege of eating in the book of Revelation (2:7; 22:2, 14, 19), see Aune, *Revelation 1–5*, 151–54.

forever" (25:4). Hence, insofar as the universal judgment marks the divide between partaking of the fragrant the tree of life and thereby receiving long life, on the one hand, and being eternally condemned, on the other, we have a similar dichotomy to that found in 2 Cor 2:14–16.

This understanding of Paul and his ministry informs our interpretation of 2 Cor 3:1–3, where the apostle continues to develop this theme in terms of the "letter from Christ."

As the latter-day, Enoch-like revelatory mediator par excellence (even greater than Moses [cf. 3:7–18]),[15] Paul obviously does not need letters of recommendation either to or from the Corinthians (2 Cor 3:1–2), such as the kind that he wrote to the Corinthians on behalf of Titus, commissioning the latter to complete the collection at Corinth (2 Cor 8:16–24).[16] The apostle works at a much higher level of authority, indeed the very highest that exists in the created order. When he speaks and acts, he channels all the authority of the divine word and power (cf., e.g., 2 Cor 10:1–6). The effects of his ministry become apparent in the Corinthians themselves, whose changed lives become in effect a letter of recommendation for Paul (3:2).

In 2 Cor 3:3, Paul continues the letter theme, but he introduces a new epistolary genre into the discussion. This is not a completely new idea, but rather a new take on Paul's aforementioned role as the Enoch-like revelatory mediator par excellence in 2:14–17. For as it turns out, Enoch was also a letter-writer, and his letter-writing can be characterized as a Jewish apocalyptic version of the Hellenistic royal letter tradition. What we are suggesting for 3:3 is that Paul has left the idea of letters of recommendation in 3:1–2 and goes on now to contrast two kinds of *royal letters*—on the one hand, the usual one that is inscribed in tablets of stone and, on the other hand, the "letter of

15. If Paul, the latter-day revelatory mediator par excellence, is an Enoch-like figure, then the apostle and his ministry are greater than Moses and his ministry. As is well known, the Enochic tradition contains no Mosaic laws, but it does use Mosaic language in order to enhance the primacy of Enoch over Moses. This use of Mosaic language by the antediluvian patriarch effectively makes Moses an echo of Enoch rather than the other way around. Cf. Nickelsburg, "Nature and Function of Revelation in 1 Enoch, Jubilees, and Some Qumranic Documents," 91–119, here 101: "It is noteworthy that the authors of 1 Enoch do not simply attribute their writings to a pre-Mosaic author. They also present them in a manner that devalues the Mosaic pentateuch. The initial oracle in chapters 1–5 is a paraphrase of part of Deut. 33, and some of the content and testamentary language in chapter 91 is reminiscent of Moses' farewell discourse in Deut. 29–32. In effect, this casts Moses into the role of a 'me-too.' In addition, the account of the events at Mount Sinai in the Animal Vision, while it allows Moses an important role as a leader of Israel and even grants him a vision of the Deity, never states that he received the Torah on Mount Sinai (89:29–32). Revelation came to Israel at Marah (89:28; cf. Exod. 15:25–26). Thus, 1 Enoch leapfrogs the Mosaic Torah and assumes for itself a prophetic authority that precedes Moses." In a similar way, Paul prioritizes his revelation over that of Moses: Just as Enoch's revelation of saving wisdom is seen in the Enochic tradition as the sole basis for withstanding the final judgment, so also the apostle's revelation of the gospel is understood as the only foundation for ultimate salvation.

16. Again, the vexed question of the unity of 2 Corinthians looms large for any study of the letter. For purposes of the present chapter, however, this issue can be sidestepped, since the interpretation of 3:3 within the context of 2:14—7:4 is hardly affected by this issue.

Christ" that is engraved in tablets of fleshly hearts. This is a crucial point that has so far eluded scholarly attention: Paul is *not yet* referring to the Mosaic Law, which was chiseled on stone tablets (cf. 2 Cor 3:7–11), although the apostle is clearly preparing for that discussion;[17] rather, he is appealing to a phenomenon that was common in the ancient cities through which he traveled,[18] including Corinth.[19] In other words, the contrast in 2 Cor 3:3 is between two kinds of glorious royal letters, with one kind (i.e., the royal letter of Christ engraved on human hearts) being much more glorious than the other (i.e., monumental royal letters inscribed on stone stelae).[20]

Hans-Josef Klauck is certainly correct: "Hellenistic royal letters have received too little attention in New Testament exegesis."[21] Part of the reason for this lack of attention among students of Paul is that the focus has been on *biblical* allusions, often to the exclusion of materials from the wider Greco-Roman culture in which the Pauline text was embedded. However, as Neil Elliott notes, "Nothing requires us to limit intertextuality to echoes from the Bible, as if we should imagine Paul and his audiences completely closed off from all the other forms of communication going on around them."[22] After listing a number of terms that could have been heard by the recipients of Paul's letters as carrying political connotations (e.g., κύριος ["lord"], ἐκκλησία ["assembly"], εὐαγγέλιον ["good news"], and παρουσία ["advent, arrival"]), Elliott concludes: "There is often no way to prove or disprove that a particular [political] connotation was intended, of course, but ruling the possibility of one or another implicit meaning out of bounds in preference for a supposedly certain 'biblical' meaning would constitute an exercise in theological special pleading." If we follow this kind of more inclusive approach to Paul's letters, we can see how a political interpretation of some key Pauline terms, such as "letter of Christ," adds significantly to our understanding of Paul's letters in terms of the political typology of assemblages. As we shall see, the apostle employs

---

17. Cf., e.g., Hafemann, *Suffering and Ministry in the Spirit*, 209, 213–16, 221–22, here 221: "In II Cor. 3:3b Paul wishes to affirm that the Corinthians' relationship to Christ has not been established by the Spirit's work in conjunction with the law, but by the Spirit's work in their hearts, pictured in terms of the promise from Ezekiel. Against the background of Ezekiel, the contrast between the two spheres of God's revelatory-salvific activity, i.e., the 'law' and the 'heart,' is best understood, therefore, as a contrast between the two basic ages in the history of salvation, which are represented by these two fundamental rubrics. While in the 'old age' the locus of God's activity and revelation was the law, in the 'new age,' according to Ezekiel, God will be at work in the heart." Hafemann is, however, correct that we should not read the allusion to Jer 38:33 LXX in 2 Cor 3:6 back into 3:3 (*Suffering and Ministry in the Spirit*, 213).

18. See further below on the evidence drawn primarily from the cities of Asia Minor in Ma, *Antiochos III*.

19. Cf., e.g., Geagan, "Letter of Trajan to a Synod at Isthmia," 396–401, referring to a Greek imperial letter inscribed on a stele of white marble, dated 98/99 CE. See further Oliver, *Greek Constitutions of Early Roman Emperors from Inscriptions and Papyri*, 58–65; Corcoran, "State Correspondence in the Roman Empire," 177–79 (on the epigraphic evidence); Millar, "Imperial Letters in Latin," 65–83.

20. Contrast Hafemann, *Suffering and Ministry in the Spirit*, 222.

21. Klauck, *Ancient Letters and the New Testament*, 78.

22. Elliott, "Paul and Empire 1," 149.

a concept drawn from state assemblages (i.e., Hellenistic royal letters) and contrasts it with his own official mediation of the "letter of Christ."

Although this section of the present chapter will focus on Hellenistic royal letters, we have elsewhere argued that these royal letters also influenced the writing of the Epistle of Enoch (1 En. 92–105), and that both of these sources have informed Paul's writing of the letter to the Galatians.[23] For this reason, we will have less to say about imperial correspondence per se, which, in any case, shows substantial continuity with Hellenistic royal letters.[24]

"Inscribed"

We begin our discussion of 2 Cor 3:3 by noticing the verbal form used to describe the "letter of Christ": ἐπιστολὴ Χριστοῦ . . . ἐγγεγραμμένη . . . ἐν πλαξίν. In the context of "(stone) tablets," the verb ἐγγράφω denotes "to inscribe." As BDAG (s.v., 270) notes,

> In the continuation of vs. 3 the imagery of a handwritten document ἐγγεγραμμένη οὐ μέλανι ἀλλὰ πνεύματι θεοῦ, *written not w[ith] ink but w[ith] God's Spirit* points to ἐγγρ[άφω] as equivalent to γράφω . . . , but the related clause οὐκ ἐν πλαξὶν λιθίναις ἀλλ' ἐν πλαξὶν καρδίαις σαρκίναις suggests engraved letters. Like the Gk. term ἐγγρ[άφω], which can be used of handwriting as well as engraving, the Eng. rendering "inscribe" does double duty for Paul's imagery and is in harmony with the official flavor (numerous official letters were inscribed on stone) of his prose in 2 Cor.

BDAG is correct that Paul's use of ἐγγράφω here invokes the image of official letters—or, as we shall see more particularly, royal/imperial correspondence. However, as a structural analysis of 2 Cor 3:3 shows (see below), it is unlikely that Paul is referring here to a handwritten document at this point. Rather, the image that he employs in verse 3 is consistently one of inscribed stone.[25]

Structural Analysis

In 2 Cor 3:3, the two contrasting sets of elements (i.e., AB and A´B´) describing how the Corinthians are a "letter of Christ" are arranged in synonymous parallelism:

23. See Scott, *Apocalyptic Letter to the Galatians*, chap. 4.

24. On the continuity between Hellenistic royal correspondence and imperial letter-writing (including their inscription on stone), see Sherk, *Roman Documents from the Greek East*, 186–97 et passim; Millar, *Emperor in the Roman World (31 BC–AD 337)*, 213–28 et passim; Ma, *Antiochos III*, 183; Lavan, *Slaves to Rome*, 222. This is in line with recent trends in the study of the Eastern Mediterranean world, in which the "long Hellenistic Age" is seen as a period extending from the reign of Alexander the Great through the reign of Hadrian. For the term "long Hellenistic Age," see Chaniotis, *Age of Conquests*, 3 (quoted and discussed in ch. 2 above).

25. The issue of how to interpret μέλανι ("with ink"), which seemingly privileges a handwritten letter, will be dealt with below.

A ἐγγεγραμμένη οὐ μέλανι

  B ἀλλὰ πνεύματι θεοῦ ζῶντος,

A´ [ἐγγεγραμμένη] οὐκ ἐν πλαξὶν λιθίναις

  B´ ἀλλ᾽ ἐν πλαξὶν καρδίαις σαρκίναις

The A elements negate (οὐ/οὐκ) one medium of inscription ("with ink"/"in stone tablets"), and the B elements, introduced by the strong adversative ἀλλά, affirm the alternative ("with the Spirit of the living God"/"in tablets of fleshly hearts").

The synonymous parallelism between the pairs is more easily seen in the B elements because of their clear allusion to Ezek 36:26–27 (cf. 11:19):[26]

> And I will give you a new heart (καρδίαν καινὴν), and a new spirit (πνεῦμα καινὸν) I will give in you, and I will remove the stone heart from your flesh and give you a heart of flesh (καὶ ἀφελῶ τὴν καρδίαν τὴν λιθίνην ἐκ τῆς σαρκὸς ὑμῶν καὶ δώσω ὑμῖν καρδίαν σαρκίνην). And I will give my spirit in you (καὶ τὸ πνεῦμά μου δώσω ἐν ὑμῖν). . . .

Based on the biblical allusion, Paul's formulations "with the Spirit of the living God" and "in tablets of fleshly hearts" obviously correspond to each other. The first phrase indicates the *mode* of inscribing, whereas the second phrase gives the *medium* of the inscription itself.

Here, it should be mentioned that the theme of the giving of the Spirit in Ezek 36:26–27 is continued in 37:1–14, Ezekiel's famous vision of the valley of the dry bones, in which the imagery appears directly to reflect and develop the scene of the creation of man in Gen 2, using a constellation of imagery that relates re-creation with creation.[27] In particular, just as in Gen 2:7, man is formed but becomes a living being only after God breathed into his nostrils the breath of life into him, so also in Ezek 37:5, the prophet is instructed to prophesy to the bones, "I [sc. the Lord God] will cause breath/spirit [רוח/πνεῦμα ζωῆς] to enter you, and you shall live."[28] The divine word proclaimed through the prophet is a performative speech-act that actually accomplishes the re-creation of the dry bones (Ezek 37:7–10). We shall return to this subject below.

For Paul, Ezek 36:26–27 evokes the image of inscribing inscriptions. Therefore, he sets up the analogy in the A elements, which, again, are in synonymous parallelism. That is, "with ink" and "in stone tablets" correspond to each other as *mode* of inscribing and *medium* of inscription. Paul is not talking about normal handwriting on perishable materials, such as papyrus or parchment, but rather about engraving stone

26. On the allusion to Ezek 36:26–27 in 2 Cor 3:3, see Hafemann, *Suffering and Ministry in the Spirit*, 209–20.

27. On the theme of creation and re-creation in Ezekiel 36–37, see Kutsko, *Between Heaven and Earth*, 124–47.

28. Cf. Kutsko, *Between Heaven and Earth*, 133.

tablets (i.e., stelae, upright stone slabs or columns typically bearing a commemorative inscription) and filling the inscribed grooves with "ink."[29] The crevices of royal stone inscriptions were commonly filled with red color,[30] so that the lettering would stand out from the white marble, even in strong sunlight that casts no shadows. Indeed, the purpose of inscribing the stone in the first place was to create deep recesses to receive the color.[31] (The same material [cinnabar] was used to paint red letters in both books and engraved stone; therefore, Paul could plausibly call it "ink.")[32]

29. Note, however, that some stones were written on with ink, which could be washed away. See, for example, the Vision of Gabriel, the text of which is written in two columns in black ink on the polished side of a grayish limestone slab. Cf. Henze, ed., *HAZON GABRIEL*, 2, 12, 25, 61, 113, 189–94 (photographs).

30. Cf. Woodhead, *Study of Greek Inscriptions*, 27: "It is well known that, for greater clarity, stone-cut letters were often also coloured with paint, as is in fact not infrequent in modern times. The colours have for obvious reasons seldom survived, but were traces do remain they suggest that red was the colour ordinarily used for the purpose. Where two colours were used, alternate lines were painted in red and black. This two-colour system may have been more widespread than the scanty remains of it so far suggest, and the chances of the survival of paint traces on an inscription are too low for hopes that more evidence will be speedily forthcoming." See also Woodhead, *Study of Greek Inscriptions*, 129; Keppie, *Understanding Roman Inscriptions*, 15, 40–41; Dušek, *Aramaic and Hebrew Inscriptions from Mt. Gerizim and Samaria between Antiochus III and Antiochus IV Epiphanes*, 50; Meiggs and Lewis, *Selection of Greek Historical Inscriptions to the End of the Fifth*, 20, 27, 65, 69; Pfeiffer, *Griechische und lateinische Inschriften zum Ptolemäerreich und zur römischen Provinz Aegyptus*, 53–56 (no. 10: Tempel und Kult auf Philae [243/242 v. Chr.?] = *OGIS* I 61); *IG* II3,1 1204; Schwitter, "Funkelnde Buchstaben," 125n31. Another color that was used for monumental inscriptions was blue. In at least one case, alternating lines of red and blue coloring were used for the lettering of the inscription. See the color photograph of one of the blocks of the Isidorus, *Hymns to Isis* (= Bernand, *Inscriptions métriques de l'Égypte gréco-romaine*, 631–52 [No. 175], here Hymn II [Pl. CVI, halftone only]), in Bresciani et al., *Medinet Madi: Archaeological Guide*, 32 (unfortunately, the coloring of the letters was restored by a team from the University of Pisa in 2004–5); cf. also Lougovaya, "Greek Inscriptions in Ptolemaic Narmouthis," 118. In the course of time, the coloring of the scored letters of monumental inscriptions often either faded or disappeared altogether. In some cases, only minute traces of the coloring is left. In other cases, the small amount of coloring that remained in the fissures was stripped away when a squeeze of the inscription (i.e., a cast impression from the inscribed surface) was taken in modern times. Cf. Duggan, "Not Just the Shadows on the Stone," 269–83. On Thucydides 6.55.4, referring to an inscription on the altar in the sanctuary of Phythian Apollo (i.e., *IG* I3 948 [521–510 BCE]), see Stanton, *Athenian Politics c. 800–500 BC*, 74n5: "Since the letters [of the inscription] are distinctly cut [cf. http://drc.ohiolink.edu/handle/2374.OX/232], Thucydides' comment about 'faint letters' [ἀμυδροῖς γράμμασι] probably refers to the disappearance of red paint which originally filled the deeply cut letters . . . ; indeed, traces of red paint may be seen in some of the grooves today." Cf., however, Dillon, "Lakedaimonian Dedication to Olympian Zeus," 60–68, here 63–64; Lavelle, "Thucydides and *IG* I3 948: ἀμυδροῖς γράμμασι," 207–12.

31. Cf. Tracy, *Lettering of an Athenian Mason*, 119–20.

32. Cf. Pliny, *HN* 33.122: "Cinnabar is also used in writing books, and it makes a brighter lettering for inscriptions on a wall or on marble even in tombs" (*minium in voluminum quoque scriptura usurpatur clarioresque litteras vel in muro vel in marmore, etiam in sepulchris, facit*). See further Eastaugh et al., *Pigment Compendium*, 105–6 (s.v., "Cinnabar"); Brecoulaki, "'Precious Colours' in Ancient Greek Polychromy and Painting," 3–35, here 17: "Cinnabar was one of the most esteemed pigments in the Classical world, the equivalent of murex purple in the mineral universe. In his *Meteorologica* (378a26), Aristotle describes cinnabar among the coloured stones, while both Pliny and Vitruvius give us detailed information about its use, classifying it among the 'bright', or *floridi* colours. Pliny

"Letter of Christ"

So far, we have discussed 2 Cor 3:3 in general terms: Paul employs the analogy of monumental inscriptions in order to conceptualize the work of the Spirit in human hearts. It is possible, however, to be more specific about what kind of inscription is involved, because, as we have seen, Paul refers here to the Corinthians as a "letter of Christ" (ἐπιστολὴ Χριστοῦ). This brings us into the realm of royal/imperial correspondence, a rich and complex subject that requires access to largely inscriptional evidence. We are fortunate that in recent decades, epigraphers, historians, and other scholars of antiquity have opened up this vast field of inquiry with helpful surveys and analyses of royal letters inscribed on stone. We will focus here especially on the seminal work of John Ma.

Crucially important for our study is the interpretation of Χριστοῦ as a genitive of authorship (i.e., a letter whose author is Christ).[33] The genitive of authorship with ἐπιστολή is very common (e.g., Polyb. 2.50.3; 2 Esdr 12:9; 2 Macc 2:13; Josephus, *Ant.* 11.97; 13:39; 14.131; 17.139, 223, 229; 18.262, 266, 277, 294; *Ap.* 2.37). The collocation is also found in the Pauline corpus (cf. 2 Thess 2:15, ἐπιστολῆς ἡμῶν). Of particular interest for our study are instances in which ἐπιστολή with the genitive of authorship either introduces the verbatim citation of a king's letter (cf. 2 Macc 11:22, 27; Josephus, *Ant.* 12.137; *Let. Arist.* 34) or refers back to a royal letter that has been quoted (cf. Thuc. 7.16; Josephus, *Ant.* 12.51; *Let. Arist.* 51). Therefore, although Χριστοῦ has sometimes been construed as an objective genitive ["a letter about Christ"]), well-established Greek usage points in a different direction.

If we take Χριστοῦ as a genitive of authorship (i.e., a letter whose author is Christ), then it is necessary to recall that Christ is presented as a royal figure in the Corinthian correspondence. The term Χριστός itself has messianic significance, referring to the end-time king of Israel.[34] Moreover, Paul preaches "Christ Jesus as *Lord* (κύριον)"

---

also recalls the use of cinnabar in writing books and inscriptions on a wall or on marble, because of its 'exceptional brightness' (*HN* 33.122). Dioscorides in his medical treatise *De materia medica* dedicates a quite extensive paragraph to the origin of cinnabar, its hues and pictorial uses. He too, like Pliny, describes its colour as εὐανθέστατον καὶ φλογωδέστατον χρῶμα (5. 94), and tell us that painters would only use it in luxurious wall decorations. Later Roman sources specify that cinnabar was the pigment kings used to sign with (τὸ κιννάβαρι ἔστι δὲ εἶδος βάμματας πυρροῦ, ἐξ οὗ γράφει ὁ βασιλεύς, Aelius Herodianus, Περὶ κλίσεως ὀνομάτων 3, 2. 767), and the epithet *kinnavarinos* is often used to evoke a saturated red hue."

33. Cf., e.g., Martin, *2 Corinthians*, 51; Thrall, *Second Epistle to the Corinthians*, 1.224.

34. Paul's use of Χριστός is a controversial issue, particularly with respect whether the term is a messianic title. It seems clear, however, that, however much Christ may have burst the bounds of traditional messianic expectations (which, in any case, were not unitary and fixed), Jesus was, for Paul, the Son of God who is of Davidic ancestry (τοῦ υἱοῦ αὐτοῦ τοῦ γενομένου ἐκ σπέρματος Δαυὶδ κατὰ σάρκα, Rom 1:3; cf. 2 Sam 7:12, 14), and "the Messiah" who stems from the Israelites (ἐξ ὧν ὁ Χριστὸς τὸ κατὰ σάρκα, Rom 9:5). See further Novenson, *Christ among the Messiahs*. See, however, "Paul and the Missing Messiah," in Zetterholm, *Messiah in Early Judaism and Christianity*, 33–55, who argues that Paul deliberately downplayed the messianic character of Jesus for gentile readers.

(2 Cor 4:5).[35] Christ is enthroned next to God in accordance with Ps 110:1 (1 Cor 15:24–28).[36] Therefore, "all of us must appear before the judgment seat of Christ (τοὺς γὰρ πάντας ἡμᾶς φανερωθῆναι δεῖ ἔμπροσθεν τοῦ βήματος τοῦ Χριστοῦ), so that each may receive recompense for what was done in the body, whether good or evil" (2 Cor 5:10; cf. Rom 14:10: "For we must all stand before *the judgment seat of God* [πάντες γὰρ παραστησόμεθα τῷ βήματι τοῦ θεοῦ]").[37] As an "ambassador for Christ" (2 Cor 5:20),[38] Paul has a ministry of reconciliation that ultimately encompasses the whole world. There is no potentate on earth with more authority than Christ. Therefore, a "letter from Christ" will be understood within the firmly established and omnipresent tradition of royal/imperial correspondence.

A sizeable number of Hellenistic royal letters has survived from antiquity because they were inscribed in stone by the grateful communities who originally received them.[39] Since the epigraphical material tells us only what the cities themselves chose to monumentalize, we do not have any threatening letters from kings, or letters refusing petitions, etc.[40]

35. Cf. "Lord Jesus Christ" in 2 Cor 1:2, 3, 5. Elsewhere, Paul proclaims "the Son of God, Jesus Christ" (1:19) and "the good news of Christ" (2:12). See further Hurtado, *Lord Jesus Christ*, 108–18.

36. The passage is saturated with the language of kingdom, ruling, power, and subjugation (e.g., τὴν βασιλείαν, πᾶσαν ἀρχὴν καὶ πᾶσαν ἐξουσίαν καὶ δύναμιν, βασιλεύειν, τοῦ ὑποτάξαντος).

37. Along similar lines, cf. 2 Cor 2:14, where Paul gives thanks to God, "who in Christ always leads us in triumphal procession, and through us spreads in every place the fragrance that comes from knowing him." For a comparable image, see the gold aureus and silver denarius issued under Nero in 55 CE: The reverse in each case shows an elephant quadriga bearing two chairs with seated figures of Divus Claudius and Divus Augustus, both radiate; American Numismatic Society: http://numismatics.org/collection/1967.153.219?lang=en and http://numismatics.org/collection/1944.100.39410?lang=en; British Museum: https://www.britishmuseum.org/collection/object/C_1964-1203-89. For commentary on the coin, see Latham, "'Honors Greater Than Human,'" 121; Hekster, *Emperors and Ancestors*, 50–51.

38. See the discussion of Paul as "ambassador for Christ" (2 Cor 5:20) in chapter 7. Cf. Paul as "apostle of Christ Jesus" (2 Cor 1:1).

39. Two websites are particularly helpful for accessing the extant royal letters: (1) The Packard Humanities Institute's "Searchable Greek Inscriptions" https://inscriptions.packhum.org, which provides the Greek text of inscriptions and some relevant bibliography; (2) an online version of C. Bradford Welles's *Royal Correspondence in the Hellenistic Period* http://www.attalus.org/docs/rc/index.html, which includes the original 75 letters in *RC*, as well as an additional 51 letters that have been discovered since the time of Welles's publication. See also Bagnall and Derow, *Hellenistic Period*. On the present state of the corpus of Hellenistic royal letters, see Ceccarelli, *Ancient Greek Letter Writing*, 304n23; Ma, *Antiochos III*, 182: "The dossier of texts concerning the relations between Antiochos III and the cities is large and consistent enough for a survey of these forms, and also of the language shared by both parties. These texts also have the advantage of being typical of Hellenistic diplomatics in general, so that their examples can be expanded with parallels, and the findings they encourage apply to the Hellenistic world in general." Ma, *Antiochos III*, 183: "Parallels are easy to find . . . , all these examples, substantially preserved, showing the same uniformity of composition (which also influenced the letters of Roman officials and emperors)."

40. Ma, *Antiochos III*, 235–36; Ceccarelli, "Letters and Decrees," 179n80; Ceccarelli, *Ancient Greek Letter Writing*, 307 with n34. Note, however, that the reference to a conquered foe's previous "sin" of rebellion and subsequent "repentance" in *RC* 54.9–10 (cited below) presupposes that threatening

These royal letters, along with the honorific civic decrees that respond to them, show us the formulaic language of euergetism that constituted the standard medium for interaction between ruler and ruled, shaping consistent communication and actions across the whole Hellenistic world.[41] As Ma shows in detail, these two forms—the royal letter and the honorific civic decree—can be considered as partners in a potentially never-ending dialogue of benefaction and gratitude.[42] Ma observes, "Both forms can be described as conducting a dialogue, because they are built around reciprocity and exchange. By their very syntax, they are structured as reactions, or motivated decisions: on the part of the king, a reaction to an embassy or to realizing a local community's good behaviour; on the part of the city, a reaction to a benefaction, real or perceived, requited through τιμαί ['honors']."[43] This dialogue is designed to be continuous—"I will give, in order that you give, in order that I will give, etc." (*do ut des*)—in a self-perpetuating spiral that both fosters and strengthens the reciprocal relationship between ruler and ruled.[44] Ma calls the promise of future benefaction, if the local community behaves well—"we will take all care of you, inasmuch as you show yourselves the better disposed and the more zealous towards the interests of King Antiochos"—a "contract clause,"[45] and such expressions of reciprocity are common in the epigraphical material throughout the Hellenistic period.[46]

communication has occurred in some form. Moreover, in 154 CE, a letter of Emperor Antoninus Pius to the Ptolemais-Barcans (i.e., the men of a single community comprising Barca and its port Ptolemais about 16 km away) rebukes the latter for sending representation to the contest of the Capitolia, although previously they had failed to send a delegation or share in the sacrifice. Cf. Oliver, *Greek Constitutions of Early Roman Emperors from Inscriptions and Papyri*, 283–84 (no. 124).

41. On the language of euergetism, see Ma, *Antiochos III*, 182–94, here 186: "The dynamic, open structure characteristic of the euergetical dialogue is reinforced by the very language in which the interaction was couched. The formalized vocabulary and syntax guarantee reproducibility; more importantly, the interaction is framed, or expressed, through generalizing idioms of consistency, which characterize any transaction as normal rather than exceptional." See also Ceccarelli, "Letters and Decrees," 169. Note, however, that in her chapter, "Poleis and Kings, Letters and Decrees" (Ceccarelli, *Ancient Greek Letter Writing*, 297–330), Ceccarelli focuses specifically on letter-writing by both Hellenistic kings and the *poleis*, without denying that a euergetical dialogue existed between royal correspondence and civic decrees (cf. 332, for a succinct description of the major differences between the latter two modes of writing).

42. Cf. Ma, *Antiochos III*, 179–242.

43. Ma, *Antiochos III*, 184–85. Cf. Ceccarelli, "Letters and Decrees," 174.

44. Cf. *Antiochos III*, 186; Ceccarelli, "Letters and Decrees," 174–75. If 2 Cor 8–9 forms part of the same letter of which 2:14—7:4 is also a part, then this might be an argument for the collection (if the Corinthians do their part in faithfully participating in the euergetical dialogue fostered by the royal letter of Christ). Once again, however, we confront the question of the unity of the letter, which is beyond the scope of the present study.

45. Cf. Ma, *Antiochos III*, 185: "In the royal letters, the contract clause . . . expresses reciprocity, linking royal benefaction and civic reaction in a self-perpetuating spiral. . . ." On the contract clause, see further Ma, *Antiochos III*, 101, 179–80, 182, 200n68, 240.

46. Ma, *Antiochos III*, 179. For the quote from the Letter of Zeuxis to the Kildarians (probably 197 BCE), see Ma, *Antiochos III*, 327–29 (no. 25), here 328 (lines 7–11). As examples of the contract clause, see, e.g., 1 Macc 10:27 ("Now continue still to keep faith with us, and we will repay you with

Very important for our present considerations is the fact that the royal side of the euergetical dialogue, particularly in Hellenistic royal correspondence, is replete with *performative utterances*, that is, language that performs an action in and by words.[47] As discussed in chapter 2, the term goes back to the book by the analytical philosopher J. L. Austin entitled *How to Do Things with Words*.[48] Words can both act on reality and inaugurate a changed state of affairs, through (or in) their very utterance. Language not only *reveals* a preexisting phenomenon or a state of affairs, it also has the power to *create* and *install* something new.

Ancient documents provide us with many examples of performative speech-acts. In terms of the euergetical dialogue we are presently discussing, performative utterances are found commonly in the grant of privileges and benefits by rulers (Hellenistic kings or Roman emperors), whenever they seek a corresponding positive response from the addressees. The whole process begins with the conquest of the city. As Ma notes, "The most important transaction that followed the takeover by the Seleukids was the regulation of local statuses. [. . .] Conquest entailed the momentary loss of the vanquished party's political existence, to be recreated by a unilateral pronouncement (a performative speech-act *par excellence*) of the conqueror, on terms of his choosing and subject to his goodwill."[49] This is the point at which the conquered peoples "entrust" (πιστεύσαντες) themselves to their conqueror.[50] From there, the ruler's performative

---

good for what you do for us"); 2 Macc 11:19 ("If you will maintain your goodwill toward the government, I will endeavor in the future to help promote your welfare"); Josephus, *Ant.* 13.48 ("Since you have preserved your friendship for us, and in spite of their tempting offers have not joined yourselves to my foes, I commend you for this loyalty on your part, and exhort you to continue in the same course, for which you shall receive a recompense from us and our favor"). For an inscriptional example, see Jonnes and Ricl, "New Royal Inscription from Phyrgia Paroreios," 1–30, here 3–4 on Letter A (after 188 BCE), lines 34–38: "As to recognizing your constitutional status [i.e., as a *polis*], I myself have addressed you (accordingly) in the second letter at the beginning. So do try, having received such great honors from me, to show your true goodwill by your deeds on all occasions." Letter B, lines 47–48: "And, in general, know that, if you preserve your goodwill towards us, you will receive many times more privileges." Cf. Bagnall and Derow, *Hellenistic Period*, 80–81.

47. For a brief summary of J. L. Austin's speech-act theory which is designed to help ancient historians read documents, see Ma, "Seleukids and Speech-Acts," 75–85.

48. Austin, *How to Do Things with Words*. For a more nuanced approach to performativity (i.e., divine/sovereign and sociopolitical forms of performative utterance), see the previous chapter on Gal 3:28.

49. Ma, *Antiochos III*, 111–12. On the king's power to define statuses, see Ma, *Antiochos III*, 100, 101, 104, 109, 113, 128, 149, 150–74, 175, 178, 179, 238, 244, here 173: "All statuses must originate with a performative speech act by the king."

50. Thus, Zeuxis's letter to Amyzon (*RC* 38), written in the immediate aftermath of the conquest of the city, is framed in the wider context of "all those who have entrusted and handed themselves over to us" (α]ὐτοὺς πιστεύσαντες ἡμῖν ἐνεχείρισαν). Cf. Ma, *Antiochos III*, 179, 292–94 (no. 5, line 2). See also the Letter of the Scipios to the Herakleians: "As for us, we happen to be well disposed towards all the Greeks, and we will try, since you have come over to our [faith] (παραγεγονότων ὑμῶν εἰς τὴν ἡμέτεραμ [πίστιμ]), to show solicitude as much as possible, always trying to be responsible for some advantage. We grant you your liberty, just as to other cities which have entrusted themselves to us, with the right to see all your own affairs conducted by yourselves according to your

speech-act decides on both the degree of subordination (ranging from "free" [in name only] to subject) and the amount of spoliation (ranging from exemption from tribute and garrisoning to heavy tribute, taxes, levies, and/or fines).[51]

As discussed in chapter 2, the ongoing euergetical dialogue between ruler and ruled can be plotted along three axes, all of which contribute to a rhetoric of *generalization*. (1) Chronologically, individual acts of euergetism or gratitude are never presented as isolated in time; they are always presented against a background of precedent and prospect. (2) In addition to a generalization of the euergetical dialogue on a temporal axis *through time*, specific acts of euergetism either to or from a specific city could be generalized on an anthropological axis, so that they are placed in the context of constant beneficence to "all Greeks" or even "all men." (3) The language of euergetism strives at generalization along a third axis by making individual transactions into paradigmatic shows of virtuous character within the relationship between the ruler and the ruled.

The foregoing considerations have important implications for our understanding of the Corinthians as a "letter of Christ" in 2 Cor 3:3. First, the letter of Christ expresses the performative utterance of the royal figure which establishes the status of the recipients on a wholly new basis. Here we need to recall that Paul's gospel is a performative speech-act—the "word of Christ" ($\dot{\rho}\tilde{\eta}\mu\alpha$ Χριστοῦ, Rom 10:17)[52] that actually effects salvation (cf. Rom 1:16).[53] As discussed in chapter 7 on Gal 3:28, Paul's gospel

---

laws, and in all other matters we will try to assist you and always be responsible for some advantage." Cf. Ma, *Antiochos III*, 366–67 (no. 45, lines 7–14).

51. The status of a community could change over time. Cf. Cotton-Paltiel et al., "Juxtaposing Literary and Documentary Evidence," 1–15, which discusses three copies of Seleucus IV's epistolary *prostagma* from 178 BCE to his vizier Heliodorus, and forwarded to other officials with the instruction to have a copy of the king's letter "engraved on stelae made of stone and set up in the most conspicuous of temples in these places." The authors argue that the king's letter created a new status for the communities affected in Coele-Syria and Phoenicia in 178 BCE, that is, an overturning and withdrawal of the charter of privileges granted by Antiochus III (Cotton-Paltiel et al., "Juxtaposing Literary and Documentary Evidence," 14).

52. Cf. Hofius, "Wort Gottes und Glaube bei Paulus," in *Paulusstudien*, 148–74, here 153–54, who helpfully discusses the complex interrelationship in Rom 10:8–17 between "faith" (πίστις) and Paul's apostolic proclamation (ἡ ἀκοή), on the one hand, and between that proclamation and the "word of Christ" ($\dot{\rho}\tilde{\eta}\mu\alpha$ Χριστοῦ) = "the gospel" (τὸ εὐαγγέλιον), on the other. The word of Christ, which is coterminous with the "word of God" (λόγος θεοῦ), is not a human word; it is divine revelation. See 1 Thess 2:13: "When you received the word of God that you heard from us, you accepted it not as a human word but as what it really is, God's word. . . ." As Hofius further observes (Wort Gottes und Glaube bei Paulus," 148–49), the salvific *word* is not a purely linguistic event; it is inextricably linked with the salvific *deed* of God's reconciliatory work in Christ (cf. 2 Cor 5:14–21).

53. Cf., e.g., Martyn, *Theological Issues in the Letters of Paul*, 220 (emphasis mine): "They [sc. the Corinthians] will have noted . . . that whereas in the context of 1 Cor 1:18 Paul speaks repeatedly of foolishness and wisdom as a pair of opposites, he does not do so in referring to the event of the world of the cross. The surprising linguistic imbalance of 1 Cor 1:18 is one of the major keys to the text. By means of that imbalance, *Paul not only speaks of the gospel as God's performative word*. He also denies that this performative word—the gospel of the crucified Christ—is subject to human evaluation, whether that of the gentiles or that of the Jews (1 Cor 1:22–24). And in this denial Paul obliterates in

is modeled on the divine speech-acts of creation in Gen 1 (cf. the citation of Gen 1:27 in Gal 3:28c); hence, Paul's proclamation of the gospel effects a new creation (cf. Gal 6:15; 2 Cor 4:6 [see further below]; 5:17).[54] In normal royal correspondence, the king's performative utterance effects a new status for the recipients of the letter. The letter of Christ does the same thing, except on a grander scale.

The second implication of Paul's analogy is that the Corinthians, as a royal letter, actually embody the usual euergetical dialogue along the aforementioned three axes in the rhetoric of generalization. Here, we highlight merely the anthropological axis in which specific acts of euergetism either to or from a specific city could be generalized, so that they are placed in the context of constant beneficence to "all Greeks" or even "all humankind." Paul had already stated in 2 Cor 3:2 that the Corinthians are an "epistle . . . read by all people" (ἡ ἐπιστολὴ ἡμῶν ὑμεῖς ἐστε, ἐγγεγραμμένη ἐν ταῖς καρδίαις ἡμῶν, γινωσκομένη καὶ ἀναγινωσκομένη ὑπὸ πάντων ἀνθρώπων). This shows that the public display of the Corinthians as "letter of Christ" is very much on his mind.

Royal letters could be known and read by all people precisely because they were inscribed in stone and displayed in a prominent place in the city. In fact, further to our earlier discussion, Hellenistic royal letters sometimes contain a "publication clause," instructing the recipients to inscribe the letter on stone and display it in a prominent place.[55] For example, the publication clause in the letter of Antiochus III to Zeuxis

---

one stroke the thought that the gospel is subject to criteria of perception that have been developed apart from the gospel!"

54. The performative speech-act of Paul's gospel results in believers receiving the adoption as sons and in God sending "the Spirit of his Son into our hearts crying 'Abba! Father!'" (Gal 4:4–6). In other words, Paul's efficacious gospel/word of Christ translates into a performative speech-act of the Spirit of God's Son, whereby believers undergo a status formation from slaves to adopted sons: Through the performative utterance of the Spirit, using the Son's own Aramaic term of address to God as Father (αββα ὁ πατήρ), believers take on the identity of Christ and all that pertains to it (e.g., Abrahamic heirship [v. 7]). Paul underwent the same status change that all believers do, but, for him, the transformation occurred by the direct, performative word of Christ rather than through human mediation.

55. Cf., e.g., RC 36.22–24: ". . . have copies of the letters, engraved on stelae (καὶ τὰ ἀντίγραφα τῶν ἐπιστολῶν ἀναγραφέντα εἰς στήλας ἀνατεθήτω), set up in the places where they may best be seen, so that both now and in the future there may be evident to all in this matter also our policy toward our sister." (The plural forms in this text can be explained by the fact that this is a circular letter.) See also RC 44.41–43, at the end of the Letter of Antiochus III to a Governor on the Appointment of a Chief-Priest at Daphne (189 BCE): "Give orders, also, to inscribe a copy of the letter on stelae and to set them up in the most prominent places" (ἀναγραφῆναι δὲ καὶ τῆς ἐπιστολῆς τὸ ἀντίγραφον εἰς στήλας καὶ ἀναθεῖνα[ι] ἐν τοῖς ἐπιφανεστάτοις τόποις). On publication/inscription clauses in Hellenistic royal letters, see further Bencivenni, "King's Words," 147–51; idem, "Il re scrive, la città iscrive," 171–75; Ceccarelli, "Letters and Decrees," 179. Cf. the royal letter of Demetrius II to the Jewish high priest Jonathan (who is addressed as "his brother" [τῷ ἀδελφῷ]) in 1 Macc 11:30–37, which embeds a letter from Demetrius to Lasthenes concerning Seleucid decisions about Jewish affairs that appends a publication clause: "Now therefore take care [Lasthenes] to make a copy of these things (τούτων ἀντίγραφον), and let it be given to Jonathan and be exposed in the Temple, in a conspicuous place on the holy mountain" (v. 37). Cf. Amitay, "Correspondence in I Maccabees and the Possible Origins of the Judeo-Spartan Connection," 83. Hofmann, "Communications between City and King in the

gives the order "to write up the copy of the letter on stone stelae and expose them in the most conspicuous sanctuaries."[56] The purpose of this clause was to ensure that even long after the letter was originally written, its accurate transmission would be guaranteed in perpetuity through public display.[57]

For Paul, then, the Corinthians themselves are like the epigraphical recording and publication of royal correspondence that broadcast the dynamics of their new communal life and their relationship with Christ to both other members of the community and visitors from abroad.

Hellenistic royal letters were often published as part of a collection of related documents and included as ἱερὰ γράμματα ("sacred writings") in the temple archives or displayed on the walls of temples.[58] The *antas*—i.e., the posts or pillars on either

---

Hellenistic East," 147: "When Mylasa finally settled the dispute with the priesthood there, it inscribed no less than six letters on an anta-block: one of Seleukos II to Olympichos, three of Olympichos to Mylasa, and two of Philip V, one addressed to Mylasa and the other to Olympichos." Sherwin-White, "Edict of Alexander to Priene," 69–89, which discusses the *anta* of the temple to Athena Polias, patron deity of Priene, on which the royal letter of Lysimachus is placed below Alexander's edict to Priene, together with many other inscriptions.

56. Ma, *Antiochos III*, 288–92 (no. 4), here 291 on lines 46–50. See also the Letter of Attalus the Brother of Eumenes II concerning the Tax-Exemption of the *Catoeci* of Apollo Tarsensus (185 BCE): "They wish that the grant be inscribed on a [stone] stele. [Give orders therefore] that it be erected by [. . .] in the temple and when this has been inscribed . . ." (*RC* 47.7–9). Cotton-Paltiel et al., "Juxtaposing Literary and Documentary Evidence," 3, 7.

57. Cf. Ceccarelli et al., *Letters and Communities*, 8: "The practice of monumentalizing official letters in stone endowed specific instances of long-distance communication relevant for communal life with special permanence: they became public sites of memory, for the purpose of symbolic display and future reference. A ready example from the Hellenistic period is the epigraphical recording and publication of royal pieces of correspondence that granted special privileges to a given city-state, broadcasting the dynamics of civic life and international diplomacy to both members of the community and visitors from abroad." See also Hofmann, "Communication between City and King in the Hellenistic East," 145–46: "Only a small portion of texts was finally inscribed on stone to create permanency and evoke the approval of the gods. Temples were favoured places for publishing documents, but the *agora*, as political center of the city, could guarantee maximum publicity. The most important benefit of thus publicizing a document, as a royal official put it when advising the publication of a royal dossier he had forwarded to the city of Illium, was the prospect that the grants mentioned in it would remain securely in their possession for all time." Chaniotis, *War in the Hellenistic World*, 69: "Its [sc. Amlada's] inhabitants, part Greek, part native, had taken advantage of the Pergamene involvement during the Third Macedonian War and of a Galatian invasion in 168 BC, and had overthrown the Pergamene garrison. When their revolt was subdued, they had to provide hostages and pay substantial sums for reparations. A few years later (160 BC?) Amlada was in a desperate financial situation. When the city appealed to the king's benevolence, Attalos, acting on behalf of his brother Eumenes II, explained why he accepted their request, released the hostages and reduced the tribute (*RC* 54): 'because I saw that you have repented of your former offences [θεωρῶν οὖν ὑμᾶς μετανενοηκότας τε ἐπὶ τοῖς προημαρτημένοις] and that you zealously carry out our orders.' Through the publication of this letter on stone, the principle of *do ut des* became an example for future generations." The practice continues in the early Roman Empire. Cf., e.g., Rhodes, "Public Documents in the Greek States: Archives and Inscriptions, Part II," 136–53, here 147: "Claudius' letter to the Alexandrians was read aloud, but because 'the whole city' could not be present the prefect had a text displayed in public (though we know it from a papyrus copy [i.e., *P.Lond.* 1912])." See also Oliver, *Greek Constitutions*, 63.

58. Cf. Welles, *Royal Correspondence*, xl–xli, 33, 56, 69–70, 89, 247, 278, 280n1; Henrichs, "*Hieroi*

side of a doorway or entrance of a Greek temple—were common places to display royal letters.[59] Moreover, Hellenistic royal letters often dealt with issues relating to temples[60] and other sacred matters (e.g., the royal letters in response to the request made by the citizens of Magnesia on the Maeander in 208/7 BCE to have their festival for Artemis Leukophryene accepted as equal in status to the Pythian games and to have their city declared sacred and inviolable).[61]

An important observation emerges from our interpretation of 2 Cor 3:3 in light of the publication of royal correspondence inscribed on stone tablets and publicly displayed in temples: The *one* letter of Christ is inscribed in tablets of fleshly hearts, implying *multiple copies* of the royal letter. Such a practice was known in antiquity where the royal letter in question applied to more than one temple within a given city.[62] Thus, each individual Corinthian believer is seen as a copy of the letter of Christ, which corresponds to Paul's conception of the Corinthians as corporately and individually the temple of the Holy Spirit (cf. 1 Cor 3:16–17; 6:19; 2 Cor 6:16).[63] Paola Ceccarelli makes the point that the arrival of the Hellenistic king in a city was "almost a divine epiphany," but that, given the vast expanses of territory controlled by a Hellenistic king, "the public reading of a royal letter by the king's friend or ambassador in the agora or in the assembly [i.e., the *ekklēsia*] functioned as a substitute for a direct appearance or epiphany, and the inscription of a royal pronouncement within the

Logoi and *Hierai Bibloi*," 239n111; Piejko, "Antiochus III and Ptolemy Son of Thraseas," 248–49.

59. Cf., e.g., Ma, *Antiochos III*, 252 (quoted above), 287, 305, 340, 344, 367.

60. For example, the letter of Seleucus IV to Heliodorus (178 BCE), a *prostagma* that regulated all temples in Coele-Syria and Phoenicia. Cf. Cotton-Paltiel et al., "Juxtaposing Literary and Documentary Evidence," 1–15; Bencivenni, "King's Words," 152.

61. Cf. Ceccarelli, "Letters and Decrees," 149–69; Ma, *Antiochos III*, 261: "To enjoy *asylia*, a city (with its territory) had to be declared 'holy' (ἱερά) to a deity—often a local decision, prompted by an oracle or an apparition. The city then asked for recognition as 'holy and inviolate,' which could only be granted piecemeal, by the members of the international community, each in a specific decree; a collection of such decrees could be referred to as 'the *asylias* (τὰς ἀσυλίας: I. Stratonikeia 7, lines 4–5). The procedure combined acknowledgement of the city's consecrated status and an agreement to refrain from spoliation against the city or on its territory."

62. For example, of the three copies of dossier that have been found containing the letter of King Seleucus IV to Heliodorus (a *prostagma* that applied to all temples in Coele-Syria and Phoenicia [see above]), two of the copies came from the town of Maresha (40 km southwest of Jerusalem) and were associated, in all likelihood, with two different Hellenistic temples there. Cf. Cotton-Paltiel et al., "Juxtaposing Literary and Documentary Evidence," 3–4. In other cases, the royal correspondence was designed from the beginning as a circular letter to various communities in the empire, so the publication clause of the letter refers to plurality of letters and copies. Cf. Welles, *Royal Correspondence*, 162: "The plural of ἐπιστολῶν, like that of ἀντίγραφα, στήλας, and τόποις below, is probably to be explained by the general tendency of Hellenistic chanceries to use plurals where they are logically inappropriate.... On the other hand, these plurals are particularly appropriate if the letter is in fact only one copy of a circular letter which was being sent, *mutatis mutandis*, to many other satrapies throughout the empire. With this in mind, the writer naturally thought of 'letters,' 'copies,' 'stelae,' and 'places.'"

63. In stating that individual Corinthian believers are copies of the letter of Christ, we are not suggesting thereby an inert system of replication. The concrete expression of the letter of Christ in each case also exhibits the creative activity of transformation by means of the Spirit.

enclosure of a sanctuary enabled a similar experience of vicarious royal presence in the act of reading."[64] On this analogy, when people "read" the lives of the individual Corinthians as copies of the "letter of Christ," they are vicariously experiencing the royal presence of Christ, the author of the letter.

No wonder, then, that Paul did not need letters of recommendation either to or from the Corinthians: Insofar as he was involved in the process of inscribing the letter of Christ on the Corinthians' hearts through the Spirit, the apostle mediated the very presence of Christ in their midst for all to see. Moreover, the self-perpetuating euergetical dialogue that has been established between Christ and the Corinthians— and, by extension, between the apostle of Christ and the Corinthian assembly—means that Paul no longer needs to be concerned with winning the assembly over to his cause for the first time.[65] The Corinthians' changed lives, as exemplified by their gratitude and loyalty in the euergetical dialogue, are proof positive of Paul's authority and

64. Ceccarelli, "Image and Communication in the Seleucid Kingdom," 231–55, here 231–32. On the effect of *parousia* caused by the reception of a letter, see Ceccarelli, *Ancient Greek Letter Writing*, vii–viii, 3, 9, 268, here 3n8: "The *graphe* ['letter'] is thus the image of the correspondent." The function of a royal letter as mediating the personal presence of the sender could explain the apotropaic function of the pseudepigraphic letter of Jesus Christ to King Abgar, which is first attested in Eusebius, *Ecclesiastical History* 1.13.4–10 and copies of which have been found inscribed in liminal spaces such as the threshold of a house and the gate of a city. Cf. Henry, "Apotropaic Autographs," esp. 173. For the Coptic text of Leiden Anastasi 9 (500–600 CE), whose original title is "The Letter of Jesus Christ our Lord to Abgar," see https://www.coptic-magic.phil.uni-wuerzburg. de/index.php/text/kyp-t-1606/. The correspondence begins with Abgar https://www.coptic-magic. phil.uni-wuerzburg.de/index.php/text/kyp-t-1479/: "Abgar, the king of Edessa, the city, writes to the great king, the son of the living God, Jesus Christ, Greetings!" Jesus is being entreated as a king, indeed "the great king." Jesus' letter responds to King Abgar's entreaty for healing for his city (emphasis mine): "The copy of the letter of Jesus Christ, the son of the living God, writing to Abgar, the king of Edessa. Greetings! You are blessed, and that which is good will happen to you, and blessed is your city, whose name is Edessa, for you have not seen <but> you have believed, you will receive according to your faith and according to your good intention. Your illnesses will be healed, and if you have committed many sins as <a> man, they will be forgiven for you, and Edessa will be blessed forever, and the glory of God will multiply among its people, and faith and love will shine in its streets. I, Jesus, it is I who commands and it is I who speaks. Because you have loved greatly, I shall preserve your name as an eternal memory and an honour and a blessing among the generations who come after you through your entire lineage, and they will hear it to the end of the earth. It is I, Jesus, who has written this letter with my very own hand. *The place to which this manuscript is affixed, no power of the Adversary nor unclean spirit will be able to approach nor to reach into that place, and forever.* Be well in peace, amen! The letter of our Lord Jesus Christ to Abgar. Amen." Since this is the only writing directly attributed to Jesus, it is surely significant that it takes the form of a royal letter. Indeed, the apotropaic power attributed to the public display of this letter is reminiscent of the status-changing, performative effect of Hellenistic royal letters on the cities to which they are addressed.

65. On reciprocity in Paul, see esp. Barclay, *Paul and the Gift*.

genuineness as an apostle.[66] In this sense, the Corinthians themselves are also Paul's letter of recommendation (2 Cor 3:2; cf. 1 Cor 9:1-2).[67]

The "letter of Christ" is subject to the usual disclaimer about pressing a metaphor too far. We certainly cannot expect this singular metaphor to provide detailed analysis for *our* questions about Pauline theology.[68] Nevertheless, seen in the context of the Hellenistic royal correspondence, the metaphor is a master stroke. It succinctly incorporates various strands of Paul's thinking about the dissemination of the gospel in all its intricate weave: the origin of the gospel as a performative speech-act of the resurrected and enthroned Lord Jesus Christ; Paul's mediation of the transformative message of the gospel to the Corinthian community; the Corinthians' reception and embodiment of the message through the Spirit; and the display of the message's comprehensive effects in the Corinthians' lives for all to see. In this sense, the royal-letter metaphoric does clarify how the communal letter is simultaneously a recommendation "to the community itself" (2 Cor 3:1, πρὸς ὑμᾶς).

"Administered by Us"

In 2 Cor 3:2-3, Paul uses the *letter* metaphor to exemplify the reciprocity between himself and the Corinthians assembly: The Corinthians are "letters" in two complementary senses, which contrast the places where the letters are inscribed (i.e., in Paul's heart and in the Corinthians' hearts, respectively) and the agency of the parties in each case. On the one hand, the Corinthians are Paul's letter of recommendation, written on the apostle's heart (v. 2). In other words, the Corinthians are the tangible evidence of Paul's genuineness as an apostle. But how they came to be such a "letter" for Paul is described in the very next verse, which highlights the apostle's important role in that process. Thus, on the other hand, the Corinthians are a "letter of Christ," which is inscribed on their own hearts (v. 3). Since, as Paul makes clear, he was involved in some way in enabling the Corinthians to become this "letter of Christ" (διακονηθεῖσα ὑφ' ἡμῶν [see further below]), the Corinthians' role as a letter in the first sense (i.e., as a letter of

66. Cf. Hafemann, *Suffering and Ministry in the Spirit*, 223: "Paul's authority is identified with and supported by the changed hearts which come about as he mediates the Spirit as *the* eschatological gift *par excellence*." In terms of the royal-letter tradition on which 2 Cor 3:3 is in part based, the giving of the Spirit in the heart is the status-changing benefaction that initiates the self-perpetuating euergetical dialogue with the Corinthians.

67. Cf. Hafemann, *Suffering and Ministry in the Spirit*, 188-99, 205, 207.

68. For example, for purposes of the present article, we remain agnostic about how our principle interpretive decision on 2 Cor 3:3 relates to Paul's opponents in 2 Cor 2:14-7:4 (e.g., οἱ πολλοί in 2:17), whether a kind of "Hellenistic sophistic" opponent (e.g., Bruce Winter and George van Kooten) or opponents who are internal to the community and not primarily taken up with the problems of Torah but with problems of "apostolic weakness" (e.g., Margaret Mitchell and Paul Duff). If we are correct that Paul is drawing on a tradition that combines the Hellenistic royal correspondence and the Epistle of Enoch, then Paul's perspective in 2 Cor 3:3 may not reveal anything particular about the opponents. The question remains open for now.

recommendation for Paul) is based on their being a letter in the second sense (i.e., as a letter of Christ mediated by Paul). Hence, we see the reciprocal relationship between the Corinthians community and its founding apostle.

By this point at the latest, we can see that Paul has moved far beyond his opening query in 2 Cor 3:1, about whether he needs letters of recommendation to or from the Corinthians. If the Corinthians themselves are the vicarious presence of Christ in "letter" form, then the genuineness of Paul's apostleship is clear. For it was the apostle himself who either "delivered" the letter or "administrated" the letter that was inscribed on the tablets of the Corinthians' hearts: ἐστὲ ἐπιστολὴ Χριστοῦ διακονηθεῖσα ὑφ᾽ ἡμῶν (2 Cor 3:3b).[69]

Evidence for the latter possibility (i.e., that Paul "administrated" the letter of Christ rather than "delivered" it) can be seen from the fact that a royal letter sometimes appears in a hierarchical dossier of letters that includes the intermediaries who are involved in carrying out the king's instructions to have his correspondence inscribed in stone.[70] For example, in the "Dossier Concerning the High-Priesthood of Nikanor: Correspondence of Philotas to Bithys, Zeuxis to Philotas, Antiochos III to Zeuxis" (209 BCE), the first letter, at the top of the dossier, is from a local official (Philotas) to a subordinate who will actually have the letter inscribed in stone (Bithys). The second letter down is from a high-ranking official (the viceroy Zeuxis) who instructs the local official (Philotas) to carry out the inscription of the letter. The last letter in the dossier is from the king himself (Antiochos III) to his viceroy (Zeuxis), the last part of which contains the initial publication clause (to write up the copy of the letter on stone stelae and expose them in the most conspicuous sanctuaries).[71] All three missives were inscribed on a large stele, surmounted by a massive semicircular pediment.[72]

Seen in this light, Paul's reference to the letter of Christ being διακονηθεῖσα ὑφ᾽ ἡμῶν (i.e., administrated by the apostle) could be comparable to a high-ranking, royal official receiving instructions from the king to have the royal letter inscribed in stone. Although he is neither the author nor the coauthor of the letter,[73] the apostle is intimately involved in the actual process of inscribing the word of Christ onto the recipients' hearts. This occurred when Paul initially proclaimed the gospel—the

---

69. For the various uses of the verb in different contexts, see Collins, "A Monocultural Usage: διακον-words in Classical, Hellenistic, and Patristic Sources," 287–309, here 301–4. Collins includes 2 Cor 3:3 under "[i] διακονεῖν [ii] τι [iii] τινα [iv] πρός / [i] deliver [ii] something [iii] at someone's behest [iv] to another" ("A Monocultural Usage," 302). See also the discussion of διακονηθεῖσα ὑφ᾽ ἡμῶν in Hafemann, *Suffering and Ministry in the Spirit*, 199–205.

70. On the nature and function of the epigraphical publication of administrative dossiers, see Ma, *Antiochos III*, 149.

71. Cf. Ma, *Antiochos III*, 288–29; cf. 122, 149. For another example of a dossier of letters, with the royal letter itself containing the initial publication clause, see Ma, *Antiochos III*, 354–56 (no. 37: Royal Enactment Concerning the State Cult for Laodike [February/March to May 193]).

72. Cf. Ma, *Antiochos III*, 122.

73. Cf. Hafemann, *Suffering and Ministry in the Spirit*, 205, who argues that "Paul is at least its [sc. the 'letter of Christ's'] 'co-author.'"

performative word of Christ—to the Corinthians, whereby they underwent a change of status in multiple respects through the work of the Spirit in their hearts.[74] As we have seen, the result is that the Corinthians are restored to the status quo ante, a status analogous to the creation of humankind in Genesis 1–2 (see the discussion of Ezek 36:26–27 and 37:1–14 above and of 2 Cor 4:6 below).

Restoration of the Status Quo Ante

In view of our discussion of the restoration of the status quo ante, the Hellenistic royal correspondence provides us with yet another interesting and important insight for our interpretation of 2 Cor 3:3. As Ma discusses in thoroughgoing detail, "the Great Idea to which Antiochos [III] devoted his life"[75] was a program of reconquest of the patrimony,[76] i.e., the territory that he considered his inherited right,[77] so that cities were restored to their former status under the Seleucids.[78] This was what Antiochus III was attempting to accomplish: the reduction of all cities of Asia Minor to "the ancient structure of sovereignty" (in antiquam imperii formulam, Livy 33.38.1).[79] Ma refers to "the palimpsestic history of Asia Minor,"[80] whereby the region was continually reconquered, each time erasing the claim of the previous regime and reasserting the ancestral claim of the new king.[81] As a result, the collections of inscribed royal letters on display in Hellenistic temples cumulatively recorded "the local epigraphical narratives": e.g., "the antas of the temple of Athena at Herakleia, where the Seleukid letters were succeeded by the letter of the Scipios, or the 'epigraphical museum' of the Amyzonian Artemision, recording the life of the city under Ptolemies, Seleukids, Rhodians, and as a free community."[82]

Seen in this light, "the letter of Christ" that the Corinthians embody presupposes a similar "epigraphical museum"—a long history of subjugation, which entails a repeated cycle of the erasure of old statuses and alliances and the imposition of new

74. Cf. Hafemann, *Suffering and Ministry in the Spirit*, 205: "As the participial phrase 'having been ministered by us' indicates, the Corinthians owe their existence as Christians to Paul's ministry in Corinth. As the 'letter of Christ,' the Corinthians are part of what Christ has accomplished through Paul. . . ."

75. Cf. Ma, *Antiochos III*, 32.

76. As we have seen, the concept was evidently common during the Hellenistic period. See on *Jub.* 8:11–12 compared with 10:37–42 in chapter 2.

77. Cf., Ma, *Antiochos III*, 217.

78. As we have seen, the performative utterance of the king himself was the sole determiner of (re) conquered city's status. Cf., e.g., Ma, *Antiochos III*, 100.

79. As discussed previously, Antiochus III's policy was broadly interpreted to include not only the parts of Asia Minor conquered by Seleucus I but, according to Appian (*Syr.* 1), also Coele-Syria, some parts of Ptolemaic Cilicia.

80. Ma, *Antiochos III*, 51, 81.

81. Cf. Ma, *Antiochos III*, 31, 252.

82. Ma, *Antiochos III*, 252.

ones to replace them. This time, however, the situation is very different: "The founding act of violence" is not conquest through military means,[83] but rather the death of the crucified Messiah, which is seen as a gracious act (cf., e.g., 2 Cor 5:14–15, 21; 8:9; 13:4; 1 Cor 15:4). Moreover, the new status brought about by the death and resurrection of the Son of God, while certainly palimpsestic,[84] is not a bid to reclaim a mundane kingdom of relatively recent origin,[85] but rather the reestablishment of the original world order through an act of "new creation" (2 Cor 5:17).[86]

Conclusion to Part 1

In 2 Cor 3:3, Paul sets up a contrast between royal letters inscribed in stone and the royal "letter of Christ" engraved on human hearts through the Spirit in order to order to emphasize his own role as an official who is involved in the engraving process. The analogy is apposite because normal royal letters are performative in nature, effecting a fundamental status change in the communities to which they are addressed. Conquest entailed the momentary loss of the vanquished party's political existence, to be recreated by a unilateral pronouncement (a performative speech-act part excellence) of the conqueror. Such royal letters also establish a euergetical dialogue in which benefaction requires a fitting response of thanksgiving and loyalty. Finally, at least in the case of the Seleucids, royal letters involved a return to the status quo ante—the reversion of the patrimony to its rightful heirs.

All of these aspects are important for understanding why and how Paul uses the royal-letter tradition in 2 Cor 3:3. First, Paul conceives of his gospel as the performative word of Christ that effects a fundamental status change in the Corinthian community to which it is addressed.[87] Thus, the letter of Christ engraved on the Corinthians' hearts through the work of the Spirit effects a comprehensive transformation, which entails a complete loss of their previous existence to be re-created by a unilateral pronouncement (*the* performative speech-act par excellence) of the Conqueror,[88] resulting from repentance and forgiveness of past sins. Paul, of course,

83. For the term "the founding act of violence," see Ma, *Antiochos III*, 33, referring to the victory of Seleucus I over Lysimachus at Corupedium (281 BCE), "when 'all of Lysimachos' kingdom became spear-won to Seleukos [Polybius 18.51.4]." Subsequent Seleucid kings used this signal victory as a pretext to "reconquer" any territory that may have been lost.

84. Cf. 2 Cor 5:16–21; 10:1–6.

85. For example, by the time that Antiochus began his program of (re)conquest, Asia Minor had become spear-won to Seleucus I only about 58 years earlier (281–223 BCE).

86. Paul had previously impressed upon the Corinthians that "for us there is one God, the Father, from whom are all things and for whom we exist, and one Lord, Jesus Christ, through whom are all things and through whom we exist" (1 Cor 8:6).

87. Compare our discussion of Paul's performative gospel as a word of Christ in the previous chapter.

88. The title of J. Christiaan Beker's book is suggestive in this context: *Der Sieg Gottes*. Within the Corinthian correspondence, see, e.g., 1 Cor 15:25 (alluding to the concluding words of Ps 110[109]:1):

was involved in the process of inscribing the Corinthians' hearts when he initially preached the gospel to them. Therefore, his own authority and veracity as an apostle are underscored by the Corinthians' changed lives. Second, the royal letter of Christ established an euergetical dialogue vastly superior to that of normal royal letters. Instead of a form of reciprocity (*do ut des*) that masks oppression on the part of the king and perfunctory tokenism by the people,[89] Paul presents the letter of Christ as fostering a genuine relationship of love and obedience from the heart through divine enablement.[90] Finally, the royal letter of Christ also returns believers to the status quo ante, because the transformation brought about by the Spirit in the Corinthians' hearts restores humanity to the originally intended will of God for creation. The new humanity in Christ thus embodies the divine will from the heart.

The result of our interpretation of 2 Cor 3:3 is to render clearer the exemplaric pragmatics of the Corinthian community as a letter on a worldwide stage. It also reinforces a counter-imperial reading of the Pauline letters, in which Christ is presented as an alternative king, whose royal correspondence does not depend on external fanfare, but on inward, communally formative proclamation.

Part II: The Use of Gen 1:3 in 2 Cor 4:6

The second part of this chapter can proceed more expeditiously, since 2 Cor 4:4–6 reinforces some of the same ideas that we have already discussed on the basis of 3:3. Given its context in 2 Cor 3–4 (and particularly 3:3), Paul's statement in 4:6 is almost certainly an allusion to Gen 1:3, as indeed most scholars recognize. It is significant, however, how much Paul's conception of his gospel is rooted in the divine performative utterances of Gen 1–2. The two creation accounts of Genesis, together with their uptake in the prophetic tradition, provide Paul with language and models for the way that God in Christ speaks things into existence, sometimes through prophetic agency.[91] The apostle argues essentially that in proclaiming the message of

---

"For he [sc. Christ] must reign until he has put all his enemies under his feet." We may add 2 Cor 2:14, where Paul refers to himself as the vanquished being led in triumphal procession by God as the victor.

89. The Hellenistic kings were primarily warlords who ruthlessly and with mechanical precision carried out their imperialistic ambitions to bring cities into their orbit and then to follow up with a post-conquest military occupation that was both oppressive and exploitative, in Ma's words, "a landscape of extortion through 'organized violence'" (*Antiochos III*, 121; cf. 105, 193–94, 243). All of this should be considered when reading the gracious letters written by the victorious Hellenistic kings and subsequently monumentalized on stone (cf. Ma, *Antiochos III*, 109–11). Hence, Polybius's contrast (5.11.6) between the tyrant (who rules by fear) and the king, whose characteristic is "to do good to all and be loved on account of his beneficence and kindness, thus ruling and presiding over people with full willingness," can be taken *cum grano salis*.

90. Of course, Paul can also use coercion in order to compel submission (cf., e.g., 1 Cor 5:3–5; 2 Cor 10:1–11).

91. Similarly, we suggested in chapter 7 the possibility that Paul understood Gen 12:3 as a further unfolding of the divine performative utterance in the original creation of the world (Gen 1).

the gospel to the Corinthians, he is an integral part of the recipients' transformation into a new creation.

"Christ, Who Is the Image of God" (2 Cor 4:4)

It stands out immediately that in describing the gospel, Paul refers to "the light of the gospel of the glory of Christ, who is the image of God" (τὸν φωτισμὸν τοῦ εὐαγγελίου τῆς δόξης τοῦ Χριστοῦ, ὅς ἐστιν εἰκὼν τοῦ θεοῦ, 2 Cor 4:4). This reference to the "image of God" (εἰκὼν τοῦ θεοῦ) clearly alludes to Gen 1:26–27:

> καὶ εἶπεν ὁ θεός Ποιήσωμεν ἄνθρωπον κατ᾽ εἰκόνα ἡμετέραν καὶ καθ᾽ ὁμοίωσιν. . . . καὶ ἐποίησεν ὁ θεὸς τὸν ἄνθρωπον, κατ᾽ εἰκόνα θεοῦ ἐποίησεν αὐτόν, ἄρσεν καὶ θῆλυ ἐποίησεν αὐτούς.

> Then God said, "Let us make humankind *according to our image* and according to [our] likeness. . . ." And God made humankind; *according to the image of God* he made it; male and female he made them.

Thus, Gen 1:26 quotes the divine performative word verbatim, and v. 27 reports that that word was efficacious in bringing about a status change from nonbeing to being.

As previously mentioned, Gal 3:28c cites Gen 1:27 (οὐκ ἔνι ἄρσεν καὶ θῆλυ) as part of the declaration of the divine performative utterance of the gospel. In other words, the framework for Paul's gospel is strongly creational. The ultimate performative speech-act, from a biblical perspective, was the series of divine utterances, which, according to Genesis 1, effected the creation of the world. Here, the powerful word of God is the means of bringing a new reality into existence:

> Day 1: "And God *said*, 'Let there be light'; and there was light" (Gen 1:3).

> Day 2: "And God *said*, 'Let there be. . . .' And it was so" (vv. 6–7).

> Day 3: "And God *said*. . . . And it was so" (v. 9). "And God *said*. . . . And it was so" (v. 11).

> Day 4: "And God *said*. . . . And it was so" (vv. 14–15).

> Day 5: "And God *said*. . . . So God created. . . ." (vv. 20–21).

> Day 6: "And God said. . . . And it was so" (v. 24). The sixth and final day of creation culminates with the creation of humankind in the image and likeness of God and as male and female (vv. 26–27).

In a similar way, Paul's gospel, sourced in divine revelation (cf. Gal 1:11–12, 15, 16), is also a performative utterance—the word of Christ—that effects a status-change by divine fiat: Believers become a new creation (Gal 6:15; 2 Cor 5:17), in that they are transformed into the image of Christ, who is the image of God (2 Cor 3:18; 4:4, 6; 5:17).

This is the recapitulation of the beginning, albeit on a new and improved basis insofar as human beings are enabled to be Spirit-directed from the heart. Alert readers will notice that Paul is here partaking of the *Urzeit-Endzeit* thematic, which we have often encountered in previous chapters. The difference here is that the role of the Spirit in that process of transformation comes to the fore, along with its biblical basis.

The Use of Gen 1:3 in 2 Cor 4:6

Second Corinthians 4:6 continues to develop the theme of the gospel and its performative effects, building on the transformation that, according to 3:2–3, takes place through the Spirit in human hearts.[92] Indeed, this passage shows that Paul's gospel is a performative speech-act that is analogous to—or possibly an instantiation of—God's performative utterances in creation: "For it is God who said, 'Let light shine out of darkness' (ὅτι ὁ θεὸς ὁ εἰπών· ἐκ σκότους φῶς λάμψει), who has shone in our hearts to give the light of the knowledge of the glory of God in the face of Christ."[93] Most scholars agree that Paul is alluding here to the *fiat lux* in Gen 1:3: καὶ εἶπεν ὁ θεός

92. As Hofius ("Wort Gottes und Glaube bei Paulus," in *Paulusstudien*, 166–67) correctly observes, 2 Cor 4:6 continues the thought developed in 3:2–3 insofar as both passages focus on the human heart as the locus of transformation. The gospel that Paul preaches mediates the "Spirit of the living God" and, through this Spirit, the gospel is written "in the tablets of human hearts." In the gospel, which impresses itself on the human heart and actually creates faith, Paul sees Ezek 36:26–27 fulfilled, whereby God himself promises to re-create the human heart through his Spirit. Hence, the Spirit-impelled gospel is a performative word that imparts life and makes the human a "new creation" (καινὴ κτίσις). See also Wort Gottes und Glaube bei Paulus," 168–69: "Das πνεῦμα is nicht 'die Gabe, die der Glaube empfängt' [so Bultmann], sondern die den Glauben allererst schaffende δύναμις Gottes, die unlöslich mit dem schöpferischen Wort Gottes verbunden ist."

93. On Paul's use of χάρις as a performative speech-act, see Joubert, "ΧΑΡΙΣ in Paul," 187–211, here 206–9. On 2 Cor 4:6, cf. Joubert, "ΧΑΡΙΣ in Paul," 196 (author's emphasis): "The event on the road to Damascus (cf. Acts 9; 22; 26), where Paul saw the face of Christ in a divine revelation (2 Cor 4:6; cf. also 1 Cor 9:1; 15:8), completely altered the direction of his life. His present cosmology [as a Pharisee], which was the result of a process of internalisation of and reflection on a complex network of knowledge over many years, proved to be irreconcilable with the new knowledge now given to him δι' ἀποκαλύψεω[ς] Ἰησοῦ χριστοῦ [*sic*] (Gal 1:12). From this moment on, the basic religious axioms of his previous life-world [were] challenged and, consequently, also adapted and altered. . . . As a result of this revelatory experience, the content of Paul's symbolic knowledge and his language system was also transformed (Phil 3:10–11). The basic building block of Paul's new symbolic world, which turned him into a καινὴ κτίσις, was his salvific knowledge concerning the death and resurrection of Christ (2 Cor 5:17). The very same Jesus, whom he previously knew κατὰ σάρκα (2 Cor 5:16) and whose followers he persecuted for spreading blasphemy, now became the centre of his existence. Paul's new knowledge of *history* (namely that God raised Jesus from the dead) and the *symbolic universe* (namely that Jesus is now the heavenly *Kyrios*, the mighty son of God through the Holy Spirit Phil 2:11; Rom 1:3), was interpreted by him as nothing less than a sovereign act of God's χάρις, *a creatio ex nihilo*, a second Genesis (2 Cor 4:6). In other words, Paul knew that it was only through God's own goodness, *extra nos*, and not out of himself that he received this new knowledge, as well as the apostolic calling to preach this message to the nations (Gal 1:16). This is also expressed in 1 Cor 15:10: χάριτι δὲ θεοῦ εἰμι ὅ εἰμι."

Γενηθήτω φῶς. καὶ ἐγένετο φῶς.[94] In both cases, we are dealing with reported speech of God himself, which is introduced by an introductory formula: καὶ εἶπεν ὁ θεός (Gen 1:3) and ὁ θεὸς ὁ εἰπών (2 Cor 4:6). In both cases, God calls forth light out of darkness.[95] Although the verbs are different in each case (i.e., the imperative γενηθήτω and the future indicative λάμψει, respectively), "the Genesis text is so foundational for the Jewish understanding of creation that the allusion can hardly be missed."[96]

The fact that Paul alludes here to God's first performative utterance on Day 1 of creation may also imply—*pars pro toto*—the culminating performative utterance on Day 6, the creation of humankind in the image and likeness of God (Gen 1:26–27; cf. 1 Cor 11:2–16), which, as we have seen, is alluded to in Ezek 36–37 (2 Cor 3:3 alludes, in turn, to Ezek 36:26–27) and in 2 Cor 4:4.[97] In that case, Paul's thought process seems to be that the performative utterance of the gospel effects a transformation into the image of Christ, who is the image of God, hence the re-creation of humankind in the image of God.

For Paul, this transformation into Christlikeness is a comprehensive process, entailing changes that are epistemological, behavioral, relational, and ontological. The Spirit plays a key role in each of these four aspects of the transformation. Let us consider, for example, the latter two aspects. Volker Rabens's study of 2 Cor 3:18 emphasizes the *relational* aspect of the Spirit's work: On the basis of the intimate relationship to God in Christ created by the Spirit, believers are transformed "into the same image," that is, their lives portray more of the characteristics of Christ (understood primarily in an ethical sense).[98] According to Rabens,

94. Cf., e.g., Thrall, *Second Epistle to the Corinthians*, 1.315–16; Hofius, "Wort Gottes und Glaube bei Paulus," 161–63. Richard B. Hays argues that Isa 9:1 LXX (ὁ λαὸς ὁ πορευόμενος ἐν σκότει, ἴδετε φῶς μέγα· οἱ κατοικοῦντες ἐν χώρᾳ καὶ σκιᾷ θανάτου, φῶς λάμψει ἐφ᾽ ὑμᾶς) also plays a role in Paul's formulation (*Echoes of Scripture in Paul*, 152–53). See, however, Guthrie, *2 Corinthians*, 244.

95. The ἐκ σκότους in 2 Cor 4:6 picks up the reference to σκότος from the verses before and after Gen 1:3: Gen 1:2 (καὶ σκότος ἐπάνω τῆς ἀβύσσου) and Gen 1:4 (καὶ διεχώρισεν ὁ θεὸς ἀνὰ μέσον τοῦ φωτὸς καὶ ἀνὰ μέσον τοῦ σκότους).

96. Hays, *Echoes of Scripture*, 153.

97. We may note here that Aristobulus—the Alexandrian Jew who wrote philosophical interpretations of works in Greek about the Jewish lawgiver Moses during the first half of the second century BCE—uses Gen 1:3 as a summarizing verse to encapsulate all of the performative speech-acts of God in the subsequent context (i.e., Gen 1:6, 9, 11, 14, 20, 24): "For it is necessary to take the divine 'voice' not as a spoken word, but as the establishment of things. Just so has Moses called the whole genesis of the world words of God in our Law. For he continually says in each case, 'And God spoke, and it came to pass' (καὶ εἶπεν ὁ θεός, καὶ ἐγένετο)" (frg. 4.3, *ap.* Eusebius, *Praep. Ev.* 13.12.3). The only question is whether Aristobulus is citing the LXX at this point (cf. Gen 1:3, καὶ εἶπεν ὁ θεός . . . καὶ ἐγένετο φῶς) or making an independent translation of the Hebrew text. Cf. Adams, "Did Aristobulus Use the LXX for His Citations?," 185–98, here 193–94. See also Ps-Longinus, *De Sublimitate* 9.9, which cites Gen 1:3, 9–10 to obtain the *pars pro toto* effect: "A similar effect was achieved by the lawgiver of the Jews—no mean genius, for he both understood and gave expression to the power of the divinity as it deserved—when he wrote at the very beginning of his laws, I quote his words: 'God said'—what? 'Let there be light. And there was. Let there be earth. And there was.'" Cf. Stern, *GLAJJ*, 1.361–65, here 364.

98. Cf. Rabens, *Holy Spirit and Ethics in Paul*, 174–203.

As believers let themselves be drawn by the Spirit into the transforming and empowering relationships with God and the community of faith and then live according to the values set forth by Paul's gospel, the depth of their relationship to God and others will increase. Believers are thus further empowered as they put Paul's imperatives (which are, in fact, aimed at deepening their relationships to God and others) into practice.[99]

Rabens's relational approach is explicitly set against a "substance-ontological approach" (based, e.g., on 1 Cor 12:13), whereby the Spirit is understood as an infusion of a substance that effects the transformation.[100] Rabens tries to bridge the two approaches: "The adjacent pairs which are often conceived as opposites (i.e., relational versus substance-ontological transformation; [functional] empowerment versus [ontological] transformation; new self-understanding versus a completely new self) thus converge in our concept of *transforming relationships*."[101] At this point, Rabens adduces 2 Cor 3:18, which

> displays lucidly how these various perspectives of the two different sides are part of the same coin (a growing relationship, a deepening of knowledge of God and self, and a "substantive" transformation). What is more, this verse also provides the answer to a tantalizing question that might be addressed to our relational model of the Spirit's work in Paul's ethics: Is it the Spirit that transforms and empowers, or is it the relationships, or is it those (i.e., Ἀββα, Χριστός, ἀδελφοί) with whom believers are brought into relation? The solution is that for Paul, these aspects cannot be set against one another. It is the Spirit (καθάπερ ἀπὸ κυρίου πνεύματος), the relationships (expressed by intimacy that is created by the unveiling of faces, as well as the beholding) and the one that "we all" are being related to (i.e., τὴν δόξαν κυρίου) who effect the transformation (μεταμορφούμεθα).[102]

If, as we are arguing, however, the gospel is a performative utterance directly analogous to (or perhaps a further unfolding of) the divine performative speech-act at creation, then the transformation effected by the gospel through the agency of the Spirit is *more than relational*; it is *ontological* as well.[103] Without referring to the

99. Rabens, *Holy Spirit and Ethics in Paul*, 252.

100. Cf. Rabens, *Holy Spirit and Ethics in Paul*, 138–39.

101. Rabens, *Holy Spirit and Ethics in Paul*, 143 (author's emphasis).

102. Rabens, *Holy Spirit and Ethics in Paul*, 143. The single quotation marks in his expression "'substantive' transformation" are telling. He is evidently still resisting the idea that the Spirit also effects an ontological transformation.

103. In a similar way, Ezek 37:1–14 entails a performative speech-act that God instructs the prophet to make to the dry bones in order to revivify them through the agency of the Spirit/spirit that was involved in creation: "Prophesy to these bones, and say to them: O dry bones, hear the word of the Lord. Thus says the Lord God to these bones: I will cause רוח to enter you, and you will live. I will lay sinews on you, and will cause flesh to come upon you, and cover you with skin, and put רוח in you, and you shall live; and you shall know that I am the Lord" (Ezek 37:4–6). Cf. Kutsko, *Between Heaven*

probable allusion to Gen 1:3 in 2 Cor 4:6, Rabens nevertheless comes close to this insight in his exegesis of 2 Cor 3:18 (τὴν αὐτὴν εἰκόνα [i.e., the image of Christ] μεταμορφούμεθα ἀπὸ δόξης εἰς δόξαν) and 4:4 (τὸν φωτισμὸν τοῦ εὐαγγελίου τῆς δόξης τοῦ Χριστοῦ, ὅς ἐστιν εἰκὼν τοῦ θεοῦ) when he interprets being transformed into the image of God/Christ as effecting a "new creation" (cf. 2 Cor 5:17) analogous to the original creation of humankind in the image of God in Gen 1:27 (καὶ ἐποίησεν ὁ θεὸς τὸν ἄνθρωπον, κατ᾿ εἰκόνα θεοῦ ἐποίησεν αὐτόν, ἄρσεν καὶ θῆλυ ἐποίησεν αὐτούς).[104] This conception of humankind's re-creation in the image of God arguably explains why Paul is able to write that "there is no longer male and female (ἄρσεν καὶ θῆλυ); for all of you are one in Christ Jesus" (Gal 3:28).[105]

As we have seen, a performative speech-act changes the world by having an effect on it and creating a new state of affairs and new relations between things. How much more does the ultimate performative create things with words, whether in the original creation or in the new creation?[106]

---

and Earth, 129–38, here 133: "The imagery of [Ezek] 37:1–8 appears directly to reflect and develop the scene of creation of man in Genesis 2, using a constellation of imagery that related re-creation with creation." It is interesting to note that Paul evidently alludes to Ezek 37:6, 14 (δώσω [sc. God] τὸ πνεῦμα μου εἰς ὑμᾶς, "I will give my Spirit into you") in 1 Thess 4:8 (τὸν θεὸν τὸν [καὶ] διδόντα τὸ πνεῦμα αὐτοῦ τὸ ἅγιον εἰς ὑμᾶς, "God, who [also] gives his Holy Spirit into you"). On the connection between 2 Cor 3:3 and 4:6, see Hafemann, *Suffering and Ministry in the Spirit*, 209: "Believers are created anew, ontologically understood (cf. I Cor. 1:26ff.; 2:5, 12–16; 3:16; 5:4f.; 6:19; II Cor. 3:17f.; 4:6; 5:17)."

104. Cf. Rabens, *Holy Spirit and Ethics in Paul*, 197–98. As we have seen, the most important transaction following a takeover "entailed the momentary loss of the vanquished party's political existence, to be recreated by a unilateral pronouncement (a performative speech-act *par excellence*)" of the conquering king (Ma, *Antiochos III*, 111–12). The divine speech-act of justification in and through the gospel works similarly. Cf. Linebaugh, "Debating Diagonal Δικαιοσύνη," 126 (emphasis mine): "The God who justifies the ungodly (Rom 4:5) is the God who gives life to the dead and calls non-beings into being ([θεοῦ τοῦ ζωοποιοῦντος τοὺς νεκροὺς καὶ καλοῦντος τὰ μὴ ὄντα ὡς ὄντα,] 4:17). The linking of these liturgical predications of God suggests an analogous form of divine activity in the acts of creation, resurrection and justification. Justification, therefore, can be said to be an act of creation, or at least a creation-like act. God does not call the sinner righteous even though he or she is not; God calls the sinner righteous and thereby constitutes him or her as such. God's forensic word is right, not because it describes the empirical, but because, as God's word, it establishes reality. Justification, then, to borrow Gathercole's borrowing of Barth, is *creatio e contrario*—a recreation of the sinner as righteous. In the context of Rom 3:21–26, however, it is clear that *the first movement of this re-creation is an act of de-creation*: the judgment of the world in the cross. The justification of the sinner takes place on the other side of judgment." We may compare Rom 4:17 and 2 Cor 4:6 with Philo, *Spec. Leg.* 4.187: "For he [sc. God] called the non-existent into existence, in that he created . . . light from darkness" (τὰ γὰρ μὴ ὄντα ἐκάλεσεν εἰς τὸ εἶναι . . . ἐκ δὲ σκότους φῶς ἐργασάμενος). On creation by God's word, see further Pss 33:6, 9; 148:5; Isa 40:26; 48:13; Wis 9:1–2 ("O God . . . who have made all things by your word, and by your wisdom have formed humankind"); Jdt 16:14; 1 En. 69:13–16; Aristobulus 4.3 (*ap.* Eusebius, *Praep. Ev.* 13.12.3 [cited above]); Philo, *Somn.* 1.75–76 (citing Gen 1:3); *Jos. As.* 12:3; *2 Bar.* 21:4–5; 48:8; John 1:3; Heb 11:3; 2 Pet 3:5; Ignatius, *Eph.* 15:1; Shep. Herm. *Visions* 1.3.4.

105. Again, see the discussion of Gal 3:28 in chapter 7.

106. From Paul's perspective, the Mosaic Law does not effect the new creation, but rather sin and death. Therefore, although Paul regards the Law as "holy," and the commandment as "holy, just, and good" (Rom 7:12), he nevertheless speaks of it as "the law of sin and death" (Rom 8:2). Similarly, in

Conclusion to Part II

Given its context in 2 Cor 3–4, Paul's statement in 4:6 is almost certainly an allusion to Gen 1:3, as indeed most scholars recognize. It is significant, however, how much Paul's conception of his gospel is rooted in the divine performative utterances of Gen 1–2. The two creation accounts of Genesis, together with their uptake in the prophetic tradition, provide Paul with language and models for the way that God in Christ speaks things into existence, sometimes through prophetic agency. The apostle argues essentially that in proclaiming the message of the gospel to the Corinthians, he is an integral part of the recipients' transformation into a new creation.

Conclusion

Second Corinthians 3–4 advances our knowledge of Paul's appropriation and creative unfolding of the Jesus revolution in several ways. First, we learn that Paul is very much involved in Jesus' project of renewing the world. It cannot be missed that Paul's gospel is rooted in the creation accounts of Gen 1–2, to which Jesus also appealed in many and sundry ways. As we have seen, the correlation between *Urzeit* and *Endzeit* means that for both Jesus and Paul, the "new creation" recapitulates the originally intended will of God for creation. Second, the royal letter of Christ that Paul administers in Corinth is an example of creating a new world *in the shell of the old*. The Jesus revolution entails creating the new and better world in the prefigurative future anterior (i.e., in the time before the consummation at the Parousia), so this construction takes place right alongside the old world, which, for Paul, is in the process of passing away. Sometimes, the Jesus revolution expresses the anticipated new world in terms of old forms which are then filled with new meaning and purpose. In chapter 3, for example, we explained Jesus' performative proclamation of the gospel of the kingdom in terms of the Hellenistic royal letter tradition. This is the very same tradition that we have used in the foregoing chapter to understand Paul's proclamation of the gospel in terms of the "letter of Christ." The similarity between Jesus and Paul at this point is not accidental. The apostle's metaphor of the "letter of Christ" constitutes his creative unfolding of Jesus' own performative proclamation of the gospel. This important observation on the nature and function of Paul's gospel and its correlation with Jesus corrects the long-standing misconception that their respective proclamations have little or nothing in common.

Second Corinthians 3:3 puts a premium on the creation of the future anterior in another important respect. The "letter of Christ" metaphor makes it clear that the Corinthians' *transformed lives* are the tangible evidence of the reality of the Spirit's working in their hearts and therefore verification of the fact that the new creation is

---

contrast to Paul's ministry of the new covenant that mediates the life-giving Spirit (2 Cor 3:6), Moses's ministry was a ministry of death and condemnation (vv. 7, 9).

in fact underway. Seen against the backdrop of the Hellenistic royal letter tradition, the "letter of Christ" as manifested in the copies of the letter on public display in the Corinthians' changed lives is tantamount to the revelation of the royal presence of Christ before the whole world. In other words, the proclamation of the gospel, as a word of Christ delivered through the apostle of Christ, continues to be projected to the world in and through the Corinthians' changed lives. Hence, personal and communal transformation is not just a matter of internal moral renewal; rather, it is an important way in which the proclamation of the gospel spreads and effects the new creation. By the same token, when believers' lives do not demonstrate the royal presence of Christ to the world, the Jesus revolution is subverted to that degree.

A final implication of the foregoing study deserves brief mention here. Judith Newman has argued that the repeated performances of 2 Corinthians by the liturgical body would have led to community formation, on the one hand, and to the scripturalization of Paul's letter, on the other: "Performing the letter constitutes an act of author construction and community formation. The reading of the letter enacts the letter as scripture."[107] This process would have been further enhanced by the reference to "the letter of Christ" in 2 Cor 3:3. Seen against the background of the Hellenistic royal correspondence, "the letter of Christ," of which the liturgical body (i.e., the Corinthian assembly) are copies, presupposes a euergetical dialogue that keeps the process going as well as the preservation and honorific public display of the textual artifact. Insofar as Paul's letters themselves were seen as royal correspondence, that would have encouraged their collection and canonization.[108] All of this goes to the thesis that Paul wrote more than occasional correspondence.[109]

---

107. Newman, *Before the Bible*, 75–105, here 105.

108. As mentioned previously, David Trobisch argues that Paul himself created the earliest edition of his letters: The apostle collected, edited, and arranged four letters—the Corinthian correspondence (in the form of two collections of fragments—1 and 2 Corinthians), Galatians, and Romans—and then sent them, together with Rom 16 as a cover letter, to the Christ-followers in Ephesus. Cf. Trobisch, *Die Entstehung der Paulusbriefsammlung*; Trobisch, *Paul's Letter Collection*. Trobisch compares the Pauline letter collection with other ancient letter collections as a literary *Gattung*, but he does not consider how Hellenistic royal letters were collected, edited, and displayed so that they could be read by a larger public. Since, as we have shown elsewhere, Paul's letter to the Galatians is modeled on the Hellenistic royal correspondence as mediated by the Epistle of Enoch (cf. Scott, *Apocalyptic Letter to the Galatians*, ch. 4), and, as the present chapter argues, Paul's concept of "the letter of Christ" in 2 Cor 3:3 has the same Hellenistic model in view, especially with respect to his role in that process, Trobisch's thesis might be enriched by examining this material.

109. Cf. Hartman, "On Reading Others' Letters," 137–46.

9

The Jesus Revolution in the Book of Revelation

Introduction

PERHAPS MORE THAN ANY other writing in the New Testament, the book of Revelation sets forth the world as it presently is in stark contrast to the world to come. In the meantime, believers are to construct the prefigurative future anterior—the new world in the shell and alongside the old (that which will have been). As the author states in Rev 1:3, "Blessed is the one who reads aloud the words of the prophecy, and blessed are those who hear *and who keep* what is written in it; for the time is near." The Apocalypse of John was meant to be read aloud and therefore to be heard.[1] Equally important is the need to *keep* what is written in the book of Revelation, that is, abide by its admonitions and persevere in the time before the consummation. The blessing pronounced at the very beginning of Revelation can be compared to the one that frames the whole Enochic corpus. As Judith H. Newman has shown, the blessing in 1 En. 1:1—"The words of the blessing with which Enoch blessed the righteous chosen who will be present on the day of tribulation, to remove all the enemies; and the righteous will be saved"—is "potent speech" or, in the terms we have been using, "performative language," a testamentary blessing that is "in effect an open-ended promissory note."[2] In other words, the potent character of this divine speech pertains

1. Cf. Rev 2:7, 11, 17, 29; 3:6, 13, 20, 22; 13:9; 22:17, 18.

2. Newman, "Participatory Past," 429. We have appealed to Newman's work several times in our developing Biblical Theology of the New Testament, and all of them are relevant for our understanding of the book of Revelation. (1) In the introduction, we used Newman's concept of liturgical practices in

to words that had power not just in the past, but that have enduring power that can become active on agents in the future. "The words of blessing pronounced to 'a distant generation' [cf. 1 En. 1:2, 'Not for this generation do I expound, but concerning one that is distant I speak'] become adopted by the contemporary audience whenever they are heard."[3] Moreover, Enoch's testamentary promise, like John's promise, is not just the word of a mortal human being; it is the reiteration of divine revelation and, as such, a divine promise. This divine promise is both *realized*, partially fulfilled at "pregnant times" when subsequent audiences hear it anew, and *unrealized*, awaiting full and final realization at some undisclosed point in the future.[4] "Pronouncing blessing locates its pronouncer in a zone of response to a revelatory interruption, in which the pronouncer participates in an atemporal order associated with the divine realm. Its temporal realization is unanticipated, but must be discerned by those with the ability to discern an inbreaking, pregnant *now*."[5] We shall argue in the present chapter that the divine promise that John reiterates is creation-based, an outworking of the original divine performative utterances in creation (Gen 1)[6] which become instantiated afresh at the "pregnant nows."[7] In other words, John's Apocalypse folds space-

---

scripturalization and of scripture in community formation in order to describe the mutual relationship between the three elements of the New Testament assemblage (i.e., condition/abstract machine, concrete elements, and agents/personae). (2) In the introduction, we noted that Newman's concept of testamentary blessing provides a possible explanation for the compositional development of the Enochic corpus as a whole: The testamentary blessing at the beginning of 1 Enoch serves not only to set up the series of visionary sub-collections that are gradually incorporated into the rolling collections, but to alert readers, or listeners, or others who engage in this collection, to their potential response to such inbreaking. (3) In chapter 7, we related Newman's concept of blessing as "potent speech" to our use of the term "performative utterance" (particularly with respect to Jesus' and Paul's "gospel"); we emphasized the connection of Paul's gospel with (re)new(ed) creation as a creative unfolding of Jesus' performative proclamation of the gospel; and we considered whether the divine promise to Abraham in Gen 12:3, which Paul identifies with his "gospel" in Gal 3:8, could be viewed as a further instantiation of the divine performative utterances emanating from the original act of creation described in Genesis 1. (4) In chapter 8, we brought together all these strands from Newman's work: Paul's metaphor of "the letter of Christ" (2 Cor 3:3) exemplifies the transformation in the Corinthians' lives as a *lux fiat* event on par with—or an actual enactment of—the creation of the world in Gen 1; the act of inscripturation in the Corinthians hearts and of Paul in writing the royal letter to the Corinthians can then be related to Newman's concept of "enacting the letter as scripture." Obviously, we are on very fertile ground here for understanding a biblical theology of the New Testament as an ongoing *process*. By the same token, these concepts are helpful for our treatment of the book of Revelation.

3. Newman, "Participatory Past," 429–30.

4. For the concept of "pregnant time" or "pregnant now," see Newman, "Participatory Past," 426, 429, 433.

5. Newman, "Participatory Past," 433.

6. In addition to the divine performative utterances that called the world into existence, Genesis 1 includes blessing speech: "God *blessed* them, saying, 'Be fruitful and multiply and fill the waters in the seas, and let birds multiply on the earth'" (v. 22); "God *blessed* them, and God said to them, 'Be fruitful and multiply, and fill the earth and subdue it; and have dominion over the fish of the sea and over the birds of the air and over every living thing that moves upon the earth'" (v. 28). Cf. Newman, "Participatory Past," 430.

7. Cf. Newman, "Participatory Past," 432: "Blessings are the only kind of prayer speech that is

time—the originary past and the recapitulatory future—at extraordinary moments of blessing appropriated in the present.[8]

The flip side of these positive concepts is the anticipated subversion of the presently prevailing reality. Many of the Jewish and Christian apocalypses are subversive and revolutionary,[9] and resistance to empire, whether Seleucid or Roman, figures prominently in some major apocalypses, notably Daniel and Revelation.[10] The ancient apocalypses arose out of crisis and persecution, amid a sense of lawlessness and existential angst. The Apocalypse of John fits within this general framework. The Apocalypse looks forward to the soon passing away of worldly empire. Thus, when the seventh angel blew his trumpet, the announcement from heaven came: "The kingdom of the world has become the kingdom of our Lord and of his Messiah, and he will reign forever and ever" (Rev 11:15). The anticipated reversal of the topsy-turvy status quo is a source of great comfort and earnest desire in the Apocalypse.

Although Revelation is often condemned for its focus on violence and schadenfreude, it must not be viewed exclusively from this standpoint. At times of crisis and social upheaval, when an apocalypse like Revelation arises,[11] the reflection on the values of the kingdom of God promotes engagement in searching critiques of the dominant political order and the promotion of positive change in social and economic relations, including advocating or actualizing equality of wealth, power, gender, or status. The full apocalyptic scenario includes the vision of a new and better world, not just revenge for injustice and judgment for the unjust.[12]

---

used both by the deity and by humans. Humans can bless other humans, as we see in the case of testamentary blessings, but they can also offer blessings to God. In that way, human blessings provide an index of divine immanence, of the awe-filled experience of the Creator as potent and privileged creator of time and space, as revealer of heavenly wisdom and cosmic mysteries. Yet these blessings are pronounced by a human mouth using the same faculty of speech in which God created and blessed animals, humans, and even sabbatarian time itself." Instead of noting simply an analogy between divine and human blessing-speech, we are suggesting a direct relationship in this case.

8. Cf. Newman, "Participatory Past," 431–32: "The word עלם . . . is flagged by the translators of 1 Enoch, Nickelsburg and VanderKam: 'No English word indicates the fact that in the Greco-Roman period 'alam is acquiring spatial as well as temporal connections (world as well as age).' Thus all of the blessings pronounced by Enoch involve an affirmation of the character of God as one who is beyond human temporality and human containment, but who reveals aspects of divine reality that are in a unique space-time, a dimension not wholly available to all humans."

9. Cf. Collins, "Temporality and Politics in Jewish Apocalyptic Literature," in Rowland, *Apocalyptic in History and Tradition*, 26–43.

10. Cf. Portier-Young, *Apocalypse Against Empire*.

11. The date of composition for the book of Revelation is disputed, although most scholars opt for a date during the reign of the Roman Emperor Domitian (81–96 CE). See, however, Cook, *Roman Attitudes Towards Christians*, 138–251, here 246–50, who dates the book to the time of Emperor Trajan (98–117 CE). On the dating of Revelation, see further Aune, *Revelation 1–5*, lvi–lxx. For our purposes, the exact dating is relatively unimportant, since we do not intend to "decode" the book's visions as referring to concrete historical events.

12. In the Enochic literature, we find a similar combination of desire for revenge against oppressors and an expression of hope for a better future. The Epistle of Enoch (1 En. 92–105), for example,

In the following, we will once again appropriate the assemblage lens of Deleuze and Guattari, applying it this time to an examination of the book of Revelation. In doing so, we are cognizant that Deleuze himself had the same kind of negative reaction to the Apocalypse as D. H. Lawrence did. Lawrence writes: "When we come to read it critically and seriously, we realise that the Apocalypse reveals a profoundly important Christian doctrine which has in it none of the real Christ, none of the real Gospel, none of the *creative* breath of Christianity, and is nevertheless perhaps the most effective doctrine in the Bible."[13] In a similar vein, Deleuze opines: "If we are steeped in the Apocalypse, it is . . . because it inspires ways of living, surviving, and judging in each of us. It is a book for all those who think of themselves as survivors. It is the book of Zombies."[14] Deleuze continues: "With the Apocalypse, Christianity invents *a completely new image of power*: the system of Judgment. The painter Gustave Courbet (there are numerous resemblances between Lawrence and Courbet) spoke of people who woke up at night crying, 'I want to judge! I have to judge!' The will to destroy, the will to infiltrate every corner, the will to forever have the last word—a triple will that is unified and obstinate: Father, Son, and Holy Spirit."[15]

In the present chapter, we certainly question the kind of view expressed by Lawrence and endorsed by Deleuze which divorces "Christian doctrine" in the Apocalypse from Christ himself, and asserts that the book has "none of the real Christ, none of the real Gospel, none of the *creative* breath of Christianity. . . ." Moreover, we should not understand the Apocalypse as inventing "a completely new image of power: the system of judgment." As we will show, the Apocalypse constitutes another example in the New Testament of a creative unfolding of the Jesus revolution.[16] If Revelation features judgment—and particularly the final judgment—in a special way, it has a powerful precursor in Jesus himself.[17] However, the positive side of Jesus' proclamation of the gospel is also strongly in evidence in the Apocalypse. Hence, despite Deleuze's reaction against the Apocalypse, his concept of revolutionary deterritorialization—creating a new and better world in the shell of the old in the prefigurative future anterior—strikes a resonant chord with the Jesus revolution as creatively unfolded in John's Apocalypse.[18]

intersperses a mixture of both elements throughout.

13. Lawrence, *Apocalypse and the Writings on Revelation*, 66 (author's emphasis).

14. Deleuze, *Essays Critical and Clinical*, 37.

15. Deleuze, *Essays Critical and Clinical*, 39 (author's emphasis).

16. Similar to the letter to the Galatians and the letter of James, the book of Revelation is presented as a circular letter, this time to the seven churches of Asia Minor. This similarity invites, once again, a comparison with the Hellenistic royal letter tradition, particularly as it was appropriated by the Epistle of Enoch, but we cannot explore that possibility further here.

17. Cf. Reiser, *Jesus and Judgment*; "The Problem of Gehenna," in Allison, *Resurrecting Jesus*, 56–110; Allison, *Constructing Jesus*, 42, 186, 219, 228–29, 246, 252, 263, 303.

18. My thinking in this paragraph has been stimulated by Dempsey, "Deleuze's Apocalypse," who argues that despite Deleuze's reaction against the Apocalypse, his concept of revolutionary

Christ as Condition / Abstract Machine

In the book of Revelation, as in the New Testament in general, Christ is the condition or abstract machine for the entire writing, that is, Jesus Christ is the vital mechanism that suffuses, animates, and creates a relationship between the constituent elements. Just as the writings of the New Testament were brought together because, in some way, they were seen to function together because of Jesus Christ, so also the many and varied revelatory visions of the Apocalypse function as a system held together by Christ. According to Rev 1:1, what has been revealed is either *from* Jesus Christ or *about* Jesus Christ, depending on how one construes the Greek genitive "of Jesus Christ": "The revelation of Jesus Christ (*apokalypsis Iēsou Christou*), which God gave him to show his servants things that must take place soon; and he made it known, having sent a message through his angel to his servant John." Either construal of the genitive works here, because the Apocalypse presents Jesus Christ both as the Lamb (5:6) and in a mediatory role (cf. 4:1; 22:6).[19] Hence, it is through the revelation of Jesus Christ that the Apocalypse conveys everything else portrayed in the writing. If, as we have seen, Jesus' proclamation inaugurates the kingdom of God by constructing the future anterior in

---

deterritorialization is itself "apocalyptic" in nature, thus radically redefining revelation as a philosophical concept of immanence. Cf. "Deleuze's Apocalypse," 78: "In the end, apocalypse seems more adequate than utopia, precisely because it is capable of being affirmative in the Deleuzian way to an extent that utopia ultimately cannot be. Whereas utopia certainly highlights the deterritorializing mode of resistance proposed and elaborated by Deleuze, apocalypse better integrates reterritorialization therewith, giving to thought—in the concept of revelation that, from out of the combination of apocalypse, also emerges fresh and charged—the power to think of Deleuzian resistance not just in terms of escape and breakdown, as flight out of this world that we care so much to affect, but in terms of increasing expansion, as the breaking of *this* world onto the plurality and potential from which there can always be *a* world. Being leftist, as Deleuze says, is first of all a matter of perception. As such, it is a matter of revelation. It is apocalyptic." While I do not think that we should confuse the term "apocalyptic" any more than it already has been by attempts at "redefinition," I nevertheless appreciate that Dempsey is thinking more in terms of continuity rather than contrast between Deleuze's concept of revolutionary deterritorialization and the book of Revelation. Cf. also Saldanha, *Space After Deleuze*, 42: "Politics is only revolutionary when it leaves all identity and place behind. 'Revolution is absolute deterritorialization even to the point where this calls for a new earth, a new people' (WP 101). What to make of this enigmatic call for a new earth and anew people? The concept of the new earth, the world to come, derives from the ancient apocalyptic trope in the Middle East monotheistic religions. It finds its clearest expression in Christian eschatology (for example, 'Then I saw a new heaven and a new earth, for the first heaven and the first earth had passed away, and the sea was no more,' Revelation 21:1)."

19. A strong case can be made that Rev 1:1 construes the genitive *Iēsou Christou* as a subjective genitive, that is, as a "revelation *from* Jesus Christ." This is shown by the immediately following relative clause *hēn edōken autō ho theos* ("which God gave to him [sc. Jesus Christ]"), in which the feminine accusative relative pronoun *hēn* expands on the term *apokalypsis* ("revelation"). In other words, God is the ultimate source of the revelation, and Christ, the mediator of that revelation, transmits it to John and thence to other believers. Cf. Aune, *Revelation 1–5*, 6, 12. Nevertheless, it is also clear that Jesus Christ himself is the central object of revelation in the Apocalypse. We face a similar issue of how to construe the genitive "of Jesus Christ Son of God" in Mark 1:1: Is Jesus Christ the author of the gospel or its contents? Once again, it is arguably both. Cf. Aune, "Meaning of ΕΥΑΓΓΕΛΙΟΝ in the Inscriptions of the Canonical Gospels," 861–62, 882.

the here and now, then the Apocalypse unfolds Jesus' proclamation through a series of revelations of Jesus Christ that encourage the presence of the future. As we have often stressed, "Jesus wants some things even now to be the way they were in the beginning because that is how they are going to be in the kingdom of God." The book of Revelation is completely in line with Jesus' creation-based agenda.

This struggle to which John gives witness in the here and now is obviously *political* in nature. Indeed, the integral interrelationship between politics and "religion" could hardly be stronger than in this case. As Richard Bauckham rightly observes, "Those who imagine early Christianity as a quietist and apolitical movement should study the book of Revelation."[20] Elsewhere, Bauckham goes so far as to say that the book of Revelation is "the most powerful piece of political resistance literature from the period of the early Empire."[21] John the seer offers Jesus as a vehicle of a robust political critique of the contemporary polity. Insofar as the book of Revelation continues the Jesus revolution, it stands in opposition to all other assemblages, whether they be territorial, state, or capitalist. Yet the book is not merely oppositional; it is *constructive* as well. Revelation is about creating the prefigurative future anterior. The revolutionary transformation that John envisions encompasses personal, corporate, and indeed universal elements. Revelation launches a thought and practice capable of expressing and instantiating a desire both to undo the prevailing world order and to continue the dominical inauguration of the world to come.

The Prefigurative Future Anterior

The book of Revelation is most often understood as *predicting future events*.[22] This is because there is so much in the text that emphasizes future time, whether imminent or ultimate. No less than four times, the book summarily declares that therein things "to take place" are being disclosed (1:1, 19; 4:1; 22:6), and in the two instances that frame the book (1:1; 22:6), the work claims to reveal what is to happen "soon."[23] In addition, it is difficult to escape the impression that for the author, the three series of sevenfold depictions of divine judgment are concerned with imminently forthcoming events: The breaking of the seals (6:1–17; 8:2), the blowing of the trumpets (8:6–9:20; 11:15–19), and the pouring out of bowls of wrath (15:5–16:21) each herald, with increasing intensity and specificity, how the wicked, who are considered allied with

20. Cf. Bauckham, *Bible in Politics*, 101.

21. Bauckham, *Theology of the Book of Revelation*, 38.

22. On the interpretation of the book of Revelation from the early patristic period through the early post-Reformation era, see Boxall and Tresley, *Book of Revelation and Its Interpreters*, esp. Rowland, "The Reception of Revelation: An Overview," 1–25.

23. Compare the temporal aspect of the summary of Jesus' proclamation in Mark 1:15: "The time is fulfilled, and the kingdom of God is *at hand*; repent, and believe in the good news." As we have seen, there is some discussion of whether this represents a "realized eschatology" or an imminent expectation.

the Roman Empire in its embodiment of Satanic power, will undergo judgment for their evil deeds. Moreover, several other announcements of judgment are concerned with the future, whether they are envisioned as punishment of the wicked (14:6–13 14–20; 18:1–24; 20:11–15), as reward of the righteous (20:4–6), or as an eschatological battle (19:11–21; 20:7–10) that will result in the triumph of God and the creation of a new world order (21:1–22:5). The emphasis on the future in John's Apocalypse is on *revolution*—a radical change in which the rule of God in heaven will be extended to the earth as well, thereby eliminating all evil. Indeed, the new world order will be fully and finally ushered in when heaven—the New Jerusalem—descends to earth, and God sets up his kingdom on the renewed earth (21:1–3).[24]

Nevertheless, to assume that the book of Revelation is solely or even primarily concerned with the future is misleading. The Apocalypse also emphasizes that the process of *actualization* of the future is already underway among an ideal audience, the people to come: "The kingdom of the world has become the kingdom of our Lord and of his Messiah, and he will reign forever and ever. [. . .] We give you thanks, Lord God Almighty, who are and who were, for you have taken your great power and begun to reign" (11:15, 17). This process of *actualization* has implications for John the seer's intended audience.[25] In terms of the categories that we have been using in our study of the Jesus revolution, John wants his audience to prefiguratively construct the future anterior in the here and now.[26] Thus, the language of revolution is not limited to ulti-

24. On the renewed world, see further below.

25. The literary means by which John invites his readers into the lived process of actualization is unique. Cf. Aune, "Apocalypse of John and the Problem of Genre," 89–90: "The second aspect of our functional definition [of apocalypses] proposes that apocalypses mediate a new actualization of the original revelatory experience through literary devices, structures and imagery which function to 'conceal' the message which the text purportedly 'reveals.' That is, the skillful apocalyptic writer may portray the revelatory experience which he purportedly had with such literary skill (particularly enhanced through public performance) that the intended audience may indeed participate in the original experience to such an extent that the experience is 're-presented' or re-actualized for them. [. . .] The central message of an apocalypse can lie at the center of or at the climax of a series of literary devices intended to protect the sacred character of the revelatory message from profane hearers and readers. Just as an initiant makes his way through various cultic barriers into the *adyton* where the focal religious experience will be staged, so the audience of such revelatory literature as the Apocalypse of John is brought through various literary structures and devices into the innermost recesses of the secrets which an apocalypse is designed to convey. The phenomenon of profound embedment of the focal message of the Apocalypse functions to conceal, as it were, that message within the innermost recesses of the composition. The movement from one level of communication to another, then, is a device utilized by the author to replicate the original revelatory experience in a literary, rather than a ritual or spatial, idiom, thereby maximizing the participation of the audience in the performance of the Apocalypse within the framework of public performance, possibly within [the] framework of worship. That is, the author does not merely *narrate* the substance of the divine revelation he has received to his audience, he provides the audience with a literary vehicle so that they can, in effect, relive the experience of the seer and thereby appropriate for themselves the revelatory message." See further below on "Worship on Earth as in Heaven."

26. Cf. Bauckham, *Theology of the Book of Revelation*, 7–8: The message of the book of Revelation "is not that the here-and-now are left behind in an escape into heaven or the eschatological future, but

mate outcomes but to the interim steps in the present leading up to the final kingdom come.[27] We are talking about a *process* that includes the active involvement of John's present addressees: "If you conquer, you will be clothed like them [sc. the minority in Sardis assembly who have remained faithful and pure] in white robes . . ." (Rev 3:5). "If you conquer, I [sc. the exalted Jesus Christ] will make you a pillar in the temple of my God; you will never go out of it. I will write on you the name of my God, and the name of the city of my God, the new Jerusalem that comes down from my God out of heaven, and my own new name" (Rev 3:12). "Those who conquer will inherit these things" (Rev 21:7). The process of conquering to which John calls his addresses is not armed resistance,[28] but rather a counterintuitive sort of "conquering"—modeled by the Lamb who was slaughtered[29]—which includes perseverance in the pres-

---

that the here-and-now look quite different when they are opened to transcendence." Compare Dale Allison's quite similar statement about Jesus, which we have already had occasion to quote (*Historical Christ and the Theological Jesus*, 112–13).

27. As we have seen, Jesus' faith in the world to come did not take him out of the world *but rather all the further into it*. In a similar way, the book of Revelation is not a call to retreat from the world or to hope for escape from the world, but rather a summons to actualize, through anticipations, the new and better world of which they have received revelatory glimpses. Cf. Portier-Young, *Apocalypse Against Empire*, 399: "Political theologian Johann Baptist Metz insists on the possibility and even necessity of a nonviolent apocalyptic theology that entails hope for one's enemy. Metz finds in apocalypticism not flight from the world but its temporalization, and deep engagement with human suffering. Out of and within this temporal awareness emerge radical hope, longing for justice, and trust in God; these in turn 'provide a foundation for the seriousness of a liberating praxis and emphasize the urgent and critical character of human responsibility.'" This means, of course, that we must eschew the idea of *Entweltlichung*. Cf. Hengel, "Salvation History," 243: "The reduction in existentialist theology of the saving event to the individual decision of faith in the here and now and the *Entweltlichung*, the 'detachment from the world' by which one achieves one's 'authenticity' (*Eigentlichkeit*) that is bound up with it, also deprives this 'history' of is reality and power of conviction, since only it preserves the indispensable *extra nos* of the revelation of God in Christ, who was active and died for our salvation at that time in Galilee and Jerusalem."

28. As we have seen in our study, the Jesus movement was never about violent revolution. If it had been, it would have been stuffed out at its inception, along with its ringleader (cf. Matt 26:52, "all who take the sword will perish by the sword"). Instead, the Jesus movement continued to flourish and expand precisely because, despite its use of provocative language (e.g., "Kingdom of God," "*Lord* Jesus Christ," "line of David") and its outspoken nonviolent resistance (e.g., proclamation of the "gospel" despite injunctions against such activity), the movement presented no immanent threat to the dominant state assemblage. Nonviolent resistance is also reflected in Daniel, 2 Baruch, Revelation, and the Testament of Moses. See further Portier-Young, *Apocalypse Against Empire*, 219, 227, 229, 234, 236, 262, 277–78, 372, 387, 399, here 274: "The writers of Daniel found Isaiah's Servant a model for nonviolent (לא חמס עשה 53:9) transformational revelatory praxis."

29. The image of the "Lamb" is one of a powerless and vulnerable animal. Its status as "slaughtered" (Rev 5:6, 12; 13:8) further underscores its underdog status as far as the world's values are concerned. We are not to think of a marshal figure here, but rather its very opposite. Nevertheless, the book presents the angels as singing in a mighty chorus, "Worthy is the Lamb that was slaughtered to receive power and wealth and wisdom and might and honor and glory and blessing!" (5:12). This is a complete reversal of what one might expect on the basis of conventional notions of wisdom and power. The *counterintuitive* aspect of the Jesus revolution has been emphasized throughout our study. For example, according to Mark 10:35–45 pars., being first in the kingdom of God is not like the usual exercise of power in mundane kingdoms; it entails becoming last, the servant of all, on the model

ent struggle by patiently enduring persecution (cf. Rev 3:8–10).[30] The outcome of the revolution is foreseen: Not only do the faithful *already* have their crowns that will have been given to them at the successful end,[31] but the Lamb (Jesus Christ) will conquer, for he *is* (*estin*) Lord of lords and King of kings (Rev 17:14).

The book of Revelation evidently sees the past, present, and future in terms of folding of space-time instead of a strictly linear understanding of time. To explain this, let us review a concept that was introduced earlier in the book: a view of history based on the mathematical field of topology, in which a single surface is composed of multiple points that are connected together by folds or morphisms in their surface (like a piece of origami). Independent of linear contiguity, succession or dialectics, topological shapes move and change by folding themselves into new networks of relations. If space-time is a topological plane of various contingent and heterogeneous processes connected together through folding and morphism, then a revolutionary intervention does not emerge dialectically or developmentally, or ex nihilo; it emerges by creating a new fold or connection between various points in space-time: a new arrangement of past, present, and future.[32]

We find this folding of time-space in Rev 12–13: the vision of the woman, the child, and the dragon (12:1–17) and the vision of the two beasts (13:1–18).[33]

"Wisdom" in Rev 13:18 not only denotes the ability to calculate the number of the beast (i.e., "six hundred sixty-six")[34] but also entails (a) the perception that this beast

---

of the Son of Man, "who did not come to be served but to serve, and to give his life a ransom for many" (v. 45). For Paul, likewise, the wisdom of God—especially the crucified Christ!—is completely counterintuitive; indeed, it is foolishness to the world (1 Cor 1:18–2:5). On wisdom in the book of Revelation, see further Stuckenbruck, "Book of Revelation as a Disclosure of Wisdom," 347–59.

30. The book of Revelation uses counterintuitive notions of power and conquering. Cf. Johns, *Lamb Christology of the Apocalypse of John*, 175–80, here 20: "John's readers are to 'overcome' in the same way that the Lamb overcame, making Jesus' death and resurrection ethically paradigmatic for the readers."

31. Cf. Rev 3:11b: "Keep what you have that no one takes away your wreath." In other words, the members of the Philadelphian assembly already have their crowns but must take care that no one take them away. Hence, the outcome of the process is still indeterminate for specific individuals and groups. We may compare the two senses of the term "adoption as sons" (*huiothesia*) in Rom 8: Believers already have "the Spirit of adoption by which they cry, 'Abba! Father!'" (v. 15), but they will receive the adoption of sons in a full and final sense, when, by means of the Spirit who raised Christ from the dead (cf. v. 11), believers' bodies are redeemed at the resurrection (v. 23). See further Scott, *Adoption as Sons of God*, 221–66.

32. The ultimate example of the folding of space-time (or at least the spatial aspect) is when the New Jerusalem comes down to earth and thereby fuses heaven and earth. See further below.

33. For the following, see Stuckenbruck, "Book of Revelation as a Disclosure of Wisdom," 347–59.

34. The number of the beast, 666, has long been recognized as the sum of the numerical equivalents for the Hebrew letters which spell the words "Neron Caesar." By this reckoning, Nero is the second beast of Revelation. This kind of numerical play was quite common in the Greco-Roman world. According to Suetonius, *Nero* 39.1, for example, we find the following saying, which was posted in pubic or circulated: "A new enumeration: Nero killed his own mother." Here, "Nero killed his own mother" is conveyed in Greek as *Neron idian metera apecteine*. Greek numbers are represented by letters of the alphabet. Hence, the numerical value of *Neron* is the same as that of the rest of the line *idian*

is merely a defeated power, and therefore (b) the confidence to resist any strictures the beast might impose, even to the point of death. This "wisdom," in other words, entails far more than what even the most discerning mind can immediately comprehend.

We can see this principle at work in Rev 12–13, where the visions convey insight into the nature of the dragon and the two beasts' activities. From the very beginning, the dragon is portrayed as posing a treat to the woman who bears a child (12:1–5); after a brief period of temporary protection for the woman and child (v. 6), the dragon "wages war" against them (12:17; cf. v. 13)—a conflict that extends, through the two beasts, until the end of chapter 13. The insight, however, that the text offers relates to the initial outcome of the conflict, as described in 12:7–9, and the immediately following proclamation from heaven (vv. 10–13). By the time the situation of conflict threatens the well-being of believers (13:7), the dragon and its minions have already been involved in a celestial war (12:7–9). This event is not simply a "battle" that marks out one phase of a prolonged struggle, but rather a decisive defeat that *from the outset* determines the status of "the great dragon." Significantly, the dragon is also called "the ancient serpent," "the devil," and "Satan, who deceives the whole world." In other words, the latter-day beasts' activities go back to a power that has *already been defeated*.

So when did the defeat of Satan take place—or when will it have taken place, if it is a future event? Some interpreters think the text refers to an eschatological event that, as yet, lies in the author and the audience's future.[35] Jan Dochhorn, by focusing narrowly on tradition history in relation to Satan (or the devil) as a single figure, argues that there is no evidence prior to John's Apocalypse that the devil was defeated in the past. Rather, if one follows the lead of parallel texts such as the *War Scroll* (1QM 17:5–8, describing the eschatological war between "the sons of light" led by the archangel Michael against the "sons of darkness" led by Belial) and John 12:31 ("now the ruler of this world will be cast out"), the victory over Satan should be considered as taking place in the eschatological future. Loren Stuckenbruck argues, however, that another case can be built on the basis of different textual evidence. For example, Luke 10:18, in which Jesus is quoted as saying, "I *saw* Satan fall like lightning," is not clearly referring to a future event. In addition, the interpretation of this text as a future event presupposes an unwarranted distinction between defeating Satan and all other forms of defeating evil. Against such a distinction, we can cite Mark 3:20–27 pars., according to which Jesus identifies his exorcisms (expulsion of demons) with the defeat of Satan himself. Stuckenbruck himself draws attention to the past defeats of evil angels, such as the rebellious "sons of God" in the Book of the Watchers (1 En. 6–16), in which, at the time of the Flood, the archangel Michael carries out the punishment against the Watchers and their leader Shemihazah (cf. 10:11–13). David Aune, who likewise regards the defeat of Satan and his minions in Rev 12:7–9 as eschatological, has dismissed any influence of the fallen angels tradition on the grounds that they were not *cast out* or forcibly

---

metera apecteine, namely 1005, suggesting that Nero is a matricide (a person who kills their mother).

35. Cf. Dochhorn, *Schriftgelehrte Prophetie*, 254–85; Aune, *Revelation*, 2:692–93.

removed from heaven (cf. *eblēthē* in Rev 12:10, 11), but rather *left* heaven on their own volition (1 En. 6:1–5). It should be noted, however, that in Rev 12:12, the summary of what has happened is described in the active voice: "the devil has come down (*katebē*) to you." Significantly, this interchange of passive verbs with an active one in Revelation is similarly found in the Animal Apocalypse (1 En. 85–90), which clearly stands under the influence of the myth of the rebellious angels in the Book of Watchers. Although the lead star (equivalent to Shemihazah in the Book of Watchers) *fell from heaven* (1 En. 86:1), those "many stars" coming after him are said not only to have come down, but also to have been *thrown down* from heaven (86:3).[36]

Where does all this leave us with the aforementioned folding of space-time in the book of Revelation? Our confusion about the time-frames in the Apocalypse is caused by the fact that Revelation does not adhere to one time-frame but freely conflates or enfolds different time-frames—past, present, and future—into one continuous, overlapping reality.[37] Seen in this light, it is unnecessary to opt for one alternative over another. Critical is the heavenly proclamation in Rev 12:11: "they [sc. the faithful] have conquered him [sc. the devil] by the blood of the Lamb and by the word of their testimony." It is tempting to regard this defeat of the devil as not having happened until Jesus' death "on the cross" (11:9 refers fleetingly to Jesus' crucifixion); however, for the writer of Revelation, what happened in Jesus' death is an all-encompassing reality that begins even before the crucifixion itself. That reality reaches back to reflect something that was inaugurated by God "at the foundation of the world,"[38] when not only is the Lamb found already in a slaughtered state, but also the names of those who are/are not written in the book of life are determined (cf. 13:8 ["everyone whose name has not been written from the foundation of the world in the book of life of the Lamb that was slaughtered"]; 17:8 ["the inhabitants of the earth, whose names have not been written in the book of life from the foundation of the world"]). In this particular case, the crucial dawn of "salvation and power and the kingdom of God and of his Messiah" (12:10) has been generated by the Lamb's blood (i.e., his sacrificial death). The new reality that has come into being is intermingled with a prior one. According to the older Jewish apocalyptic tradition, a formative perspective is lent to the present on the basis of the defeat of Satan at the time of the Flood, which expelled evil

36. Similarly, 1 En. 88:1 refers to the lead star as having fallen, followed by a description of how one of the archangels bound him hand and foot and threw him into the abyss, as also happens to the other stars (88:3).

37. We see the same kind of conflation or enfolding of time-frames in the Epistle of Enoch (1 En. 92–105). Since the whole Apocalypse is framed as a letter (cf. Rev 1:4–5; 22:21; see further Aune, *Revelation 17-22*, 1238–41), it is possible that the book of Revelation can be understood as directly influenced by the Epistle of Enoch. Preliminary work on this possibility has been carried out on the relationship between Paul's letter to the Galatians and the Epistle of Enoch. See Scott, *Apocalyptic Letter to the Galatians*, ch. 4. A similar analysis seems feasible for Revelation as well.

38. As mentioned above, the temporality of the Apocalypse is creation-based.

from the heavenly sphere.[39] Though images from this primordial defeat of Satan can still be identified in Rev 12:7–9, the language of triumph is ultimately absorbed into a christological framework. The advent of Jesus (12:1–5) and its culmination in his death, resurrection and ascent (12:11; cf. the reference to the son's being taken away to God and God's throne in v. 5b) become the new foci around which the primordial defeat of Satan is defined. At the same time, the new context is not simply a matter of reassigning the primordial defeat of Satan to the more recent past; *even Jesus' death in the recent past is but an outworking of a reality that existed in primordial time as well.* By the same token, the most recent beast to arise out of the earth, who speaks like a dragon (Rev 13:11) and whose encrypted name takes "wisdom" to discern (v. 18), is merely the latest manifestation of the long-defeated Satanic foe.

Creation of a New People

Premise #1: The Jesus revolution entails absolute positive deterritorialization—the process of creating a new and better world in the shell of the old in the prefigurative future anterior. This process also calls forth a new people who currently do not exist. Where, then, will these people come from? The new people will not come from any majority; instead, they will come from the world's marginalized minorities.[40] To be on the right side of history, therefore, means to make common cause in the name of Christ with those marginalized minorities.

Premise #2: As an apocalyptic seer, John is a "fabulation artist," a becomer.[41] With larger-than-life images that metamorphose conventional representations and conceptions of collectivities, he evokes and enables the creation of the people to come. If the book of Revelation (7:9–17) conceptualizes this people to come—"from every nation, from all tribes and peoples and languages" (v. 9)—as unified with respect to language (v. 10), dress (vv. 10, 13, 14), and worship of the one, true God (vv. 10, 15), such unity is not evidence of the retrograde reterritorialiation of a new nationalism,[42] but rather

39. On the notion of the prior defeat of evil in Second Temple apocalyptic literature, see Stuckenbruck, *Myth of Rebellious Angels*, 1–35, 161–86, 240–56.

40. What constitutes "minorities" is not their absolute count, which may in actuality be greater than that of the "majority," but rather their position within asymmetrical power relationships that are reinforced by and implemented through linguistic codes and binary oppositions. All creativity and revolutionary transformation necessarily comes from a minoritarian position. The majority is intent on the maintenance of the status quo.

41. "Fabulation" is the artistic practice of evoking and fostering the creation of a people to come. Fabulation is related to story-telling and myth-making. The can be accomplished in many ways: the painter creates with color; the musician creates with sound; the writer creates with words; and the philosopher creates by inventing concepts.

42. Cf. Sharon Jacob, "Face-ing the Nations: Becoming a Majority Empire of God—Reterritorialization, Language, and Imperial Racism in Revelation 7:9–17." Although, as of the present writing, Jacob's essay has not yet been published and therefore could not be consulted, the online blurb provides the following summary https://api.equinoxpub.com/chapter/show/30151: "Sharon Jacob's chapter . . . illustrates the ways in which linguistic imperialism helps construct a homogenous subjectivity of

a matter of the revolutionary becoming-indistinguishable that breaks down linguistic codes and binary oppositions that normally divide and stratify people in the mundane world.[43] Whereas nationalism *excludes* based on a single criterion (e.g., race, ethnicity, or language) and legitimates itself by claims based on linear history, the Jesus revolution actually opposes the kind of standardization imposed by state assemblages and fosters instead complex, heterogeneous inclusivity.

In the book of Revelation, the people to come is always latent, dormant, ready to mobilize, when popular forces push against the forces of constraint and homogenization that would compel everyone to strive to conform to a single and uniform set of norms.[44] At that moment, the people become a creative community that is open to innovation and a wholly new future and their own creative potential. They reject the mentality that is the basis of all narrow-mindedness and exclusivity, the ant-hill mentality that leads to conformism (conformity to a single set of universal norms) and populism (appeal to conservative instincts of tribalism and obligation rather than to openness and creative becoming). The problem with populism, nationalism, and sectarianism is that they are all retrograde movements that seek to either maintain or reestablish closed societies, thus making the Other into a virtual enemy and excluding everything but homogeneity and sameness. These regressive movements are defensive and reactionary rather than opening out and moving forward toward a new universal humankind.

It is impossible to become an "open" people by gradually enlarging the closed society that claims it is pure and dominant. Rather, becoming an "open" people happens only by a sudden, revolutionary leap in response to exceptional individuals who provide us with a unique example to emulate, a force so attractive and compelling that it inspires us to form a new and more inclusive social entity. We see before us the creative life-force made manifest. We see someone who is already excluded from the status quo and is compelled to think and act ahead of their time, and for that reason already entwined with a people to come, invoking and awaiting that people. In John's vision, the model to be emulated is provided by Jesus Christ, the

the colonized other in the empire. Using D&G's theories on deterritorialization, reterritorialization, facialization, and language to interpret Revelation 7:9-17, Jacob suggests that the image of the nations speaking in one language constructs them into pliable, compliant, recognizable, and comprehensible entities. At the same time, the insertion of heterogenous nations into a single, unified, homogenous vision of the empire of God can be viewed as the beginnings of the nationalistic vision of the divine empire of God. The new divine order 'is a multinational, multicultural, multilinguistic multitude that speaks in one language. The facialization of these nations, illustrated through an overt and deliberate reterritorialization of their language and dress, racialized in order to familiarize, constructs a nationalized vision where only one nation, speaking one language, wearing one dress, gathers to worship only the one and true God.'"

43. See the discussion of Gal 3:28 in chapter 7. As discussed there, becoming-indistinguishable in our sense of the term is related to the recapitulation of humankind to the originally intended will of God for creation. See further below.

44. Key points in the following are adapted from Baugh, "Open Society and the Democracy to Come," 352–66.

Lamb of God who was slain. As in the Gospels, Jesus Christ's self-sacrificial leadership of love for humankind (cf. Mark 10:45), in obedience to the will of the Father (Mark 14:36), sets the agenda.

Jesus Christ calls into being a new creation, a new kind of human being,[45] which changes one's relationship not just to the whole of humanity, but with the rest of creation as well. This new creation of humankind is perpetually open to a future of further innovation and transformation—believing that a new world *is* coming and needs to be actualized even now, albeit in preliminary form—rather than trying to go back to or preserve the past of the hidebound majority, the repressive norms that would impede rather than free.[46] The majority is not about becoming; becoming is *creation* and continually connects with the real potentiality of revolution. The new species of human being resists the conditions of a closed society—the already-constituted power, institutions or peoples, everything that crushes or imprisons, all that is intolerable in the present—by replacing authoritarianism, hierarchization, and exclusion with liberty, equality, and fraternity. Renewed humanity is thus in the process of being liberated from the world as it is presently constituted in order to allow the individual to once again become a co-creator, commensurate with the whole movement of creation, that is, resonating with a wholly different historical trajectory, toward the recapitulation of the originally intended will of God for creation. Until that ultimate goal is reached at the consummation, however, renewed humanity is

45. Cf. Eph 2:15: "he [sc. Christ Jesus] created in himself one new humanity" in place of the hostile duality of Jews and Gentiles. We leave open at this point how to characterize the people to come in the book of Revelation. Cf., e.g., Korner, *Reading Revelation after Supersessionism*, who argues that John's extensive social identification with Judaism(s), Jewishness, and Jewish institutions does not reflect a literary program of replacing Israel with the *ekklēsiai* ("churches"/"assemblies"), that is the Jewish and non-Jewish followers of Jesus as Israel's Messiah. Rather, John is emplacing his Christ-followers further within Israel, without thereby superseding Israel as a national identity for ethnic Jews who do not follow Jesus as the *Christos*. There are three primary roads travelled in this investigative journey. First, Korner explores ways in which a Jewish heritage is intrinsic to the literary structure, genre, eschatology, symbolism, and theological motifs of the Apocalypse. Second, he challenges the linear chronology of (generally) supersessionist dispensational readings of Revelation's visionary content by arguing for a reiterative/repetitive structure based on certain literary devices that also provide structure for visions within Jewish apocalypses and Hebrew prophecies. Third, he incorporates the most recent research on *ekklēsia* usage, especially in Asia Minor, to assess how John's *ekklēsia* associations might have been (non-supersessionally) perceived, especially by Jews in Roman Asia. In our study, by contrast, we are asking whether Jesus Christ, as the condition/abstract machine of the revolutionary New Testament assemblage, represents a rupture with previous assemblages, such that a new species of human being is in the process of formation. This new species of human being was already anticipated by the Enochic tradition, which has the characteristics of a Jewish revolutionary movement of the Second Temple period (see especially the expected transformation of humankind at the end of the Animal Apocalypse [1 En. 90:37–38]). Therefore, although the book of Revelation represented a major break with the territorial assemblage of the dominant form of contemporary Judaism, it was still within Judaism, broadly conceived. A similar argument is developed for Paul's letter to the Galatians in Scott, *Apocalyptic Letter to the Galatians*, chap. 3.

46. A majority always presents itself, not as a specific group or contingent assemblage, but as representative of humanity in general. In contrast, a minoritarian politics does not see itself as the expression of the people but as the creation of a "people to come."

necessarily always virtual and perpetually in the process of becoming. As such, it will always be "the people to come," that is, a minor people, a despised, inferior, and dominated people, which is always incomplete and yet completely devoted to the radical inclusion of all races and continents. From the perspective of the Apocalypse, *anything less than this trajectory is* not *the Jesus revolution*.

This new species of human being sustains completely new social relations. No longer does it relate on the basis of established norms, such property, family, nation, and the particular qualities that belong to the individual and serve to separate them into competing interests (e.g., ephemeral notions of beauty, popularity, productivity, and success that are perpetually stoked at the speed of social media). Instead, the new humanity relates to others by recognizing their equality in virtue of their *creative potential* rather than their identifying and actual characteristics. This is obviously not how the "real world" works, and it may therefore seem counterintuitive. As we have seen throughout our study, the Jesus revolution is not about maintaining the status quo but about overturning it. We may recall, however, that Jesus did not handpick his most intimate followers on the basis of their superior qualities, but rather in spite of their almost total lack of qualifications. He saw in these marginal people what they would *become*,[47] rather than what they *were* at the present time.[48] If we extrapolate this *principle of transformation* to the rest of the burgeoning Jesus movement, we see the potential for an unbounded, open society which includes within itself the Other—the misfit, the mistreated, the miscreant, the outcast, the downcast, the weak and lowly things of the world—in a continuously open and creative becoming-Other that engenders active solidarity. This is a community of friends that is open to each other, to change, to all contacts, and to the possibilities of yet more friendships.

Premise #3: Although John's images and impulses are novel in certain respects, they are not completely without precedent. They are influenced in many cases by antecedents drawn from the Old Testament, early Jewish literature, and Greco-Roman sources. Some of these antecedents refer to the eschatological creation of a new people composed of Israel and the nations. Take, for example, the assemblage of Jewish writings collectively called 1 Enoch, in which we have already identified the Epistle of Enoch as a possibly major influence on the Apocalypse. The Enochic authors believed that they were members of the eschatological community of the chosen constituted

47. As we have seen, however, most of the Twelve are not much more than names in a list of disciples, perhaps signifying that they did not really amount to all that much in the end (and in one case, a disciple actually became a traitor).

48. Douglas Hyde, a leader in the Communist Party in London during the 1930s and 1940s who defected to the Catholic Church in the late 1940s, tells the story of a stuttering, obese communist who, despite a severe disability and glaring lack of qualifications ("the most unpromising-looking piece of human material that ever came my way"), went on to become a national union organizer within his own industry. Cf. Hyde, *Dedication and Leadership*, 62–72, here 69: "Jim's story says much of what can be said about the training of a leader as the Communists see it. First, I inspired him, gave him the clearly defined goal of a new and better world and the belief that he and others could between them achieve it provided that they prepared themselves sufficiently for the moment of opportunity."

by revelation.[49] This revelation—although it was the possession of a select group of Israel that arose at the threshold of the dawning eschaton—was to be proclaimed to "all the sons of the earth" (1 En. 100:6), in the hope that they too would be saved at the end time of the final judgment. The conversion of the human race is a prominent theme in both the Enochic corpus as a whole and the Epistle of Enoch in particular. First Enoch is presented as the sacred writing of a revelation in primordial antiquity, before the division of humankind into Israel and the gentile nations, thus giving the Enochic books an inherently universal significance.[50] Through a long transmission process, the writing was to be conveyed from the revelatory mediator, Enoch, through his son Methuselah, to "the generations of the world" (82:1). The Enochic corpus views two different men as pivotal in this transmission process on the way toward the universalization of the revelation, although both men occupy similar functions in that process. In the Book of the Watchers, on the one hand, the focus is on Noah, who receives divine revelation that teaches him "how he may preserve himself alive and escape forever" (10:3). It is Noah's seed that will be propagated: "From him a plant will be planted, and his seed will endure for all the generations of eternity" (10:4). Hence, in the eschaton, when Michael renovates the earth and eliminates evil, "the plant of righteousness and truth" will again appear and flourish (10:16–17). After this, "all the sons of men will become righteous, and all the peoples will worship" God (10:21). In the Epistle of Enoch (particularly the Apocalypse of Weeks that is embedded in the Epistle), on the other hand, the line of transmission runs through *Abraham* and Israel, rather than through Noah. Abraham is chosen as "the plant of righteous judgment," and from him, stems Israel, "the plant of righteousness forever and ever" (93:5). Hence, in the eschaton (at the conclusion of week 7), Israel becomes the basis for a righteous remnant: "the chosen will be chosen, as witnesses of righteousness from the everlasting plant of righteousness, to whom will be given sevenfold wisdom and knowledge" (93:10). After this (in week 9), "righteous law will be revealed to all the sons of the whole earth . . . , and all humankind will look to the path of everlasting righteousness" (91:14). As George W. E. Nickelsburg notes, "Thus revelation is universalized and becomes the source of righteousness of the whole human race."[51] The rest of the Epistle of Enoch envisions a similar process of transmission of the Enochic revelation. Enoch's wisdom is written down for "the last generations who will observe truth and peace" (92:1). In the eschaton, Enoch's books will be given to "the righteous and pious and wise," and they will learn from those books "all the paths of truth," and then, instruct "the sons of the earth" (104:12–105:2). According to 100:6, "the wise among men will see the truth, and the sons of the earth will contemplate

49. Cf. Nickelsburg, *1 Enoch 1*, 86; Nickelsburg, "Revealed Wisdom as a Criterion for Inclusion and Exclusion," 73–91. The following is based in part on Scott, "Comparison," 193–218.

50. Thus, 1 Enoch represents a salient example of the fact that a universal perspective is not the product of Christian invention.

51. Nickelsburg, *1 Enoch 1*, 53.

these words of this epistle, and they will recognize that their wealth cannot save when iniquity collapses."

Like the Epistle of Enoch, the Apocalypse of John constitutes a new people through revelation, and this new people is decidedly universal in scope. The events anticipated in the book of Revelation are a way of construing the world that is shaped by what has been revealed.

Creation of a New World

The book of Revelation holds out hope for a gloriously transformed material existence *on earth*. What is perhaps somewhat unique is that the future is expected to unfold in two stages (Rev 21:1–22:5). One might have thought this would mean that the first stage, during which the reign of Christ or God is established on the earth, would be followed by the final consummation in heaven (as in Jewish apocalypses, 4 Ezra and 2 Baruch, which were more or less contemporary with the Apocalypse of John). For the book of Revelation, however, *both* stages are conceived as taking place on earth. This is very significant for our discussion of the creation of the new and better world in the prefigurative future anterior. We are talking about a this-worldly transformation.

Here, a "Jewish-Christian"[52] witness deserves brief mention. If a concrete earthly expectation was a central feature of the thought world of Jesus and the early community of Christ-followers in Jerusalem, one would expect it to live on in the hopes of those who are the most likely heirs of the early community, that is, the Jewish-Christian circles (often called Ebionites). We do indeed find such expectations in a Jewish Christian source within the *Pseudo-Clementine Recognitions* 1.27–71.[53] In this source, the land (of Israel) is of particular importance. At the time of composition (ca. 200 CE), the occupation of Judea by Jewish Christians is seen as in continuity with the promise to Abraham of return to the land. The present occupation "would issue into an earthly kingdom of heaven, in which the believers would be filled with food and drink." This terrestrial kingdom would be followed by the resurrection of the dead.[54] Thus, we have an early expectation that entails two successive stages of fulfillment in which the traditional land of Israel is central.

---

52. The term "Jewish Christian" is problematic, because it embeds all sorts of assumptions that we have worked hard to avoid in this study (e.g., "Christianity" as a "religion" separate from "Judaism"). Nevertheless, we reluctantly use the term as a convenient shorthand for a group of Christ-followers who were Jewish in composition and territorial in outlook.

53. Cf. Jones, "Jewish-Christian Chiliastic Restoration in *Pseudo-Clementine Recognitions* 1.27–71," 529–47.

54. Jones specifically quotes 1.55.4 and 1.61.2 ("Jewish-Christian Chiliastic Restoration," 544–45). In the former passage, "the kingdom of heaven" and the "resurrection of the dead" appear as successive stages in the future. In the latter, Jesus is said to have "called the poor blessed and promises earthly rewards" so that they "would inherit the earth and would be filled with food and drink."

The first surviving document to present a two-stage fulfillment scenario, however, is the book of Revelation. In that apocalypse, even the final consummation is located on *earth*, albeit on a re-created earth. Before this final stage is reached, however, a number of things will have happened. An intense period of plagues and tribulations, the escalation of evil, will introduce the final battle between Christ and his enemies. Then there will be a resurrection to life. Satan will be bound, and the faithful (martyrs?) will, after the "first resurrection," reign with Christ for a thousand years in Jerusalem. The millennial reign of Christ with the saints is not described in any detail.

When the thousand years is completed, Satan is set loose to deceive the nations and mount a last attack. A new period of tribulation will ensue, eventually followed by the consummation (now enjoyed by *all* the faithful of all generations) after a new creation. The heavenly New Jerusalem will come down to earth (21:2, 10), so that God's will is done on earth as in heaven. Thus, eternal life will be life on a renewed earth (rather than in heaven as conventionally thought).[55] The twelve tribes will have reassembled in the resurrection (21:12).[56] Even "the kings of the earth shall bring their glory" (21:24, 26) to this New Jerusalem. The leaves of the tree of life there will be "for the healing of the nations" (22:2).[57] This worldwide focus and centripetal movement of the nations to Jerusalem as the center of the new world order correlates well with our understanding of the Jesus revolution, which is outwardly expanding and radically inclusive but also Jerusalem-centered and recapitulatory as in the Animal Apocalypse (1 En. 85–90).

In subsequent Christian tradition, depictions of the millennium abound, especially in Asia Minor (e.g., Papias and Melito). For Justin Martyr, belief in the millennium is a criterion of orthodoxy, though he admits that not all "pious and pure Christians" think in this way (*Dialogue with Trypho* 80.4). In this millenarian tradition, the vagueness of the book of Revelation gives way to graphic depictions of a most concrete kind. Irenaeus cites a fragment from the lost work of Papias, who in turn cites a purported word of Jesus Christ himself about the glorious future to come in the new creation after the resurrection:[58]

> There will be a time when the righteous shall bear upon their rising from the dead; when also the creation, having been renovated and set free, shall bring forth an abundance of all kinds of food (simply) from the dew of heaven, and from the fertility of the earth . . . the Lord used to teach, saying, "The days will come in which vines shall grow each having 10,000 branches, and in each

55. On the eschatological breaking in of heaven to earth, whereby the present ontological dualism between heaven and earth will be overcome, resulting in the full and final manifestation of the kingdom of heaven, see Alexander, "Dualism of Heaven and Earth in Early Jewish Literature and Its Implications," 169–85.

56. Recall our discussion of the presumed reason for Jesus' choosing *twelve* disciples.

57. Note how the mention of "the tree of life" entails an implied correspondence between *Urzeit* and *Endzeit*. See further below.

58. Such a citation of Jesus from outside the Gospels is called an *agraphon* (literally, "not written").

branch 10,000 twigs, and in each twig 10,000 shoots, and in each shoot 10,000 clusters, and on every cluster 10,000 grapes, and every grape when pressed will give 25 measures of wine. And when any one of the saints shall lay hold of a cluster, another shall cry out: 'I am a better cluster, take me; bless the Lord through me.' All the animals, feeding only on the produce of the earth, shall in those days live in peaceful harmony together, and be in perfect subjection to man." (cited in Irenaeus, *Against Heresies* 5.33.3)

This graphic portrayal of the millennium has both Old Testament and early Jewish antecedents. The Papias fragment obviously reflects the eschatological renovation of the world expected in Isa 65:17–25, where the earth's fertility is restored and the world is once again at peace.[59] At the same time, the graphic portrayal of the millennium in the Papias fragment is clearly derived from the Enochic Book of the Watchers: "They will plant vines on it [sc. the renewed earth], and every vine that will be planted on it will yield a thousand jugs of wine, and of every seed that is sown on it, each measure will yield a thousand measures, and each measure of olives will yield ten baths of oil" (1 En. 10:19).[60] In other words, the Papias fragment bears witness to a Jesus logion that insinuates the Jesus himself thought in terms of the Enochic expectation of a renewed world, the restoration of the creation to its pristine state. The Apocalypse ascribes to the same worldview.

Worship on Earth as in Heaven

While waiting for the renewed world, there is something to be done. The idea that John's visions are not just about the distant future but rather about their prefigurative actualization in the here and now can be illustrated by the theme of worship in the book of Revelation. The singing or chanting of hymns was an integral part of the worship of early Christ-followers.[61] The Philippian hymn (Phil 2:5–11), for instance, uses the story of Christ's voluntary self-humiliation and exaltation by God as an example to believers to "let the same mind be in you that was in Christ Jesus" (v. 5). Notice how the text gathers up past, present and future. In other words, through their present worship and their following of Christ's example, believers are to construct the future anterior—the new and better world in the shell of and alongside the old. This revolutionary prefiguration heralds the universal acknowledgment of Jesus Christ as Lord: "Therefore God also highly exalted him and gave him the name that is above

---

59. See chapter 3 for our discussion of the eschatological return of universal peace as a recapitulation of the beginning.

60. See also 2 Bar. 29:5: "The earth will also yield fruits ten thousandfold. And one vine will be a thousand branches, and one branch will produce a thousand clusters, and one cluster will produce a thousand grapes, and one grape will produce a cor of wine."

61. Cf. 1 Cor 14:26; Col 3:16; Jas 5:13; Pliny, *Epistle* 10.96 (referring to *carmen Christo*); *Odes of Solomon*. Col 3:16 and Eph 5:19 refer to "psalms," "hymns," and "spiritual songs."

every name, so that at the name of Jesus every knee should bend, in heaven and on earth and under the earth, and every tongue should confess that Jesus Christ is Lord, to the glory of God the Father" (vv. 9–11).[62]

We see something similar in the book of Revelation. An important feature of the book is the presence of sixteen hymns or hymn-like compositions at various points in the narrative.[63] Many of these hymns gather up past, present, and future: for example, "the Lord God the Almighty, who was and is and is to come" (Rev 4:8); "You [the Lamb, Jesus Christ] are worthy to take the scroll and to open its seals; for you were slaughtered and by your blood you ransomed for God saints from every tribe and language and people and nation; you have made them a kingdom and priests serving our God, and they will reign on earth" (5:9–10).[64] In Rev 7:9–12, John has a revelation of the universal worship of God: "After this I looked, and there was a great multitude that no one could count, from every nation, from all tribes and peoples and languages, standing before the throne and before the Lamb, robed in white, with palm branches in their hands. They cried out in a loud voice, saying, 'Salvation belongs to our God who is seated on the throne, and to the Lamb!'" (vv. 9–10). Then the angels join in with their own worship of God (vv. 11–12). Of particular interest is Rev 15:3–4, which again combines past, present and future elements in the hymn and emphasizes the universal worship of God: "And they sing the song of Moses, the servant of God, and the song of the Lamb: 'Great and amazing are your deeds, Lord God the Almighty! Just and true are your ways, King of the nations! Lord, who will not fear and glorify your name? For you alone are holy. All nations will come and worship before you, for your judgments have been revealed." In the hymnic finale of the book (Rev 19:1–8), a voice from the heavenly throne enjoins, "Praise our God, all you his servants, and all who fear him, small and great" (v. 5), and in response a great multitude sings a hymn: "Then I heard what seemed to be the voice of a great multitude, like the sound of many waters and like the sound of mighty thunderpeals, crying out, 'Hallelujah! For the Lord our God the Almighty reigns. Let us rejoice and exult and give him the glory, for the marriage

62. Cf. Hengel, "Hymns and Christology," 78–96; Hengel, "Song about Christ in Earliest Worship," 227–91; Bauckham, *Jesus and the God of Israel*, 135–39. As Hengel has shown in detail, the earliest hymns celebrated the saving death and heavenly exaltation of Jesus as the one who now shares the divine throne and, as God's pleniopotentiary, receives the homage of all creation. In offering praise to Christ, they anticipate the eschatological consummation, when all will acknowledge Christ's lordship and worship him.

63. Cf. Rev 4:8c, 11; 5:9b–10, 12b, 13b; 7:10b, 12; 11:15b, 17–18; 12:10b–12; 15:3b–4; 16:5b–7b; 19:1b–2, 3, 5b, 6b–8.

64. See also Rev 12:10b–12: "Now have come the salvation and the power and the kingdom of our God and the authority of his Messiah, for the accuser of our comrades has been thrown down, who accuses them day and night before our God. But they have conquered him by the blood of the Lamb and by the word of their testimony, for they did not cling to life even in the face of death. Rejoice then, you heavens and those who dwell in them! But woe to the earth and the sea, for the devil has come down to you with great wrath, because he knows that his time is short!" Other hymns emphasize present and past: "You are worthy, our Lord and God, to receive glory and honor and power, for you created all things, and by your will they existed and were created" (4:11; 5:12).

of the Lamb has come, and his bride has made herself ready; to her it has been granted
to be clothed with fine linen, bright and pure'—for the fine linen is the righteous deeds
of the saints" (vv. 6–8). The upshot of all this is that the revelation to John unveils the
present practice of worship in heaven and the expected practice of worship by the nations and the faithful in the future, so that when John's readers and hearers participate
in worship in direct response to these revelations, the readers and hearers are presently
constructing the revolutionary future anterior, anticipating the coalescence of heaven
and earth in a new space-time (cf. Rev 21:1–4).[65]

The Dangers of Relative Negative Deterritorialization

Where is another side of the message of the Apocalypse that needs attention. The positive construction of prefigurative future anterior has its potential pitfalls as well. For
example, the intended audience of Revelation, the Christ-assemblies of Asia Minor,
may have been merchants in the economic trade that chapter 18 critiques. As Richard
Bauckham argues in his detailed analysis of Rome's economic exploitation, "it is not
unlikely that John's readers would include merchants and others whose business or
livelihood was closely involved with the Roman political and economic system."[66]
Along these lines, Harry O. Maier suggests that the imagery of merchants mourning at
Babylon's demise (Rev 18:15–19) is a deliberate critique of the seer's opponents within
the churches, such as the wealthy at Laodicea who may have been sympathizers with
empire.[67] For Christ-followers, therefore, the allure of riches achieved through coop-
erating with the state-capitalist system of the empire-Whore, which is fundamentally

---

65. Note again the relevance of Newman's discussion of liturgy and ritual for the construction of a
new communal temporality: the access to עלם, a time-space in which the present, past, and future of
finite human experience are overcome. Cf. Newman, "Participatory Past," 434.

66. Bauckham, "Economic Critique of Rome in Revelation 18," 47–90, here 84. See further Royalty, *Streets of Heaven*. Extraction of wealth from conquered territories is documented for the Hellenistic empires. Cf., e.g., Ma, "Hellenistic Empires," 324–57, here 343–44, 346–48; Ma, *Antiochos
III*, 134–35. Aelius Aristides's *Encomium of Rome* (*Or.* 26), delivered to Emperor Antoninus Pius in
155 CE, shows that the extractive practices of the Hellenistic empires continued right into the early
Roman Empire: "Around it [sc. the Mediterranean Sea] lie the great continents greatly sloping, ever
offering to you in full measure something of their own. Whatever the seasons make grow and whatever countries and rivers and lakes and arts of Hellenes and non-Hellenes produce are brought from
every land and sea, so that if one would look at all these things, he must needs behold them either by
visiting the entire civilized world or by coming to this city. For whatever is grown and made among
each people cannot fail to be here at all times and in abundance. And here the merchant vessels
come carrying these many products from all regions in every season and even at every equinox, so
that the city appears a kind of common emporium of the world. Cargoes from India and, if you will,
even from Arabia the Blest one can see in such numbers as to surmise that in those lands the trees
will have been stripped bare and that the inhabitants of these lands, if they need anything, must
come here and beg for a share of their own." Cf. Oliver, "Ruling Power," 896 (with commentary on
910). Cf. Evans, *Utopia Antiqua*, who considers the cultural effects of importing luxury goods and
the way that it gives rise to a rhetoric of Roman decline.

67. Maier, "Staging the Gaze," 147, 150.

irreconcilable with Christ and his kingdom, threatens to recapture the loyalties of his followers through relative negative deterritorialization.[68]

The Roman Empire presents another pathway to relative negative deterritorialization for Christ-followers, this time in the matter of worship. Whereas, as we have seen, worship of God and the Lamb is part and parcel of the Jesus revolution and a harbinger of things to come on earth as in heaven, there is a distinct possibility that individuals or groups can be derailed by worshiping the breast. The two forms of worship are mutually exclusive alternatives.[69] The "saints," of course, refuse to worship the (second) beast (13:15). However, those who refuse to comply with the activities of the beast's image are condemned to death, so that the very existence of the community of Christ-followers is threatened. While in Rev 13 two beasts representing Roman rule are the immediate source of the threat, its ultimate source is the dragon, who is unequivocally identified as "the devil, Satan, and the deceiver of the whole world" (12:9). This deceiver and his henchmen have the potential of causing relative negative deterritorialization, that is, rejection of the proper worship of God in favor of the worship of the breast.

Not just the saints, but John himself is in danger of relative negative deterritorialization. In Rev 17, the interpreting angel informs the seer that the vision he will be given of the whore of Babylon concerns her "judgment" (v. 1). Although he sees her "drunk with the blood of the saints and the blood of the witnesses to Jesus" (v. 6a), he nevertheless marvels at her appearance: "Seeing, I admired her with great wonder" (v. 6b). This response (as in the seer's reaction to the interpreting angel in 19:10 and 22:8–9) is misguided: far too much, it resembles the response to the beast by the inhabitants to the earth immediately thereafter: "seeing the beast, they will admire it" (17:8). Before proceeding to explain the meaning of the vision, the angel wastes no time in reprimanding John with the question, "Why do you show (her) admiration?"

---

68. A revolutionary assemblage that results from absolute positive deterritorialization is, as we have seen, never a complete process and, in any case, always contains the other three assemblages to some degree. In this case, the state assemblage of the Roman Empire looms large and may precipitate redeterritorialization.

69. Cf. Stuckenbruck, "Book of Revelation as a Disclosure of Wisdom," 353: "In chapter 13, it is precisely the act of *worship* that functions as a determinative criterion for religious identity; those who refuse to worship the image of the beast (v. 15, ὅσοι ἐὰν μὴ προσκυνήσωσιν τῇ εἰκόνι τοῦ θηρίου)—these are the very ones whose understanding is appealed to in verse 18—are under threat, and closely aligned to this, are excluded from participating in commercial buying and selling (v. 17). 'Here (ὧδε) is wisdom' does not simply introduce the following calculation [of the beast's name], but may very well link what follows to the consequences for the faithful of the true worship just described [i.e., in 7:11], that is, to their refusal to have anything to do with the second beast and the image it has erected. The decoding of the number thus takes on the exhortatory function *if* what precedes in verses 15–17 marks out what loyalty to God means; in a world of stark contrasts between one kind of loyalty and another, the identification of 666 with Nero boldly underscores the audience's awareness of a system with which there can be no effective or reasonable negotiation. The number is not merely one to decode, but also, as because clear within the text to follow, one to *conquer* 15:2, those with harps in their hands have 'conquered the beast and its image and the number of its name')."

(17:7). This correction of the seer, which is absent in chapters 12 and 13, serves to add a dimension to the wisdom mentioned in 17:9. If we remember that the book was to be read aloud (1:3) and therefore to be *heard* (1:3; cf. 2:7, 11, 17, 29; 3:6, 13, 20, 22; 13:9; 22:17, 18), then what the seer presents as having been learned through the vision is to be pondered and absorbed by the book's recipients, as indicated in the words, "Here is the mind that has wisdom" (17:9; cf. 13:18, which likewise presupposes a direct interactive participation of the audience with the vision of the beast).[70] In other words, the way of wisdom is to be careful not to succumb to the seductive appeal of state capitalism. Thus, the State assemblage is essentially a mechanism of capture through carrot-and-stick methods; that is, the form of capture entails either attraction through the offer of inducements or control through the exercise of violence.

Correspondence between *Urzeit* and *Endzeit*

Throughout this introduction to a Biblical Theology of the New Testament, we have emphasized the correspondence between *Urzeit* and *Endzeit*. According to Mark's Gospel (10:2–12), Jesus, citing Gen 1:27 and 2:24, appealed to the originally intended will of God for creation as the answer to the question of whether it is lawful for a man to divorce his wife, even though Moses allowed a man to divorce (Deut 24:1–4). Paul, in his own way, continues to unfold this idea of the originally intended will of God for creation when he declares that "All of you are one in Christ Jesus" in the context of an allusion to Gen 1:27 ("male and female"), or when he identifies his proclamation of the gospel with the divine performative utterance in Gen 1:3, whereby light was called out of darkness (2 Cor 4:6). Now we turn to the Apocalypse of John and notice a similar correspondence between protology and eschatology based on the creation accounts of Genesis 1–2.

According to Gen 3:22, Adam and Eve were cast out of the garden of Eden and barred from returning so that they would not be able to eat of the tree of life, which had been planted in the midst of the garden, and thereby live forever.[71] The book of

70. Rev 13:18: "Here is wisdom. He who has a mind let that person calculate the number of the beast (*thēriou*), for it is the number of a person. Its number is six hundred sixty-six." The second beast, from the earth, has horns like a lamb and speaks like a dragon. It controls the earth on behalf of the first beast, performs miracles, and by a mixture of force and persuasion induces the people of the earth to worship the image of the first beast. Most important, the second beast marks everyone, from the highest to the lowest, with its own mark, and no one without the mark can buy or sell (13:11–17). This is an excellent example of State overcoding, which is characterized by centralized accumulation and forced resonance of diverse points of order. Recall the examples of State overcoding that were given earlier of the Ara Pacis Augustae and the US Wilderness Act of 1964.

71. Cf. Gen 2:9: "Out of the ground the Lord God made to grow every tree that is pleasant to the sight and good for food, the tree of life also in the midst of the garden, and the tree of the knowledge of good and evil." Gen 3:22, 34: "Then the Lord God said, 'See, the man has become like one of us, knowing good and evil; and now, he might reach out his hand and take also from the tree of life, and eat, and live forever. [. . .] He drove out the man; and at the east of the garden of Eden he placed the cherubim, and a sword flaming and turning to guard the way to the tree of life."

Revelation, however, holds out the hope that the faithful will one day be given access to the tree of life (and hence to eternal life):

> Let anyone who has an ear listen to what the Spirit is saying to the churches. To everyone who conquers, I will give permission to eat from the tree of life that is in the paradise of God. (Rev 2:7)

> Then the angel showed me the river of the water of life, bright as crystal, flowing from the throne of God and of the Lamb through the middle of the street of the city [i.e., the New Jerusalem]. On either side of the river is the tree of life with its twelve kinds of fruit, producing its fruit each month; and the leaves of the tree are for the healing of the nations. (Rev 22:1–2)

> Blessed are those who wash their robes, so that they will have the right to the tree of life and may enter the city by the gates. (Rev 22:14)

> I warn everyone who hears the words of the prophecy of this book: if anyone adds to them, God will add to that person the plagues described in this book; if anyone takes away from the words of the book of this prophecy, God will take away that person's share in the tree of life and in the holy city, which are described in this book. (Rev 22:18–19)

Hence, the book of Revelation looks forward to the restoration of the status quo ante—the return to the pristine conditions before the Fall of humankind in the garden. This time, however, there will be no sin and death.

The book of Revelation is not the only ancient writing that shows interest in the tree of life. A number of ancient sources specifically refer to enjoying the tree of life—smelling its fragrance or eating its fruits—as the essence of the reward for the righteous in the eschatological future:[72]

> [Enoch relates:] And there was among them a tree such as I have never smelled, and none of the other [trees] was like it. It smells more fragrant than any fragrance, and its leaves and its flowers and its wood never wither; its fruit [is] good, and its fruit [is] like the bunches of dates on a palm. (1 En. 24:4)

> [The angel Michael explains to Enoch:] "And as for this fragrant tree, no creature has the authority to touch it until the great judgment. . . . This [fruit] will be given to the righteous and the humble. From its fruit life will be given to the chosen." (1 En. 25:4-5; cf. 32:3-6)[73]

---

72. Cf. Kugel, *Traditions of the Bible*, 136–37.

73. Cf. Newman, "Participatory Past," 431: "After witnessing the mountain of God on which grows the tree of life that will be transplanted to the house of God, the King of eternity, he [sc. Enoch] recounts, 'Then I blessed the God of glory, the King of eternity, who has prepared such things for people (who are) righteous, and has created them and promised to give (them) to them' (25:7)."

[God says to Adam:] But when you have come out of Paradise, if you guard yourself from all evil, preferring death to it, at the time of the resurrection I will raise you again, and then there shall be given to you from the tree of life, and you shall be immortal forever. (Apoc. Mos. 28:4)

The tree of life will give them [sc. God's new people] fragrant perfume, and they shall neither toil nor become weary. (4 Ezra 2:12)

Paradise . . . whose fruit does not spoil and in which are abundance and healing . . . (4 Ezra 7:123)

Paradise is opened, the tree of life is planted, the world to come is prepared, delight [in Hebrew, ʿēden] is prepared. (4 Ezra 8:52)

And I saw there the earth and its fruit . . . and the garden of Eden and its fruits, and the source and the river flowing from it, and its trees and their flowering, making fruits, and I saw righteous men therein, their food and their rest. (Apoc. Ab. 21:3, 6)

And He shall open the gates of paradise; He shall remove the sword that has threatened since Adam, and He will grant to the righteous to eat of the tree of life. (T. Levi 18:10)

[In a vision of paradise:] And in the midst was the tree of life, at that place where the Lord rests when He goes into paradise. And that tree is indescribable for pleasantness and fine fragrance, and more beautiful than any other. (2 En. 8:3)

Then Gabriel and Uriel will become a pillar of light leading [the righteous] into the holy land. It will be granted to them to eat from the tree of life. (Apoc. El. 5:5–6)

Clearly, then, the book of Revelation is not alone in its expectation of renewed access to the tree of life.

For another example of the correspondence between *Urzeit* and *Endzeit*, let us consider the solemn warning at the end of the book of Revelation relating to adding or subtracting anything from the words of the prophecy of this book (Rev 22:18–19).[74] As we have seen, the reference in that warning to the tree of life takes us back to the very beginning of the Bible, to the book of Genesis, where "the tree of life" is first mentioned (Gen 2:9; 3:22, 34). The end corresponds to the beginning. According to the Bible, who was the first one to add to God's words of prophecy? According to Gen 2:16–17, when God first told Adam the rules of the garden, he did so in these terms:

74. The following is based on Kugel, *Traditions of the Bible*, 102–3.

> And the Lord God commanded the man, saying, "You may freely eat of every tree in the garden; but of the tree of the knowledge of good and evil you shall not eat, for in the day that you eat of it, you shall die." (Gen 2:16–17)

The curious thing is that when the serpent later comes along to tempt the woman to eat of the forbidden tree, *the woman adds to what God has said*. Thus, according to Gen 3:2–3, when the serpent asked Eve about the same rules, she had a slightly different answer:

> And the woman said to the serpent, "We may eat of the fruit of the trees of the garden, but God said, 'You may not eat of the fruit of the tree which is in the midst of the garden, *neither shall you touch it*, lest you die.'" (Gen 3:2–3)

Why would the woman add the words "neither shall you touch it"? It could hardly have been an accident. For later interpreters this puzzling question required an answer. According to one interpretation, the extra words "neither shall you touch it" contained a very subtle hint about (1) how the serpent managed to trick Eve into eating the forbidden fruit and (2) who was ultimately responsible for the extra words:

> The text says, "And God commanded Adam, saying, 'Of the tree of the knowledge of good and evil you shall not eat, for in the day that you eat of it you shall die' (Gen 2:17)." But Adam did not choose to tell God's words to Eve exactly as they had been spoken. Instead, he said to her, "God said, 'You shall not eat of the fruit of the tree which is in the midst of the garden, neither shall you touch it, lest you die' (as per Gen 3:3)." Whereupon the wicked serpent said to himself, "Since I seem unable to trip up Adam, let me go and try to trip up Eve." He went and sat down next to her and started talking with her. He said: "Now you say that God has forbidden us to touch the tree. Well, I can touch the tree and not die, and so can you." What did the wicked serpent then do? He touched the tree with his hands and feet and shook it so hard that some of its fruit fell to the ground. . . . Then he said to her, "[You see? So likewise] you say that God has forbidden us to eat from the tree. But I can eat from it and not die, and so can you." What did Eve think to herself? "All the things that my husband has told me are lies" . . . Whereupon she took the fruit and ate it and gave to Adam and he ate, as it is written, "The woman saw that the tree was good to eat from and a delight to the eyes" (Gen 3:6). (*Abot deR. Natan* [A] ch. 1)

> The error lay in [Eve's] report of the commandment. . . . We ought not to make any addition to a commandment even for the purpose of instruction, for any addition or qualification of a commandment is the nature of a falsification. . . . What is objectionable, therefore, is the addition made by the woman, ". . . neither shall you touch it." God had not said this, but rather, "You shall not eat of it." . . . Now many believe that all this was really Adam's fault, not the woman's. They reason that Adam, in his desire to make her more cautious, had said to the woman that God had given this additional

instruction, "Neither shall you touch it." For we know that it wa t Eve, but Adam, who had initially received the commandment from God, because Eve had not yet been created. Of course, Scripture does not reveal the exact words that Adam used when he disclosed to her the nature and content of the commandment. . . . What opinions others have offered should be taken into consideration, but it seems to me that the initial violation and deceit was due to this woman. (Ambrose of Milan, *On Paradise*)

The extra words, according to this interpretation, did not come from Eve. She did not change God's words *because she did not hear them in the first place*. When God spoke to Adam about the tree in Gen 2, Eve had not yet been created. (God's words appear in Gen 2:16–17; Eve is not created until Gen 2:22.) So it must have been *Adam* who, in telling Eve about God's prohibition after she was created, added the words "neither shall you touch it." Perhaps he did so in order to make absolutely sure that she would not even come close to eating the fruit. But if so, the plan backfired. The serpent came to her and first touched the tree himself. Then he invited Eve to touch it as well and so see for herself that nothing bad would happen. Then the serpent actually took a piece of the fruit and ate it, and urged her to do the same thing. At this point she began to doubt the truth of everything Adam had told her: "All the things that my husband told me are lies." And so she decided to take a bite. The harrowing consequences their actions are spelled out in Gen 3:14–24, including expulsion from the garden, so that they could not eat from the tree of life and thereby live forever. Thus, the first humans were condemned to an untimely death.

It is against the backdrop of this kind of interpretation of Genesis that the book of Revelation ends with the solemn warning against adding to or taking away from the prophecy contained in its book. *Adding* to the prophecy would have harrowing temporal consequences similar to those that were inflicted on the first man and woman as the result of their violation of the divine prohibition against eating of the tree of knowledge: "if anyone adds to them [sc. the words of prophecy in the book], God will add to that person the plagues described in this book" (Rev 22:18). However, *taking away* from the prophecy would result in even more dire consequences: "if anyone takes away from the words of the book of this prophecy, God will take away that person's share in the tree of life" (v. 19). If, in the beginning, adding to God's words is what led to the first sin and its disastrous consequences, then, conversely in the end, subtracting from God's words will lead to exclusion from eating from the very tree of life that will undo the death to which the first humans and their progeny had been subjected through the ages. In the final section of Revelation, the New Jerusalem is described (Rev 21:2–27), and the tree of life in its midst is mentioned (22:2). In contrast with the *temporal* punishment referred to in v. 18, exclusion from the tree of life and the Holy City must be regarded as an *eternal* punishment.

At the beginning of the present chapter, we set forth the thesis that the divine promise that John reiterates is creation-based, an outworking of the original divine performative utterances in creation (Gen 1) which become instantiated afresh at "pregnant nows." In this section, we learn how the Apocalypse's emphasis on the correspondence between *Urzeit* and *Endzeit* adds a thick description of what the book's creation-based vision entails.

Conclusion

The book of Revelation motivates followers of Christ to continue to creatively unfold the Jesus revolution in the midst of extremely challenging times. John's visions spark the imagination not only to anticipate the future consummation—the people to come and the world to come—but also to actualize intimations of that future already in the present. At the same time, the Apocalypse warns Christ-followers not to be diverted by the worldly empire, which, by turns, can be so seductive and coercive. Those who are in the process of becoming must be steadfast and persevere.

CONCLUSION

Lines of Flight and the Beginnings
of Revolutionary Change

Introduction

WE HAVE MENTIONED THE term "line of flight" several times in the course of our study, and in this final chapter we use it again in order to come back full circle to the beginnings of revolutionary change.[1] How does a revolutionary assemblage emerge from a relatively stable assemblage, whether territorial, state, or capitalist? A revolutionary assemblage is one that is undergoing transformation and is in the process of creating the prefigurative future anterior (the people to come and the world to come). A "line of flight" escapes from the assemblage of which it is a part, connecting up with other escapees and potentially creating a new revolutionary assemblage. In the following, we will provide several concrete illustrations of the concept and then show how it relates specifically to Jesus and the revolution to which he gave rise. These considerations inevitably prompt us to reflect on the state of affairs in our world today and to evaluate what kind of course correction is necessary.

---

1. The following has benefited substantially from Thornton, "On Lines of Flight," 433–56.

Example #1: The Transmutation of Wolves into Dogs by Natural Selection

Our first illustration of "line of flight" is drawn from the annals of evolutionary biology.[2] During the middle part of the Stone Age, people lived by hunting, gathering, and fishing. Most importantly for our purposes, this period also saw the domestication of the dog. Scientists have debated how the domestication of the dog came about, whether by direct human intervention (wolf puppies were snatched from their dens and then selectively bred for desired characteristics) or by passive means, such as genetic mutation. The theory that has gained prominence in recent years is the Village-Dog Theory: a natural-selection theory in which wolves self-selected into dogs very rapidly during an approximately four-thousand-year period.[3] These individuals were the "line of flight" that led to the transformation of wolves into dogs. A line of flight reaches outside the original assemblage: the parts that escape the structure of which they are members and connect with other assemblages. This initiates a mutual process of becoming whereby transformation occurs. The Village-Dog Theory presupposes that the line of flight was *always latent within the regular wolf assemblage*; all the line of flight needed was suitable conditions to express itself. The means of evolution of wolves into domesticated dogs can be summarized as follows:

1. Mesolithic people create a new niche—the village.

2. Some wolves invade the new niche, scavenging in refuse dumps at the edge of the villages. They thereby gain access to a dependable food source that requires far less effort to obtain than hunting large, powerful animals on their own. The humans do the difficult work for them.

2. Compare Deleuze and Guattari's discussion of the mutual becoming of the orchid and the wasp (*ATP*, 10, 12, 238, 293–94, 314 [snapdragon and bumblebee]). See further Bennett and Posteraro, *Deleuze and Evolutionary Theory*.

3. Cf. Coppinger and Coppinger, *Dogs*, 37–96: Part I: The Evolution of the Basic Dog: Commensalism; Ch. 1: "Wolves Evolve into Dogs" (39–68). See also Pete Chinn and Jacob Thompson, "Dog Tales," PBS *Nova* (Season 47, Episode 2, aired February 12, 2020): "It's now widely accepted that selection for behavior can rapidly domesticate a wild animal. But in the journey from wolf to dog, who made that selection? Most scientists now believe it was the wolves themselves. Wolves are extraordinarily adaptable. Different packs specialize in hunting different types of prey. It's thought that when humans first arrived, some packs may have adopted a novel survival strategy. [Evolutionary geneticist Greger Larson, University of Oxford:] 'It's not crazy to think that there may have been a population of wolves that found themselves attracted to people and started following people, in the same way that other wolf populations have started following caribou.' Rather than hunting, these wolves would thrive by scavenging close to human encampments. But only the boldest would hang around for long. These adventurous wolves would breed and, over generations, evolve into an increasingly human-tolerant sub-species, the domestic dog. 'Survival of the fittest' turned out to be 'survival of the friendliest.'" Cf. Deleuze and Guattari, *ATP*, 238 (authors' emphasis): "Finally, becoming is not an evolution, at least not an evolution by descent and filiation. . . . It concerns alliance. If evolution includes any veritable becomings, it is in the domain of *symbioses* that bring into play beings of totally different scales and kingdoms, with no possible filiation. There is a block of becoming that snaps up the wasp and the orchid, but from which no wasp-orchid can ever descend."

3. Those wolves that use the new niche are genetically predisposed to show less "flight distance" that those that don't. (Flight distance refers to how close humans can come to animals before the animals will flee. Normally, wild wolves are highly averse to any human contact and will run away even before a human is seen.)

4. The "tamer" wolves gain selective advantage in the new niche over the wilder ones, because they have food, safety, and more opportunities for reproduction and survival. This increased reproduction allows the wolves to rapidly adapt to their new environment. Since eating refuse does not require as much brain and brawn as hunting large animals, the scavenger wolves gradually develop smaller heads, teeth, and brains than those of wild wolves.

In our first example, then, the wolves that could tolerate human presence constitute the line of flight from their original wolf assemblage. The subsequent transformation took place because the individual wolves that escaped from their own wolf assemblage connected up with a human assemblage living in a village.

Example #2: *Parable of the Sower* by Octavia E. Butler

Our next example is drawn from Octavia E. Butler (1947–2006), one of the most prolific science fiction authors of the twentieth century and winner of numerous awards, including the MacArthur "Genius" Fellowship in 1995.[4] Butler is a visionary writer who uses fiction as a test flight, allowing the reader to imagine and prepare for a future together, to generate ideas that we want to see more of in the world. Butler gives us the practice, and then she provides us with case study after case study of our imaginary futures and examines how we will behave. Butler built new words in the shell of the old. She imagines a liberated future and concretely portrays the realm of the possible.

For example, Butler's dystopian novel, *Parable of the Sower*, which was published in 1993, tells the story of a teenage Black girl who lives in a place called Robledo, which is a stand-in for Pasadena, a city northeast of downtown Los Angeles. The protagonist, Lauren Oya Olamina, is fifteen going on sixteen, so it's a coming-of-age novel. It's also the story of a teenage girl in the year 2024 watching society crumble before her very eyes and desperate to find a way to survive. What Lauren experiences in the story is exactly what we readers have experienced over the past four years—global warming, ecological devastation, drug epidemic, fascist politics, white nationalism, rampant misogyny and racism, corporate greed, dysfunctional government, police brutality, miscarriage of justice, mass migrations, human trafficking, homelessness, the rich getting richer, abject poverty, deteriorating public education,

---

4. On Octavia E. Butler's work in light of Deleuze and Guattari's philosophy, see further Bogue, "Deleuze and Guattari and the Future of Politics," 77–97, esp. 90–94. *Parable of the Sower* is a good example of Deleuze and Guattari's aforementioned concept of fabulation and minor literature. Cf. Bogue, "Deleuze and Literature," 286–306.

a pandemic, mass shootings, drought, wildfires, frustration, polarization, hopelessness, rage, and insurrection.[5] But Lauren's story goes beyond our present situation to show us the cataclysm that awaits us in the not too distant future if we blithely continue on the current trajectory.[6] By 2024, Southern California and much of the rest of the United States have become a parched, burnt-out, and pillaged wasteland. The fabric of human society is broken. The better-off are living in walled communities of ten or twelve homes, and they risk their lives whenever they venture out of their fortresses. Most people, however, are indigent, living on the street and needing to steal from others just in order to survive. Everyone has guns. The jobless rate is through the roof, and, even if one can get a job, the pay is hardly enough for food, let alone housing. Under these conditions, people willingly put themselves into indentured servitude, just to have food on the table and a roof over their heads. Things like cars, television, computers, and phones are luxuries of a forgotten past, although the super-rich enjoy new technologies such as immersive VR, which caters to every bodily appetite. The disparity between rich and poor could not be more pronounced.

In the midst of this chaos, Lauren knows that if she is going to survive at all, she needs a plan of escape. To go it alone would be suicide. She could already see that from the few times that she dared to go outside the compound in the company of an armed group of her friends, and observed what happens to a vulnerable young woman in that hostile environment. Lauren realizes, in other words, that a successful

5. Dystopian novels are usually set about a generation ahead of their own time (e.g., George Orwell's *Nineteen Eighty-Four*, published in 1949, was set 35 years ahead of its own time and now appears prescient). These days, however, reality is rapidly outpacing our imaginative capacity to write dystopian fiction. When she wrote *Parable of the Sower*, Butler thought that having her main character and the Earthseed community relocate to Northern California would enable them to easily escape the expected extreme drought of Southern California. Now, several years before the setting of the novel in 2024, climate change is so severe that Northern California and Southern Oregon are also running out of water, and this situation is leading to major social upheaval in those places. Even the regions further north, in British Columbia, are experiencing severe drought conditions.

6. Cf. Snyder, *On Tyranny*, 124–25, referring to the United States during the early Trump presidency (emphasis mine): "The danger we now face is of a passage from the politics of inevitability to the politics of eternity, from a naive and flawed sort of democratic republic to a confused and cynical sort of fascist oligarchy. The politics of inevitability is terribly vulnerable to the kind of shock it has just received. When something shatters the myth, when our time falls out of joint, we scramble to find some other way to organize what we experience. The path of least resistance leads directly from inevitability to eternity. If you once believed that everything always turns out well in the end, you can be persuaded that nothing turns out well in the end. If you once did nothing because you thought progress is inevitable, then you can continue to do nothing because you think time moves in repeating cycles. Both of these positions, inevitability and eternity, are antihistorical. The only thing that stands between them is history itself. History allows us to see patterns and make judgments. It sketches for us the structures within which we can seek freedom. It reveals moments, each one of them different, none entirely unique. To understand one moment is to see *the possibility of being cocreator of another*. History permits us to be responsible: not for everything, but for something." This dovetails with the aforementioned concept of human beings as "created cocreators" in the wisdom tradition. Cf. Fretheim, *God and the World in the Old Testament*, 215–16: "The goal for human beings is to be caught up in the task of cocreating, participating creatively in the continuing becoming of the world."

escape would be possible only if it is done in collaboration with others. She would need to gather up a community of fellow survivors who would adopt her vision for starting a new life in a new and better world. Hence, Lauren starts to write down her thoughts and dreams of a better future. She calls her notes *Earthseed*, which becomes her religion. Those thoughts become the motivational basis for all that she says and does in preparation for her escape. They would also provide a kind of roadmap for her conception of the new people and new world to come. So, *Parable of the Sower* is not only a coming-of-age novel or a post-apocalypse nightmare;[7] it is also a quest for a new and better life, a new way of being in the world. It is a seedbed of hope, a reason to keep going and a reason to continue believing in the world.[8]

Lauren's compound had often been raided and looted in the past, but as time went on, the pattern was one of ever-increasing violence, destruction, and, eventually, even individual cases of murder. Therefore, when the fateful day came that her compound was completely overrun by marauders, who killed her family and most of the other inhabitants, she had her backpack ready to go, stuffed with survival gear, food, and seeds to plant crops. She had picked out a new home in Northern California, which was sparsely populated, had cheap, abundant water, and offered an opportunity to start over. In the immediate aftermath of the attack, she was able to link up with two other people from her compound who had survived—a neighbor boy about her same age with whom she had grown up and a young woman whom another neighbor had bought on the slave market as a third "wife." As the three traveled together ever northward, they continued to encounter clusters of people who wanted or needed to join them, at first for protection and sustenance but eventually also to share in the group's growing Earthseed vision.[9] It was a motley crew that included a wide variety of races, ages, genders, socioeconomic classes, and backgrounds. There was nothing that would normally bind these people together into a cohesive whole. Nevertheless, through much adversity and many setbacks, the necessity of survival and the common vision provided by Lauren helped them to overlook their enormous differences, to overcome their innate distrust of each other, and to bond with one another as a new people.[10] Without Lauren, who was turning eighteen by the end of the story, they could not have survived, let alone thrived. The secret to their success was the ability

7. The term "apocalypse" is used here in its popular sense (i.e., an event involving destruction on a catastrophic scale) rather than as a technical term (i.e., a genre of revelatory literature with a narrative framework, in which a revelation is mediated by an otherworldly being to a human recipient, disclosing a transcendent reality which is both temporal, insofar as it envisages eschatological salvation, and spatial insofar as it involves another, supernatural world).

8. Cf. Shakespeare, *Hamlet* Act 1, Scene 5, where Hamlet bemoans the responsibility he carries: "The time is out of joint: O cursed spite, | That ever I was born to set it right!" Yet Hamlet continues: "Nay, come, let's go together."

9. The people whom Lauren encounters along the way become, in effect, to borrow an expression from Deleuze, "the seed of a people to come." Cf. Deleuze, *Cinema 2*, 216; also 221.

10. As Lauren puts it in *Earthseed*, "Embrace diversity. / Unite— / Or be divided, / robbed, / ruled, / killed / By those who see you as prey. Embrace diversity / Or be destroyed."

to imagine the prefigurative people to come and world to come and then to antici-pate that future through concrete action in the present. At every stage, people were encouraged to think about what kind of world they wanted to live in and then to take steps to enact it. They might not achieve the perfection of an ideal society—with total liberty, equality, benevolence, harmony or justice—but they endeavored nonetheless to envision the goal and then to actualize it. And hitting the target would require an ongoing process of individual and communal transformation.

In short, Lauren formed the nucleus of a line of flight that became the basis for a new, revolutionary assemblage. This revolutionary assemblage has the usual three basic components: (1) Lauren herself—her life and teachings—became the abstract machine/condition for the assemblage. (2) Lauren's *Earthseed* writings became the concrete elements of the assemblage, along with other emblems, such as Acorn—the name of the undeveloped land that they eventually choose to settle on in a secluded part of Northern California—and the actual acorns they plant in memory of all their dead relatives and friends.[11] Lauren wants to use Earthseed "verses to pry them [sc. people] loose from the rotting past, and maybe push them into saving themselves and building a future that makes sense."(3) The Earthseed community founded by the people who had joined Lauren on the road to Acorn become the personae/agents of the assemblage. Lauren consistently calls them "her people." Their self-conception transcends biological heredity and all their inherent differences.

Earthseed doctrine is perfectly adapted to meet the challenges that the com-munity will encounter. Earthseed teaches two basic lessons: (1) "God is Change,"[12]

11. In actuality, Acorn is merely an intermediate destination for the Earthseed community. Ac-cording to *Earthseed*, the ultimate destination for the people to come was to live among the stars, which is analogous to heaven in Christian theology (although *Earthseed* expects actual space travel during life rather than supernatural translation after death). When Lauren first discusses the title of her book of verses, she refers to it as *Earthseed: The Book* [singular] *of the Living*, whereas elsewhere it is always subtitled *The Books* [plural] *of the Living*. In the same passage, Lauren explains: "There are the Tibetan and the Egyptian Books of the Dead. . . . I've never heard of anything called a book of the living, but I wouldn't be surprised to discover that there is something." This explanation is strange because Lauren is the daughter of a Baptist pastor and has even preached sermons in his stead on occasion. Therefore, Butler seems to be testing the reader's Bible knowledge here, since Ps 69:28 explicitly refers to "the book of the living," and there are also references elsewhere to "the book of life" (Phil 4:3; Rev 3:5; 13:8; 17:8; 20:12, 15; 21:27).

12. This line recurs throughout the novel. Chapter 18 includes a discussion of Lauren's conception of God. "'How did you get your ideas about God' 'I was looking for God,' I said. 'I wasn't looking for mythology or mysticism or magic. I didn't know whether there was a god to find, but I wanted to know. God would have to be a power that could not be defied by anyone or anything.' 'Change.' 'Change, yes.' 'But it's not a god. It's not a person or an intelligence or even a thing. It's just . . . I don't know. An idea.' I smiled. Was that such a terrible criticism? 'It's a truth,' I said. 'Change is ongoing. Everything changes in some way—size, position, composition, frequency, velocity, thinking, whatever. Every living thing, every bit of matter, all the energy in the universe changes in some way. I don't claim that everything changes in every way, but everything changes in some way.' Harry, coming in dripping from the sea, heard this last. 'Sort of like saying God is the second law of thermodynamics,' he said, grinning. He and I had already had this conversation. 'That's an aspect of God,' I said to Travis. 'Do you know about the second law?' He nodded. 'Entropy, the idea that the natural flow of heat is from something hot to

and being shaped by and shaping God are the sole means of becoming-other in a productive fashion in this new world; (2) humanity's ultimate destiny is to leave earth ("this dying place") and colonize other planets: "The Destiny of Earthseed / Is to take root among the stars."[13] This component of the Earthseed project came from the belief that humans can only form a viable community by uniting in a struggle against an alien and challenging environment. Hence, the community of the people to come issues in a creative line of flight, but that line of flight is to other worlds, since humans cannot coexist peacefully on this world alone. In the meantime, "There's so much to do before it can even begin. I guess that's to be expected. There's always a lot to do before you get to go to heaven."[14]

---

something cold—not the other way—so that the universe itself is cooling down, running down, dissipating its energy.' [...] 'I still can't see change or entropy as God,' Travis said, bringing the conversation back to Earthseed. 'Then show me a more pervasive power than change,' I said. 'It isn't just entropy. God is more complex than that. Human behavior alone would teach you that much. And there still more complexity when you dealing with several things at once—as you always are. There are all kinds of changes in the universe.' He shook his head. 'Maybe, but nobody's going to worship them.' 'I hope not,' I said. 'Earthseed deals with ongoing reality, not with supernatural authority figures. Worship is not good without action. With action, it's only useful if it steadies you, focuses your efforts, eases your mind.'" From this and other passages in the novel, it becomes clear that Earthseed is a philosophy similar to early Stoicism, in which an impersonal "god" (sometimes called Zeus) was identified with "universal law." On early Stoicism, see further my *Apocalyptic Letter to the Galatians*, ch. 2.

13. This aspect of Butler's novel should not be viewed as merely a flight of fantasy. Presently, the billionaire Elon Musk is seriously looking at Mars as a bailout planet if, for whatever reason, earth becomes uninhabitable at some point in the near future. Cf. Musk, "Making Humans a Multi-Planetary Species," 46 (emphasis mine): "By talking about the SpaceX architecture, I want to make Mars seem possible—*make it seem as though it is something that we can do in our lifetime.* There really is a way that anyone could go if they wanted to. Why Go Anywhere? I think there are really two fundamental paths. History is going to bifurcate along two directions. One path is we stay on Earth forever, and then *there will be some eventual extinction event.* I do not have an immediate doomsday prophecy, but eventually, history suggests, *there will be some doomsday event.* The alternative is to become a space-bearing civilization and a multi-planetary species, which I hope you would agree is the right way to go. So how do we figure out how to take you to Mars and create a self-sustaining city—a city that is not merely an outpost but which can become a planet in its own right, allowing us to become a truly multi-planetary species?" By suggesting that relocating to Mars is "something that we can do in our lifetime," Musk seems to entertain the possibility that the need to relocate to Mars may be relatively soon, even though he does not want to be an alarmist and therefore also says that "I do not have an immediate doomsday prophecy." Why else would a multi-billionaire put so much time and effort into the Mars project if he did not think that the threat was potentially imminent? Clearly, then, Musk is a "revolutionary" in the sense that we are using the term, because he envisions a new world in the shell of the old and, like Lauren, he is creatively constructing that world in the present. Over and over again, Butler's vision of the future is turning out to be prescient. At the same time, her vision parallels that of Deleuze and Guattari's insofar as their call for a new earth and a new people moves from "the forces of earth" and its territorialization toward lines of deterritorialization that leave the earth—"the cosmic 'breakaway.'" Cf. Deleuze and Guattari, *ATP*, 337, cited in Lundy, "Call for a New Earth, a New People," 128.

14. Similar remarks from *Earthseed* are scattered throughout the novel: "We are Earthlife maturing, Earthlife preparing to fall away from the parent world. We are Earthlife preparing to take root in new ground, Earthlife fulfilling its purpose, its promise, its Destiny." "Now is a time for building foundations—Earthseed communities—focused on the Destiny. After all, my heaven really exists, and you don't have to die to reach it." "A unifying, purposeful life here on Earth, and the hope of heaven

To fully appreciate the origin of Lauren's newfound Earthseed religion, we need to realize where she began her journey. She was raised in the home of her father and stepmother, both PhDs, and her father was a Baptist pastor and college professor.[15] Weekly church services took place in the Olamina home, and Lauren would preach the sermon when her father was unable to be there. The parishioners were the few families who lived within their walled compound. Although for reasons that are not described in the novel, Lauren felt herself more and more alienated from her Baptist roots, she continued to try to please her father by attending church and even submitting to baptism. Here is how Lauren herself puts the matter in an entry dated Sunday, July 21, 2024:

> At least three years ago, my father's God stopped being my God. His church stopped being my church. And yet, today, because I'm a coward, I let myself be initiated into that church. I let my father baptize me in all three names of that God who isn't mine any more. My God has another name [i.e., Change].

The reason for Lauren's alienation from her roots seem clear. Although she loves her family and especially her father, with whom she has so much in common (e.g., intelligence, natural ability, love of learning, and a muscular physique), Lauren nevertheless views her father as a stodgy patriarch who is presiding over a failing assemblage with a fortress mentality, an assemblage that is unable to respond effectively and decisively to the impending threat that their walled community clearly faces. From her perspective, the father's Baptist religion merely maintains the status quo at all costs. It offers only an anesthetizing opiate—a comforting hymn, a stabilizing sermon, a prayer chain and support group—for a people who are waiting to be overrun, rather than a catalyst for the creative, transformational change that is so desperately needed. Indeed, Lauren's father has done his best to keep his daughter from spreading what he considers fearmongering by forbidding Lauren from speaking out in the community about the need to form a plan of escape. Hence, this gifted, but tortured, teenager comes to the conclusion that the God of her father—the do-nothing God of the self-destructive status quo—is not the God she needs. She needs the God of *Change*.

The point that we need to see clearly from this story is that the line of flight is *latent* within the status-quo assemblage itself, just as the wolves that would become the "tamer" dump-scavengers feeding at the edge of the village were *latent* within the wild wolf pack. In other words, Lauren already exists within the assemblage of her father's community, even though she has not yet fully developed or manifested as a line of flight. The fact that she now plans her escape from her own assemblage is a torturous decision. But she wants to survive, so she carries out her plan with exacting detail.

---

for themselves and their children. A real heaven, not mythology or philosophy. A heaven that will be theirs to shape."

15. Interestingly enough, Butler herself grew up a Baptist, although she subsequently abandoned her roots. Butler remarks that early on, she did not see herself in the stories she was reading, so she decided to write herself into stories of her own.

In doing so, she takes many elements from the existing assemblage and carries them with her into what will become a revolutionary (transformational) assemblage. Some of what she will carry with her can fit into a backpack as the physical basis for a new assemblage. Other things are less tangible but nevertheless real. For example, there are some structural similarities between her new-found, Earthseed religion and the Baptist religion of her father, including the concepts of God, community, scripture, ritual, heaven, etc. Obviously, all of the elements that Lauren carries over from the old assemblage need to be adapted to their new, revolutionary application, but we should not miss the significant correspondences.

All this causes us to wonder whether what Lauren was seeking all along was really the *true* religion of her father after all. At one point in the narrative, a character makes the point that, as a religion, Earthseed will change over time, just as all religions do:

> "All religions change. Think about the big ones. What do you think Christ would be these days? A Baptist? A Methodist? A Catholic? And the Buddha—do you think he'd be a Buddhist now? What kind of Buddhism would he practice?" He smiled. "After all, if 'God is Change,' surely Earthseed can change, and if it lasts, it will."

This is a crucial statement in the novel, because it hints at a solution to Lauren's original conundrum that the teen herself did not even consider. She rejected her father's *Baptist* religion wholesale because it did not meet her need for change in a world that was falling apart.[16] The Baptist church had, in other words, become

16. Laura's rejection of her father's church may seem surprising, given the historic role of the Black church in revolutionary activism to create the prefigurative future anterior. Cf. Gates, *Black Church*, xx–xxi: "What sustained our ancestors under the nightmare of enslavement to build families and survive their being ripped apart and sold off in the domestic trade (the dreaded 'Second Middle Passage'); to carry on despite not being able to ward off the rapacious sexual advances of their masters (a verity exposed by DNA, which shows that the average African American is more than 24 percent European); to acquire skills; to create a wide variety of complex cultural forms; to withstand torture, debasement, and the suffocating denial of their right to learn to read and write; to defer the gratification of freedom from bondage—all without ever given ever giving up the hope of liberty, as one enslaved poet, George Moses Horton, put it, if not for themselves, then for their children or grandchildren, when slavery had no end in sight? What gave them the belief in the future, and by that I mean the future not just in the clichéd 'world to come' in heaven , but *here, in this world to come on earth*—the future that their sacrifices enabled us to occupy today? What empowered them with 'hope against hope'? Darryl Pinckney . . . notes that 'if a person cannot imagine a future, then we would say that that person is depressed.' To paraphrase Pinckney's next line, if a people cannot imagine a future, then its culture will die. And Black culture didn't die. The signal aspects of African American culture were planted, watered, given light, and nurtured in the Black Church, out of the reach and away from the watchful eyes of those who would choke the life out of it. We have to give the church its due as a source of our ancestors' unfathomable resiliency." Gates, *Black Church*, xxiii: "The Black Church was the cultural cauldron that Black people created to combat a system designed in every way to crush their spirit. Collectively and with enormous effort, they refused to allow that to happen. And the culture they created was sublime, awesome, majestic, lofty, glorious, and at all points subversive of the larger culture of enslavement that sought to destroy their humanity. The miracle of African American survival can be traced directly

largely *irrelevant* to her life.[17] But she did not reflect on what Jesus himself might have been about in his own day and time. For it is entirely possible that the latter-day Baptist church of Lauren's upbringing had lost the original, revolutionary vision of Jesus Christ, replacing it with something much more mundane, comfortable, and "safe." What would have happened, then, if Lauren had decided to go back to the ancient roots of the Jesus movement, that is, to its very wellspring, Jesus Christ himself? Would she have discovered the revolutionary whom she so desperately wanted and needed? Would she have found the impetus for creative transformation that she was looking for all along? Not just some sort of inner, spiritual solace, but rather the resources for decisive action? Would she have been able, on that basis, to create the people to come and the new and better world in the prefigurative future anterior? To ask the question is almost to answer it.

Jesus as a Line of Flight and the Beginnings of the Revolution

We have identified Jesus as the inaugurator of a movement that became a revolutionary assemblage. How, then, did it all begin? How did Jesus become a line of flight resulting in a revolutionary assemblage? A line of flight is always *latent* within the assemblage from which it attempts to escape: for example, the friendly wolves that formed a line of flight from the wild wolf pack or Lauren and her companions who formed a line of flight from the disintegrating communities of Southern California. As

to the miraculous ways that our ancestors—across a range of denominations and through the widest variety of worship—reinvented the religion that their 'masters' thought would keep them subservient. Rather, that religion enabled them and their descendants to learn, to grow, to develop, to interpret and reinvent the world in which they were trapped; it enabled them to bide their time—ultimately, time for them to fight for their freedom, and for us to continue the fight for ours. It also gave them the moral authority to turn the mirror of religion back on their masters and to indict the nation for its original sin of allowing their enslavement to build up that 'city upon a hill.' In exposing that hypocrisy at the heart of their 'Christian' country, they exhorted succeeding generations to close that yawning gap between America's founding ideals and the reality they had been forced to endure." Interestingly, Gates frequently uses the terms "revolution" and "revolutionary" throughout his book. See, e.g., Gates, *Black Church*, xvi–xvii, 56–61, 96, 131, 141, 143, 152.

17. Cf. "5 Trends Shaping the Next Season of Next Gen Discipleship" https://www.barna.com/research/five-themes-to-frame-next-gen-discipleship/: "Historically, Gen Z and Millennials are less likely than older generations to be connected to a church. In *Faith for Exiles[: 5 Ways for a New Generation to Follow Jesus in Digital Babylon* (2019)], [Barna president David] Kinnaman and [former executive director of Youth Specialties Mark] Matlock share that the church dropout rate among 18–25-year-olds has increased from 59 percent to 64 percent in the past decade. Data featured in *Gen Z* [vol. 1, *The Culture, Beliefs and Motivations Shaping the Next Generation* (a Barna report produced in partnership with Impact 360 Institute)] also sheds light on the fact that the emerging generation is less likely to see church as important, with those who hold this perspective admitting 'Church is not relevant to me personally' (59%), 'I find God elsewhere' (48%) and 'I can teach myself what I need to know' (28%)." All three of these reasons accurately reflect Lauren's attitude toward the Baptist church of her upbringing. Amazingly, Octavia Butler saw this trend coming already before 1993 (the year of the novel's publication) and presciently projected it onto 2024.

we have seen, Jesus escapes simultaneously from a territorial assemblage (his ancestral roots in Mosaic Judaism) and from a state assemblage (the prevailing Roman Empire). And the leaders of both assemblages conspire to do away with him in the end. Nevertheless, Jesus was *latent* within both assemblages at one point. Here, we are most interested in Jesus' escape from a form of early Judaism (although, as we have seen, he did not entirely escape from every form of Judaism). There is no question that Jesus was a Galilean Jew and that he would have observed Torah during at least part of his life, even if he later flouted some of its rules (e.g., Sabbath observance and purity laws). What led him to escape from the Mosaic Judaism of his upbringing? We cannot know all of the factors, because our sources are virtually silent on the early development of Jesus.[18] But two major influences seem to have contributed to Jesus' breakout. First, at some point, Jesus came under the influence of a form of apocalyptically oriented wisdom tradition *within early Judaism* that can rightly be called "Enochic." This does not mean that he was necessarily a member of some sort of social group, but he did imbibe the atmosphere of the Enochic perspective, which, as George W. E. Nickelsburg has shown, was centered in northeastern Galilee.[19] In particular, Jesus came to understand from this perspective that becoming right with God did not entail adherence to the Mosaic Law, but rather a creation-based reorientation to the will and ways of God that were inscribed in the world from the beginning of creation. Under this influence, Jesus' vision expanded from the more narrowly focused territorial assemblage of the dominant Jewish culture to a creation-wide, apocalyptic perspective. Hence, to survive the final judgment would entail becoming realigned with the originally intended will of God for creation and all that that entailed. Second, Jesus came under the influence of John the Baptist, the fiery preacher of repentance and the imminent final judgment of humankind: "*Even now* the ax is lying at the root of the trees; every tree therefore that does not bear good fruit is cut down and thrown into the fire" (Matt 3:10//Luke 3:9 [Q]). This gave Jesus a real *urgency* to his already deep-seated perspective on humankind's need for comprehensive transformation in order to survive the final judgment. Putting these two influences together, Jesus set out, after the death of

18. Luke's Gospel describes a little about Jesus' formative years, portraying him as a twelve-year-old in the Jerusalem temple (Luke 2:41–52). The Apocryphal Gospels seek to fill the gap in Jesus' life story. For example, the *Infancy Story of Thomas* tells what Jesus did or said at the ages of five (2:1), six (11:1), eight (12:2), and twelve (19:1–5, which elaborates the Lukan story). For the text, see Schneemelcher, *New Testament Apocrypha*, 1:392–401. Some of the stories of Jesus' early childhood are quite fantastic. In the *Infancy Story of Thomas* (Schneemelcher, *New Testament Apocrypha*, 1:439–451), we find the following account (9.1–3): "Jesus was playing in the upper storey, and one of the children who were playing with him fell down from the roof and died. And when the other children saw it, they fled, and Jesus remained alone. And the parents of him that was dead came and accuse him of having thrown him down. And Jesus replied, 'I did not throw him down.' But they continued to revile him. Then Jesus leaped down from the roof and stood by the body of the child, and cried with a loud voice: 'Zenon'— for that was his name—'arise and tell me, did I throw you down?' And he arose at once and said, 'No, Lord, you did not throw me down, but raised me up.' And when they saw it they were amazed. And the parents of the child glorified God for the miracle that had happened and worshipped Jesus."

19. Cf. Nickelsburg, *1 Enoch 1*, 238–47.

John the Baptist, on a campaign of preaching repentance and proclaiming the performative gospel message of the kingdom, in order to call forth the people to come, to prefiguratively create a new and better world in the shell of the old, and to institute a revolutionary new kind of leadership. Jesus' violent death as a royal pretender did not extinguish this vision in the least, but rather—counterintuitively as usual—served only to accelerate it, as more and more people believed his performative word and advanced it beyond the narrow confines of Galilee and Judea, creatively unfolding it in ever-new situations. In time, Jesus' world-encompassing vision of revolutionary transformation became a world-encompassing reality. The question remains as to how faithful the Jesus movement has remained over the centuries to the original Jesus revolution and his vision for comprehensive change.

The present volume is merely an *introduction* to *a* Biblical Theology of the New Testament. The answers we have found only serve to raise a whole set of new and pressing questions. We invite readers to become involved with us in seeking answers to those questions. Our goal in all of this is to advance the relationship between the abstract machine/condition (Jesus Christ), the concrete elements (the Scriptures), and the agents/personae (the community of Christ-followers and their fellow travelers) in process of creating the prefigurative future anterior.

Bibliography

Achenbach, Reinhard et al., eds. *The Foreigner and the Law: Perspectives from the Hebrew Bible and the Ancient Near East.* Wiesbaden: Harrassowitz, 2011.

Adams, Sean A. "Did Aristobulus Use the LXX for His Citations?" *JSJ* 45 (2014) 185–98.

Adkins, Brent, and Paul R. Hinlicky. *Rethinking Philosophy and Theology with Deleuze: A New Cartography.* Bloomsbury Studies in Continental Philosophy. London: Bloomsbury, 2013.

Alexander, Philip S. "The Dualism of Heaven and Earth in Early Jewish Literature and Its Implications." In *Light Against Darkness: Dualism in Ancient Mediterranean Religion and the Contemporary World*, edited by Armin Lange et al., 169–85. JAJSup 2. Göttingen: Vandenhoeck & Ruprecht, 2011.

———. "Geography and the Bible (Early Jewish)." In *ABD* 2:977–88.

Allison, Dale C. *Constructing Jesus: Memory, Imagination, and History.* Grand Rapids: Baker Academic, 2010.

———. *The Historical Christ and the Theological Jesus.* Grand Rapids: Eerdmans, 2009.

———. *The Intertextual Jesus: Scripture in Q.* Harrisburg, PA: Trinity, 2000.

———. *Jesus of Nazareth: Millenarian Prophet.* Minneapolis: Fortress, 1998.

———. "Q 12.51–53 and Mk 9:11–13 and the Messianic Woes." In *Authenticating the Words of Jesus*, edited by Bruce Chilton and Craig A. Evans, 289–310. NTTS 28/1. Leiden: Brill, 1998.

———. *Resurrecting Jesus: The Earliest Christian Tradition and Its Interpreters.* New York/London: T. & T. Clark, 2005.

Amedick, Rita. "'Iesus Nazarenus Rex Iudaiorum': Hellenistische Königsikonographie und das Neue Testament." In *Picturing the New Testament: Studies in Ancient Visual Images*, edited by Annette Weisenrieder et al., 53–66. WUNT 2.193. Tübingen: Mohr Siebeck, 2005.

Amitay, Oray. "The Correspondence in I Maccabees and the Possible Origins of the Judeo-Spartan Connection." *SCI* 32 (2013) 79–105.

Anderson, Gary A. *The Genesis of Perfection: Adam and Eve in Jewish and Christian Imagination.* Louisville: Westminster John Knox, 2001.

Andrejevs, Olegs. *Apocalypticism in the Synoptic Source: A Reassessment of Q's Stratigraphy.* WUNT 2.499. Tübingen: Mohr Siebeck, 2019.

Appiah, Kwame A. *Cosmopolitanism: Ethics in a World of Strangers.* New York: Norton, 2006.

Ashford, Bruce. "Augustine for the Americans: Lessons on Christianity & Public Life from a Fifth-Century North African Theologian." The Ethics & Religious Liberty Commission of the Southern Baptist Convention (April 20, 2015). https://erlc.com/resource-library/articles/augustine-for-the-americans-lessons-on-christianity-and-public-life-from-a-fifth-century-north-african-theologian/.

Ashton, John. *Understanding the Fourth Gospel.* 2nd ed. Oxford: Clarendon, 2007.

Aune, David E. "The Apocalypse of John and the Problem of Genre." *Semeia* 36 (1986) 68–96.

———. "The Meaning of ΕΥΑΓΓΕΛΙΟΝ in the Inscriptions of the Canonical Gospels." In *A Teacher for All Generations: Essays in Honor of James C. VanderKam*, edited by Eric F. Mason et al., 2.857–82. JSJSup 153. Leiden: Brill, 2012.

———. "Oral Tradition and the Aphorisms of Jesus." In *Jesus and the Oral Gospel Tradition*, edited by H. Wansbrough, 211–65. JSNTSup 64. Sheffield: JSOT, 1991.

———. *Revelation 1–5.* WBC 52. Dallas: Word, 1997.

———. *Revelation 17–22.* WBC 52C. Nashville: Thomas Nelson, 1998.

———, ed. *The Westminster Dictionary of New Testament and Early Christian Literature and Rhetoric.* Louisville: Westminster John Knox, 2003.

Austin, J. L., *How to Do Things with Words.* 2nd ed. Cambridge, MA: Harvard University Press, 1975.

Baasland, Ernst, *Theologie und Methode: Eine historiographische Analyse der Frühschriften Rudolf Bultmanns.* Wuppertal/Zürich: Brockhaus Verlag, 1992.

Badiou, Alain. *Saint Paul: The Foundation of Universalism.* Stanford: Stanford University Press, 2003.

Bagnall, Roger S., and Peter Derow, eds. *The Hellenistic Period: Historical Sources in Translation.* Blackwell Sourcebooks in Ancient History. Oxford: Blackwell, 2004.

Bar-Asher Siegal, Elitur. "Who Separated from Whom and Why? A Philological Study of 4QMMT." *RevQ* 25 (2011) 229–56.

Barber, Daniel C. *Deleuze and the Naming of God: Post-Secularism and the Future of Immanence.* Edinburgh: Edinburgh University Press, 2015.

Barclay, John M. G. "Ἰουδαῖος: Ethnicity and Translation." In *Ethnicity, Race, Religion: Identities and Ideologies in Early Jewish and Christian Texts, and in Modern Biblical Interpretation*, edited by Katherine M. Hockey and David G. Horrell, 457–512. London: T. & T. Clark, 2018.

———. *Paul and the Gift.* Grand Rapids: Eerdmans, 2015.

Baron, Lori et al., eds. *The Ways That Often Parted: Essays in Honor of Joel Marcus.* Early Christianity and Its Literature 24. Atlanta: SBL, 2018.

Bash, Anthony, *Ambassadors for Christ: An Exploration of Ambassadorial Language in the New Testament.* WUNT 2.92. Tübingen: Mohr Siebeck, 1997.

Bates, Dawn, et al. *Lushootseed Dictionary.* Seattle: University of Washington Press, 1994.

Bauckham, Richard. *The Bible in Politics: How to Read the Bible Politically.* 2nd ed. Louisville: Westminster John Knox, 2011.

———. "The Economic Critique of Rome in Revelation 18." In *Images of Empire*, edited by Loveday Alexander, 47–90. Sheffield: JSOT, 1991.

———. "For Whom Were Gospels Written?" In *The Gospels for All Christians: Rethinking the Gospel Audiences*, 9–49. Grand Rapids: Eerdmans, 1998.

———. "James and the Jerusalem Church." In *The Book of Acts in Its First Century Setting*, edited by Richard Bauckham, 4:415–80. Grand Rapids: Eerdmans, 1995.

———. *Jesus and the God of Israel: God Crucified and Other Studies on the New Testament's Christology of Divine Identity.* Grand Rapids: Eerdmans, 2008.

———. "Jesus and the Wild Animals (Mark 1:13): A Christological Image for an Ecological Age." In *Jesus of Nazareth, Lord and Christ: Essays on the Historical Jesus and New Testament Christology*, 3–21. Grand Rapids: Eerdmans, 1994.

———. *Jude and the Relatives of Jesus in the Early Church.* Edinburgh: T. & T. Clark, 1990.

———. "Kingdom and Church according to Jesus and Paul." *HBT* 18 (1996) 1–27.

———. *The Theology of the Book of Revelation.* New Testament Theology. Cambridge: Cambridge University Press, 1993.

Baugh, Bruce. "G. W. F. Hegel." In *Deleuze's Philosophical Lineage*, edited by Graham Johns and Jon Roffe, 130–46. Edinburgh: Edinburgh University Press, 2009.

———. "The Open Society and the Democracy to Come: Bergson, Deleuze and Guattari." *Deleuze and Guattari Studies* 10 (2016) 352–66.

Bautch, Kelley Coblentz. *A Study of the Geography of 1 Enoch 17–19: "No One Has Seen What I Have Seen."* JSJSup 81. Leiden: Brill, 2003.

Beard, Mary. *SPQR: A History of Ancient Rome.* New York: Norton, 2015.

Beker, J. Christiaan. *Der Sieg Gottes: Eine Untersuchung zur Struktur der paulinischen Denkens.* SBS 132. Stuttgart: Katholisches Bibelwerk, 1988.

Bencivenni, Alice. "Il re scrive, la città iscrive. La pubblicazione su pietra delle epistole regie nell'Asia ellenistica." *Studi Ellenistici* 24 (2010) 149–78.

———. "The King's Words: Hellenistic Royal Letters in Inscriptions." In *State Correspondence in the Ancient World: From New Kingdom Egypt to the Roman Empire*, edited by Karen Radner, 141–71. Oxford Studies in Early Empires. Oxford: Oxford University Press, 2014.

Bennett, Michael J., and Tano Posteraro, eds. *Deleuze and Evolutionary Theory.* Deleuze Connections. Edinburgh: Edinburgh University Press, 2019.

Bermejo-Rubio, Fernando. "Jesus and the Anti-Roman Resistance: A Reassessment of the Arguments." *JSHJ* 12 (2014) 1–105.

Bernand, Etienne. *Inscriptions métriques de l'Égypte gréco-romaine: Recherches sur la poésie épigrammatique des Grecs en Égypte.* Annals Littéraires de 'Université de Besançon 98. Paris: Les Belles Lettres, 1969.

Betz, Hans Dieter. *Galatians: A Commentary on Paul's Letter to the Churches in Galatia.* Hermeneia. Philadelphia: Fortress, 1979.

Bloch, René. "Jew or Judean: The Latin Evidence." In *Torah, Temple, Land: Constructions of Judaism in Antiquity*, edited by Markus Witte et al., 229–40. TSAJ 184. Tübingen: Mohr Siebeck, 2021.

Bockmuehl, Markus. "James, Israel and Antioch." In *Jewish Law in Gentile Churches: Halakhah and the Beginning of Public Ethics*, 49–83. Edinburgh: T. & T. Clark, 2000.

———. "The Noachide Commandments and New Testament Ethics." *RevQ* 102 (1995) 72–105.

———. *Seeing the Word: Refocusing New Testament Studies.* Studies in Theological Interpretation. Grand Rapids: Baker Academic, 2006.

Bogue, Ronald. "Deleuze and Literature." In *The Cambridge Companion to Deleuze*, edited by Daniel W. Smith and Henry Somers-Hall, 286–306. Cambridge: Cambridge University Press, 2012.

———. *Deleuzian Fabulation and the Scars of History*. Plateaus—New Direction in Deleuze Studies. Edinburgh: Edinburgh University Press, 2010.

———. "Search, Swim and See: Deleuze's Apprenticeship in Signs and Pedagogy of Images." In *Deleuze's Way: Essays in Transverse Ethics and Aesthetics*, 53–67. London: Routledge, 2007.

Bollobás, Enikő. "Biblical Word Power from a Performative Perspective: A Reinterpretation." In *Schöner Alfréd hetven éves: Essays in Honor of Alfred Schöner*, edited by Oláh János and Zima András, 87–88. Budapest: Gabbiano, 2018.

Bormann, Lukas. "Barbaren und Skythen im Lykostal? Epigraphischer Kommentar zu Kol 3:11." In *Epigraphical Evidence Illustrating Paul's Letter to the Colossians*, edited by Joseph Verheyen et al., 161–98. WUNT 2.411. Tübingen: Mohr Siebeck, 2018.

Boundas, Constantin V. et al. "Encounters with Deleuze: An Interview with Constantin V. Boundas and Daniel W. Smith." *Symposium* 24 (2020) 139–74.

Bourdieu, Pierre. *Ce que parler veut dire. L'économie des échanges linguistiques*. Paris: Favard, 1982.

Boxall, Ian, and Richard Tresley. *The Book of Revelation and Its Interpreters: Short Studies and an Annotated Bibliography*. Lanham, MD: Rowman & Littlefield, 2016.

Brande, David. "Not the Call of the Wild: The Idea of Wilderness in Louis Owens's 'Wolfsong.'" *American Indian Quarterly* 24 (2000) 247–63.

Brassier, Ray. "Concrete Rules and Abstract Machines: Form and Function in *A Thousand Plateaus*." In A Thousand Plateaus *and Philosophy*, edited by Henry Somers-Hall et al., 260–79. Edinburgh: Edinburgh University Press, 2018.

Brecoulaki, Harikleia. "'Precious Colours' in Ancient Greek Polychromy and Painting: Material Aspects and Symbolic Values." *RAr* 57 (2014) 3–35.

Breed, Brennan W. "Nomadology of the Bible: A Processual Approach to Biblical Reception History." *Biblical Reception* 1 (2012) 299–320.

Bremmer, Jan N. "Virgil and Jewish Literature." *Vergilius* 59 (2013) 157–64.

Bresciani, Edda et al. *Medinet Madi: Archaeological Guide*. Verona: Geodia Edizioni, 2010.

Breytenbach, Cilliers. "Taufe als räumliche Metapher in den Briefen des Paulus." In *Spatial Metaphors: Ancient Texts and Transformations*, edited by Fabian Horn and Cilliers Breytenbach, 127–43. Berlin Studies of the Ancient World 39. Berlin: Edition Topoi, 2016.

———. *Versöhnung: Eine Studie zur paulinischen Soteriologie*. WMANT 60. Neukirchen-Vluyn: Neukirchener Verlag, 1989.

Brookins, Timothy A. "The (In)frequency of the Name 'Erastus' in Antiquity: A Literary, Papyrological, and Epigraphical Catalog." *NTS* 59 (2013) 496–516.

Brueggemann, Walter. *The Land: Place as Gift, Promise, and Challenge in Biblical Faith*. 2nd ed. Minneapolis: Fortress, 2002.

Brughmans, Tom. "Ancient Greek Networks." *Classical Review* 63 (2013) 146–48.

Bryson, Bill. *The Body: A Guide to Occupants*. New York: Doubleday, 2019.

Buckley, Emma. "Ending the *Aeneid*? Closure and Continuation in Muffeo Vegio's *Supplementum*." *Vergilius* 52 (2006) 108–37.

Bultmann, Rudolf, *Theologie des Neuen Testament*. 9th ed. Tübingen: Mohr Siebeck, 1984.

Butler, Octavia E. *Parable of the Sower*. New York: Grand Central, 1993.

Campbell, Douglas A. *The Quest for Paul's Gospel: A Suggested Strategy*. London: T. & T. Clark, 2005.

Caneva, Giulia. "The Augustus Botanical Code: The Message of the *Ara Pacis*." *Bocconea* 23 (2009) 63–77.

———. *The Augustus Botanical Code: Rome—Ara Pacis. Speaking to the People through the Images of Nature.* Rome: Gangemi, 2010.

Capper, Brian J. "The Judaean Cultural Context of Earliest Christian Community of Goods, Parts I–V." *QC* 24–27 (2016–19) 29–49, 501–45, 39–75, 129–52, 53–82.

Carter, Warren. "The Question of the State and the State of the Question: The Roman Empire and New Testament Theologies." In *Interpretation and the Claim of the Text: Resourcing New Testament Theology*, edited by Jason Whitlark, 197–211. Waco, TX: Baylor University Press, 2014.

Catchpole, David R. "The 'Triumphal' Entry." In *Jesus and the Politics of His Day*, edited by Ernst Bammel and C. F. D. Moule, 319–34. Cambridge: Cambridge University Press, 1984.

Catmull, Ed. *Creativity, Inc.: Overcoming the Unseen Forces That Stand in the Way of Inspiration.* New York: Random House, 2014.

Ceccarelli, Paola. *Ancient Greek Letter Writing: A Cultural History (600 BC–150 BC).* Oxford: Oxford University Press, 2013.

———. "Image and Communication in the Seleucid Kingdom: The King, the Court and the Cities." In *The Hellenistic Court: Monarchic Power and Elite Society from Alexander to Cleopatra*, edited by Andrew Erskine et al., 231–55. Swansea: The Classical Press of Wales, 2017.

———. "Letters and Decrees: Diplomatic Protocols in the Hellenistic Period." In *Letters and Communities: Studies in the Socio-Political Dimensions of Ancient Epistolography*, edited by Paola Ceccarelli et al., 147–84. Oxford: Oxford University Press, 2018.

Ceccarelli, Paola, et al., eds. *Letters and Communities: Studies in the Socio-Political Dimensions of Ancient Epistolography.* Oxford: Oxford University Press, 2018.

Chaniotis, Angelos. *Age of Conquests: The Greek World from Alexander to Hadrian.* Cambridge: Harvard University Press, 2018.

Chrubasik, Boris. *Kings and Usurpers in the Seleucid Empire: The Men Who Would Be King.* Oxford: Oxford University Press, 2016.

Cohen, Shaye J. D. *The Beginnings of Jewishness: Boundaries, Varieties, Uncertainties.* Berkeley: University of California Press, 1999.

Colebrook, Claire. *Understanding Deleuze.* Cultural Studies. London: Routledge, 2020.

Coleman, Katherine. "Fatal Charades: Roman Executions Staged as Mythological Enactments." *JRS* 48 (1990) 44–73.

Collins, Adela Yarbro. *Mark.* Hermeneia. Minneapolis: Fortress, 2007.

———. "No Longer 'Male and Female' (Gal 3:28): Ethics and an Early Christian Baptismal Formula." *Journal of Ethics in Antiquity and Christianity* 1 (2019) 27–39.

Collins, Adela Yarbro, and John J. Collins. *King and Messiah as Son of God: Divine, Human, and Angelic Messianic Figures in Biblical and Related Literature.* Grand Rapids: Eerdmans, 2008.

Collins, John J. *The Apocalyptic Imagination: An Introduction to Jewish Apocalyptic Literature.* 3rd ed. Grand Rapids: Eerdmans, 2016.

———. "Before the Fall: The Earliest Interpretation of Adam and Eve." In *The Idea of Biblical Interpretation: Essays in Honor of James L. Kugel*, edited by Hindy Najman and Judith H. Newman, 293–308. JSJSup 83. Leiden: Brill, 2004.

———. *The Bible after Babel: Historical Criticism in a Postmodern Age.* Grand Rapids: Eerdmans, 2005.

———. *Encounters with Biblical Theology.* Minneapolis: Fortress, 2005.

———. "The Genre Apocalypse Reconsidered." *ZAC* 20 (2016) 21–40.

———. *The Invention of Judaism: Torah and Jewish Identity from Deuteronomy to Paul.* Berkeley: University of California Press, 2017.

———. "Temporality and Politics in Jewish Apocalyptic Literature." In *Apocalyptic in History and Tradition*, edited by Christopher Rowland and John Barton, 26–43. Journal for the Study of the Pseudepigraph Supplements 43. Sheffield: Sheffield Academic, 2002.

Collins, John J., et al. *Ancient Jewish and Christian Scriptures: New Developments in Canon Controversy.* Louisville: Westminster John Knox, 2019.

Collins, John N. "A Monocultural Usage: διακον-words in Classical, Hellenistic, and Patristic Sources." *VigChr* 66 (2012) 287–309

Conio, Andrew, ed. *Occupy: A People Yet to Come.* London: Open Humanities, 2015.

Conniff, Richard. "Unclassified." *Discover* 31 (2010) 52–57.

Cook, Johann. "The Septuagint as a Holy Text: The First 'Bible' of the Early Church." *HvTSt* 76 (2020) 1–9.

Cook, John Granger. "Chrestiani, Christian, Χριστιανοί: A Second Century Anachronism?" *VigChr* 74 (2020) 237–64.

———. *Roman Attitudes Towards Christians: From Claudius to Hadrian.* WUNT 261. Tübingen: Mohr Siebeck, 2010.

Coppinger, Raymond, and Lorna Coppinger. *Dogs: A New Understanding of Canine Origin, Behavior and Evolution.* Chicago: University of Chicago Press, 2002.

Corcoran, Simon. "State Correspondence in the Roman Empire: Imperial Communication from Augustus to Justinian." In *State Correspondence in the Ancient World: From New Kingdom Egypt to the Roman Empire*, edited by Karen Radner, 172–209. Oxford Studies in Early Empires. Oxford: Oxford University Press, 2014.

Costa Malufe, Annita. "Free Indirect Discourse and Assemblages: Literary Procedures in Deleuze and Guattari's Style." In *Machinic Assemblages of Desire: Deleuze and Artistic Research 3*, edited by Paulo de Assis and Paolo Giudici, 261–71. Opheus Institute Series. Leuven: Leuven University Press, 2020.

Cotton-Paltiel, Hannah M., et al. "Juxtaposing Literary and Documentary Evidence: A New Copy of the So-Called Heliodoros Stele and the Corpus Inscriptionum Iudaeae/Palaestinae (CIIP)." *BICS* 60 (2017) 1–15.

Courtwright, David T. *The Age of Addiction: How Bad Habits Became Big Business.* Cambridge: Belknap Press of Harvard University Press, 2019.

Crossan, John Dominic. *The Birth of Christianity: Discovering What Happened in the Years Immediately after the Execution of Jesus.* San Francisco: HarperSanFrancisco, 1998.

———. "Josephus and Nonviolent Resistance to Romanization: The Immediate Jewish Matrix of Jesus of Nazareth." Paper presented at Virtual Annual Meeting of Biblical Meeting of the Society of Biblical Literature. 2020.

Culpepper, R. Alan. *Mark.* Smyth & Helwys Bible Commentary. Macon, GA: Smyth & Helwys, 2017.

Davies, W. D. *The Territorial Dimension of Judaism.* Berkeley: University of California Press, 1982.

Davis Bledsoe, Amanda M. "Throne Theophanies, Dream Visions, and Righteous(?) Seers: Daniel, the Book of Giants, and 1 Enoch Reconsidered." In *Ancient Tales of Giants from*

Qumran and Turfan: Contexts, Traditions, and Influences, edited by Matthew Goff et al., 81–96. WUNT 360. Tübingen: Mohr Siebeck, 2016.

Deleuze, Gilles. *Cinema 2: The Time Image*. Translated by Hugh Tomlinson and Robert Galeta. Minneapolis: University of Minnesota Press, 1989.

———. *Difference and Repetition*. Translated by Paul Patton. New York: Columbia University Press, 1994.

———. *Essays Critical and Clinical*. Translated by Daniel W. Smith and Michael A. Greco. Minneapolis: University of Minnesota Press, 1997.

———. *Negotiations, 1972–1990*. Translated by Martin Joughin. New York: Columbia University Press, 1995.

Deleuze, Gilles, and Félix Guattari. *Kafka: Toward a Minor Literature*. Translated by Dana Polan. Minneapolis: University of Minnesota Press, 1986.

———. *A Thousand Plateaus: Capitalism and Schizophrenia*. Translated by Brian Massumi. Minneapolis: University of Minnesota Press, 1987.

Dempsey, Grant. "Deleuze's Apocalypse." MA thesis, University of Western Ontario, 2014.

deSilva, David A. *The Jewish Teachers of Jesus, James, and Jude: What Earliest Christianity Learned from the Apocrypha and Pseudepigrapha*. Oxford: Oxford University Press, 2012.

de Ste. Croix, G. E M. *Christian Persecution, Martyrdom, and Orthodoxy*. Edited by Michael Whitby and Joseph Streeter. Oxford: Oxford University Press, 2006.

Dillon, Matt. "Gods in Ancient Greece and Rome." *Oxford Research Encyclopedia of Religion* (2019).

Dillon, Matthew P. J. "The Lakedaimonian Dedication to Olympian Zeus: The Date of *Meiggs and Lewis* 22 (*SEG* 11, 1203A)." *ZPE* 107 (1995) 60–68.

Dinkler, Michal Beth. "Beyond the Normative/Descriptive Divide: Hermeneutics and Narrativity." In *Verstehen und Interpretieren: Zum Basisvokabular von Hermeneutik und Interpretationstheorie*, edited by Andreas Mauz and Christiane Tietz, 127–45. Hermeneutik und Interpretationstheorie 1. Göttingen: Schöningh, 2020.

Dochhorn, Jan. *Schriftgelehrte Prophetie: Der eschatologische Teufelfall in App Joh 12 und seine Bedeutung für das Verständnis der Johannesoffenbarung*. WUNT 268. Tübingen: Mohr Siebeck, 2010.

Doering, Lutz. "Marriage and Creation in Mark 10 and CD 4–6." In *Echoes from the Caves: Qumran and the New Testament*, edited by Florentino García Martínez, 133–63. STDJ 85. Leiden: Brill, 2009.

———. "'Much Ado about Nothing?' Jesus' Sabbath Healings and Their Halakic Implications Revisited." In *Judaistik und Neutestamentliche Wissenschaft: Standorte—Grenzen—Beziehungen*, edited by Lutz Doering et al., 213–41. FRLANT 226. Göttingen: Vandenhoeck & Ruprecht, 2008.

———. *Schabbat: Sabbathalacha und -praxis im antiken Judentum und Urchristentum*. TSAJ 78. Tübingen: Mohr Siebeck, 1999.

———. "Urzeit-Endzeit Correlation in the Dead Sea Scrolls and Pseudepigrapha." In *Eschatologie—Eschatology: The Sixth Durham-Tübingen Research Symposium. Eschatology in the Old Testament, Ancient Judaism and Early Christianity (Tübingen, September, 2009)*, edited by H.-J. Eckstein et al., 19–58. WUNT 272. Tübingen: Mohr Siebeck, 2011.

Dohmen, Christoph, and Thomas Söding, eds. *Eine Bibel—Zwei Testamente: Positionen biblischer Theologie*. Paderborn: Schöning, 1995.

Doole, J. Andrew. "Could Paul Refer to Himself in the Plural?" Paper presented at Virtual Annual Meeting of the SBL. 2020.

Doroszewski, Filip, and Dariusz Karłowicz, eds. *Dionysus and Politics: Constructing Authority in the Graeco-Roman World.* Routledge Monographs in Classical Studies. London: Routledge, 2021.

Drawnel, Henryk. *Qumran Cave 4: The Aramaic Books of Enoch: 4Q201, 4Q202, 4Q204, 4Q205, 4Q206, 4Q207, 4Q212.* Oxford: Oxford University Press, 2019.

Dreyfus, Hubert, and Mark A. Wrathall, eds. *A Companion to Heidegger.* Malden, MA: Blackwell, 2005.

Duggan, T. M. P. "Not Just the Shadows on the Stone: The Greek, Lycian and Roman Craft of Encaustica (ἔγκαυσις) and the Polishing (γάνωσις) of Coloured Inscriptions, That Is, of Graphō (γράφω) and Its Study—Epigraphy." *Phaselis* 2 (2016) 269–83.

Dunn, James D. G. *Christianity in the Making, Vol. 1: Jesus Remembered.* Grand Rapids: Eerdmans, 2003.

———. *A Commentary on the Epistle to the Galatians.* London: Black, 1993.

———. *The Theology of Paul the Apostle.* Grand Rapids: Eerdmans, 1998.

———. *The Theology of Paul's Letter to the Galatians.* New Testament Theology. Cambridge: Cambridge University Press, 1993.

Dunne, John Anthony. *Persecution and Participation in Galatians.* WUNT 2.454. Tübingen: Mohr Siebeck, 2017.

Dušek, Jan. *Aramaic and Hebrew Inscriptions from Mt. Gerizim and Samaria between Antiochus III and Antiochus IV Epiphanes.* Culture and History of the Ancient Near East 54. Leiden: Brill, 2012.

Eastaugh, Nicholas, et al. *Pigment Compendium: A Dictionary of Historical Pigments.* Oxford: Elsevier Butterworth-Heinemann, 2004.

Ego, Beate et al., eds. *Gemeinde ohne Tempel = Community without Temple: Zur Substitutierung und Transformation des Jerusalemer Tempels und seines Kults im Alten Testament, antiken Judentum und frühen Christentum.* WUNT 118. Tübingen: Mohr Siebeck, 1999.

Ehrman, Bart D. *The Triumph of Christianity: How a Forbidden Religion Swept the World.* New York: Simon & Schuster, 2018.

Elliot, J. K., ed. *The Apocryphal New Testament: A Collection of Apocryphal Christian Literature in English Translation.* Oxford: Clarendon, 1993.

Elliott, Neil. "Paul and Empire 1: Romans, 1 Corinthians, 2 Corinthians." In *An Introduction to Empire in the New Testament*, edited by Adam Winn, 143–64. SBLRBS 84. Atlanta: SBL, 2016.

———. "The Question of Politics: Paul as a Diaspora Jew under Roman Rule." In *Paul within Judaism: Restoring the First-Century Context to the Apostle*, edited by Mark D. Nanos and Magnus Zetterholm, 203–43. Minneapolis: Fortress, 2015.

Esler, Philip F. *God's Court and Courtiers in the Book of the Watchers: Re-Interpreting Heaven in 1 Enoch 1–36.* Eugene, OR: Cascade Books, 2017.

Esterhammer, Angela. *Creating States: Studies in the Performative Language of John Milton and William Blake.* Toronto: University of Toronto Press, 1994.

Evans, Craig A. "Daniel in the New Testament: Visions of God's Kingdom." In *The Book of Daniel: Composition and Reception*, edited by John J. Collins and Peter W. Flint, 490–527. VTSup 83. Leiden: Brill, 2001.

Evans, Rhiannon. *Utopia Antiqua: Readings of the Golden Age and Decline at Rome.* Routledge Monographs in Classical Studies. London: Routledge, 2007.

Ferguson, B. A. et al. "Course-Scale Population Structure of Pathogenic *Armillaria* Species in a Mixed-Confer Forest in the Blue Mountains of Northeast Oregon." *Canadian Journal of Forest Research* 33 (2003) 612–23.

Fraade, Steven D. "To Whom It May Concern: 4QMMT and Its Addressee(s)." *RevQ* 76 (2000) 507–26.

Franco Beatrice, Pier. "The Word '*Homoousios*' from Hellenism to Christianity." *CH* 71 (2002) 243–72.

Fredriksen, Paula. *From Jesus to Christ: The Origins of New Testament Images of Jesus.* New Haven: Yale University Press, 1988.

———. *Paul, The Pagans' Apostle.* New Haven: Yale University Press, 2017.

Fretheim, Terence E. *God and the World in the Old Testament: A Relational Theology of Creation.* Nashville: Abingdon, 2005.

Freyne, Seán. "Jesus in Jewish Galilee." In *Redefining First-Century Jewish and Christian Identities: Essays in Honor of Ed Parish Sanders*, edited by Fabian E. Udoh, 197–212. Christianity and Judaism in Antiquity Series 16. Notre Dame, IN: University of Notre Dame Press, 2008.

Gabrielson, Timothy A. "Parting Ways or Rival Siblings? A Review and Analysis of Metaphors for the Separation of Jews and Christians in Antiquity." *CBR* 19 (2021) 178–204.

Gaskin, Richard. "On Being Pessimistic about the End of the *Aeneid*." *HSCP* 111 (2022).

Gassman, Mattias. "On an Alleged *Senatus Consultum* against the Christians." *VigChr* 75 (2021) 1–8.

Gates, Henry Louis, Jr. *The Black Church: This Is Our Story, This Is Our Song.* New York: Penguin, 2021.

Gatz, Bodo. *Weltalter, goldene Zeit und sinnverwandte Vorstellungen.* Spudasmata 16. Hildesheim: Olms, 1967.

Geagan, Daniel J. "A Letter of Trajan to a Synod at Isthmia." *Hesperia* 44 (1975) 396–401.

Gerstenberger, Erhard S. *Theologies in the Old Testament.* Minneapolis: Fortress, 2002.

Gilbert, Jeremy. "Deleuzian Politics? A Survey and Some Suggestions." *New Formations* 68 (2009) 10–33.

Goff, Matthew. "Recent Trends in the Study of Early Jewish Wisdom Literature: The Contribution of 4QInstruction and Other Qumran Texts." *CBR* 7 (2009) 376–416.

Goldenberg, David. "Scythian-Barbarian: The Permutations of a Classical Topos in Jewish and Christian Texts of Late Antiquity." *JJS* 49 (1998) 87–102.

Goodman, Martin. "Galatians 6:12 on Circumcision and Persecution." In *Strength to Strength: Essays in Honor of Shayne J. D. Cohen*, edited by Mary Glück, 275–79. BJS 363. Providence, RI: Brown Judaic Studies, 2018.

———. "Nerva, the *Fiscus Judaicus* and Jewish Identity." *JRS* 79 (1989) 40–44.

———. *The Ruling Class of Judaea: The Origins of the Jewish Revolt against Rome, A.D. 66–70.* Cambridge: Cambridge University Press, 1987.

Goward, Trevor. "Twelve Readings on the Lichen Thallus V—Conversational." *Evansia* 26 (2009) 31–37.

Graf, Fritz. "What Is New about Greek Sacrifice?" In *Kykeon: Studies in Honour of H.S. Versnel*, edited by H. F. J. Horstmanshoff et al., 113–26. Leiden: Brill, 2002.

Green, Joel B. "Kingdom of God/Heaven." In *The Dictionary of Jesus and the Gospels*, edited by Joel B. Green et al., 468–81. Downers Grove, IL: IVP Academic, 2013.

———. "Scripture and Theology: Uniting the Two So Long Divided." In *Between Two Horizons: Spanning New Testament Studies and Systematic Theology*, edited by Joel B. Green and Max Turner, 23–43. Grand Rapids: Eerdmans, 2000.

Green, Joel B., et al., eds. *The Dictionary of Jesus and the Gospels*. 2nd ed. Downers Grove, IL: IVP Academic, 2013.

Green, Joel B., and Max Turner, eds. *Between Two Horizons: Spanning New Testament Studies and Systematic Theology*. Grand Rapids: Eerdmans, 2000.

Gruen, Erich S. *The Construct of Identity in Hellenistic Judaism: Essays on Early Jewish Literature and History*. Deuterocanonical and Cognate Literature Studies 29. Berlin: de Gruyter, 2016.

Guthrie, George H. *2 Corinthians*. Baker Exegetical Commentary on the New Testament. Grand Rapids: Baker Academic, 2015.

Hacham, Noah. "Exile and Self-Identity in the Qumran Sect and in Hellenistic Judaism." In *New Perspectives on Old Texts: Proceedings of the Tenth International Symposium of the Orion Center for the Study of the Dead Sea Scrolls and Associated Literature, 9–11 January, 2005*, edited by Esther G. Chazon et al., 3–21. STDJ 88. Leiden: Brill, 2010.

Hacht, Sydney von. "The Spotify Assemblage: Why your playlist shapes both your Saturday night and the application itself." *Salience* (2020). https://www.salienceatsydney.org/blog/2020/08/11/the-spotify-assemblage-why-your-playlist-shapes-both-your-saturday-night-and-the-application-itself/.

Hafemann, Scott J. *Biblical Theology: Retrospect and Prospect*. Downers Grove, IL: InterVarsity, 2002.

———, ed. *Suffering and Ministry in the Spirit: Paul's Defense of His Ministry in II Corinthians 2:14–3:3*. Grand Rapids: Eerdmans, 1990.

Hahne, Harry Alan. *The Corruption and Redemption of Creation: Nature in Romans 8.19–22 and Jewish Apocalyptic Literature*. LNTS 336. London: T. & T. Clark, 2006.

Hall, Jonathan. *Hellenicity: Between Ethnicity and Culture*. Chicago: University of Chicago Press, 2002.

Harder, Annette. "Spiders in the Greek Wide Web?" In *Hellenic Studies at a Crossroads: Exploring Texts, Contexts and Metatexts*, edited by Richard Hunter et al., 259–71. Berlin: de Gruyter, 2014.

Hardie, Philip. *The Last Trojan: A Cultural History of Virgil's Aeneid*. London: Tauris, 2014.

Harnack, Adolf. *Die Mission und Ausbreitung des Christentums in den ersten drei Jahrhunderten*. 4th ed. 2 vols. Leipzig: Hinrichs, 1924.

Harris, M. "History and Significance of the Emic/Etic Distinction." *Annual Review of Anthropology* 5 (1976) 329–50.

Harris, Tracy, and Chris Rushton. "Hong Kong artists: Should I stay or should I go?" *BBC*, December 11, 2021. https://www.bbc.co.uk/programmes/w3ct1ptn.

Hartman, Lars. "On Reading Others' Letters." *HTR* 79 (1986) 137–46.

Hatina, Thomas R. *New Testament Theology and Its Quest for Relevance: Ancient Texts and Modern Readers*. London: Bloomsbury, 2013.

Hauptmann, Deborah, and Andrej Radman, eds. "Signifying Semiotics: Or How to Paint Pink on Pink." *Footprint: Delft Architecture Theory Journal* 14 (2014). https://journals.open.tudelft.nl/footprint/issue/view/392.

Hayes, Christine. *Gentile Impurities and Jewish Identities: Intermarriage and Conversion from the Bible to the Talmud*. Oxford: Oxford University Press, 2002.

Hays, Richard B. *Echoes of Scripture in the Letters of Paul*. New Haven: Yale University Press, 1989.

Heil, John Paul. "Jesus with the Wild Animals in Mark 1:13." *CBQ* 68 (2006) 63–78.

Heilmann, Jan, and Matthias Klinghardt, eds. *Das Neue Testament und sein Text im 2. Jahrhundert*. TANZ 61. Tübingen: Narr Attempto, 2018.

Hekster, Olivier. *Emperors and Ancestors: Roman Rulers and the Constraints of Tradition*. Oxford Studies in Ancient Culture and Representation. Oxford: Oxford University Press, 2016.

Hengel, Martin. *The Atonement: The Origins of the Doctrine in the New Testament*. Philadelphia: Fortress, 1981.

———. "Aufgaben der neutestamentlichen Wissenschaft." *NTS* 40 (1994) 321–57.

———. *The Four Gospels and the One Gospel of Jesus Christ: An Investigation of the Collection and Origin of the Canonical Gospels*. Harrisburg, PA: Trinity, 2000.

———. "Hymns and Christology." In *Between Jesus and Paul*, 78–96. London: SCM, 1983.

———. "Jakobus der Herrenbruder—der erste 'Papst'?" In *Glaube und Eschatologie: Festschrift für Werner Georg Kümmel zum 80. Geburtstag*, edited by Erik Grässer and Otto Merk, 71–104. Tübingen: Mohr Siebeck, 1985.

———. *The Pre-Christian Paul*. London: SCM, 1991.

———. "Salvation History: The Truth of Scripture and Modern Theology." In *Reading Texts, Seeking Wisdom: Scripture and Theology*, edited by David F. Ford and Graham Stanton, 229–44. London: SCM, 2003.

———. "The Song about Christ in Earliest Worship." In *Studies in Early Christology*, 227–91. Edinburgh: T. & T. Clark, 1995.

———. *Studies in the Gospel of Mark*. London: SCM, 1985.

Hengel, Martin, and Anna Maria Schwemer. *Jesus und das Judentum*. Tübingen: Mohr Siebeck, 2007.

Henrichs, Albert. "*Hieroi Logoi* and *Hierai Bibloi*: The (Un)Written Margins of the Sacred in Ancient Greece." *HSCP* 101 (2003) 207–66.

Henry, Andrew Mark. "Apotropaic Autographs: Orality and Materiality in the Abgar-Jesus Inscriptions." *Archiv für Religionsgeschichte* 17 (2016) 165–86.

Henze, Matthias. *HAZON GABRIEL: New Readings of the Gabriel Revelation*. SBLEJL 29. Atlanta: SBL, 2011.

Herzer, Jens. "'Alle Einer in Christus'—Gal 3,28b und kein Ende. Ein Vorschlag." In *Spurensuche zur Einleitung in das Neue Testament: Eine Festschrift im Dialog mit Udo Schnelle*, edited by Michael Labahn, 124–42. FRLANT 271. Göttingen: Vandenhoeck & Ruprecht, 2017.

Hillenkam, Oliver. "Becoming Fungal: Humans and Mushrooms at the 2018 Radical Mycology Convergence." *Radical: Reed Anthropological Review* 4 (2019) 1–6.

Hofius, Otfried. *Paulusstudien*. WUNT 51. Tübingen: Mohr Siebeck, 1989.

Hofmann, Vera. "Communication between City and King in the Hellenistic East." In *Official Epistolography and the Language(s) of Power: Proceedings of the First International Conference of the Research Network Imperium & Officium*, edited by Stephan Procházka et al., 139–52. Papyrologica Vindobonensia 8. Vienna: Austrian Academy of Sciences, 2015.

Hofstadter, Douglas, and Emmanuel Sander. *Surfaces and Essences: Analogy as the Fuel and Fire of Thinking*. New York: Basic, 2013.

Hogan, Pauline Nigh. *No Longer Male and Female: Interpreting Galatians 3:28 in Early Christianity.* LNTS 380. London: T. & T. Clark, 2008.

Holton, Gerald. "Einstein, Michelson, and the 'Crucial' Experiment." *Isis* 60 (1969) 132–97.

Hope, David, and Julian Limberg. "The Economic Consequences of Major Tax Cuts for the Rich." *The London School of Economics and Political Science Working Paper* 55 (2020). http://eprints.lse.ac.uk/107919/1/Hope_economic_consequences_of_major_tax_cuts_published.pdf.

Horbury, William. "The Twelve and the Phylarchs." *NTS* 32 (1986) 503–27.

Horsfall, Nicholas. "Virgil and the Jews." *Vergilius* 58 (2012) 67–80.

Horsley, Richard A., ed. *Paul and Politics: Religion and Power in Roman Imperial Society.* Harrisburg, PA: Trinity, 1997.

Houten, Christiana van. *The Alien in Israelite Law.* JSOTSup 107. Sheffield: JSOT Press, 1991.

Hurtado, Larry W. *Lord Jesus Christ: Devotion to Jesus in Earliest Christianity.* Grand Rapids: Eerdmans, 2003.

Hyatt, Millay Christine. "No-where and Now-here: Utopia and Politics from Hegel to Deleuze." PhD diss., University of Southern California, 2006.

Hyde, Douglas. *Dedication and Leadership: Learning from the Communists.* Notre Dame, IN: University of Notre Dame Press, 1966.

Iossif, Panagiotis P. and Catharine C. Lorber. "Celestial Imagery on the Eastern Coinage of Antiochus IV." *Mesopotamia* 44 (2009) 129–46.

Jacob, Sharon. "Face-ing the Nations: Becoming a Majority Empire of God—Reterritorialization, Language, and Imperial Racism in Revelation 7:9–17." In *Critical Theory and Early Christianity*, edited by Matthew G. Whitlock. Sheffield: Equinox, forthcoming.

Jensen, Erik. *Barbarians in the Greek and Roman World.* Indianapolis: Hackett, 2018.

Johns, Loren L. *The Lamb Christology of the Apocalypse of John: An Investigation into Its Origins and Rhetorical Force.* WUNT 2.167. Tübingen: Mohr Siebeck, 2003.

Johnson, Ryan J. *Deleuze, a Stoic.* Edinburgh: Edinburgh University Press, 2020.

———. "On the Surface: The Deleuze–Stoicism Encounter." In *Contemporary Encounters with Ancient Metaphysics*, edited by Abraham Jacob Greenstine and Ryan J. Johnson, 270–88. Edinburgh: Edinburgh University Press, 2017.

Jones, F. Stanley. "Jewish-Christian Chiliastic Restoration in *Pseudo-Clementine Recognitions* 1.27–71." In *Restoration: Old Testament, Jewish, and Christian Perspectives*, edited by James M. Scott, 529–47. JSJSup 72. Leiden: Brill, 2001.

Jonnes, Lloyd, and Marijana Ricl. "A New Royal Inscription from Phyrgia Paroreios: Eumenes II Grants Tyriaion the Status of a Polis." *Epigraphica Anatolica* 29 (1997) 1–30.

Joubert, Stephan J. "ΧΑΡΙΣ in Paul: An Investigation into the Apostle's 'Performative' Application of the Language of *Grace* within the Framework of His Theological Reflection on the Event/Process of Salvation." In *Salvation in the New Testament: Perspectives on Soteriology*, edited by Jan G. Van der Watt, 187–211. NovTSup 121. Leiden: Brill, 2005.

Justaert, Kristien. *Theology After Deleuze.* Deleuze Encounters. London: Continuum, 2012.

Kahn, Yoel. *The Three Blessings: Boundaries, Censorship, and Identity in Jewish Liturgy.* Oxford: Oxford University Press, 2011.

Käsemann, Ernst. *On Being a Disciple of the Crucified Nazarene.* Grand Rapids: Eerdmans, 2010.

———. "Rechtfertigung und Heilsgeschichte im Römerbrief." In *Paulinische Perspektiven*, 108–39. Tübingen: Mohr Siebeck, 1968.

Keener, Craig S. "Greek versus Jewish Conceptions of Inspiration and 2 Timothy 3:16." *JETS* 63 (2020) 217–31.

Kelhoffer, James A. *Miracle and Mission: The Authentication of Missionaries and Their Message in the Longer Ending of Mark.* WUNT 2.112. Tübingen: Mohr Siebeck, 2000.

Kennedy, Dorothy Irene. "Threads to the Past: The Construction and Transformation of Kinship in the Coast Salish Social Network." PhD thesis, Oxford University, 2000.

Kennell, Nigel M. "New Light on 2 Maccabees 4.7–15." *JJS* 56 (2005) 10–24.

Keppie, Lawrence. *Understanding Roman Inscriptions.* Baltimore, MD: Johns Hopkins University Press, 1991.

Kim, Seyoon. *"The 'Son of Man'" as the Son of God.* Wissenschaftliche Untersuchungen zum Neuen Testament 30. Tübingen: Mohr Siebeck, 1983.

Kimber Buell, Denise. *Why This New Race: Ethnic Reasoning in Early Christianity.* New York: Columbia University Press, 2005.

Kinman, B. "Jesus' Royal Entry into Jerusalem." In *Key Events in the Life of the Historical Jesus*, edited by Darrell L. Bock and R. L. Webb, 383–427. WUNT 247. Tübingen: Mohr Siebeck, 2009.

Kirk, Ruth. *Tradition and Change on the Northwest Coast: The Makah, Nuu-chah-nulth, Southern Kwakiutl and Nuxalk.* Seattle: University of Washington Press in association with The Royal British Columbia Museum, 1986.

Klauck, Hans-Josef. *Ancient Letters and the New Testament: A Guide to Context and Exegesis.* Waco, TX: Baylor University Press, 2006.

Kloppenborg, John S. "Associations, Christ Groups, and Their Place in the Polis." *ZNW* 108 (2017) 1–56.

———. *Christ's Associations: Connecting and Belonging in the Ancient City.* New Haven: Yale University Press, 2019.

Kooten, George H. van. "Ἐκκλησία τοῦ θεοῦ. The 'Church of God' and the Civic Assemblies (ἐκκλησίαι) of the Greek Cities in the Roman Empire: A Response to Paul Trebilco and Richard A. Horsley." *NTS* 58 (2012) 522–48.

Korner, Ralph J. *The Origin and Meaning of Ekklēsia in the Early Jesus Movement.* Ancient Judaism and Early Christianity 98. Leiden: Brill, 2017.

Kosmin, Paul J. "A Short Introduction to the Seleucid Era." *Center for Hellenic Studies Research Bulletin* 4 (2016). http://nrs.harvard.edu/urn-3:hlnc.essay:KosminP.Introduction_to_the_Seleucid_Era.2016.

Koulakiotis, Elias, and Charlotte Dunn, eds. *Political Religions in the Greco-Roman World: Discourses, Practices and Images.* Cambridge: Cambridge Scholars, 2019.

Kugel, James L. *How to Read the Bible: A Guide to the Bible, Then and Now.* New York: Free, 2007.

———. *Traditions of the Bible: A Guide to the Bible As It Was at the Start of the Common Era.* Cambridge, MA: Harvard University Press, 1998.

———. "Wisdom and the Anthological Temper." *Prooftexts* 17 (1997) 9–32.

Kuhn, Thomas. *The Structure of Scientific Revolutions.* 4th ed. Chicago: University of Chicago Press, 2012.

Kutsko, John F. *Between Heaven and Earth: Divine Presence and Absence in the Book of Ezekiel.* Biblical and Judaic Studies from the University of California, San Diego 7. Winona Lake, IN: Eisenbrauns, 2000.

Lambers-Petry, Doris. "Verwandte Jesu als Referenzpersonen für das Judenchristentum." In *The Image of Judaeo-Christians in Ancient Jewish and Christian Literature*, edited by

Peter J. Tomson and Doris Lambers-Petry, 32–52. WUNT 158. Tübingen: Mohr Siebeck, 2003.

Last, Richard. "Ekklēsia outside the Septuagint and the Dēmos: The Titles of Greco-Roman Associations and Christ-Followers' Groups." *JBL* 137 (2018) 959–80.

Latham, Jacob A. "'Honors Greater Than Human': Imperial Cult in the *Pompa Circensis*." In *Performance, Memory, and Processions in Ancient Rome: The Pompa Circensis from the Late Republic to Late Antiquity*, 105–45. Cambridge: Cambridge University Press, 2016.

Lavan, Myles. "The Foundation of Empire? The Spread of Roman Citizenship from the Fourth Century BCE to the Third Century CE." In *The Crucible of Empire: The Impact of Roman Citizenship upon Greeks, Jews and Christians*, edited by Katell Berthelot and Jonathan J. Price, 21–54. Leuven: Peeters, 2019.

———. *Slaves to Rome: Paradigms of Empire in Roman Culture.* Cambridge Classical Studies. Cambridge: Cambridge University Press, 2013.

Lavan, Myles, et al., eds. *Cosmopolitanism and Empire: Universal Rulers, Local Elites, and Cultural Integration in the Ancient Near East and Mediterranean.* Oxford Studies in Early Empires. New York: Oxford University Press, 2016.

Lavelle, Brian M. "Thucydides and *IG* I3 948: ἀμυδροῖς γράμμασι." In *Daidalikon: Studies in Memory of Raymond V. Schoder*, edited by R. F. Sutton, 207–12. Wauconda, IL: Bolchazy-Carducci, 1989.

Lawrence, D. H. *Apocalypse and the Writings on Revelation.* New York: Cambridge University Press, 1980.

Le Donne, Anthony. *Historical Jesus: What Can We Know and How Can We Know It?* Grand Rapids: Eerdmans, 2011.

Lembke, Anna. *Dopamine Nation: Finding the Balance in the Age of Indulgence.* New York: Penguin Random, 2021.

Lieu, Judith. *Neither Jew nor Greek? Constructing Early Christianity.* Edinburgh: T. & T. Clark, 2005.

Lin, Yii-Jan. "Junia: An Apostle before Paul." *JBL* 139 (2020) 191–209.

Lincoln, Bruce. *Holy Terrors: Thinking about Religion after September 11.* Chicago: University of Chicago Press, 2003.

Llewelyn, S. R., and D. Van Beek. "Reading the Temple Warning as a Greek Visitor." *JSJ* 41 (2010) 1–22.

Lockett, Darian R. *Letters from the Pillar Apostles: The Formation of the Catholic Epistles as a Canonical Collection.* Cambridge: James Clarke, 2017.

Long, A. A. "The Concept of the Cosmopolis in Greek and Roman Thought." *Daedalus* 137 (2008) 50–58.

Long, A. A., and D. N. Sedley. *The Hellenistic Philosophers.* 2 vols. Cambridge: Cambridge University Press, 1987.

Longenecker, Bruce W., and Mikeal C. Parsons, eds. *Beyond Bultmann: Reckoning a New Testament Theology.* Waco, TX: Baylor University Press, 2014.

Longenecker, Richard N. *Galatians.* WBC 41. Dallas: Word, 1990.

Lougovaya, Julia. "Greek Inscriptions in Ptolemaic Narmouthis." In *Vor der Pharaonenzeit bis zur Spätantike: Kulturelle Vielfalt im Fayum. Akten der 5. Internationalen Fayum-Konferenz, 29. Mai bis 1. Juni 2013, Leipzig*, edited by Nadine Quenouille, 103–22. Wiesbaden: Harrassowitz, 2015.

Lundy, Craig. "The Call for a New Earth, a New People: An Untimely Problem." *Culture and Society* 38 (2021) 119–39.

Lynch, Patrick Michael. *The Internet of Us: Knowing More and Understanding Less in the Age of Big Data*. New York: Liveright, 2016.

Ma, John. *Antiochos III and the Cities of Western Asia Minor*. Oxford: Oxford University Press, 2000.

———. "Epigraphy and the Display of Authority." In *Epigraphy and the Historical Sciences*, edited by John Davies and John Wilkes, 133–58. Proceedings of the British Academy 177. Oxford: Oxford University Press, 2012.

———. "Hellenistic Empires." In *The Oxford Handbook of the State in the Ancient Near East and Mediterranean*, edited by Peter Fibiger Bang and Walter Scheidel, 324–57. Oxford: Oxford University Press, 2013.

———. "Kings." In *A Companion to the Hellenistic World*, edited by Andrew Erskine, 177–95. Oxford: Blackwell, 2003.

———. "Paradigms and Paradoxes in the Hellenistic World." *Studi Ellenistici* 20 (2008) 371–86.

———. "Re-examining Hanukkah." *Marginalia* (July 9, 2013). http://marginalia.lareviewofbooks.org/re-examining-hanukkah/.

———. "Seleukids and Speech-Acts: Performative Utterances, Legitimacy and Negotiation in the World of the Maccabees." *SCI* 19 (2000) 71–112.

Macaskill, Grant. "Apocalypse and the Gospel of Mark." In *The Jewish Apocalyptic Tradition and the Shaping of New Testament Thought*, edited by Benjamin E. Reynolds and Loren T. Stuckenbruck, 53–77. Minneapolis: Fortress, 2017.

MacMullen, Ramsay. "How to Revolt in the Roman Empire." In *Changes in the Roman Empire: Essays in the Ordinary*, 198–203. Princeton: Princeton University Press, 1990.

Macquarrie, John. *An Existentialist Theology: A Comparison of Heidegger and Bultmann*. London: SCM, 1955.

Maier, Harry O. "Staging the Gaze: Early Christian Apocalypses and Narrative Self-Representation." *HTR* 90 (1997) 131–54.

Malkin, Irad, ed. *Ancient Perceptions of Greek Ethnicity*. Center for Hellenic Studies Colloquia 5. Cambridge, MA: Harvard University Press, 2001.

———. "Between Collective and Ethnic Identities: A Conclusion." *Dialogues d'histoire ancienne* supplément 10 (2014) 283–92.

———. "Networks and the Emergence of Greek Identity." In *Mediterranean Paradigms and Classical Antiquity*, edited by Irad Malkin, 56–74. London: Routledge, 2005.

———. *A Small Greek World: Networks in the Ancient Mediterranean*. Oxford: Oxford University Press, 2011.

Manu, Joseph. *Serious Men*. New York: Norton, 2010.

Marcus, Joel. *Mark 1–8*. AB 27. New York: Doubleday, 2000.

Martin, Dale B. "The Queer History of Galatians 3:28: 'No Male and Female.'" In *Sex and the Single Savior: Gender and Sexuality in Biblical Interpretation*, 77–90. Louisville: Westminster John Knox, 2006.

Martin, Ralph P. *2 Corinthians*. WBC 40. Waco, TX: Word, 1986.

Martyn, J. Louis. *Galatians*. AB 33A. New York: Doubleday, 1997.

———. *Theological Issues in the Letters of Paul*. London: T. & T. Clark, 1997.

Mason, Steve. "Jews, Judaeans, Judaizing, Judaism: Problems of Categorization in Ancient History." *JSJ* 38 (2007) 457–512.

Massa-Pairault, Françoise-Hélène, and Claude Pouzadoux, eds. *Géants et gigantomachies entre Orient et Occident*. Naples: Centre Jean Bérard, 2017.

Mathews, Mark D. *Riches, Poverty, and the Faithful: Perspectives on Wealth in the Second Temple Period and the Apocalypse of John.* SNTSMS 154. Cambridge: Cambridge University Press, 2013.

Matthes, Claudia. *Die Taufe auf den Tod Christi: Eine ritualwissenschaftliche Untersuchung zur christlichen Taufe dargestellt anhand der paulinischen Tauftexte.* Neutestamentliche Entwürfe zur Theologie 25. Tübingen: Narr, Francke, Attempto, 2017.

Maxey, James. "The Power of Words in Mark: Their Potential and Their Limits." *CurTM* 37 (2010) 296–303.

Mayshar, Joran. "Who Was the *Toshav?*" *JBL* 133 (2014) 225–46.

McKnight, Scott, and Joseph B. Modica, eds. *Jesus Is Lord, Caesar Is Not: Evaluating Empire in New Testament Studies.* Downers Grove, IL: IVP Academic, 2013.

Meeks, Wayne A. *The First Urban Christians: The Social World of the Apostle Paul.* New Haven: Yale University Press, 1983.

Meier, John P. "Jesus, the Twelve, and the Restoration of Israel." In *Restoration: Old Testament, Jewish, and Christian Perspectives*, edited by James M. Scott, 365–404. JSJSup 72. Leiden: Brill, 2001.

———. *A Marginal Jew: Rethinking the Historical Jesus.* Vol. 1, *The Roots of the Problem and the Person.* ABRL. New York: Doubleday, 1991.

———. *A Marginal Jew: Rethinking the Historical Jesus.* Vol. 3, *Companions and Competitors.* ABRL. New York: Doubleday, 2001.

Meiggs, Russell, and David Lewis. *A Selection of Greek Historical Inscriptions to the End of the Fifth.* Rev. ed. Oxford: Oxford University Press, 1989.

Millar, Fergus. *The Emperor in the Roman World (31 BC–AD 337).* London: Duckworth, 1992.

———. "Imperial Letters in Latin: Pliny and Trajan, Egnatius Taurinus and Hadrian." *SCI* 35 (2016) 65–83.

Miller, Riel, ed. *Transforming the Future: Anticipation in the 21st Century.* London: Routledge, 2018.

Mukherjee, Siddhartha. *The Gene: An Intimate History.* New York: Schribner, 2016.

Müller, Christel. "Globalization, Transnationalism, and the Local in Ancient Greece." *Oxford Handbooks Online: Scholarly Research Reviews* (2016). https://www.oxfordhandbooks.com/view/10.1093/oxfordhb/9780199935390.001.0001/oxfordhb-9780199935390-e-42.

Musk, Elon. "Making Humans a Multi-Planetary Species." *New Space* 5 (2017) 46–61.

Nail, Thomas. "Deleuze, Occupy, and the Actuality of Revolution." *Theory and Event* 16 (2013). https://muse.jhu.edu/article/501858.

———. *Returning to Revolution: Deleuze, Guattari and Zapatismo.* Edinburgh: Edinburgh University Press, 2012.

———. "What Is an Assemblage?" *SubStance* 46 (2017) 21–37.

Najman, Hindy. *Losing the Temple and Recovering the Future: An Analysis of 4 Ezra.* Cambridge: Cambridge University Press, 2014.

Nanos, Mark D., and Magnus Zetterholm, eds. *Paul within Judaism: Restoring the First-Century Context to the Apostle.* Minneapolis: Fortress, 2015.

Nasrallah, Laura Salah. "Paul's Letters: The Archaeology of Their First Recipients and the Responsibility of Their Modern Readers." *Theological Review* 40 (2019) 85–104.

Nawotka, Krzysztof. "Apollo, the Tutelary God of the Seleucids, and Demodamas of Miletus." In *The Power of Individual and Community in Ancient Athens and Beyond: Essays in Honour of John K. Davies*, edited by Zosia Archibald and Jan Haywood, 261–84. Swansea: Classical Press of Wales, 2019.

Neusner, Jacob. *Judaism as Philosophy: The Method and Message of the Mishnah*. Eugene, OR: Wipf & Stock, 2004.

Neutel, Karin B. *A Cosmopolitan Ideal: Paul's Declaration "Neither Jew Nor Greek, Neither Slave Nor Free, Nor Male and Female" in the Context of First-Century Thought*. LNTS 513. London: Bloomsbury T. & T. Clark, 2015.

Newman, Judith H. *Before the Bible: The Liturgical Body and the Formation of Scriptures in Early Judaism*. Oxford: Oxford University Press, 2018.

———. "The Participatory Past: Resituating Eschatology in the Study of Apocalyptic." *Early Christianity* 10 (2019) 415–34.

Nickelsburg, George W. E. *1 Enoch 1: A Commentary on the Book of 1 Enoch, Chapters 1–36; 81–108*. Hermeneia. Minneapolis: Fortress, 2001.

———. "Enochic Wisdom: An Alternative to the Mosaic Torah?" In *Hesed ve-Emet: Studies in Honor of Ernest S. Frerichs*, edited by Jodi Magness and Seymour Gitin, 123–32. BJS 320. Atlanta: Scholars, 1998.

———. "The Nature and Function of Revelation in 1 Enoch, Jubilees, and Some Qumranic Documents." In *Pseudepigraphic Perspectives: The Apocrypha and Pseudepigrapha in Light of the Dead Sea Scrolls. Proceedings of the International Symposium of the Orion Center for the Study of the Dead Sea Scrolls and Associated Literature, 12–14 January, 1997*, edited by Esther G. Chazon and Michael E. Stone, 91–119. STDJ 31. Leiden: Brill, 1999.

———. "Revealed Wisdom as a Criterion for Inclusion and Exclusion: From Jewish Sectarianism to Early Christianity." In *"To See Ourselves as Others See Us": Christians, Jews, "Others" in Late Antiquity*, edited by Jacob Neusner and Ernest S. Frerichs, 73–91. Chico, CA: Scholars, 1985.

Novenson, Matthew V. *Christ among the Messiahs: Christ Language in Paul and Messiah Language in Ancient Judaism*. Oxford: Oxford University Press, 2012.

Novick, Tzvi. "Peddling Scents: Merchandise and Meaning in 2 Corinthians 2:14–17." *JBL* 130 (2011) 543–49.

Ober, Josiah. "The Athenian Revolution of 508/7 B.C.: Violence, Authority, and the Origins of Democracy." In *The Athenian Revolution: Essays on Ancient Greek Democracy and Political Theory*, 32–52. Princeton: Princeton University Press, 1996.

O'Brien, Renee Nicole, and Frederik Juliaan Vervaet. "Priests and Senators: The *Decemviri Sacris Faciundis* in the Middle Republic (367–104 BCE)." *REA* 122 (2020) 85–106.

Oliver, James Henry. *Greek Constitutions of Early Roman Emperors from Inscriptions and Papyri*. Memoirs of the American Philosophical Society 178. Philadelphia: American Philosophical Society, 1989.

———. "The Ruling Power: A Study of the Roman Empire in the Second Century after Christ through the Roman Oration of Aelius Aristides." *Transactions of the American Philosophical Society* 43 (1953) 871–1003.

Ono, Ken. "The Nature of a Math 'Eureka!'" https://www.youtube.com/watch?v=eLIRAy9xBpI.

Orian, Matan. "The Purpose of the Balustrade in the Herodian Temple." *JSJ* 51 (2020) 487–524.

Orlin, Eric M. "Augustan Religion: From Locative to Utopian." In *Rome and Religion: A Cross-Disciplinary Dialogue on the Imperial Cult*, edited by Jeffrey Brodd and Jonathan L. Reed, 49–59. SBL Writings from the Greco-Roman World Supplement Series 5. Atlanta: Society of Biblical Literature, 2011.

Osborne, Robin et al. "Polarities in Religious Life and Inclusions/Exclusions." In *Thesaurus Cultus et Rituum Antiquorus (ThesCRA)*, 247–82. Los Angeles: The J. Paul Getty Museum, 2012.

Owens, Louis. "Mapping, Naming, and the Power of Words." In *Mixedblood Messages*, 205–13. Norman, OK: University of Oklahoma Press, 1998.

———. *Wolfsong*. American Indian Literature and Critical Studies Series 17. Norman, OK: University of Oklahoma Press, 1994.

Paddock, Alisha. "Βασιλεία τοῦ θεοῦ and ἐκκλησία τοῦ θεοῦ: Boundary Markers for the Corinthians Believers." Paper presented at Virtual Annual Meeting of the Society of Biblical Literature. 2020.

Pars, Adrian ed. *The Deleuze Dictionary*. Rev. ed. Edinburgh: Edinburgh University Press, 2010.

Pedersen, Nils Arne. "The New Testament Canon and Athanasius of Alexandria's 39th *Festal Letter*." In *The Discursive Fight over Religious Texts in Antiquity*, edited by Anders-Christian Jacobsen, 168–77. Aarhus: Aarhus University Press, 2009.

Pelikan, Jaroslav. "Luther and the Liturgy." In *More About Luther*, 3–62. Decorah, IA: Luther College Press, 1958.

Pennington, Jonathan T. *Heaven and Earth in the Gospel of Matthew*. NovTSup 126. Leiden: Brill, 2007.

———. "Heaven, Earth, and a New Genesis: Theological Cosmology in Matthew." In *Cosmology and the New Testament*, edited by Jonathan T. Pennington and Sean M. McDonough, 28–44. LNTS 355. London: T. & T. Clark, 2008.

Pérez i Díaz, Mar. *Mark, A Pauline Theologian: A Re-Reading of the Traditions of Jesus in the Light of Paul's Theology*. WUNT 2.521. Tübingen: Mohr Siebeck, 2020.

Pesch, Rudolf. *Das Markusevangelium*. 2 vols. Freiburg: Herder, 1984.

Pfeiffer, Stefan. *Griechische und lateinische Inschriften zum Ptolemäerreich und zur römischen Provinz Aegyptus: Einführungen und Quellentexte zur Ägyptologie*. Berlin: Lit, 2015.

Piejko, Francis. "Antiochus III and Ptolemy Son of Thraseas: The Inscription of Hefzibah Reconsidered." *L'Antiquité Classique* 60 (1991) 245–59.

Poli, Roberto. *Introduction to Anticipation Studies*. Anticipation Science 1. Cham, Switzerland: Springer, 2017.

Popović, Mladen, ed. *The Jewish Revolt against Rome: Interdisciplinary Perspectives*. JSJSup 154. Leiden: Brill, 2011.

Portier-Young, Anathea E. *Apocalypse Against Empire: Theologies of Resistance in Early Judaism*. Grand Rapids: Eerdmans, 2011.

Posteraro, Tano. "Assemblage Theory and the Two Poles of Organic Life." *Deleuze and Guattari Studies* 14 (2020) 402–32.

Potters, David. *Prophets and Emperors: Human and Divine Authority from Augustus to Theodosius*. Revealing Antiquity 7. Cambridge, MA: Harvard University Press, 1994.

Pratscher, Wilhelm. "Der Herrenbruder Jakobus bei Hegesipp." In *The Image of the Judaeo-Christians in Ancient Jewish and Christian Literature*, edited by Peter J. Tomson and Doris Lambers-Petry, 147–61. WUNT 158. Tübingen: Mohr Siebeck, 2003.

Price, Simon R. F. "Rituals and Power." In *Paul and Politics: Religion and Power in Roman Imperial Society*, edited by R. A. Horsley, 47–71. Harrisburg, PA: Trinity, 1997.

———. *Rituals and Power: The Roman Imperial Cult in Asia Minor*. Cambridge: Cambridge University Press, 1983.

Rabens, Volker. *The Holy Spirit and Ethics in Paul: Transformation and Empowering for Religious-Ethical Life*. 2nd ed. Minneapolis: Fortress, 2013.

Räisänen, Heikki. *Beyond New Testament Theology: A Story and a Programme*. London: SCM, 1990.

———. *The "Messianic Secret" in Mark's Gospel*. Edinburgh: T. & T. Clark, 1990.

Reinhold, Theodore. *Classica Americana: The Greek and Roman Heritage in the United States*. Detroit: Wayne State University Press, 1984.

Reiser, Marius. *Jesus and Judgment: The Eschatological Proclamation in Its Jewish Context*. Translated by Linda M. Maloney. Minneapolis: Fortress, 1997.

Renwick, David A. *Paul, the Temple, and the Presence of God*. BJS 244. Atlanta: Scholars, 1991.

Reynolds, Benjamin E., and Loren T. Stuckenbruck, eds. *The Jewish Apocalyptic Tradition and the Shaping of New Testament Thought*. Minneapolis: Fortress, 2017.

Rhodes, P. J. "Public Documents in the Greek States: Archives and Inscriptions, Part II." *Greece & Rome* 48 (2001) 136–53.

Richter, Daniel S. *Cosmopolis: Imagining Community in Late Classical Athens and the Early Roman Empire*. Oxford: Oxford University Press, 2011.

Riesner, Rainer. *Jesus als Lehrer*. WUNT 2.7. Tübingen: Mohr Siebeck, 1981.

———. "Jesus as Preacher and Teacher." In *Jesus and the Oral Gospel Tradition*, edited by H. Wansbrough, 185–210. Sheffield: Sheffield Academic, 1991.

Rives, James B. "Animal Sacrifice and Political Identity in Rome and Judaea." In *Jews and Christians in the First and Second Centuries: How to Write Their History*, edited by Peter J. Tomson et al., 105–25. CRINT 13. Leiden: Brill, 2014.

Robinson, H. Wheeler. "The Hebrew Concept of Corporate Personality." In *Werden und Wesen des Alten Testament*, edited by Johannes Hempel et al., 49–62. BZAW 66. Berlin: Töpelmann, 1936.

Robinson, James M. et al., eds. *The Critical Edition of Q: Synopsis*. Hermeneia. Minneapolis: Fortress, 2000.

Rogerson, John. *A Theology of the Old Testament: Cultural Memory, Communication, and Being Human*. Minneapolis: Fortress, 2010.

Rooney, Sally. *Beautiful World, Where Are You*. Toronto: Knopf Canada, 2021.

Rowe, Kavin. *World Upside Down: Reading Acts in the Graeco-Roman Age*. Oxford: Oxford University Press, 2010.

Royalty, Robert M. *The Streets of Heaven: The Ideology of Wealth in the Apocalypse of John*. Macon, GA: Mercer University Press, 1998.

Rüger, Hans Peter. "Mit welchem Maß ihr meßt, wird euch gemessen werden." *ZNW* 60 (1969) 174–82.

Ruiten, Jacques T. A. G. M. van. "The Creation of Man and Woman in Early Jewish Literature." In *The Creation of Man and Woman: Interpretations of the Biblical Narratives in Jewish and Christian Traditions*, edited by Gerard P. Luttikhuizen, 34–62. Themes in Biblical Narrative 3. Leiden: Brill, 2000.

Runia, David. "Philo of Alexandria and the Greek *Hairesis*-Model." *VigChr* 53 (1999) 117–47.

Russell, Frank. "Roman Counterinsurgency Policy and Practice in Judaea." In *Brill's Companion to Insurgency and Terrorism in the Ancient Mediterranean*, edited by Timothy Howe and Lee L. Brice, 248–81. Leiden: Brill, 2016.

Sahraoul, Nassima and Caroline Sauter, eds. *Thinking in Constellations: Walter Benjamin in the Humanities*. Newcastle upon Tyne, UK: Cambridge Scholars, 2018.

303

Said, Edward. *Representation of the Intellectual: The 1993 Reith Lectures.* New York: Pantheon Books, 1994.

Saldanha, Arun. *Space After Deleuze.* Deleuze Encounters. London: Bloomsbury, 2017.

Sanders, E. P. *Comparing Judaism and Christianity: Common Judaism, Paul, and the Inner and Outer in Ancient Religion.* Minneapolis: Fortress, 2016.

———. *Paul and Palestinian Judaism: A Comparison of Patterns of Religion.* Philadelphia: Fortress, 1977.

Savalli-Lestrade, Ivana. "Ambassadeurs royaux, Rois ambassadeurs. Contribution à l'étude du 'métier de roi' dans le monde hellénistique." *Dialogues d'histoire ancienne* supplément 17 (2017) 695–718.

Schiavone, Aldo. *Spartacus.* Revealing Antiquity 19. Cambridge, MA: Harvard University Press, 2013.

Schlatter, Adolf. "Atheistische Methoden in der Theologie." In *Zur Theologie des Neuen Testaments und zur Dogmatik: Kleine Schriften,* 134–50. TB 41. Munich: Kaiser, 1969.

Schnabel, Eckhard J. "The Persecution of Christians in the First Century." *JETS* 61 (2018) 525–47.

Schneemelcher, Wilhelm, ed. *New Testament Apocrypha.* Rev. ed. 2 vols. Louisville: Westminster/John Knox, 1991.

Schnelle, Udo. *Die getrennten Wege von Römern, Juden und Christen: Religionspolitik im 1.Jahrundert n. Chr.* Tübingen: Mohr Siebeck, 2019.

———. "Römische Religionspolitik und die getrennten Wege von Juden und Christen." *EvT* 80 (2019) 432–43.

Schröter, Jens et al., eds. *Jews and Christians—Parting Ways in the First Two Centuries CE? Reflections on the Gains and Losses of a Model.* Berlin: de Gruyter, 2021.

Schwartz, Daniel R. "'Judaean' or 'Jew'? How Should We Translate IOUDAIOS in Josephus?" In *Jewish Identity in the Greco-Roman World,* 3–28. AJEC 71. Leiden: Brill, 2007.

———. *Judeans and Jews: Four Faces of Dichotomy in Ancient Jewish History.* Toronto: Toronto University Press, 2014.

Schweitzer, Albert. *The Quest for the Historical Jesus.* 1st complete ed. Minneapolis: Fortress, 2000.

Schwitter, Raphael. "Funkelnde Buchstaben, leuchtende Verse: Die Materialität der Inschrift und ihre Reflexion in den *Carmina Latina Epigraphica.*" In *Antike Texte und ihre Materialität,* edited by Cornelia Ritter Schmalz and Raphael Schwitter, 119–38. Materiale Textkulturen 27. Berlin: de Gruyter, 2019.

Scolnic, Ben. "Heliodorus and the Assassination of Seleucus IV according to Dan 11:20 and 2 Macc 3." *JAJ* 7 (2016) 354–84.

Scott, James M. *Adoption as Sons of God: An Exegetical Investigation into the Background of ΥΙΟΘΕΣΙΑ in the Pauline Corpus.* WUNT 2.48. Tübingen: Mohr Siebeck, 1992.

———. *The Apocalyptic Letter to the Galatians: Paul and the Enochic Heritage.* Minneapolis: Fortress, 2021.

———. "A Comparison of Paul's Letter to the Galatians with the Epistle of Enoch." In *The Jewish Apocalyptic Tradition and the Shaping of New Testament Thought,* edited by Benjamin E. Reynolds and Loren T. Stuckenbruck, 193–218. Minneapolis: Fortress, 2017.

———. "Galatians 3:28 and the Divine Performative Speech-Act of Paul's Gospel." *ZNW* 112 (2021) 180–200.

———. *Geography in Early Judaism and Christianity: The Book of Jubilees.* SNTSMS 113. Cambridge: Cambridge University Press, 2002.

———. "Jude the Obscure: The Letter of Jude and the Enochic Heritage." *JTS* (forthcoming).

———, ed. *On Earth as in Heaven: The Restoration of Sacred Space and Sacred Time in the Book of Jubilees.* JSJSup 91. Leiden: Brill, 2005.

———, ed. *Paul and the Nations: The Old Testament and Jewish Background of Paul's Mission to the Nations with Special Reference to the Destination of Galatians.* WUNT 84. Tübingen: Mohr Siebeck, 1995.

———. "Second Corinthians 3–4 and the Language of Creation: The Citation of Genesis 1:3 in 2 Corinthians 4:6." In *Scriptures, Texts, and Tracings in 2 Corinthians and Philippians,* edited by A. Andrew Das and B. J. Oropeza, 51–69. Lanham, MD: Lexington Books/ Fortress Academic, 2022.

———. "The Speech-Acts of a Royal Pretender: Jesus' Performative Utterances in Mark's Gospel." *JSHJ* 20 (2021) 1–37.

Scurr, Ruth. *Fatal Purity: Robespierre and the French Revolution.* New York: Metropolitan, 2006.

Searle, John R. "How Performatives Work." *Linguistics and Philosophy* 12 (1989) 549.

Sheldrake, Merlin. *Entangled Life: How Fungi Make Our Worlds, Change Our Minds, and Shape Our Future.* New York: Random, 2020.

Sherk, Robert K. *Roman Documents from the Greek East: Senatus Consulta and Epistulae.* Baltimore, MD: Johns Hopkins, 1969.

Sherwin-White, A. N. *The Roman Citizenship.* 2nd ed. Oxford: Clarendon, 1973.

Sherwin-White, S. M. "The Edict of Alexander to Priene, a Reappraisal." *JHS* 105 (1985) 69–89.

Siegert, Folker. "Vermeintlicher Antijudaismus und Polemik gegen Judenchristen im Neuen Testament." In *The Image of the Judaeo-Christians in Ancient Jewish and Christian Literature,* edited by Peter J. Tomson and Doris Lambers-Petry, 74–105. WUNT 158. Tübingen: Mohr Siebeck, 2003.

Sim, David C. "The Gospels for All Christians: A Response to Richard Bauckham." *JSNT* 84 (2001) 3–27.

Simard, Suzanne W. *Finding the Mother Tree: Discovering the Wisdom of the Forest.* Toronto: Allen Lane, 2021.

Simard, Suzanne W., et al. "Mycorrhizal Networks: Mechanisms, Ecology, and Modelling." *Fungal Biology Reviews* 26 (2012) 39–60.

Sly, Liz. "The Unfinished Business of the Arab Spring." *Washington Post,* January 25, 2021. https://www.washingtonpost.com/world/interactive/2021/arab-spring-10-year-anniversary-lost-decade/.

Smith, Jonathan Z. *Map Is Not Territory: Studies in the History of Religions.* SJLA 23. Leiden: Brill, 1978.

Smith, Julien. *Paul and the Good Life: Transformation and Citizenship in the Commonwealth of God.* Waco, TX: Baylor University Press, 2020.

Smith-Christopher, Daniel L. "The Outlaw David Ben Jesse: Reading David as Geronimo in Exile?" *OTE* 31 (2018) 757–77.

Snodgrass, Klyne R. *Stories with Intent: A Comprehensive Guide to the Parables of Jesus.* Grand Rapids: Eerdmans, 2008.

Snyder, Timothy. *On Tyranny: Twenty Lessons from the Twentieth Century.* New York: Tim Duggan, 2017.

———. *The Road to Unfreedom: Russia, Europe, America.* New York: Tim Duggan, 2018.

Stanley, Christopher D. "Paul the Cosmopolitan?" *NTS* 66 (2020) 144–163.

Stanton, G. R., comp. *Athenian Politics c. 800–500 BC: A Sourcebook.* London: Routledge, 1990.

Stern, Menahem, ed. *Greek and Latin Authors on Jews and Judaism.* 3 vols. Jerusalem: The Israel Academy of Sciences and Humanities, 1974–84.

Stevens, Kathryn. "The Antiochus Cylinder, Babylonian Scholarship and Seleucid Imperial Ideology." *JHS* 134 (2014) 66–88.

Stordalen, T. *Echoes of Eden: Genesis 2–3 and Symbolism of the Eden Garden in Biblical Hebrew Literature.* Contributions to Biblical Exegesis and Theology 25. Leuven: Peeters, 2000.

Strait, Drew J. "Proclaiming Another King Named Jesus? The Acts of the Apostles and the Roman Imperial Cult(s)." In *Jesus Is Lord, Caesar Is Not: Evaluating Empire in New Testament Studies,* edited by Scott McKnight and Joseph B. Modica, 130–45. Downers Grove, IL: IVP Academic, 2013.

Strootman, Rolf. "Hellenistic Court Society: The Seleukid Imperial Court under Antiochos the Great, 223–187 BCE." In *Royal Courts in Dynastic States and Empires: A Global Perspective,* edited by Jeroen Duindam et al., 63–89. Rulers and Elites 1. Leiden: Brill, 2011.

Stroumsa, Guy G. *The End of Sacrifice: Religious Transformations in Late Antiquity.* Translated by Susan Emanuel. Chicago: University of Chicago Press, 2009.

Stroumsa, Guy G., and Markus Bockmuehl, eds. *Paradise in Antiquity: Jewish and Christian Views.* Cambridge: Cambridge University Press, 2010.

Stuckenbruck, Loren T. "The Book of Revelation as a Disclosure of Wisdom." In *The Jewish Apocalyptic Tradition and the Shaping of New Testament Thought,* edited by Benjamin E. Reynolds and Loren T. Stuckenbruck, 347–59. Minneapolis: Fortress, 2017.

———. "The Eschatological Worship of God by the Nations: An Inquiry into the Early Enoch Tradition." In *With Wisdom as a Robe: Qumran and Other Jewish Studies in Honour of Ida Fröhlich,* edited by Károly Dániel Dobos and Miklós Kőszeghy, 188–206. Hebrew Bible Monographs 21. Sheffield: Sheffield Phoenix, 2009.

———. "Johann Philipp Gabler and the Delineation of Biblical Theology." *SJT* 52 (1999) 139–57.

———. *The Myth of Rebellious Angels: Studies in Second Temple Judaism and New Testament Texts.* WUNT 355. Tübingen: Mohr Siebeck, 2014.

———. "Overlapping Ages at Qumran and 'Apocalyptic' in Pauline Theology." In *The Dead Sea Scrolls and Pauline Literature,* edited by Jean-Sébastien Rey, 309–26. Leiden: Brill, 2014.

Stuhlmacher, Peter. *Biblische Theologie: Gesammelte Aufsätze.* WUNT 146. Tübingen: Mohr Siebeck, 2002.

———. *Biblische Theologie des Neuen Testaments.* 2 vols. Göttingen: Vandenhoeck & Ruprecht, 1992–1999.

———, ed. *The Gospel and the Gospels.* Grand Rapids: Eerdmans, 1991.

———. *How to Do Biblical Theology.* Allison Park, PA: Pickwick, 1995.

Theissen, Gerd. "The Sacrificial Interpretation of the Death of Jesus and the End of Sacrifice." In *A Theory of Primitive Christian Religion,* 139–60. London: SCM, 2003.

———. *The Social Setting of Pauline Christianity: Essays on Corinth.* Philadelphia: Fortress, 1980.

Thom, Brian David. "Coast Salish Senses of Place: Dwelling, Meaning, Power, Property and Territory in the Coast Salish World." PhD diss., McGill University, 2005.

Thonemann, Peter. "Pessinous and the Attalids: A New Royal Letter." *ZPE* 194 (2015) 111–28.

Thornton, Edward. "On Lines of Flight: The Theory of Political Transformation in *A Thousand Plateaus*." *Deleuze and Guattari Studies* 14 (2020) 433–56.

Thrall, Margaret E. *A Critical and Exegetical Commentary on the Second Epistle to the Corinthians, Vol. 2: II Corinthians VIII–XIII.* ICC. Edinburgh: T. & T. Clark, 1994.

Tolmie, D. F. "Tendencies in the Interpretation of Galatians 3:28 since 1990." *AcT* 19 (2014) 105–29.

Tomasino, Anthony. "Oracles of Insurrection: The Prophetic Catalyst of the Great Revolt." *JJS* 59 (2008) 86–110.

Tracy, Stephen V. *The Lettering of an Athenian Mason.* Hesperia Supplement 15. Princeton: American School of Classical Studies at Athens, 1975.

Trebilco, Paul. *Self-Designations and Group Identity in the New Testament.* Cambridge: Cambridge University Press, 2012.

Trobisch, David. *Die Entstehung der Paulusbriefsammlung: Studien zu den Anfängen christlicher Publizistik.* NTOA 10. Göttingen: Vandenhoeck & Ruprecht, 1989.

———. *The First Edition of the New Testament.* Oxford: Oxford University Press, 2000.

———. *Paul's Letter Collection: Tracing the Origins.* Minneapolis: Fortress, 1994.

Tuckett, Christopher. "Does the 'Historical Jesus' Belong Within a 'New Testament Theology'?" In *The Nature of New Testament Theology: Essays in Honour of Robert Morgan*, edited by Christopher Rowland and Christopher Tuckett, 231–47. Oxford: Blackwell, 2006.

———, ed. *The Messianic Secret.* London: SPCK, 1983.

Udoh, Fabian E. *To Caesar What Is Caesars: Tribute, Taxes, and Imperial Administration in Early Roman Palestine (63 B.C.E.–70 C.E.).* BJS 343. Providence, RI: Brown Judaic Studies, 2020.

Uzukwu, Gesila Nneka. *The Unity of Male and Female in Jesus Christ: An Exegetical Study of Galatians 3.28c in Light of Paul's Theology of Promise.* LNTS 531. London: Bloomsbury T. & T. Clark, 2015.

VanderKam, James C. *From Joshua to Caiaphas: High Priests after the Exile.* Minneapolis: Fortress, 2004.

———. *Jubilees: A Commentary in Two Volumes.* Hermeneia. Minneapolis: Fortress, 2018.

———. "Putting Them in Their Place: Geography as an Evaluative Tool." In *Pursuing the Text: Studies in Honor of Ben Zion Wacholder on the Occasion of his Seventieth Birthday*, edited by John C. Reeves and John Kampen, 47–69. JSOTSup 184. Sheffield: Sheffield Academic, 1994.

VanderKam, James C., and Peter Flint. *The Meaning of the Dead Sea Scrolls: Their Significance for Understanding the Bible, Judaism, Jesus, and Christianity.* San Francisco: HarperSanFrancisco, 2002.

Via, Dan O. *What Is New Testament Theology?* Guides to Biblical Scholarship: New Testament Series. Minneapolis: Fortress, 2002.

Vogt, Kari. "'Becoming Male': A Gnostic and Early Christian and Islamic Metaphor." In *Women's Studies of the Christian and Islamic Traditions: Ancient, Medieval and Renaissance Foremothers*, edited by Kari Elisabeth Børresen and Kari Vogt, 217–42. Dortrecht: Kluwer Academic, 1993.

Vorster, W. S. "Jesus: Eschatological Prophet and/or Wisdom Teacher?" *HvTSt* 47 (1991) 526–43.

Wagner, A. *Sprechakte und Sprechaktanalyse im Alten Testament: Untersuchungen in biblischen Hebräisch an der Nahtstelle zwischen Handlungsebene und Grammatik*. Berlin: de Gruyter, 1997.

Wall, Robert W., and David R. Nienhuis, eds. *A Compact Guide to the Whole Bible: Learning to Read Scripture's Story*. Grand Rapids: Baker Academic, 2015.

Ward, Jacob. *The Loop: How Technology Is Creating a World without Choices and How to Fight Back*. New York: Hachette, 2022.

Wearne, Gareth. "4QMMT: A Letter to (Not from) the Yaḥad." In *Law, Literature, and Society in Legal Texts from Qumran: Papers from the Ninth Meeting of the International Organisation for Qumran Studies, Leuven 2016*, edited by Jutta Jokiranta and Molly M. Zahn, 99–126. STDJ 128. Leiden: Brill, 2019.

Wedderburn, A. J. M. "Paul and Jesus: The Problem of Continuity." *SJT* 38 (1985) 189–203.

Weinfeld, Moshe. *The Promise of the Land: The Inheritance of the Land of Canaan by the Israelites*. Berkeley: University of California Press, 1993.

Weissenberg, Hanne von. *4QMMT: Reevaluating the Text, the Function, and the Meaning of the Epilogue*. STDJ 82. Leiden: Brill, 2009.

Welborn, L. L. *Paul's Summons to Messianic Life: Political Theology and the Coming Awakening*. Insurrection: Critical Studies in Religion, Politics, and Culture. New York: Columbia University Press, 2015.

Welles, C. Bradford. *Royal Correspondence in the Hellenistic Period: A Study in Greek Epigraphy*. New Haven: Yale University Press, 1934.

Wenham, David. "Jesus Tradition in the Letters of the New Testament." In *Handbook for the Study of the Historical Jesus*, edited by Tom Holmén and Stanley E. Porter, 2041–57. Leiden: Brill, 2011.

———. *Paul: Follower of Jesus or Founder of Christianity?* Grand Rapids: Eerdmans, 1995.

Westermann, Claus, *Genesis*. BKAT 1. Neukirchen-Vluyn: Neukirchener Verlag, 1968.

White Crawford, Sidnie, and Cecilia Wassen, eds. *The Dead Sea Scrolls at Qumran and the Concept of a Library*. STDJ 116. Leiden: Brill, 2016.

Whitlock, Matthew G., ed. *Critical Theory and Early Christianity*. Studies in Ancient Religion and Culture. Sheffield: Equinox, 2022.

Witte, Markus et al., eds. *Torah, Temple, Land: Constructions of Judaism in Antiquity*. TSAJ 184. Tübingen: Mohr Siebeck, 2021.

Woodhead, A. G. *The Study of Greek Inscriptions*. 2nd ed. Cambridge: Cambridge University Press, 1981.

Wrede, William. *Das Messiasgeheimnis in den Evangelien, zugleich ein Beitrag zum Verständnis des Markusevangeliums*. Göttingen: Vandenhoeck & Ruprecht, 1901.

Wright, Nicholas. "Seleucid Royal Cult, Indigenous Religious Traditions, and Radiate Crowns: The Numismatic Evidence." *Mediterranean Archaeology* 18 (2005) 67–82.

Yon, J.-B. "De Marisa à Byblos avec le courrier de Séleucos IV. Quelques données sur Byblos hellénistique." *Topoi* Supplement 13 (2015) 89–105.

Young, Arthur. *Travels in France during the Years 1787, 1788, 1789*. Edited by C. Maxwell. Cambridge: Cambridge University Press, 1926.

Yu, Kenneth W. "The Divination Contest of Calchas and Mopus and Aristophanes' *Knights*." *GRBS* 57 (2017) 910–34.

Zack, Andreas. "Forschungen über die rechtlichen Grundlagen der römischen Außenbeziehungen während der Republik bis zum Beginn des Prinzipats. VIII. Teil: Die juristische Form und der rechtliche Zweck der intergesellschaftlichen *deditio* und die Bedeutung der *fides* im Zusammenhang mit der *deditio*." *Göttinger Forum für Altertumswissenschaft* 19 (2016) 89–163.

Zetterholm, Magnus. *The Messiah in Early Judaism and Christianity*. Minneapolis: Fortress, 2007.

Zimm, Michael. "The *Chrēsmologoi* in Thucydides." *SCI* 29 (2010) 5–11.

Zimmermann, Ruben. *Die Logik der Liebe: Die "implizite Ethik" der Paulusbriefe am Beispiel des 1.Korintherbriefs*. Neukirchen-Vluyn: Neukirchener Theologie, 2016.

Ziolkowski, Theodore. *Virgil and the Moderns*. Princeton: Princeton University Press, 1993.

Index of Authors

Index of Ancient Sources

4QMMT

53n21, 72n69

Messianic Apocalypse 4Q

4Q521 — 91n47

Songs of the Sabbath Sacrifice

4Q400–407 — 71n67
11Q17 — 71n67

Temple Scroll

51n14

War Scroll

51n14
1QM 17:5–8 — 253

Ancient Jewish Writers

Josephus

55

Against Apion
1.54 — 7n19
2.37 — 223
2.47 — 7n19

Antiquities of the Jews
11.97 — 223
12.51 — 223
12.137 — 223
12.142–144 — 105n105
12.253 — 82n15
13.39 — 223
13.48 — 226n46
13.257–58 — 180n26
13.274 — 86
13.318 — 70n60, 180n26
14.18 — 87n32
14.19 — 87n32
14.131 — 223
17.139 — 223
17.223 — 223
17.229 — 223
17.295 — 112n129
18.23–25 — 160
18.63–64 — 111
18.136 — 52n18
18.262 — 223

18.266 — 223
18.277 — 223
18.294 — 223
20.17–96 — 205
20.168 — 109n120
20.169–72 — 109
20.200 — 112

Jewish War
1.304–16 — 159
2.56–65 — 159
2.57–59 — 109
2.75 — 112n129
2.118 — 160
2.403–404 — 106n109
2.408–409 — 57n29

Life of Flavius Josephus
113 — 70n60

Philo of Alexandria

133n60

De somniis
1.75–76 — 241n104
2.127 — 7n19

De specialibus legibus
4.187 — 241n104

De Vita Mosis
2.216 — 7n19

Embassy to Gaius
245 — 7n19
356 — 57n29

New Testament

Matthew

42, 47n2, 99n82, 114n1,
115n1, 118, 151n5, 154,
163n31
2:1–12 — 121
2:13–21 — 123n25
3:10 — 282
5:3–12 — 123, 123n27
5:4 — 136n68
5:5 — 188n44
5:12 — 124
5:17–18 — 157n20
5:21–26 — 189n46
5:21–44 — 40n104
5:33–37 — 123n25, 131

John

	39n102, 42, 44n119,
	122n23, 139, 139n7, 141,
	151n5, 152, 152n6, 153,
	154
1:3	241n104
1:29	44n119, 57n32
2:1–11	139n7
2:13–17	136n68
2:18	139n7
2:18–21	109, 110n124
2:19	99n83
3:3	144, 174
3:3–4	141
3:5	144, 174
4:22	158
4:46–54	139n7
4:54	139n7
5:1–9	139n7
5:37	122n23
6:5–13	139n7
6:14	139n7
6:19–21	139n7
6:30	139n7
7:41	160
7:42	160
10:20	75n78
11:1–44	139n7
11:42–42	53n20
12:1–8	43n115
12:15	94n59
12:18	139n7
12:31	253
13:1	152n7
13:13–14	138n4
13:20	39n102
14:12–13	153
18:28	152n7
18:39	152n7
19:12	82n12, 121n22
19:12–16	121n22
19:14	152n7
19:15	121n22
19:19	81n10
20:21–22	152
20:30	xivn6
20:30–31	28n65
21	122n23
21:1–11	139n7
21:22–23	122n23
21:24–25	28n65
21:25	xivn6

Acts

	35n86, 38, 39, 39n102, 54,
	115n2, 151, 152, 152n6,
	153, 153n10, 154, 154n11,
	155, 156, 156n16, 158,
	158n21, 161, 161n28,
	162n30, 172, 172n1,
	175n9, 177, 211n86
1	152
1:1	154n11
1:1–11	152
1:3	174
1–7	156, 158
1:8	115n2, 152
1:8a	156
1:8b	156
1:13–14	155
1:14	154, 211n86
1:15–26	163
1:21–22	163
2	152
2:1–4	154, 211n86
2:14–18	211n86
2:17–18	211n86
2:36	107
2:38	39n102
2:41	152
2:44–45	161
2:46	161
3:1	161
3:1–10	154
3:6	39n102, 153
3:16	39n102, 153
4:1–22	154, 166
4–5	161n29
4:10	39n102
4:12	154
4:13	160
4:17–18	153
4:18	39n102
4:30	153
4:32	162
4:34—5:11	162
5:9	35n86, 153n10
5:11	161
5:17–42	154, 166
5:20–21	161
5:25	161
5:28	153
5:40	39n102
5:45	161
6:1–6	162
6:5	162